'TERROR TO EVIL-DOERS':
PRISONS AND PUNISHMENTS IN
NINETEENTH-CENTURY ONTARIO

This is the history of the foundations of modern carceral institutions in Ontario. Drawing on a wide range of previously unexplored primary material – including the papers of prison inspectors and officials and the correspondence of those who wrote to the authorities – Peter Oliver provides a narrative and interpretative account of the penal system in nineteenth-century Ontario.

In a century of massive social change, the penal system remained rural, local, decentralized, and resistant to transformations that were affecting other areas of society. Despite the efforts of reformers, neither the political elites nor Ontarians in general paid much attention to the inadequacies of a system plagued by neglect, penny-pinching, and the vagaries of local control. In the 1830s, the Kingston penitentiary and punishment by incarceration became the cornerstones of the system, and these elements, however flawed, dominated the Ontario correctional system until the late twentieth century.

'Terror to Evil-Doers' focuses on the purposes and internal management of particular institutions. By synthesizing a wealth of new material into a comprehensive framework, Oliver's seminal study lays the groundwork for future students and scholars of Canadian history, criminology, and sociology.

PETER OLIVER is a professor in the Department of History at York University and Editor-in-Chief of The Osgoode Society for Canadian Legal History.

PATRONS OF THE SOCIETY

Aird & Berlis

Blake, Cassels & Graydon

Blaney, McMurtry, Stapells, Friedman

Borden & Elliot

Davies, Ward & Beck

Fraser & Beatty

Gowling, Strathy & Henderson

McCarthy Tétrault

Osler, Hoskin & Harcourt

Smith, Lyons

Tory Tory DesLauriers & Binnington

Weir & Foulds

BENEFACTOR OF THE SOCIETY

Bastedo Stewart Smith

The Society also thanks The Law Foundation of Ontario and The Law Society of Upper Canada for their continuing support.

'Terror to Evil-Doers': Prisons and Punishments in Nineteenth-Century Ontario

PETER OLIVER

Published for The Osgoode Society for Canadian Legal History by
University of Toronto Press
Toronto Buffalo London

© University of Toronto Press Incorporated 1998
Toronto Buffalo London

Printed in Canada

ISBN 0-8020-4345-3 (cloth)
ISBN 0-8020-8166-5 (paper)

Printed on acid-free paper

Canadian Cataloguing in Publication Data

Oliver, Peter, 1939–
'Terror to evil-doers': prisons and punishments in nineteenth-century Ontario

Includes index.
ISBN 0-8020-4345-3 (bound)   ISBN 0-8020-8166-5 (pbk.)

1. Prisons – Ontario – History – 19th century.   2. Punishment – Ontario –
History – 19th century.   I. Title.

HV9504.O55 1998   365'.9713'09034   C97-932589-7

This book has been published with the help of a grant from the Humanities
and Social Sciences Federation of Canada, using funds provided by the
Social Sciences and Humanities Research Council of Canada.

University of Toronto Press acknowledges the support of the Canada Council for
the Arts and the Ontario Arts Council for our publishing program.

For Donna and Michael

Contents

Part III: Alternative Sanctions and Reform Initiatives

Tables

Foreword

THE OSGOODE SOCIETY
FOR CANADIAN LEGAL HISTORY

The purpose of The Osgoode Society for Canadian Legal History is to encourage research and writing in the history of Canadian law. The Society, which was incorporated in 1979 and is registered as a charity, was founded at the initiative of the Honourable R. Roy McMurtry, former attorney general for Ontario and now Chief Justice, and officials of the Law Society of Upper Canada. Its efforts to stimulate the study of legal history in Canada include a research support program, a graduate student research assistance program, and work in the fields of oral history and legal archives. The Society publishes volumes of interest to the Society's members that contribute to legal-historical scholarship in Canada, including studies of the courts, the judiciary and the legal profession, biographies, collections of documents, studies in criminology and penology, accounts of significant trials, and work in the social and economic history of the law.

Current directors of The Osgoode Society for Canadian Legal History are Jane Banfield, Tom Bastedo, Brian Bucknall, Archie Campbell, J. Douglas Ewart, Martin Friedland, Charles Harnick, John Honsberger, Kenneth Jarvis, Allen Linden, Viginia MacLean, Wendy Matheson, Colin McKinnon, Roy McMurtry, Brendan O'Brien, Peter Oliver, Paul Reinhardt, Joel Richler, James Spence, Harvey Strosberg, and Richard Tinsley. The annual report and information about membership may be obtained by writing to The Osgoode Society for Canadian Legal History, Osgoode Hall, 130 Queen Street West, Toronto, Ontario, Canada M5H 2N6. Members receive the annual volumes published by the Society and may also choose to receive optional volumes.

We are delighted that Peter Oliver has agreed to include his seminal work on prisons and punishments in nineteenth-century Ontario in The Osgoode Society's Publications Series. Professor Oliver's book draws on a wide range of previously unexplored primary sources to offer a narrative and interpretative account of the origins and early development of Ontario's penal system. It should be emphasized that this study was undertaken quite independently of The Osgoode Society, of which Professor Oliver is editor-in-chief, and publication was already in progress through the University of Toronto Press before The Society's directors requested that 'Terror to Evil-Doers' become a Society publication.

'Terror to Evil-Doers' is the first Society publication to deal in an extended fashion with the theme of prisons and punishments. Its focus is on the purposes and internal management of Ontario's gaols, intermediate prisons, and penitentiary. By synthesizing a wealth of new material into a comprehensive framework, this important book lays the groundwork for future students and scholars of Canadian history, criminology, and sociology.

R. Roy McMurtry
President

Martin Friedland
Director

Acknowledgments

This book has been a labour of many years and it has undergone several major transformations. Over the years I have incurred innumerable heavy debts.

I am deeply grateful to the Ontario Ministry of Correctional Services (as it then was) and to the Ministry of the Solicitor General and Correctional Services for the support they have given to this project. I began my research independently. Mr Archie Campbell (now Mr Justice Archie Campbell), the deputy minister, offered me working space in Ministry offices and full access to Ministry files and records. Some months later a new deputy minister, Mr George Podrebarac, wishing to expedite the project, had me seconded to his Ministry for a two-year period and also provided generous research assistance. Without this support, the project would have taken even longer than it has. Many other staff members also assisted, and I am particularly indebted to Mr Donald G. Evans, former assistant deputy minister in the Ministry of the Solicitor General and Correctional Services. I appreciate too the Ministry's ready agreement when I decided, after a year's labour, to cut back on the work and to focus entirely on the nineteenth-century period. Finally, I thank Mr Neil McKerrell, assistant deputy minister, Ministry of the Solicitor General and Correctional Services, for providing support at the publication stage. I wish to emphasize especially that this remained in every essential way an independent academic project and the Ministry never sought in any way to influence the shape of my research or the nature of my interpretation.

I owe a huge debt to four outstanding research assistants who played a major role in gathering materials and, especially, in assisting with the quantitative dimensions of the project. I am delighted to thank John Choules, Michelle Corbett, Michael Whittingham, and Patrick Connor not only for their hard work and skill but also for their dedication and commitment to the project. I also thank the Graduate Program in History at York University, which over the years supplied me with several graduate assistants who worked faithfully on particular aspects of the research.

In addition to support from the Ministry of the Solicitor General and Correctional Services, my work was aided financially by the H.F. Guggenheim Foundation, the Social Sciences and Humanities Research Council of Canada, the Solicitor General's (Canada) Fund for Independent Research, and York University, and I am deeply grateful. I also thank the staff of Secretarial Services, York University, for typing the first draft of the manuscript.

As is true of every work of historical scholarship, this one would not have been possible without the dedicated efforts of the staff of numerous libraries and archival facilities and I particularly thank the National Archives of Canada; the Archives of Ontario; the library of the Ministry of Correctional Services; the Great Library, Law Society of Upper Canada; the University of Toronto Criminology Library; and the Queen's University Archives.

Several colleagues, with a minimum of grumbling, agreed to give a very long manuscript a careful and critical reading and their assistance so generously given was simply indispensable. A big thank you therefore to Paul Romney, Jim Phillips, Bob Gidney, Russell Smandych, John Choules, Susan Lewthwaite, and David Murray. I thank also the two anonymous readers for the Humanities and Social Science Federation of Canada for their frank yet supportive reading. Finally, Marilyn MacFarlane, my colleague of many years at the Osgoode Society for Canadian Legal History, has helped and participated in the preparation of this book in many ways over the years and I believe she knows how much I appreciate her assistance and many kindnesses.

I am delighted to be publishing once again with the University of Toronto Press, whose editorial and production standards are unexcelled in this country. It is good to be working with Bill Harnum, Gerry Hallowell, Emily Andrew, Anne Forte, and the other outstanding members of the Press staff on my own book for a change and not someone else's. I thank them for the interest they showed in my manuscript over the years and for the integrity and skill they have brought to its publication. I am fortunate indeed to have had as my copy editor Allyson May, who contributed not only superb editorial skills but the knowledge and insights of a fine legal historian.

My family, of course, was long-suffering and I am deeply grateful to them and to Maureen Hyland. I thank them for the support they offered in so many ways. I will never fully be able to make up to them the time which might better have been spent on family pursuits, but I promise to try.

Introduction

This book uses a range of primary sources to offer a narrative and interpretative account of the history of prisons and punishments in nineteenth-century Ontario. Because of its wide scope, both chronologically and topically, 'Terror to Evil-Doers' is intended to provide a general perspective and to suggest several initial lines of interpretation. Throughout, its focus is on the institutions themselves: gaols, the penitentiary, and two intermediate prisons.

For practical reasons, the punishment of juveniles is considered only tangentially, and the establishment and administration of separate prisons for juveniles is excluded. Because there is so little literature on these subjects, and because I believe an introductory account is necessary before attempting more comprehensive analysis, I have not essayed a social history of punishment, much less of crime. No doubt a more local study of a county, for example, or of several counties, would have offered the opportunity for more social analysis. But because so much of the story is of the interplay between provincial policy and local authority, between emerging bureaucratic structures and other forms of governance, a more micro-analytic account would have obscured too much that was of vital importance. I decided therefore to study prisons and punishments in the entire province, from its origins to the end of the nineteenth century. This temporal choice allowed me to deal with the essential transition from old-regime shaming punishments to a new modern regimen, which focused on imprisonment.

Partly because of these broad parameters, *'Terror to Evil-Doers'* is not a history of daily life in the various institutions. Rather, its focus is on the carceral politics of the state, the challenges of institutional governance and administrative imperatives, and, perhaps most of all, on that great nineteenth-century contest which characterized emergent nation states: conflicts between central power and local authority in an era of social change and industrialization.

The years chosen for study were the critical formative period for Ontario society, and the shape which the province had assumed by 1900 would endure for much of the twentieth century. Certainly this was true of the criminal justice system. The fundamental alterations that took place during this period in court structure, the criminal law, and methods of policing reflected the frenetic pace of change and, particularly, the transition from a rurally based traditional society to the modern industrial one which emerged fully in the years prior to the First World War. From a wilderness at the beginning of the period, Ontario assumed its richly diverse modern guise. Prosperous farms co-existed with factories and large cities, with Toronto secure as the pre-eminent metropolis. These transformations took place within an intellectual framework marked by an overweening confidence that economic advance, technological innovation, and moral improvement marched together. This characteristically Victorian faith in progress infused all aspects of provincial life, and it would have been strange if the province's citizens had seen their criminal justice system as an exception.

One theme of this book, however, is that nineteenth-century Ontarians did indeed treat the field of criminal justice differently from other aspects of social endeavour. Some writers have suggested that the province's citizens at certain points seemed preoccupied by the extent of crime in their midst. My own sense is that concern over crime occupied a small place in the collective Ontario mind. Certainly most citizens were unwilling to make much effort to engage directly or indirectly in efforts to shape and refine the instruments of punishment, preferring to leave this task to small groups of elected and appointed officials. And they were unwilling to reconsider their social priorities so as to allot any larger proportion of community resources to improving the conditions of imprisonment or to meeting the challenge of rehabilitation. In numerous ways, this public indifference shaped the approach of nineteenth-century Ontarians to criminal justice issues broadly defined.

It is argued here that the critical turning point in the evolution of criminal sanctions from those of an 'old regime' that deployed shaming punishments to a 'modern' approach based on incarceration occurred primarily in the 1830s. This transition took place well before the new industrial system and the middle-class values which it reflected had come to the fore. By this date, it is true, the province had already experienced considerable 'pauper migration,' and this had its effect on such institutional initiatives of the 1830s as the decision to erect poorhouses, an asylum, and the penitentiary. Nonetheless, it is the thesis of this book that transformations in the criminal justice system were made primarily in response to elitist views and influenced only indirectly by economic change and class tensions. And they were achieved by that small group within the governing class which had the most direct contact with criminal justice institutions, a fact which seems obvious but has not been grasped by some students of the subject.

My approach has been to focus on prisons and punishments, while referring briefly to such related aspects of the criminal justice structure as are necessary to understand correctional developments. It has been difficult to exclude abundant material which emerged in the course of the research on crime and criminals. In the routine study of gaol registers, prison records, and other documentation, the study of prisons and punishments invariably shades over into the equally fascinating subject of crime itself. Sometimes, the relationship is so intimate that issues of correctional history demand a considerable knowledge of the nature and extent of crime. The most obvious example of this is the relationship between crime rates and the decision to establish Kingston Penitentiary. The topic of crime, however, is so vast and complex that a conscious decision has been made not to make any extensive excursion into it here.

As for the penitentiary, its opening initiated a new era in the colony's criminal justice system. However, it is critical to understand that this institutional transformation was complemented, indeed made possible, by a concerted effort at gaol reform and by extensive changes in the criminal law. The new commitment to incarceration must be placed in relation to other legal and judicial processes. Although judges had been making increasing use of the gaol as a means of punishment from the mid-1820s, the changes of the 1830s were radical in the sense that they led to the virtually complete elimination of all other forms of punishment for serious criminal offences. It should be understood, however, that imprisonment at this time by no means became monolithic in nature. The older experience of incarceration in local gaols remained as a prominent and distinctive form of provincial justice. It is true, nonetheless, that by the end of the 1830s incarceration in whatever form dominated the punitive structure and would continue to occupy that place for more than a century. In Ontario, more than in some neighbouring jurisdictions, the triumph of incarceration left little room for old alternatives or, more significantly, new experiments.

One predominant theme in the narrative presented here is the relationship between local communities and the political elite in their respective efforts to shape and control the levers of punitive power. There were far-ranging implications to the fact that the penitentiary was promoted primarily by a small group within the Tory elite. In Upper Canada, Tory tradition identified criminal justice issues as critical components of political and social order, and the Tory leadership took the initiative to reshape both the law and the instruments of punishment to legitimate and extend social control. During the Union years, however, those who put the penitentiary in place and who instigated both legal and gaol reform were displaced in power by others – both reform and conservative – representing the forces of political modernization. In the 1850s and 1860s processes of state formation and bureaucratic evolution brought to the fore a new cadre of civil servants and administrators who endeavoured with mixed success to place their own mark on gaol and penitentiary discipline. In the era of the Canadian Union, 1841–67, the processes of politics left a broadly popular imprint on correctional policy, one which was generally negative in its consequences. At first glance, the gaols suffered most from political parsimony and public hostility, but a closer look demonstrates that the penitentiary fared little better.

This book makes no attempt to provide a complete institutional history of nineteenth-century Kingston. Rather, I have chosen to assess the penitentiary at three critical points in its history, arguing that the very structure and nature of this facility throughout the century, as well as its situation in the Canadian state, determined that it must be narrowly custodial in nature.

The penitentiary story was repeated, with minor variations, in every other aspect of the adult system of prisons and punishments. In the two intermediate prisons for men and women opened in Toronto later in the century, the Central Prison and the Mercer Reformatory, there was the same story of neglect, constraint, and punishment prevailing over every other possible approach. This was equally true of the gaols, the foundation of the system, and those who fought for better physical conditions and correctional improvements achieved agonizingly little.

These defeats and failures, however, cannot be attributed to any single cause. Certainly they did not represent the deliberate policy imposed by a middle-class elite intent on achieving deterrence through harsh and punitive punishments. Most assuredly, they were not the consequence of deliberate cruelty on the part of penitentiary officers or local gaolers. Public indifference, competition for scarce resources, the competing influence of local and centrist political cultures, the failure of emerging bureaucratic imperatives to become entrenched in such a way as to challenge more traditional political influences, and the essentially rural and conservative values of a society still close to its pioneer origins are all important parts of the story that unfolds here.

There is one other determining circumstance. Ontario's prisons and punishments were the product of a particular society. They were shaped by the needs, the resources, and the ideas of Ontarians of the nineteenth century. The most difficult challenge of criminal justice history is to relate a society's penal practices to its social structure and political culture. For this reason, the study of a society's penal regimes offers insights into many aspects of that community's history. When he was British Home Secretary, Winston Churchill observed that one test of a society's character was how it treated its criminals. This remark has since become a cliché, but it still has the ring of truth to it. In nineteenth-century Ontario, however, the difficulty of relating social change to evolving penal regimes is compounded by the dynamic pace of change throughout the period. In the 1790s, Upper Canada was a wilderness peopled by a few thousand Aboriginal peoples and white settlers. When war with the United States broke out in 1812, there were only about 60,000 people in the colony, some four-fifths of whom were immigrants from south of the border. In 1841, when Upper Canada was joined politically with Lower Canada in the Province of Canada, with the sections now called Canada West and Canada East, it contained about 480,000 people. Predominantly rural in nature, its settlements were scattered along a vast territory linked only by primitive roads and often treacherous water communication. But population growth was steady. Canada West underwent another political transformation in 1867, and emerged as the Province of Ontario in the new Dominion of Canada. By 1871, it contained 1,621,000 people, almost half of the country's total population. As Douglas McCalla has demonstrated, there was remarkable economic growth in this period.[1] Ontario had a dynamic and diverse economy, firmly rooted in the staple industries of farm and forest, but propelled as well by a forceful commercial class, by the transportation revolution of the 1850s, which saw the construction of over one thousand miles of railway, and by the beginnings of industrialization.

Throughout the century, the rural–urban balance was shifting continuously. Although McCalla argues that agriculture continued to dominate the provincial economy, the steady rise in the urban population had a social significance out of proportion to its numbers. And the numbers themselves were impressive. In 1851 only 14 per cent of the Canada West population was classified as urban; twenty years later it had reached 20.6 per cent and by 1901 it stood at 40.3 per cent. Most striking was the growth of large urban centres, especially Toronto, Hamilton, Ottawa, and London. Toronto far outdistanced all other cities, becoming a truly metropolitan centre. Yet the 1850s and 1860s saw a balanced and widely distributed urban growth, with Hamilton moving from 10,300 in 1850 to 27,500 in 1856, and London growing from 5,000 to 15,000. Toronto's population increased from 30,000 in 1851 to 44,000 in 1861 and 56,000 a decade later. In the 1880s this steady pace of urban growth escalated into a tumultuous rate of change that was disorienting to those who lived through it. Hamilton, for example, grew from 35,000 in 1881 to 49,000 in 1891, and Toronto's population mushroomed in the same period from 86,000 to 181,000, reaching 208,000 by 1901.

The forces that propelled this urban concentration were accompanied by social dislocation and considerable human suffering. In urban communities, slums emerged in some inner-city areas. In the Ontario countryside, some counties, especially those closest to the urban centres, experienced an actual population decline in the later decades of the century. Change and dislocation naturally affected the conditions of employment, the housing of transient and more permanent populations, and a host of other social conditions. These in turn were reflected in the circumstances of criminality and the nature of punishments. In a general study such as that which follows, it is not usually possible to delve deeply into complex social relationships, but the overall nature and pace of change must be kept in mind as determining influences on both crime rates and patterns of punishment.

The province's political culture, which evolved over the course of the century in a manner equally as dramatic as the province's physical and social circumstances, must also be borne in mind. Throughout the century there were intimate connections between the political climate of the day and the administration of criminal law and penal regimes. The little Tory province established in the 1790s, with its governing elite threatened on all sides by republicanism and democracy, to say nothing of war and rebellion, might have been expected to administer its criminal justice system with a stern hand and with the frequent application of severe punishments. As we shall see, this was not necessarily the case. Oligarchic rule was challenged in the 1840s and undermined in the 1850s as political modernization and increased popular participation accompanied social change and economic growth. Although a high degree of turbulence and a measure of extremism characterized the politics of the Union period, by Confederation moderation was beginning to emerge and the post-Confederation era was a period of political stability. The Liberal party governed from 1871 to 1905, achieving its greatest successes under the astute leadership of Oliver Mowat between 1872 and 1896. During the Mowat administrations class and regional interests were skilfully balanced, and there was a gradual but persistent extension of a wide variety of social and political reforms, including full manhood suffrage, legal adjustments, factory acts, and a host of other progressive measures.

Although the period saw some real advances in the field of women's rights, especially property rights, women in Ontario did not achieve the franchise until the First World War. More to the point, opportunities for remunerative employment for women remained severely restricted. Contemporary moral values, especially relating to sexuality, propelled by a powerful but rigid evangelistic impulse, were equally narrow and confining. These circumstances would be fully reflected in changing patterns of female incarceration, and in particular in the establishment in 1880 of the province's first penal facilities for adult females and young girls.

The late-century political equilibrium achieved by Mowat Liberalism and the middle-class values it expressed might have been expected to lead to more liberal approaches to criminal law and penal policy. But Ontario, despite the shift in the rural-urban balance, remained a province dominated by older values. Life was hard, many remained on the margins of existence, and a degree of affluence, except for a very few, would not emerge until the next century. In these circumstances, Ontarians continued to believe that those who broke the law should be subjected to severe punishments. As a result, the penal system reflected both parsimony and authoritarianism, which remained characteristics of Ontario life for years to come. In the pages that follow, the relationships between econcomic structures, social circumstances, and the character of nineteenth-century Ontario penality are necessarily more often assumed than demonstrated. Nonetheless, these connections were the enduring reality that shaped and reshaped prisons and punishments over the course of the century.

In Ontario the heritage of the nineteenth century would be long-enduring. The shameful facts uncovered by the provincial Ross Commission inquiry into Ontario's welfare facilities in the late 1920s and by the more famous Archambault Royal Commission investigation of Canada's penitentiary system in the 1930s leave no doubt of that. The prisoners in Ontario's gaols and penitentiaries consequently suffered greatly and in a variety of ways, but so too did many other Ontarians. The consequences of ongoing failures of policy, humanity, and social imagination were far-reaching, and many paid the price, including both the guilty and the innocent. In the mid-1950s, John Foote, V.C., a well-meaning minister of reform institutions in the Conservative government of Leslie Frost, uttered the following lament about the attitude towards convicted criminals taken by his Cabinet colleagues:

I don't think there was one person within Cabinet that was enthusiastic about the Department [of Reform Institutions]. They had no use for the people who were committed to prison and they didn't think society owed them a great deal. They liked to see people reformed and changed and so on but they weren't very hopeful about it and they didn't want to spend very much money on it. We were short of money and the Cabinet just felt that the less they heard of the prisons the better.

His fellow ministers, Foote believed, were humane enough and willing to see him effect improvements, so long as they were accomplished 'with a minimum of expenditures.' Their priorities, Foote believed, reflected those of most members of the legislature and public opinion generally across Ontario.[2] By the mid-1950s, it seemed, nothing had changed in Ontario, in this field at least.

Neglect and a sense of hopelessness, however, did not constitute the whole story. In some important ways, achievements were made in the penal enterprise which redounded to the benefit of all, and there were many examples, some of which became institutionalized, of benevolence, humanity, and efficiency. This book is an account not only of failure, but also of the accomplishments of caring individuals at all levels of Ontario society. If, finally, the conclusion must be that prisons and punishments were to some extent out of step, both in intent and in achievement, with other nineteenth-century social endeavours, the record was never entirely bleak.

One final note. The tale told here is not a comprehensive one and I have cut into the story of punishment only at several critical points. As such, the chapters may be read as separate essays which I hope will provide enlightenment on discrete aspects of a large topic.

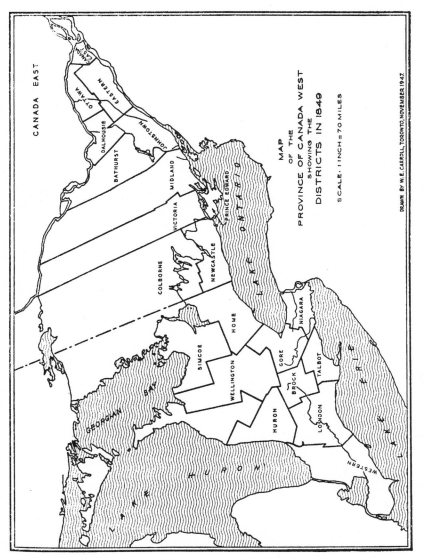

Source: the Ontario Historical Society, *Profiles of a Province*, drawn by W.E. Carroll

Part I

Colonial Origins

1

Upper Canadian Punishments

THE CRIMINAL LAW

At its origins in 1791 and for the first four decades of its existence, Upper Canada, as a British colony and an old-regime society, punished crime by means of a traditional mix of punishments. These included the so-called shaming punishments, whipping and the pillory; fines for minor transgressors; banishment and transportation; imprisonment; and finally, execution, which was generally restricted to those convicted of high treason or murder. Although the unreformed English criminal law was in effect at the colony's establishment, that law, the notorious 'bloody code,' with its more than two hundred capital offences, was ill-suited for a North American society established at the end of the eighteenth century. Consequently, in a statute passed in 1800, Upper Canadian legislators moved to adapt English law to local needs. Since 1774, they noted, when English criminal law had been confirmed in the Old Province of Quebec, 'divers amendments and improvements' had been made in the criminal law of the mother country, 'which it is expedient to introduce and adopt in this Province.' To that end, the legislature declared the criminal law of England as it stood on 17 September 1792 – the date of the opening of the first legislature of Upper Canada – to be the criminal law of Upper Canada.

The intent of the statute of 1800 was to ensure that the representatives of the province would henceforth accept and adapt English criminal law as they felt appropriate. As it turned out, however, the fledgling legislators had little desire to enact their own criminal law and, except for the statute of 1800 itself, they effected few significant changes before 1833. The Act of 1800 gave judges the authority to dispense with the plea of benefit of clergy and its accompaniment of burning on the hand, on the grounds that such burning 'is often disregarded and ineffectual, and sometimes may fix a lasting mark of disgrace and infamy on offenders, who might otherwise become good subjects.' As an alternative, judges received the authority to impose 'a moderate pecuniary fine' on all cases previously subject to clergy (except manslaughter) and also to order the offender to be whipped. The next clause affirmed that nothing in the new Act was intended to deprive any court of the authority to sentence offenders to prison or to the workhouse. And finally, the statute noted that because it would be difficult to carry transportation into effect, banishment should be used as a convenient alternative, and that any person convicted of returning from such a sentence should 'suffer death.'[1] The law reform of 1800 provided the framework for the decisions of the Assize judges for most of the Upper Canadian period. The judges followed its letter and spirit and regularly imposed the range of punishments it prescribed. As time passed, however, sharp variations emerged in both the nature and balance of punishments. The eventual opening of an Upper Canadian penitentiary in 1835 – a truly significant point of departure – served only to carry forward changes in punitive practices that were gradually introduced after 1800.

THE EARLY GAOLS

Throughout the Upper Canadian period, 1791–1840, local government was administered by appointed justices of the peace who served in each of the districts into which the province was divided. The district authorities were obliged by law to make due provision for both gaols and courthouses. This legal requirement, however, did not take into consideration the relative poverty and scarcity of resources which beset local authorities. Moreover, the problems facing gaol construction in this early period did not not disappear as the community grew in wealth and resources. Throughout the course of the entire nineteenth century the local gaols would retain the dubious distinction of being the neglected orphans of provincial society.

This situation was not a result of indifference on the part of the political elite. In 1792, at the first session of the Upper Canadian legislature, a statute was passed directing that 'a Gaol and Court House shall be erected ... in each and every District' throughout the province. This was to be accomplished by authorizing the justices meeting together at Courts of Quarter Sessions 'by such means as shall to them seem most fitting and convenient' to procure plans and to select one of them by vote. Any two or more of the justices were then authorized to let tenders and contract for construction. Specifically this legislation enacted that a gaol and court-house be erected in New Johnstown (Cornwall) for the Eastern District, Kingston for the Midland District, Newark (Niagara-on-the-Lake) for the Home District, and L'Assomption (Sandwich) for the Western District, these constituting the four original districts.[2]

The same statute established several procedures that did much to shape – and misshape – the gaols in the Upper Canadian period and beyond. It placed the power to appoint and remove the gaoler in the sheriff. It made it the responsibility of the justices 'to ascertain and appoint a reasonable yearly salary ... to be paid to the Gaoler,' which put this employee at the mercy of the most poorly funded level of government. More positively, the Act incorporated several recent English reforms when it asserted that the gaoler's salary was to be 'in place of all fees, pre-requisites, or imposition of any sort' and that no licence would be granted to retail spirituous liquors in any gaol. And the Act empowered the justices at Quarter Sessions 'to frame and draw up ... rules and regulations to be observed and obeyed within the said Gaols.' Once these rules received the approbation of one of the judges of the soon-to-be-established Supreme Court, they were to be binding. The statute emphasized that the gaols were local institutions and ensured that the influence of the provincial central authority was minimized. Although some districts carried out the admonition to put rules in place, others felt no urgency and an opportunity to institute province-wide standards of staffing and administration had been missed. Over one hundred and fifty years would pass before the problems to which this contributed would be fully remedied. However, given the state of the colony and the weakness of the little government at Newark, there was no alternative to local initiative.

The early passage of a gaols statute indicated that the colony's leaders believed that the institutional structures of a criminal justice system included not only courts but penal facilities, and that these were essential for every civil polity. The statute's preamble expressed a sense of urgency, noting that 'great inconveniences have been suffered by the inhabitants of this Province, from the want of Prisons and Court Houses in the several districts thereof, and ... such buildings are manifestly necessary for the regular administration of justice.' Inconveniences, to be sure, had existed for some years already and despite the passage of the Act would continue for many more. In his definitive study of local government in Upper Canada, J.H. Aitchison concluded that the fiscal challenge imposed on the districts by the need to provide gaols and courthouses was simply 'the most serious governmental problem the magistrates had to face' and that the burden thus imposed was 'the greatest single strain on the district budget.'[3] This must be kept in mind before the districts are too severely condemned because their efforts fell short of the standards of a later and incomparably more affluent age. In these early years resources were slight and there were many pressing demands, including those of schools, churches, and roads. Just as important, the mother country, in recognition of the principle of no taxation without representation, had placed severe limits on the fiscal capacity of the appointed justices. Furthermore, the districts, continually subdivided as the result of population growth and shifts, were a perpetually unstable unit of government.

In these circumstances the story of the early gaols is a tale of local needs, competing demands, and inadequate resources. For the first decade and more of their existence the districts relied on makeshift expedients and ramshackle structures intended to be replaced when circumstances changed. At times, persons were confined for brief periods in private homes. Naturally, the penalties assessed by judges reflected these circumstances, and resort was had more frequently to fines and whippings than to imprisonment. But to a considerable extent this sentencing pattern was more a reflection of prevailing practices than a response to the inadequacies of the gaols. At this point in time, the gaols were used primarily to house accused persons awaiting trial and those who had been found guilty and were awaiting execution or some other form of punishment. Judges seldom sentenced convicted persons to gaol as punishment. In colonial New York, for example, Douglas Greenberg could discover only nineteen instances in which individuals received a prison term as punishment for the commission of a crime in the period 1691 to 1776.[4] Adam Hirsch, in his recent study of prisons in Massachusetts, confirms that 'the central function of the jail in early Massachusetts was to facilitate pretrial and presentence detention.'[5] But by the end of the first decade of the nineteenth century this had changed. Most American states amended their criminal laws, limited capital punishment to a relatively few offences, and replaced some forms of physical punishment with brief terms of incarceration. In Massachusetts in 1785 the legislature established a prison on Castle Island in Boston harbour for convicted prisoners and simultaneously 'revised the criminal code to permit judges to impose long-term incarceration as an alternative to public punishments.'[6] Similarly in Britain as Margaret DeLacy demonstrates, the number of persons committed to gaols as punishment remained small in the 1780s, but it was increasing. Towards the end of the century, 'the number of prisoners in all categories, including debtors, began a steady rise that would last until the mid-nineteenth century.'[7] As we shall see, Upper Canada was affected by this increasing willingness to use the gaol for punishment and to hold debtors, and the important law reform statute of 1800 furthered a trend already in existence.

For these reasons it was a matter of urgency for the Upper Canadian authorities, local and central, to put the terms of the 1792 gaols statute into effect with all possible speed. This proved to be no easy task. In 1789, the judges of the Court of Common Pleas in what was soon to become the Midland District reported that 'as the District is unprovided with either Court House or Prison we need not mention how inconvenient and in some cases how impossible it will be to carry the laws into effect.' A room owned by the Kingston garrison was used temporarily but it had 'neither floor, chimney or Glazing in the Windows' and in the winter no one could be confined there 'without manifestly endangering his life.'[8] Notwithstanding a special grant of taxing power made to the districts in 1793, things were slow to change.

Peter Russell, who became administrator of the province following the departure of John Graves Simcoe, the first lieutentant-governor, worried a great deal about the absence of gaols and courthouses. In 1796 he asked district officials how far the people 'may be capable of bearing the whole or part of the Expence' for building at least one gaol in each district. In 1798, with the little village of York soon to become capital of the Home District as well as the seat of government for the province, he decided to treat its needs as especially urgent. In May of that year he informed the sheriff, Alexander Macdonell, that he had asked the Executive Council 'to take the Police of York into their Consideration and digest some economical plan for preserving Order among its Inhabitants.'[9] The matter was discussed by a committee of Council which decided that it would 'be most economical to erect a District Jail at once.' Russell had in mind 'a small log building ... of sufficient strength and size to secure three separate Prisoners, and accommodate the Keeper.' Macdonell was further instructed 'to provide Handcuffs and other Irons for binding gross Offenders, and stocks for punishing those who may deserve such Chastisement.' All expenses were to be 'discharged on your Requisition by my

Warrant on the Receiver General of the Province.' This facility – Toronto's first gaol – was opened on King Street east of Yonge Street early in 1799. Built of squared logs ten inches thick with the lower floor beneath the surface of the earth, it measured thirty-four by twenty feet and was divided into three rooms. A few years later, the building was enclosed by a wood stockade.[10]

Having given the district its gaol, the province on 30 June 1799 transferred all financial responsibilities to Quarter Sessions. The consequent reluctance or inability of the magistrates to shoulder the burden was a clear warning that Upper Canadian districts were ill-equipped to pay gaol costs. From the beginning parsimony prevailed and in January 1801 the justices directed that a prisoner's diet should be 'one pound of wheaten bread' per day 'and no more.'[11]

The district's financial woes affected the state of the gaol in every imaginable way. In September 1804 the sheriff noted that the facility was entirely inadequate 'to secure prisoners' and he warned against 'the consequences which might thence ensue.' The magistrates in turn blamed the gaoler and a committee of JPs reported in 1806 that the gaol was 'in such a state of Disorder & filth as denotes great negligence' on his part. In April 1807 a new sheriff, Miles McDonell, formally protested 'against the insufficiency' of the facility and presented a report on urgently needed repairs. The strongest note of protest in the pre-war period came from Sheriff John Beickie. On 13 April 1811 Beickie reported that many of the cells were rotten. He felt it unsafe for the attendants to confine anyone therein, as several hearths were so decayed as to threaten the inmates' well-being. Some repairs were made but eight months later Beickie noted that the prisoners 'suffer much from Cold and Damp.'[12]

In 1801 Quarter Sessions asked the sheriff to set aside two rooms for use as a 'bridewell,' presumably to house needy persons who were deemed also to require an element of correction, but the district's chronic financial incapacity must have eroded the will to use the gaol for this purpose. Instead of being paid in money both the gaoler and the high constable for a time received certificates which gave their claims priority whenever the treasurer should succeed in collecting enough taxes to liquidate some of the district's debts. In October 1803 when the long-suffering gaoler resigned, the court ordered that his successor receive £30 'and no more.' In these circumstances, magistrates hesitated to place the poor and the idle in the gaol, if only because of the cost.[13]

Notwithstanding the financial constraints which beset all districts, the legislature in 1810 passed 'An Act to declare the Common Gaols to be

Houses of Correction for certain purposes.'[14] In Upper Canada there was no statutory provision to take care of the poor and in 1792 the legislature had specifically decided not to adopt any of the provisions of the English poor law. Presumably it was sometimes cheaper to house the poor and the idle in gaol than to provide assistance in the community and the new Act had the virtue of extending the magistrates' options. Apart from money, however, the 1810 Houses of Correction Act was significant because in effect it was the colony's first vagrancy statute. According to this measure, it was expedient that every gaol should so serve 'until Houses of Correction shall be erected.' Since such institutions were never built, the spirit of this provision remained for the rest of the century and beyond to help justify the use of the gaols as congregate institutions to house the poor, the elderly, the insane, and other unfortunates. The Act swept a wide net, defining the type of person to be incarcerated as 'all and every idle and disorderly person, or rogues and vagabonds, and incorrigible rogues, or any other person or persons who may by law be subject to be committed to a House of Correction.'[15] No reference was made in this statute to hard labour, persumably because it was assumed that persons confined in 'Houses of Correction' must somehow be put to work.

It was some time before the districts chose to make much use of the gaols as poorhouses and asylums. Upper Canadian magistrates seemed to expect that with an abundance of work available no family need face want except perhaps a few unfortunates who could be assisted by friends, the church, or family. Even into the 1820s, as David Murray has demonstrated, the magistrates of the Niagara District provided public funds for the deserving poor through a 'pauper list' only with the greatest of reluctance.[16] Given these attitudes, it would not have been surprising to find the gaols pressed more frequently into service for welfare needs. The use of correctional facilities for such purposes implied that those who came through their doors were partly responsible for their condition and stood in need of correction.

Given English precedent and colonial need, one would expect to find Upper Canadian magistrates committing unfortunates to the local gaols in some numbers. Yet following the 1801 minutes suggesting the use of the Home District gaol as a bridewell, there was no further mention of such use in district minutes until 1811. Apparently the magistrates continued to prefer outdoor relief as less of a burden to the community. But abundant evidence from Quarter Sessions records demonstrates a growing reluctance to pay the costs of outdoor relief, and in these circumstances the gaol sometimes became the only alternative to starvation. No doubt individual magistrates made commitments without reference to Quarter Sessions and such commitments, given the absence of gaol registers for this period, are impossible to trace. The decision of the Home District Sessions in 1811 to implement the 1810 statute by appointing William Knott, the gaoler, as keeper of the House of Correction and to pay him a salary for that purpose suggests that the intent was to use the facility for broad social and corrective purposes.

Perhaps the magistrates felt a greater sense of responsibility for the insane than they did for the poor. On 22 November 1806 the Home District minutes record that Aaron Allworthy, who had been confined to gaol 'for a disordered mind,' was 'brought up and it appearing that his mind was perfectly composed, he was discharged.'[17] In 1807 'sundry inhabitants of Yonge Street' petitioned that one William Copland, 'a man disordered in his Senses' who was going from house to house threatening the occupants, be dealt with. Two magistrates were directed to issue an order committing Copland to gaol, where 'his actions & his state of mind will be fully investigated.'[18] But overall there were few cases of either poor or ill people being confined, at least according to the Home District minutes. Similarly in the London District there is no mention at all of welfare matters until 1815, at which point one Frederick Steinhoff was allowed 7s.6d. a week 'for the maintenance of George Fisher a pauper.'[19] The explanation lies partially in the fact that the large-scale migration of indigents to Upper Canada did not begin until the mid-1820s.

The progress of gaol construction in early Upper Canada is a chronicle of how political incapacity and sectional wrangling intersected with confusion as to purpose and use. No other district was as fortunate as the Home District in having the Executive Council foot the bill and most struggled to find the funds and harness their political will to conform to statutory demands. In Kingston, where there was no dispute over the location of the district capital, the process worked smoothly. By 1793 the Midland District was provided with a solid two-storey stone structure which was used as both gaol and courthouse until 1833, when a second substantial gaol and courthouse were built at Church and Clarence Streets.[20] Similarly in the Niagara District, created in 1798, a large building was erected which at one stage during the War of 1812 held about 300 prisoners but became itself a casualty of war, being destroyed by fire in 1813. The replacement, completed in 1818 and used until 1847, was a rather grand structure built in part with relief funds raised in Nova Scotia and Great Britain and using soldier-artisans from nearby Fort George.[21] In the Western District a small pre-existing blockhouse served in the very early days but the district had to struggle to secure a more adequate structure. Finally in 1799 a contract was let and a frame structure erected which served the district until a stone building was provided in 1870.[22] The situation in the Eastern District was complicated by rivalry between New Johnstown (Cornwall), located in the eastern part of the district, and the growing population in the western part, around what later became Prescott. This was resolved in 1798 with the creation of the Johnstown District and gaols and courthouses were established in both locations.[23]

The districts which suffered most severely from sectional rivalry were London, created in 1798, and Gore, created in 1816. Originally the London District town was Turkey Point, located in Charlotteville Township on Lake Erie. A tiny facility was built there under contract with Lieutenant James Munro, with a courthouse constructed separately. In 1815 the district capital moved north to Vittoria and by 1818 a gaol and courthouse were constructed there, but these facilities were subsequently destroyed by fire. With the population again shifting, London was chosen as the district capital and commissioners were appointed to supervise the construction of a gaol and courthouse. Work began in 1826 on a two-storey frame building with the gaol on the ground floor and the court on the second. Poorly built, with small and inadequate cells, described in one report of the early 1840s as 'loathsome,' it was replaced in 1844 by a large, fortress-like building which was used into the twentieth century.[24]

Following the establishment of the Gore District with its capital at Hamilton, a log and frame structure with dimensions of twenty by thirty feet was promptly erected. Apparently prisoners were housed below ground, debtors on the ground floor, and the court was situated on the second floor. Before long some citizens were petitioning for the legislature to move the district town elsewhere and to construct new and improved facilities. The matter excited intense controversy. It was referred to a select committee of the legislature chaired by Attorney General John Beverley Robinson, which reported in 1827 that the opinions of the district inhabitants were 'much at variance with respect to the measures to be adopted for providing a suitable gaol and court house.' The opposition of citizens of Dundas, Ancaster, and other competing centres was finally defeated and a handsome new building which served as gaol and courthouse opened in Hamilton in 1832.[25]

In 1831 the government decided that no new district could be proclaimed until a gaol and courthouse had been erected.[26] By the date of the Union of 1841, there were twenty districts in Upper Canada and an equal number of gaols, and most districts were on their second or third gaol.

The story of their construction is that of struggling new communities facing uncertain futures and hard-pressed to meet their obligations. No doubt each succeeding gaol was an improvement on its predecessor; yet these new or rebuilt facilities were often ill-designed and poorly constructed, contributing thereby to suffering on the part of prisoners and causing anxiety for gaolers who struggled to prevent escapes and keep their charges healthy. Gaols continued to be built without attention to any particular rehabilitative or even penal purpose. They were erected on practical lines to hold prisoners until their trial or until punishment could be carried out. By the early 1830s increasing numbers of inmates were being retained in gaol for purposes of punishment, but this change in function had little impact on Upper Canadian gaol design. There was no official in the early period whose duty it was to consider and act upon the relationship between prison architecture and penal objectives. The early gaols reflected that fact in their structure and arrangements.

Typically the gaols consisted of several large cells for criminal prisoners, several cells for debtors, and quarters for the gaoler and his family. There was also a hallway or corridor where inmates might congregate during the day to while away time in conversation, sometimes playing cards or other games. No effort was made to supply workshops, and only the most primitive classification separated the sexes from each other and debtors from criminals. Most important, these facilities were not designed on the cellular principle, which would have segregated the prisoners at least at night.[27] Thus they slept several to a cell and behaved as they saw fit.

The other feature that shaped the quality of prison life was the existence in almost every facility of fundamental problems of construction. Sometimes the criminal cells were placed partly underground; many gaols lacked proper heat and ventilation; the air in most gaols was contaminated by the fumes from the primitive facilities for the disposal of human waste. Almost as common was the need to employ irons and similar instruments on dangerous prisoners to prevent them from escaping from ramshackle facilities. Despite often-heroic efforts to carry out the terms of the 1792 and 1830 statutes requiring the erection of gaols and courthouses, the districts proved incapable of providing solid buildings and secure cells. The alternative, frequently resorted to, was to chain dangerous prisoners to the walls and floors.

PATTERNS OF PUNISHMENT

In Upper Canada the early decades of the nineteenth century saw a continuing infliction of the shaming punishments, together with a gradual expansion of imprisonment. Justice William Campbell at the Eastern Circuit Assizes in 1816 demonstrated that by that date gaol imprisonment had moved firmly to the foreground. Of sixteen individuals found guilty of offences, three were sentenced to be hanged and another, guilty of manslaughter, was burned in the hand and discharged. Another man was fined twenty pounds and in the event of non-payment was to be imprisoned until the fine was paid. The remaining eleven were sent to gaol, one receiving a straight six months' sentence, while six were sentenced to gaol and a fine and four to gaol and a whipping. Three of the whippings consisted of thirty-nine lashes; the longest term of imprisonment was six months.[28]

Other circuit reports confirm that the most common sentence delivered at the Upper Canadian Assizes was a combination of gaol with a fine or whipping. A total of 1,119 sentences were handed down at the Assizes between 1792 and 1835, with 83 (7.42 per cent) of those sentenced being female and 1,036 (92.58 per cent) male. Looking first at the 737 sentences handed down to 1830, that is, prior to the establishment of a penitentiary, it is startling to discover that only three individuals received corporal punishment as their sole penalty. One hundred and nine were sentenced to corporal punishment plus gaol; 132 received a fine plus gaol; and 63 were sentenced to just a fine. A few were also sentenced to stand in the pillory, as well as given some combination of gaol and fine. No fewer than 162 (21.98 per cent) offenders were sentenced just to gaol, and this is the largest single total by far. Looked at another way, in the period up to 1830, 403 of 737 offenders, or 54.68 per cent, were sentenced to either gaol alone or gaol plus a fine or whipping. Throughout the Upper Canadian period prior to the establishment of the penitentiary, the gaols provided the most common means of punishing offenders tried at the Assizes (see Table 1.1).

If we break the figures down further, there is a distinctly different pattern before and after 1825. This is especially clear if we look only at the four five-year periods from 1816 to 1835. In the periods 1816–20 and 1821–5, thirty-seven and thirty-nine individuals respectively were sentenced to corporal punishment plus gaol. From 1826 to 1830 the number whipped and gaoled dropped dramatically to fifteen and by the period 1831–5 it was only four. On the other hand, imprisonment in gaol as the sole penalty rose dramatically, moving in five-year segments from 16 to 28 to 87 to 167. For the period 1816–25, 44 persons out of a total of 334, or 13.47 per cent, were sentenced to gaol only; for the years 1826–35 this reached 254 out of a total of 494 persons sentenced, or 51.42 per cent. The

TABLE 1.1

Sentences Handed Down at the Criminal Assizes of Upper Canada, 1792–1835*

Punishment		1790–1810	1811–15	1816–20	1821–25	1826–30	1831–35	Total
Corporal punishment	f							
	m	2	1					3
Corporal punishment and gaol	f	2	1	6	5			12
	m	2	15	31	**34	15	4	***101
'Burning on the hand'	f	1		1	1			1
	m	5	1	1	1			8
Stock/pillory (includes those who also received gaol sentences and fines)	f	2		2	4	1		9
	m	6	6	6	15	6		39
Banishment (includes those who also received gaol sentences and fines)	f	2	1	1	2	1	3	10
	m	13	3	11	31	16	50	124
Imprisonment (local gaol)	f	5	1	1	4	7	15	33
	m	17	8	15	24	80	152	296
Imprisonment (penitentiary)	f						4	4
	m						63	63

TABLE 1.1—(*Concluded*)
Sentences Handed Down at the Criminal Assizes of Upper Canada, 1792–1835*

Punishment		1790–1810	1811–15	1816–20	1821–25	1826–30	1831–35	Total
Imprisonment and fine	f			4		1		5
	m	13	18	29	30	43	52	185
Fine	f				2		1	3
	m	24	12	6	5	14	11	72
Capital punishment	f	1		1	4			6
	m	13	16	17	34	28	24	132
Total	f	11	3	15	21	10	23	83 females
	m	95	80	116	174	202	356	1023 males
								1106 total

Table prepared by Michelle Corbett. Compiled from AO, RC22, Series 134, Assize Minutebook Criminal. Totals do not include those gaoled prior to banishment or those sentenced to pillory who also received combinations of gaol and fines. A computerized study of the Assizes for this period was carried out under the supervision of Dr Robert Fraser (copy in my possession) and this work confirmed in quite a striking fashion the accuracy of the earlier work done by hand by Michelle Corbett. The Assize records themselves are terribly incomplete and we have located scores of cases that simply do not appear in the records. There is serious doubt as to whether the extent of Upper Canadian crime can be reconstructed from them. However, the patterns of punishment reflected in this table would probably not be greatly affected by such omissions.

 *Between 1836 and 1841 virtually all offenders convicted at the Assizes were sentenced to imprisonment

 **Includes one person who was also sentenced to the pillory

 ***Includes eight people who were also to be banished after their sentences increase is dramatic. Imprisonment experienced a gradual increase up to about 1825, and then emerged unequivocally as the dominant form of punishment.

The same figures also demonstrate that the traditional punishments, especially capital punishment, banishment, and the fine, retained a significant place until Kingston Penitentiary was opened. While 167 persons (out of a total of 280 sentenced) were sent to gaol between 1831 and 1835 as their sole punishment, and 52 had fines added to their gaol terms, 12 received only a fine, 24 received a death sentence, and, perhaps surprisingly, 53 were banished.

THE QUARTER SESSIONS

The Quarter Sessions offer a substantially different picture of penal practice. It is in the work of the Sessions that we are able to get closest to the daily life of local communities and to comprehend how minor offenders were dealt with at the local level. The early records of the London and Home District Quarter Sessions, for the periods 1800–9 and 1813–18 for the former and 1800–11 for the latter, demonstrate a pattern of punishments distinctly different from those handed down at the Assizes.

The penalties at the early London and Home District Sessions confirm that the justices did not for the most part believe that the guilty parties deserved harsh punishment. In 87 of the 140 cases dealt with in the London District, the only penalty imposed was a fine. The fines varied in amount from the trivial (one shilling) to the relatively substantial (twenty pounds). In most cases, the fine was small, at most a few pounds, but court costs of an additional pound or two would have added to the burden, particularly in a cash-poor society. Frequently attached to the sentence were the words 'to be imprisoned until paid,' but Attorney General Robinson insisted that such a clause was not legal with respect to misdemeanours.[29] One creative instance of the use of the fine occurred in July 1816 in two cases of selling liquor without a licence. Both men were fined twenty pounds, one half of which was paid to the King, while the other half went to the informer.[30] Another unusual sentence was handed down in an 1818 swindling case. A fine of four dollars plus costs was imposed, the prisoner was to return a watch to the owner, and he was to be imprisoned one week and to remain in prison until the fine and costs were paid.[31] Another interesting monetary device frequently used was to require offenders, especially those convicted of assault, to give recognizances to keep the peace for a specified period, often six months or a year, and to find two other persons willing to serve as sureties for them. In a sense, they were being put on probation.

In such cases the justices were acting creatively to settle community and family disputes and to provide a measure of security for the aggrieved party. In a typical case, on 14 June 1809 John Winegarden was fined 2s.6d. for an assault and battery and was 'recognized for the peace and good behaviour ... towards His Majesty and all his Liege Subjects and in particular towards Philip Sovereign for Six Months.'[32] His recognizance was set at twenty pounds and each of two sureties posted ten pounds. In one 1817 case the magistrates dealt with a 'breach of the peace' between James Hutchinson and his wife Esther by ordering that the couple 'each enter into a Recognizance to keep the Peace and be of good behaviour towards each other ... for twelve months,' the principals in the amount of £100 each and their sureties to post fifty pounds each.[33] When the trial of serious offences was held over to the Assizes, recognizances were commonly taken from all parties, including prosecutors and witnesses, to ensure their appearance.

What is noteworthy about the punishments levied by the London Quarter Sessions is the regular use of small monetary penalties and the reluctance to resort to whipping, the pillory, or imprisonment. As one of their initial acts, in 1800 the London magistrates ordered that a 'movable stock and a whipping post be erected' and paid for out of the first district assessment.[34] But they usually left these unpleasant instruments for the almost exclusive use of the Assize judges, preferring to function as a dispute settlement tribunal rather than to assign punishment. One man was placed in the stocks in 1805 for creating a disturbance in court, but over the entire period there was no other case of stocks or pillory being used. The only case of whipping in these records occurred in 1805 when Peter Combs, guilty of petty larceny, was ordered to receive 'twenty lashes upon his bare back, well laid on, the Sheriff being ordered by the Court, to have the sentence put into immediate execution.'[35]

Nor did the justices favour sending guilty parties to gaol. A few people were 'committed to the custody of the sheriff' until their fines were paid, but almost no one was sent to gaol as punishment. The first such case was that of William Rice, who spoke in contempt of court and was 'committed to prison for two hours' to cool his heels. There was an exceptional case in 1818 in which five men convicted of riot were fined ten pounds each and sentenced to a week in gaol, to be kept there until the fine and costs were paid. For some reason, perhaps because it was planting season, the week's imprisonment was remitted, as was two pounds of each of the fines.[36]

The twelve years covered by the Home District records confirm the London experience. Of the assault cases, it would seem from the punishment imposed (usually a small fine) that none of these was of an aggravated nature. In the Home District Sessions records there is little indication of the lawlessness that caused some citizens in remote and frontier areas to live in fear of their lives. In a few cases, nonetheless, the magistrates did not hesitate to use their authority to protect citizens from their neighbours. In 1810 for example, Ephraim Payson told the court that he lived 'in continual bodily fear' of one Stillwell Willson and asked that Willson be 'bound under recognizance.' The magistrates ordered the fearsome Mr Willson to 'find forthwith good and sufficient security for him to keep the peace towards all His Majesty's subjects for 1 year, himself in £100 and each surety in £50.'[37] When such guarantees were breached, the court moved swiftly. In 1801 when Joseph Harrison deposed that Charles Willcocks had violently assaulted him, 'the said Charles being then under a recognizance to keep the peace,' the court issued a bench warrant and Willcocks soon found himself in gaol.[38]

Of a total of ninety cases, there were fifty-six findings of guilty, thirty-two not guilty verdicts, and two cases were settled by negotiation. Fines were imposed in thirty-nine of the fifty-six guilty cases, on a total of forty-five individuals. Of these, twelve were for one shilling, nine for five shillings, and only eight were for five pounds or more, with the largest fine being twenty pounds. The usual accompaniment of a fine, or indeed of any other penalty, was a requirement that the guilty party find sureties for good behaviour, and in several cases this was the only penalty imposed. Acting pragmatically, the justices were more interested in achieving constructive solutions than in imposing penalties.

Nonetheless, a gaol penalty was levied in nine cases, rather more than in the London District, although still fewer than one per year. Since there seems little to distinguish cases drawing a gaol sentence from those in which only a fine was imposed, we can only speculate as to the explanation for the different sentences. In 1802 Abraham Gordin was sentenced to one month in gaol and fined forty shillings for leaving the service of a brewer without permission.[39] Perhaps Gordin provoked this sentence by refusing in court to work out his employment term, or perhaps the justices were making a point about the seriousness with which they regarded master-servant relations in a society with a notorious labour shortage.

Similarly, brief gaol sentences were imposed in several assault and battery cases, obviously because of special circumstances. In the family violence case of Mary versus Benjamin Runnell, Benjamin was required to find sureties, fifty pounds for himself and twenty-five pounds each from two others, and was sent to gaol for a month.[40] Gaol sentences were also imposed in other assault cases, the usual penalty being one month plus a fine. In 1808 Baptiste Renaud, convicted of petty larceny, was sent to gaol for a day and was required to give security of twenty pounds for himself and to find two sureties each for ten pounds.[41] Why a day in gaol? Was a French Canadian and a stranger receiving harsher treatment than a resident, or was this kindness in lieu of a fine which he had no means of paying? In another unusual case, three men in 1809 were convicted of assault and riot and given fourteen days in gaol plus a fine of ten shillings and costs. And in an offbeat case in 1810, four men were convicted of nuisance and keeping a disorderly house. They were given fourteen days in gaol and ordered 'to remove out of the House called the yellow house, with their things and never return.'[42]

About all that can be said to explain why a few cases attracted gaol sentences is that each must have been unusual in some way, and thus caught the attention of the magistrates. Gaol sentences were used in about 10 per cent of the cases in the Home District and fewer in London. In all cases, the period of confinement was brief. It cost the hard-pressed justices money to lodge someone in the gaol and they preferred to use other sentencing options. In five of the nine cases in the Home District in which a gaol sentence was imposed, it was accompanied by a fine.

There was not a single case of whipping, nor were the pillory, banishment, or transportation ever mentioned. The only reference to whipping was an attempt to frighten a poor woman into returning to service, and she was told it would be remitted if she returned to her master; she refused and was sent to gaol to ponder her decision. In both London and the Home Districts, whipping and the pillory were regarded as best left for the Assize judges, despite the fact that in the Home District, as in London, pillory and stocks were provided for use when necessary. In the Home District it was ordered in July 1811 that a carpenter be employed 'to make Moveable stocks' to confine two persons at once, to be erected where the magistrates 'may think most proper.'[43]

The final point about the criminal business of the Sessions for this early period is that little stigma was attached to those who were convicted. Some of the best-known people in the two districts, including Ryersons, Jarvises, Boultons, Mahlon Burwell, and many others – not excepting magistrates themselves – were hauled up, fined, and required to find sureties for good behaviour. There is no evidence, however, that any of these prominent persons were subjected to the pillory or whipped by order of either Sessions or Assizes. It was unthinkable for one of the 'regularly bred' to be subjected to such an indignity, and no judge, it seems safe to say, would impose a shaming punishment on someone of 'quality.' In this sense, then, the criminal work of both levels of court was fully expressive of the class values of a hierarchically ordered community.

CORPORAL PUNISHMENT AND THE ASSIZES

If the preferred judicial instrument of the magistrates was the fine, the Assize judges resorted to the full range of punishments. Their effectiveness, however, varied over time, with the role of the shaming punishments gradually declining in significance.

Whipping played a prominent role in the old regime penal systems of England and the United States. Michael Ignatieff notes that 17 per cent of all punishments at the Old Bailey in 1775 were whippings; Douglas Greenberg found that for the period up to 1750 in colonial New York 70.9 per cent of those convicted of larceny were whipped.[44] In Upper Canada too this was the preferred punishment for petty thieves. In common law petty larceny, the theft of an item with a value of a shilling or less, was punishable by whipping. But the Assize judges almost never used corporal punishment on its own; instead they combined it with a term in gaol. In the entire period 1792 to 1835, there were only three instances in which corporal punishment stood on its own, while there were 113 cases of corporal punishment and gaol. In twelve of these the person being punished was female. The continued infliction of whippings was used to justify relatively brief gaol sentences. Almost everyone regarded this as desirable, both because of the cost of keeping prisoners in gaol and because of the abominable conditions in most gaols. Fully eighty-seven of the offences punished before 1835 by whipping were larceny, both grand and petty, and the remaining categories of offences which attracted this penalty – horse stealing, sheep stealing, forgery, and assault – were numerically insignificant. Under English law, several other offences, including counterfeiting and vagrancy, were also punishable by whipping but with few exceptions the Upper Canadian judges reserved this punishment for the thieves.

This is somewhat puzzling, since petitions against whipping make it clear that it was greatly feared and presumably an effective deterrent. For the first twenty years of the colony's existence there were only two cases at the Assizes in which whipping was imposed as the sole penalty. Both were heard in 1798 and reveal much about what the authorities intended to achieve by such a punishment. The first occurred at the Home District Assizes, still held at Newark, when two men were convicted of petty larceny. The first received five months in gaol, the other six months, and both were 'to be publicly whipped on the first Monday of the last three months of their imprisonment.' The judge intended to achieve the maximum amount of public benefit by directing that the first whipping be inflicted at the landing of Queenston, the second 'at the fork of the road near James Forsythe's in Stamford, being the place where the larceny was committed,' and the third at the mouth of either the Chippewa or Welland Rivers. William Hawkins, found guilty of grand larceny at the Home District Assizes in the same year, was sentenced to be publicly whipped in the market place at York, and the *Upper Canada Gazette* noted that the whipping had taken place.[45]

In order to attract spectators, times and locations were often announced in court. In Brockville, for example, the offender was to be 'twice publicly whipped in the most conspicuous part of the main street of the village.'[46] Often the punishment was inflicted during Quarter Sessions at the noon hour, either in the marketplace or the courthouse square. Sometimes the place chosen was where the crime was committed or in the offender's home community. In 1815 James Paine, convicted of grand larceny, was sentenced to a month in gaol and two public whippings in Edwardsburgh township; larcenist William Ogden in 1830 received three months in gaol and three public whippings to take place in Prescott.[47]

In the period prior to 1812 the judges resorted to the fine far more frequently than the whip. Whipping and whipping plus gaol were used four times while the fine or fine combined with gaol were used thirty-seven times. It might be suspected that the fine was preferred to whipping because it brought in some revenue. For some reason, in 1812 the judges began to resort to the whip with greater frequency. Twelve people were sentenced to whipping that year and the numbers whipped remained substantial until the early 1830s, when they dropped sharply.[48]

The petitions against whipping manifest a sense of desperation and sometimes panic. William Stoutenburgh in the Home District gaol demonstrated an excess of both these emotions. Sentenced to two months' imprisonment and twenty-five lashes, he appealed the whipping. Chief Justice Powell told the governor's secretary that the man's own application made it 'evident that the whipping is the most exemplary part of the punishment and likely to have the most effect in deterring others.'[49] The terrified Stoutenburgh responded by breaking out of gaol. He then demonstrated remarkable effrontery by submitting another petition justifying his escape. As his father explained, he had received a letter from William claiming that 'the ignominy of being publicly whipped, which would eternally stigmatize not only him but stamp disgrace on his brothers and sisters also ... was the irresistible impulse which induced him to break prison.' If His Excellency the Lieutenant Governor would reconsider the whipping, Stoutenburgh was willing to submit to 'any period of confinement which to your Excellency's wisdom may seem correct.' Judge Boulton, speaking for all his colleagues, indignantly rejected this proposal. He was 'aware of the feelings of parents' whose children were whipped in public, but there would be no judicial bargaining with a culprit like William Stoutenburgh.[50]

The old regime pardoning system was never restricted to appeals against death sentences. Clemency was requested and granted in all sorts of cases. The grounds included age, health, and, significantly, protestations as to the effect of a whipping on a family's pretensions of respectability. In 1816 the chair of the Home District Sessions supported clemency for one prisoner after the gaol doctor certified that he was 'so much reduced in his strength as to be incapable of suffering the infliction of corporal punishment without danger to his life.'[51] Another prisoner, John Willson, who appealed for mercy 'to appease the tender honour of an affectionate wife and child,' avoided whipping on condition that he make restitution for the property he had stolen.[52] In 1822 one Blewett, whose parents lived in Nova Scotia, told Archdeacon John Strachan it would 'break their hearts' were they to discover 'that their child was doomed to an ignominious punishment of being publicly whipped in the public market.' On finding that Blewett had been well behaved in gaol, Judge Campbell supported remission of 'the disgraceful part of the punishment.'[53] That same year from the Kingston gaol William Laird pleaded that he came from a respectable family and asked that the whipping be remitted to save 'him and his from everlasting disgrace.'[54] In 1824 one Hoffman convicted of larceny gained the sympathy of William Campbell who dispensed with 'the usual corporal infliction' because of the prisoner's military service and out of concern for his family.[55] Such remissions suggest that the judges believed that corporal punishments were a deterrent precisely because they did indeed serve to shame the prisoner's entire family.

Apart from the shaming aspect, the infliction of pain was deemed to be a powerful deterrent for all who observed the actual infliction of the strokes. Since the newspapers seldom described these events, it is difficult to assess the extent of the pain or the impact on witnesses. According to one account, the sheriff of the Gore District often eased the suffering by providing the offender with a pint of whisky prior to the infliction.[56] There was no false sense of chivalry to exempt women from the shaming punishments. Although only 7 per cent of those convicted at the Assizes between 1800 and 1835 were female, they were subjected to whipping in a proportion somewhat greater than men. Twelve women were whipped, compared with 104 men, all for either larceny or stealing;[57] women found guilty of morals offences were more likely to be sentenced to the pillory. Nor did youth save offenders from the lash. In 1818 eleven-year-old Mary Smith, convicted of stealing, was sentenced to a month in gaol, during which time she was to be publicly whipped twice in the presence of at least two women. The Upper Canada *Gazette* commented that Mary had been 'instructed and encouraged in [a] nefarious mode of life by her parents.'[58]

The absence of any public outcry against the whipping of women and children suggests that Upper Canada, as a less developed society, was moving more slowly than either England or the United States to reform old-regime punishments. In both these countries in the early nineteenth century there was significant opposition to corporal punishment, which critics suggest was both cruel and ineffective.[59] The sense of anger and resentment that whipping induced was believed to create a desire for revenge, while the public humiliation made it more difficult for the offender to find future employment or to achieve rehabilitation. Michael Ignatieff testified to the influence of such campaigns in noting that by 1805 only 4.5 per cent of sentences handed down at the Assizes and Quarter Sessions in England included corporal punishment.[60] The movement to abolish whipping in Britain, however, was unsuccessful.

In Upper Canada the resort to whipping would not peak until the 1820s. In 1825 John Rolph, who represented Middlesex, presented a bill which would have limited the use of whipping but this was not proceeded with. In 1826 Marshall Spring Bidwell, a lawyer who represented Lennox and Addington, introduced a bill for the total abolition of corporal punishment. Corporal punishment, Bidwell argued, tended to debase the offender rather than to reform him. Attorney General Robinson was sympathetic to Bidwell's measure but he pointed to the absence of viable alternative punishments. Fines, he said, were not a practical penalty as most of those who offended lacked the means to pay them, and the gaols had no means to classify prisoners. He could not support any bill to abolish the lash until a penitentiary was built as an alternative punishment. Bidwell countered by urging the government at least to prohibit the whipping of women, as had been done in England in 1820. His bill, although amended to that effect and also to exclude women from the pillory, was not proceeded with.[61]

Despite the timidity of the legislators, the judges themselves gave practical effect to those suggestions. In 1824 Mary Wiley of Kingston became the last woman, in the Upper Canadian period at least, to be sentenced to whipping by an Assize judge, and the ten lashes she received were to be administered in private.[62] That changes were occurring in social attitudes, which extended to men as well, is demonstrated by the sharp decrease in whipping sentences after 1825. As Michelle Corbett notes, 'when the whipping post and pillory were destroyed by rioters in York in 1834, no attempt was made to replace them.'[63] The law reform of 1833 singled out only two offences, forgery and impersonation, for which whipping might be imposed. With the penitentiary about to be opened, whipping effectively ceased to function as a significant punishment in Upper Canada.

THE STOCKS AND PILLORY

Resort to the stocks or pillory served a similar purpose to whipping, and their use followed a similar pattern. Their effectiveness, however, was even more dependent on societal response. The Assize judges awarded the stocks or pillory as punishment between 1792 and 1835 for forty men and nine women and it is probable that the magistrates were more likely to resort to them than to whipping.[64] Nonetheless there are relatively few appeals against their use and they played a far lesser role in punishing offenders than did the whip. Almost a quarter of those sentenced by the Assizes to be pilloried were women, confirming that they were used on occasion to punish women convicted of morals offences.

Unfortunately few newspaper or other accounts have come to light to convey an impression of what it was like to be pilloried in Upper Canada. One description appeared in *The Farmers' Journal* of 7 October 1829. Two men, William Gray and Edward Keon, were placed in the pillory for one hour:

Keon appeared trembling and penitent, he did not lift his hand nor raise his eyes to gaze on the assembled multitude. Not so with Gray, he came forward with a bold and unblushing effrontery, assisted in moving the iron clasp which bound the planks through which his head and arms were protruded – and looked around and smiled upon the crowd! – his appearance was that of a man with a hard and unfailing heart, incapable of being affected with a sense of shame.

The paper concluded by advocating hard labour in a penitentiary as a more efficacious punishment for criminals of this type. There are no accounts which effectively portray the nature of crowd participation in the pillory ceremony, and certainly no descriptions of individuals suffering death as a result of crowd action, as is known to have occurred in England.[65]

The few appeals of pillory sentences that exist, however, demonstrate that offenders felt a strong repugnance, if not fear, of being put on display in this manner. In 1835 Elliot Buck claimed that his sense of shame if pilloried would be such that 'if I have to stand as a public example I must leave the country and fly to some distant place.' The gaoler at York supported another petition against pillorying, because the prisoner 'has conducted himself in so very becoming a manner while in custody.'[66] After 1830 the Assize judges simply stopped sentencing offenders to the pillory, although the magistrates did not, and as late as 1835 several offenders were pilloried in the Niagara District.[67] In 1841 a statute abolished the use of these instruments, finally ending a method of punishment which had by that date become an anachronism and a curiosity.[68]

BANISHMENT AND TRANSPORTATION

The place of banishment in Upper Canadian punishments has been underestimated, in part because it was denounced in H.C. Thomson's well-known 1831 report as utterly ineffective.[69] Thomson was wrong. Banishment as a punishment is better described as severely flawed. It was greatly feared by those occasional offenders who turned to stealing to provide food or some other necessity for their families, if not by professional criminals. For such ordinary persons, being forced to remove themselves from their homes and sometimes to relocate their families in a foreign jurisdiction often resulted in enormous suffering. This was true as well of those convicted of homicide who received pardons conditional on perpetual banishment. On the other hand, hardened criminals, many of whom frequently operated on both sides of the border, must have been encouraged in their operations by the knowledge that if apprehended they would not be sentenced to long terms of confinement. For other classes of offenders, especially soldiers trying to desert to the United States, the penalty ludicrously embodied the very objective they were endeavouring to accomplish. That is why Samuel Smith, as administrator of the province in 1817, was inclined to recommend transportation rather than banishment for a soldier sentenced to death for highway robbery. Banishment, Smith informed Sir John Sherbrooke, 'substituted here by law, for transportation, would operate as encouragement to Soldiers to commit Crimes in order to be released from the Service.'[70]

Banishment was resorted to more frequently between 1821 and 1835 than in the earlier period. Up to 1820, thirty-one sentences of banishment were handed down by the Assize judges. This increased to fifty for the decade 1821 to 1830 and in the five-year period 1831 to 1835 the number reached fifty-three.[71] Undoubtedly this rapid acceleration represented an effort on the part of the judges to deal with the growing number of serious offences. Evidently the judges believed that banishment had considerable deterrent and punitive effect. Throughout this period to return from banishment was a non-clergyable felony punishable by death, although no instance has come to light of such a sentence being imposed.

Like corporal punishment and the pillory, banishment had several uses and purposes. It was the customary secondary punishment in capital cases in which the offender's life was to be spared but a free pardon was not merited. For such offenders, banishment was a welcome alternative and Thomson was not alone in regarding it as altogether too light a punishment for serious offenders. In pointing on 14 September 1833 to the prevalence of horse stealing, the Niagara *Gleaner* suggested that 'further depredations' must be expected so long as banishment remained the usual penalty. And the Brockville *Recorder* of 11 October 1832 joined an increasingly loud debate over Upper Canadian punishments when it proclaimed a strong preference for transportation over banishment. A year in Van Dieman's Land, it suggested, would disabuse anyone who believed that transportation offered 'a state of ease and advantage.' 'If we are not greatly deceived, the infliction of transportation ought to satisfy even those critics of our criminal code who are most clamorous for efficient secondary punishment.'

Banishment was also used to punish relatively minor offences and in such cases seemed extremely cruel. For example, the well-known Methodist preacher Henry Ryan was sentenced in 1819 to fourteen years' banishment and ordered to quit the country within eight days, all for solemnizing matrimony. Ryan successfully appealed this sentence.[72] By the 1830s there was some evidence that the device was being used more flexibly. One woman fined for keeping a disorderly house was ordered to leave not the province but the neighbourhood; another woman was sentenced to one week's imprisonment and banished five miles beyond the limits of her district; a third convicted of larceny was banished from her district for twelve months. Banishment like other punishments affected the offender's entire family. In December 1834 a woman petitioned from Norwich on behalf of her son who had been sentenced to banishment. She asked His Excellency to 'relieve the solitude of a poor widow' by informing her whether her son might be pardoned. For such persons, banishment remained an awful and much feared penalty.[73]

If the place of banishment as a sentence option is relatively clear, that of transportation is less so. Although formally abolished by the 1800 criminal law statute, it continued to be used from time to time and reappeared legally in the law reform statute of 1833.[74] This measure asserted that for all felonies previously punishable by death and which now ceased to be capital offences, the court could order the offender either to be imprisoned or 'banished or transported for life or for a term of years not less than seven.' The provincial authorities rightly considered transportation to be a far more fearsome deterrent. Attorney General Robert Jameson in an 1834 letter to the lieutenant-governor's office noted that banishment 'offers no parallel in fact to transportation, which involves hard labour.'[75] In 1837 'the crimes for which one could be transported were increased' by 'An Act respecting the Transportation of Convicts' but this did nothing to ease the continuing logistical problems which transportation sentences created.[76] As W.J. Blacklock notes in his study of the Niagara region, one offender, George Martin, petitioned the Sessions in 1834 for release from gaol. 'He had been earlier ordered transported but was still confined in the common gaol 8 months later.' In both Canadas transportation emerged fully as a terrible response to the rebellions of 1837–8.[77]

FINES

Fines were employed far less frequently at the Assizes than by Quarter Sessions. Up to 1835 the Assize judges awarded straight fines in only 75 cases and imprisonment plus a fine in another 190.[78] There were hundreds of cases of use of the fine at the Sessions. The fine was a useful instrument of social control, but it also provided a means of promoting social harmony and attaining reasonable settlements without resort to shaming punishments or gaol. Despite H.C. Thomson's scorn for its use and occasional comments by Assize judges that the lack of pecuniary means of offenders limited its value, the fine remained as a flexible and creative part of the Upper Canadian system, especially for the type of minor offences dealt with at the Sessions.

Yet the potential for abuse was large. A common sentence included

confinement until the fine and costs had been paid and numerous petitions attested that for many this would have meant imprisonment for life.
Since that was never the intention, it is clear that the provision 'until paid'
was deployed as an arbitrary device by the judges and the provincial
executive. The power which this placed in the hands of a few men was
hardly mitigated by evidence that in most cases the authorities acted
humanely. The potential for arbitrary abuse remained a danger to all
Upper Canadians. To his credit, Attorney General Robinson appears to
have been sensitive to this issue and in an opinion handed down in 1824
told the lieutenant-governor's office that 'the Justices when passing sentence in cases of misdemeanor, can not legally order that the Defendant
shall remain in custody, until costs are paid.'[79]

Yet this did not itself touch the matter of unpaid fines. The numerous
petitions of those imprisoned indefinitely for non-payment demonstrate
that the abuse of power was not merely potential. In one notorious case,
the editor of the *Canadian Freeman*, Francis Collins, was prosecuted for
libel after having made remarks about the 'native malignancy' of the
attorney general. Judge Sherwood sentenced Collins to a year in gaol plus
a £50 fine, and he was to remain in gaol until he put up £600 as security
for future good behaviour.[80] These sums were enormous and both the
House of Assembly and the law officers in England condemned the penalty. After serving his full prison term, 'Collins' fine was paid by public
subscription,' and he was released.[81]

The injustice of this provision of the law was revealed innumerable
times over the years in ordinary criminal matters. In 1809 the justices at
Niagara informed the governor that seven individuals who could not pay
their fines would suffer perpetual imprisonment without His Excellency's interposition. They added that had they known this prior to sentencing 'the fines would not have been imposed, or at least greatly
lessened.'[82] In 1810 Judge Powell informed His Excellency that he was
submitting the case of several convicted forgers to his consideration, in
order 'to obviate the possibility of their sentence operating a perpetual
imprisonment in case of inability to pay the fine imposed on them.' Sensitive to their economic status, he urged that the part of the sentence imposing imprisonment be replaced by security for good behaviour.[83] In 1810
the Niagara District magistrates expressed concern about four forgers
who had been fined, gaoled, and pilloried. Their term of imprisonment
had expired some time previously but they remained behind bars
because of their inability to pay the fine. Emphasizing that the district
found this ongoing detention to be expensive, the magistrates recom-

mended that the prisoners be released 'to prevent any attempt they might make to break gaol.'[84] However extraordinary this may seem at first glance, it was logical to expect that men confined indefinitely would attempt such a break, probably with the assistance of indignant friends and family members.

In many cases, remission of the fine was granted on condition of banishment for a period of time. Another solution was indicated in the 1821 case of Thomas Davison. According to the fiat of Attorney General Robinson, 'Davison being wholly unable at present to pay the said fine we have been pleased to assent that upon his entering into recognizance with sufficient sureties for the payment of the said fine to us within one year, he should be discharged from custody.'[85] Another fiat from Robinson addressed the case of the unfortunate William Stoutenburgh, who had been fined twenty pounds in addition to his other punishments and who protested he could not pay. 'Since he is wholly unable to do so, he is to be released on providing sufficient sureties to pay within the calendar month.'[86] Even when the judges had a bad opinion of the convict, they sometimes showed flexibility, as did Judge Powell in another case when he asserted that he could 'see much good from the remission of that part of the imprisonment for the fine, which shall ever hang over him if he is discharged from confinement only.'[87] William Lyon Mackenzie took a similar position in 1834 in the case of a poor tradesman who had already lost the best part of his work year by being imprisoned for a month. To insist on payment of the fine after release 'might abridge his family of many comforts, and perhaps ruin, or greatly discourage himself in time to come.'[88] In 1835, in the case of an aggravated assault in the Gore district, the magistrates assisted the prisoner by directing that the District take over payment of the costs and asked the governor to remit the fine.[89] That same year, the chairman of the Gore Quarter Sessions expressed concern that several prisoners remained in gaol beyond the expiry of their sentence only because they were poor. 'They have all remained over the period sentenced one month – some two months – and some even more.' Such detention, the magistrate pointed out, made 'their poverty if not a crime, at least a very serious inconvenience to them.'[90]

CAPITAL PUNISHMENT

Statistical evidence confirms Robert Fraser's assertion that the gallows did not cast a long shadow in Upper Canada. Chief Justice Robinson's 1833 estimate that roughly a person a year had been executed throughout the colony's history seems about right. In the absence of a central registry of executions it is impossible to be certain, but preliminary research in Assize records and in the Upper Canada sundries and the press has turned up 392 persons sentenced to death between 1792 and 1869, when public executions were abolished, 92 of whom were actually executed. Out of the 392, 115 were convicted of homicide, usually murder. Of this group, 58 were executed and 57 had their sentence commuted, usually to banishment for life or, after 1835, to a life sentence in the penitentiary.[91] Not only were few people hanged, but almost no one was executed for property offences. Except for the state trials of 1814 and 1837–8, only seven persons were executed for crimes other than murder. Although rape remained a capital offence even after the law reforms of 1833 and 1841, apparently only one man was executed for this offence, Robert McIntyre, who led a brutal gang rape in 1820.[92] Infanticide was not a crime which led to execution in Upper Canada, even though a punitive English statute of 1624 remained in effect in the colony until replaced by a more humane provincial statute in 1831.[93] As the evidence presented in Table 1.2 demonstrates, there was a remarkably low rate of persons charged with homicide for a frontier community which some historians have characterized as lawless and violent.

Nonetheless, as in England, Upper Canada retained both capital punishment and public executions until 1869, and about half of those convicted of homicide became unwilling actors in the fearsome rites of execution. Large crowds gathered to observe the condemned person deliver what was expected to be a carefully rehearsed scaffold speech relating how he or she had reached the awful moment by living a life of idleness and dissolution, neglecting religion, ignoring parental guidance, and progressing inexorably from minor transgressions to capital offence. Such a performance in this theatre of guilt was intended to demonstrate the susceptibility of all citizens to evil and to emphasize the need to conform to the dictates of morality to avoid a similar fate. The admission of guilt, the conversion to religion – symbolized by the cleryman praying on the scaffold beside the condemned – and the plea for forgiveness constituted the dramaturgy of death. All was reinforced by the horror of the occasion and the pain and suffering of the lead performer, who experienced death by agonizing suffocation.

The execution was supervised by the sheriff, who employed a hangman, usually lacking in experience, and not even the introduction of the long drop in the late 1830s prevented some horrid spectacles of botched executions and sustained suffering. In London in 1830 during the hang-

TABLE 1.2
Persons Charged with Homicide:
Estimated Rate per 100,000 Population,
1806–1849 (Selected Years)*

Year	Provincial population	Number of murder charges	Rate per 100,000
1806 K	70,700	2	2.8
1811 K	77,000	2	2.6
1814 K	95,000	3*	3.2
1824	150,066	3	2.0
1825	157,923	3	1.9
1826 E	166,379	2	1.2
1827	177,174	4	2.2
1828 E	186,488	4	2.1
1829 E	197,815	4	2.0
1830 E	213,156	5	2.3
1831	236,702	6	2.5
1832 E	263,554	1	0.4
1833 E	295,359	4	1.3
1834	321,145	4	1.2
1835 E	347,099	5	1.4
1836	374,099	3	0.8
1837 E	390,929	6	1.5
1838	399,422	14	3.5
1839	409,048	12	2.9
1840	432,159	5	1.6
1841	455,688	12	2.6
1842	487,053	23	4.7
1843 E	526,857	15	2.8
1844	566,661	4	0.7
1845	606,465	3	0.5
1846	646,269	6	0.9
1847 E	686,073	9	1.3
1848	725,879	5	0.6

Table prepared by John Choules. Derived from *Court of King's (Queen's) Bench Assize Minutebooks*, 1811–48; the 1824, 1825, 1827, 1831, 1834, 1836, 1838, 1839, 1840, 1841, 1842, and 1848 censuses of Upper Canada in *Censuses of Canada, 1665–1871* vol. iv (Ottawa 1876); and population estimates for 1806, 1811, and 1814 (marked by a 'K') in Warren E. Kalbach and Wayne W. McVey, *The Demographic Bases of Canadian Society* (Toronto 1971), 24 and 25. Population estimates for other years (designated by an 'E') are extrapolation of missing data by dividing the number of missing years by the population growth.
*Because of disruptions caused by the War of 1812 some of the 1814 murder trials were postponed until 1815. Further research will uncover additional cases, but the above rate is a reasonably accurate estimate.

ing of Cornelius Burley, the rope broke and the terrified man tumbled to the ground and had to await the return of the sheriff who went off to purchase a new, hopefully stronger, cord. At the execution of Michael Vincent in Hamilton in 1828, the knot slipped under his chin and he struggled desperately for fifteen minutes. The newspapers reported the pain and contortions of these final agonies. In 1835 the Sandwich *Western District Advertiser* described how Richard Bird writhed in agony for nine minutes. Edward Kennan, executed in Milton in 1862, 'struggled hard for a few minutes and managed to get a toe hold on the trap door of the scaffold which he shook violently.'[94]

Did the Upper Canadian authorities truly believe that these execution rites served to deter potential murderers? Were such scenes appropriate for a society in which murder was so rare an occurrence? In one sense the public execution found its legitimacy as the ultimate shaming punishment. This was clear, for example, in an 1817 petition of non-commissioned officers and soldiers on behalf of a comrade sentenced to death for highway robbery. The administrator of the province, Samuel Smith, informed Sir John Sherbrooke that the soldiers desperately wanted to avoid the disgrace which would attach to the regiment from a public execution, and he reported that they begged the imposition of any other penalty, 'however severe.' Then Smith added the telling comment that 'the public sentiment revolts at capital punishment in this young colony unless for very great atrocity.'[95]

The judges themselves were cautious about criticizing what was after all the ultimate weapon in their judicial arsenal. In pronouncing the death sentence, they invariably mixed expressions of personal anguish with the sternest of admonitions about the horror of the crime and the justice of the sentence. In sentencing William Kain to death in 1830, Chief Justice Robinson shared his distress with those present in the courtroom: 'Short time as I have presided in this office, not once or twice has it become my unpleasant task to discharge this most painful part of my judicial duty.' In so doing he could only 'hope to God that the dreadful example which the law makes for the crime of murder should have its due effect.' The purpose of the law, said Robinson, was to punish, and it 'will punish, as long as necessary, until men of violence are restrained.' In sentencing Kain, the chief justice employed the language of carefully calibrated terror:

Unhappy man – you have brought yourself by your shameful conduct to the brink of eternity. I cannot say to spare you for the grave, for the laws of your country deny sepulchre to those standing in your situation. By your own heinous, vicious, vindictive and blood-thirsty conduct, you oblige those of the community under which you live, and by whom you have been hitherto protected – to cut short your earthly existence in a few days.[96]

Although an 1826 statute made it unnecessary to pronounce sentence in open court on those who were likely subjects for a pardon, the 1833 law reform statute reaffirmed the value of such pronouncements. The sentence, it stated, should express 'not only the usual judgment of death, but also the time appointed for the execution thereof, and the mark of infamy hereby directed for such offenders, in order to impress a just horror in the mind of the offender, and in the minds of such as shall be present.' As an additional deterrent, the statute directed that the murderer's body be delivered 'to a Surgeon, for the purpose of being dissected and anatomized.'[97] The condemned person was forthwith returned to gaol, ironed to the floor, fed bread and water only, and after a few days brought out to face the gawking crowd and to play out his final moments before, in the expressive language of the day, being 'launched into eternity.'

Of the 115 persons convicted of murder between 1800 and 1869, only 58 were executed. The question therefore arises as to why the province retained the gruesome spectacle of the public execution until 1869. In the United States the movement to abolish public executions had made considerable progress by the 1840s. By that time executions in most northern states were carried out within the confines of a gaol or prison and three states, Michigan, Rhode Island, and Wisconsin, abolished capital punishment entirely.[98]

In Canada, few questioned the value of the existing system. One exception was the Kingston *Chronicle*, a paper which often commented on criminal justice issues. In an 1833 editorial the *Chronicle* insisted that 'the hundreds of dying speeches which have fallen from the lips of ill-fated men, while they have seldom caused abhorrence of the crime, have generally created a sympathy' with the offender. Why, asked the *Chronicle*, should a murderer be provided with an opportunity to glorify himself? 'No sooner is the penalty of the law carried into effect ... than the culprit becomes a brilliant but unfortunate hero. His murders are looked upon as little else than feats of chivalry.' Worse still, his account of his criminal career 'is read and admired by the sympathetic and aspiring youth' and sometimes adopted as a model for future action. The impressionable young man is given to understand that it was possible to live a life of undeviating crime and when the moment of reckoning came, 'he dies the object of universal sympathy and heir to immortality.'[99]

The manner in which religious ministrations held out the hope of life everlasting was a sore point with some. Many condemned persons, said the *Chronicle*, seemed so taken up with the redeemer's message that they failed to demonstrate the requisite fear and trembling. 'Has it ever occurred to the servants of the church who officiate at public executions that this powerful sanctifying of a murderer whose hands are reeking with the blood of his victim, must tend to impair the force of religious and moral obligation?' It was not strange then, the newspaper concluded, 'that a life of crime loses its terrors, whenever it is rewarded with such a blissful termination, and such rich hopes of future happiness.'

By the 1840s another growing concern was the behaviour of the spectators. Most contemporary accounts of the audiences found them in a festive mood, drinking and singing, with vendors selling their wares, pickpockets plying their trade, and women and children jostling with the men to gain the best view of the final agonies. Press reports of these events often condemned the crowd for its prurient interest and holiday spirit. In 1847 the Anglican journal the *Church* complained that one would have thought the crowd was attending a fair or a horse race, 'instead of the entrance of two poor creatures into the dark valley.' The *Church* believed the effect must be to 'blunt and petrify the finer feelings' and 'to create a fierce thirst for whatever was savage and revolting. It would act as a gluttonous draught to the hereto unfleshed tiger.' In short, the tendency of public executions was 'to degrade and brutalize the mind.'[100] Following the execution in Toronto of Julia Murdoch in 1837, the *Christian Guardian* found it revolting to discover so many women among the spectators. By the late 1850s George Brown's *Globe* was one of several secular papers condemning 'the morbid curiosity' of those who attended such events.[101]

Although no direct evidence has come to light, many of the judges must have had reservations about the execution spectacle. Nonetheless, no concerted campaign developed to abolish these unedifying performances until the late 1840s and then in the context only of a brief spurt of public sentiment against capital punishment itself. In a meeting in Montreal in January 1849 speakers denounced both. Several communities in Canada West forwarded petitions to the governor general modelled on the Montreal document, and a few newspapers published editorials to the same effect.[102] The most significant political initiative came in 1850 when William Buell Richards, a lawyer and member on the government side of the House, presented a bill to hold all executions at Kingston Penitentiary. Richards also advocated the system adopted in Maine whereby no execution could take place until one year after the date of the sentence and then only on the basis of a new warrant from the executive. Richards's bill did not emerge out of committee.[103]

A commitment to tradition along with lethargy probably accounts for the continuation of public executions. There seems to have been no strong feeling among the public about the matter and a decision in Britain in 1856 to continue public executions appears to have brought a temporary end to any possibilities at the political level. When the British in 1868 passed a statute requiring executions to take place behind prison walls, Canada followed suit the following year. The last public execution in Canada was not that of the assassin of D'Arcy McGee, but that of Nicholas Melady, who was hanged in Goderich, Ontario, in December 1869 for the murder of his parents. As the Toronto *Globe* described it, 'about two hundred people stood in the cold with a half satisfied, half disgusted look, on the last public hanging which will be witnessed in Ontario.'[104] In a real sense, this marked the end of a system in which governments and people cooperated together in carrying out punishments intended to shame or terrify.

THE MEANING OF A GAOL SENTENCE

There was a steady increase throughout the Upper Canadian period in numbers sentenced to gaol by the Assize judges. As we have seen, even in the period prior to the opening of the penitentiary, the judges were turning to imprisonment, either alone or in combination with some other sanction, as their principal secondary punishment. This fact helps explain why the judges emerged in this period as the loudest advocates of gaol reform.

A gaol sentence in the Upper Canadian period continued to lack the stigma which would later attach to a long term in the penitentiary. Sentences were brief, the prisoner was not removed from his own community, and the gaols held a congregate population including debtors, the insane, and the needy. Nonetheless the populace understood, as did the judges, that even a brief period in the local gaol was a serious punishment which might well mean financial ruin for the prisoner and the prisoner's family and which could also undermine the individual's health and break his spirit. For these several reasons the judges never felt the need to award long sentences. This was the saving grace of a system of confinement which had little else to recommend it.

Travelling about the province to preside over the Assizes, coming into close contact with all types of people and conditions, the judges understood the implications of even brief gaol confinement. The demands of hewing out a farm, planting and harvesting a crop, and surviving long, cruel winters meant that the labour of all family members was critical for survival. The absence for a few weeks – or sometimes even days – of the adult male often brought family disaster, as the petitions of numerous prisoners testified. From the Gore gaol in 1816 a prisoner lamented that 'there is not a sufficient succour or nourishment for my poor bereft family, which adds to my other troubles more than I can bear.'[105] Another prisoner enduring a one-month sentence begged for his release after eleven days because 'his innocent children are the real sufferers, in as much as they are deprived of the means of living when deprived of his industry.'[106] Many who sent these poignant appeals seemed desperate. Confined in the Brockville gaol for six months, William Orr begged for clemency because 'as a husband and father his sufferings since his confinement have been indescribable, almost too much for human nature to bear.' This was the case not so much because of his own hardships but because he had 'always before his eyes the deplorable situation of his suffering wife and helpless children.'[107] With no welfare cushion or prisoners' aid society, and where existence for many was a struggle under normal circumstances, incarceration could bring severe emotional hardship. These included feelings of deep guilt and mental anguish for the suffering experienced by innocent family members.

Even when friends, private charities, or understanding officials provided succour, the families of prisoners were placed in painful and humiliating situations. Desperate need often induced victims of family violence to plead for the early release of brutal husbands. Anne O'Bryon, beaten by her husband while he was in a drunken stupor, was 'willing to forgive him the assault upon me' because 'I have no means of subsistence for myself during his confinement.'[108] In 1834 Toronto's mayor, William Lyon Mackenzie, responded to the petition of John Bedford by denying that Bedford's wife was destitute. 'The day I put him in prison I sent her two dollars. A few days ago I sent again for her, gave her another two, and told her that if she suffered for want she was to come again.' Bedford had been imprisoned for 'a cruel and most wanton and unprovoked assault upon his wife.' By pleading for release after a brief confinement he may well have been cynically exploiting his wife's unhappy circumstances to avoid serving the rest of his sentence. In this case the petition failed and Mrs Bedford had some reason to be content with the decision.[109]

The provision of a few dollars from a charity fund did not always address the financial consequences of even a few weeks in gaol. People living from day to day faced economic disaster. On 10 September 1835, during a harvest, Moses Pattison was sentenced to three weeks in gaol for participating in a brawl. Appealing on the grounds that his crops would be lost and that the loss of his farm was threatened, he was released immediately.[110] In 1821 a widow in Vaughan Township begged for the release of her son-in-law. She had no other means 'to have her harvest saved,' the rest of the family being small children.[111] In these circumstances the judges made allowances for the fact that even brief sentences constituted severe punishment.

They also knew that the suffering of the prisoners was increased immeasurably by the appalling conditions in most gaols. In the early days, such conditions might be attributed to the difficulties faced by small populations in finding the money needed to erect gaols and courthouses. But similar conditions continued to exist throughout the entire Upper Canadian period, and they were exacerbated by increasing populations, often composed of indigent immigrants, and larger numbers sentenced to confinement. The demands of the districts for services of all kinds were great and revenues small, and it is not surprising that gaol conditions remained crude. Some districts into the 1830s were spending no less than about 20 per cent of their total revenues on the gaols and it must have seemed unthinkable to many ratepayers to even consider spending more when roads and schools and other social services were suffering similar privations.[112] After all, these relatively poor pioneer communities were expending a far larger proportion of their revenues on gaols than twentieth-century Canadian society.

These hardships were attested to in literally hundreds of reports, letters, and petitions. In 1811, for example, the sheriff of the Home District complained to the chairman of Quarter Sessions that the prisoners 'suffer much from cold and damp, there being no means of communicating heat from the chimnies' nor were there any bedsteads 'to raise the straw from the floors.' Complaints about the Home and Gore District gaols were voluminous and no gaol in the province was exempted from a stream of plaintive and sometimes desperate criticism. The situation of female prisoners was often particularly desperate. In November 1823 Catherine Sharply in the Brockville gaol complained that she had been confined for several weeks in a fourteen-foot cell with four men 'where she still languishes in irreligious indecency, misery and horror.' Without assets or friends, and unable to get bail, she was awaiting trial.[113]

Many prisoners feared that their health was being destroyed by cold, damp, heat, and virtual starvation. In the Midland gaol in 1826 a prisoner reported that for a year no one had assisted him with either food or garments, 'excepting the gaol allowance' and he was 'almost exhausted for want of more substantial diet.'[114] From the Gore gaol in 1835 John Wirick complained that his health was greatly impaired from long confinement 'in a cold and damp cell' and that he 'could not survive much longer under the excruciating pain [he] then felt.'[115]

The suffering brought by a gaol sentence was further increased for prisoners considered dangerous and for those awaiting trial on capital charges. This was because prisoners were always breaking out and the only way to ensure that the prisoner would actually be there to face trial was to iron him to the floor or wall. Although prisoners suffered horribly from ironing, even this did not always work and in the classic tradition some prisoners managed to file through or otherwise remove their fetters. The case of Edward McSwiney, a sergeant in the Leeds militia convicted of murder in 1813, suggests other possibilities of escape. McSwiney had been fettered to the floor of the Johnstown District gaol when American troops liberated the prisoners from the Elizabethtown gaol. According to McSwiney's petition, he had spurned the thought of becoming 'a fugitive ... amongst enemies of his King and Country.' The gaoler was unimpressed. He reported that 'it was impossible for him to make his escape unless rescued as he is kept in Irons and chained.' Although Judge Campbell could find no legal reason to support a pardon, McSwiney's shrewd appeal on the basis of patriotism succeeded. The case went to Britain and a pardon was recommended by the Prince Regent and the Privy Council.[116]

In 1815 a Dr Wood, a Canadian equivalent of the notorious English escape artist Jack Sheppard, made off for the third time from the Kingston gaol, along with several other prisoners. One distraught official reported that the use of irons had required Wood to 'break the bolt of about an inch long and an inch and a half in diameter and must have caused a great deal of noise.' He suspected that 'their escape was connived at' because the prisoners 'broke through a thick outer wall without being heard.'[117] The use of irons did not always guarantee secure detention. In 1823 the justices for the Eastern District told His Excellency the governor that the Cornwall gaol had for many years been 'in so insecure a state that it is incapable of detaining within its walls either criminals or debtors.' Even the use of irons 'from the practicability of conveying tools through the gaol are no security.'[118]

While gaol officers might sympathize with some of their charges, they also lived in fear of them. In several disticts gaolers and sheriffs expressed grave concern that they might be overwhelmed and murdered by prisoners assisted by accomplices who remained at large. In the pre-war period, Sheriff Thomas Merritt of Niagara was continually alerting the authorities in York to the threat posed by desperate prisoners with friends on both sides of the border. In 1809 he told Samuel Street, the chairman of Quarter Sessions, that the gaol was 'crowded with prisoners,' many of whom were charged with forgery, an activity often organized from the United States. Merritt feared that confederates of the prisoners would storm the building and murder the gaoler. The gaol, he warned, was insecure and its timber decayed. Merritt refused to be 'responsible for the safekeeping of the prisoners.' It must 'be obvious to the Bench,' he lamented, 'that the sheriff with his ordinary means has not the power of effectually guarding the prisoners.' Samuel Street responded by asking the lieutenant-governor to order a special commission of oyer and terminer to deliver the gaol (i.e., try and sentence the prisoners) because of the threat posed by 'the daring gang of desperadoes' operating in the area.[119] This exchange highlighted the fear of many magistrates that the decayed state of the gaols and the facility with which escapes were effected would undermine respect for the law.

Facing desperate situations, local justices often appealed for a military guard. In 1810 the clerk of the peace at York made such a request 'as there are several prisoners confined therein, whom the Magistrates are afraid will make their escapes.'[120] With troops garrisoned in the principal towns, requests for military aid could be met with little cost or inconvenience but they were received with a marked lack of enthusiasm. With the St Lawrence river frontier as open to cross-border depredations as Niagara, the chairman of the Quarter Sessions at Cornwall expressed alarm that 'several threats and attempts' had been made by persons on both sides of the border 'to break the gaol of the District and liberate a number of prisoners.'[121] In this case no troops were readily available, so the chairman asked for a special session of oyer and terminer. Even communities far from the border lived in fear of the gaol officers being overwhelmed. In 1821 the sheriff at York told the governor's secretary there was reason to believe an attempt would be made 'by some persons unknown' to free the notorious William Stoutenburg confined on a capital charge. He asked for 'a sentinel at the gaol, during the night time, till after the approaching assizes were over.'[122] Here was another reason why judges allowed only a few days to pass between the imposition of a capital sentence and execution.

Since the gaols often held soldiers, the military authorities had a considerable stake in the system. The gaol at Kingston was especially important to the military and many soldiers were imprisoned there for drunkenness and brawling and some for the serious offence of desertion. The Kingston gaol was one of the most secure in the province and for that reason dangerous prisoners were sometimes transferred there from other districts. Ironically, four such desperadoes escaped in 1815 while being transferred to Kingston from the York gaol.[123] But Kingston itself was not immune from the escape virus. In April 1815 three prisoners escaped and two months later so did another four. Major General F.F. Robinson, reporting in 1815 to the lieutenant-governor, blamed the laxity of gaol officials and magistrates. Faced with so many soldiers deserting to the United States and with others enticing soldiers to desert, he warned that the situation was critical. 'It is with some difficulty,' he told the lieutenant-governor, that he was able to get such individuals committed even upon the clearest deposition, 'owing to timidity in the Magistrates.' For the military, the sad state of the gaol was contributing to the collapse of military authority. 'If the escape of the delinquents is passed over in silence, one half of our men will be enticed from us in the course of the summer.'[124]

Not even the exigencies of the military led to a solution of the problem. Debtors, persons awaiting trial, and those expecting an early execution continued to hack, cut, climb, and sometimes merely walk away from these ramshackle facilities. The courts did what little they could to assert the authority of the state. When the Western District gaoler was prosecuted and fined in 1819 following a 'negligent escape,' William Campbell showed no sympathy for the impecunious official's request for a remission of the fine. Campbell reported to the governor that the prisoners, although kept six in a cell, had not been fettered, and one prisoner had testified that only once in three weeks had the gaoler inspected the cell, and that 'prisoners' victuals was always handed to them through a small hole in the door.' Yet in the Home District, as in every other gaol in the colony, funds simply were not available to build and staff secure facilities. As late as April 1836, the Home District grand jury reported that since July 1832 no fewer than thirty-one prisoners had escaped.[125] In such circumstances gaol officers had no alternative but to resort to methods that caused suffering and distress.

The prisoners were frantic to escape the life-threatening physical conditions of local prisons; desperate conditions created desperate men. In 1819 a prisoner testifying before Judge Campbell following the escape of several fellow-prisoners claimed that they had been quite prepared to kill the gaoler and the sheriff.[126] Reporting in 1830 on an escape attempt at York, Sheriff Jarvis drew a picture of a fearful scene of a threatened mass uprising. Bludgeons had been forged from fuel and wood and a large bolt wrenched from the wall. The intent was 'to murder the turnkey if necessary.' The cell wall was poorly built and easily breached and the magistrates had rejected Jarvis's request to build a perimeter wall because there were no available funds. Again Jarvis, supported by the magistrates, pleaded for a military guard. Although aware of the reluctance 'to impose a duty upon the military which comes more within the province of the civil power,' he emphasized that the situation was critical. The gaol contained individuals charged with 'manslaughter, horse stealing, larcenies, perjury etc. who rather than meet their trial would not hesitate to add murder to the number of crimes.' To Jarvis's dismay the gaoler, fearing for his life and that of those assisting him, had resigned.[127]

Similar accounts from just about every district confirmed that while the gaols at times functioned as relatively friendly neighbourhood institutions harbouring a diverse and congregate population, their character could change swiftly to become threatening and even explosive. The gaol in Niagara exemplified the frequently desperate situation of the local officers. In June 1829 Sheriff Leonard appeared panic-stricken to learn that the military guard 'which for two years past has been mounted at the gaol' was soon to be withdrawn. He reminded His Excellency that the period before military assistance had been extended had witnessed numerous escapes 'which from the frontier situation and insecurity of the Gaol, were unavoidable.' Worse yet, 'in some instances the Gaoler was overpowered and severely injured by the prisoners in the act of escaping.' He pointed to 'the immediate vicinity of the American frontier' and to the 'desperate and lowly character' of much of the population, employed on public works. Like other sheriffs before him, Leonard abjured responsibility, 'unless the guard is continued.' A sympathetic Sir John Colborne minuted on the correspondence that he had no objection to Leonard's request, yet he noted that the same considerations might be advanced by other districts. While Colborne hesitated, the guard was withdrawn. That very evening, Leonard told the governor, 'four desperate fellows made their escape.' 'I trust,' he concluded with a flourish, 'His Excellency will now see the necessity of restoring the Guard.'

Apparently Colborne did this, but the following year the guard was again withdrawn and Leonard expressed fear for the lives of his officers. A few years later, in 1834, the Niagara authorities reported on the crowded state of the gaol due to the recent apprehension of a number of persons engaged in forging bank-notes: 'from the desperate character of some of those prisoners who have already broken gaol several times, and above all from the insufficiency of the gaol itself, it is much to be feared' that they would succeed in escaping 'unless we have the assistance of a military guard.' Colborne ordered such a guard to be posted so long as the forgers were confined.[128]

Such were the circumstances of Upper Canadian gaols throughout the Upper Canadian years. In sentencing offenders, the judges were alert to these often abominable conditions. They understood that it would be cruel and probably futile to sentence prisoners to long periods in such facilities. Yet the judges clearly wished to deploy imprisonment as a sentencing alternative in preference to the traditional shaming punishments. In this, then, as in other areas, the criminal justice system by the mid-1830s was feeling increasing strains and stood in need of substantial reform and modernization.

2

The Gaol and the Community

GAOLS AS WELFARE FACILITIES

Upper Canadian gaols were not used solely to house convicted criminals. Many of the inmates were harmless citizens confined because they were old, sick, poor, or in debt. Imprisonment emerged in the late 1820s and the 1830s as the colony's principal secondary punishment, but the goals also became increasingly important as congregate facilities serving a wide array of social needs. The districts had been slow to take advantage of the 1810 statute designating gaols as houses of correction. With a burgeoning population and the spread of social problems, it was less feasible and more expensive to provide assistance for the disadvantaged through outdoor relief. As Margaret Angus and David Murray have demonstrated, by the early 1820s the districts were endeavouring to reduce expenditures for social assistance.[1] Sometimes this took the form of cutting down or eliminating the pauper list; sometimes it meant pushing social responsibilities onto the townships, which were even less equipped to shoulder the burden. The socially disadvantaged were often lodged in the local gaols by default. Although of doubtful legality and even more dubious propriety, the transformation of the gaols into all-purpose community facilities would prove to be of enduring significance in Ontario. Indeed, this use of the gaol went far to shape its character, and helped thereby to determine that hardened criminals deemed to require some harsher form of punishment would be sent elsewhere. The consequencences of this social differentiation had a significant long-term impact on both the province's welfare programs and its penal policies.

Some of the difficulties facing the magistrates during this process were highlighted in the Niagara District by the sad case of Mary Buggins. One day in 1836 several citizens went to magistrate John Alma to ask him, as he put it, to remove Buggins 'from one of the public streets of the town, where it appeared she was in a dying state.' The previous night she had collapsed, drunk and almost nude. There were few in the town, Alma continued, who 'did not feel for the unfortunate creature,' notwithstanding 'her well known depraved character, as well as her indecent, immoral, and truly disgusting appearance.' At the same time, no one could be 'induced to let her into his house.' A doctor concluded Buggins would be dead in a few hours unless given assistance, and he urged Alma to place her in gaol as a vagrant. Some of his fellow magistrates opposed this course of action, fearing contagious disease, but Alma produced a certificate from the doctor to the effect that Buggins's condition was 'nothing more than what might be expected' from poverty and filth, and he committed her to gaol as 'a most notorious prostitute.' Buggins was permitted to remain there only for a day or two, however, after which four other magistrates 'turned her out, in the same state of nakedness' as when she was committed.[2]

THE INSANE

Throughout the nineteenth century, many Ontarians were saved from death or misery in the streets by being confined in the gaols. One such group was the insane. For several decades the mentally unbalanced had occasionally been lodged in the local gaols in an informal way, without legal authority. Early in 1830, following a 'petition of the Prisoners in York Gaol,' this practice was challenged. A committee of the legislature chaired by W.L. Mackenzie investigated and discovered that three insane women were locked in the basement. One of the debtors complained that 'their incessant howlings and groans were annoying in the extreme,' while the committee itself found that 'the smell from the dungeon in which these poor lunatics' were locked was 'most disagreeable.' Their confinement, concluded the committee, 'is severe beyond that of the most hardened criminal.' The Home District Quarter Sessions asked that the practice be ended, and that 'some place may be provided as an asylum for lunatics, and funds to maintain the same.' But the Assembly not only refused to assume this responsibility, it passed an Act, applicable only to the Home District, authorizing the magistrates to use the gaol 'to provide for the relief of insane destitute persons in that District.'[3]

This statute led to increased numbers of mentally ill people being confined in gaol. Soon the magistrates were complaining that the Home District was becoming a dumping ground for 'persons afflicted with this malady from other parts of the province, in which no district provision is made.' Protesting that the situation was inconvenient and unsafe, they again asked for the establishment of a general asylum. In 1833 Attorney General Robert Jameson presented a bill 'for procuring plans and estimates for an asylum for insane persons.' But the legislature instead extended the terms of the 1830 statute to allow all districts to use their gaols to house the insane.[4] The effect of this unfortunate measure was soon apparent, and petitions and complaints poured in from across the province. In 1835, for example, the grand jurors of the Johnstown District reported on one Evans, confined as insane. Describing his case as 'most deplorable,' they urged the justices to place Evans in an apartment separate from the criminals, or to take other means to alleviate his situation. That same year the York magistrates reported that £216 out of a total expenditure on the gaol of £516 had been incurred to lodge four insane persons.[5]

Tom Brown has argued that only John Macaulay of the Midland Sessions seemed alive to the fact that 'the greatest "inconvenience" was for the insane themselves.' Macaulay rightly observed that 'our common gaols do not afford the requisite accommodation for the successful treatment of the insane persons.'[6] But this was the view of magistrates and other officials across the province. Understandably worried about the impact of the presence of insane persons on gaol administration, they were equally concerned with the suffering of the mentally ill.

By the mid-1830s there was a heightened dissatisfaction with the 1833 legislation. Gaolers, sheriffs, grand juries, and judges all urged the province to remedy the situation. One powerful critic was Judge James B. Macaulay. Following the Assizes in 1836 on the Eastern circuit, Macaulay reported that he had 'found maniacs confined, as the only means of restraining them from acts of violence,' in each district gaol. Macaulay asserted that it was 'manifest that a common gaol is not the place in which persons so unhappily afflicted ought to be confined.' He believed the opinion was 'very generally entertained' that a lunatic asylum was 'much wanted for the reception and care of the insane, especially such as may be without friends, or destitute.' The case for an asylum was further strengthened by the fact that some lunatics remained in gaol for long periods; one poor soul had been incarcerated in the Home District gaol, the grand jury noted in 1840, since 1832.[7]

Officials administering the gaols were at a loss to know what to do about mentally ill persons believed to be a danger to themselves or to the community.[8] Part of the problem was the confusing lack of clarity in both law and practice with respect to those deemed 'criminally insane.' There was, for example, the notorious case of Patrick Donally, confined in the early 1830s to the Niagara gaol on a charge of murder. Donally had been a prisoner awaiting trial at the 1832 Assizes. Chief Justice Robinson reported that all who encountered him, including doctors who visited him during confinement, came to the conclusion that he was 'decidedly insane.' Robinson and the petty jury concurred. Although an indictment had been found against him, Robinson believed himself 'compelled' to remand Donally and to leave him in custody untried at the termination of the Assizes. Some two years later, Donally was still in the Niagara gaol, much to the disgust of a grand jury, which asked that he be removed to the penitentiary 'or some other place, where he may be confined in safety.' He might have remained in gaol indefinitely had not the grand jury jogged Robinson's memory. 'I had not heard of him since,' the chief justice admitted, 'but I observe the Grand Jury speak of him unhesitatingly as still insane.' The Donally case left the usually resourceful Robinson in a quandary: 'He cannot be discharged. The Penitentiary is clearly not a place in which he will be received, and I can point out no other to which he can properly be removed.'[9]

The treatment, trial, and incarceration of the mentally disturbed constituted an intractable problem. In 1840, the Johnstown District grand jury was at a loss to know how to deal with two unfortunates confined to the gaol: 'although they commisserate their unfortunate situation ... they nevertheless dare not recommend them to be set at liberty.' Until some 'insane asylum' could be erected for the 'protection and security' of this 'unfortunate class of our fellow beings,' the jury advised that they be confined in the district gaol.[10]

In dealing with this case, Justice Macaulay adopted the same legal position as Robinson had in 1832. When one of the two individuals, indicted for stabbing, had been arraigned, he did not plead, 'but muttered some incoherent matter.' A jury impanelled to enquire whether he was insane determined that he was, both 'at the time of committing the offense and also of his arraignment.' Macaulay therefore 'did not feel that he had any option but to detain the man in close custody.[11] Many individuals placed in this legal limbo were detained in gaol for indefinite periods, with little attention paid to their legal rights and with no provision for regular review or treatment.

By the end of the Upper Canadian period, however, some progress had been made. The sheriff of the Home District helped lead the reform effort. Following a critical 1834 presentment of the district grand jury on existing practices, Sheriff William Botsford Jarvis had responded that a noxious odour would spread throughout the prison so long as 'maniacs' were therein confined. A few years later he urged the magistrates to establish a separate facility for the insane. The chairman of the district sessions, J.N. Gamble, applauded the sheriff's proposal and argued in favour of a temporary asylum. The 1833 statute, Gamble suggested, had intended that the gaol be used only as a last resort and had given magistrates the option of establishing some other facility. 'I most heartily wish,' Gamble told Jarvis, 'that your present application to the Executive may succeed and that ... the stain upon our character as a Christian community, for our barbarous treatment' of the afflicted, 'may at last be effaced.'[12]

Jarvis's proposal appears to have influenced the 1839 decision to convert the old district gaol into a temporary asylum for the province, once the criminal prisoners and debtors were removed to a new building. The Assembly had appointed a commission in 1835 'to obtain information on the best method of managing and establishing' an asylum, and in 1836 Dr Charles Duncombe, spokesman for the commission, tabled a report in the House in which he outlined developments in Europe and the United States. In those countries, new reformed asylums employed moral treatment – amounting really to little more than kindness and the isolation of inmates from the community – and reformers were claiming that asylum treatment led to the cure of the vast majority of patients. In a scathing condemnation of Upper Canadian practices, Dr Duncombe alleged that 'no other portion of America' lodged their insane in the gaols. He recommended that the colony establish a model asylum similar to that which opened in 1833 in Worcester, Massachusetts. Political circumstances – including Duncombe's own flight as a rebel to the United States – postponed action, but asylum legislation was passed in 1839,[13] and in 1846 Chief Justice Robinson presided over a ceremony formally opening the provincial asylum in Toronto. By the late nineteenth century, as Sam Shortt has demonstrated, Ontario was spending about 16 per cent of its total budget on an extensive system of asylums spread across the province.[14] Despite the opening of these asylums, however, many insane individuals continued to be confined in the district gaols. For a variety of reasons, as we shall see, the situation continued and was given legal sanction. Well into the twentieth century commissions of inquiry would protest against the practices which had so offended Duncombe, Jarvis, and many others in the colonial period.

DEBTORS

If the presence of the insane in the gaols had an adverse impact on those facilities, that of another non-criminal population, debtors, created even greater problems, since far larger numbers were involved. Scattered returns presented to the legislature in 1836 for twelve districts, covering one year for one district, two years for three, three years for six, and four years for two, show a total of 2,304 debtors confined out of a prisoner population of 4,726, or 48 per cent of the total.[15] By comparison J.M. Fecteau reports that debtors made up only 8 per cent of the prison population in Quebec City between 1823 and 1834, and Evelyn Kolish concludes that in Quebec imprisonment for debt 'was a relatively marginal phenomenon.'[16] The Upper Canadian experience conforms more closely to English and American norms, although Upper Canada did not possess the equivalent of the great English debtor prisons, King's Bench and the Fleet.

In Upper Canada, as elsewhere, the overwhelming majority of those imprisoned for debt were men: the 1836 return showed only six female debtors. In the Midland, Home, and Gore District gaols, the numbers involved were substantial. In the Midland gaol in the period 1832–5, 333 debtors were confined out of a total of 601 prisoners; in the Home District during the period 1833–5, 379 prisoners out of 943 were debtors; and in the Gore District during the same period, 282 prisoners out of a total prison population of 510 were confined as debtors.[17]

While there were differences in law and circumstances, the most important contrast between England and Upper Canada was the absence of a separate debtors' prison.[18] Debtors were lodged in the same local gaols as criminal prisoners and suffered the same privations – and worse. The need for the financially pressed districts to lodge non-criminal prisoners in substantial numbers had a significant impact on the institutional arrangements and the social role of these facilities. Richard Splane has suggested that the presence of debtors had both positive and negative consequences. While it 'made for extra costs in the construction of gaols, complicated their management, and made classification of other prisoners even more difficult,' debtors 'frequently drew attention to conditions in the gaols and in so doing gained a more sympathetic hearing from the public than might other classes of offenders.'[19]

The debtors in Upper Canadian gaols were better educated and more able to articulate complaints than were criminal prisoners. On the whole, their letters and petitions confirm the sense of gaol conditions gained from criminal petitions. But many of the debtors felt a deeper sense of injustice and greater anger. Confined frequently for longer and indefinite periods, and often regarding themselves as the victims of an unjust system, their petitions conveyed feelings of the deepest anguish and misery. Debtors consequently contributed disproportionately to the emergence in the 1830s of a powerful movement for gaol reform. When, in 1829, John Rolph presented an abortive bill to end imprisonment for debt, he added the cause of the debtors to what Robert Fraser has argued was a growing chorus of discontent with the colonial legal system.[20] In Upper Canada, as in England and the United States, the insolvency laws also became an important political issue.[21]

The insolvency laws were an attempt to protect the interests of creditors, which were vital to the functioning of a colonial economy based to a large extent on borrowing, without subjecting honest but impecunious debtors to unduly harsh treatment. The law sought to differentiate between those willing to pay their bills and those who sought to avoid doing so, by flight or other means. In 1805 an 'Act for Relief of Insolvent Debtors' effected one significant improvement. There was no provision, it pointed out, 'for the support of insolvent debtors detained in execution,' as opposed to those awaiting trial. The statute held that it was 'inexpedient' that the support of such persons should depend on the districts or on private charity. Any person detained for debt might therefore apply to the court and, after that debtor swore 'that he or she [was] not worth five Pounds,' it became the responsibility of the creditor to pay five shillings a week to maintain the debtor in gaol.[22]

The objective was to ensure not only that debtors did not starve, but also that creditors would not detain debtors lightly. The creditor was not, however, obliged to make this payment if he could prove to the satisfaction of the court 'that the defendant ha[d] secreted, or conveyed away, his or her effects, to defraud his or her creditors.' A supplemental Act of 1822 provided for the rigorous legal examination of debtors to ascertain whether property was being hidden in order to receive the gaol allowance. If the creditor did not pay the allowance, the prisoner could apply to the court to be discharged, although this would not deprive the creditor 'of any remedy thereafter' against the goods of the discharged prisoner. The purpose of the law was to detain dishonest debtors only so long as to force them to disgorge themselves of the wealth they were believed to have secreted away.[23]

The circumstances of debtors were further ameliorated by a second 1822 statute, which assigned limits within which debtors might have freedom of movement if someone would post a bond on their behalf.[24] Justices in Quarter Sessions were empowered to establish such limits, 'not exceeding six acres.' Any debtor so released lost his right to receive the weekly maintenance allowance from the creditor, but he was allowed to seek employment to support himself and pay off his debt. It is unclear how this system worked in practice. The limits are seldom referred to in the numerous debtors' petitions, so perhaps they did not significantly alter the experience of the majority of prisoners confined for debt. One vivid account was offered by Judge J.F. Pringle in his classic study, *The Old Eastern District* (1890), in which he described the boundaries of the limits in Cornwall. They included parts of several streets and most buildings on those streets. 'The fact that these limits included two churches and one tavern, proves that the magistrates considered not only the spiritual but the spirituous needs of the prisoners.' In 1826 the limits were extended to include the district schoolhouse; in 1830 and 1847 they were further extended, with posts erected to mark out the boundaries, and by 1890 they were the same as the boundaries of the county.[25]

Many debtors suffered severely under the insolvency Acts, as numerous petitions confirm. Consider the case of Captain Matthew Leech of Lanark, confined in the Brockville gaol. In January 1821 Leech had signed a promissory note for £400 on behalf of a friend, and when a dispute arose over whether this note had been discharged, Leech was imprisoned. Civil process respected neither status nor personal situation. Leech, who had served in His Majesty's forces for thirty-five years, was severely disabled by war wounds; he also had a wife and nine children. The court was indifferent to personal circumstances. Still in gaol several years later, Leech petitioned the Assembly in 1825 for 'relief in the premises.' A select committee found no irregularities in the trial procedure but authorized the Court of King's Bench to take appropriate action.[26] If Leech, with his nine children and long-term military service, had been held on a criminal conviction, he might have gained his freedom expeditiously, but the King's mercy did not extend to debtors.

Many debtors professed to believe that they were experiencing lengthy imprisonment because of improper, if not illegal, measures taken by their creditors. In 1823, for example, one Jackson begged the civil secretary for assistance in 'getting the situation of insolvent debtors ameliorated.' His creditors would extend no mercy because they expected his father to pay, but, Jackson wrote, 'it is utterly out of his power to assist me were he ever so willing but he is not.'[27] Another man asked for assistance in 1825 because he had stood bail for a Mohawk Indian who then refused to budge from the Mohawk village.[28] In 1834 James Gray faced an eight-month wait in the Brockville gaol before trial. Claiming he would be financially ruined were he detained much longer, he requested a special Assize. Unsuccessful at trial, Gray was still in gaol four-and-a-half years later, and he claimed that he owed his prolonged detention to 'the malicious but sneaking inveteracy of Mr. Jonas Jones, aided by his friends and relations on the Bench.'[29]

Although imprisoned debtors frequently lashed out at those they believed responsible for their situation, sheriffs and gaolers were seldom in their line of fire. James Gray had no complaint to make 'with respect to the gaoler,' while another debtor thanked the sheriff who, 'on his own responsibility,' had permitted him 'to be at large and perfectly unmolested.'[30] Common complaints were made in Canada, as in England, however, against lawyers. From the Hamilton gaol a debtor protested that his lawyer, Charles Durand, had 'neglected and deceived him and now won't do any more for him until he gets three pounds fees.'[31] Frequently, too, debtors fell victim to inefficiencies in the system. In 1833 three debtors in the Kingston gaol claimed that they had applied to be released through their own attorney and the plaintiffs but remained in gaol because of the absence of the judge, 'who does not reside in this District.'[32]

Some debtors did find reason to complain about gaol officials. In 1827 several debtors said they had been mistreated by Elias Dulmage of the Kingston gaol, who had placed one of their number in shackles following an escape attempt. When the civil secretary requested a full report from Sheriff John Maclean, Maclean responded that the matter had been already investigated by a magistrate, with the petitioners questioned under oath. According to Maclean, the inquiry had confirmed that Dulmage had been 'as attentive and lenient to them' as it was in his power to be, considering 'the nature of the place in which they were confined.'[33]

Debtor complaints contributed to an exacting legal scrutiny of gaol conditions and administration. Several letters from Midland District magistrates confirm that debtors were treated respectfully and given every opportunity to make their case. In November 1826 Magistrate Pringle visited the Kingston gaol at the request of debtor Peter Grant, and engaged in a lengthy discussion with him, principally over complaints against Dulmage. That same month Pringle reported that he 'attended with Thomas Markland and John Macaulay' to hear the complaints of the debtor who had been placed in irons after attempting escape. Here was an assemblage of very considerable local power gathered in the gaol to ensure fair treatment. Pringle reported that the debtor in question, in contradiction to his written complaint, had admitted that he deserved his punishment. Dulmage, for his part, 'humanely proposed' to remove the man's shackles and place him back in the debtor's apartment.[34] Pringle, it is clear, was a regular visitor to the gaol, and he reported that he had 'frequent opportunities' of observing Dulmage's conduct.

Another prominent Midland magistrate, the clerk of the peace, James Nickalls, also confirmed that he had 'occasion very frequently to visit the gaol on business with the debtors there.' Nickalls 'never found any difficulty in getting access to them, at all times.'[35] Details concerning the legal circumstances of the debtors frequently brought magistrates, and especially the clerk of the peace, to the gaol, and the criminal prisoners cannot help but have benefited from their presence. Elias Dulmage himself pointed to the regularity of magisterial inspections. There had been numerous complaints from the debtors, he admitted, but these had 'always been attended to by the Magistrates' and his own conduct had been proven to be faultless. It was a further protection, he noted, that the conduct of the gaol was governed by specific regulations formulated by the magistrates.[36] In effect, the magistrates played the role of gaol inspectors until the 1850s. Their frequent visits served in many districts to contribute to the humanity and efficiency of gaols in the pre-bureaucratic era. The ongoing involvement of magistrates of the stature of Nickalls, Pringle, Markland, and Macaulay ensured that the district gaols could never be what Kingston Penitentiary would soon become: isolated, cut off from the community, places to inspire fear and loathing.

Such interventions did not prevent severe suffering on the part of debtors as well as criminals. Many of the debtors who petitioned complained of long periods of close confinement. In 1821 Lester Farrand from the Johnstown District, in gaol for over a year and half, wrote of 'the bitter hardships and grievances, which debtors have always had to suffer since my confinement here.' In the Niagara gaol Charles Walsh, severely ill and for five months unable to rise from bed, claimed that his life was in danger 'from the impure atmosphere ... and being denied salutary exercise in the open air.' The yard was too insecure to be used. Nor did the gaol have even the most primitive classification: 'Debtors and criminals, insane and mad persons and prostitutes are almost comingled.' From Brockville, James Gray, subject to 'all the annoyances of a crowded room and the most objectionable associates,' pleaded desperately for relief. The gaol was without a yard and he had passed four-and-a-half years 'within iron bars, without the opportunity of enjoying the light of heaven or fresh air.' Gray was confined with six others, 'one of whom is literally rotten with the itch, and another is infected with lice,' in a single room. He described the room as a 'horrid den,' rendered unbearable by a constant fire on a cooking stove, 'while the effluvia from a privy in the room ... causes the eyes to water.'[37]

Gray and other debtors contrasted the treatment they received with that meted out to the criminals. 'While prisonment for debt continues,' he pleaded, 'whatever accommodation is provided for prisoners at the public expense should not be withheld from them.' Debtors not in receipt of the legal allowance, often because it was believed they were concealing assets, were usually in desperate circumstances. Sometimes, as Gray reported, they could bring work to the debtors' apartment, and two men imprisoned with Gray were allowed to work as shoemakers. From the Midland District John Maclean reported in 1827 that 'the debtors in the gaol are obliged to furnish themselves with everything, there being no allowance whatever from the District.' Even though 'the doors are opened very often, and every facility afforded them of supplying themselves with necessities,' many lacked friends and received no assistance from the outside. In these circumstances, many debtors were dependent 'upon the gaoler's bounty.' It became the gaoler's reponsibility to ensure that they did not starve to death. Maclean repeated that he always directed the gaoler to be 'as lenient and humane with them as possible.'[38]

A grim picture emerged in the Home District. Debtors in 1832 pointed out that several of them were strangers in the community and that some time must pass before relatives even learned where they were. Some of them would 'have been actually starved was it not for the humanity of their fellow prisoners.' Similarly, in the Kingston gaol in 1833 three debtors reported that the five shilling allowance had been cut off after four weeks, and they were obliged to apply 'for support of the District funds forthwith.'[39] In the Home District, at least, the legal provisions, however harsh, were ruthlessly enforced, whatever the consequences in human suffering.

In 1835, fourteen debtors from the Newcastle gaol claimed to be 'entirely destitute of the means of support.' They had petitioned 'the magistrates at various times for relief from their sufferings,' which were 'too painful to relate,' but to little avail; many of them had been 'for several days without any kind of sustenance whatever.' They would have perished but for 'the kind hospitality of our worthy and humane sheriff, and some other who has frequently contributed to our wants.' They requested 'His Excellency's intervention,' but there seemed to be no legal remedy at hand. The clerk of the peace was instructed by Quarter Sessions to report that the debtors 'had no cause to complain.' They might be starving, but the funds of the district could not legally be expended 'to furnish provisions to the debtors,' although 'in some extreme cases bread has been furnished.' Why were the magistrates so hard-hearted? They professed to believe that 'most if not all of the prisoners subscribing to the petition are able to support themselves or have friends that are able to assist them.' Furthermore, if they were genuinely unable to pay their debts, the prisoners had only to demonstrate that they were not worth five pounds in order to 'be discharged under the several statutes passed for the relief of insolvent debtors or be allowed five shillings.'[40]

In most cases, debtors survived with the assistance of the gaoler, other prisoners, or private charity until the legal machinery came to their aid. But while they survived, they hardly flourished, and many had their health undermined, as case after case confirmed. In 1835 John Newall, a farmer who had fought for His Majesty in Egypt, had been imprisoned on the writ of a Cobourg storekeeper for a debt 'that he was obligded [sic] to contract for the support of 9 of a small family.' From the Newcastle gaol he wrote that he was in fear of dying 'for want of support and likewise his poor small family that he left naked and starving in the bush.' His plea to Colborne was not only on behalf of himself but for all 'poor debtors who has [sic] not the means of supporting themselves when in gaol.' When Newall's request for assistance was referred to the local authorities, the sheriff responded that there was 'no law to authorize either His Excellency or the Magistrates' to make any provision and even if there were, 'the small amount of the District assessments' would permit no such expenditure. Nonetheless, 'in some very peculiar hard cases' the magistrates, on their 'personal responsibility,' had ordered some bread. Whether Newall had ever received this allowance, 'my gaoler does not recollect.'[41]

Criminal prisoners might retain their health on a bread-and-water diet for brief sentences, but the same fare for debtors confined for far longer periods must have had devastating effects. Debtors also lived in constant fear of being denied medical assistance by prison doctors because they could not pay. In 1832, when the Home District gaol experienced an outbreak of cholera, the debtors petitioned that they were terrified that 'death may put a stop to our present suffering before we could obtain the necessary medical aid.' Their 'lamented friend Mr. Wallace' had been almost dead 'before he could get the slightest assistance.' In another petition, the debtors pointed out that while 'closely confined in the cells' they were without means of preventing contact 'with persons of filthy habits.' They believed they were in great danger and begged for their freedom.[42]

Although the lieutenant-governor claimed he had no authority to release them even during a cholera epidemic, he asked Sheriff Jarvis to ensure that they had medical attention and adequate food. By contrast, criminals facing the cholera could be released, and Colborne ordered this to be done except in the case of two condemned to death, conditional on banishment.[43]

The legislature addressed some of these anomalies and injustices in 1834 and 1835. An Act of 6 March 1834 provided relief for those confined on mesne process, i.e., pending trial and unable to procure bail. If such persons demonstrated they were not worth five pounds, the court might order the creditor to pay the weekly allowance 'in the same manner as if the defendant were in custody upon final process.' In default of such payment, the court was to discharge the defendant. Anyone confined for sums under ten pounds might, after thirty days in gaol, swear that he was not worth the sum for which he had been arrested, and be discharged from imprisonment by the court. In 1835, a statute addressed the issue of imprisonment for debt more generally by declaring such imprisonment to be not 'otherwise justifiable than as a means of compelling such persons' to apply any money or property they possessed to satisfy their creditors. Henceforth no person was to be arrested 'when the cause of action shall not amount to ten pounds,' and writs were no longer to be issued for costs only. Most important, the length of time for which debtors could be incarcerated was specifically limited: 'it might tend greatly to the relief of certain debtors in execution for small debts, and at the same time occasion no material prejudice to trade and public credit if such debtors should, after a limited period of imprisonment, be allowed to be discharged.' Therefore all persons in execution upon any judgment for a debt not exceeding twenty pounds, and who had been in prison for three months or confined to the limits for a year, might apply to the court to be discharged from custody. This did not provide any relief from the debt itself. Persons imprisoned for between twenty and one hundred pounds might apply for discharge after six months, and if the debt exceeded a hundred pounds, after a year. The debtor's application had to include an affidavit stating that he was not possessed of any moneys, goods, or effects of any description in excess of five pounds; in effect, he had to declare bankruptcy. The creditor had the right to show cause against any such application. If a discharge was granted, it was not to affect any other remedy available to the creditor.[44]

These statutes alleviated but did not solve a glaring social problem. In 1836 the masses of data gathered in response to the lieutenant-governor's request for information on the gaols revealed that many debtors continued to fare worse than criminal prisoners. In the Ottawa District George Hamilton, chair of Quarter Sessions, reported that all prisoners except those confined for debt were provided with bread, meat, firewood, and blankets.[45] For the Home District the magistrates asserted that the gaol had held 174 debtors compared to 295 criminals over the previous year, and 21 of these had no means of support. They provided some interesting additional information as to how debtors sometimes survived. The gaoler had paid some of them to help him run the gaol. It also appeared that the gaoler's losses 'in boarding debtors generally amounted to more than his profits.'[46] From the Midland District John Macaulay reported that debtors, like the criminal prisoners, were funished with food, clothing, and bedding, a result possibly of recent changes in attitude to non-criminal prisoners. Similarly, the prison doctor 'never hesitate[d] to extend his professional aid to unfortunate and pennyless debtors when required.' As for debtors without means of subsistence, Macaulay specifically noted that under prison rules the gaoler provided food and reported thereon to the magistrates in Sessions, 'who direct it to be continued if it is ascertained that the party thus relieved, is actually destitute.'[47]

By the late 1830s both law and practice seem to have undergone a change for the better, although in some districts humane treatment of debtors is apparent from an earlier date. William Young of the London District, for instance, claimed that debtors in his district had been treated humanely from shortly after the district's establishment. Even though 'not expressly authorized by legislative enactment,' the magistrates had supplied medicines, bedding, and clothing 'even to indigent debtors.' They believed it to be 'an imperative duty' to do so. As for food, the London Sessions in 1830 ordered a pound of meat a day, plus vegetables, 'to indigent debtors previous to their obtaining the usual order for payment by the plaintiff' of a dollar a week. Even so, Young noted, 'within the last year several successful attempts at escape by debtors have occurred.'[48]

In Prince Edward District, too, the chair of Quarter Sessions claimed that regulations adopted in 1834 and approved by Chief Justice Robinson ensured humane treatment. As was the case in many gaols, the lower cells were set aside for the criminals, while the second floor apartments, free from from the dreaded dampness of being partially underground, were reserved for debtors. As in most gaols, debtors could entertain visitors for most of each day. In all cases in which the sheriff was satisfied that the prisoner lacked other means, he was authorized to furnish meat, bread, and potatoes, and was to report these cases to the Sessions, 'when such allowance shall be confirmed or withheld according to the evidence.' Another regulation provided that prisoners confined for debt or being held for trial might be supplied by friends with a pint of wine or a quart of beer or cider daily. The temperance movement had as yet made little impression on the Prince Edward District sheriff's office. The debtors were also allowed use of a light until ten in the evening.[49]

Other districts similarly granted the gaoler considerable discretion to supply needy debtors with provisions, reinforcing the impression that by the late 1830s a more humane attitude prevailed towards this class of prisoner. But as the Upper Canadian period drew to a close, debtors still suffered many privations. In an 1839 petition to Sir George Arthur from the Gore gaol, the debtors begged to be allowed a brief period each day of exercise in the yard. 'Some of us,' the petition read, 'have been confined from seven to fifteen months' in rooms adjacent to a noisome privy, and Sheriff Alan Macdonell agreed that this was 'in hot weather perhaps unhealthy.' But the sheriff hesitated to give the debtors access to the open air because this space was insecure and he would be liable to plaintiffs in the event of an escape. Even so, the sheriff sometimes allowed such liberties to those whose health was in danger, 'on the plea of humanity.'[50]

Although John Rolph had not succeeded in his 1829 attempt to abolish imprisonment for debt, and several subsequent bills had likewise failed to gain passage, the reformers did not abandon their efforts. In 1836 a committee of the legislature enquiring into the administration of justice argued that 'the laws relating to debtor and creditor are very unsatisfactory.' During the Union years there were calls for reform both from debtors and from municipalities burdened with charges that more properly belonged to creditors. As late as 1857, the municipal council of Lambton County made this point in a petition to the governor general. They considered it 'a great grievance that the County should be made to afford sustenance to prisoners incarcerated by Creditors,' and asked that a provision be made to require creditors to pay all support charges.[51] In 1858 a public meeting in Galt expressed 'regret and alarm' at the operation of the law of imprisonment for debt; experience taught them that it was 'greatly abused and perverted from its original intention and has thus been rendered an instrument of oppression.' In the view of these citizens, the law had caused 'many honest but unfortunate debtors to abscond from the Province rather than remain and undergo the disgrace of imprisonment.' Had no such law been in operation, 'these parties might have remained amongst us, and liquidated their debts to the benefit of their Creditors and the community at large.' The petitioners asked for the abolition of imprisonment for debt except when fraud was proven, and for 'the passage of an equitable Bankrupt Law.'[52]

Grand juries also continued to protest both the law and the conditions of confinement. In 1857 the grand jury of Middlesex County pointed to the crowded accommodation for debtors, the lack of opportunity for exercise, and the abominable state and offensive smell of the privies. The jurors noted that thirteen persons were confined for debt: 'Many of these are totally unable to satisfy the demands for which they are incarcerated, and the keeping them there is but a piece of cruelty, some of those confined were among the most respected in the city and county.' After noting that a confined debtor could neither support his family nor pay his debt, the jurors emphasized that they viewed the matter as one of grave concern. It had 'the most dire consequences to the well being of the country and of the province,' by driving to a neighbouring republic 'those who might otherwise be useful and respected citizens.' The law, they said, was 'shameful.'[53]

Of course, debtors themselves continued to submit petitions, and frequently these were pitiful. From the gaol in Hamilton Elizabeth Hart in 1852 complained that she had been imprisoned for upwards of two years. Supported by one of her daughters, she had four younger 'helpless' children, and she did 'not know what to do with them.' She had applied to her creditors for a discharge. They knew she had no assets but they refused, 'thinking this is the only way they have of punishing her.' As a result, she had 'been punished more than if she had stolen the amount,' a claim that was literally true for Elizabeth and many others.[54]

By the 1850s there were fewer debtors in gaol suffering from this kind of treatment. An 1851 return to the assembly listed the numbers of those in the county gaols for debt and the number bailed to the limits. Waterloo, for example, reported one debtor in gaol and one on the limits. From Hamilton, Sheriff Cartwright-Thomas reported the confinement, in addition to Elizabeth Hart, of three men. But he did not know how many were bailed to the limits, 'as the Debtors are discharged from close confinement, and admitted to bail by judges' order, and no notice of their discharge from the limits is ever given to the Sheriff.' This casual attitude suggests that release to the limits had become tantamount to complete freedom. The sheriff was not expected to keep track of the numbers bailed, and certainly the judges were not about to do so. From another large gaol, Sheriff James Hamilton of Middlesex reported two debtors in custody and ten registered as on the limits. Some had been discharged without Hamilton's knowledge. From Kingston, Thomas Corbett reported none in gaol and seven on the limits. Similarly, there were none in the Niagara gaol and the sheriff was uncertain as to how many were on the limits.[55]

The 1851 return, however, dealt primarily with the situation on a given day as opposed to numbers confined over a longer period. A massive return to the legislature printed in 1857 demonstrated that between 1855 and May 1857 substantial numbers continued to be confined.[56] In Carleton County Sheriff Simon Fraser reported ninety-six cases of imprisonment for debt for the period, nine of which were for amounts of one hundred pounds or more. In Frontenac, Lennox, and Addington Counties there were fourteen cases. For Grey County there were no cases in 1855 or 1856, and ten to May 1, 1857. From the United Counties of York and Peel, Sheriff Fred Jarvis reported from 1 January 1855 to 1857 a total of 176 cases from the Courts of Queen's Bench and Common Pleas, and another 149 from County Court. In Huron and Bruce Counties from 1 January to 16 May 1857, the clerk of the County Court issued twenty-three writs of *capias*, for sums varying from ten to twenty-five pounds, 'averaging about £16 or £17 each.' As deputy clerk of Crown Pleas he issued eight writs of *capias*. Most striking was the brevity of the period of detention, usually a month or less. It was deemed worthy of special note when one man in Grey County spent 111 days in confinement before being discharged by Judge Hagarty upon swearing he was not worth five pounds. The debt was not paid.

On any given day, at least into the early 1840s, Upper Canadian gaols probably housed more non-criminals than criminals, and their governance reflected that important reality. Clearly no system of prison rules could ever distinguish adequately between such disparate groups as had come together in these ill-built structures, and reformers, with an irresistible logic, demanded that other facilities be built to house the insane, the poor, the old and, above all, hardened criminals. With the passage of the Penitentiary Act in 1834, the House of Industry Act in 1837, and the Asylum Act in 1839,[57] Upper Canadians finally moved to establish purpose-built facilities to house distinctive deviant populations. Whether propelled by fear of political upheaval, by genuine humanitarianism, or by fiscal reasons, these changes had far-ranging consequences: the penitentiary, the asylum, and the poorhouse profoundly affected Canadian society's treatment of the criminal, the deviant, and the ill. Ironically, however, the establishment of these new segregative institutions did surprisingly little to alter the established congregate character of the gaols.

The new era of segregative control did not, as we shall see, lead to the effective reform of the gaols, or to the systematic removal of these populations to facilities better adapted to their needs and circumstances. The gaols continued to house the poor, the insane, the debtor, and all those awaiting trial, in addition to the convicted criminal. These populations in turn continued substantially to shape, if not determine, the character of those facilities.

The onging use of the gaols for multiple social purposes reflected the community's persisting shortages of social capital. Some have argued that the 'new urban middle class' was 'acutely aware of the social dangers' inherent in the transition to a capitalist market economy, with its inevitable accompaniment, the creation of a class of property-less wage-labourers and of a new urban poor.[58] But there is little evidence in contemporary documents to support the argument that Upper Canadian capitalists created new, segregative social institutions to head off the threat posed by the poor and the deviant. To the contrary, the debate over gaol conditions suggests not the existence of any sweeping social crisis, but rather points to the challenge posed by the colony's inadequate political and administrative apparatus. As early as the late 1820s, the machinery of the Upper Canadian state, and especially of local administration, had become so anachronistic as to be almost non-functional. The administrative structure that situated the gaols within this flawed political system was a long time tottering to final collapse. In the 1840s, another generation of public men would find creative new approaches to political and administrative management. What was achieved in the 1840s and 1850s, however, was less a social revolution than a political reordering. In the event, the gaols would not only survive side by side with the new institutions, but in many respects they maintained and even extended the congregate role they had assumed in the Upper Canadian period.

THE GRAND JURIES ON GAOL CONDITIONS

The most voluminous source documenting contemporary concerns over the condition of the gaols is the reports of grand juries. In the absence of appointed inspectors, the regular inspection of the gaols by citizens of standing in the community served to prevent some of the worst abuses and to remedy a few others. Since the Assize juries were composed largely of magistrates, while those of Quarter Sessions were selected from a list prepared by the sheriff, there was room for some official manipulation. Still, magistrates were notoriously individualistic in their opinions and the content of their presentments reveals a striking independence of mind. Their reports demonstrated considerable diversity in conditions from district to district. Taken together, they also suggest that there was no uniform deterioration of gaol conditions in most districts from the 1820s to the 1830s.

It is equally true, in the earlier decade, however, that jurors were more accepting of primitive conditions, and tended to speak positively of what they encountered. In 1821, for example, the Johnstown District jurors believed that new regulations laid down by the magistrates had removed many causes of complaint. These simple regulations required gaolers to cook for felons and for those incarcerated for being unable to pay fines; debtors were required to pay 1s.3d. a week for the same service. The gaoler was to furnish water and wood for the stove, and to empty the tubs 'once each day.' In a comment that appeared in many reports, the Johnstown jurors found that prisoners were subject to 'many inconveniences and sufferings,' but they attributed these to structural deficiencies in the gaol itself, rather than to the neglect of the gaoler.[59]

Many jury reports alleged genuine distress, and sometimes the magistrates concurred. From Cornwall in 1825 a petition of magistrates and jurors asserted that a new gaol was essential because the prisoners suffered 'the most dreadful privations' and it was impossible, especially during the winter, to make the cells fit for their reception. Often jurors championed the cause of a specific individual. In 1831, the London jurors reported on an Indian, Canesco, suffering a long confinement for horse stealing. Disease, 'originating probably from the change in his habits of life,' had made 'frightful ravages on his constitution' and only 'immediate liberation' could save his life.[60] In these efforts, the jurors emerged as the most vociferous advocates of prisoners' rights in the nineteenth century.

In addition, the jurors fulfilled the inspectoral function of investigating and reporting on the general state of the facilities. From their comments, which sometimes consisted of bold condemnation, sometimes cautious praise, it is apparent that these were plain and honest citizens performing an important civic duty. A typically balanced report was delivered in 1831 by the London jurors. After identifying a common and horrendous problem of this era, in noting that the sewer leading from the privy was so foul as to infest the air, they described the rest of the gaol as clean and comfortable. And, like jurors across the province, they pointed out that 'the prisoners express themselves satisfied with the Gaoler's treatment.'[61]

From scores of reports from this period and later, it is incontestable that gaolers usually treated their charges with humanity and even respect. Little is known about the social class of the gaolers. The appointment fell within the jurisdiction of the sheriff, and since those officials were legally responsible for many aspects of gaol management, it would appear that the choice of gaolers was made with some care. There are few references in this early period to the employment of matrons; apparently when female prisoners were present the gaoler's wife made herself available as necessary. It is perhaps surprising, considering the lack of training and poor remuneration of the gaolers, that jury reports repeatedly confirmed that prisoners attested that gaol staff were doing all in their power to assist them. 'The persons confined,' said the Johnstown jurors in 1835, 'have stated their entire satisfaction at the treatment of the Gaoler, whose conduct they represent as uniformly kind and obliging.'[62]

But this assessment was frequently a convenient point of departure used by jurors about to launch into a condemnation of the physical state of the facility, and of the failure of the magistrates to provide for minimal human needs. The Gore jurors in 1834 struck the common balance. They found, ambiguously, that the cells and other apartments were 'as clean and as well ventilated as the construction of the building will admit.' The interior, however, urgently needed a complete whitewash and some 'powerful preparation' was required to purify the air. The food was deemed adequate. However, 'the straitened state' of district funds – the usual lament – prevented the construction of a wall which would have allowed the prisoners to exercise in the open air.[63]

Three of the largest gaols – those of the Niagara, Gore, and Home Districts – posed all but overwhelming problems. In Niagara a state of semi-permanent crisis dated back to the turbulent conditions of the 1790s. This border community attracted more than its share of local and American riff-raff, and remained a focus of the operations of gangs of organized hooligans and thieves. The population pressures of the 1830s made matters worse. In 1835 John Clark, as chair of Quarter Sessions, informed the lieutenant-governor that the gaol held even more than its usual allotment of debtors and desperadoes. The situation seemed beyond the capacity of the district to control. Clark told a sad tale of prisoners, including 'women and young children, and many of the men, in a state of starvation and nakedness.' In communication with Sir John Colborne, Clark was responding to the indignant presentment of the grand jury. The jurors, he noted, had appealed to the humanity of the magistrates 'for the temporary relief of the prisoners,' but this was beyond the means of the district. He begged Colborne to grant a special Assize to deliver the gaol.[64]

Despite frequent subsequent appeals from magistrates and jurors, no action was forthcoming from provincial officials. The rage of the Niagara jurors culminated in 1839. 'Notwithstanding the strongest representations' made by the grand jury over many years, 'nothing [had] been done' to remedy appalling circumstances. When the jurors appealed to the magistrates, they had claimed to have no authority over the sheriff, 'who arranges all in connection with the gaol.' And that official was of course appointed by the government in York. Conditions were so horrendous that 'prisoners committed for first offence, or petty trespasses' had to be confined 'with the most atrocious criminals, the accused with the convicts, and all occupying a day room, only separated by an open railing from the unfortunate debtors.' Such total absence of classification was 'an outrage.'[65]

The Niagara jurors joined a common chorus in offering a searing indictment of one of the most widespread problems of Upper Canadian gaols, their horrid stench: 'from the want of ventilation and the state of the necessaries, a most noxious and abominable effluvia is produced.' This was so 'highly injurious' to the health of the prisoners that it was impossible in warm weather 'to contemplate their situation without shuddering.' The jurors were furious 'that the presentments made for many years on this subject' had not been attended to by the magistrates. As a result, the facility was 'in a state not only disgraceful to the district but to a civilized people.'[66]

The Home District experienced a similar conflict between jurors and magistrates, but one with political implications which contributed to increasing polarization between Tory and Reform factions. The 1830s began symbolically with William Lyon Mackenzie chairing a legislative committee investigating the 'petition of the Prisoners' in the York gaol. In addition to complaints about the harmful presence of several insane persons, the prisoners without exception pointed to the scanty food allowance, 'only three half pence worth of bread per diem.' While the committee emphasized that it had no desire to convert the gaol into a place of comfort, 'it should not be a place of starvation.' Finally, the lack of classification deserved 'severe reprobation'; about a dozen of the criminals were mixed together all day in the same ward.[67] The magistrates resented these comments, especially from a committee headed by Mackenzie.

In 1834 the struggle again pitted the future rebel against the Tory magistrates, but by this time the fiery little Scot was Mayor of Toronto, and feuding with the district over the sharing of gaol costs. By its Act of incorporation, Toronto was required to pay the district for the use of the gaol and courthouse an amount that has been calculated at about a third of the city's total assessment. As one of its first acts, the new city council dispatched a committee on justice and prisons to tour this expensive facility. The committee reported 'many shortcomings, noting too that the magistrates had ignored critical presentments on the subject by several grand juries.' The magistrates ignored this report as well, and the confrontation escalated when the first grand jury of the Mayor's Court returned another highly critical presentment. In a devastating critique, the jurors charged that confinement in the district gaol was so debilitating that some prisoners on release were incapable of 'earning by manual labour an honest livelihood.' To their claim that want of a regular medical attendant 'appears to be greatly felt,' Sheriff W.B. Jarvis responded that the medical needs of the criminals were well cared for, and if the debtors were unable to pay, they had 'never to [Jarvis's] knowledge been refused assistance.' To the jurors' complaint that no sufficient effort had been made to introduce 'a regular system of divine service,' he pointed out that the Archdeacon of York and his assistant attended regularly, although clergymen of other denominations had been notably absent.[68] When Mackenzie forwarded the jurors' statement to the lieutenant-governor, he drew Colborne's attention to the high cost to the city of a facility which in any case was in an 'insecure and unwholesome' state.

Colborne readily concurred. As the recipient of petitions from prisoners across Upper Canada and grand jury reports from every district, he knew more than Mackenzie about the condition of the gaols. He may also have been reacting to the growing disapproval of colonial office officials over Canadian conditions. That very day he wrote to Sheriff Jarvis, insisting that 'immediate measures' be taken to bring before the magistrates 'the disgraceful state of the Gaol,' and he demanded that the condition of the prisoners be ameliorated. Colborne also instructed the sheriff to report back on how 'the evils complained of' might be remedied.[69] The gleeful Mackenzie published an account of this exchange in the *Colonial Advocate*. Feeling betrayed by Colborne, Jarvis and Grant Powell, chair of Quarter Sessions, wrote to the governor with detailed rebuttals. With some justice, they made the customary magisterial disclaimer that their hands were tied by lack of funds. This alone had prevented 'the attainment of so desirable' an improvement as the construction of a perimeter wall. Similarly, the gaol could not be whitewashed quarterly instead of annually because of the cost.[70]

Despite their anger at what they regarded as the lieutenant-governor's uninformed letter, Jarvis and Powell did not place all the blame on Colborne and his advisers. One of the most revealing aspects of their response is what they had to say about the attitudes and behaviour of the prisoners. If the gaol was not whitewashed more often, claimed Jarvis, it was owing to 'the utter impossibility of preventing the idle and dissolute by every means in their power from wantonly' desecrating the walls and floors and smashing the windows. While the grand jury recommended that indoor privies be erected, it had failed to inform itself about what had happened when this had been tried earlier: the prisoners had deliberately plugged the pipes and the gaol had been flooded with filth. The privies 'were of necessity removed and tubs used in place thereof.' The jurors had been critical because the prisoners suffered from the want of bedsteads and their bedding lay on the floor, accumulating 'all manner of filth and vermin.' But in the past, good quality bedding had frequently been destroyed by the prisoners and the district had been put to considerable expense in replacing it. Grant Powell condescendingly endeavoured to enlighten Colborne about the recalcitrant nature of Upper Canadian prisoners. Gaols, he lectured, 'cannot be always in a state of perfect neatness and order, since it is impossible to restrain those reckless and dissolute individuals who take pleasure in wantonly defacing and destroying.' It must be remembered, he told Colborne, 'that the front windows of the building open directly on the street and there is not even a fence to keep persons from approaching.' It was not to be wondered at, echoed Jarvis, that 'in a building exposed as the gaol of the district is,' liquor should reach the prisoners. Every care was taken and the gaoler had seized large quantities of liquor.[71]

Numerous other sources confirm the bleak and miserable state of the physical condition of most contemporary gaols. When Isaac Hoff died while serving a brief sentence in the Niagara gaol, a coroner's jury found that close confinement in a cell with little air had been the cause of death. In York Francis Collins of *The Canadian Freeman*, himself a former prisoner, published frequent horror stories. Commenting in an 1830 editorial on an attempted escape, he described the new gaol as an abomination to both health and safety. 'In winter the stench ... is enough to knock down a butcher's dog – in summer it is enough to poison ... a rattlesnake.' The following year, after receiving 'several anonymous communications from prisoners,' Collins claimed that many of the evils 'exist through the sheer stupidity of the magistrates.' What punishment, he asked, 'can exceed that of being obliged to inhale confined or foul air, and to drink rotten water off putrid bodies?' As for the poor debtors, they were even worse off than the criminals, with no provision for their upkeep. 'What terrible crime is there in getting a few dollars into debt that warrants a man without means of support' to be so treated 'that he may perish from want.'[72]

Misery and privation created a prison subculture shaped by anger and characterized by resistance and brutality. Some prisoners refused to be intimidated by authority or to behave docilely in the expectation of early release or pardon. Although relatively powerless, they were not impotent, and at times they combated those who ran these poorly staffed and weakly built facilities on almost equal terms. In their resistance to authority, prisoners destroyed the toilets, bedding, and other objects that would have added to their own comfort. It is clear that turnkeys and gaolers frequently lived in a state of intermittent terror. In such circumstances, most gaolers did their best to treat prisoners as kindly as possible, lest they themselves suffer from the rage of their charges and excite some lust for vengeance. Yet it is not clear that the portrait drawn by Jarvis and Powell and others was typical of all gaols for most of the Upper Canadian period. More likely, the situation they described existed primarily in the larger gaols, and then only when those gaols were occupied by convicted felons and other notorious characters.

In any case, Powell and Jarvis believed they had suffered a grievous wrong at the hands of the lieutenant-governor. The magistrates, Powell told Colborne, felt that the state of the gaol and its inmates 'so far as it has depended upon them or upon the Sheriff and his officers does not deserve the epithet which ... has been applied to it in your letter.' In the *Colonial Advocate* Mackenzie crowed that 'their worships read His Excellency a pretty round lecture ... We advise our readers to peruse it – it is quite edifying.'[73]

The Gore District gaol, the third focal point of troubles, was a dank, dark dungeon and suffered from severe overcrowding. In the early spring of 1835, an incident in this disgraceful facility transformed the politics of Upper Canadian gaols and led directly to the most serious effort ever undertaken to achieve fundamental reform. On 30 May one James Owen McCarthy, a Catholic Irish immigrant who had been convicted of murder, died a violent death in his cell. Before that transpired, his case had become a *cause célèbre*, engaging the attention of the British authorities, causing great excitement among the Irish Catholics, and involving many prominent political and judicial figures.

The episode that led to the conviction of McCarthy and his friend, hotel owner John Rooney, occurred in May 1834. McCarthy and his wife were badly beaten in a brawl in a Dundas tavern. McCarthy left to find reinforcements; when he and Rooney returned they used clubs and stones to beat one William Forden, who died the next day. Tried before James Macaulay, both McCarthy and Rooney were found guilty and the judge, satisfied that murder, not manslaughter, was the proper charge, did not support an appeal for mercy. McCarthy then appealed to prominent friends he had made while a tailor in Dublin, and the colonial secretary, Lord Stanley, forwarded material on the case to Sir John Colborne. The local Irish community and McCarthy himself gathered petitions with hundreds of names, and a decision was made in Britain to grant a conditional pardon.[74]

In the meantime, McCarthy complained that he and Rooney were confined in a cell '9 feet square with two bed sheets in it and only four inches square to receive the air through a narrow slit.' They were 'full of pains all over without the heat of any kind of fire ... in this cold season of the year.' The sheriff responded that there was a large stove in the hall and that their cell was as large as any other. He also claimed that McCarthy's wife had confided that he was a drunk and had 'many times beaten her' severely. The sheriff alleged that McCarthy's language was foul and that 'there has never been in this gaol a worse character.' He feared that McCarthy's friends would mount an escape attempt. When McCarthy was told that his sentence had been commuted, conditional on banishment for life, he apparently 'fell into a great passion,' and further abused his keepers. During an attempt to place him in irons, made the day before his scheduled release, McCarthy experienced a seizure and died.[75]

Although the degree of fault on either side cannot be determined, the colonial office was vastly displeased. Probing questions began to be raised about gaol conditions in Upper Canada. A grand jury concluded that McCarthy's own recalcitrant behaviour had led to his death; they absolved the gaoler and all others who assisted 'in ironing the unfortunate James Owen McCarthy from all blame.' In a separate report, the jurors resorted to the common formula. They found the prisoners generally healthy, 'perfectly satisfied' with the treatment of the gaoler, and as comfortable as their circumstances would permit. As usual, this covered a host of sins. The jurors added that the small cells were not adequately ventilated, that a separate room was urgently needed for the sick, and that classification was impossible. 'The indiscriminate mixture of the most abandoned felons with those who are confined for minor offences tends materially to prevent the reformation of the latter.' During repeated recent attempts to break gaol, one of which was successful, extensive damage had been done to the facility.[76]

When Macaulay visited the prisoners, he found a building which, although new, was too small, insecure, and lacking a yard: 'each of the cells will accommodate from four to six persons tolerably well – but of late twice that number have been confined in Debtors Rooms.' Because of numerous escape attempts, many prisoners were 'kept locked up constantly – and some are bound to the floor with leg-irons.' Macaulay was appalled by the lack of classification in this newly constructed old-style prison. But for him, the solution had to be a provincial one. Most Upper Canadian gaols were already too small and he believed the legislature should provide plans for new buildings and establish rules and regulations for their governance. When Colborne reported on this matter to the colonial secretary, Lord Glenelg 'expressed his displeasure at the state of the prisons and the Gore gaol in particular.'[77]

Further confirmation of the abominable conditions in the Gore gaol came from Lewis A. Norton, who was imprisoned there for some months after the 1837 Rebellion. 'Every hall was crowded full,' he related, 'and there were no blankets or other covering save what the prisoners had on.' But conditions in the winter may have been preferable to those experienced by another arrested rebel, Elijah Woodman, who was there during the summer of 1838. 'The cells were very much crowded which, with the hot summer weather, came nearly suffocating us. At night we took turns at a hole called a window, eight inches square, to get a little air.'[78]

REFORM EFFORTS, 1835–1840

Following the death of James Owen McCarthy, the King's Bench judges collectively determined to achieve change. In a statement dated 22 December 1835, they issued a ringing call for reform. Their first concern was diet. Some districts, they noted, supplied meat and vegetables, but they were 'not sure that this is the case generally.' They strongly disapproved of the Home District's practice of feeding prisoners only bread and water, describing this as insufficient for prisoners' health. Some prisoners in the York gaol were 'in a state of suffering' from want of 'the absolute necessaries of life.' No claim upon district funds could take precedence over providing whatever might be necessary 'for preserving prisoners from absolute suffering.' In all cases, the districts must provide adequate medical attendance, fuel, bedding, clothing, and food. If the districts could not pay for these needs, the legislature must do so. The treatment of prisoners, they insisted, 'appears to call for the establishment, by Legislative authority, of more precise and satisfactory regulations than are at present provided.'[79]

This judicial clarion call was the first demand of many made over the course of the nineteenth century that the central government take the initiative. The lieutenant-governor and the colonial office shared the views of the judges and their report was printed. In a circular of the same date, 22 December 1835, Colborne directed district officials to submit full reports on the practices followed in their gaols. The material brought forward in response to the lieutenant-governor's direction provides the most comprehensive data ever gathered on Upper Canadian gaols. It includes grand jury presentments, reports for the 1832–5 period prepared by sheriffs and gaolers, and documents submitted by clerks of the peace and magistrates. Although much of this data reflected the views of those responsible for gaol administration, this did not mean that it was biased in favour of the status quo. Many of those who provided information knew conditions first-hand, and believed there was an urgent need for change. Magistrates continued to complain that the law tied their hands and that the funds available for gaol administration were entirely inadequate. Sheriffs, legally at risk for escapes which they lacked the means to prevent, and faced with the problem of finding competent gaolers to perform a poorly paid function, had their own grievances. And gaolers, constantly subject to danger, aggravation, and never-ending work, wanted reform most of all. Colborne's request for information provided an opportunity for local officials to make their case for change.[80]

District officials first addressed the judges' shocking assertion that some prisoners were suffering from want of 'the absolute necessaries of life.' Were prisoners given adequate food, clothing, bedding, and medical attention? Were the cells properly ventilated? Had gaol imprisonment effectively replaced the old shaming punishments, such as whipping and branding, as a means of inflicting physical pain? And, perhaps most important, was it the intention to maintain prisoners in a state of deprivation as part of a system of condign punishment designed to achieve the maximum measure of deterrence?

Although responses varied from district to district, the information supplied clearly indicates that the judges were correct in suggesting that physical suffering, pain, and deprivation were common consequences of gaol imprisonment. But it also emerges that this was more a result of district parsimony and unplanned circumstances than of any coherent punitive approach. There is virtually no evidence of a consistent intention to impose pain as part of the punishment, although there was an element of this in the response of D'Arcy Boulton of the Home District, and of a few others. The overwhelming impression arising from this documentation is of well-meaning and humane officials who believed that prisoners confined in the local gaols had a right to reasonable standards of care. There was little in the responses to indicate that sheriffs, magistrates, and gaolers had any desire to impose a harsh or punitive regimen. To the extent that suffering was allowed to exist, it was a consequence not of any determination to punish in order to deter, but of inadequate resources, administrative and political weaknesses and, occasionally, of human inefficiencies. Nonetheless, the standards of care that were deemed adequate and humane in the 1830s were far below those which a later age of prisoners would receive as basic rights. This was revealed most fully in an extended discussion of prison dietary. Of the districts reporting on this issue, five said they supplied bread and water only; seven said they supplied bread, meat, and vegetables. The question of cost was a large consideration.

Sir John Colborne, John Beverley Robinson, and those who read these reports would not have been reassured by what they learned of existing practices in such other areas as heating, ventilation, clothing, bedding and medical attention.[81] These were provided for inadequately in all of the gaols some of the time, and in several gaols most of the time. Diversity was the rule and some districts tried harder than others. According to William Young, the chair of London Sessions, his district, even in the absence of legislative authority, had supplied medical aid, bedding, and clothing for all prisoners, including those awaiting trial and indigent debtors. The magistrates 'felt it an imperative duty ... to order all such and other necessary expenses to be paid out of the funds,' if it were required 'for the health and comfort' of prisoners. Magistrates willing to spend scarce funds, which many citizens would have preferred to allot to schools or roads rather than to 'the comfort' of prisoners, did not possess a punitive attitude towards gaol confinement.

Young and many of his colleagues were by no means satisfied with the status quo. 'The gaol in this District,' he noted, 'and I believe it is the case with many others throughout the Province, is ill constructed, badly ventilated, and without yards,' which he considered essential to prisoner health. Grand juries, he added, had 'invariably presented our gaol as most insecure and wholly unfit for the purpose.' Several debtors had recently escaped and the magistrates wished to remedy 'so serious an evil.' But costs of improvements 'exceed any funds at the disposal of the magistracy,' and it would be impossible to build a new gaol unless the legislature provided financial authorization. For Young, the ideal solution would be a statute applicable across the province to allow districts to raise funds commensurate with their responsibilities.

The information that emerged about other necessaries of life offered compelling reasons in favour of such a legislative initiative. The sheriffs of every district asserted that bedding was provided, but conditions were often attached. In the Ottawa District, there was a standing order to provide bedding and blankets when 'actually necessary.' In the Johnstown and Prince Edward Districts bedding and clothing were provided only for the destitute. The Niagara District allowed one straw bed for two prisoners, 'with 4 small blankets, clothing in extreme cases,' and in the Gore District two prisoners shared each straw bed. In the Western District, as in most others, no clothing was allowed, but bedding was supplied. In the Home District, the ever-intransigent D'Arcy Boulton maintained his hard line. Bedding was supplied, but 'the destruction of them by refractory prisoners in a wanton manner has been the cause of repeated complaints.' Any suffering on the part of prisoners was 'confined to such of them as from their own intemperate conduct and insubordination' could not be trusted with the usual allotment. Boulton had nothing to say as to why prisoners might destroy bedding and other amenities necessary for their own health.

Prisoners in Upper Canadian gaols, as these reports documented, suffered grievously from heat, cold, and dreadful ventilation. The sheriffs' returns for some reason seldom referred to the provision of wood for winter heat. The Johnstown sheriff indicated that ten pence a week was supplied for fuel, but possibly this was for cooking. The magistrates said more. In the Midland District, long-time Sessions chair John Macaulay reported that prisoners and debtors were well supplied with stoves and fuel. On receiving the lieutenant-governor's communication, the Midland magistrates in Special Session toured the gaol and asked every inmate 'whether any of them had suffered from the recent severity of the weather, or from want of necessary sustenance.' Macaulay was 'gratified' to report that 'the result of this inspection was most satisfactory.' The prisoners and debtors had adequate food, clothes, and bedding. Given his reputation for integrity and his interest in penal matters, including his leading role in the establishment of the penitentiary, Macaulay's assessment must be treated with respect.

Although most other magistrates also claimed, as did the Ottawa sheriff, that 'an adequate supply of firewood' was always provided, this did not prevent much suffering from the cold. Often whatever heat did come from inefficient stoves, usually located in the halls, did not penetrate the cells. In summertime fetid air and abominable ventilation were an even greater threat to prisoner health. In many gaols, the mere act of breathing was a serious hazard. Regulation 8 of the Prince Edward District rules that 'as much air shall be allowed the prisoners as the situation and plan of the Gaol will allow' was a bad joke.

With more justification, magistrates and sheriffs claimed that the medical needs of the prisoners were well provided for, but again conditions varied locally. Ottawa reported that medical attendance was 'seldom hitherto required' and it appointed no regular physician to attend. In Bathurst, 'a surgeon attends when required' and this was also the case in the Eastern, Johnstown, and most other districts. Some doctors were paid a retainer and appear to have had fairly formal obligations. John Macaulay reported that in Kingston the doctor made quarterly reports on the health of the prisoners and was given fifty pounds per annum. Though paid to attend the criminal inmates only, he 'never hesitate[d]' to help the debtors when required. Among his duties was the supervision of the diet, and he was expected to recommend any changes required for reasons of health. Several other districts had similar requirements, although none appear to have been as comprehensive as those of Midland. In London, a doctor was appointed in 1832 at the rate of fifteen pounds per annum. By Prince Edward District Regulation 16, a doctor was to attend regularly and to make formal reports twice a year to the magistrates. And D'Arcy Boulton used the opportunity to rebut what he regarded as earlier slurs on the Home District gaol. The district, he reported, employed a doctor of high standing, who was 'ever prompt in giving his immediate attention' to every call made on him. As proof of medical efficiency, he boasted that there had been only three deaths in the gaol over the previous three years, the period covered by the cholera visitation. The magistrates, he concluded, knew of no case in which a prisoner's health had been so impeded that his ability to labour after discharge had been affected in any way. On balance, it would seem that prisoners lodged in Upper Canadian gaols probably received as good, if not better, medical attention than they would have received if not imprisoned.

The situation respecting discipline appears even more positive. Without exception, punishments inflicted by gaol officers were infrequent and light. Regulation 4 of the Prince Edward District rules directed that no prisoner was to be put in irons 'except in cases of absolute and unavoidable necessity.' The particulars of every such case were to be entered into a journal and submitted to the magistrates at the next sessions. No prisoner was to be kept in irons 'longer than may be found strictly necessary.' Such explicit rules ensured that few prisoners, if any, were ironed as a form of punishment. Ironing was used for security reasons only and was strictly regulated.

For prisoners who broke the rules or who were otherwise guilty of refractory behaviour, the Prince Edward District rules authorized the keeper 'to put the offender into solitary confinement, and keep him on bread and water' for a period not exceeding twenty-four hours, each punishment again to be entered in a journal. The sheriff's reports suggest that actual punishment practices largely adhered to the benevolent intent suggested by such rules. Districts reporting that solitary confinement, whipping, and irons were never resorted to included Ottawa, Johnstown, Newcastle, and Western. The Western District reported that the prisoners always behaved with propriety, evidently exhibiting none of the rebelliousness that outraged D'Arcy Boulton at York. The apparent lack of need to impose harsh punishments is suggestive. In an age of brief sentences, in which the gaol experience was not expected to impose a disciplinary regimen or to achieve behavioural changes, the need to inflict penitentiary-style punishments simply did not exist. In the absence of hard labour, and with no attempt made to enforce a rule of silence, the gaols retained much of the informality of the prisons of an earlier day, an ambience which was reinforced by their continuing congregate and communal nature. The absence of brutal punishments in most gaols was probably beneficial not only for gaoler and gaoled, but served the community well, too. Those sentenced to brief terms of imprisonment were more likely to enter upon and leave their confinement punished, to be sure, but not embittered, and less likely to seek to revenge on society than they were after the infliction of penitentiary-style corporal punishments.

Yet several districts did report that they resorted to a range of physical punishments. In the Eastern District, solitary confinement, whipping, and irons were all used, as was the case in the Midland Distict. The London District said that solitary confinement, whipping, and irons were resorted to because there was no legislative provision to the contrary. The several reports, however, offered no details as to frequency, and generally sheriffs did not seem anxious to inflict such punishments, taking pride instead in their avoidance. In the Gore District, the sheriff commented that 'when a prisoner is quarrelsome and abuses other prisoners, or from his riotous conduct attempts to escape, or abuses the gaoler, he is put in irons, but is never whipped, except by sentence of a Court of Justice.' Sheriff Richard Bullock confirmed that the Prince Edward rules were strictly adhered to. The gaoler, he reported, was authorized by Quarter Sessions to put an offender in solitary and to keep him on bread and water (for not more than twenty-four hours) 'for disregard of prison rules, assaults in prison, profane cursing and swearing, or indecent or refractory behaviour.' One prisoner, he noted, 'was whipped by order of the magistrates in Quarter Sessions.'

In Upper Canada the continuing existence of the gaols as community facilities, the brevity of sentences, and restraint in the imposition of punishments all helped to ensure that no convict class existed in Canada until after the opening of Kingston penitentiary. On the other hand, the same limited purposes that allowed the gaols to retain some communitarian values also helped to ensure that these facilities could never be anything other than places of confinement, with narrowly circumscribed objectives. There was seldom any thought that the gaols could be organized either to impose sentences of hard labour or to provide prisoners with an opportunity to perform work that would be of value both to themselves and to the district. In the Ottawa District, the sheriff reported that no arrangement had been made to put prisoners to work, because individuals were 'seldom ... in custody'; in the Bathurst District, prisoners were not employed because they were 'not sentenced to labour'; and in the Eastern and Johnstown Districts, no regulations pertained to labour. In the Home District, however, male prisoners broke stone while females did washing and scrubbing. The stones broken by prisoners were used on city streets. D'Arcy Boulton complained nonetheless that there was no means for putting most prisoners to work and he loudly regretted that it seemed impossible to use their labour to pay the costs of maintaining them. Nowhere was there any suggestion that labour might serve rehabilitative purposes. In Niagara, however, it was reported that 'prisoners are allowed to work for their own benefit at harmless trades when tools may be safely entrusted to them.' Even there it was admitted that generally 'prisoners [are] not employed because of the danger of entrusting them with the necessary tools.'

Still more surprising was the absence in most gaols of minimal provisions for religious needs. If district officers believed that crime was to some extent explained by the absence of moral or religious feelings, it would have been reasonable to expect that more effort would have been made to inculcate religious values. Few gaols had their own chaplain, and some did not even possess a copy of the Bible. There was no regular ministry to the gaols, and dissenting clergymen were notable by their absence. Even in the well-run Prince Edward gaol it was reported that 'no clergyman [was] appointed to perform divine service ... nor has any Minister performed service therein' and there were no Bibles or other books. In Newcastle, however, a chaplain managed to attend about once a fortnight to preach and read prayers, and a few Bibles were supplied by the Society for the Propagation of the Gospel. In the Home District John Strachan did yeoman service. Strachan's dedication extended beyond formal preaching and he often wrote and worked on behalf of prisoners.

The lack of provision for religious instruction, which contrasts sharply with developments later in the century, may reflect the weakness of the evangelical spirit at this point in the colony's history or the shortage of clergymen in many communities. It also confirms that neither the churches nor the secular authorities anticipated the conversion or rehabilitation of prisoners. Not even John Macaulay, who was committed to providing chaplaincy services as an integral part of the rehabilitative apparatus of the penitentiary, had much to say at this point about religion in the local gaols. It was not Macaulay but William Young of the London District who suggested that religious instruction should be offered in all gaols, and that if the districts could acquire the necessary funds, a room in each should be set aside as a chapel. 'Not a gaol in England,' said Young, 'is without this, and not one in Canada supplied with anything of the sort.' Magistrates should also be 'empowered to appoint and remunerate a chaplain.' But few Upper Canadians shared Young's commitment, and few clergymen seemed anxious to perform on a voluntary basis.

The deepest resolve held by the reformers of the mid-1830s was to achieve more effective classification. The phrase 'nurseries of crime' was on the lips of every reformer, and if the gaols could not be expected to rehabilitate, at least they should no longer contaminate. No one expected that the districts would immediately be able to convert their old ward-style facilities (in which prisoners slept together in large rooms) to new cellular models, but something had to be done: the 1836 returns confirmed that the most hardened and dissolute offenders were lodged side-by-side with the young and the innocent of both sexes.

Thus both the Eastern and the Johnstown Districts reported three rooms for criminals, two for debtors, and 'no classification of criminals.' The large Kingston gaol had the most complete classification. Although it did not operate on the cellular system, the prisoners were divided into five classes: convicted felons, convicted misdemeanants, those charged in either category or committed for want of sureties, and vagrants. The sexes were segregated and debtors were housed in separate apartments. But Kingston had no day rooms, workrooms, or exercise yard. In Niagara, in contrast, there was 'one large hall where all the prisoners are allowed to assemble during the day time.' With only rails separating debtors from criminals and prisoners from the gaoler, there was a potential for routine chaos, which helps to explain the frequent requests from Niagara that the army be sent. At night the felons were separated from misdemeanants in cells when practical, but no other classification was attempted.

The occasional pregnancy threw officials into a tizzy, confirming as it did the failure to impose even the most essential form of classification. Soon there would be several complaints from officers of the new penitentiary that women were arriving from the gaols *enceinte* and claiming that conception had occurred during gaol confinement. On this subject there was consensus as to the harmful effects, but no agreement on a remedy. All new construction, said D'Arcy Boulton, should be carried out so as to 'enable a proper degree of attention in classification.' For John Macaulay, it was 'important to prevent our Common Gaols from becoming schools of vice,' which occurred when prisoners were 'associated in large rooms or cells.' But Macaulay had limited expectations where the gaols were concerned. A better classification, he concluded, 'is perhaps all that can be accomplished by any improvement in the architecture and discipline of Common Gaols.' Evidently Macaulay was advocating reconstruction along cellular lines, but as one of the most experienced magistrates in the province, he understood the problems lying in the way of significant gaol reform, and did not expect that classification could be designed as part of a rehabilitative program.

Most magistrates believed that change required strong leadership from the central government. D'Arcy Boulton appealed for 'a general revision of the laws on the subject of prisons,' while the Bathurst District magistrates called for 'a legislative enactment for the maintenance of prisoners and insane persons in each District.' Gore District magistrates similarly desired either comprehensive instructions from the judges, 'or otherwise that the whole arrangement shall be refined and regulated by the Legislature.' And from London, William Young urged that gaol management be made 'a general measure throughout the province.' Newcastle District Quarter Sessions chair John Steele told the lieutenant-governor that more should be done by legislative enactment to increase the food allowance and to improve the general treatment of prisoners.

The magistrates stopped short of recommending a complete provincial takeover of gaols. A hundred and thirty years would pass before that would occur. But they pleaded for help and direction, and especially for legislation that would provide increased taxing authority for their level of government. The agreement that a crisis existed which called for executive leadership is significant. The magistrates were asserting in the clearest possible way that the traditional machinery of local government was inadequate. Equally significant is the consensus about the nature of the crisis. No one even hinted that it had been caused by the rampant spread of crime. D'Arcy Boulton, to be sure, did contrast 'the comparative absence of crime' in the early years of the colony with the situation brought about by population growth, but he regarded this as normal and lauded the many benefits accruing from recent immigration. The magistrates without exception were convinced that the gaol crisis had little to do with increases in the amount of crime and everything to do with inadequacies in district governance. Repeatedly they protested, like Fraser of the Bathurst District, that they had treated prisoners 'with the greatest humanity' and made them 'as comfortable as circumstances and their unfortunate situation would admit of.' But, warned Fraser, the funds of the district were simply 'inadequate to the maintenance of so many prisoners.' Like so many of his colleagues, he recommended that 'some provision may be made by a Legislative enactment for the maintenance of prisoners and insane persons in each District.

This was not an early case of different levels of government attempting to escape responsibility. Magistrates, sheriffs, and grand jurors all understood the extent of human suffering caused by the inability of the districts to manage the gaols adequately, and they desperately wished to remedy the situation. In 1835, James Fitzgibbon, foreman of the Home District grand jury, petitioned the assembly on the grounds that prisoners were suffering horribly. The crisis in gaol management had led to increased rigour towards the prisoners, 'debtors as well as criminals, causing them to suffer more than the law would sanction or humanity approve.' This state of affairs, said Fitzgibbon, had existed for eight years and was getting progressively worse. The district had made repeated applications to the legislature 'for an Act to increase the taxation of property,' and to allow the magistrates 'to apply the needful remedies' but to no avail.

District authorities readily admitted their difficulties and begged the province to effect the necessary changes. The extensive documentation generated in 1836 underlines the political and administrative nature of the Upper Canadian crisis. There was a lack of interest at this point in either the causes of crime or the social context of law enforcement. If social turmoil had been a concern to local authorities, they would have used the lieutenant-governor's query of December 1835 as an opportunity to express their concerns and vent their fears. Overwhelmingly, the problem was perceived as one of governmental structures.

The body of evidence collected in 1836 also testifies to the existence of deeply rooted humanitarian attitudes towards those confined in the gaols. What stands out in this discourse is the language sheriffs and magistrates chose to describe their prisoners. George Hamilton of the Gore District, for instance, said it had been an object of the highest priority with the justices to keep the gaol 'clean and comfortable,' and added that the district was trying to provide 'as much comfort' as was compatible with safekeeping. From the Western District Charles Eliot confirmed that his colleagues were doing their best not only to prevent prisoners from suffering, but to render them 'comfortable.' Such language would not have been used by magistrates who held gaol prisoners in contempt, nor was it the language of a class expressing fear over rising crime rates and social upheaval. These were the words of men who still viewed the prisoners as individuals, who could address them familiarly by name, and who often knew other members of their families. Many of them would soon be resuming normal lives and those who could not, the very old perhaps, or the insane, were deserving of pity, not contempt. Not only in the 1836 documentation but throughout the Upper Canadian period, the discourse was carried on at this level. There were of course a few exceptions. Occasionally a D'Arcy Boulton would demonstrate contempt for the prisoners, and Sheriffs Jarvis and Merritt might express fear that some hardened characters would not stop short of murder. Sometimes desperate men resorted to desperate deeds, sometimes sheriffs and gaolers had to deal with the dregs of humanity. But that was not the rule, and throughout the period the local and congregate character of the gaols ensured that it would not be so. As this communitarian discourse confirmed, until the opening of Kingston Penitentiary there were no convicts in Upper Canada, just unfortunate men and women briefly detained.

JUDICIAL LEADERSHIP

The most influential advocate of gaol reform was John Macaulay's old friend, the chief justice. Operating smoothly behind the political scene, John Robinson suggested to the Home District grand jurors in 1835 that they ask the legislature to institute an inquiry into 'the general state of all the gaols.' In 1836 he again urged the jurors to act, informing them that 'the representation of a respectable Grand Jury' must carry great weight with the politicians. The jurors did what the chief justice asked, and soon a copy of Robinson's charge was before the assembly for its consideration.[82]

In this thoughtful document, Robinson again justified his reputation as the most talented Upper Canadian. Demonstrating an intimate familiarity with both local conditions and recent British legislative changes, he also revealed a shrewd grasp of the politics of correctional reform. A few people, he suggested, might be indifferent as to what happened to prisoners, but more people were simply preoccupied with their private lives and unwilling to take the time to study the question. Nonetheless, said Robinson, the amelioration of public prisons, was 'a subject worthy of inquiry in every enlightened community.' To discharge prisoners in a morally worse condition than they had been in when they entered the gaol was thoroughly pernicious, especially in the case of those found innocent of all charges.

In the Tory tradition, Robinson argued that improvements would best be achieved by an expansion of the role of the central government. He wanted the legislature to appoint commissioners to inspect all the gaols and to make suggestions for improvement, thereby enabling the legislators to acquire the requisite information to proceed with what Robinson termed 'the necessary work of reform.' Long the province's most important Tory, and speaking now as chief justice, Robinson's powerful advocacy meant that gaol reform moved immediately to the foreground of the public stage. In his charge to the jury Robinson outlined his own thinking, acquired through close familiarity with every gaol and close acquaintance with all of the sheriffs and most of the working magistrates. His first point was that two paramount objects must predominate in the erection of gaols: security and discipline. Robinson believed that most of the suffering prisoners endured resulted from physical conditions such as overcrowding, poor ventilation, and dampness, and the necessity of placing high-risk prisoners in chains.

Pointing to recent British statutes, Robinson applauded the way in which these enactments applied to all gaols across England. He especially approved of the requirement that those committed for trial receive adequate food, and that no labour be required of this class of prisoner. Combining his faith in the rule of law with a generalized humanitarianism, Robinson insisted that it was the gaoler's duty to preserve order and decency by rigorously enforcing all prison rules and punishing every breach of them. Reacting to a recent claim of Lord Brougham that English gaols were becoming nurseries of crime, he particularly emphasized that the local authorities must carry out a system of classification, again to be achieved 'by some general enactment' applicable across the province.

Speaking as the outstanding leader of the emerging bureaucratic state, Robinson explained why such an assertion of centrist authority had become essential. 'I have reason to believe that prisoners in some of the gaols do not receive the allowance which in my opinion, they should have.' Equally shocking, 'the frequent use of irons in every gaol, amounts in my opinion to a presumption of mismanagement in the gaoler, or insecurity in the gaol.' Robinson was not persuaded by sheriffs' returns and other documentation that the province's gaols were humane or that they achieved minimal standards of efficiency. As a former attorney general, a lawyer, and a judge, he had strong views on the relationship between the duties of the state and what he termed the rights of all prisoners. Emphasizing again that problems would continue until every gaol was made secure, he deployed the language of prisoners' rights, especially clean air, exercise, food and clothing, and proper medical attention. 'There can be no time or circumstances in which a prisoner accused or convicted of crime has not a right to all things indispensably requisite for the preservation of health and life.' Beyond that, 'prisoners of every description have a right to be protected, as far as possible, from bad examples and bad society.' They should also receive religious instruction, and he suggested that the expense required to ensure the regular attendance of a minister 'must appear trifling indeed when compared with the social advantages.' On one subject he said little, but insisted it was worthy of future consideration. The employment of prisoners at constructive labour could divert the minds of prisoners 'from evil to good habits,' and he hoped the topic would be pursued elsewhere.

As chief justice, Robinson's rhetoric of rights assumed enormous significance. There were some he knew who shared his vision and his understanding, but others did not, and many more were indifferent and ignorant. Robinson spoke strongly, loudly, and often because he regarded it as his duty to do so, and because he believed the politicians would listen to a chief justice. Most assuredly, Robinson's program was consonant with the traditional Tory faith in the use of central authority to address societal issues. Beyond that, gaol reform was a subject of importance for Robinson because he believed that these facilities must play a leading role in reform of the Upper Canadian system of criminal justice. Robinson's wide-ranging reform program included, as we shall see, not only the gaols but the law reforms of 1833 and the statute of 1834 establishing a penitentiary.

For a while, with the lieutenant-governor, the colonial office, and the judges leading the parade, the momentum towards gaol reform seemed irresistible. Aside from Robinson, one of the most influential voices was that of John Macaulay. As chair of the Midland Sessions, Macaulay had in December 1835 forwarded a return to the lieutenant-governor that included rules for the Midland gaol, which proved influential in later efforts to establish a province-wide set of gaol rules. As co-chair of the legislature's 1833 committee studying the need for a penitentiary, Macaulay had been impressed by William Powers, an official of New York state's Auburn penitentiary. Powers soon would become deputy warden of Kingston Penitentiary and he and John Macaulay worked together to prepare a plan for a model district gaol. Macaulay promised to submit this plan to the judges to 'determine whether it may not be well to recommend it for general adoption on all future occasions of construct-ing District Prisons.' Under the existing system, Macaulay explained, the justices at the district level would go to considerable expense to build a gaol which 'turns out to be defective,' and the same thing would then be repeated 'in the very next District, in which a Gaol is to be built.' Macaulay believed that 'this evil might be remedied' if the executive gov-ernment would adopt a general plan for all gaols and allow no deviation, 'except by consent of an Inspector of Prisons.'[83]

Briefly, at least, the Tory elite had achieved a consensus. The province had reached a size and complexity that demanded the implementation of formal structures devised and regulated by the executive government. In the 1836 throne speech, the lieutenant-governor asserted that 'the state of the Gaols, and the treatment of Prisoners confined in them, I shall have occasion to bring to your notice: for it appears to me that to relieve the Magistrates from an undue responsibility, as well as to ensure the humane care, and safe custody of the prisoners, it is desirable to frame more particular provisions than have hitherto been made.' The result was the important 1838 Act 'to regulate the future erection of Gaols in this Province.' This measure established a Board of Gaol Commissioners, composed of the judges of the Court of King's Bench, the vice-chancellor, all of the district sheriffs, and others appointed by the lieutenant-governor. It became the responsibility of this board, which was to report annually to the legislature, to supervise the building of new gaols and the rebuilding of old ones. The objectives to be achieved were those of the chief justice. The purpose of imprisonment was described as 'the reforma-tion of convicts, as far as may be practicable, and ... their employment, in order that the common gaols may really serve for places of correction.' The board was instructed to meet without delay and to formulate rules and regulations for the government of all gaols. Specifically, the rules were to deal with diet, clothing, bedding, medical attendance, religious instruction, restraint and punishments, and 'the treatment and custody of the prisoners generally.' The commissioners were authorized to deal with 'all such matters' connected with the gaols that they considered 'expedi-ent,' and they were to pay particular attention to the great issue of classification. The proposed regulations were to be submitted to the legislature for consideration at the next session and to take effect at the end of that session.[84]

Notwithstanding the Rebellion and post-Rebellion turmoil, John Robinson and like-minded colleagues had succeeded in giving gaol reform a leading place in the governmental agenda. And they achieved this at a time when Durham, Arthur, and later Sydenham were developing the most far-reaching program for governmental restructuring that would emerge in the first half of the nineteenth century. The promise of genuine prison reform had never been brighter. But with so many issues demanding government attention, and with the colony soon to be merged in a wider union, it would prove difficult to keep prison reform in the foreground of the provincial agenda. As Robinson recognized, this subject was of pressing interest to few. For a variety of reasons, including costs and the complexities of the relationship between central and local governments, gaol reform demanded continuing resolve and commitment on the part of reformers, locally as well as at the centre. Regrettably, events would soon reveal that too few Upper Canadians shared in the liberal vision and commitment to prisoner's rights, and the moment would pass with little real achievement.

At first the new board moved ahead with considerable energy. In 1839, it submitted a report signed by Robert Jameson as vice-chancellor, by Queen's Bench judges Sherwood, James Macaulay, Jones, and McLean, and by a few others, including John Macaulay.[85] In accordance with the statute, the commissioners approved plans for new gaols in Woodstock, Peterborough, Guelph, Barrie, and London, and authorized the magistrates to proceed. They also presented for legislative approval a comprehensive list of rules and regulations. Most basic was a call for classification, so far as the state of the buildings allowed, to place prisoners in five distinct categories. But the proposed rules also expressed Robinson's belief that the state had an obligation to supply all the basic necessities of life, including food, clothing, bedding, medical care, heating, ventilation, and 'as much exercise' as needed for the health of the prisoners, and as the plan of the gaol would allow. This last expression was an escape clause, but at least the districts were to be placed on notice as to their responsibilities.

The rules went well beyond the proclamation of minimal standards. Provision was to be made, 'as far as practicable,' to enforce hard labour when imposed by the court and, more innovatively, to provide work for other prisoners. Mechanics were to be allowed to practice their trades when that could be done without a threat to security. Bibles were to be supplied to each cell and divine service performed each Sunday, with attendance compulsory. Provision was to be made, again 'as far as practicable,' for the religious instruction of the prisoners, and for their instruction in reading and writing. Here can be discerned the influence of the Assize judges, especially Robinson, and that of penitentiary advocates like John Macaulay, who were committed to achieving not only the punishment but the rehabilitation of prisoners. Many local gaolers must have gasped with disbelief when they learned the extent of these provisions.

Nor did the commissioners ignore prisoners' rights. Beyond providing for all physical needs, the sheriffs and gaolers were to put no prisoner in irons, 'except in case of urgent and absolute necessity.' When done, the particulars of every case must be described in writing and notice sent to the sheriff and to one of the justices. Special procedures were to be followed if any prisoner was ironed for more than four days. Upon the death of a prisoner, notice was to be sent to the sheriff, the coroner and, if practicable, the nearest relative of the deceased. Impressed by the importance that the English had recently attached to regular inspections, the commissioners required the justices at every Quarter Sessions to nominate two or more justices to act as gaol visitors, and one or more of the visitors was to inspect the gaol at least three times in each quarter, and monthly if necessary.

Finally the duties of gaolers and keepers were laid out more fully than ever before, although nothing was said about qualifications for these positions. The keeper was to see every prisoner and inspect every cell at least twice a day. He was to hear prisoner complaints and to punish offenders by placing them in solitary cells and on a bread and water diet 'for any time not exceeding three days.' In every case, he was to note the particulars in his journal and 'immediately' inform the sheriff. He was to keep a register of all those confined and the magistrates were to inspect this register at each Quarter Sessions. The proposed register included fifteen pieces of information, including age, occupation, education, place of birth, religion, offence, and the prisoner's conduct. The commissioners prepared a sample annual return to be submitted by each district gaol, which would record thirty-one pieces of information.

These regulations went much further than the rather primitive rules adopted by some districts in the 1820s and early 1830s. They included all of the reform proposals desired by Robinson, and incorporated British and American improvements with which Robinson and Macaulay in particular were familiar. This sophisticated program, to be imposed province-wide, fully embodied the utilitarian administrative advances associated with Durham, Arthur, and Sydenham. But in common with some other reform proposals of the late 1830s and early 1840s, the gaol commissioners' program was primarily elitist in nature, lacking popular support, or even interest. The bureaucratic/administrative origins of many of the Sydenhamite reforms did not undermine the effectiveness of change, if only because most of the structural adjustments of the period had the powerful political backing of Lord Sydenham. But Robinson increasingly lacked an effective political base and by the early 1840s was in disfavour with Sydenham himself.[86] Beyond that, the program was costly, there was little public interest in the welfare of prisoners, and the implementation of the program depended on local politicians with other priorities.

Some of these considerations were apparent in the 1840 report of the commissioners appointed to consider 'the state of the several Public Departments of this Province.'[87] This document presented the results of a comprehensive study of provincial government and administration undertaken after the Rebellion, and its recommendations inspired some of Sydenham's famous reforms. The membership of the committee over-lapped substantially with the Board of Gaol Commissioners, and included Judges Sherwood, Macaulay, Jones, and McLean. Not surprisingly, the committee expressed itself as being 'deeply sensible of the imperative necessity' of placing the gaols under a well-regulated discipline, subject to 'some active and efficient inquisitorial power.' After visiting thirteen gaols the committee reported that eight were wanting 'in accommodation and other requisites.' The London gaol, for example, was judged to be too small and its cells were described as loathsome; the Niagara gaol was offensive and insufficient; Toronto's gaol, soon to be replaced, was well managed but too small. More generally, the committee regretted that the provisions of the 1838 gaols statute 'do not seem to have been regularly complied with,' and were deficient in any case. They especially pointed to the failure to supply the gaol commissioners with any clerical or secretarial assistance.

It was obvious that the gaol commissioners had been politically stranded, lacking both the political support and the logistical assistance to carry out their responsibilities. Yet the 1840 committee, doubtless influenced by its judicial membership, was unwilling to accept defeat. It called for the appointment of commissioners to carry out an investigation of every gaol in the province and to make recommendations for improvement. Possibly, they thought that any such commission would encounter such horrendous conditions that it could shock the government into action. They also recommended that the executive government, on receipt of this report, should direct the magistrates in each district to carry all necessary improvements into effect and, if necessary, to impose a rate to cover the costs. Yet by recommending another investigation the members of the committee seem to have been grasping at straws. Perhaps reformers hoped that the recent statutes dealing with houses of industry and establishing a provincial asylum would reduce the number of gaol prisoners and make additional expenditures unnecessary. The promise of Kingston Penitentiary may also have diverted attention from the gaols. Sadly, the gaol reform movement in Upper Canada had lost all momentum. It ended in anti-climax and confusion. The conditions which had been so well documented by the reformers of the 1830s would continue to prevail to the end of the century and beyond.

3

'Order Is Heaven's First Law':
The Tory Origins of Upper Canada's
Penitentiary

THE BIRTH OF KINGSTON PENITENTIARY

In June 1835 the Upper Canadian penitentiary at Portsmouth, about a mile west of Kingston, received its first prisoners. In establishing a penitentiary, the citizens of the small and predominantly rural colony were following the example of the mother country and of many other nations, including the United States, whose famous penitentiary at Auburn, New York, provided the immediate inspiration for the Upper Canadian initiative. Few Upper Canadians can have suspected that the institution they were creating would dominate their criminal justice system for a century and more. Indeed, those who lived in the Kingston area seem to have paid little attention to the imposing edifice that was rising in their midst, perhaps because they were 'watching with pride the early beginnings of a little school called Queen's College, and had no concern in what went on behind the grim walls of the other institution at Portsmouth.'[1]

Such indifference did not endure for long. Not only was the new penitentiary too important an addition to the local economy, but citizens, ever fascinated by those who commit 'dark and evil deeds,' soon flocked to Portsmouth where, for a small fee, they could observe at first-hand the pain and suffering of their fellow creatures. In short order, Kingston Penitentiary, as it was soon known, became an indispensable part of the itinerary of a succession of luminaries, from governors and chief justices to the celebrated novelist Charles Dickens who, in 1842, commented in his *American Notes* that 'there is an admirable jail here, well and wisely governed, and excellently regulated in every respect.'[2]

Quite apart from any prurient interest in the perpetrators of evil deeds, the new penitentiary excited contrasting emotions among the citizenry. There were those, including such political opposites as William Lyon Mackenzie, Mayor of Toronto, soon to flee the country as a rebel, and ermine-robed John Beverley Robinson, chief justice of the Court of King's Bench, who applauded the penitentiary as a long-needed and invaluable innovation. Others denounced the enormous structure, four-pronged and five-tiered, by the 1850s replete with a great dome which served as the heart of the massive facility, as a palace for evil-doers. For a brief period some Upper Canadians, disgusted by the contrast between the apparent opulence of the penitentiary and the living conditions of many artisans and rural folk, or alarmed at the threat posed to their livelihoods by the anticipated sale of prison-made products, challenged the very need for such an institution. But opponents of the penitentiary were unsuccessful and construction, following a few assurances as to the deployment of convict labour, proceeded more or less on schedule.

The failure of the opponents of the penitentiary to delay its construction or to alter its design has obscured the contemporary concerns that led in the first place to the decision to build a facility along Auburn-style lines. The question of a penitentiary in British North America seems to have been raised initially in Lower Canada in 1822 by Governor Dalhousie, who was familiar with Britain's national penitentiary, Millbank, which had opened in 1816.[3] In Upper Canada the matter was first presented in the legislature in 1826 by Hugh Thomson, then sitting as a Reformer for Frontenac. Thomson, a local businessman, published the Kingston *Herald*, but another Kingston journal, *The Chronicle*, a Tory paper once owned by John Macaulay, proved to be more influential. The punishments available to the courts, and especially banishment or transportation, said the *Chronicle*, were sadly ineffectual as deterrents. 'For any offence short of murder,' the paper lamented, the guilty party knew that his sentence would be commuted to one of banishment, which 'is not only in its very worst form no punishment at all, but is even ... in nine cases out of ten, entirely disregarded.' But an alternative was at hand. Already tested in the United States and Britain, the penitentiary system would render 'the punishment of offenses *real* and *certain*' and 'be productive of essential benefit in checking the progress of crime.'[4]

For the next decade, a debate sputtered sporadically in the legislature and in the press over two issues: the need for a penitentiary and the type of discipline it should implement. At times it proceeded with some passion, especially over the issue of competition between prison and free labour. But in the stormy period leading up to the Rebellion of 1837 the penitentiary question never became one of the burning issues of the day. It remained a matter of concern primarily to members of the small governing elite.

Both the decision to build a penitentiary and the related commitment to an Auburn-style discipline were made on somewhat narrow and technical grounds by a very few prominent individuals. This is an important point, given that it has been argued elsewhere that Upper Canadians were experiencing some collective malaise and that they built a penitentiary because rampant crime and turbulent social change presented the threat of social collapse and possibly political revolution. The construction of the penitentiary, it has further been argued, was but one prong of a broad attack led by middle- and upper-class elements on all forms of deviance, encompassing not only crime but poverty and insanity as well. According to this analysis, the decision to establish a penitentiary and other purpose-built and segregative instruments of social control represented a radical new departure. Indeed, taken together, the argument continues, these developments constituted a social revolution, breaking sharply from century-old practices and contributing substantially to the transition from pre-modern to early modern structures of social organization.

If such an explanation is valid, other conclusions logically follow. If elite and bourgeois members of Upper Canadian society working in concert truly turned to the penitentiary solution as a part of a widespread movement to reimpose social control, then it is hard to believe that such urgent origins would not fundamentally affect the nature of the new institution, at least during the early formative years of its development. If Upper Canadians deployed their new penitentiary as a mechanism to control an unruly and threatening underclass, then surely this harsh disciplinary purpose must largely account for the triumph of punitive over rehabilitative influences, which apparently dominated penitentiary governance under the first warden, Henry Smith. And most of all, it must at least partially explain the brutality and sadism of the institution, revealed by the famous Royal Commission of 1848. All these propositions, it is argued here, are of dubious value; all are based on slight research and less analysis. As this chapter proposes, the origins of Canada's first penitentiary lie primarily in a technical adjustment secured by a small but powerful group of law reformers.

It readily becomes apparent that the crime control/social control interpretation of the origins and early history of Kingston Penitentiary was developed on a narrow evidentiary base. One widely quoted writer, who argued that Upper Canada was beset by rising crime rates, based his entire argument on a few cases reported in the daily press.[5] In another effort, Tom Brown, also on slim evidence, claimed that by the early 1830s a new middle class had emerged in the larger towns and cities of Upper Canada, which viewed with dismay the threat suddenly posed by 'a class of propertyless wage-labourers, the new urban poor, casualties of the transition to capitalist market economy.' Members of the governing elite, too, Brown argues, feared imminent social and political collapse. He cites Tory lawyer Christopher Hagerman's 1832 comment that 'everything seems leading towards revolution,' and John Strachan, who believed 'revolution to have virtually commenced.'[6] After noting similar concerns expressed by Reform MPP Charles Duncombe and in the Methodist weekly, the *Christian Guardian*, in 1834, Brown concludes that Reformers as well as Tories were persuaded that 'the very survival of Upper Canadian society' was at risk.

The eminent historian of criminal justice John Beattie is much less moved by Strachan's political nightmares, although he too has asserted that large numbers of Upper Canadians were disturbed by a vision of burgeoning crime and disorder. For Beattie, while 'serious crime was not a problem in Canada in the 1830s and 1840s,' this did not mean that 'crime was not thought to be a serious problem.' Crime in the colony was a frequent topic of public discussion and accounts of criminal activity appeared regularly in the press. Even more important, for Upper Canadians 'crime was regarded not simply as acts of theft or violence, but more broadly as one aspect of a much larger social question.' An increasing incidence of crime in a society, says Beattie, was seen to reflect moral weakness and social malaise. It was this conviction 'that underlay a number of striking changes in the criminal law and in penal practice in this period.'[7] In either form, these arguments locate legal and penal reform, and particularly the birth of the penitentiary, in the context of a powerful movement which united elements of the old elite with the emerging middle class.

Such an interpretation assumes plausibility when the extent of social change in the colony is taken into consideration. This was, after all, the period leading up to the Rebellion of 1837, and the decision to build Kingston Penitentiary was made at a critical juncture in Upper Canada's development. With the population burgeoning between 1820 and 1840 from about 100,000 to 400,000, and with thousands of destitute immigrants, primarily Irish in origin, settling in Upper Canada, the colony faced for the first time what might genuinely be described as a social crisis. According to a report prepared in 1831 by Archdeacon Strachan, many arrived seriously ill, the hospital in York was continually full, and the town was 'overwhelmed with widows and orphans.' In these circumstances, York's small population faced the problem 'of furnishing bread to upwards of four hundred mouths.' As York's population mushroomed from 2,860 in 1830 to 9,765 in 1835, shanties sprang into existence along the waterfront and beggars appeared everywhere.[8] In 1836, leading citizens called a public meeting to find ways to provide for the basic needs of the indigent, who would otherwise perish 'from cold and hunger.' One response was the establishment the following year of a poorhouse, the House of Industry. The purpose of the House of Industry was not only to provide poor relief but, as a Citizen's Committee put it, to achieve 'the total abolition of street begging' and 'the putting down of wandering vagrants.'[9] With the poorhouse and the penitentiary in place, the legislature in 1839 passed an Act that authorized the erection of an asylum for the insane. The new institution, officially opened in 1846 on Queen Street, was a structure almost as massive as the penitentiary and equally forbidding. In the period before it was fully operational in 1850, the old Home District gaol was converted into a temporary asylum.[10]

Thus within a brief span of years three new institutions of fundamental importance had been established in Upper Canada. Together they addressed the widest possible range of social problems, and they did so by rejecting older approaches common in pre-industrial societies, whereby the poor and ill remained in the community (sometimes helped in their own homes, sometimes boarded out), while criminals were fined, scourged, or confined briefly in small gaols located in local centres. The era of the 'total institution,' it seemed, had begun. Although the evidence was not always there to link social transformations to the decision to build poorhouses, asylums, and penitentiaries, it seemed plausible that it was just such linkages that had moved the middle class and the elites to act.

Most students of the period seem to have found the class conflict and crime control interpretation of institutionalization persuasive, but it has been challenged by the scholar who has looked most closely at criminality and distress in Upper Canada, Rainer Baehre. In several much-cited articles on poverty, poor relief, and the origins of the penitentiary system, in his thesis on the nineteenth century asylum, and in more recent work which focuses on the extent of external influences on Upper Canadian decision-makers, Baehre finds not class conflict but consensus among Upper Canadians, consensus in favour of institutional approaches to social control. In Baehre's analysis, members of all classes and political groupings, including Reformers and Tories, were strongly influenced by an international milieu in which institutional solutions were adopted for a complex mix of motives, partly humanitarian, partly coercive.[11] Baehre's incrementalist perspective, which places less emphasis on class conflict and demonstrates a sensitive understanding of the complexities of human motivation, provides a thoughtful corrective to the crudities of earlier social control analyses.

There can be no doubt that Upper Canadians would not have implemented such a range of institutional controls had it not been for their prior adoption in Britain and the United States. The 'ideological origins' of the Canadian penitentiary system were undeniably British and, as Baehre's recent work confirms, American. Yet while the foreign adoption of the penitentiary solution was a necessary condition for its implementation in Upper Canada in 1834, it was hardly a sufficient condition on its own. Empirical research into the circumstances accompanying the Upper Canadian decision makes the inadequacies of the class conflict analysis clear, but it is equally true that Baehre misses a great deal about the extent to which actual agency accounts for the penitentiary's establishment, about the timing of the process, and about the specific forces that shaped Kingston's subsequent disciplinary structure. And finally, he fails to account for the strong elements of ideological continuity between the early Upper Canadian social vision, as it emerged under Simcoe, Powell, Strachan, and other Tory leaders, and those who held sway in the 1830s, especially Colborne, Macaulay, and Robinson.

To comprehend the development of Kingston Penitentiary, including the forces that caused the collapse of its disciplinary system and the real nature of the scandal documented in the 1848 Royal Commission, it is essential to understand who in Upper Canadian society demanded the penitentiary, and what they expected to achieve by it. In the late 1820s there had been some discussion in Upper Canada of how best to punish criminals. On this issue men of differing political persuasion and from contrasting social groupings were found on all sides of the debate. It was the prominent Reformer Marshall Spring Bidwell who introduced the bill of the late 1820s, for example, 'to abolish the punishment of whipping and the pillory,' an initiative which, in the absence of alternatives punishments, failed to garner support.[12] Nonetheless, it was primarily those directly involved with the criminal justice system who were most concerned with the issue and were in a position to influence policy. Most of all, it was the judges of the Court of King's Bench, and especially the for-

midable chief justice, John Beverley Robinson, who were the most determined advocates of penal reform. The Tory elite demanded such a
reform, and the Tory elite, acting with little reference to other groups,
achieved it. Neither the statistics of crime, as represented by gaol committals, nor the experience of the judges, either at the Assizes or in the Quarter Sessions, gave any indication that society was wracked by fear of
social disorder or of a rising crime rate.

To begin at the top of the legal pyramid, the King's Bench judges, better
placed than anyone else to know the extent of crime in the colony, simply
did not believe any substantial increase in the numbers of serious
offences to have taken place. Their opinions assume even greater importance since their charges to grand juries at Assizes were usually published in the newspapers, and consequently influenced public opinion. In
the early 1830s, when the penitentiary idea was receiving serious consideration, the judges did sometimes express concern about the spread of
crime in the colony, yet they were more apt to congratulate the community on the lightness of the criminal calendar. In 1830, Judge James B.
Macaulay was reported in the Kingston *Chronicle* to have commented that
'the extent of crime which sometimes casts a shade over the fair character
of portions of the Province is deeply to be deplored,' but in 1833 the
Kingston *Herald* reported Macaulay as saying that 'the Criminal Calendar, exhibited an amount of crime quite small in proportion to the population of the District, and very creditable to its inhabitants. We perceive
this Province,' he concluded, 'fortunately not fruitful in crime.'[13] Chief
Justice Robinson was even more sanguine. In 1831, for example, the
Brockville *Recorder* reported him as telling the grand jurors that the criminal calendar was so light, considering the extent of the population, 'as to
be almost a subject of congratulation.' Comments from the chairs of the
Quarter Sessions reinforced the prevailing sense that crime of whatever
variety was not a problem in Upper Canada. Charles Eliot, chair of the
Western District Sessions, told the grand jury in January 1832 that 'there
is nothing for your deliberation ... beyond the common minor offences.'[14]
John Robinson's close friend John Macaulay, as chair of the Midland District Sessions, concluded in May of that year that the number of offences
had not increased even in proportion to the growth of population, clear
evidence that the increased numbers of indigents in the colony had not
led to any outbreak of pilfering or more serious offences. From this evidence, Macaulay believed, 'it may be inferred that public morals are
improving,' a result he attributed to 'the diminished frequency of intemperance.' These views, coming from one of the most influential men in the

province, a Kingstonian who was soon to become one of the founders of the penitentiary, are significant.

Literary evidence of this type is not, however, conclusive on its own. Preliminary research into the Home and London District Quarter Sessions records for the period up to 1818, as indicated earlier, reveals an astoundingly small amount of petty crime, but a fuller analysis of archival records awaits further research. Nonetheless, an attempt has been made, using a mix of Assize records and Quarter Sessions materials for the Home, Newcastle, Johnstown, Western, London, and Midland Districts, to prepare some crude estimates of Upper Canadian crime rates. The absence of gaol registers until the 1830s and the failure of most Sessions records to take into account offences dealt with by a single magistrate or by petty sessions must render all such efforts highly suspect. Even so, the results of the analysis seem accurate enough to delineate some general trends.

One significant finding is that up to 1820, assault and assault and battery constituted fully 36.1 per cent of all prosecuted crimes (737 cases), followed by petty and grand larceny at 18.1 per cent (368 cases). All other offences were numerically insignificant. With population growth, municipal incorporation, and a somewhat more extensive commitment to policing, this pattern changed radically. In the 1825–49 period, drunk and disorderly had emerged as the leading offence numerically, constituting 31 per cent of recorded cases (3,797 cases), with larceny at 22 per cent (2,688 cases) and assault dropping to 15.6 per cent (1,906 cases). Clearly the social changes of the period, including the aggressive enforcement of new municipal by-laws, had led to the rise of what a later generation would describe as 'victimless offences.'

Looked at from another perspective, and using as the study area the Home, Gore, Newcastle, and Wellington Districts, the rate of committals to gaols for crimes against property increased from 42.5 per 100,000 of population in 1824 to only 54.6 in 1838. The rate for crimes against the person actually dropped from 136.5 per 100,000 in 1824 to 31.7 in 1838. What was most dramatic was the astounding increase in public order and moral offences, from a four-district average of 27.4 per 100,000 in 1824 to 246.2 in 1838.

While these figures must be treated with extreme caution, a few tentative conclusions may be suggested. With respect to property crime, and considering the large social and demographic changes that marked the 1830s, the gradual rise in the property crime rate is moderate indeed. Far more striking is the substantial drop in crimes against the person. As the the frontier phase of development passed, Upper Canada appears to have been becoming a less violent society. Most significant of all, and what would have the greatest long-term implications for attitudes to punishment across the rest of the nineteenth century, was the new propensity to punish those who were deemed to represent a threat to public morals and social harmony. But this expansion in the prosecution of petty offences hardly represented a serious threat to public safety or private property. These were not the types of crimes that placed basic security in jeopardy or the type to which the judges of Assizes were referring when they raised questions about the relationship between the incidence of crime and the health of society. And most of all, the petty criminals, the drunks, vagrants, and prostitutes who increasingly occupied the local goals, did not excite the imagination of those who were the foremost advocates of a penitentiary. The penitentiary was never intended to hold the drunk or the vagrant.

Despite the relative absence of serious crime and judicial consensus that no threat existed to the security of life and property, the public may have had a rather different perception of the state of affairs. What local crime did exist was reported in flamboyant terms in the newspapers, which also seized upon every opportunity to publicize violence and criminal activities in the mother country and in foreign jurisdictions. The Sessions, and especially the Assizes, received extensive publicity, doubtless because of the large place they occupied in the social calendar of early nineteenth century jurisdictions, but also because they provided the fledgling colonial press with a cheap and ready source of news. The same entertainment value explains the enormous amount of space given to crimes in far away places. It would be surprising if the prevalence of lurid crime reporting did not in some way prepare the public mood for so drastic a remedy as the construction of a penitentiary. This is far from suggesting, however, that the institution was established in response to a widespread or urgent public demand. It is frustratingly difficult to argue from scattered newspaper accounts, but what can be discerned seems to suggest that the penitentiary idea was never an urgent or popular cause. To the extent that there was comment in the press, it was advanced as an aspect of legal reform far more than as a remedy for rampant crime.

When Hugh Thomson raised the issue in the House in 1826, he took pains to emphasize that he was not motivated by any increase in the amount of crime. Indeed, he noted, the incidence of crime did not exceed in proportion the increase in population, and further, 'we cannot say that the offenses committed are often of an aggravated or atrocious nature.' Thomson could not have stated his position more clearly. He was acting entirely from the conviction that 'the necessity of some melioration of our criminal law is very manifest.' In many respects, he argued, the law as it existed in the statute books was far too severe, but 'everyone knows that it is administered with much leniency.' To demonstrate this, Thomson pointed to a case during the recent Midland District Assizes of a man convicted of returning from transportation (probably banishment) who, when condemned to execution, 'showed by his deportment that he had no dread of suffering under his awful sentence.' There were strong grounds, said Thomson, for believing that some culprits sentenced to banishment did not bother to leave the province, so deep was their disdain for the colony's system of criminal justice. To Thomson this intolerable situation was fraught with danger to the community, and the remedy was clear. The penitentiary, already used 'with good effect' in England and the United States, would render punishment *real* and *certain.*' This was sound Beccarian doctrine; the influence of Cesare Beccaria, the creative Italian thinker of the 1760s, had penetrated deeply into the psyche of Upper Canadian law reformers. The penitentiary, Thomson was persuaded, would check the contempt for the law demonstrated by convicted criminals, especially the growing number of repeat offenders. A treadmill, he added, must be an essential part of the new institution.[15] Not crime, then, but the demonstrated lack of respect for the legal system was the motivation for Thomson's initiative.

In the absence of significant public concern, Thomson's proposal was premature. A committee established to look into the penitentiary question never reported and perhaps never even met. For the time being, the penitentiary received little notice in press or legislature. One exception was a comment in the *Farmer's Journal* in March 1829, which praised New York's Auburn prison for actually making a profit through convict labour, while turning the vast majority of discharged convicts into 'good and useful citizens.'[16] Not until 1830 was the penitentiary idea again advanced in Upper Canada, and then it was put forward by no less a figure than lieutenant-governor Sir John Colborne. In his January address at the opening of the legislature Colborne pointed to the need for such an institution and urged members to prepare legislation to give it effect. The governor's comments were brief and it is unclear what provoked them. By this time John Robinson had been functioning for some months as chief justice and his efforts to achieve legal and gaol reform were greatly admired by Colborne. In Robinson's mind those several changes in the criminal justice system were intimately interrelated. He made precisely this point to a grand jury in Niagara in September 1832, arguing that the critical issue of criminal law reform depended upon the establishment of a penitentiary, a position he had held from at least 1829.[17] It is likely, then, that Colborne's remarks at the opening of the House in January 1830 represented the joint vision of himself and the chief justice, the two most powerful men in Upper Canada.

Even with such august sponsorship, the idea was not taken up by a rather penurious and sceptical Assembly. Evidently the government now turned to Hugh Thomson, well known as the House's most zealous penitentiary advocate, to introduce a motion in February 1830 for funding to be provided for a penitentiary. The motion, however, attracted little interest, only four members bothering to speak on it. Three members, including the Speaker, Marshall Spring Bidwell, leading reformer Peter Perry, and Tory Thomas Dalton, publisher of the York *Patriot*, feeling little concern about the amount of crime in the colony, dismissed the idea as beyond the financial capacity of the province. William Lyon Mackenzie, who provided a full account of the debate in his *Colonial Advocate* of 18 February, also doubted that sufficient money could be raised to pay for a penitentiary, but Mackenzie felt such a reform was greatly needed and urged that a 'small sum' be provided so that at least a start could be made. There was no discernible division in the House along party lines. An Assembly with a majority of Reformers was not immediately responsive to an initiative advanced by Colborne and Robinson;[18] nonetheless, the members did establish another committee to investigate 'the expediency of erecting a penitentiary.' As it turned out, the major difference between this committee and the abortive one of 1826 was that this time the penitentiary had strong support from the Tory elite. Thomson, the committee's dominant voice, proceeded on that basis in 1831 to bring down his strongly argued report condemning and ridiculing the existing system of punishing criminals.

In the meantime there were other significant developments. As a result of the October 1830 election, the Tories held a majority in the Assembly; this new political reality probably encouraged Robinson in December 1830, as speaker of the Legislative Council, to urge the administration to proceed with a penitentiary. Arguing that 'the exposure of property and the facility of depredation in certain Districts requires a system of secondary punishment,' Robinson, in the same terms as Thomson in 1826, further insisted that the frequent pardon of capital offenders had undermined the deterrent power of the criminal law.[19] For the chief justice, this was the critical point. Deterrence encompassed the most essential purpose of the criminal law; its absence suggested weakness which, if unchecked, must, as Robinson believed, eventually undermine law, order, and the entire social structure. Here was a state of affairs that the Tory leadership could not tolerate. For Robinson, failure to act would constitute a contemptible abdication of authority. With the Tories in control of both houses of the legislature, and with Colborne and Robinson providing firm direction from the top, Hugh Thomson received his marching orders. Not surprisingly, his report recommended that Upper Canada proceed at once to build its penitentiary.

THE PLACE OF LAW REFORM

For Robinson and his colleagues the penitentiary remained as only one part of a three-pronged program of penal reform. The related parts included a radical restructuring of the criminal law and reform of the colony's gaols. In 1830 the Legislative Council, chaired by newly appointed chief justice Robinson, had prepared a bill 'to mitigate the severity of the criminal law, and provide more effectively for the certain punishment of offenders.' This effort did not win the support of the Assembly and in 1833 Robinson tried again. At that point a problem arose when prominent Reformer Marshall Spring Bidwell carried an amendment that no sentence of death should be carried out within less than a month.

The Bidwell amendment worried Robinson, who was attempting to make punishment speedy and certain. A delay of a month, he insisted, would undermine the deterrent effect of these changes. The purpose of the 1833 law reform was to effect a great mitigation in the criminal law by eliminating scores of capital offences, but there was nonetheless 'reason to fear the effect of postponing executions in all cases.' Members of the council could not 'but observe with pain, that in this Province cases of murder have of late years been numerous' and they hesitated therefore 'to adopt a relaxation in respect to this heinous crime, which might deprive the Laws' of any portion of their deterrent power. They especially noted that crimes of treason in wartime, murder, and arson 'may call for a prompt execution of the Law to restore peace and security.' Although the council referred to a higher murder rate, there is little evidence of significant increases in this crime. Nonetheless, the principal effect of the Tory law reform would be to end capital punishment for over a hundred offences. It is understandable, then, that members of the council were somewhat nervous, and felt that this was not the time to experiment with the procedures for carrying out the execution of those capitally convicted. The Assembly backed down and the bill *sans* amendment was assented to on 13 February 1833.[20]

This legislation marked a turning point in the administration of criminal justice in Upper Canada. The statute reduced the number of offences subject to capital punishment from about 150 to 12, substituting other punishments, especially long-term imprisonment in the penitentiary, for the dealth penalty. The statute also abandoned the system of discretionary justice, in which the awe and terror provoked by the threat of execution was balanced against a judicial application of royal mercy. Robinson's wide experience as attorney general and his more recent role as chief justice had left him utterly persuaded that the discretionary system had never worked effectively in Upper Canada. The less severe penalties imposed by the 1833 legislation were intended to be applied in all cases of conviction. This firmly Beccarian statute pronounced in favour of certain and proportionate punishment, uniformly applied. As its preamble asserted, 'it is fit that it should be plainly declared in the Statutes of this Province, for what crimes offenders shall be punished with death.' Here was a conscious effort to abandon the old English system, long since gutted by the activities of English reformers, by which the ruling class in the eighteenth century had manipulated the law to select from the hundreds available for execution the relative few who would actually die. 'It does not seem to be indispensable,' concluded the preamble 'for the security and well being of society, that punishment of death should be inflicted in any other cases than those hereinafter mentioned.'

Having reduced the sense of gratuitous brutality associated with the old code, the Act laid down the procedures and punishments to be followed in non-capital felonies. One loophole was closed with the abolition of benefit of clergy – by which those able to demonstrate their literacy had been able to avoid the full force of the law for many first offences – which had been ended by statute in Britain in 1827 and was seldom used in Upper Canada. But most important, for all offences not mentioned in the Act but previously punishable by death, the penalty with a few exceptions became banishment, transportation, or long-term imprisonment. Banishment or transportation were to be for life or for not less than seven years. Alternatively, imprisonment only, or imprisonment at hard labour, in solitary confinement in the common gaol, or in any penitentiary or house of correction, was to be 'for any term not exceeding fourteen years, except persons convicted of returning from transportation or banishment,' in which case the term might be extended to life. The penalty for manslaughter was a fine or imprisonment or both, the term not to exceed one year. The final clause in this landmark statute specified which felonies were punishable by whipping or the pillory. These included forgery, a common crime and one which caused considerable difficulty in a colony that used several forms of currency, and 'falsely personating any person.' Whipping and the pillory could be imposed in addition to or instead of any other penalty, as the court might decide. Because larceny was not mentioned, this statute signalled a radical reduction in the use of the whip for penal purposes.

The drastic reduction in the scope of capital punishment and the central place given to imprisonment in anticipation of the opening of the penitentiary had a wide-ranging and immediate effect. The Act might be regarded as transitional in nature because it retained the old-regime shaming punishments, whipping and the pillory. Banishment, which had been largely abandoned in the United States after independence, was also specifically retained, and transportation, which, despite the 1800 statute, had never been entirely discontinued, was restored. In this sense the statute seemed to look backward as much as forward. But the traditional elements of the 1833 law were not particularly important. The cautious Robinson was not about to make a clean sweep of one penal system until another was securely in place and tested over time. The penitentiary had not yet opened and the numerous changes the chief justice was demanding in the administration of the unreformed gaols had yet to be implemented. In these circumstances, Robinson was reluctant to abandon the shaming punishments entirely before the new modes of imprisonment could be implemented and shaped to Upper Canadian conditions.

In giving royal assent, Sir John Colborne, Robinson's old ally, emphasized the extent of the departure from old-regime traditions: 'The enactment which you have just sanctioned for the amendment of the Penal Code, must while it renders the administration of justice more efficacious, prevent that frequent recurrence of mitigation of punishment appointed by the Statutes, which has hitherto necessarily taken place through the intervention of the power of the Crown and which enervated the general authority of the law.' Colborne's comments cut to the heart of the question. It has usually been assumed that the discretionary power of the Crown was a cherished weapon deployed by a shrewd ruling class to pardon many, execute a few, and keep the general populace in a supine state of awe and trembling. Instead, the lieutenant-governor was bluntly insisting that mercy, when it pertained to scores of offences, had become a burden to the Crown and had served to 'enervate the general authority of the law.'[21] Now the slate was being wiped clean. A new beginning might commence.

In working to achieve these far-ranging legal changes, Robinson was acting in a manner utterly consistent with long-standing Tory principles of paternalism and commitment to statist activities. Under Simcoe and his successors, the Upper Canadian government, supported by like-minded local leaders, had always demonstrated an unbending faith in its ability to use institutional structures to shape the polity and control human activities. The Constitutional Act of 1791,[22] reacting to the perceived weaknesses in authority structure that the British ruling elite believed had contributed to the American Revolution, had greatly reinforced the powers of both the lieutenant-governor and the Legislative Council, the appointed upper house of the local legislature. Upper Canadian Tories believed that the threat to social stability posed by republicanism and democracy as expressed in the American and French Revolutions could only be held back by a powerful ruling class, able to shape and control the political process through the traditional institutions of the British state. Of the numerous means crafted to achieve these ends, none was more important than the legal-judicial apparatus. In the face of strong protest from some early settlers and from much of the merchant community, the government, through its 1794 Judicature Act, imposed the full weight of the British legal system upon the colony. The powerful Court of King's Bench had created a new elite of lawyers and judges, and at the local level appointed justices of the peace became the rulers of the districts. In the economic sphere, the Tory commitment to strong leadership and institutional growth meant a ready willingness to deploy governmental powers to establish banks, build roads and canals, and to commit scarce resources to wide-ranging developmental programs.

The values of Tory activism also infused provincial social policy. Here it took the form of a Christian paternalism, which operated more through provincial aid and succour than by direct executive involvement. When the Upper Canadian leadership explicitly rejected the English poor law in 1792, their intention, as Richard Splane argues, was more to reject a particular means of offering assistance as inappropriate to Upper Canadian circumstances than to turn their back on those in need of assistance.[23] From the beginning, some support was provided at the local level by the magistracy, but more significant was the proliferation of charitable bodies, including churches, national societies, immigrant-aid groups, and agencies established to offer assistance to widows, children, the disabled, and others unable to help themselves. In the teens and twenties of the nineteenth century, as Russell Smandych demonstrates, it had been predominantly Tory community leaders who established such organizations in the principal towns, and it is notable how frequently the prominent members of the Family Compact served as long-time officers of the entire range of Upper Canadian charitable endeavours. In Kingston as well as York, Compact Tories, including Christopher Hagerman, John Macaulay, and Thomas Markland dominated the principal charity organizations.[24]

Such organizations, described by Smandych as 'pre-segregative institutions of social control,' existed for purposes that inseparably combined humanitarian and social control purposes. Such a prominent Tory as John Strachan worked tirelessly at a host of charitable endeavours, preaching most Sundays at the local gaol and doing all in his power to ensure that those in genuine need were fed and housed. As a church leader, he acted out of an unbending conviction that those who possessed wealth and education had a Christian obligation to assist the poor; as a leader of the community, he regarded the performance of such obligations as essential to the maintenance of a peaceful and well-ordered society.

Initially, Tory paternalism operated primarily through private subscriptions and by offering out-of-doors relief. There was no ideological objection to governmental funding, as the assistance offered by magistrates through the rates demonstrated, and as the 1810 House of Corrections statute seemed to confirm.[25] Nonetheless, as the extent of poverty and distress increased in response to urban growth and pauper migration, there was a tendency to make distinctions between the 'deserving' and the 'undeserving' poor, and to restrict relief to an institutional environment. In 1828 an Emigrant Asylum was established at York and those needing help were forced into it before receiving relief.[26] The organizers of private charitable societies turned more than ever to government for assistance. They found a ready friend in John Colborne and under his leadership public funds were forthcoming for numerous worthy causes, including the York Emigrant Asylum, of which he was a founder. Perhaps because of the governor's encouragement, other prominent Tories in the 1830s worked to persuade the state to play a larger role in social endeavours. It was that high Tory, Sheriff Jarvis, for example, who led the movement to build a provincial asylum for the insane, while other Tory paternalists, including Strachan himself, were zealous advocates of a house of industry.

If strong leaders steeped in a Christian activism best expressed by Strachan and his many acolytes turned easily to state intervention and looked to purpose-built institutions to deal with the social concerns of the 1830s, it is in the attitude of the elite toward the criminal law that we encounter some of the most characteristic values of Upper Canadian Toryism. No one ever articulated those values or explained their place in the Tory mind as well as chief justice Robinson. As deeply Christian in outlook as Strachan himself, Robinson never regarded the legal system as some kind of secular faith which could replace the church as the ultimate sanction enforcing morality and protecting life and property. For Robinson, the law was divinely inspired and the judges were secular priests meting out justice according to the highest precepts of God and man. The rule of law was sacred and law and God together inspired and informed the constitution of Upper Canada.

Robinson's lofty conception of the rule of law was first demonstrated when he served as prosecutor at the wartime treason trials at Ancaster in 1814. Although only twenty-three years old, as acting attorney general he courageously resisted pressure from the military command to proceed swiftly to make an immediate example of those who had been charged. Robinson insisted that the accused receive every right and protection under the law, in order to ensure, as a recent biographer puts it, that it was 'apparent to all that the condemned had not been judged by a harsh or hasty tribunal.'[27]

Robinson's adherence to the rule of law was conveyed more routinely in the socially turbulent 1830s in a series of thoughtful charges to grand juries. The picture that emerges of Chief Justice Robinson from these charges is of a man utterly committed to the centrality of law to Upper Canadian peace and progress. Robinson used the charges to share that understanding with the magistrates who dominated the grand juries, and through them with the larger society. It is clear from these documents that Robinson believed that Upper Canada was a good society, law-abiding and secure, a community with excellent laws enforced by high-minded judges. But by the early 1830s the system was encountering glaring problems which might undermine public faith in the law, with disastrous consequences for the colony.

Firstly, Robinson established that Upper Canadians although generally law-abiding were nonetheless faced with a relatively high level of crime. He believed that Upper Canada offered ample opportunity to all who were willing to work, and found it 'lamentable' that crimes should be relatively numerous in a society 'where there are no other temptations to dishonesty than the profligate desire to indulge in idleness.'[28] Raised without the benefit of proper religious instruction, such persons commonly advanced from bad habits to criminal activities. For the Tories, there was no contradiction between pointing to the increase of crime while at the same time congratulating the community on its relatively limited extent. For Robinson, who believed that the potential for sin was the common lot of mankind, the existence of crime was only part of nature's order. Occasionally, even in a land of plenty, simple want and economic necessity could account for wrong-doing. As a judge he was prepared to take such circumstances into account, and as a leading advocate of economic development, he believed that increased material prosperity must lead to less crime.[29] But Upper Canada, he believed, was a land of opportunity and for the most part the guilty parties he encountered at the Assizes could not plead necessity. 'The plea of necessity, if it could be admitted in any order of society can with no degree of reason be urged here, and therefore the folly of such offenders is scarcely worse than their guilt.'[30]

Because human folly and sin could lead to crime, judges and others who held responsibility for upholding the law must be eternally vigilant. Just as individuals could gradually fall from grace and through sin and depravity come to a tragic end, so too the social order, dependent on the efficient administration of the law, might falter and fall. While not believing that revolution was at hand or even that Upper Canada was beset by crime, Robinson was convinced that society's natural leaders, the *regularly bred*, as he described them to Macaulay, must check and punish the evil few to ensure that their malign example not be emulated by the many.[31] In charge after charge, Robinson drove the point home. The security of the community, the integrity of the constitution, and the social system which buttressed all, depended on the respect placed by citizens on the fearless administration of justice. For 'it must never for a moment be forgotten, that the security of *all that is worth enjoying* depends not *partly* but *wholly* upon supremacy of the Laws,' a supremacy that he deemed integral to 'maintenance of the social system.'[32]

The chief justice was at pains to explain that all of Upper Canada's citizens, regardless of rank or status, were equal before the law.

Without desiring to speak disparagingly of the institutions of any other people we need not hesitate to say that we shall find no country whose laws are more *just* in principle or more *mild* in their actual administration, none in which the innocent are more effectually and certainly protected, or in which the distinction between the rich and the poor, the powerful and the humble has less weight in the scales of justice – I need not have said *less* weight, for I should not be warranted in conceding that it has *any*.

For Robinson, one of 'the most powerful securities' for the maintenance of order was the good conduct and example of magistrates, judges, and other community leaders. Upper Canadians, he told successive grand juries, were well served by their natural leaders. 'It is happy for such persons, and for others, when this influence is beneficially exerted, and when empowered with the important truth that order is heaven's first law.'[33]

In articulating this vision of Upper Canada's allegedly benign and near-idyllic legal orthodoxy, the chief justice understood the social utility of the message he was conveying to the populace and that he was giving authoritative expression to a great and noble myth. Robinson, better than any other Upper Canadian, was well aware of the many defects of the legal structure he praised instinctively. But unlike the Reformers, who were often unrestrained in their verbal abuse of the existing system, Robinson lauded the system even as he worked to reform it. From the earliest days of his judicial career he was deeply disturbed at its actual operations. In his jury charges, one student notes, 'one of the most frequently repeated themes is the need to bring wrongdoers to account and to punish them effectually.'[34] For several years before the criminal law reform of 1833, however, Robinson and his fellow judges had been forced to work within the sentencing procedures of the old criminal code. In applying these antiquated rules they had participated in the farce of sentencing criminals to death knowing they would be pardoned, and had resorted to fines, whippings, and brief gaol sentences, none of which Robinson regarded as satisfactory punishments for serious felonies. In numerous cases, the majesty and dignity of the law had been mocked. While Robinson would not have concurred in all the views of old-regime sanctions expressed by Hugh Thomson in his 1831 report, he knew better than any other Upper Canadian that reform was desperately needed to stem the disrespect for the law, disrespect that was rooted in the irrationality of and abuses inherent in the old system.

In undertaking reform, Robinson was thoroughly modern in his attitudes. Closely in touch with recent English legal reforms inspired by Mackintosh, Bentham, Peel, and others, which had been largely carried into law in the 1820s, he regarded the English experience as the model for Upper Canada. Like the English reformers, the Upper Canadian chief justice had accepted Cesare Beccaria's condemnation of old-regime legal codes, and especially discretionary justice. 'It is an admitted truth,' he told the Home District jurors in October 1831, 'that it is the *certainty* more than the *severity* of punishment which deters offenders.'[35] By eliminating the element of indeterminacy and by imposing severe but fair punishments, the law would be restored to that degree of respect and awe which Robinson deemed essential for the well-governed society. The changes that Robinson and his colleagues effected in the criminal law in 1833 thus represented the essential foundation for all subsequent changes in the nature and conditions of punishment.

OPENING THE PENITENTIARY

With law reform achieved in 1833, all that remained was to work up a detailed blueprint for the Upper Canadian penitentiary. This was no simple task. Although generally familiar with the principles of penitentiary discipline, Robinson had no special expertise and left the details to his colleagues. As it turned out, this required not one but two legislative investigations, which proceeded at the same time as Robinson's work on the criminal law. The committee appointed by the legislature in 1830 was dominated by Hugh Thomson, and its report in 1831 added considerably to the impulse for legal reform. Thomson's recommendations for a penitentiary, however, were relentlessly punitive, and his approach was thus somewhat at variance with the more benevolent and flexible strain that infused Tory paternalism. The harsh model propounded by Thomson could not gain the unconditional support of either Robinson or Sir John Colborne.

Nonetheless, Thomson's report revealed much about attitudes towards crime and punishment in Upper Canada. Most striking is the absence of any expression of public fear of increased crime or even of popular demand for a penitentiary; the vision which inspired the Thomson committee was that of the law reformer. The substance of the report contributed substantially to the 1833 law reform statute. Capital punishment, it noted, was never implemented for crimes less than murder, 'so that the law as practised at present amounts very nearly to an act of indemnity for all minor offenses.' Furthermore, no satisfactory system of secondary punishment had yet been established. Fines were unjust because of the varying capacity of individuals to pay. Imprisonment in the common gaols, with their lack of classification, was 'inexpedient and pernicious in the extreme.' Corporal punishments should be employed only where they did not degrade and in cases of great atrocity. Banishment was 'nonsensical' for it was no punishment at all to order a man 'to live on the right bank of the Niagara River instead of the left.'[36]

Nowhere in this recital was there any mention of the penitentiary's potential as a rehabilitative institution, which had once excited British and American reformers. The Canadian legislator was blunt and brutal about the purpose of penitentiary discipline. The penitentiary, the Thomson report submitted, 'should be a place to lead a man to repent of his sins and amend his life, and if it has that effect, so much the better,' but such a prospect was dismissed contemptuously. While reform was problematic, deterrence must be certain, and 'it is quite enough for the purpose of the public if the punishment is so terrible that the dread of a repetition of it deters him from crime, or his description of it, others.'[37]

In emphasizing primary deterrence (aimed at the criminal himself) and secondary deterrence (aimed at the entire population), the Thomson report, one suspects, was in harmony with the views of most members of the public, who saw harsh punishments as the best means of protecting their persons and their property. For Thomson, the penitentiary would exist not as punishment but for punishment, and prisoners must be subject to a regimen of pain and deprivation, as they were in New York's Auburn and Scotland's Glasgow penitentiaries. Both were run on systems of solitary confinement when not at work, hard labour, and 'privation of all superfluities,' and both, Thomson believed, maintained themselves financially on the basis of the labour of the prisoners. Of the two, Thomson preferred Glasgow (apparently he had visited there), because it imposed unrelenting hardships while Auburn tended by comparison to be 'indulgent.' The Auburn diet included meat and vegetables, while at Glasgow the prisoners were fed oatmeal and meatless soup: 'That the food was unpalatable, adds to the punishment.' On the other hand, the Scots worked to inculcate moral and religious values and provided some education for 'such as require it, particularly juvenile delinquents.' Such leniency, the Canadian committee believed, was unwise and at Auburn such matters were confined to a sermon on Sunday. This was 'vastly preferable,' because 'a penitentiary is not a school for education.' It was, the report argued, a serious error to attempt punishment and reformation in the same institution and any efforts at rehabilitation should be confined to a house of refuge, 'when their punishment is at an end.' There was little hope of making the prisoner any better in any penitentiary, but 'you certainly make him no worse, which can't be said of confinement as practised at present.'

Thomson may be applauded for his candour and lack of hypocrisy, but his unrestrained pessimism about the prospect of rehabilitation marked an interesting stage in informed opinion about the penitentiary experience. By this date, widespread scepticism had emerged in the United States about the prospects for rehabilitation. In 1834, officials of New York State's Sing-Sing Penitentiary informed a committee of the state legislature that most reformers had already abandoned the notion of a 'general and radical reformation of offenders through a penitentiary system.' In the language of less eligibility – the idea that the most favoured prisoner must be treated no better that the worst-off individual in free society – they contended that a prison 'should not be governed in such a manner as to induce rogues to consider it a comfortable home.'[38]

The Upper Canadian legislature, under Tory domination, responded to the Thomson report by accepting the penitentiary in principle and passing in 1832 a statute authorizing an expenditure to obtain plans and estimates for such an institution. Recognizing the need for more information about foreign systems, it appointed Hugh Thomson and John Macaulay to carry out this task. By making John Macaulay co-chair with Thomson the legislators ensured that whatever recommendations ensued would be fully reflective of Tory values and practices. As long-time chair of the Midland District Quarter Sessions and intimate friend of the chief justice, Macaulay was experienced and reliable and Robinson was content to leave matters in his hands. Nor did it make any difference to the Tory leadership that the Thomson–Macaulay investigation was carried out primarily in the United States. The penitentiary had European roots and a long history, but it had been effectively reinvented by the Americans in the 1820s. Thomson and Macaulay made the trek south and their report, which was presented later in 1832, brought Upper Canadians fully in touch with recent American approaches to penology. While Robinson and his friends abhorred republicanism and democracy, they were far too sophisticated to hesitate to learn from American successes in a wide range of fields.

Not surprisingly, the Thomson–Macaulay report differed substantially from Thomson's solo effort of the previous year.[39] Without abandoning the punitive model, it expressed the traditional Tory faith in the possibility of effecting changes in human behaviour through the careful inculcation of a rigid if not ruthless institutional discipline. More flexible too about means, the 1832 document, through the instrumentality of the astute Macaulay, drew on decades of Tory ruling class experience and values. What makes the Thomson–Macaulay report most interesting is the skill with which it wedded Tory ideology to American practice. In their tour of American penal facilities, the Upper Canadians encountered two rival systems, Auburn and Philadelphia, both of which had earned international acclaim.[40] The former, called the silent or congregate system, placed emphasis on convict labour. The prisoners worked together in shops but a strictly enforced rule of silence kept them from conversing amongst themselves and at night they returned to separate cells. The supporters of the so-called separate system at Pennsylvania's Eastern Penitentiary were sceptical about the possibility of enforcing silence under congregate conditions without resorting to a brutal regimen of corporal punishment, and they denounced the Auburn system for putting convict earnings ahead of rehabilitation. At Philadelphia, the system of solitary confinement was rigidly enforced and it was claimed that this kept each convict entirely apart from potential evil influences and provided every opportunity for reflection and repentance. Each system put forward its own discipline with unrelenting zeal as representing the model which others should emulate, and each proselytized aggressively on its own behalf. The Canadians soon found themselves pouring over a plethora of printed materials supplied by proponents of the rival systems, and in particular, booklets prepared by the Boston Prison Discipline Society, which was campaigning for the Auburn method. Macaulay established a good working relationship with several members of the Boston society.

The spread of the cholera prevented Thomson and Macaulay from journeying to Philadelphia but they did visit Auburn, Sing-Sing, the New York City facility at Blackwell's Island, and the penitentiary at Wethersfield, Connecticut. They also studied an extensive literature which documented the rival American systems and traced the European origins of the penitentiary idea from the Maison de Force at Ghent through the work of Howard and Bentham. Between reading and inspection, the Upper Canadians gained a sound grasp of the historical development of the penitentiary as well as of the most recent thinking both of theorists and of prison administrators.

Like many of their contemporaries, Thomson and Macaulay were excited by the prospects for rehabilitation offered by the separate system. They seemed awe-struck by Philadelphia's architecture, which kept the convicts totally separated, and they were astounded at the expense of the structure, noting the 'magnificence' of a prison in which the yard wall alone cost over $200,000. Most importantly, they grasped the essence of the Philadelphia discipline. The first objective, they noted, was to cause the convict to turn his thoughts inward upon himself and to reflect on the causes of his fall. Having had time to reflect, before long every convict begged to be allowed to work in his cell. Both work and moral and religious books were granted as a reward and withheld as punishment. Before long, this treatment would break the convict's unruly spirit and allow the discipline to work on 'a contrite heart.' Solitary confinement was a fail-proof solution to the old problem of lack of classification, which had turned the gaols into schools of vice and misery. In Philadelphia, the delighted Canadians noted, 'no prisoner is seen by another after he enters the walls.' Years later, with his sentence served, the convict's old associates would be 'scattered over the earth' and he may truly begin life anew, a reformed man. They pointed with approval to the fear that the separate system inspired in all who knew of it: 'Great terror is known to have been impressed upon the minds of the convict community by this Institution; and ... the most knowing rogues avoid committing those offenses that would subject them to its discipline.' The emphasis on fear and deterrence that had shaped Thomson's 1831 report thus remained prominent in the 1832 analysis of the Philadelphia system.

It was Auburn and the other Auburn-style institutions that the commissioners saw at first hand that received the most detailed analysis. At Auburn, prisoners experienced 'absolute solitude during the night: joint labour during the day.' Even though meals were communal and religious instruction on Sunday was given to the convicts in a group, there was an absolute prohibition of any conversation. The silent system thus solved the great problem of classification: 'by this system every prisoner forms a class by himself.' The rule of silence, the breaking of the convict's will, the pervasive order and regularity imposed by prison rules, and the constant surveillance made possible by architectural design all led to this remarkable achievement. 'The strictness with which these rules have been enforced,' applauded the Canadians, 'is such ... that among thirty or forty working together for years, in the same shop, no two of them know each other's names. Nothing (it is well said) can be more imposing than the view of a prison conducted on these principles.'[41]

To anyone with experience, such claims were incredible, but Thomson and Macaulay had become true believers. They had been sold a bill of goods! Significantly, their report said nothing about the punishments needed to enforce an Auburn-style discipline. Yet John Macaulay at least had nagging doubts. A few years later he told a colleague that he had had difficulty in deciding whether to recommend the separate or the silent system to the legislature. While he had considered the Philadelphia system 'the most effective, as respects the reformation of culprits,' he opted for Auburn as 'most suitable for our Province under all circumstances.'[42] In their 1832 report the commissioners, somewhat disingenuously, claimed they had decided on Auburn because Upper Canadians 'or at least such of them as had directed their attention to the subject,' favoured the New York approach, which 'was in action under their immediate view.' Somewhat elusively, they added that Auburn was 'a beautiful example of what may be done by proper discipline, in a prison well constructed. Here it was said, of officials as well as convicts, "there is a place for every man, and that every man is in his place." We regard it as a model worthy of the world's imitation.'[43]

What did this mean? Reading between the lines, it is likely that the commissioners selected Auburn because of the expense involved in constructing a prison based on solitary confinement, and because the system of congregate labour brought in a vastly greater revenue than could be achieved by convicts labouring apart in their own cells. It strains credulity to believe that the enormously expensive Philadelphia system could ever have been sold to the financially strapped colony, and it is equally hard to believe that Thomson and Macaulay were sufficiently committed to rehabilitative theory as advanced by the Philadelphia Quakers to risk presenting so radical a notion to conservative Upper Canadians. For Upper Canadian Tories, deterrence and punishment retained pride of place as rehabilitative mechanisms. The commissioners, swept up by the spirit of advocacy, presented the prospect of the penitentiary becoming self-sufficient as though it were a certainty. In both systems, they claimed, this objective had been achieved, yet 'the profits resulting from joint labor are found to be greater than those which are derived from solitary labor.' Thus it was not rehabilitation but the prospect of avoiding truly debilitating costs that determined the decision of the Upper Canadian Tories.

If this is clear enough, the assertion that an Auburn-style prison was 'a model worthy of the world's imitation' is problematic. Did the notion of 'every man in his place' harken back to Benthamite panopticism? Bentham's model prison was to be constructed around a central inspectoral tower, by means of which the prisoners would be kept under constant surveillance. Bentham made the utopian claim that the penitentiary could demonstrate and apply principles which were integral to all forms of social organization. Undeniably the suggestion is there, but the idea as now enunciated reflected too the fundamentalist Tory belief in the possibility of reshaping human character through strong institutionalism. A ruling class which, in 1791, had shown its faith in the ability of a new constitution to mould an entire future society in the image of the mother country could readily believe that those sentenced to long years of imprisonment at hard labour would emerge from prison very different than when committed. And they were right in some senses, as we shall see.

What is most significant about these decisions is that the Thomson–Macaualy analysis said little about how to promote reform and rehabilitation. It was the disciplinary institution itself, including the rule of silence, the opportunity for reflection, and the rigour of enforced labour, which most impressed the commissioners and explained for them the evident contrast between the unreformed American prison and the new penitentiary. In the former, they noted, recidivism was rife and reformation infrequent. In Auburn, however, out of 206 discharged convicts, there were only 17 second commitments, no third, and 146 'well authenticated' cases of reformation. The commissioners did not record how such cases were authenticated but, having decided in favour of Auburn, they placed themselves to an astounding extent in the hands of American expertise in the person of Colonel William Powers, Auburn's deputy warden.

THE AUBURN SYSTEM

Powers, an extreme partisan of the Auburn system and a man brimming with Yankee self-confidence, praised Auburn in the most exalted way, while assuring the impressionable Canadians that if they followed his advice they could build an even more perfect institution. An understanding was reached between Powers and the commissioners when they visited Auburn in June 1832; the following month they formally asked him to provide detailed plans and cost estimates for a penitentiary that could hold 200 convicts in an initial wing, and which could be expanded to hold 800. In response, Powers assured his clients (for such they had become) that he was providing them with an Auburn-style plan, but one altered so as to 'bring that system into complete and perfect operation.'[44] Powers's advice covered everything from how to heat the facility to how to cook the food. If nothing else, the need for this kind of detail about the working of a large prison brings to our attention how inexperienced Upper Canadians actually were in funding, building, and operating the total institution. In this sense, the next decade and a half, the period of Kingston's first wardenship, was primarily a learning experience.

The central issues in Powers's vision fell into two categories: the cost of building and administering the penitentiary, and the way in which moral architecture should shape the discipline. On the former Powers provided totally misleading assurances that did more than anything else in the years ahead to place the very existence of the penitentiary in jeopardy. The penitentiary, Powers promised, would be entirely self-supporting. It would cost $45,000 a year to run a prison that would hold 800 convicts. If 100 convicts were used for domestic tasks, the labour of the other 700 could be sold on the open market and would bring in $63,000 a year, leaving a clear profit even 'after making every reasonable deduction for unforeseen embarrassments, accidents, etc.' As well, convict labour could be used to build the entire penitentiary, keeping costs down to about $50,000. The assertive American was equally definite about how convict labour should be employed. Powers believed that the so-called state account system, by which the administration supplied materials and disposed of the finished articles, too often led to graft and peculation; he strongly recommended that convict labour be let out under contract. Again Powers promised there would be no problems; it would 'undoubtedly always be the case' that contracts would be available once it became known that the prison discipline ensured 'that the work will be performed reliably and well.'

There was not a word in all this about potential pitfalls, not a hint that the sale of goods produced by convict labour would meet opposition in the community or that the costs of building and running such a substantial institution might conceivably exceed returns, not a word about the implications for discipline of extending the building period over years in order to save money by using the convicts in construction. It seems not to have occurred to Powers that convicts used in construction could not be employed by contractors. Most of all, nothing was said about how men could be forced to work together twelve to fourteen hours a day, month after month, year after year, without ever speaking to each other, or about the punishments that such a system would require.

The commissioners can only have believed such American bumpf because they were inexperienced. This was equally true of the members of the legislature who readily accepted the facile assurances presented to them as the voice of American experience. Was there ever a more glaring example of the folly of listening to 'expert' advice, especially when that advice came from a foreign source that was anything but disinterested? Because they believed convict labour in a congregate institution would make the facility self-supporting, the organization of such labour took priority over every other consideration. All other disciplinary possibilities, such as the inculcation of religious values and the provision of educational training, received lip service at most. The defective assumptions on which the legislature acted would bedevil the penitentiary's administration for almost two decades, and they contributed enormously to its tragic failure.

The other great principle of penitentiary administration, Powers assured his clients, was moral architecture. Descended directly from Benthamite panopticism, this sort of thinking had become familiar to Thomson and Macaulay through the publications of the Boston Prison Discipline Society, which argued eloquently that 'there are principles in architecture, by the observance of which great moral changes can be more easily produced among the most abandoned ... There is such a thing as architecture adopted to morals' and 'the prospect of improvement, in morals, depends, in some degree, upon the construction of buildings.'[45] Kingston Penitentiary was to be the outstanding example in nineteenth-century Canada of a purpose-built facility designed to transform the human condition. For Colonel Powers, as for Bentham, the key was the all-seeing eye. The Auburn system, he explained, based as it was on convict labour and the rule of silence, depended entirely on the prevention of all communication among the convicts. To achieve this, 'it is necessary that they should be under the most vigilant and strict surveillance.' To facilitate inspection Powers recommended that the size of the cells, which in Auburn were three and a half feet wide and seven feet long, be reduced to two and a half feet by nine. This would so contract the length of each cell range as to allow a keeper 'standing in the center to see and hear through every part of the Prison' and the chaplain to be heard by all at once. Powers did not believe that such small cells could be called inhumane, because a space of thirty inches was 'amply sufficient for the largest man to lie down in' and in any case the convicts, except on Sunday, would be in the cells only to sleep. Thanks to such thinking Canadian convicts for most of the nineteenth century were housed in cells more suited to small domestic animals than to human beings.

An even more critical design point was the inspection avenue. These were interior corridors which gave guards access to viewing apertures that could not be reached by the prisoners. At Auburn, Powers explained, they allowed a guard to pass from shop to shop and cell to cell throughout the whole prison and to keep the convicts under constant surveillance without their knowing when they were being watched. An almost perfect order and industry was 'maintained almost solely by means of the Argus-eyed avenue, and which we have every reason to believe, would continue without interruption for hours, if every Keeper were secretly to leave the Prison.' In the improved plan Powers offered the Canadians, all four prison work shops could be seen in a moment, allowing for the maintenance of perfect discipline. In this way punishments would be fewer because offences could be readily detected, and costs would be less because fewer guards would be needed. And not only the convicts would be subject to this perfect discipline. The guards, likely to be men of little education or training, could thereby be subject to a 'complete supervision' and, equally important, their direct contacts with the prisoners would be minimized. 'Facility of inspection,' Powers concluded with a flourish, 'is everything.' Beyond the inspection avenues and convict labour, Powers showed astonishing little interest in programs to improve the convicts. With superior inspection facilities in place, he suggested, the convicts could 'spend the long winter evenings in reading religious,

moral and scientific books.' Rather vaguely, he added that the appointment of chaplains and the establishment of a sabbath school would be 'a
useful, benevolent object.' In reality, the movement from the punitiveness
of Thomson and 1831 seemed slight but only the actual experience of penitentiary life would determine its true extent.

The legislature accepted these recommendations unquestioningly. In
1833 it passed an 'Act to Defray Expenses of Erecting a Penitentiary.'[46]
Macaulay, Thomson, and Henry Smith, a Kingstonian businessman and
magistrate, were appointed as commissioners to superintend the project.
The sum of £12,500 was appropriated, payable in equal sums over three
years. Their first report, dated 19 November 1833, recommended that the
facility be built at Portsmouth near Kingston on a hundred-acre site with
a fine harbour on Lake Ontario and containing 'abundant quarries of fine
limestone.'[47] Soon there was another trek south. Colonel Powers was
hired, at a generous salary of £350 a year, to supervise construction, and
another American, John Mills of Auburn, was engaged as master builder
and foreman.

In contrast to Auburn, which had been built without a coherent plan,
Kingston would be a carefully designed facility, erected around four radi-
ating wings joined by an impressive central rotunda. The cell blocks
would be five tiers in height, with a hospital, kitchen, and other administrative facilities placed in the north wing. The intention, announced by
the commissioners in a November 1833 report, was to build the south
wing first, with 270 cells, and then the rotunda, with 130 cells, and to erect
temporary work shops and administrative facilities. They estimated a
total cost on completion of £56,850 for a penitentiary that would hold 810
male convicts and include a separate female wing. The commissioners
assured the politicians that this amount of money would be required only
over a period of years, and once the south wing and rotunda were in
place, the construction task would be assumed by convicts. In the meantime, the decision was taken to begin construction by hiring workers
under the supervision of Powers and Mills instead of putting the project
out to contract. The commissioners reported that it was unlikely that convict labour could bring in enough money during the first two or three
years of construction to relieve the legislature from the necessity of making an annual appropriation.[48] By late 1833 construction had begun.

Earlier that same year, however, opposition to the penitentiary had
emerged from an unexpected quarter, no less an establishment figure
than James Buchanan, the British consul in New York. Buchanan, an
interested observer of American penitentiaries for some years, had been

asked by the British government to report on the American experience. From his New York perspective he had been influenced by the many reservations that American reformers had developed about penitentiary discipline. In a letter to John Colborne written in March 1833 and published in Thomas Dalton's York *Patriot* of 5 April he offered a devastating critique in which he claimed that the penitentiary had become notorious in America as a school for crime. These 'Schools of Vice,' he insisted, by bringing together desperate felons from all over the country had effectively furnished 'inmates for the State Colleges of Crime, where villainy attains its highest degree.'

Having positioned himself as the Upper Canadian penitentiary's best informed opponent, Buchanan moved to give the lie direct to the claim that the institution could ever be self-supporting. Far from this being the case, it must prove 'a continually absorbing gulf of expenditure,' to the extent that its cost to the public, 'independent of the crime it will generate,' would be sufficient 'to carry railroads from one end of the province to the other.' He warned all Upper Canadians, and especially 'all possessors of property that they are laying an egg which will produce a monster, that will absorb the taxes that we or our children must pay.' Worst of all, Buchanan claimed, the massive costs of the penitentiary diverted the attention of reformers from such effective means of preventing crime as the support of Sunday schools and other means of promoting religion. And he warned that the province must guard against the claims of many penitentiary advocates who were frequently motivated by their own economic interests, since 'all advocates for, gainers by, and officers connected with an institution, cheerfully award praise' for a facility that 'affords patronage or gain' for themselves. Buchanan could not say that prisons never rehabilitated offenders, yet, despite incessant inquiries, he had never 'found a clear decided case of amendment and restoration to society.'

Here Buchanan offered what he regarded as his most devastating criticism, one that would resound throughout the province and gain weight over the years. The penitentiaries, he pointed out, pretended to achieve reform by tutoring inmates in trades, but these already were occupied by honest mechanics. The free labourer, unlike the convict, had only his own labour to rely on 'to sustain his family, and must suffer severely.' Further, even those who did learn a trade in prison would be so stigmatized that they would never be 'admitted among respectable mechanics.' Having been in a penitentiary, he claimed, marked a man for life and created 'a degree of degradation not to be purged,' but one which 'clings to the third and fourth generation.'[49]

It is testimony to the strength of their commitment to the penitentiary idea that Buchanan's letter did not shake Upper Canada's Tory leadership in their resolve. They must have reflected that many in America and Britain disagreed with him, as the ever-growing numbers confined in penal institutions demonstrated. More importantly, Robinson and Colborne never needed to be disabused of any grandiose expectations about the penitentiary experience: as Tories they were never utopians. They believed only that the penitentiary must act as a more certain deterrent to crime than the existing system, and if some felons were reformed, as Hugh Thomson had put it, so much the better. From the beginning, the Tory prison was based on limited expectations for the institution and on considerable confidence in the state's capacity for efficient management and administration. If anything, Buchanan's views probably put the colony's politicians on the alert about potential costs, and reinforced their determination to maximize the returns from prison labour.

The opinions of so prominent an individual as the British consul in New York did stir up a wider debate, which began in earnest with the onset of construction in the late summer or early fall of 1833. As the carceral presence began to loom forebodingly, it excited apprehension and indignation among increasing numbers of Upper Canadians. Many of the critics, familiar with the intent that the penitentiary become self-supporting through the sale of cheap prison-made goods, were apprehensive about how this would affect their own livelihoods. Sometimes they restricted their criticism to the labour question; often their concerns led them to object to the entire endeavour. The opposition took the form of public meetings, debates in the press, and mass petitions, and it acquired political drive during the 1834 and 1836 elections.[50] Once again, however, the Tory commitment to the penitentiary could not be shaken by popular agitation. With law reform achieved – or about to be achieved – the penitentiary was perceived as essential to public safety in Upper Canada. During the 1834 election, Kingston Tory Christopher Hagerman offered assurances that he would do all in his power to see that local businesses were not hurt by the sale of products made in the penitentiary. A March 1834 editorial in the conservative Kingston *Chronicle and Gazette* argued that penitentiary labour should never be carried on in such a way as to injure the livelihood of free workers. To this end it suggested that the products of prison labour must not be sold below prevailing prices, and that they be sold not in one place but across the province.[51]

Such assurances sufficed for a while, but in January 1835 a group of Kingstonians, primarily working men and mechanics, met to renew the struggle and to organize a committee to contact sympathizers about the province. Another group, apparently small and also described as mechanics, organized at the same time to offer support for the penitentiary.[52] Subsequent meetings on behalf of the anti-penitentiary cause took place in Toronto as well as Kingston. That the movement had developed some momentum was demonstrated when the legislature created a committee, chaired by Hagerman, to consider several petitions on the subject. One such document, signed by 380 persons, describing themselves as 'inhabitants, mechanics and others of the Town of Kingston and vicinity,' took the view that 'crime is on the increase in the Province and ... the Penitentiary system is the one best calculated to promote reformation.' Having supported the penitentiary idea, the petitioners addressed the issue of convict labour. They noted that there was a wide sale in the province of articles manufactured in United States prisons, and this 'to the prejudice of honest British mechanics.' They demanded protection against this situation but made no reference to goods manufactured in Kingston Penitentiary.[53]

A second petition, signed by 871 persons from Toronto, described as 'tradesmen and mechanics,' expressed hostility to efforts to teach trades to prisoners because this would 'have a tendency to act as a *premium* to the commission of crime, and most materially affect the credit and interests of the honest and industrious artisan and mechanic by bringing immoral characters into competition with them.'[54] In a third petition, signed by 579 persons from Kingston, there was no indication as to occupation but the large numbers of signatures makes it clear that all levels of society were represented. This document complained of the 'monopoly' of the penitentiary and prayed that 'the different branches of business carried on or about to be carried on in the Penitentiary ... may not be allowed to interfere with the interests of the inhabitants' of that town.[55]

The Hagerman Committee's report, which appeared on 28 March 1835, expressed the 'decided opinion' that convict labour 'should never be permitted under any circumstances, to come into injurious competition with the honest and industrious mechanic.' If at any future date it should be thought advisable to permit the manufacture of articles of any description in prison, they should be exported. The committee recommended that 'the chief, if not the only labour' of the convicts should be breaking stone to be used for the highways and quarrying stone in the rough for building purposes.[56]

The penitentiary opened in June 1835 and by early 1836 some believed that their worst fears had been realized. At a public meeting of mechanics in Kingston, it was claimed that Hagerman's promises notwithstanding, 'their hopes [were] blasted by the witnessing of the said injurious system now in active operation,' and they resolved 'to counteract the evil with every effort in their power.'[57] In another petition, this one from Kingston and the surrounding area and bearing 2,000 signatures, the legislature was asked to restrict convict labour to breaking stones, pumping water, and other efforts that could not injure the interests of free labour.

The opposition movement cut across class and party lines. From newspaper descriptions of the participants, however, it is safe to conclude that mechanics and tradesmen were in the foreground of the agitation. For that reason and because of the subsequent determined opposition of organized labour to convict competition, the actual nature of worker protest in this early period assumes some significance. The most persistent theme that runs through the movement is the hostility of members of the working class to the prisoners. As early as 1830 someone styling himself 'Mechanicus' condemned convict labour in a Kingston paper as a system which, 'instead of punishing evil doers, becomes a scourge for them that do well.'[58] The mechanics were not alone in these attitudes. As the century progressed and the penitentiary confined ever larger numbers of the 'criminal class,' attitudes hardened across society. Middle-class officials developed ever harsher and nastier structures to discipline, deter, and punish those in breach of the law. Nonetheless, there was a special virulence and urgency present in working-class attitudes. After all, mechanics and tradesmen, living far closer to the subsistence level than did businessmen or professionals, stood to suffer most from the ruinous competition anticipated from convict labour. In many ways they were most vulnerable to the depredations of criminals.

In these circumstances, rumours that the criminals in this imposing new institution were better lodged and fed than many of those leading marginal lives in Upper Canada's pioneer society created indignation and a huge sense of grievance. Thus the radical reformer William Lyon Mackenzie, his earlier support for the penitentiary notwithstanding, declaimed against 'sending down our rogues and vagabonds to the Kingston Penitentiary, to be fed like Lords in idleness, or only to work to the injury of honest mechanics.'[59] And Kingston tradesmen set out to organize 'a combination not to employ any artisan taught in the Penitentiary.' These actions expressed disdain for members of the convict class, which was a continuing influence in shaping nineteenth-century penal policies. Before the establishment of the penitentiary, there may or may not have been a criminal class, but a convict class as such did not exist in Canada. Among the many negatives arising out of the birth of the penitentiary, none was more influential in contributing to the creation of community and especially to working-class hostility to convicts than the prospect of economic ruin.

In the meantime, the building process continued. The construction commissioners' second report, dated 1 December 1834, was their last. Construction had proceeded well; forty-four cells were already completed in the south wing and this wing, with cells planned for 220 would be 'capable of accommodating as many convicts as will probably be sentenced to the Penitentiary' during the next six or seven years. To some extent, the original plan had already been amended. The American, Mills, had been replaced by an English mechanic, William Coverdale, destined for a long career as an architect in Upper Canada. The commissioners assured the government that the central block, which had not yet been started, could be built when needed, with east and west wings to be added even later. In the meantime, the north wing with its urgently needed facilities would be built as soon as possible, and a temporary wooden wall would be put in place for security until a permanent stone one could be erected.[60]

The next step was the establishment of laws and procedures to govern the new institution. These were provided by an 1834 statute and by rules and regulations issued in 1836.[61] Together they present a picture of confused purpose and more confused governance. In July 1834, with the arrival of the first prisoners imminent, John Macaulay urged the government to appoint a Board of Inspectors and to hire a warden and other officers. He assured Colborne that Colonel Powers had devised a plan to build a temporary kitchen, keepers' hall, hospital, and offices to serve until the north wing could be constructed, and told him that funding would be necessary to clothe and maintain the prisoners.[62] In fact, only bad health had prevented the earlier appointment of Hugh Thomson as warden, and his death in April 1834 required the government to look elsewhere. Dr James Sampson, a prominent Kingston physician, recommended Henry Smith as one whose services as 'an active Magistrate and man of business are highly appreciated by the public.'[63] Smith, already familiar with the institution through his work as building commissioner, was appointed at the first meeting of the new Board of Inspectors.

In accordance with the statute, the penitentiary's governing body took office on 28 July 1834. The board, composed of five prominent Kingstonians – John S. Cartwright, C.W. Grant, Alexander Pringle, W.H. Grey, and John Macaulay – met for the first time on 2 August and chose Macaulay as chair. Its most urgent tasks were to prepare for the reception of convicts and to make the 1834 statute operational by promulgating rules and regulations. Under the statute the key officers of warden, deputy warden, physician, and chaplain were to be appointed by the government and to hold office during pleasure. The inspectors, all unpaid amateurs, received enormous power, including full authority 'to make all necessary rules and regulations respecting the discipline and police' of the institution. Holding office during pleasure, they were to 'examine and inquire into' every aspect of penitentiary life, including the punishment and employment of the prisoners and the conduct of all officers of the institution. They were to carry out regular inspections every two months, to keep minutes of their meetings, and to submit an annual report to the legislature. In theory, their authority was absolute; they were not even directed to consult with the warden in carrying out their duties.[64]

Much would depend on how the inspectors exercised these powers, and on their relationship with the warden. Even so, the extent of their authority from the beginning called into question the role of the warden as full-time head of the institution. Over the next decade and a half, until the appointment in 1851 of permanent paid inspectors, there were frequent clashes between that official, the deputy warden, and the inspectors, which threatened to disrupt, if not destroy, any possibility of running an efficient and secure facility. Why did the government create a situation with such potential for conflict? In the era before the achievement of responsible government and prior to the Sydenhamite political and administrative reforms of the early 1840s, Upper Canada's governmental structure was simplistic, even chaotic. Among its deficiencies was the absence of any department or agency to assume responsibility for such welfare functions as health, poor law policy, or penal systems. In this void, it had become customary to appoint *ad hoc* bodies in which such positions were filled by leading citizens, most of whom had genteel pretensions and who assumed such responsibilities without pay and as part of their social and political obligations. It was convenient for the government to draw in this way on the services, offered in spirit of *noblesse oblige*, of local worthies. As J.F.C. Harrison has argued in his study of the early Victorians, 'What was most clearly expected of a gentleman was public service, given voluntarily and at his own expense.' In return for taking on the obligations of service, the worthy citizen expected commensurate rights. As Harrison put it, the gentleman 'was accorded immense respect and his authority and privileges were accepted.' The concept of gentility, he concludes, functioned 'as an agency of social discipline.'[65]

In the history of Canadian public administration, the reliance on boards of local worthies led to frequent conflicts between trustees vested with far-ranging legal powers and administrators charged with the daily responsibility of running large, and often dangerous, new institutions. Such problems bedeviled the administration of the provincial lunatic asylum, as trustees battled superintendents amid charges of incompetence and cruelty to patients, and several commissions of inquiry kept the asylum problem in the foreground of public debate. In asylum administration, however, the medical superintendents were assisted in their struggle to gain more control over staff and management by the prestige derived from their status as doctors and men of science and, in the United States by the existence of a professional organization of asylum superintendents. Even so, the struggle in Canada continued, at considerable cost to the quality of asylum care, until the passage in 1853 of a statute that gave the asylum superintendents fuller control over the institutions they headed.[66]

In the penitentiary, the warden had to work under the absolute legal authority of citizen inspectors, and Kingston's first warden, Henry Smith, was placed in a position of unrelieved tension. Unlike the medical superintendents, Smith lacked both formal training and professional prestige and, as the only prison warden in Canada, he worked in total isolation. In contrast to the doctors, who had custody of patients deemed ill and for whom society had considerable sympathy, Smith knew that his charges had few claims on public generosity. He soon discovered that as warden he would not be provided with the staff or the facilities to do more than restrain and punish the convict population. In these circumstances, the penitentiary for the first decade and a half of its life was treated contemptuously by successive governments, and wracked by frequent conflicts between inspectors and warden.

The conflict between warden and inspectors was fuelled by an equally ill-advised division of responsibility for the institution's daily management, which was split between the warden and the deputy warden. The relevant clauses in the 1834 statute and the 1836 rules[67] confirm that the warden was to function as the prison's business manager and his deputy was responsible for discipline, with both subject to the authority of the inspectors. The Act required the warden or his deputy to 'attend constantly' at the penitentiary, and to exercise 'a general supervision over the government, discipline and police' by directing the keepers and examining daily into the state of the prison and the health, conduct, and safekeeping of the prisoners. Other clauses focused on the warden's role as business manager. He was to furnish the prisoners with employment, make contracts at the direction of the inspectors to sell their labour, to 'superintend all the manufacturing and mechanical businesses' within the penitentiary and, when convict labour was not let under contract, to receive and sell all articles they manufactured. He was also in charge of purchasing all supplies, and required to keep 'a regular and correct account' of all money received and paid out. (A clerk, Francis Bickerton, was hired to perform the latter task.) The warden was to ensure that the inspectors received a monthly accounting, and a full annual return with vouchers was to be made to the government, including an inventory of all goods, raw materials, and other penitentiary property. The warden was to report annually on all aspects of penitentiary life, including numerous details about the convicts. The 1836 rules and regulations placed a similar emphasis on the warden as business manager.

It seems unlikely that this division of responsibility could have worked in any circumstances, and the problems were exacerbated by the background and personalities of the first warden and deputy warden. Perhaps it made sense, given the job definition, to attempt some division of functions. Smith's talents as a businessman and his local knowledge would allow him to act as a sort of general manager, while his lack of experience in a penal facility might encourage him to leave control of the discipline to his deputy. In a July 1834 letter to Governor Colborne, Macaulay made it clear that it was 'essential' to the successful introduction of the Auburn system 'that Mr. Powers or some other experienced individual' be placed in the position of deputy warden. In the same letter, he cited Powers on several aspects of penitentiary management, making it clear that the American had become his choice for the deputy's position. There was opposition to the appointment of an American colonel and later Henry Smith claimed that he had used his own influence to lobby on Powers's behalf.[68]

Since the prison had been built largely according to his design and under his supervision, it is understandable that Powers should chafe at any effort by the novice Smith to challenge his authority. At the same time, however, his salary had been reduced from the £350 he had received as supervisor of construction to a mere £150 while Smith received £200. These circumstances virtually ensured clashes between the two, and over the next five years they broke out with such frequency that soon the two men were no longer on speaking terms, much to the detriment of institutional discipline.[69]

The destructiveness of this situation was intensified by ongoing problems with the rest of the staff. There were two classes of subordinate officers, keepers and guards, but neither the statute nor the rules and regulations said much about their qualifications. The keepers received considerable responsibility. They were to enforce all rules and regulations, especially the silent system. They were given wide latitude to inflict punishments for 'wilful violations' of the rules and were directed to do so 'with discretion' and in such manner as would 'convince the convict that his conduct has rendered punishment necessary.' Only after the punishments had been inflicted were they to report such infliction in writing to the deputy warden. There was no specification in the regulations of what type of behaviour merited punishment, or of how much or what type of punishment was to be inflicted. The keepers were also charged with supervision of the workshops. Their deportment towards the convicts at all times was to be 'grave, manly and discreet, in order to inspire the convicts with respect towards them.' In turn, 'they must require from the convicts great deference and respect, not suffering the least degree of familiarity to be displayed.' Their salary was set by the inspectors at £80 per annum, and the intention was to hire respectable yeomen or mechanics skilled in some trade.[70] The role of the guards or watchmen, who received £60 a year, was more restricted. They were to watch over the convicts and prevent disturbances and escape. They were to have 'no intercourse or conversation with, or control of any kind over convicts.' The guards were regarded as cheap labour, fit only to follow orders and with no correctional responsibilities whatsoever.[71] Consequently this position attracted men of little education and lacking any skilled trade, and, to a considerable extent, the penitentiary experience was shaped and limited by this fact.

Prison routine from the beginning expressed John Robinson's dictum that 'order is heaven's first law.' The officers were expected to enforce a system whose rigid discipline was designed to break the convict's will, and to establish a machine-like regularity and efficiency. On arrival, the new convict was stripped and his person thoroughly cleansed, his hair cropped, beard shaven, 'and the prison dress put on him.' A record was made that described his personal appearance, age, occupation, place of birth, and other available information. The convicts were then informed of how they must behave. They were 'to yield perfect obedience and submission,' 'to labour diligently and preserve unbroken silence.' They were not to 'exchange looks, wink, laugh, nod or gesticulate to each other' and, perhaps most of all, they were 'not to stop work nor suffer their attention to be drawn from it.' They were forbidden to carelessly or wilfully injure their work, their clothing, bedding, or anything else, nor were they to 'execute their work badly when they have the ability to do it well.' The violation of any of these duties would result in 'corporal punishment, 'instantly inflicted.'[72] From its very beginning the life and daily rhythms of Kingston Penitentiary were dependent on the lash and fear of the lash.

From the first day in the penitentiary, every convict was subjected to an unceasing routine of slave labour, kept at his particular task for every hour of daylight. Henceforth he would move through every moment in response to the incessant regimen of bells and orders. From April to September a bell would ring at 5 a.m. and the guards and keepers would muster in the Keepers' Hall; another bell would ring, the guards would repair to their posts, and then the cells were opened. The convicts were to 'come out of their cells in regular order,' all facing one direction, and proceed to where they were to empty and clean their night tubs, then 'each Company proceed[ed] in the same regular order to its respective shop' to begin the labour of the day. After about an hour the bell would sound again and the convicts would march in a line to the mess room for breakfast, where the meal commenced at the sound of yet another bell. The mess tables were narrow and the convicts were seated along one side only, so as never to face other convicts. After breakfast, a few convicts received some instruction in spelling and reading, but most returned directly to work. The daylight hours were spent in unrelieved drudgery. Once in the cell for the night, there was a brief opportunity for reading before a bell signalled the convicts to retire to bed. This routine was interrupted only on Sundays by the provision of religious services. Being forced to spend almost the entire Sabbath in a confining dungeon could hardly have been preferable for most convicts to the time spent at routine labour.

In providing for food, clothes, and other needs, the statute and the rules ensured that the penitentiary was a place of deprivation. Bedding and clothing were to be of coarse materials manufactured, 'when it can be done,' in the penitentiary. Convicts were supplied with a 'sufficient quantity of inferior and wholesome food.' Each convict who could read was to receive a Bible. There was no reference to a library, although many British prisons were so equipped. There was no reference to hiring a teacher and no intention to do so; the chaplain was to spend some time organizing brief periods of instruction, primarily for illiterate convicts, while those able to read and write would tutor others. Reflecting the intention that one purpose of imprisonment was to separate the convict from all contact with the outside world, the statute forbade any person from bringing any letter into or out of the penitentiary without consent of the warden. The prisoner was cut off from contact with friends and family.

Not only the prisoner but the institution itself was isolated by the system. One of the most characteristic aspects of the Upper Canadian gaol was its role as a community institution. Often situated near the centre of town and with easy access permitted to friends and relatives, visited regularly by magistrates and sheriffs, and inspected frequently by grand juries of both the Sessions and Assizes, the gaol had become a familiar abode, assuming for some the aspect of a shelter in time of need or a haven from the worst consequences of cold and want. The penitentiary systematically obliterated this sense of communal familiarity. Located in the countryside, surrounded by a wall, and containing large numbers of desperate felons serving lengthy sentences, the penitentiary at once became a forbidding, fearful place. Not only were friends and relatives denied access, but magistrates and other community officials were also strangers to the facility. Regrettably, no tradition developed of grand jury inspection, probably because this would have been seen as conflicting with the role of the inspectoral board and with the overriding purposes of isolation and punishment. As a result, the facility was deprived of regular visits by independent or objective outsiders.

The statute did permit officials, such as King's Bench judges and members of the legislature, to visit 'at pleasure,' but few proved anxious to avail themselves of such a dubious pleasure. The clause permitting such visits was restrictive in intent, as it laid down that 'no other persons' were to be allowed to enter the walls, except by permission of the warden or inspectors. One clause ran counter to this secretive trend: admission was permitted to respectable persons on payment of a small fee. The intent here was to raise revenue. The warden was to direct an officer to conduct guided tours, and visitors were to have no contact with the prisoners. The admission of large numbers who wished to stare at the convicts or to satisfy some prurient curiosity was out of harmony with the penitentiary's stated purpose. The gawking of the curious did nothing to dispel the prisoner's essential isolation and it made it more difficult for the officers to maintain order.

The final significant aspect of institutional life dealt with in the statute and regulations was the vexed question of rehabilitation. In the Thomson–Macaulay report, as we have seen, reform of the prisoner was dealt with briefly and within the context of the punitive prison and forced labour. The statute did make provision for the appointment of a chaplain, at a salary to be fixed by the inspectors but nothing was said of his status or intended role. (In contrast, the duties of the prison physician were enumerated at length.) And the government failed at first to make any appointment at all.

The inspectors were neither opposed nor indifferent to the appointment of a chaplain; on the contrary, in their first report to the legislature, dated 2 November 1835, they discussed approaches to rehabilitation at some length, and had a good deal to say about the chaplain's role.[73] John Macaulay had recently read the report of William Crawford, a merchant and prison reformer who had just investigated the American prison system on behalf of the British government. What impressed Macaulay about Crawford's report was his emphasis on the role of a chaplaincy service in England, where 'far greater efforts' were being made than in the United States 'to impress on the minds of the unhappy and deprived inmates of prisons, a suitable sense of religion and virtue.' In their report to the legislature the inspectors expressed regret that no chaplain had yet been appointed and asserted that the existing arrangement, which required the warden to read prayers each day to the assembled convicts, was unsatisfactory. Not only was a chaplain 'most important,' but his labours must be 'unremitting.' Any appointee should possess not only learning but also 'zeal and devotion to the cause he is engaged in.'

The Crawford recommendations to the government of the United Kingdom, if adopted in Canada, would have had a significant impact on early Canadian penal practices. Crawford insisted that, to be effective, a chaplaincy service must be full time and that the chaplain should have access to every convict in his cell. He told the British authorities that prison discipline should be based on systematic religion instruction, a condition which did not yet exist in much of the United Kingdom, where many chaplains had other duties beside prison work. Significantly, Crawford would have placed certain constraints on the exercise of the chaplain's authority: 'A convict should not be allowed to hope for any temporal advantage, during confinement, from religious professions: nor ought a chaplain to be exposed to deception, by having it in his power to procure for a prisoner any species of indulgence or reward.' With such safeguards in place, Crawford believed there were few limits on what a pious and active clergymen might accomplish. He was sure that the minds of convicts, 'however hardened, may be raised from degradation and reclaimed by the power of the gospel.'[74]

The Upper Canadian inspectors seemed to agree. They recommended that the chaplain receive 'as many opportunities of private communication with each convict, as the general arrangements of discipline will admit of.' Convicts, they advised, 'should on no account be left without instruction or admonition' and they noted that many American prisons were deficient in this respect. The inspectors boldly suggested that the chaplain should be given a reformative role, protected in some degree even from interference by the warden. It 'may be advisable,' they wrote, to authorize the chaplain (as at the Massachusetts State Prison) 'to take an individual aside at his discretion, and confer with him in private.' Even more daring was the suggestion that this might be done 'during the usual hours for labour.' Most important of all, the chaplain should be a full-time official with 'a salary liberal enough for the support of himself and his family.' The inspectors concluded by expressing the 'trust' that they would be 'enabled to introduce' such regulations.[75]

Perhaps the government intervened to prevent it or perhaps the inspectors changed their collective mind, but the 1836 Rules made no mention of a full-time chaplain. Their emphasis was on ensuring that the chaplain remain a subordinate officer whose activities were directed and controlled by the administration: 'The Chaplain, in all cases and under all circumstances, shall strictly conform to the rules and regulations of the prison.' He was to furnish the convicts with 'no intelligence other than what his profession requires' and to give them no aid in securing pardons. Although granted 'free access to the convicts at all times,' this was strictly for the purpose of imparting religious instruction. The strongest evidence that the Chaplain's office was intended to be part of a disciplinary machinery conceived and controlled by the administration was the instruction that he was to 'endeavour to convince the prisoners of the justice of their sentence, and explain to them the advantages of amendment and enjoin upon them strict obedience to the Rules and Regulations of the Penitentiary.'

The regulations did not seek to establish the strong chaplaincy that Crawford envisioned, and the government felt no urgency to proceed with even a subservient chaplaincy. In their 1836 report the inspectors pointed out, as they had the previous year, that the absence of a chaplain left the prison system sadly incomplete. They told the government that the efforts of the warden and his deputy to awaken the moral feelings of the convicts could hardly be expected to leave a lasting impression. And they pointed to the view of the London-based Society for the Improvement of Prison Discipline that it was a sacred obligation to provide for the religious needs of the convicts. Henry Smith joined the inspectors in a campaign to persuade an indifferent and probably hostile government to act. 'Reformation,' Smith asserted, was 'the primary object to be kept in view in the management of convicts,' and knowledge of scripture was 'the principal means to attain that end.' Smith's deputy read evening and morning prayers to the convicts who remained in their cells, while Smith himself read a sermon, prayers, and scripture on Sunday. But his own efforts, he pointed out, could only be directed at the convicts collectively; 'to effect a permanent good, it is necessary that the moral and religious welfare of the inmates ... should be studied and watched over individually.'[76]

The government failed to respond to this and other entreaties. In the fall of 1836 John Macaulay proposed the appointment of the Reverend William Herchmer, a Kingstonian recently returned from Oxford and about to be ordained. Macaulay, however, was less than hopeful about the possibilities of the position. He advised that Herchmer might accept it, rather than go to a remote parish, 'and if he succeeds in reclaiming many of the convicts, it may be an inducement for him to continue in this not very pleasant duty which will only bring him in to contact with the most degraded portion of the community.'[77] A few weeks later three of the other inspectors also put Herchmer's name forward. Weeks later Macaulay made another inquiry as to when a chaplain was to be appointed but Herchmer did not begin his duties until early in 1837, and even then he served only on a part-time basis. This foot-dragging on the government's part did not augur well for the influence of those who regarded the penitentiary an instrument of reformation.[78] Kingston Penitentiary, it confirmed, was not viewed by the government as a rehabilitative facilty, other than in the narrowly deterrent sense.

For Macaulay, Smith, and those directly responsible for running the new prison, there was little opportunity in this early period to give adequate thought to anything but the most basic considerations of confining the prisoners in a secure way and putting them to hard labour at essential tasks. An even more urgent need was adequate funding. In August 1834, with the south wing roofed and ready to receive convicts, there was no money available to open the new prison.[79] The board instructed Smith to inform the lieutenant-governor that the prison could not be opened until money was available to pay staff and purchase supplies. With his own salary unpaid, Smith complained to the lieutenant-governor that he could not 'for a moment imagine that the service of anyone for so long a period ... can be expected without a moderate compensation for them.'[80] Considering the disorganized state of government in the colony, the failure to provide operating funds did not necessarily mean that the Assembly was hostile. The problem was solved temporarily in April 1835, when the legislature voted £3,000 for the completion of the penitentiary and the maintenance of convicts, and in June of that year the first convicts were received.[81] By September 1835 there were 55 convicts confined; a year later this figure had risen to 81 and by September 1837 the penitentiary housed 123 convicts. While the institution's financial woes were far from over, Kingston Penitentiary was fully operational and a new era in Upper Canadian criminal justice had begun.

RECONSIDERATIONS

There were two final episodes that called into question Kingston's very existence and that properly mark the end of this discussion of the penitentiary's ideological origins and physical foundation. For the third time, the provincial legislature embarked upon an investigation of the penitentiary's anticipated role. Although it is not entirely clear what the politicians had in mind when they established the commission whose report was published in 1836 under the name of Charles Duncombe, a Reform member of the legislature, it is hard not to conclude that some members of the Assembly were having second thoughts about the penitentiary. It is also apparent that these doubts deepened during yet another investigation, this time into the penitentiary's labour system, which seriously raised the possibility of shutting down the Kingston facility and moving the convicts north to the rugged bushland around Marmora, where they would perform in effect slave labour, mining iron in a penal colony.[82] Both episodes reflected divisions in Upper Canada along traditional Reform and Conservative lines, and both offer an opportunity to reflect on the ideological significance of the original decision to build a penitentiary in a relatively new and pre-industrial society.

In 1835, with the penitentiary already an established fact, an Assembly with – it should be emphasized – a Reform majority appointed a commission to investigate 'the subject of Prisons, Penitentiaries, etc.' The commissioners appointed to the task, Drs Bruce and Morrison, were well-known Reformers, but for some reason, when the commission's report appeared in 1836, it took the form of a statement of Dr Charles Duncombe to the commissioners. Duncombe, a vigorous man of firm views, soon to be a leader in the 1837 Rebellion, had pre-empted the commissioners' task. Following an extensive tour of American facilities, he submitted reports on three subjects: prisons, asylums, and education. Duncombe's prison report has been dismissed by Rainer Baehre as differing only in degree from the 1831 and 1832 reports, and therefore as being of little importance.[83] The same author questions Duncombe's humanitarian commitment, on the grounds that he supported the Philadelphia system, with its more ruthless approach of complete solitary confinement over the allegedly more humane Auburn system, and because he favoured as a means of discipline a 'tranquillizing chair' that forcibly submerged the prisoner in water. Baehre's arguments reflect both a belief that the penitentiary was the common ideological heritage of British and American societies and the premise that there were no significant differences in approach in Upper Canada between Reformers and Tories. In fact, a closer analysis of the Thomson–Macaulay position, which formed the basis for the 1834 legislation and the 1836 rules and regulations, with what Duncombe had to say reveals profound differences. If the Rebellion had not intervened to discredit the Reform approach, it is likely that some fundamental changes would have been made in prison discipline, changes along lines which Kingston's warden and inspectors would consistently try but fail to achieve for almost a decade, primarily because of resistance by the Conservative governments of the 1840s.

Macaulay, Thomson, and the Tories, as we have seen, regarded the penitentiary as part of the larger system of criminal justice, an essential instrument of social control designed to maintain a well-ordered and hierarchical society. For the Tories, wrong-doing was a reality in every society and it was the right of society to take all necessary means to deter wrong-doers and protect itself. But for Charles Duncombe, it was not the individual sinner who was at fault but society itself. In language evocative of American civic humanism and Christian evangelism, he argued that government had a positive obligation not merely to punish the offender but to rectify the conditions that had led to his offence in the first place. To achieve this, 'no pains should be spared to remove the causes of the offence, and to diminish, as far as possible, the sources of temptation and corruption.' The great object of government, he asserted, was 'to advance the prosperity, and to increase the happiness of its subjects.' 'The agents of government' in pursuing these ends were no less than 'the fathers of the people.' No Tory account of criminal causality would have placed the onus on the state to create conditions not only of prosperity but of happiness as well. Although Duncombe did not refer specifically to the virtues of republican governance, which American legal thinkers liked to contrast with the failings of monarchical judicial systems, the Lockeian nature of his account is abundantly apparent. While Robinson and his colleagues gave greatest weight to human sinfulness and the failures of individuals facing a hostile environment, Duncombe placed far less influence on the culpability of the individual than on some wider social responsibility. And he relied heavily on an interpretation of criminal causality that focused on neglected juveniles, more sinned against than sinning, young people who traditionally could not be held responsible in law for actions that they were too young to understand or control.[84]

The obligation of the state to remove the causes of offences and to diminish temptation applied, said Duncombe, 'with peculiar force' to such young persons. Here was a class whose increasing numbers and deplorable situation 'loudly calls for more effective interposition, and the benevolent interference of the legislature.' Anyone who walked the streets of Toronto, Duncombe was sure, 'must be struck with the ragged and uncleanly appearance, the vile language, and the idle and miserable habits' of large numbers of children. Their parents, in all probability, were 'too poor, or too degenerate' to provide them with clothing or schooling. It was inconsistent with justice that such delinquents should be 'consigned to the infamy and severity of punishments' that could only 'perfect the work of degradation.' No Christian community, he concluded, could possibly 'lend its sanction to such a process, without any effort to rescue and to save.'

Duncombe did not hide his disdain for the penitentiary itself. Having made the rounds of numerous American institutions, he was appalled by the punishment model in place in most western states. He was hardly more enthusiastic about the famous Philadelphia and Auburn systems. At Auburn, he noted with disapproval such institutional practices as the notorious lock-step system of marching from place to place and the use of striped jackets, trousers, and caps. Nonetheless, he was pleased at the efforts of the chaplain, the workshops seemed well managed, and the agent had 'strong hopes' that many convicts were reformed. Duncombe, however, expressed some preference for Philadelphia, where rehabilitation seemed a more central concern than at Auburn, which emphasized producing a revenue for the state. But he found more evidence of failure than success in the American penitentiaries.

Any careful reader of Duncombe's report must have reflected on how different it was in tone and substance from the Thomson-Macaulay report. Duncombe's scepticism contrasted starkly with the almost arrogant assurances so recently provided by William Powers. In itemizing the abuses that he believed had undermined the hopes of penitentiary promoters, Duncombe pointed first to the want of classification. In the penitentiaries, he had encountered 'the indiscriminate assemblage of all ages and degrees of guilt.' and he had seen the 'inevitably corrupting tendency' of such intercourse. Society, Duncombe believed, would pay a terrifying price for its practice of throwing hundreds of felons together in one great prison for punishment rather than reform. By so doing, officials were creating a school for criminals, with results too horrible to contemplate. The cost to the community, he warned, would be incalculable; there would exist 'a well trained and organized corps of depredators constantly on the increase and destructive of the object of society and government.' For Duncombe this was no idle threat. In Upper Canada as much as in the United States, he alleged, overcrowding and architectural deficiencies were 'evil influences' that 'most powerfully counteract the reformatory influence of imprisonment.' Equally corrupting was the excessive use of corporal punishment, which Duncombe regarded as leading inexorably to the degradation of the convict. Flogging in penitentiaries, he insisted, was 'highly reprehensible,' and it was for that reason that he considered the use of a 'suspended animation chair' as a more humane means of punishment. Observing its use in Kentucky, he found it much less brutalizing than the whip. Fear, he continued, 'should not be the only incentive to action – convicts should feel a respect for themselves; for the good opinion of their keepers; and even of their fellows.'

Duncombe's reservations called into question the very existence of the penitentiary. There were so many defects in state prisons and so much injury done, especially the contamination of younger prisoners, that it had become a question 'in the estimation of many persons' whether the penitentiary, 'with all its expensive apparatus, and all its show of lenity, and moral treatment,' should not be abandoned in favour of a return to simple incarceration and the corporal punishments and pillories of former times. In his critical analysis, Duncombe sounded like no one more than James Buchanan. Perhaps he had Buchanan's letter before him as he wrote. But then he drew back. In all the basics of his critique, Duncombe would be proven right. But reformers like Duncombe would not turn back the clock in favour of a system they had campaigned so hard to abolish. Instead, he urged society to progress towards a truly reformed criminal justice system, in which a remodelled penitentiary would be only one element. Society, he insisted, must institute speedy trial after arrest and apply thorough classification of all prisoners in the common gaols. In the penitentiary, rigidly enforced hard labour must never be allowed to obliterate systematic efforts at rehabilitation. When a sentence of hard labour was passed, it should be carried into effect 'in the manner least calculated to debase the human mind, and most calculated to produce the *reformation* of the convict.'

While there is nothing original in any of this, Duncombe's position was profoundly different from the Tory approach. The influences that shaped Duncombe's thinking and the tenor of his recommendations were distinct in critical respects from the program enunciated by Thomson and Macaulay and put into effect in 1834 and 1836. Duncombe's vision was altogether more critical of harsh institutionalism and of deterrence theories; it focused more on society's responsibility for crime and on the prospects of actually accomplishing individual reformation and, above all, it warned of the dangers of the penitentiary experience. In Duncombe's somewhat limited understanding can be discerned the outline of an alternative and reformist approach to criminal justice. As Duncombe himself expressed it, in the florid language typical of much liberal discourse, it was essential that 'all our literary, civil and political institutions be so conducted that the organs of benevolence, veneration, conscientiousness and hope may predominate.' In an expression of the faculty psychology widely accepted in the 1830s, he argued that 'the energies of the law in the suppression of crime, are most potent and availing, when directed with a constant reference to the moral faculties of our nature.' For penitentiary discipline, this emphasis on the moral as opposed to the emotional faculty required that the convict be dealt with at all times as 'an accountable being, both to God and society.' As such, his treatment must be 'just and consistent and as lenient as his situation would admit of.' Above all, the convict must be taught 'that upon himself, to a certain extent, depended his future prospects in life.'

With those insights, Charles Duncombe was pointing unmistably in the direction of a new penology. In his commitment to evangelical and humanitarian objectives and in his focus on reformation through self-respect and positive reinforcement, he foreshadowed the work of Joshua Jebb in England and Walter Crofton in Ireland, whose achievements revolutionized penal practices. He was also pointing towards that great beacon of American reform penology, the Cincinnati Declaration of 1870. For the moment, however, Duncombe's impact was slight, although his report probably had some influence, as we shall see, on Kingston's warden and inspectors in the late 1830s and early 1840s. But there were few who grasped the meaning of his approach, and Duncombe himself was soon to flee to the United States as a fugitive from British justice. For the moment, the Tory vision of the penitentiary as a punitive institution committed to deterrence, to forced labour, and to harsh punishments, with only lip service paid to rehabilitation by more benevolent means, remained intact.

The only significant challenge to the Thomson–Macaulay penitentiary came not from a Reformist direction but from a commission appointed when the Tories dominated all branches of government. Three commissioners were in 1839 directed to examine the iron works at Marmora to ascertain the cost of transferring the penitentiary to that location 'should such a measure be decided upon by the legislature.' This initiative was motivated by concerns over the operating costs of Kingston and by continuing sensitivity to community opposition to convict labour. Two of the three commissioners found that the use of convict labour at Marmora to produce iron would be of enormous economic benefit to the province and they insisted that such a move would be the best way to ensure that the interests of honest mechanics would not be injured. By moving the penitentiary, 'the operations of the convicts themselves would be found productive of an increasing revenue, instead of being as at present a public and unprofitable charge.' The third commissioner agreed that such a proposal might help protect the interests of the mechanics, but he professed himself willing to defer to the view of the Warden and deputy warden as to whether the same objective might better be achieved in some other way. On this matter Smith and Powers for once agreed. Powers, with typical self-confidence, ridiculed the mechanics' agitation, describing their concerns as 'entirely groundless.' If an increase in mechanical labour was a public detriment, he argued, then so too was the migration to Upper Canada of every skilled worker.[85] Doubtless the penitentiary was already too firmly rooted in the Kingston area for a move to be seriously contemplated, and the investigation was probably a sop to placate some of its enemies. There would be no more talk for a very long time indeed of moving or closing Kingston Penitentiary. The penitentiary system, the commission confirmed, had come to stay.

The rejection of the 1839 commission recommendations, the fourth study of the penitentiary question during the 1830s, brings to a close the first stage in the history of the Canadian penitentiary, the period of origins. Throughout this chapter it is argued that the decision to establish the penitentiary was not a response to fears of a rising crime rate or even to a perception that crime was a serious problem. It was not the result of a popular movement, embracing upper- and middle-class elements of various political persuasions. And it did not, at least in its early stages, represent a sharp and complete break with earlier methods of dealing with crime and deviance. Although strongly influenced by British and American reforms, the Canadian decision, both in its content and its timing, was a response to indigenous needs and perceptions that cut across Upper Canada's entire criminal justice system, and as such was part of a tripartite program of legal and prison reform. It was also a considered measure of change undertaken by leading members of Upper Canada's Tory elite, and as such fully expressive of the values and methods of the province's traditional leaders and of conservative political culture.

Finally, the establishment of the penitentiary was not an isolated but decisive act of social control; it was part of a coherent measure of criminal justice reform, planned and advanced by the most powerful figures in Upper Canada responsible for the administration of justice. If there is a single key to this significant change, it must be located in Chief Justice John Beverley Robinson's understanding of the centrality of law to British governance and constitutional practice, and in his resolve that the defects in law and practice that had developed over many decades must not be allowed to bring the legal system crashing down. For with it, or so Robinson believed, the rest of the delicately balanced political and social mechanism he so revered would also fall.

Part II

In the Penitentiary

4

'The Reformation of Convicts Is Unknown': The Penitentiary under Henry Smith, 1834–1848

THE BROWN COMMISSION

'The Reformation of Convicts is unknown.' So in 1849 pronounced the famous *Commission Appointed to Inquire into the Conduct, Discipline and Management of the Provincial Penitentiary*. Popularly known as the Brown Commission, after George Brown, the Toronto publisher and rising politician who was commission secretary and dominated its work, this organization conducted a massive and sensational investigation and delivered a searing indictment of early Canadian penitentiary administration. In words no doubt penned by Brown himself, the commissioners stated their findings forcefully: 'We have found the Warden guilty on all the charges preferred against him; and the case is so fully established – whether as regards indifference to the success of the Institution – neglect of his duties – incapacity – mismanagement – cruelty – falsehood – peculation – that the only course left us, is to recommend Mr. Smith's permanent removal.'[1]

The commission's verdict on the Smith administration stands today as the conventional wisdom about early Canadian penal administration. The commission's investigation seemed so comprehensive and its recommendations so unequivocal that subsequent students have done little more than echo its findings. Thus, in 1954 criminologist J. Alex Edmison wrote that Kingston's early years were marked by 'discord and turbulence,' and in 1966 his colleague Sidney Shoom focused on the inhumane treatment of convicts and the horror of frequent punishments. Discussing the agitation against convict labour, Bryan Palmer refers to the 'corrupt and inhumane' administration of Henry Smith and repeats earlier assessments to the effect that this 'would be proven all too true with the report of George Brown's 1849 Commission inquiry.'[2]

George Brown and his colleagues had done their job well. Their report, all 280 double-column pages, published in the journals of the legislature, was devoured hungrily by a sensationalist press which fed it in turn to a public avid for the gory details of public corruption and private horror. The report was characterized by massive and seemingly irrefutable amounts of evidence presented in an unfaltering certitude of tone. Most Canadians who know anything of the penitentiary's early years have learned of it, directly or indirectly, from this impressive document.

Even Donald Creighton and Maurice Careless, the two eminent Canadian historians who dealt with Henry Smith and the penitentiary inquiry incidentally as they touched the lives of their respective subjects, John A. Macdonald and George Brown, did no more than nibble at the edges of the commission's work. Creighton clearly found Brown's prosecutorial zeal distasteful, and he is accurate enough in his comment that the commission 'moved in upon the Provincial Penitentiary with all the horrid purposefulness of an armoured regiment,' and in his conclusion that it 'carried out a minute, particular, uncompromising and exhaustive inquiry.' Creighton interpreted the inquiry through the eyes of Macdonald who, as a Kingston politician, was closely allied with the Smith family, both the warden and his son Henry Jr, who in 1841 became the Tory member for Frontenac. But Creighton did not pursue the matter in depth, and his sceptical attitude to the commission seems unpersuasive. Perhaps more revealing is Maurice Careless's instinctive understanding that Brown and his colleagues pressed too hard and that by acting as prosecutors rather than members of a commission of inquiry they weakened 'sound arguments by making them appear extreme and arbitrary.'[3]

Careless himself did not claim that their arguments were unsound, and the prevailing sense that the commission's case was unanswerable seemed confirmed and extended by the work of Christopher Norman, the most careful student of the penitentiary's early history. In his comprehensive study of penitentiary administration in the Smith years, Norman even argues that Careless perhaps 'all too readily concedes' that Brown's overbearing methods weakened his case. Based on his own thorough examination of penitentiary letter books and minutes, Norman arrived at conclusions that confirmed in minute detail the ringing condemnation of

Henry Smith reached more than a century earlier by George Brown and his colleagues. In Norman's account, we meet once again bad Warden Smith, guilty of neglect, stupidity, corruption, and hideous cruelties against the helpless men, women, and children entrusted to his care. Norman argues that 'judging from Smith's record as Warden, and his defensive tactics during the inquiry,' the procedural firmness, not to say ruthlessness, of the commissioners was more than justified.[4]

Given this historical consensus, peculation, cruelty, and mismanagement, the issues considered and defined by the commissioners, have remained the focus of later analyses of the penitentiary's early history. Listen to Peter Hennessy, the most recent writer to take up the subject, who described the penitentiary as 'a cesspool of political corruption, cruelty, and depravity' and attributed it all to 'the disastrous and terrible tenure of Warden Smith.'[5]

George Brown would be delighted. His commission shaped the common vision of Kingston's early history for a hundred years and more. On reflection, this seems astounding. From the beginning, the penitentiary faced profound problems and challenges which transcended by far the administrative and moral deficiencies of its first warden. In fact, many of its problems were external to the prison administration and encompassed a range of issues that were broadly political in nature, including weaknesses in the will to support the penitentiary, the under-financing of the institution, and the underdeveloped apparatus of the Canadian state, both politically and administratively, which rendered it unequipped to manage an institution of the complexity of the new penitentiary. Internally, too, severe limits were placed on the warden's power and authority, including critical flaws in the statutory and regulatory provisions for penitentiary governance; basic miscalculations about the value of convict labour and the nature and duration of the construction process; and an utter confusion of purpose about the very essence of the penitentiary experience, institutional discipline, including the vital relationships between punishment and deterrence on the one hand and rehabilitation on the other. In short, Kingston Penitentiary possessed problems that no penitentiary administration could have overcome.

When the institution's early history is considered from this broader perspective, the nature of the enquiry must depart in the most basic ways from the investigatory structure imposed by the Brown Commission. One might speculate, for example, as to why Kingston Penitentiary, even in its long-uncompleted state, avoided the number of escapes, disturbances, and prisoner violence that characterized some American institutions, while at the same time achieving a record of good convict health and safety which surpassed that of many contemporary prisons. But before such an inquiry can be successfully pursued, it is useful to look at the institution one more time in terms of the investigation carried out by the Brown Commission, in order to dispel as far as possible the obfuscatory myths perpetrated by Brown and his colleagues. In doing so, it is well to keep in mind the views offered on the Brown Commission in the unpublished account of Ontario's early prison history written by A.E. Lavell, the son of a later nineteenth century Kingston warden, who himself had wide experience in prison and prison-related work. Lavell concluded that the commissioners did 'not appear to have had the judicial ability to separate the wheat from the chaff in the evidence they heard, nor had they the time to digest it.' He insisted that they 'lacked the scientific knowledge, the philosophical basis, and the administrative qualifications' needed to allow them to understand 'what was really the matter' and to propose practical solutions. Nor was Lavell impressed by the commission's evidentiary base. There were, he pointed out, over a hundred witnesses, including officers, discharged officers, convicts, and discharged convicts. 'In the evidence there was much animus, exaggeration, loose gossip, and no little lying, together with some facts and truthful intent.' The many pages, he concluded, were 'only of value in the general impression they make on the reader. No one acquainted with prisons of any age or place will read them with surprise.'[6]

This is a fair assessment. By focusing their inquiry on the sins of Henry Smith, the commissioners neglected issues of far greater import. And by seeking to discredit further an exhausted and morally bankrupt administration, they never developed any real insight into the critical challenges facing all penitentiary systems in mid-century. Their failure to read widely, to think critically, and to gain any deeper understanding of the penitentiary's ambiguous place in the emerging industrial and social order had profound consequences, affecting penitentiary administration in Canada for more than a hundred years. Partly because they found it convenient to blame Henry Smith for just about everything, the commissioners felt no need to question any of the determining characteristics of Kingston's Auburn system of discipline. Because they engaged in their task at a point of fundamental crisis, the commissioners had been given an opportunity to truly shake the old order, but it was an opportunity missed and their recommendations did little more than shore up that order. They endorsed the existing structure and advised changes intended not to challenge but to bolster that structure. In 1938, nine decades later, the report of the Archambault Commission, another great study of Canadian penitentiaries, demonstrated some of the consequences of the tragic failings of the earlier inquiry.

The Brown commissioners were handicapped by the circumstances of their origins, especially by the Reform government's willingness to allow its 'trusted servants' to shape the extent and nature of the investigation. The commission did not arise out of any awareness on the part of the Reform administration of Baldwin–LaFontaine that the government was failing to provide reasonable support or adequate supervision for the country's penal faculties, or even that matters of correctional administration were sufficiently important to merit an investigation of newer developments or foreign practices. In their second report (a relatively slim document), the commissioners did make significant suggestions for improvements and alterations in Canadian practices, but both the space allotted to this side of their work and the relative time spent on investigating the Smith regime, as opposed to looking to the future, made their priorities clear. The commission owed its origins entirely to the emerging scandal, uncovered largely by newspapers, which brought public attention for the first time to the state of affairs in the penitentiary. With frequent reports of penitentiary brutality, especially the infliction of horrible punishments, the government was forced to act. George Brown's Toronto *Globe* led the charge and the tenor of the press campaign was captured by its editorial entitled 'Kingston Penitentiary – Lash! – Lash!! – Lash!!!,' in which it made the calculation, based on 200 to 300 prisoners given corporal punishments a month, that '1300 lashes were given in a month and 50,000 in a year.'[7]

Interestingly, Henry Smith responded to the public clamour by asking the legislature to conduct an investigation. Even though a friendly government still held a majority, he must have known that this would give opposition members every opportunity to attack his administration. It was, however, the Reform government that appointed the commission. In his letter of instructions to the commissioners, Provincial Secretary R.B. Sullivan directed them to 'exercise the most rigorous impartiality,' but Sullivan's actions belied his words.[8] All five of those appointed to the commission were members of the Reform party: Chairman Adam Fergusson and Narcisse Amiot were politicians, E. Cartwright-Thomas of Hamilton was sheriff of the Gore District, and William Bristow of Montreal and George Brown of Toronto were journalists. Brown was a notorious partisan; the hue and cry against the Smith administration raised by the *Globe* should have prohibited his appointment, but instead he was also given the position of secretary. It is hard not to suspect that the government, aware of his enormous energy and overweening ambitions, gave him the position to keep him out of the way and busy.

Thus a pre-existing commitment to the view that the penitentiary had become a house of horrors and extreme partisanship were outstanding characteristics of the penitentiary commission. Utter lack of experience in all penitentiary matters was another. That the government felt no need to appoint anyone with some prior understanding of penitentiary administration speaks yet again to contemporary attitudes about prisons and prisoners. Yet the formal document establishing the inquiry was sufficiently broad in its terms to allow for a wide-ranging inquiry. Sullivan's letter of authorization, although it stated that the commissioners' first priority would 'probably be the various charges and complaints' preferred against some of the officers of the institution, added that there was 'another and, as regards the public, a much more important branch of the present inquiry, viz.: The general system of Discipline and Management of the Penitentiary.'⁹ The commissioners were directed to give this part of their work the 'most serious attention' and to suggest any modifications to either the discipline or the system of management they felt appropriate.

Unfortunately, the commissioners treated the two questions – the charges against the Smith administration and their duty to make recommendations for change – as largely distinct. As Sullivan had instructed, they carried out their investigation of the Smith regime as their first priority and never conducted any wide-ranging inquiry into those forces that had shaped the entire system, except through specific charges against Smith and his son Frank. Then, late in their work, they made a quick tour of American facilities and in a second report submitted proposals for changes in the penitentiary system. Proceeding in this manner, they failed even to consider a wide range of obvious and fundamental factors of primary importance to the experience of the Smith years. It is difficult to find any reason other than partisanship or ignorance based on inexperience to account for their failure to look beyond the role played by a few individuals to the looming structural problems that bedeviled the Smith regime. Yet these larger issues, far more than the role played by Warden Smith, are critical to understanding the development of the penitentiary between 1834 and 1848.

POLITICS AND GOVERNANCE

The penitentiary was not well served in its early years by the state of

Canadian politics or by the mechanisms which then existed for governing an institution of such novel design and purpose and vast physical and moral dimensions. The penitentiary suffered severely from general governmental debility. As an appalled Lord Durham noted in his brilliant Report, and as J.E. Hodgetts confirmed in his classic study of the colonial bureaucracy, Upper Canadian government was immature and chaotic. The malaise started at the top and extended through all branches of the system. There was no Cabinet to focus executive authority, merely an Executive Council which contained some heads of departments and not others, and whose officers, while technically responsible to the lieutenant-governor, often acted irresponsibly and without his knowledge. As well, the council was not responsible to the legislature, but existed in theory only for the governor to consult, or not, as he so chose. Some increasingly important functions of government possessed neither an executive head nor even a departmental apparatus, and this included most areas pertaining to welfare, which were either dealt with locally, or by ad hoc boards appointed for specific purposes, and reporting, if at all, directly to the legislature. This had been true of the Board of Gaol Commissioners, and was now the case for the Board of Inspectors of the Penitentiary. Not until after the Union did the government of Lord Sydenham create the Office of the Provincial Secretary, which gradually became responsible for a potpourri of functions including, over time, penitentiary affairs. Prior to this, no particular member of council assumed authority over the penitentiary; penitentiary matters were likely to be addressed directly to the governor or to reach him through the civil secretary, an officer 'closely affiliated with the Governor' who tended to a morass of business on behalf of his superior. Of course, too, there was no line of authority between the legislature and the Executive Council, a grievance which, in the late 1830s and much of the 1840s, occupied most Canadian politicians through the struggle for responsible government.[10]

The absence of any formally responsible authority was but a part of the broader structure of debility. In a system lacking any reasonable measure of financial control, each member of the legislature was free to introduce money bills to the benefit of his own constituents, with the result, as Durham noted, that the great business of the colonial assemblies 'is literally parish business,' the log-rolling effort of each member to make deals to get roads, bridges, and other patronage favours for the local voters. When the members 'come to their own affairs, and, above all, to money matters,' Sydenham reported, 'there was a scene of confusion and riot of which no one in England can have any idea. Every man proposes a vote for his own job; and bills are introduced without notice, and carried through all their stages in a quarter of an hour.' The lack of executive control over the raising of funds and the lack of system for presenting estimates of future needs were paralleled by the absence of proper audit and control mechanisms. This profligacy over local expenditures and the absence of even minimally efficient financial procedures existed in a colony faced with inadequate public revenues and a rising public debt, caused in part by the amount of public money that went to assist the Welland Canal and numerous local jobs.[11]

In addition to these structural weaknesses of government, which became the object of Sydenham's reforms in the early 1840s, the penitentiary suffered as well from a lack of political support. In 1831 the colonial secretary had decided that in future no judges should be appointed to the Executive Council. John Robinson, who to that point had presided over the council as chief justice, took the hint and resigned, although he continued to exercise political influence as long as Colborne remained as governor. When Colborne was replaced by Bond Head in 1836, the penitentiary, in effect, lost its two greatest champions, and the well-known dislike between Sydenham and Robinson meant that Robinson's voice was heard less and less in political matters in the 1840s. In its early years the penitentiary lacked a champion to give it a voice in high places.

By August 1834 Kingston Penitentiary should have been ready to open for business. The warden and Board of Inspectors were in place, cells in one wing were ready to receive prisoners, and judges were anxious to provide the necessary clients. Under the 1834 statute, any court in the province could sentence to the penitentiary any convict convicted of any offence.[12] This open-ended committal clause suggested that no thought had been given as to whether the penitentiary should be restricted to those convicted of serious felonies. Some time would pass before there was a clear trend to reserve penitentiary confinement to those sentenced to longer periods of imprisonment. In the minds of many legal officers, the question of hard labour seemed more relevant than sentence length. In Toronto, the mayor, William Lyon Mackenzie, a firm believer in making prisoners work for their upkeep, was anxious to relieve the city of the charge of sending prisoners to the Home District gaol. On 4 September the Mayor's Court sentenced four prisoners to the penitentiary, including two to four months', one to six months', and one for a year's imprisonment. Mackenzie soon learned to his disappointment that the penitentiary was not yet available to relieve the distressed Toronto taxpayer. There was no money to permit it to open. Similarly, in August the chair of the Gore District Quarter Sessions had been instructed by Judge James B. Macaulay to inform the government that at the recent Assizes he had sentenced a number of guilty parties to the penitentiary, but he received the same reply.[13] And on 31 October two convicts and an accompanying constable arrived from the Niagara District, only to be told that there were no funds to open the prison.[14]

It would be almost another year, June 1835, before the penitentiary was given enough money to allow it to receive prisoners. And the initial shortage of funds was not just some temporary aberration. The penitentiary's financial woes would endure for a decade and more, and constitute a bizarre tale of the vagaries of early institutional management. Time and again the warden lacked enough money to pay salaries and bills. Construction of the penitentiary dragged on until the mid-1850s, partially owing to financial shortages which made it difficult to purchase essential construction materials. Consequently, a stone wall, permanent workshops, a proper hospital, a chapel, adequate rooms for women prisoners and houses for staff were unavailable,[15] and the warden and his poorly paid staff were somehow expected to maintain the strict discipline of the rule of silence for a workforce spread across an enormous area and inadequately supervised. Perhaps most serious of all, convict labour could not be sold on the open market to pay many of the bills of the penitentiary. Colonel Powers had promised in 1832 that it was 'impossible' that the facility should not be run at a large profit from the sale of contract labour. At Kingston, the impossible had become the norm, and the hapless Warden Smith received full blame.

In view of this extended financial crisis, it seems ironic that the Brown Commission put financial maladministration and profligacy high on the list of Henry Smith's sins. George Brown and his colleagues regarded the penitentiary as a bloated and financially corrupt enterprise that wasted vast amounts of public money. Complaining that the penitentiary drew 'large and increasing sums of money annually' from the public treasury, they calculated that in the period from its establishment to the appointment of the commission it had received £128,387 12s.8d. for the erection of buildings and the maintenance of prisoners. These costs, said the commissioners, 'attracted general attention, and in view of the economic administration of similar institutions in the neighbouring Republic, an investigation into the cause of so heavy an expenditure was urgently desired.'[16]

To peculation and extravagance the commissioners added the warden's failure to manage the sale of convict labour as a principal cause of this staggering public burden. In an era when convict labour in many

American institutions was paying a large portion of the costs, the total income from labour at Kingston over this extended period was a meagre £16,118.2s.10d. As the commissioners noted, 'the small amount of productive labour obtained from the Convicts ... excited much notice.'[17] What the commissioners did not choose to notice was that the extended construction program consumed by far the largest amount of convict labour throughout the Smith period, a choice made not by Smith but by the inspectors and the government.

Henry Smith came face to face with the funding problem on his first day on the job. Instructed by the inspectors on 2 August 1834 to inform the governor's secretary that the penitentiary could not open unless funds were immediately received, he received an answer on 7 August in the form of a minute of the Executive Council, which read: 'if the funds of the Penitentiary have been exhausted the Council are not aware of any which can with propriety be taken, after the refusal of the Assembly to make further appropriation.'[18] An exasperated board told Smith to reiterate yet again that the prison could not open without money, and to ask what to do 'in the event of application being made ... for the reception of convicts that may be sentenced during the present Assizes.' Even the arrival of prisoners that year failed to move the government or legislature to provide the wherewithal. All prisoners who arrived were returned to their home districts.

This embarrassing situation could not endure. The following spring, in April 1835, Sheriff Jarvis of the Home District informed the civil secretary that once again the court had sentenced several persons to the penitentiary and no doubt other courts were doing the same. Yet as late as 30 April after almost a year of service, Smith had not been paid his salary and had to remind the inspectors that he had discontinued all his mercantile pursuits and was suffering severe losses. On 23 April the clerk, Francis Bickerton, was instructed to let the governor know that the prison had been ready since the previous August but it had not opened because the inspectors had no funds 'for the maintenance and clothing of convicts.'[19] Nor did they have such basic information as how many convicts might be sentenced to the penitentiary. It was a planner's nightmare. The board itself had been forced to remain inactive until April 1835, when a grant of £3,000 was finally made.

'Thus supplied with means,' the board now instructed Smith to prepare to accept convicts. At this point Powers was hired as deputy, and three keepers and six watchmen were taken on at salaries of £80 and £60 a year respectively. The money available, however, was less than the inspectors believed necessary to ensure the security of the institution. In a letter of 7 May to Colonel Rowan, the governor's secretary, Macaulay expressed the fear that the inadequacy of funds might jeopardize the safety of the officers. He hinted strongly that if disaster should occur, responsibility must lie with the legislature, which 'at its last session refused the appropriation that was requested for prosecuting the original plan of the Prison by the construction of the North wing, and the yard wall.' Macaulay feared that the weakness of the temporary plank wall might contribute to a prisoner revolt and great bloodshed.[20] Security was also weakened, Smith told the inspectors on 4 May, by the need to economize to ensure that the limited funds available were not exhausted before the legislature resumed sitting; therefore, 'great care should be taken ... that too many persons are not employed whether as Keepers, Watchmen, or otherwise.'[21] The same stringency extended to the purchase of supplies. For a time, Smith was unable to purchase such essential materials as timber, but by October 1835 dire necessity caused the inspectors to allow him to make purchases on credit.

With the penitentiary operational as of June 1835 and prisoners received, the inspectors anticipated that the financial situation would be regularized. But the problems continued, exacerbated by the financial deadlock in 1836 between the new lieutenant-governor, Bond Head, and the Assembly and, in 1837–8 by the upheavals of the Rebellion and its aftermath. In April 1836, with £216 on hand and bills of £165, Smith feared that the legislature once again might make no appropriation and he would 'be altogether without funds.' It was therefore essential that he be in Toronto when the legislature opened, 'in order to attend to the affairs of this Establishment.' His presence would 'tend to a speedier settlement' of any questions respecting the penitentiary.[22] Evidently, Smith thought that procrastination or inefficiencies, rather than outright opposition to the penitentiary, were the root cause of the problem. He underestimated the difficulties involved. That same month Smith reported that all the officers were 'in immediate want of the amounts due to them' and that he was unable to pay tradesmen and suppliers. In early May, Macaulay reiterated these points to the governor's secretary, emphasizing that 'the Keepers and Watchmen are subjected to very serious inconvenience by the suspension of their pay.' They were paying exorbitant prices to buy on credit, 'and are becoming so disheartened that if exposed to continued embarrassment many of them will probably abandon their places.' The inspectors, Macaulay warned, could not be responsible 'for the consequences.'[23]

And so it went. Year after year, the inspectors' minute books and the warden's letter books told the story of an institution inadequately supported, deeply in debt, living from day to day, unable to plan effectively, never knowing what the government's pleasure might bring. In the early 1840s, following the Union of Upper and Lower Canada, Lord Sydenham effected a brilliant modernization of government structures, but somehow the penitentiary continued to lurch from crisis to crisis, as if excluded by special decree from the influence of Sydenham's magic wand.

One continuing problem was the low salaries paid the guards. Discontent was rife. In December 1836, Smith reported sympathetically that the guards' pay was not adequate to support them, being much less than guards at Auburn received, and he found their complaints 'well founded.'[24] A second problem was the occasional lack of money even to carry out the statutory requirement that convicts be given a pitifully small sum on release, to enable them to travel to their homes. In April 1838, for example, with thirteen convicts scheduled for release, Smith had to ask the inspectors to borrow twenty pounds on their personal credit.[25] A third pressing problem that continued year after year was the absence of money to pay those who provided the penitentiary with food and other supplies. By late 1838, John Counter of Kingston, one of the principal suppliers, was owed a total of £300, but the amount available for all purposes was only £265. A desperate board directed the warden to negotiate credit in the amount of £1,000, but in February 1839, when the warden's note became due, there were no funds on hand and it had to be renewed for another ninety days. The penitentiary records of the Smith years contain innumerable letters from the warden to suppliers complaining of poor quality and sometimes rotten food.[26] With suppliers unpaid, Smith had greatly reduced leverage to insist upon acceptable standards; if prisoners sometimes received food of unacceptable quality, this was directly related to the fact that the institution was frequently unable to pay for good quality produce, and too often did not pay at all.

Perhaps these difficulties can be attributed to William Powers's promise to the politicians that it was 'impossible' that Kingston not be run at a profit. No one in authority was anxious to look too closely into whether the assurances laid down by the Hagerman Committee that prison products must never be sold on the market in competition with those of free labour were being adhered to. It was up to Henry Smith to fulfil the assurances offered so carelessly by Powers and accepted too readily by John Macaulay. Despite Smith's best efforts, it was a hopeless situation. At some point in 1837 penitentiary officials realized they had no choice but to produce and sell more products on the open market. James Nickalls, then chairman of the board, described the situation frankly in a letter dated 19 July. The penitentiary being 'left without funds for support, the system of which the mechanics complained was followed as a matter of absolute necessity.'[27]

By 1838, the penitentiary was producing more items for sale on the open market as Smith scrambled to garner a small revenue for institutional purposes. One of the most popular items produced was 'Cobourg boots' and in February 1839 we find him telling his customers that early payment would be appreciated: 'I should not have troubled you at this time had not the penitentiary funds been exhausted.'[28] A more lucrative item was stone from the rich local quarries, and several district gaols, W.H. Merritt's Welland Canal Co., and Archdeacon John Strachan of Toronto were among the penitentiary's customers.[29] In late June 1839 Smith reported to James Nickalls that stone cutting and rope making would be the principal source of income from convict labour for the rest of the year, but he also anticipated profits from blacksmiths, shoemakers, and carpenters. In a rare moment of fiscal optimism, he expressed confidence that the debt, then almost £900, could easily be made up by convict earnings and that 'no apprehension need be entertained of any deficiency in the funds of the institution.'[30]

The euphoria was short-lived. The rope walk which had been introduced with much fanfare was a failure, and the total of all convict earnings remained pitifully small. With the majority of convict labour devoted to construction and much of the rest to institutional housekeeping, it was out of the question for Smith to raise an income comparable to that of Auburn and other American prisons. Within weeks of making his optimistic statement, Smith again was reduced to informing Nickalls that after paying a promissory note he had only seventy-three pounds on hand, and once more was 'unable to pay the salaries and wages due this day.'[31] In response, just at the moment Kingston was poised to become the official penitentiary for the United Canadas and to begin a vast expansion of convict numbers, there was a determined effort to downsize. Nickalls ordered Smith to dispense with the services of several keepers and guards, and to 'place the Establishment on a reduced scale'; Smith dismissed the two most recent appointees and two others who were in poor health. There was an almost desperate effort to economize following a board minute of February 1840 directing that 'as a means of reducing expenses ... every economy be used.'[32]

In February 1841, Smith was again reduced to going cap in hand to the

TABLE 4.1

Numbers in Penitentiary at End of Each Fiscal Year, 1835–1866

Year	Number	Year	Number	Year	Number	Year	Number
1835	55	1843	256	1851	448	1859	801
1836	81	1844	384	1852	463	1860	784
1837	123	1845	478	1853	496	1861	764
1838	154	1846	480	1854	512	1862	765
1839	148	1847	468	1855	557	1863	823
1840	153	1848	454	1856	668	1864	729
1841	151	1849	410	1857	683	1865	774
1842	164	1850	397	1858	778	1866	815

Source: compiled by Splane, 137

Commercial Bank to request an extension on the penitentiary loan. By this point, penitentiary officials were being forced into a dangerous choice between the demands of economy and security. When Governor General Sydenham visited on 20 August 1840, he was annoyed to discover that scarcely any progress had been made on the stone wall and he pointed out that he had made a special grant specifically for that purpose. Smith too had urged the board to press ahead with the wall and this had become a point of contention between the warden and the Nickalls board. But now an equally exasperated Nickalls responded bluntly, telling Sydenham that they too were anxious to build the wall, but that because the legislative grant had been substantially less than requested, it had to be used for the support of the prisoners.[33]

James Buchanan's prediction of a financial morass had become all too true. The Kirkpatrick board, which took office in 1840, was shocked to learn that it was saddled with a two thousand pound debt and naively hoped that this could be reduced by increased use of convict labour. But little changed. At a time when the institution was purchasing vast quantities of construction materials, Smith was furiously trying to collect debts from those who had purchased stone, boots, and other penitentiary products. Juggling competing demands, the board in February 1841 decided that institutional salaries must take precedence over other obligations and Smith was ordered to try to borrow up to three thousand pounds from the Commercial Bank.[34] In a heartfelt lament to the government, the Kirkpatrick board in 1842 expressed the hope that it would never again be placed in the position it had occupied for much of the previous year when, with no funds available, 'a period of nine months elapsed during which the Inspectors were obliged on their individual responsibility to borrow a large sum of money.'[35] This had been necessary, the board members emphasized, to supply the most basic needs of the prison, the payment of salaries and the support of the prisoners, while all other claims were postponed.

The board laid its problems out before a probably indifferent government. Given the unfinished state of the prison, almost the entire amount of convict labour went to construction and few convicts could be devoted to profit-making activities. Most important, the expense of funding the prison 'must continue to be provided by the Province.'[36] Was anyone in government listening? Did anyone in government care? Apparently, for once again conditions improved, reasonably adequate funding was provided, and the 1842 annual report proudly noted the prison was out of debt, its credit re-established, and contracts for supplies eagerly sought.[37]

But as always, relief was temporary and by 1843 financial problems again loomed. In September 1842, the board put in place procedures which might induce the legislature to be more receptive to institutional needs, and it prepared estimates up to December 1843. The effect of this move is unclear. In September 1844, with funds again almost exhausted, Smith was directed to apply for an advance.[38]

What did it all mean? On the one hand, as the Brown Commission pointed out, the penitentiary had received substantial sums of money each year, enough at least to run the facility and to carry out an impressive construction program. On the other hand, none of it came easily and warden and inspectors struggled with debts, loans, underpaid staff, and a pervasive sense of impending financial collapse. At the very least, it is evident that the Canadian state was unable to estimate costs and to transfer large sums of money in an orderly fashion. But the problem seemed so severe and so extended that clearly more was involved than a technical deficiency over the timely estimating of costs and transferring of funds. The simplest explanation is that the legislature expected more of the costs to be borne by convict labour. On several occasions, the politicians simply chopped 20 or 30 per cent off the funds requested. They were doing this for other funding requests as well, and perhaps their action did not imply any hostility to the institution. Of course, too, all budgets were tight, and American state legislatures in this period were also notoriously short of funds, especially for social expenditures.[39] In efforts to economize, the penitentiary was a tempting target. There were still those in Canada who believed that the structure represented a palace for criminals: old notions of less eligibility, the conviction that the living standard for convicts must never exceed that of the lowliest free worker, would endure to the end of the century and beyond.

When all is said, however, it remains true that the penitentiary's funding problems were serious and prolonged. They affected in many ways the efficient management of the institution and the nature and quality of life within it. The facts were all there in the annual reports, letter books, and minute books for any interested party to examine and interpret. That the Brown Commission chose to ignore so much pertinent evidence and instead to blame the warden for reckless extravagance and unexampled peculation is incontrovertible proof of the commissioners' bias and partisanship. A fairer jury would have indicated that Smith and his colleagues had been handicapped from the beginning by a system that placed a constant and unreasonable burden on penitentiary management.

Equally harmful to penitentiary operations was the ongoing three-pronged internal power struggle which pitted warden against deputy warden, inspectors against warden and, on several stormy occasions, inspectors against government. The circumstances that inspired these disputes led to the resignation or dismissal under conditions of great controversy of the first three Boards of Inspectors and finally, of the warden himself, and they culminated in the Brown Commission. During this crisis of management, conditions were so inflamed that warden and deputy warden did not speak to each other for some two years. Finally, the institution divided into two factions, pro-Smith and anti-Smith, which included, incredibly, even large numbers of the convict population. It would be difficult to conceive of circumstances more foolish or more dangerous to the safe and secure administration of a penitentiary. It is an axiom of correctional management that convicts sense weakness and always take advantage of it. It seems a minor miracle, attributable perhaps to luck or even to a measure of skill on the part of management, that the institution did not explode in an orgy of riot and violence.

The problems of governance that developed were predictable from the terms of the 1834 Act and the 1836 regulations. As we have seen, these measures initiated a rigorous disciplinary structure and attempted to implement such a system by dividing power between an inexperienced warden who was authorized to act as business manager and an ambitious American penitentiary 'expert,' who was placed in charge of discipline. The entire structure was ultimately controlled by an unpaid and untrained inspectorate of local worthies with some vague responsibility not to a department of government but to the legislature itself. The locus of power and authority was dangerously indeterminate. Christopher

Norman has argued that the warden's powers far outweighed the board's. 'In theory,' he writes, 'the Board of Inspectors was the primary restraint' to the warden's 'ubiquitous control' over staff and convicts, but 'in practice, its check was negligible since the Warden was its main adviser and link with the penitentiary. The Warden's powers were pervasive.'[40] In fact, the tortuous struggles between Smith, his deputy, and successive boards demonstrated conclusively that no individual or group possessed control to that degree. In an institution as potentially explosive as a penitentiary, the division of authority is likely to have disastrous consequences. The Brown Commission made this clear in its second report, when it demanded reforms to strengthen the warden's power.[41]

The nature of the recurrent administrative strife and its consequences for the life of the prison can be understood by looking briefly at the work of successive inspectoral boards and at their relationships with the warden and the government. There were four separate boards during the Smith years, each of which developed its own characteristic relationship with the warden. The first board was chaired initially by Macaulay and then, from 1836 until its abrupt dismissal by the Sydenham administration in 1840, by James Nickalls. The succeeding board, chaired by another prominent Kingstonian, Thomas Kirkpatrick, resigned in disgust in 1846 when a new Penitentiary Act was passed without reference to its views. Its successor, chaired by Thomas Corbett, sheriff of the Midland District, worked in complete harmony with Warden Smith and was unceremoniously dismissed in 1848 during the Brown Commission hearings, to be succeeded in turn by the commissioners themselves, at which point Smith was dismissed in disgrace.

Smith's relationship with the Macaulay–Nickalls board was at first unexceptionable. By 1837 several issues had arisen that created difficulties, especially over construction priorities. Unhappy with progress, the warden, as Nickalls reported to the government, had claimed 'a seat at the board as a member jointly with the Inspectors, in matters connected with the erection and completion of the Buildings.'[42] If Nickalls accurately stated the situation, Smith's claim was in contravention of the 1834 statute, and this was soon confirmed by Attorney General Hagerman.[43] Yet Smith was responsible for institutional security, which the construction process affected in innumerable ways, and his desire to participate made sense. Despite this disagreement, there seems to have been no sense of impending crisis in 1836 or 1837, and the annual reports were positive and upbeat. In 1836 the inspectors pointed out that the amount of punishment needed to enforce discipline had been less than anticipated; in 1837 they commented that there had been 'a visible improvement in the discipline' over the year, attributable to 'the unremitting vigilance of the Warden and Deputy Warden.' As the discipline improved, they reported, the need for inflicting punishments had declined further.[44]

Within two years, this apparent state of harmony had disappeared and several inspectors claimed that the prison had descended from a state of calm to one of crisis. By this point, the jealousies and animosities between Smith and Powers had peaked and the two men had ceased speaking to each other. In an endeavour to have his deputy dismissed, Smith twice brought charges against him. On the first occasion, the charges were petty and the inspectors, except for Grant, who consistently supported the warden, simply dismissed them. The inspectors used the opportunity to affirm their belief that authority in the prison was correctly divided between deputy and warden. 'The authority of the deputy,' they insisted, 'should be properly and strictly maintained, as the police of the Establishment is greatly entrusted to him.'[45] This did nothing to dispel the friction. By mid-July, the inmates had sensed the weakness and bickering of those in authority and the potential for disaster took the prison to the edge of the abyss. An agitated Inspector Pringle told the government on 14 July that 'nothing but a sense of duty could at present prevail on me to remain at the board.' Pringle, who had become Smith's most outspoken opponent, claimed the penitentiary 'to be at this moment in a very critical State.' Its welfare, he continued, could 'only be promoted by the establishment of a proper discipline under a judicious and discreet managing Warden, capable of enforcing the discipline and encouraging the labour of the convicts.'[46]

From Toronto John Macaulay was equally disturbed. Referring in a letter to the lieutenant-governor to his role in establishing the penitentiary, he claimed a proprietary interest in its success, which 'at this moment' he considered 'in great jeopardy.' But Macaulay was cautious about remedies. First he asserted that 'a change in management is, I fear indispensable,' but then he drew back, concluding that 'upon this point I forbear to enter.'[47]

As chair of the board, James Nickalls was unable to resolve the situation. He, too, agreed that a crisis existed and he reported as much to S.B. Harrison, Sydenham's provincial secretary. After outlining details of the dispute between Pringle and Smith, he advised that the government appoint a commission 'to investigate and report upon the nature and extent of the differences' between the warden and the deputy. He also reported that in response to Inspector Grant's motion that Powers should be dismissed, the board had voted that if one man should be dismissed, both should, but that it had not recommended such a move.[48]

The dispute at this point was primarily one of management, and the ongoing feud between deputy and warden was replicated by division on the board itself. But the crisis in governance was felt throughout the institution. Nickalls now made it clear, in an extraordinary report to the government, that personally he had little confidence in the penitentiary discipline he had sworn to uphold: 'having no faith in the efficacy of the Auburn system of discipline in effecting a moral reformation of the convict, and deterring from the commission of future crime.' Nickalls was convinced nonetheless that were Powers to be dismissed, 'before the system is more matured and established on a firmer basis, the experiment as a means of punishment in Upper Canada will prove a failure.' The difficulties between warden and deputy, he concluded, were so serious as to 'imperil the best interests of the system.'[49]

What could the government have thought of this astounding letter? The chair of the inspectors had just confessed not only to having no faith in the Auburn system to achieve reformation, but, of incomparably greater importance, he did not even believe that it could 'deter' from the commission of future crime. Could Nickalls really mean it? If this were true, why should the government pay huge sums of money to maintain a failed facility? Further, if disputes between warden and deputy imperilled the institution, why did the inspectors not take decisive action to end an intolerable state of affairs? The Nickalls letter was an abdication of responsibility and the government interpreted it as such. Top management was in chaos.

The matter could not stand, with the two top officers, each with some support in the board, working every day to undermine each other. On 14 February 1838 Smith had preferred serious charges, claiming that Powers, in conversations with other officers, was challenging his authority. If true, this was appalling, and true or not, the situation was explosive. The leadership crisis had to be resolved. Instead, the board again merely dismissed Smith's case and the poisonous atmosphere continued. At this point, in June 1838, Inspector Pringle joined the game, charging Smith with making a personal profit from a horse and team paid for by the penitentiary. It was this, together with Smith's counter-claim, that occasioned Nickalls's anguished letter to the government.[50]

The 1839 penitentiary report offered confirmation of institutional malaise. It contained a complaint from Smith that the board had not responded to his urgent advice that priority be given to the erection of a stone wall, and a response by the board that it was pressing ahead with the west wing, which was urgently required to house the permanent workshops. The inspectors emphasized that so long as detached parties of convicts were employed at construction about the prison, discipline could not be 'kept up to the point required.' The unhappy consequence, they admitted, was not only that a greater force of guards was required, but that 'communications do take place between the convicts.'[51] In this sense, too, the Auburn discipline was failing.

By this point, with anti-Americanism inflamed by the incursions from south of the border in the aftermath of the 1837 Rebellion, William Powers's position was untenable. A deal was cut, Powers was given a financial settlement and allowed to resign quietly. Some months later, on 12 September 1840 the government, unimpressed by the inspectors' performance, dismissed the board. Bitterly, Nickalls asked Provincial Secretary Harrison to convey his thanks to Sydenham for releasing him 'from the responsibility of seeming to have a control of the Institution when its management was not always satisfactory even to myself.' All involved in the penitentiary's management would have agreed with Nickalls that the system of institutional governance was severely flawed. 'Here are five gentlemen,' Nickalls continued, 'elected to perform a most onerous and gratuitous duty (at least if there are any emoluments ... I have never yet discovered them),' a board perpetually divided against itself by votes of four to one. Even worse, the majority 'have found that their views have not been carried out by the principal officers as they could have wished,' and the board's own proceedings 'are considered unsatisfactory to the government.' Nor was he optimistic that matters would improve, given that 'His Excellency should have felt reluctant to do an act which the welfare of the Institution seemed so imperiously to require, in making a radical change in the whole administration.'[52] Nickalls seemed to feel that the removal of Smith and Powers would have solved the problem; he made no recommendation for larger administrative reform. Instead, the government, with Powers already banished, fired the board. Like Nickalls himself, it perceived no need for significant amendments to the Penitentiary Act.

The new board went some distance towards justifying the government's decision. It was chaired by Thomas Kirkpatrick, a former Kingston mayor and a businessman active in philanthropic endeavours, who has been described as a person of probity and independence of mind.[53] Other active members included Anthony Manahan, a moderate conservative politician and an Irish Catholic, and Henry Sadleir, a retired army major and local magistrate. The 'state of crisis' of 1838–9 seemed to fade away with the assertion of strong authority at the top and in the absence of a deputy inclined to challenge the warden. This was not because the new

board was lax or subservient to Smith; if anything it was more determined and more interventionist than Nickalls had ever been. Nonetheless, the Kirkpatrick board early in its tenure offered unstinting praise for
Smith's 'efficiency and zeal,' reporting that 'the regularity and discipline'
apparent throughout the penitentiary were 'the best evidence of the cor-
rectness with which he fills the duties of his office.'[54] Perhaps influenced
by this attitude to Smith, Richard Splane has described the Kirkpatrick
board as 'quite tractable,' but Christopher Norman more accurately
admits that they 'jealously guarded' their independence.[55]

Such praise of Smith is significant. The Kirkpatrick board was determined to enforce discipline strictly and fearlessly and it conducted regular and thorough inspections of the keepers and guards. Perhaps this zeal
would have brought about a clash with Smith sooner or later, for the warden favoured a more relaxed approach to prison rules and regulations,
allowing for give and take among both officers and inmates. But the
mood changed dramatically with the selection of Edward Utting as assistant (as the position was now described) warden. The board agreed with
Smith that the assistant must clearly be 'subordinate to the warden.' But
Utting, as the *Globe* described him, was 'not the man Smith expected. He
turned out to be an old soldier of the most determined spirit; somewhat
of a martinet in carrying out the discipline of the Prison and exceedingly
sharp in spying out what was going on around him.'[56] In implementing
the board's instructions to tighten up discipline, Utting between 1842 and
1846 brought numerous charges of negligence and incompetence on the
part of officers before the board, for such offences as sleeping on duty,
intoxication, or general laxity. Some dismissals and numerous reprimands followed, with the result that an angry warden, according to the
Brown Commission scenario, saw control of the prison once again slip-
ping from his grasp. In retaliation, he began what Brown described in his
newspaper as 'a deliberate system of annoyance and persecution to drive
Mr. Utting from the establishment.'

Other problems also pressed between 1842 and 1846, especially the
need to move ahead as rapidly as possible with the construction program
to cope with unprecedented increases in convict numbers. In his 15 October 1845 report to the inspectors, Smith noted that 687 prisoners had been
confined since 30 September 1844, 213 of whom were military prisoners,
and that 478 convicts were then in confinement. Because of the shortage
of cells, Smith reported, with so many prisoners being admitted, 'at times
it has been necessary to confine several of them together.'[57] Keeping in
mind the size of a cell, with no room even to stand up unless the bunk

was hooked to the wall, such double-bunking led to untold miseries. There could be no more dramatic evidence of the collapse of Auburn principles, and through no fault of the warden or the inspectors. As a makeshift, the female prisoners were removed from the west wing to the assistant warden's quarters, a move that was not inclined to improve Edward Utting's always testy temper.

Then, too, the chaplain who had succeeded Herchmer, Robert Rogers, chose this period to become an increasingly disruptive force. In 1845, much to Rogers's resentment, an officiating Catholic clergyman had been appointed in the person of Angus MacDonell. Numerous board meetings, to the annoyance of Kirkpatrick, were forced to deal with Rogers's efforts at proselytization and his determination to introduce anti-Catholic literature.[58] Rogers was outraged by the constant reprimands he received from the board and complained persistently that the administration was failing to support him in the work of convict reformation. By the time he appeared before the Brown Commission, Rogers was in a constant temper and his abuse of Henry Smith at that inquiry was no surprise.

Clearly, the institution had travelled some distance away from the Auburn ideal by 1845. One problem was the large proportion of inmates sentenced to life or to very long terms. The inspectors addressed this intractable issue in their 1845 report. In the United States, political pardons and other circumstances reduced the numbers of long-serving prisoners. In Kingston, the existence of so many lifers placed great stress, the inspectors argued, on all the officers. With no incentive to the prisoners for good behaviour, no hope for a remission of their sentences, 'despair takes possession of their minds.' In these circumstances, the prison became a terrifying place. These 'hardened and reckless characters,' said the inspectors, 'would willingly risk their lives, and sacrifice those of their Keepers, in attempts to escape.' Such convicts required constant vigilance, and from their 'degraded and dispirited state,' neither 'moral reformation' nor the full benefit of their labour could be expected.[59] In these crowded conditions and facing the ever-present disruption of the construction program, the absence after a decade of prison life of indispensable facilities, and a state of overcrowding which made a mockery of the rule of silence, the Kirkpatrick board tightened the screws. They urged the warden to do whatever was necessary to enforce the disciplinary system imposed by the statute. In March 1845 the board minutes noted 'its general dissatisfaction at the laxity of the discipline and the degree of communication permitted among the convicts.'[60] In these circumstances, the board could see no alternative but to increase the numbers of punishments.[61]

Despite these grave difficulties, and notwithstanding the tension between Smith and Utting, there was no indication of dissatisfaction with the warden. Neither the reports of the Kirkpatrick board to the government nor its own internal minutes pointed the finger at Henry Smith, who continued to manage the facility without riot or even serious disturbance. In its 1845 report, with the numbers crisis at its peak, the board retained its confidence in Smith. But it was far less satisfied with the government itself. As in earlier years, the inspectors pointed to problems that urgently required the attention of the government. They expressed their dismay that youths as young as eight were still being sent to the penitentiary, and they regretted that the government had ignored their frequent requests for an enactment defining the respective duties of Catholic and Protestant clergymen.[62]

Until 1845, too, both the chaplain and the surgeon were fully supportive of the Smith administration. Given the role that Dr Sampson would soon play in the downfall of Henry Smith, his comments are especially significant. In 1842 he reported, 'in the usual terms of satisfaction,' that every suggestion he had made respecting the health of the prisoners had received 'the prompt attention' of the warden. As the growing number of convicts strained facilities, Sampson became increasingly irritable, although this was not directed at Smith. His principal complaint was the failure to build an adequate hospital, for which he blamed the government, and in 1844 he also found the quarters for female prisoners deficient. But he remained pleased at the low death rate, which he attributed to 'the ventilation and cleanliness of the Prison' being 'most strictly attended to.' He attested as well to the 'good and wholesome' quality of the food, and added that 'as soon as any deviation from furnishing the rations of proper quality was ever observed, means were taken to remedy the evil.'[63] Dr Sampson would soon lead the attack on Henry Smith's errant son, Frank, the prison's kitchen keeper, but even under the persistent questioning of the Brown Commission, he refused to retract this high opinion of the warden's administration.

Over the next two years, however, several forces undermined Smith's long-standing hegemony. The first serious problem came with a new and ill-advised Penitentiary Act passed in 1846.[64] This measure was promoted by Warden Smith and his son Henry Jr, the member for Frontenac. The second was a series of charges and countercharges involving Dr Sampson and Frank Smith, a rogue if ever there was one. These incidents exacerbated the institution's difficulties and polarized staff, officials, and convicts into two hostile camps. The new Act increased the salary of the warden from three hundred to five hundred pounds, reduced those of the chaplain, assistant warden, and architect, William Coverdale, and it also, the Brown Commission claimed, 'greatly increased' the powers of the warden. According to the commission's scenario, the Act was framed by the two Smiths and put through the House by government leader W.H. Draper with no reference to the inspectors. The Kirkpatrick board, for its part, angrily charged that the salary changes were unjust to all involved, especially to the assistant warden, who had 'the most onerous' duties of any officer in the penitentiary, and to the architect, because of the amount of construction still to be carried out. The new statute, they claimed, made 'very important changes in the interior economy' of the prison, which would be 'productive of great confusion.' They greatly regretted the 'impolicy' of lessening the influence of the assistant warden 'by reducing him in grade and title ... to the position of Keeper.' Like the Nickalls board before them, the Kirkpatrick board members pointed to the 'unremitting attention' they had paid to penitentiary affairs 'without any remuneration whatever, and often to the detriment of their private affairs.' Furious that they had not been consulted, they exaggerated the effect of the new Act on the prison's internal arrangements, claiming that 'the authority of the Board of Inspectors is superseded and rendered a nullity.' Concluding that 'His Excellency has no confidence in them,' they resigned.[65]

It is difficult to see in the actual changes made how board authority had been undermined to such an extent. Yet for the government to pass a new statute which implemented significant changes with no reference to the board served to lessen its prestige, if not its power. It may be that the warden himself was taken by surprise by Attorney General Draper's precipitate actions. Both the warden and Henry Smith Jr endeavoured to have the government rescind the salary decreases, but to no effect. No doubt there was a large element of self-aggrandizement in the Smith family's manoeuvres, but the new bill was hardly one that they would have written. For example, Draper removed a clause in the Smiths' draft to give the warden a seat on the board, and he struck out another clause the Smiths desired to establish remission procedures.[66] The statute was probably less a conspiracy against the Kirkpatrick board on Smith's part than another example of the slipshod and thoughtless way the government tended to proceed whenever the affairs of the penitentiary were dealt with.

Although the incident embarrassed Smith, he must have been pleased by the appointment of a new board. Smith's approach to discipline was far more lenient and relaxed than that which the Kirkpatrick board and its enforcer, Edward Utting, aspired to achieve. It is not clear whether this was because Smith was lax and irresponsible, as the Brown Commission argued, or because he had developed insight into techniques of managing convict populations through co-option and conciliation.[67] Whichever the case, and there is evidence to support either perspective, the new board was more to Smith's taste. Its chairman, Thomas Corbett, the sheriff of the Midland District, was an old associate of the Smith family; George Yarker had been one of Smith's sureties for the wardenship; James MacFarlane, of the Kingston *Chronicle and Gazette*, was a magistrate; and James Hopkirk, the former assistant provincial secretary recently appointed collector of customs in Kingston, was a strong man who emerged as a staunch supporter of the warden. Brown's *Globe* was quick to denounce the new board as subservient to the Smith interest. It was, sneered the *Globe*, 'an extremely snug little board' whose meetings were held in the warden's dining room.[68] As events would soon prove, the Corbett board's approach to governance was to give Henry Smith his head and to follow his advice wherever it might lead.

Even before the Corbett board took office, Smith launched a preemptive strike. Taking advantage of a clause in the new statute giving him authority to remove the head keeper, as the assistant warden was now called, he preferred charges against Utting. The most prominent of these was that Utting had employed convicts without authority and for his private advantage. Utting's removal was accepted by the government and the Corbett board at its first meeting confirmed Smith's appointment as head keeper of Thomas Costen.[69] Costen lacked the qualifications of Powers and Utting. He had served as a guard and kitchen keeper and his principal attribute was loyalty to Smith. At last Smith had achieved his long-standing objective of unified command.

The board's second decision set the penitentiary on the road to disaster: it confirmed the warden's appointment of his son Frank as kitchen keeper. Why his father tolerated Frank's destructive activities remains a mystery. Possibly worn out by a decade of strenuous activity, or just bored with it all, he seems to have believed he could trust Frank to look after things. In these circumstances, with Costen's weak hand on discipline; an inexperienced board, overly deferential to the Smith family's growing political influence; and a government, fighting for its own political survival, even more indifferent than usual to penitentiary affairs, Frank Smith ran amok. The fallout from the 1846 Penitentiary Act, combined with ongoing and debilitating management problems evident since 1842, reduced penitentiary affairs to a chaos incomparably worse than the crisis Macaulay and Nickalls had pinpointed nearly a decade before.

While the notoriety given to the increasing resort to corporal punishments finally brought matters to a head, the precipitant was the disgust felt by Dr Sampson, the one powerful independent force in the prison, for Frank Smith's puerile and destructive activities. Sickened by Frank's abuse of the convicts, the surgeon brought formal charges against the warden's son.[70] Dr Sampson accused Frank of shooting arrows at convicts, leading to the loss of one convict's eye; employing convicts for his own profit and amusement; immoral behaviour towards convicts; and selling penitentiary stores and provisions for his own profit. One can hardly imagine more serious charges. Incredibly, the Corbett board determined to acquit Frank and after a perfunctory investigation found him innocent. Dr Sampson immediately appealed to the new Baldwin–LaFontaine government. With the newspaper clamour against the 'lash, lash, lash' administration now in full cry, the government appointed the commission which in short order ended what its secretary, George Brown, believed to be a reign of iniquity.

Beyond helping to understand the evolution of events, what does a narrative of developments under the several boards contribute to understanding the penitentiary's early history and governance? The Brown Commission would soon weigh in with its version, but there is reason to stand back from and qualify the conclusions reached by so partisan and inexperienced a group. The answer is as simple in statement as it was far-reaching in consequences. The old system of dealing with social and welfare matters through the appointment of ad hoc boards of gentlemen who subsequently enjoyed minimal supervision and wide latitude from a generally indifferent government no longer worked. It had been undermined by all those influences that were then transforming Canadian society, including population growth, the spread of the market economy and, specifically, the greater complexity, extent, and cost of all social institutions. New forms of organization were urgently needed.

In the penitentiary the deficiencies of the 1834 statute and the 1836 rules had been apparent from the beginning. Power divided between warden and deputy, between board and warden, and between government and board, with no clear demarcation of order and authority, could not serve the needs of a volatile institution such as a penitentiary. Governance of the penitentiary demanded administrative reform and political and bureaucratic rationalization. The indefensible finding of not guilty brought by the Corbett board to Sampson's charges against Frank Smith drove home once again the urgent need for modernization in penitentiary governance.

THE MORAL MACHINERY

If issues of finance and of governance can be broadly identified as incapable of solution without fundamental structural change, the third problem contributing to the ills of the early penitentiary would prove even more intractable. It related to confusion about the very purpose of the penitentiary. Did it exist for punishment, deterrence, or rehabilitation? Or was it intended somehow to achieve all three? If so, which had priority? And how was each to be achieved? Of the three, the goal of reform was most elusive and most weakly supported. Few of those associated with the penitentiary ever articulated it as foremost among institutional objectives. The chaplains were the outstanding exception, and for Reverend Robert Rogers in particular there was no doubt as to the overriding objective of confinement. 'It should ever be remembered, the safekeeping of the convict is not the end proposed, but his safekeeping in order that certain means may be adopted for his moral transformation.' Everything about this 'House of Correction,' Rogers insisted, should impress on the convict that the objective of the discipline was to achieve 'his restoration to character and to his forfeited station in society.'[71]

Smith had, as we have seen, emerged as a strong supporter of establishing an effective chaplaincy. The penitentiary's first chaplain, William Herchmer, had moderate expectations. Born in Kingston and educated locally and then at Oxford and ordained in England, Herchmer, twenty-five years of age at his appointment, also served as chaplain to the garrison and headmaster of the Kingston Grammar School.[72] His reports as penitentiary chaplain expressed satisfaction with the opportunities provided to meet and instruct the convicts in a way that he described as surpassing the opportunities provided by 'any similar institution.' Speaking to convicts in the solitude of their cells, Herchmer believed he was able to supply precisely that element of personal attention the warden had called for and he was delighted by what he termed an almost universal willingness 'to receive religious instruction when communicated in private.' He was cautiously optimistic about the effect of this instruction: 'Something it is hoped has been done to ameliorate the moral condition of the prisoners – much more indeed might have been done.'[73] In particular, he recommended that enquiries be made into the life of the prisoners prior to conviction and into what happened to them after release.

From Herchmer's interviews with individual convicts some sense emerges that for a few at least the experience of imprisonment had salutary results. Herchmer reported that while 'effects produced do not equal the labour bestowed,' he found it 'gratifying to learn that very favourable accounts have been received of discharged convicts, who regard their imprisonment as the happy means employed by an overruling Providence to rescue them from misery.'[74] Several, he reported, had told him of the great change effected by their penitentiary experience and in such cases of reformation he found reason for hope. He warned, however, that when he questioned convicts on their liberation, many told him that the fear of punishment would not lead to reformation unless accompanied by fear of God. 'To encourage this principle has been my earnest endeavour.'[75]

The inspectoral board chaired by John Macaulay, while supportive of the efforts of the chaplain and the warden to reform convicts, would never have proclaimed, as Henry Smith did, that reformation was the institution's principal goal. In their 1837 report, the inspectors applauded 'the faithfulness and zeal' with which Herchmer had entered on his duties. They believed his 'conversational instruction' with individual inmates had served effectively to 'bring to light' the disposition and temperament of each convict. As well, the chaplain's ministrations had worked 'to soften and subdue' the convict's 'natural pride,' which often stood in the way of reformation.[76] But John Macaulay, who probably penned these words, continued to regard the chaplain as an instrument put in office first and foremost to help the warden enforce discipline. The inspectors suspected that once the restraints of prison life had been removed, hardened criminals would likely fall back to their old ways. All they would allow for the chaplain's achievement was that, however 'short and evanescent as may be the moral and religious impressions' made on the convicts, they 'may have a salutary influence' while confinement continued. But after release, they were likely to effect a permanent change only 'on the minds of a few.'[77] Nor could the inspectors discover any practical way to assist the chaplain's wish to gain more knowledge of the convicts' lives prior to commitment or after release.

In the 1850s, Attorney General John A. Macdonald would make numerous pointed comments about the primacy of punishment and deterrence over the chimera of rehabilitation; for the Smith years such political comment is scarce, but there is no reason to believe that members of the provincial government were any more optimistic than the inspectors about the results to be achieved by efforts to rehabilitate the prisoners. As time went on, first Herchmer, and then to a far greater extent his successor, Reverend Rogers, became disheartened by this prevailing attitude. When no fewer then three of the first five convicts to be released from Kingston became recidivists in short order, the inspectors reported that this group repented of their conduct only to the extent that it was 'productive of further punishment.' Herchmer argued that it was unrealistic to expect that the convicts' moral feelings and the habits of a lifetime could be substantially altered in sentences, often of a year or less. 'The prospect of a speedy liberation naturally checks the rise of serious reflection.'[78]

The inspectors joined Herchmer in arguing for longer sentences, but they did so from an entirely different perspective. If it were true, they began, that under even the best system of prison discipline 'there are but very few criminals truly reformed, and that the great majority of convicts are only prevented from a repetition of crime so long as they are under the restraints of imprisonment,' then it was in society's interest to impose longer sentences. Noting that many offenders had doubtless committed numerous crimes before finally being apprehended and sentenced, the inspectors drove their case home by arguing that short sentences led to 'new trials, new convictions, and new sentences passed upon old offenders, at great expense to the country.'[79] For his part, Herchmer through interviews with convicts had become persuaded that not inmate sin but acquired habits accounted for the vast majority of crime. 'I have found that *Intemperance* is the prevailing cause.' Out of 90 convicts admitted in the current year, '71 were certainly the victims of this ruinous propensity.'[80] In his 1842 report, his last as chaplain, Herchmer recorded his regret that 'in a great majority of cases, that sincere reformation has not followed, which all connected with the institution so heartily desired.' But Herchmer, who profusely thanked the warden for his support, insisted that it was not the penitentiary's discipline which was at fault, but what happened to the convict after release. He blamed 'the sudden transition from close restraint to uncontrolled freedom; the free access to every indulgence, the meeting of old associates, the remembrance of old scenes, the feeling of disgrace impressed on their minds.' In these circumstances, he believed it 'not strange that good resolutions and holy desires should be sacrificed.'[81]

The disillusionment expressed by this mild-mannered man came as the culmination of several years' effort to persuade someone in authority that the system was urgently in need of reform. In 1839, Herchmer had reported to the inspectors that his contacts with recidivists had led him to conclude that many of them were motivated by a spirit of revenge. In prison, they had been forced to perform hard labour for the financial benefit of the state while they and their families, usually living in abject poverty, received nothing in return. 'Some have even so far acknowledged, that ... had [they] been assured that a *moiety* of *their earnings* would be paid them, after a stated period of probation, they would have had some *inducement* to continue in the path of honesty.'[82]

The inspectors were fearful that if they endorsed Herchmer's bold proposal to return a portion of their earnings to ex-convicts after a satisfactory period of probation, they would lose all credibility with the government. Yet they concurred with Herchmer's opinion that the critical moment in convict rehabilitation was at the point of release. 'With great deference,' therefore, and fearful of the public reaction to so blatant a breach of less eligibility, the inspectors asked the government to consider a scheme by which ex-convicts who received certificates of good behaviour from two magistrates and a minister might receive small sums as an inducement to good behaviour. Then, terrified by their own boldness, they added that so many objections might be raised to such a scheme that they preferred to revert to their earlier recommendation for longer sentences. They were now 'inclined to think' no sentence should be for less than three years.[83]

William Herchmer was not impressed, and in June 1843 he resigned to assume duties at St George's Church in Kingston. It was revealing of the inspectors' priorities that their minute book did not contain so much as a notice of his departure, even though the most trivial matters affecting labour or discipline received extensive attention. Herchmer was succeeded by a very different kind of man. Reverend Robert Vachon Rogers had served as acting chaplain in 1840–1, when Herchmer was absent in England. His nature, writes Thomas Wilson, the closest student of the Kingston chaplaincy and an admirer of Rogers, 'could be likened to a dog with a bone, or a man of great and deep conviction and belief.'[84] Born and ordained in England, he studied at Cambridge and served as a travelling missionary in the United States 'until his strong anti-slavery sentiments made his ministry very difficult.'[85] Rogers came to Canada in 1836 and from 1839 he was headmaster of the Midland District Grammar School. About thirty-six years of age when he began his work in Kingston, he was aggressive and accustomed to expressing his opinions fearlessly.

In his first stint in Kingston, Rogers demonstrated unbridled enthusiasm. The office of prison chaplain, he wrote, 'has opened a new page in the book of men,' and was second to none in its importance to the penitentiary's success.[86] For Rogers, rehabilitation was foremost among the penitentiary's goals. Because the convict entered prison depraved in mind and body and lacking in moral and religious training, his reclamation must be 'a work of time and patient persistence.' To that end everything about this 'House of Correction' must impress on the convict that the aim of all was to achieve 'his restoration to character and to his forfeited station in society.'[87]

For the bulk of his time in Kingston this single-minded zealot was a persistent supporter of Warden Smith. During his period as Herchmer's replacement, Rogers was almost euphoric about the opportunities for good works offered by Smith and his colleagues. He pointed warmly to 'an admirable plan ... lately adopted' to allow convicts during the long winter evenings to read to 9 p.m. He was pleased, too, to initiate a short service resembling a Bible class twice a week after dinner. Like Herchmer, Rogers was delighted that he was allowed every opportunity to meet with the convicts privately, and from these encounters he believed 'many a heart has been made to feel, which never felt before.'[88] At this point Rogers accepted many, if not all, of the fundamentals of the Auburn system, firmly believing, as he expressed it, that 'the very air of the Penitentiary should inspire submission to constituted authority.'[89] In 1840 his judgment of conditions in the institution was outspokenly supportive. He expressed confidence that rehabilitation could be achieved, but understood that time alone would determine the extent of success. Nonetheless, of this he was sure: '*here is good* – crime is restrained; the *ignorant are taught*; time and opportunity are allowed for serious reflection ... *here is a place in which a man, if ever, may reform.*'[90]

Rogers's disillusionment came gradually. Like Herchmer and the inspectors, he regretted that the government refused to provide greater assistance for the convicts after release. From time to time the inspectors argued that the allowance given to prisoners on discharge was so small that they were often forced to remain in the Kingston area, far from friends and family, where, unable to secure employment, they returned to crime. Rogers was more vehement, insisting in 1843 that it should occasion no astonishment that 'our fairest prospects are sometimes blasted' when once-hopeful convicts became repeat offenders. Rogers attributed this backsliding to the overwhelming problems facing liberated convicts. 'To be known is to be shunned by the respectable portion of society! No one will employ a man who has been in the Penitentiary; and I believe it to be in no way improbable, that some have no alternative besides a recommitment or starvation.' Such claims by a responsible official were astounding. Rogers amplified his concerns by noting the progress in aftercare work in several American states. In Boston, for example, former inmates of the house of correction were sent to work for a period on area farms. Without some early action in Canada, he warned, the penitentiary system 'must in a great degree, fail of its end.'

Apparently undaunted, Rogers went to work, reading American and British prison reports, pouring over the records of foreign philanthropic societies. In his 1844 report he urged that a correspondence be initiated with such organizations as a step towards the establishment of a Canadian aftercare facility, 'suited to our peculiar circumstances.' As usual, the inspectors urged caution. While such an organization might receive governmental assistance, including the use of some of the penitentiary land, they believed it could be established only thorough voluntary effort 'by the exertions of benevolent individuals.'[91]

Rogers knew that such timidity could lead nowhere. In 1845, he reported that in the absence of official action he had prevailed on the charitable instincts of several steamboat captains, without whose kindness 'many a convict could not have left Kingston.'[92] In 1846, with three years of experience behind him, Rogers reiterated his claim that the assistance provided the liberated convict was 'so scanty,' and the prejudice against him in the community 'so strong,' that circumstances 'all but compel him to resort to unlawful means for the supply of his necessities.' Once again he pleaded for the establishment of a 'House of Refuge, under strict superintendence, offering a temporary asylum.'[93] The chaplain's repeated claims that the penitentiary had created a class of persons feared and shunned by society, who turned again to crime to avoid starvation, was a stunning condemnation of the penitentiary system. The government's failure to respond reflected a customary indifference to the welfare of the convict population.

Rogers was especially insightful in discussing the elusive relationship between convict and community. Writing in 1840, he argued that the sympathetic understanding of the convict's condition demonstrated by prison officers should not stop on release. The community 'ought to welcome his return from the error of his ways' and, if his reformation were sincere, should strengthen his good resolve. Instead, Rogers observed, society acted in the most appalling fashion, and this was the case 'not with the ignorant only, but among the intelligent and respectable classes' which 'too frequently' repulsed 'the unhappy convict ... in his honourable endeavours after a life of honest industry.'[94] Rogers's most virulent condemnation was directed at those mechanics who had been so outspoken in their opposition to all efforts to assist the convict class. 'All combinations ... against the employment' of released convicts, he insisted, were not only cruel but foolish and ran directly contrary to the self-interest of society. The state, he urged, should intervene 'to protect the weak, when necessary.' And private benevolence, he suggested, should establish a subsidiary institution to provide temporary employment for the newly released convict.[95]

In his 1844 report, Rogers made his definitive statement of the changes needed to transform Kingston, in his words, from a penitentiary to a school of reform. The list was a long one. It included a separate facility for juveniles, an after-care institution, the separation of military prisoners from convicts, the pursuit of close relations with foreign benevolent societies, an end to the admission of paying visitors, and the urgent need to attract a better quality of officer to work as guards and keepers. Most of all, there must be a full recognition of the critical role of chaplain. 'It must be evident to the board, he declaimed, that 'the Chaplain must be the main spring' of the moral machinery. To that end, there must be a permanent full-time chaplain. 'For if there is a place on earth where a Minister of the Lord Jesus Christ may contend with sin, it is in a great prison.'[96] None of these recommendations was attended to. In 1846 Rogers, feeling impotence and rage, offered his harshest assessment of Kingston, calling it 'a penitentiary in Name, a Jail in Fact!!'[97]

HENRY SMITH AND THE REFORMATORY IDEAL

As Herchmer and Rogers struggled to give some substance to the reformatory side of the penitentiary ideal, Henry Smith was carrying on his own campaign to achieve similar objectives. In his work on the Kingston chaplaincy, Thomas Wilson has asserted that for Smith 'reformation was the prime purpose in the management of prisoners.'[98] Despite the anti-Smith strictures of George Brown and his fellow commissioners, the published reports and official minutes of the penitentiary during the first decade of its existence confirm the accuracy of that observation. They provide a portrait of a warden whose reformist recommendations were rebuffed year after year by an indifferent government that had only two ideas about the provincial penitentiary, the need for harsh punishments and economical administration. Finally, of course, Henry Smith simply collapsed into indifference and lassitude.

Smith worked persistently for years to acquaint himself with a wide range of foreign innovations in penitentiary administration in order to understand and implement the most hopeful developments at Kingston. His annual reports are replete with innumerable recommendations for improvement which, taken together, far exceed the proposals for change finally recommended by the Brown Commission. Frequently, the changes Smith proposed were similar to those advocated by the chaplains, often he managed to carry with him the support of the inspectors, but almost without fail his recommendations met with hostility or indifference at the hands of a negligent government.

One of Smith's earliest concerns was the extent of recidivism. Of 148 convicts in confinement in 1839, 15 were on their second and 2 on their third conviction. Several of these had been sentenced to a year or less, a period that Smith described as too short for either punishment or reformation. Pointing out that in some American states recidivists were imprisoned for life, Smith suggested that the inspectors ask the legislature to consider passing such a law, 'not merely as punishment, but with a view of deterring discharged convicts from following their former vicious courses.'[99] Two years later, still worried about recidivism, he noted that thirty-six convicts, about a quarter of the population, were repeat offenders. The courts, he urged, should make a greater effort to identify ex-convicts and to take their records into consideration when handing down sentences. If the courts proved unable to act, then penitentiary officers should receive the authority to add a further term for recidivists once they were committed.[100] Interestingly, this area, with Smith urging a more punitive approach, proved an exception to official indifference and the legislature established longer sentences for recidivists. Soon, however, Smith was complaining that the statute was ineffective. As he told his son, Henry Jr, 'I fear that in 99 cases out of 100 this will prove a mere nullity from the circumstance that discharged convicts generally change the scene of their operations and are consequently, when arraigned for their subsequent offences, unknown to the judge, jury or officers of the District in which they are about to be tried.'[101]

Another theme to which Smith would return year after year was the desirability of being able to reduce the number of corporal punishments. Smith was obliged by statute to use such punishments to enforce the rule of silence and other aspects of the harsh Auburn program, but he believed that excessive punishments demoralized everyone. They also suggested that his own management was defective, when the discipline was breached so regularly. When the number of punishments was cut in half between 1838 and 1839, Smith cited this as 'a certain indication' that the discipline had improved, 'and that the officers of the situation had become more vigilant in their duties.' Smith's efforts to reduce punishments earned him a reprimand in 1840 from the new Kirkpatrick board. A board minute of 7 July called his 'particular attention to the strict enforcement of the discipline,' because from the list of punishments inflicted 'it would appear to be somewhat relaxed.'[102] In the years ahead, Henry Smith would not once be criticized by any of the successive boards under whom he served for being too severe in the infliction of punishments, but from time to time he would be questioned sharply about his lenience and urged to sterner efforts. In this area, at least, inspectoral punitiveness reflected the wishes of the government that discipline be unrelenting to ensure convict docility and maximum productivity.

Smith accepted the necessity of corporal punishment, as he explained privately to Henry Jr, especially because it was needed in order to enforce the labour regimen 'when any relaxation in the regulations of the Institution might prove fatal to the Establishment.' In such cases, he continued, 'it has been usual to have recourse to the whip, which in some instances tended rather to harden the offender than to convince him of his error,' but it was used so that 'no less of labour' should be obtained from the prisoners, as would be the result 'were solitary confinement adopted in lieu of it.' One answer to this dilemma, Smith told Henry, was to add five days to the length of the sentence for every day of solitary, 'and no doubt the fear of additional imprisonment will go much further to produce good behaviour, than any dread the whip can inspire.'[103] With respect to the desirability of limiting corporal punishments, however, Smith found few converts.

In numerous reports, Smith tried to explain to his superiors how important it was to exchange information with officials in other jurisdictions to keep informed of new theories and practices. He seems from the onset of his duties to have understood the dangers imposed by his lonely situation as the only prison warden in Canada, and to have tried to avoid being intellectually isolated. In 1838, the Assembly had ordered the printing of 200 copies of the Kingston report and he carefully noted that this had enabled him 'to exchange this document with those of several other Penitentiaries in the United States.' If this practice were continued, he emphasized, 'much useful information may be derived.'

Regrettably, it was not. In December 1844, Smith told Henry Jr that the reports had been printed on only two occasions since the prison opened, even though regular publication had been intended by the statute, partly so that the warden could be supplied with a sufficient quantity for his own purposes. 'I am constantly receiving useful information from the several Penitentiaries in the United States as well as from the Prison Discipline Society of Boston.' Smith wanted to reciprocate. Then, significantly, he pointed to another reason for publication: 'the public has a right,' he informed his son, to know 'how the affairs of the Penitentiary are conducted, as it requires so much money for its support and completion, and will do so, until all the Buildings are finished.' Smith believed this matter to be important enough to be attended to by legislation.[104]

Equally valuable was the personal contact Smith developed with the American prison reformer, the Reverend Louis Dwight, whose Boston

Prison Discipline Society was the most active such organization in the United States and the most determined advocate of Auburn principles. Members of the Boston Society had been in touch with Canadians since the day of the Thomson–Macaulay report, and Smith's relationship with Dwight was close. In January 1837, we find him looking forward to a visit from Dwight and telling him he had prepared a plan of Kingston suitable for publication in the Society's next report. The two men for years exchanged information on developments. One of Smith's most revealing letters to Dwight was written in early 1843 to bring the American up to date on how Kingston was functioning now that it served Canada East as well as Canada West. Dwight was especially interested in understanding the causes of crime, and Smith reported that Kingston's convicts were still being questioned closely at the time of release, 'and the same results in 99 cases out of a hundred are constantly experienced, viz: that they attribute their crimes to the use of ardent spirits which consequently led them to associate with persons of loose character, by whom they have been tempted to commit the offences.' Smith had done his best to persuade 'the more intelligent' of them to let him know what happened to them after release, 'but in no one instance have they complied.'[105] Smith found it much more difficult to establish relations with British prison reformers. His letter book is sprinkled with requests to the governor-general for assistance in obtaining British prison reports, but even such a simple request seemed beyond the inclination of His Excellency's office.

Like the chaplains, Smith in many of his reports sounded the alarm about the relationship between recidivism and the lack of aftercare assistance. He lamented to Henry Jr that the 'want of a proper place of reception for discharged Convicts on their liberation from the Penitentiary until they can procure respectable employment is most seriously felt. Some of the unfortunate creatures, particularly females, after leading a short dissolute course of life have been found dead in this neighbourhood.' And perhaps, he speculated, the same had happened to others who had managed to leave the Kingston area. 'Very probably,' he told his son, the erection of a house of industry 'into which they might be received ... would have the desired effect.' Smith had no doubt that 'the want of such a retreat is one, and the principal, cause of so many being sent here a second and a third time.' In his 1845 report, Smith formally recommended that a house of industry be established on land donated by the penitentiary. In the same report, the inspectors expressed their full agreement with the analyses offered by the warden and the chaplain, but the government turned its customary deaf ear to all such pleas.[106] In a similar vein, Smith expressed his regret that he was required to receive some convicts 'who are more fit subjects for a hospital than a prison,' although every care was taken of them until release. He was sometimes, he lamented, required by law to release very sick persons, and he suggested to his son Henry that a law be passed whereby convicts of bad health need not be released unless they so desired it.

Smith's most thoughtful commitment to a reform penology that was then emerging only slowly in Britain and the United States was his support for earned remission. The only way for convicts to receive an early release was through a pardon, but Smith complained of how the process worked. Prisoners could not apply for themselves and those with family or influential friends had an unfair advantage. Smith also believed the existing process tended to weaken his own authority and ability to manage the institution. The matter had real implications for institutional management. Up to 1842, no fewer than 72 convicts had been released through pardons, as compared to 292 at the expiry of their sentences.[107] While the number pardoned was much smaller than in most American prisons, it was large enough to preoccupy convicts and affect their behaviour in prison, especially through cases of perceived injustice.

Smith did have some influence on the pardoning process, because the government usually asked him to provide a report on the individual's behaviour in prison. Smith's correspondence in such cases suggests that he was anxious to be as positive as possible when sending reports to the government. In March 1839, for example, he noted in his letter book that he could find little that was good to say about two applicants but, not wanting to deprive them of any possible benefit, he checked with the chaplain who indicated that their behaviour had recently improved. The most interesting facet of the early pardoning process was the practice, analogous to the procedure made familiar in the courts, of requiring the individual to post a bond and find sureties for good behaviour. Henry Smith was zealous in his efforts to assist candidates in this endeavour, often writing letters on their behalf.[108]

Clemency for the few, however, fell far short of being a policy of earned remission to which every prisoner might reasonably aspire. Smith, early in his wardenship, courageously embarked on a determined campaign to involve himself more actively in the processes of convict assessment and early release for all. In support of earned remission, he pointed to the work of Captain Alexander Maconochie. Years later, the innovative methods employed by Maconochie in the British penal colony of Norfolk Island in the South Pacific would earn him legendary status.

Maconochie's administration was short-lived, because his humane methods and imaginative treatment techniques excited the hostility of traditionalists who refused to believe that hardened criminals could be reformed by such methods. Smith, however, was an early supporter. He noted carefully that Maconochie had recommended that prisoners receive time off for good behaviour and to this end had awarded 'marks' for praiseworthy conduct. 'This recommendation has been adopted, and no evil has been found to arise from the system now in operation.' Smith cited with approval Maconochie's claim that a mark system was an important tool of reformation, and aided those convicts who were sincerely endeavouring to reform. A similar law existed in Tennessee, he pointed out, and there a further period of confinement could be added to the sentences of convicts who behaved badly.

Smith's strongest expression of support for earned remission was made in a private letter to Henry Jr. 'Nothing in my opinion,' he confided to Henry, 'would have a greater tendency to produce obedience and humility on the part of the convict than holding out to him the prospect of shortening his imprisonment by means within his own power.' Smith even gave thought to how a remission law might be used to alleviate the growing problem posed by the large number of prisoners sentenced to life. Such a law, he told Henry, could not affect a lifer, but 'still something might be done to hold out a hope even to such a one' if there might be some prospect of release after a number of years.[109] Such radical doctrine was unlikely to win support from many Canadian politicians.

In view of Smith's distaste for corporal punishment, he may also have regarded a mark system as a partial alternative to the lash. He formally asked the inspectors to consider whether 'some such alteration in our Penitentiary system of punishment ... might not advantageously be made, as at present the convict has nothing to incite him to good behaviour while undergoing his sentence, but the avoidance of disciplinary punishment, which too frequently is not sufficient to deter him from the commission of offences within prison walls.'[110] Smith saw the mark system and good behaviour remission as contributing to his ability to enforce order within the institution. It is remarkable that a warden whose duty it was to implement the Auburn system could assert that nothing existed to encourage the convict to good behaviour. Two decades later, the essentials of the Maconochie system would be taken up by another great penal reformer, Sir Walter Crofton; not until then would aspects of the system Smith proposed in the early 1840s receive partial implementation in Canada.

One of the most shocking findings of the Brown Commission about the

Smith administration related to the presence at Kingston of child prisoners, who were subjected to the same harsh regimen as the adults. Perhaps more than any other feature of Smith's wardenship, the abuse of children shocked the public and blackened Smith's reputation. Yet for years Smith and his colleagues expressed their revulsion at the presence of children and did all in their power to persuade the government to make other provisions. 'The admission of children and their subjection to adult discipline,' the chaplain asserted in 1844, was 'not calculated to reform, but to injure. Should not some respect be paid to the peculiarities of youth, even in a place of confinement? Would not the desired end be more effectually secured by a judicious mixture of school, labour and recreation?' Smith thought so too and emphasized that he had previously deplored the practice of sentencing boys fifteen and under to the penitentiary at all. This issue had been taken up by the legislature and 'there are some hopes that, in future, culprits of tender age will be otherwise provided for in regard to punishment than they have hitherto been.' In his December 1844 letter to Henry Jr, Smith explained that any attempt to carry out a hard labour sentence with children would ruin their health. He was persuaded that 'the sending of them here takes away in great measure the chance of reformation' by introducing them to hardened offenders 'whom they meet in after life and join with in future depredations.'[111]

To assist the politicians in their deliberations, Smith informed them of recent advances in England and France. There the question of juvenile crime was being actively discussed and strikingly different solutions were being tried. In England, he noted, a separate facility, Parkhurst, had been established for juveniles but the success of this method had not yet been ascertained. A more complex system was being essayed in France. There children continued to be sentenced to ordinary imprisonment but after nine months, if their behaviour was good, they were released and placed in a trade as apprentices, where they remained until their original sentences had expired. In other countries, separate places of confinement were provided for young offenders. In these facilities the child was able to gain admittance to higher grades through good behaviour until he could achieve remission and be released for the remainder of his sentence. He was submitting this information to the inspectors, Smith said, in the hope that it would be brought to the attention of the legislators.[112]

In their belief that a prison must strive to rehabilitate as well as to punish, the Kingston management, while by no means unique, stood in contrast to that which existed in many American prisons by the late 1830s. In New York State, for example, wardens such as Elam Lynds and Robert Wiltse were arguing that rehabilitation was unlikely if not impossible:

'the best prison,' said Wiltse, 'is that which the inmates find worst.'[113] Such views were held in Canada too. The rhetoric of those opposed to prison labour had always encompassed a large measure of hostility to convicts themselves. Kingston officials were appalled at the repulsion former convicts encountered when they tried to re-establish themselves in the community. Far from believing in rehabilitation, most Canadians had little sympathy or understanding of the concept, or for the heartbreak and failure experienced by prisoners after release.

There was a prominent class dimension to this reactionary perspective. If mechanics were in the foreground of the less eligibility crowd, there were also some, who considered themselves to be individuals of education and breeding, who rejected not only trade training but even the simplest kinds of schooling for convicts. In 1847, the officiating Roman Catholic clergyman, Angus MacDonell, expressed fear lest convicts be too well-fed and clothed: 'if you employ schoolmasters to give them a genteel and liberal education,' and if their condition was known to be 'far better in every respect' than the vast majority of honest workers, then 'you hold out an inducement to every poor person in the country to commit some crime.'[114] The prevalence of such beliefs among the largely rural population, together with the deeply ingrained view that only harsh punishment could deter criminals, ensured that the efforts of Smith, Rogers, and a few others must fail.

CONVICT LABOUR

There was a final barrier, the most pervasive of all, to the effort to introduce sensible rehabilitative practices into the institution. The 1834 statute had placed hard labour in the dominant position in the disciplinary regimen, and the financial needs of the prison ensured that it remained there. The labour routine, because it occupied the convicts from dawn to dusk six days of the week, served to overwhelm every other possible activity. No other aspect of penitentiary life could begin to compete; convict labour was the essential element in the Auburn discipline to which everything else must conform. Every other aspect of the penitentiary experience was judged and assessed primarily as it advanced or impeded the productive capacity of the convict workers.

The promises held out for convict labour seemed to conform to every possible state interest and to fulfil every possible public need. For those who supported the penitentiary as a vehicle of punishment and deterrence, the arduous effort of breaking stone or performing similar tasks for fourteen hours a day could hardly be improved upon. Beccaria himself had proposed in 1764 that hard labour be deployed as a punitive alternative to the death penalty. 'It is not the terrible yet momentary spectacle of the death of a wretch, but the long and painful example of a man deprived of liberty, who, having become a beast of burden, recompenses with his labour the society he has offended, which is the strongest curb against crime.'[115] In England, Beccarian notions informed the national Penitentiary Act of 1779, while Jeremy Bentham's Panopticon would have modelled the penitentiary on the factory by organizing it around the profit motive. In the United States, New York prison reformer Thomas Eddy claimed once again in 1801 that perpetual labour would deter crime more effectively than the death penalty, and this belief dominated the American prison experience for most of the nineteenth century.[116] In many North American communities, including Ontario, the assurance that the convict labourers would earn enough to support the entire cost of their own detention proved an irresistible attraction. To those who believed that labour was a vital resource in a young and underdeveloped society, the Auburn approach, which maximized productivity, could be justified on mercantilist and nationalist grounds. Increasingly, too, in the nineteenth century, as the numbers of urban poor emerged as a critical social problem, prison labour was regarded as a powerful means of eradicating the habits of idleness and sloth that were seen to contribute to the spread of pauperism and vice. Not only would workers become imbued with habits of regularity and industry, but they would be provided with the skills needed to earn a living. And finally, for prison officers there was the irresistible appeal of being able to keep the prisoners continuously occupied in a way that would consume their energies and prevent dangerous liaisons. In these circumstances, Henry Smith and the inspectors made every effort to maximize productivity and offered frequent reassurances that the golden day of institutional self-sufficiency must soon arrive. There was little room to refine the concept of labour to provide for systematic trade training or to attend to other potentially rehabilitative aspects of a labour regimen. In nineteenth-century Kingston, productivity was everything, rehabilitation nothing.

Smith and his colleagues did about as well as could be expected, given these circumstances. At first, they professed to be operating within the 1835 constraints imposed by the Hagerman Committee, a task facilitated by the reality that penitentiary construction and housekeeping must occupy most convicts for the foreseeable future. In 1836, warden and inspectors reported to this effect, noting nonetheless that most bedding, prisoners' clothing, boots, and even many tools and utensils were being made at Kingston.[117]

To what extent were any of these tasks even minimally rehabilitative? Smith claimed that he tried to match convict and task by giving prisoners a choice as to employment. He also reported that he found them anxious to gain a knowledge of various trades, and that they were making 'surprising progress.'[118] It is common to denigrate prison labour as boring and menial and stone breaking certainly fits this description. Nonetheless, the variety of tasks being performed could not help but give some prisoners the opportunity to acquire important skills. As for female prisoners, the matron Smith hired as a supervisor soon had them engaged in making and repairing bedding and clothing.

There is overwhelming evidence, however, that the need to raise revenue far outweighed the provision of specialized training. In 1836, John Macaulay told the government that once the north wing was completed, a decision would have to be taken as 'to what objects the labour of the convicts shall be directed.'[119] While Macaulay was confident that this could be done without hurting free workers, he announced that the inspectors would be pleased if the government would relieve them from taking the responsibility of deciding upon work priorities by dealing with the matter by statute.[120] Macaulay was anxious to throw this political hot potato back to the hands of the government. Obviously, politics and financial imperatives from the beginning took priority in the inspectors' minds over the opportunity to establish a labour program that emphasized rehabilitation.

With few prison-made articles sold on the market, the warden in 1836 reported convict earnings of only £145.[121] In 1837, the inspectors reported that they continued to pay 'scrupulous attention' to the legislature's insistence that nothing be sold that might 'injure the business of individual tradesmen.'[122] But by 1839 they were complaining that the deployment of convict labour overwhelmingly on institutional construction had most harmful consequences for discipline. It added to costs by spreading workers across the prison and requiring more guards. More seriously, in the face of unremitting vigilance, 'communications do take place between the convicts,' who had thereby acquired extensive knowledge of events beyond prison walls.[123] Once again, John Macaulay's vision of a prison bloodbath loomed large; once again, the primary objectives of Auburn discipline could not withstand the beguiling attraction of saving some money. The convicts talked to each other easily and frequently, they hatched schemes, and they were developing an inmate subculture to serve their own peculiar needs.

Rehabilitation could not compare to economy in the hierarchy of governmental priorities. Throughout the Smith years most labour was disposed of in institutional maintenance or, to a much lesser extent, in producing a limited range of products for sale externally.[124] The sale of labour under contract which William Powers had favoured played an insignificant role and some critics complained that great financial benefits were thereby lost to the province.

'GUILTY AS CHARGED'

With the benefit of hindsight, the problems the penitentiary faced during the Smith years seem readily apparent if not inevitable. For an underdeveloped colonial society, the establishment and administration of a penitentiary was a venture of no common difficulty. The most critical problems to beset Kingston in its early years arose out of and remained closely related to the province's political, financial, and administrative circumstances, and would be addressed only gradually and as reform and modernization reshaped the Canadian political and governmental structures. More specifically, the administrative and support systems provided for the penitentiary by the 1834 statute and the 1836 rules and regulations were severely flawed, but only time and experience could reveal the source of the defects and point to the nature and extent of the reforms required. Most of the problems of the penitentiary under Smith's leadership were structural in nature, and far beyond the ability of any of the prison officers to remedy.

This judgment does not diminish the importance of the Brown Commission or whitewash Henry Smith, who in his final years as warden all but abandoned his responsibilities and stood by complacently as ignorant or evil underlings threatened to reduce the institution to chaos. It is intended, however, to alert students of correctional history to the glaring defects in the Brown Commission analysis and to suggest that the early years of the Canadian penitentiary can be understood only by endeavouring to look at the period anew. There is of course much to learn from the commission's work, which did constitute a turning point in the history of the Canadian penitentiary. On its investigative side and in its first report, the commission brought for the first time a huge body of pertinent material to the attention of a shocked public. The inner workings of the penitentiary had previously remained secret, free of scrutiny by grand juries and subject to inspection only by the boards of local gentry, themselves co-opted by the system. After Brown, penitentiary officers were always acutely aware that at any moment their actions might similarly be subject to public scrutiny. On its constructive side, in a second, much briefer

report released a few weeks after the first, the commissioners made recommendations that formed the basis of the 1851 Penitentiary Act. For that
reason alone, it is impossible to understand the penitentiary in the Smith
years without coming to terms with the Brown Commission's dramatic
and unequivocal assessment of that period.

Let us begin with the case against Frank Smith, which was dealt with in
pages 15 to 98 of the Report. In proceeding against Frank, and later
against his father, the commissioners paid little attention to the written
records of the institution, including minute books and letter books. Their
preferred method was to put questions to officers and convicts, past and
present, and to other interested parties, and then to give them an opportunity to respond. The commissioners began the inquiry against Frank by
reopening the charges Dr Sampson had made against him, which the
Corbett board had dismissed. They took note of how that board, even
while Sampson was appealing the case to the government, had raised
questions about Dr Sampson's own conduct, especially in dealing with
mentally disturbed convicts James Brown and Charlotte Reveille. In the
Reveille case, they charged him with behaving improperly while examining a female convict; in the case of Brown, who had received numerous
whippings, they censored him for certifying Brown as fit physically for
punishment while refusing to comment on his mental state. Both cases
seem to have been trumped up by the inspectors, who were angered by
the independent role Sampson was playing. They regarded Sampson as
disruptive and appear to have concluded that he must be forced to resign.
Sampson refused to appear before them on these matters and took his
case to the government.[125]

The commissioners took great pains with the Frank Smith–Dr Sampson
dispute, while not doubting for a moment which of the two was the
guilty party. When they served Smith with formal charges, he declined to
appear before them, claiming he had already been found innocent by the
previous board. The evidence against Frank was some of the most shocking of the entire inquiry. He had taken delight in perpetrating acts of
petty cruelty against the convicts, taunting them outrageously for his
own amusement. As kitchen keeper, Frank pilfered from the supplies,
evidently selling them to other officers. And he engaged in frequent acts
of disorderly conduct, such as taking male convicts out to fish with him
and consorting while inebriated with female convicts. Frank Smith was
out of control, a lawless force in an institution supposedly governed by
law, and his nonsense would not have been tolerated for a moment in any
well-managed facility. The commissioners recommended his immediate

dismissal. Frank's abuses went far to discredit not only his father but the Corbett board as well.[126]

The case against the warden covered pages 114 to 256 of the first report. Of the fifty-four witnesses, sixteen were convicts or ex-convicts and many others were officers or ex-officers of the penitentiary. The commissioners treated Smith's numerous procedural objections contemptuously, intimating that an innocent man should have nothing to complain about. When Smith appeared with a lawyer, that lawyer was not allowed to remain because the commissioners 'could see no propriety' in such representation. 'Had the Warden been an illiterate person, unfit to conduct his own case,' there might have been some justification for allowing him counsel.[127] Smith complained vehemently that 'the witnesses are, generally speaking, persons who have no friendly feelings towards me, many of them having held offices ... from which they have been discharged for misconduct.' Others were convicts or former convicts 'who have been punished under my directions.' It had never been intended, responded the commissioners, that any charge should be considered established on convict evidence alone. To his plea that the commissioners had been preparing their case for months and he needed time to prepare his, the commissioners responded that Smith must proceed forthwith. And they chose to ignore his complaint that it was grossly unfair to charge him with alleged abuses which might have occurred many years previously, with no effort being made to determine when such events might have occurred.

Henry Smith had good reason to insist that he participated 'under protest that I am not fairly dealt with, in having been denied that measure of justice accorded to the lowest criminal.'[128] The commissioners had decided to put Smith on trial, find him guilty, and punish him. They acted as judge and jury and as prosecuting attorneys as well.

Eleven separate charges were brought against the warden, each of which was divided into separate counts. On 103 of the 119 counts, and on every major charge, the commissioners pronounced Smith guilty and removed him from office. No appeal was open to him. Donald Aeneas Macdonell, who had served as acting warden during Smith's suspension, was appointed warden. During the inquiry the Corbett board had resigned and the commissioners were appointed as inspectors.[129] They continued to function in that capacity for a time after the inquiry was complete, partly in order to remove from the prison all vestiges of the Smith influence. The new broom had swept clean.

Interestingly, while the charges of which Henry Smith had been pronounced guilty included many matters that were criminal in nature, no charges were brought before him in a court of law, where he would have had opportunity to defend himself through counsel and where he would have had every other benefit of legal process. There seems to have been no explanation for this.

Was Henry Smith guilty as charged and on virtually every single count brought against him? He faced three types of charges: first, neglect, venality and mismanagement; second, horrible abuse of the convicts; and third, no demonstrable rehabilitation of a single convict. On the first group of charges, numerous witnesses testified that Smith had neglected his duties and shown an astonishing indifference to penitentiary affairs. The architect William Coverdale testified that for months at a time Smith had not spoken to him about the vast and expensive construction projects, and others said that he was seldom seen in the workshops. Coverdale also claimed there was great carelessness in managing prison property, which led to much pilfering. Generally, numerous criticisms were made of the management of convict labour in the shops and on construction; material was bought in too small quantities and work stoppages for want of materials and tools occurred frequently. The commissioners were scathing in their condemnation of Henry Smith as a business manager. To some extent, the case seemed persuasive and there is no doubt that Smith had become lax and negligent. But Coverdale, still smarting over his salary reduction in 1846, was wrong to blame the warden for the decision taken years earlier by the inspectors and approved by the government not to build the prison under a comprehensive contract. And similar criticisms of convict labour were made in just about every prison in North America, as numerous inquiries would demonstrate. To accuse Smith of personal dishonesty for making use of such customary perquisites as feeding his own livestock from prison slops was nothing more than pettiness and to argue that Smith was personally responsible for inefficient accounting procedures was palpably unfair. The inspectors and the government had every opportunity each year to challenge or query the official figures.[130]

The most shocking matter dealt with in the report was the massive and increasing incidence of physical punishments inflicted on men, women, and children. The lurid accounts offered by the press painted a picture of a sadist ruling by the whip alone and leaving a bloody trail of broken bodies in his wake. Once again, the commissioners had no doubt at all that the responsibility was the warden's. They compiled a table that showed that the number of punishments of all description had risen from

770 in 1843 to 2,102 in 1845, 3,445 in 1846, and 6,063 in 1847. In 1845 and 1846, 'the number of corporal punishments alone, averaged between four and five' each year for every man, woman, and child, with seven corporal punishments inflicted each day. This proved 'beyond cavil' that the system was one 'of the most frightful oppression.' The commissioners believed it fed on itself, and 'the moment excessive punishment commenced,' it served to harden the offender and produced the need for an escalation. According to the commissioners, the fault lay with the warden, and 'where it would have stopped, had the Government not interfered and restrained it, it is impossible to say.' The majority of punishments were 'for offences of the most trifling character; and the truth of the complaint resting solely on the word of a Guard or Keeper.'[131]

Convict Maurice Phelan described the routine:

Each morning the entries on the punishment Book are read over by Francis W. Smith; the offenders who are to be placed on bread and water, are brought forward to the front rank; after breakfast, those who are to go into the boxes are marched to them; those to be flogged with the cats are so at dinner time, before all the other prisoners, when the Surgeon and Warden are present; those flogged with the raw-hide (but that punishment is now done away) used to be punished at once, after breakfast.[132]

The commissioners believed that such a display of official brutality defeated all hope of reformation: 'to see crowds of full grown men, day after day, and year after year, stripped and lashed in the presence of four or five hundred persons' because they whispered, or lifted their eyes, or laughed, 'must have obliterated ... all perception of moral guilt, and thoroughly brutalized all their feelings.'[133]

The hypocrisy of the commissioners was nowhere more apparent than in their determination to blame the warden personally for all the excesses of the brutal Auburn discipline. Instead of denouncing the absurdities of the rule of silence, including the unnatural requirement that convicts work side by side day after day, year after year, without uttering a word to each other, they proceeded to ignore the notorious system that provoked such excessive punishments wherever it was applied. As relentless prosecutors, they moved to forestall the logical defence that such punishments were necessary to maintain the discipline. Such a defence, they insisted, was 'quite untenable' because discipline had not been maintained and because 'the history of Penal Establishments throughout the world' demonstrated that excesses of punishment and bad discipline went hand in hand. Such special pleading from commissioners who knew little of practices 'around the world' did not ring true; in any case the commissioners themselves would refuse to recommend either the abolition of corporal punishment or the ending of the rule of silence.[134]

The record of nineteenth-century Canadian corporal punishments is a sorry one, but no careful analysis yet exists of its extent or its significance. From 1835 to 1842, the only punishments inflicted were flogging with cat or rawhide. Then ironing, solitary, and bread and water were added to the prison's repertory, and the numbers of punishments increased disproportionately to the greatly expanding numbers confined. Yet it was the crisis of overcrowding and the need to confine more than one prisoner to a cell that contributed most to the breakdown of discipline, as Kingston's officials became increasingly desperate to maintain control. In this situation the Kirkpatrick board, as we have seen, considered Smith too slack in his approach and ordered him to enforce the rules more strictly.[135]

From October 1846, as a result of sensationalist press stories, the cat and the rawhide were suspended, but in February the cat was restored and the instrument known as the box, a coffin-like structure that inflicted hideous pain by forcing the convict to stand erect without any movement of the limbs, was instituted. A rule was passed in October 1847 enforcing the presence of both warden and surgeon at every corporal punishment and requiring a signed certificate from the surgeon before punishment could be inflicted.[136] There was much convict evidence on physical punishments, including that inflicted on convicts of unbalanced mind, especially James Brown who, between 1841 and 1847, received 1,002 lashes of the cats and 216 of the rawhides. Dr Sampson, however, testified that he did not begin to have suspicions of any mental aberration on Brown's part until December 1847 and former inspectors Hopkirk, Corbett, and even Kirkpatrick all said there had been no suspicion that he was unbalanced.[137]

The testimony that most horrified contemporaries was of the punishments inflicted on children for behaving like children. The commissioners dealt in detail with four cases, eleven-year-old Alexis Lafleur, committed in 1842 and pardoned in 1845; ten-year-old Peter Charboneau, committed in 1845 for seven years; eight-year-old Antoine Beauché, committed in 1845 for three years; and twelve-year-old Louis Beauché, committed in 1845 for three years. All received repeated punishments, including the rawhide, the cat, the box, the dark room, and bread and water. Peter Charboneau 'was stripped to the shirt and publicly lashed 57 times in eight and half months.' Antoine Beauché received forty-seven corporal punishments in nine months for child-like activities 'of the most trifling description – such as were to be expected from a child.' Noting that Alexis LaFleur's whippings had started within three days of his arrival, the commissioners said that this proved that 'no mild treatment' had been tried 'before the last resort.' During his first committal, LaFleur was flogged thirty-eight times with rawhide, six times with cats. 'It is horrifying to think of a child of 11 to 14 years of age, being lacerated with the lash before 500 grown men; to say nothing of the cruelty, the effect of such a scene, so often repeated, must have been to the last degree brutalizing.'[138] Perhaps it was significant that all of these children were French Canadians, but this did not become an issue at the time.

The commissioners' indignation was genuine, but the case against Smith on the punishment counts seems particularly weak. Smith was administering a system established by statute and insisted upon by his superiors. The inspectors and government never saw fit, until excessive punishments became a public scandal in late 1846 and early 1847, to address the issue in a serious way. Nor did officials, including inspectors, government, and the Brown commissioners themselves, seem willing to alter in any way the Auburn silent system from which they received such substantial returns through convict labour. Although the commissioners chose to fix responsibility on the warden, all those responsible for establishing the penitentiary along Auburn lines, and who continued to insist that the warden administer its horribly flawed discipline, would have provided a more just target.

The attitude of the broader public, indifferent to Kingston's excesses until scandal erupted, should also be considered. Corporal punishment was widely accepted by most contemporaries, as testimony before the commission of such key witnesses as James Sampson and James Hopkirk confirms. Even Rogers, by this time an outspoken opponent of the Smith regime, who claimed that its use was in conflict with the prison's objectives, could not say whether punishments were less severe at any other Auburn-style institution. Many guards and even convicts claimed that the punishments were fair and not brutal. Dr Sampson took the commissioners by surprise when he testified that he had never found the punishments 'greater than the alleged offence.' He pointed out that he could not speak from personal experience of punishments inflicted prior to the regulation requiring his presence, but added gratuitously that he was sure Henry Smith would never be 'guilty of wanton cruelty.' He had frequently witnessed similar punishments in the army, he told the bemused commissioners. He had observed one man get 500 lashes, while so small a punishment as was usual in Kingston 'would hardly require any dressing.'[139]

When Kirkpatrick, Hopkirk, and Corbett also testified, it became unmistakably clear that in administering punishments Henry Smith was carrying out official policy. Thomas Kirkpatrick pointed out that under his leadership the board had studied the number of punishments, 'but they conceived that they were often too light, and that had they been more, the number of infractions of the rules would have been diminished.' Speaking for the Corbett board, James Hopkirk confirmed that Kirkpatrick's stern policy had continued to prevail. He also emphasized that the punishment book had been submitted to the board at every meeting. Given such testimony, no unbiased observer could have singled out Henry Smith for blame over excessive punishments, but the commissioners, aware that public opinion was, for the moment, inflamed, did precisely that.[140]

Testimony about 'starving the convicts' was equally ambiguous. Experienced prison officers understand that complaints about food are a perennial aspect of prison life. Often they are justified, but complaints may be made even if the food is superior to that consumed by much of the general public. Given mid-nineteenth-century methods of preservation and the difficulties in that period of preparing food for hundreds daily, complaints were unavoidable. The task of prison officers was made even more difficult by the lack of funds to pay prison suppliers such as John Counter.[141]

Once again, the witnesses offered conflicting testimony. William Coverdale told the commissioners that convicts were frequently too weak to work and that the keepers told him this was for lack of food. Several ex-keepers told disgusting stories about what some convicts would eat in desperation. Edward Utting said the prisoners were often unable to work because of insufficient food, and when the warden asked him how it was, then, that the convicts performed such substantial construction tasks, he responded that perhaps some received more than others. Several keepers claimed the rations were more than ample. Dr Sampson reported that it was regularly, but not frequently, his duty to examine the food supply, that he often tasted it and he had found it 'very good.' Further, he could not recollect a single case of sickness arising from want of food; if he had, he would certainly have made a report to that effect. Once, when the bread was sour, he had told the warden and believed it had been attended to. Not only was there no starvation but, most astounding, he had never encountered a single case of malnutrition.[142]

The evidence provided by a professional man of integrity, and one who had been to the fore in reporting abuses, posed a problem for the commissioners. So too did the intervention of Sir Richard Armstrong, commander-in-chief of the forces in Canada West for more than six years, who reported of the numerous military prisoners that he had never received a complaint 'of cruelty, oppression, or starvation.' Armstrong informed the commissioners that the troops under his command would not have had the slightest hesitation in complaining if they had been given cause. Instead, the men returned 'in good condition, affording a satisfactory proof they have been well fed.' Armstrong added that he had personally examined their food and found it 'of wholesome good quality and abundant.'[143]

Such evidence from witnesses like Kirkpatrick, Sampson, and Armstrong presented the commissioners with serious difficulties. So too did the fact that many witnesses from the prison supported the warden on every charge, while those who condemned him, as Smith was at pains to note, had often been the subject of punishment or disciplinary action.[144] George Brown, however, was not a man to be daunted in pursuit of his causes by unruly facts, and it was probably Brown who devised the commissioners' strategy. Referring to the issue of food, the commissioners declaimed that 'the explicit testimony of seventeen credible witnesses to what they have seen, cannot be overturned by any number of witnesses, proving that they have not seen the same circumstances.'[145] Armed with this flexible rule, the commissioners simply ignored all the contrary evidence to find Smith personally guilty of starving the prisoners. In doing so they had formulated a novel legal doctrine, which fortunately never found a place in any court in the land.

The same combination of bias and ignorance on the part of the commissioners was equally apparent in the third group of charges, the failure to maintain discipline and achieve rehabilitation. Several officers testified to the disorder caused by the constant coming and going of teamsters, suppliers, and contractors. Among the evil results of this traffic, the convicts sold tools and whatever else they could pilfer in exchange for favours, especially tobacco. James Hopkirk pointed out that so long as construction continued, this evil could be checked only if the government chose to hire more guards, which they refused to do. Other witnesses, including Utting, testified to the existence of an extensive blackmarket. Convicts readily traded in tobacco, occasionally obtained liquor, and one convict inhaled mortar fumes to become intoxicated. Hopkirk and other former inspectors argued plausibly that contraband tobacco was a temporary evil which could be checked only on the completion of construction.[146]

The commissioners pretended to be outraged by this lenient attitude. Such abuses, they insisted, should have been halted at once; their existence 'to a great extent frustrated the primary object of the Institution.'

What was at issue here between the commissioners on the one hand and some former inspectors and the warden on the other was of fundamental importance. At stake was much more than whether Henry Smith had neglected his responsibilities. While the evidence is not at all conclusive, it would seem that Smith, some of the inspectors, and James Sampson had developed through actual experience in penitentiary governance a sense that the facility was run best be allowing the convicts, and perhaps even the officers, a certain latitude. It appears that Smith and some of the inspectors were prepared to demonstrate a degree of flexibility and to wink at some convict practices while coming down hard on others. In effect, by permitting the trade in tobacco, by giving some convicts special privileges, and even by trying to persuade the government to let the officers recommend some convicts for early release, Henry Smith was in effect co-opting the convict subculture to his own sense of the needs of institutional management.[147]

It is equally clear that some officers, for example Powers and Utting, and some inspectors, especially perhaps the Kirkpatrick board in its early days, were more traditional and did not accept Smith's approach to penitentiary management. The unresolved tension between Smith's managerial style and that of the strict disciplinarians seems most apparent in the critical 1846–7 period of mounting punishments and general institutional confusion.

But even if the Smith style had not broken down, the Brown commissioners, for several reasons, especially their lack of practical experience, were incapable of grasping the relationship between institutional success and security and the vigorous convict subculture. In their eyes, what existed in Kingston was not clever management but abominable laxity. And if they were scathing in their condemnation of the extent of disorder and indiscipline, they equally condemned the all-too-evident failure to achieve rehabilitation. It mattered not at all to the commissioners that this failure, as they themselves would recognize in their second report, was characteristic of almost all nineteenth-century penal facilities. Instead, they seized on the testimony of the disaffected chaplain, who pointed to the absence of a chapel, schoolrooms, and a library when there had been money enough to build handsome stone stables to house the horses. For years, said Rogers, he had not seen either warden or inspectors present to observe religious services or to demonstrate any interest in the rudimentary educational training provided. The chaplaincy was held in such low regard, said the embittered Rogers, that his salary had been reduced to the point where he was forced to spend less time at the prison, he had been forced to pledge in writing that he would not write letters on behalf of the convicts, and the warden had never asked to see his register of conversations with the convicts.[148]

As A.E. Lavell might have noted, this type of testimony foreshadowed that of countless treatment personnel in all the prisons to follow, who would complain that they lacked authority commensurate with their own sense of their place in the institution. It was enough nonetheless for another finding by the commissioners of guilty as charged. 'None of the witnesses,' they pointed out, 'have alleged that any convicts have been reformed by the discipline of the Prison, and the Warden has not alleged that he knows of any such.'[149] As is true of much of their report, it is difficult to determine whether the commissioners were being malicious or naive. The state, of course, had no means of tracing the post-release activities of convicts, something Smith had noted with regret. In any case, the commissioners must have been aware of the pervasive attitude, shared by politicians and the general public, that the penitentiary's primary purposes were punishment and deterrence and any rehabilitation must be a consequence of this disciplinary system. This objective had been unmistakably clear in the Thomson and Macaulay–Thomson reports and everyone who had anything to do with the institution understood perfectly the order of priorities.

There was no hypocrisy or effort to dissemble in the testimony on this point offered by members of the pro-Smith party. James Hopkirk asserted that while he and the other inspectors desired the penitentiary to be a place of reform, 'they do not consider it has been as much so as they could have wished' and they had been unable to make it so. He had never, Hopkirk said, 'seen anything' on the part of the warden to prevent reform, and Smith had always carried out the inspectors' orders in that regard. Sheriff Corbett went further, claiming that he had always regarded the penitentiary as a place for reform and that the inspectors had never given Reverend Rogers any reason to believe otherwise. The commissioners would have none of this. They contemptuously dismissed the school as a reproach to the institution. And with no morning or evening prayers, no grace at meals, no Sabbath school, and Smith absent from religious services, they censured him for neglect of his duties. These points were well taken, but the most reasonable conclusion would have been that neither warden, inspectors, nor the government had ever given any priority to schooling or religious instruction.

The next charge was most critical in understanding Kingston's failure to enforce the Auburn regimen. 'The silent system,' Reverend Rogers exclaimed, 'is not at all carried out; the men talk and laugh in groups together through the yard constantly; they know everything going on outside, and the want of discipline is quite notorious and often noticed by strangers.'[150]

Exactly. Everyone, even casual visitors, could observe the total failure of the silent system. According to Keeper James McCarthy, 'the convicts talk constantly among themselves, and they hear pretty much all that goes on outside.' Keeper John Swift testified that 'the convicts talk a great deal to one another; to say that the silent system is carried out is humbug.' The convicts, said another witness, got news from outside from new convicts, soldiers, and teamsters. As for the rationale that the silent system would prevent that convict familiarity with each other that would lead to the development of a dangerous criminal culture, there was ample testimony to prove how nonsensical such an expectation actually was. No one could doubt the truth of ex-convict John Freedland, who reported that 'the convicts told their histories to one another, and the men generally knew what their fellows were in prison for.' Information sped from one convict to another and through all the different work gangs. Worst of all was Freedland's claim that 'the chance of escape was very much the topic of conversation,' although he added that 'it is now considered almost hopeless.'[151]

The commissioners rightly concluded that the convicts had 'easy and continual' opportunities of communicating with each other. They were also correct to emphasize how totally this practice destroyed part of the rationale for the penitentiary's existence: all the prisoners 'not thoroughly contaminated when they arrived were exposed to very injurious influences.'[152] But they drew back just a little from reaching the obvious conclusion that Kingston Penitentiary was far more a 'school for crime' than the old gaols had ever been. To assert the obvious would have required them to ask far-reaching questions about why Canada should have a penitentiary at all, or at the very least about the viability of continuing an Auburn-style institution. For the commissioners it was just so much easier, so much more comfortable, to hold firmly to their preconceptions about bad Warden Smith. For them, Henry Smith had failed to enforce the unenforceable, Smith had turned the penitentiary away from its potential as a school for reform into a finishing school for criminals.

Guilty on all counts. Guilty of gross mismanagement and corruption; guilty of great cruelty; guilty of failing to rehabilitate a single convict. But it was really the commissioners who were guilty. They had failed in their responsibility to carry out, as instructed by the Baldwin–LaFontaine government, an inquiry with 'the most rigorous impartiality,' one which would do 'entire justice to all the parties concerned' and which would give priority to understanding and reporting on 'the general system of Discipline and Management of the Penitentiary.' Perhaps it was their bias and partisanship, readily apparent in the pages of Brown's *Globe*, which prevented their carrying out this mandate. Certainly A.E. Lavell is correct to attribute their failure to understand that Kingston's problems were structural far more than personal to their naiveté and inexperience. To a limited degree, when Brown and his colleagues doffed their prosecutorial role to look at alternatives to the existing system, they showed more insight and moved, in a few areas, in a more progressive direction. But even here, as we shall see, they were generally conservative, unimaginative, and repressive.

What did their failure signify? Here one must be tentative, even speculative. In the late 1840s the penitentiary remained a relatively new experiment in Canada, and perhaps for that reason it was vulnerable. The voluminous testimony before the Brown Commission, if accurately interpreted, would have demonstrated conclusively that the creation of Kingston had led to all of the fearful costs, the social evils and other dangers articulated in the 1830s by James Buchanan and others who had warned Canadians against establishing such an institution. If the commissioners had offered a more penetrating critique of the institution itself, truly significant change might have resulted. Not that the penitentiary, even in its early days, could have been abolished outright – but in the 1840s institutional structures were softer, weaker, more open to change.

By their unthinking acceptance of the existing institution, and in their determination to blame a single individual for most institutional problems, the commissioners effectively ruled out all alternatives. In their failure, at the penitentiary's moment of crisis, to ask the right questions or to probe the range of alternatives, they closed a door that would not open again until another famous royal commission, the Archambault Commission in the late 1930s, demonstrated more insight and far greater courage. But this was almost a century later. A great opportunity had been lost.

5

New Beginnings: The Penitentiary in the 1850s

The penitentiary in the 1850s was shaped largely by the work of the Brown Commission and by the 1851 statute that embodied many of its recommendations. The resulting changes in penitentiary governance, essentially conservative in nature, were nonetheless significant. Taken together, they promised to propel the Canadian penitentiary in some genuinely new directions. It is testimony to the intractability of the problems of penitentiary management that they failed to lead to a more progressive era in Canadian penology.

COMMISSION RECOMMENDATIONS

It was with 'sincere pleasure,' the Brown commissioners asserted, that they turned from the investigatory tasks that dominated their first report 'to the far more agreeable subject' of recommending improvements in the penal system.[1] Their agenda for change was based primarily on information gathered by George Brown and Adam Bristow during a fact-finding mission to the United States between 6 November and 10 December 1848. At this time there had been few advances in American penitentiaries beyond the original achievement of the rival Auburn and Philadelphia systems, and the commission's recommendations largely reflected the stagnant condition of the American institution. Once again, therefore, Canadian commissioners pondered the relative merits of the old rivals and once again, and not surprisingly, they opted for the practical advantages of Auburn over the more expensive and idealistic approach of the Philadelphia Quakers.

Yet the renewed commitment to Auburn was not made uncritically. Led by Brown, the commissioners regarded themselves as enlightened reformers, determined to bring to bear the shining light of mid-Victorian liberalism on the dark, dank dungeons of the state's punitive apparatus. In its evangelical zeal and its vision of a rehabilitative penology, the Brown Commission's second report had more in common with the liberal perspective advanced in 1836 by Charles Duncombe than with the disciplinary regimen proposed in 1832 by Thomson and Macaulay. Deploying a rhetoric similar to Duncombe's, the commissioners pronounced that prisons were no longer merely places of punishment, where 'fear was deemed the only passion by which prisoners could be swayed, and the law of terror the only rule of discipline.' Through the labour of penal reformers, 'great ameliorations' had been effected. The dungeon had been replaced by 'the well regulated apartment' and 'healthful labour' had replaced vicious idleness. The objective of the criminal justice system, they claimed, was now to determine how crime could be prevented and the criminal reformed 'without the appearance of revenge.' The commissioners offered an analysis of the causes of crime that seemed to encourage the possibility of carrying out this agenda. A 'large portion' of the inmates of a prison, they asserted, were 'the victims of circumstances.' Many had been sentenced for a first criminal act and many more for a moment of passion or intemperance. Also, echoing Duncombe, they argued that 'the great majority of prisoners' had been raised 'in ignorance of everything but vice.' It was therefore the duty of a Christian people to ensure that their prisons become 'schools where the ignorant are enlightened' and where 'the permanent moral reform of the Convict is the chief aim.'[2]

If the goals were lofty, the commissioners reported that Canadian practices remained sadly deficient. There was as yet no separate asylum for children, the common gaols were lacking in every respect, and the penitentiary had achieved little success in the reformation of its inmates. In their tour of seven American states, the commissioners had encountered a situation of far greater complexity, encompassing a rich range of institutions and organizations that had no parallel in Canada. Yet at the penitentiary level, Brown and Bristow found little to praise in the Auburn-type institutions they visited. At Auburn itself, they noted approvingly that convict labour was hired out to contractors and 'brings a high rate,' but judged that little attention was paid to the moral reform of the convicts. At Sing-Sing, too, they found that the various branches of manufacture had been 'brought to great perfection,' but corporal punishment was employed to a frightful extent. At Wethersfield, in Connecticut, the silent system was strictly enforced but the Canadians were suspicious as to how this could be achieved apparently with little corporal punishment.[3]

The only congregate institution that impressed the Canadians was Charlestown, Massachusetts. Charlestown was under the superintendence of Frederick Robinson, who propounded the most humane and optimistic penal philosophy that Brown and Bristow encountered. The worse the crime, said Robinson, the more the convict was to be pitied, and in his treatment of the prisoners he preferred 'to err on the side of kindness, clemency and humanity, than on that of severity of punishments.' Silence was not enforced 'and smiling and looking at strangers are not forbidden.' The convicts received privileges forbidden at other penitentiaries. They could see their friends and relatives more frequently and receive letters and gifts; they had a debating society and a choir; 'their hair is allowed to grow'; they had better clothes for Sunday and access to musical instruments. The commissioners correctly perceived the rationale behind such privileges. 'The great aim of the system is to raise the self-esteem of the Convict, to rouse his ambition, and to prove to him the beneficial results of morality and industry.' The prisoners looked 'cheerful, healthy and happy' and the kind treatment they received 'must enable the officers to exercise a strong influence over them for good.'

Here, it seemed, was a model for the progressive Canadians to emulate, but the commissioners found one insuperable objection to the Charlestown system: the moment the convict entered its walls, punishment ceased. The only objective was reformation, and the convict suffered no other 'inconvenience' than 'his restriction within the walls of the prison.' Such a system could deter neither the convict from repeating his offence nor 'the evil-doer outside' from the commission of crimes. 'Everything,' they complained, 'is done to make the prisoner comfortable and happy, and remove from his mind all feeling of degradation.' Brown and Bristow seemed genuinely shocked to be left with the 'impression that the majority of them are far better off, have more true enjoyment, and are happier than they are ever likely to be outside.' This defiance of the doctrine of less eligibility would never do.[4]

If Auburn-style institutions offered no ready model for Canadian emulation, all that remained was the famous Philadelphia program of solitary confinement which John Macaulay had considered before rejecting it a decade and a half earlier. The Canadian commissioners were equally intrigued. In 1832, Macaulay had been reluctant to recommend that his province adopt a system which remained largely untried, but by the late 1840s the separate system had gained considerably in prestige, largely through its use in such European institutions as the famous English model prison, Pentonville. The commissioners, after briefly examining its operation in the state penitentiary at Trenton, New Jersey, moved on to Philadelphia itself, where they spent almost a week in a minute inspection of its operations. They were greatly impressed. After speaking to many prisoners, they reported that they found them respectful and subdued, with no bitterness and little sullenness: the separate system had the approval of the convicts themselves. The commissioners concluded that this system was 'highly humanizing,' that it gave the officers much influence over the convicts' minds, 'and generally affords a good opportunity for effecting the moral reformation of the criminal.'

However, they could not recommend its adoption for Canada for one compelling reason. There was 'insanity to a fearful extent' at Philadelphia. The prisoners had a sallow, worn-out appearance; their eyes were deeply sunk and their eyeballs 'glare[d] with a feverish brightness.' The more educated convicts seemed better able to resist the onset of insanity, 'but there is a class, and a larger one it is feared' which soon sank from listlessness to imbecility and then into 'dementia.' Brown and Bristow were satisfied that fully 50 of 300 convicts in the prison had been driven to insanity. Whereas Charlestown had only 7 cases of insanity in the years 1837–46 and Kingston reported only 11 since 1835, Philadelphia admitted to 119 in nine years. Comparison of the respective death rates in all three prisons between 1837 and 1846 proved equally alarming. Charlestown reported 35 deaths with an average prisoner population of 295; Kingston had 41, with a population averaging 250; while Philadelphia recorded the astounding total of 155, with a population of 364. Of course the death-in-prison rate could be manipulated by the pardoning process, so the commissioners also noted that in the same period the number of pardons were: Charlestown, 144; Kingston, 142; and Philadelphia, 210. Because of 'the admitted direful effects of unmitigated solitude,' the commissioners firmly rejected the separate system. Significantly, they failed to comment on the favourable insanity and death rates in Henry Smith's Kingston as compared to that in Charlestown, the most progressive of American prisons.[5]

George Brown looked for straightforward solutions to social problems, and he must have been puzzled by the failure of either of the rival American systems of prison discipline to offer a model for Canada. The commissioners ultimately responded to this conundrum by recommending 'the combination of the two systems, the Separate and the Congregate.'

This was to be done by the erection of a sufficient number of new cells in Kingston to house every newly arrived convict. While confined in a separate cell and isolated from other prisoners, the convict would be 'furnished with secular instruction and labour, and ... earnestly dealt with by the Chaplain and Warden.' In no case, said the commissioners, should this 'ordeal' exceed six months. By limiting the time in seclusion, the worst dangers of insanity would be avoided, while the separate experience in this form, already used in some European prisons, would prepare the prisoner in mind and body for the remainder of his prison term. They recommended that fifty separate cells be constructed at once.[6]

Beyond this proposal, the commissioners were unable or unwilling to suggest any significant modification of the traditional Auburn system. They recognized that there was considerable force to frequent arguments that convict classification was an essential stage in the rehabilitative process. But classification, they maintained, whether by age, the nature of the crime, conduct in prison, or the prospect of achieving reformation, depended on so many diverse elements that it was 'almost impossible, if not absolutely so' to put into effect. After expressing the pious hope that some modified system of classification might be established 'in amelioration of the congregate system,' the commissioners made recommendations that effectively ensured that prisoners must continue to be treated as an undifferentiated mass. In the all-important area of convict labour, for example, they proposed that 'the employment selected for the prisoners, be as little diversified as possible.'[7]

Equally critical was the commissioners' adamant rejection of all suggestions that convicts be given differential treatment according to behaviour. Much had been written, they noted, 'in favour of a graduation in the severity of the Penitentiary discipline, founded on the conduct of the Convict during his confinement.' They pointed to proposals that a record of the conduct of each prisoner be kept and a classification adopted based on behaviour in prison. 'Exemplary obedience would thus purchase privileges,' while convicts who habitually violated the rules would be 'subjected to a greater rigor.' Any such system, they argued, 'would open a wide door to favoritism' whereas all convicts should be 'placed on the footing of perfect equality.' In opting for what they called the 'inflexibility' of the Auburn system, the commissioners rejected the widely acclaimed good behaviour or mark system developed by Captain Maconochie and other penal reformers and advocated so strongly by Henry Smith during his wardenship. Several jurisdictions, American and European, were experimenting along these lines, but the commissioners' failure to grasp their significance closed this door in Canada for the immediate future.[8]

The commissioners were similarly unwilling to consider a more creative use of the pardoning process to add equity to the system and to facilitate institutional management. They were appalled at the politicization of the process in the United States and unable to understand how a reform that would locate more authority in the institution itself could redress the evils of political influence and favouritism. The indiscriminate use of the pardoning power in response to good behaviour in prison, they wrote, 'tends to make the men hypocrites, and when the interest is so strong to deceive the officers, the most wily villain is most likely to be successful.' This kind of cant would be repeated ad nauseam by those opposed to good conduct remission schemes. 'It is well known,' said the commissioners, 'that the worst men commonly make the best conducted Convicts.'[9]

But there was a still more compelling reason why the principle of differential treatment leading to remission must be resisted. Nothing, claimed the commissioners, could do more 'to obliterate the distinctions between right and wrong in the minds of the convicts.' To confound the infraction of prison rules with disobedience to the laws of God and the laws of the land, and to make obedience to rules of the prison the means of mitigating penalties pronounced in courts of law was dangerous to the very idea of the rule of law. Any mitigating circumstances to justify mercy would have been taken into consideration by the trial judge.[10]

In taking this position, the commissioners demonstrated a lack of faith in the abilities of prison officers to deal with matters that extended beyond the narrow enforcement of the rules. Equally, they refused to give any credence to the dangers inherent in prison government and the consequent need to offer every reasonable support to the warden and his colleagues. The commissioners were inflexible and reactionary and the result of their judgments was to deprive Canadian penitentiary managers for many years of what would soon be regarded in other jurisdictions as indispensable tools of penitentiary governance.

Having pronounced in favour of a modified yet still rigid Auburn system, the commissioners in their other recommendations could address only the subsidiary elements of the system. Of these, the most important was punishment. The system administered by Henry Smith, they maintained, had served to 'render callous and to harden' the prisoners, and each additional punishment had merely resulted in an increase in the number of infractions. In an admission that should have mitigated the condemnation of Smith made in their first report, the commissioners pointed out that the history of the principal congregate institutions in the United States revealed great 'harshness and cruelty,' which produced the very disorders punishments were intended to prevent. George Brown, in particular, seems to have recognized that such punishments as whipping, the box, and solitary confinement hardened offenders and guards alike. Brown and his colleagues admitted that sometimes severe punishments would continue to be necessary, but they were certain that in a properly managed prison the deprivation of comforts and the occasional use of solitary confinement could largely replace the harsh corporal punishments.[11]

But it was in their treatment of the issue of convict labour that the commissioners demonstrated most completely their dependence on the principles of Auburn. They refused to break with the expectation raised by Macaulay, Powers, and others that the prison would soon be self-sustaining, and closed their eyes to the lessons of the Smith years on that score. 'We can see no reason,' they asserted, 'why the labour of able-bodied men should not produce sufficient to pay for their sustenance; and we consider that Penitentiary ... as ill-managed, that does not make its revenue nearly equal to its expenditure.' The need to make the prison self-supporting may account for their refusal to consider any plan to appropriate to the convict a share of the proceeds of his labour, although the reason given was that all such systems were 'directly calculated to foster deception among the prisoners.'[12] There was little faith here in the reformability of the convicts and none at all in the abilities of prison officers to perform any function other than the most narrowly custodial one.

In pointing to the types of labour most suitable for prisoners, the commissioners recommended those trades which required the least conversation among prisoners, those for which there was a ready market for the product produced, and which the prisoner might practice after release. They offered no example of any such trade. As for the three modes of organizing convict labour – manufacturing articles for sale at the risk of the penitentiary (the system then prevailing), letting out contract labour for hire by contractors, and manufacturing articles under contracts – they favoured the last, probably because they believed it had the potential to be the most profitable. The commissioners admitted that it was 'difficult to meet with persons disposed to enter into such contracts.'[13] But whichever system was adopted, Brown in particular was determined to reorganize the penitentiary's labour program to emulate the financial achievements of the most successful Auburn facilities in the United States. It is difficult to discern in this emphasis much interest in organizing a prison labour program around the purpose of teaching convicts useful trades or in achieving rehabilitation.

But George Brown was too good a Victorian liberal to let pass the opportunity of proclaiming both the moral and the social significance of rehabilitating as many convicts as possible. For Brown and his colleagues, the means were at hand and relatively simple. At mid-century the evangelical zeal of Protestant Christianity and an aggressive and crusading Catholicism had never been stronger. Not coincidentally, the promotional work of common school advocates (in Canada West most notably the determined cleric Egerton Ryerson) expressed the middle-class belief in universal education as a social panacea. The same social and intellectual currents that informed this aggressive mix of religious and social ideologies led the prison commissioners to conclude that reform was to be achieved through 'moral, religious and secular instruction.' Such instruction, they proclaimed, must 'occupy much greater prominence' than it did at Kingston or in any American penitentiary. The more closely the subject is studied, they asserted, 'the more forcibly is the truth pressed home to our conviction, that ignorance is the parent of crime.'[14] Nor should the pecuniary interests of the penitentiary ever be allowed to stand in the way of rehabilitation. As desirable as economy might be, 'it is a sad mistake to sacrifice for that consideration, all the higher objects' of prison discipline.[15]

For the commissioners, then, Kingston had to become a truly Christian institution. Divine services should be performed twice each Sunday in separate Catholic and Protestant chapels, 'also prayers morning and evening daily.' Forms of grace and thanksgiving should be offered at the beginning and close of every meal. A Sabbath school must be established, and from it 'the most beneficial influence' over the minds of the convicts was anticipated. Most important, full-time Catholic and Protestant chaplains should be appointed, who should 'devote their time exclusively to the duties of their office.'[16]

To complement the work of the chaplains, the commissioners recommended the appointment of a full-time schoolmaster. Under the existing system, in which convict taught convict, little time was set aside for education and there was so little supervision that the convicts used the opportunity for 'unrestricted conversation,' rendering the rule of silence 'a farce.' Recommending about an hour of school time for each convict every second day, the commissioners 'would not hesitate to carry instruction beyond the ordinary studies of reading and writing.' In another remark that echoed Dr Duncombe, they urged 'the cultivation as well of the intellectual as of the moral faculties of the convicts,' and the establishment of a small library consisting principally but not solely of religious works.[17]

Except for the proposal that convicts undergo an initial period in solitary confinement, which in any case was never acted upon, these rather slight proposals did little to challenge any of the rudiments of the Auburn discipline. The commissioners pointed to the work in Boston, for example, of the Prison Discipline Society, and noted how many distinguished citizens took an interest in prison affairs. These influences inspired the commissioners' strongly expressed hope that a similar philanthropic society would soon exist in Canada. Such a society was urgently needed because, if the convict on release was met with harshness and refused employment, 'poverty and the force of circumstances will too often drive him back to the haunts of crime.'[18] The commissioners' remedies, however, did almost nothing to achieve this vital goal. For some reason they believed that in the United States philanthropic societies had turned the tide of public opinion 'towards the helpless outcast.' They concluded that governments could do little to assist in aftercare efforts and that 'the force of public opinion will alone effectually remove the evil.'[19]

In another area, the wait would be briefer. Brown and Bistow had been fascinated by the work done by the Boston House of Reformation for Juveniles. This institution was divided into two departments, one for children 'snatched from the purlieus of vice before the commission of crime, and the other for early transgressors.' The magistrates were empowered to place the children of both classes under the control of trustees to age twenty-one. Both groups received the same treatment but were physically separated. The system, Brown reported, 'combined strict discipline, with good education, invigorating relaxation and healthful labour.' On graduation, the children were apprenticed. The commissioners were persuaded that this system had achieved great success and 'many valuable citizens' had once been wards of the House of Reformation. Like Duncombe and many others, they proclaimed that in efforts to combat crime, there was no approach so encouraging 'as the rescue and reformation of the young.' Therefore 'immediate action' must be taken to save children then being consigned 'to the utter contamination of the common gaol' and sent on to penitentiary. They recommended the establishment of a House of Refuge in each of Canada West and East, organized along lines of the Boston facility, with separate divisions for children already convicted and for those out of control or whose parents requested assistance from the state.[20]

The commissioners' anxiety to save children from the horrors of the gaols reflected their negative opinion of those facilities. Describing them as 'nurseries of crime and vice' they suggested that gaol discipline be placed under the control of government inspectors who would be required to make annual reports.[21]

These several recommendations exhausted the commissioners' recommendations for effecting convict rehabilitation. Taken together, their proposals were surprisingly conservative and conventional. Full-time chaplains and a separate facility for juveniles had been proposed many times before, by Warden Smith and successive inspectoral boards. Advances in the worthy cause of gaol reform would indeed be achieved through the mechanism of central inspection, but the commissioners gave little time or space to this issue and significant change would be delayed for many years. And with respect to the central issues of penitentiary discipline and convict reform, the commissioners' intellectual timidity, combined with their inexperience, led them no further than to endorse the Auburn system with minor improvements. In their unwillingness to consider small payments for convict labour, earned remission, or early release programs they were rigid and reactionary. In their failure to understand what was required to stimulate philanthropic efforts or to develop effective after-care programs, they were naive and remiss.

The most significant contribution of the Brown Commission was to the reform of penitentiary governance and administration. After cleaning house of most of the key officers of the old Smith regime, the commissioners examined the critical question of how authority should be reconstituted. 'It must be conceded,' they began, 'as a general principle of government in a Penitentiary, almost an absolute authority should exist somewhere.' Both the safety of the institution and the well-being of the inmates required that the institution possess a clear and unequivocal locus of power. The only question was 'in whose hands can that be vested with the greatest safety, or rather with the smallest probability of its being abused.' One possibility, the commissioners pointed out, was to divide authority between the warden, and other principal officers, but this would lead, they feared, to such clashes and divisions that the institution 'could scarcely be carried on for a single day.' Doubtless they had the struggles between Henry Smith and Powers and Utting in mind when they made this comment. A second possibility would be to give power to the warden, closely supervised by the inspectors. But this system, also comparable to that established by the 1834 statute, was equally dangerous, as the institution's recent history demonstrated. Concurrent authority, therefore, must also be rejected and full power placed in the hands of the warden. By concentrating authority in his hands, it would be possible to achieve uniformity of discipline, prompt action, firm control over subordinates, and the business-like management of the institution.[22] Irony of ironies. For over a decade Henry Smith had engaged in battles with deputy wardens and sometimes with inspectors over the locus of authority. Now, it seemed, his greatest enemies, the Brown commissioners, had endorsed his position, but without admitting as much.

At the same time, the commissioners professed to be alert to possible abuses of authority. Before entrusting powers so extensive to a single individual, they advised that they be conferred only on someone possessing all the qualifications to carry out the duties 'of so responsible and honourable an office.' And what were these qualifications? The commissioners did not mention experience, training, or professional abilities, but only 'character, manner, and habits.' The best safeguard against abuse of power was that the warden be 'imbued with the spirit of philanthropy, and deeply interested in the moral welfare of those under his charge.'[23] The commissioners had gained considerable insight into the demands made on the warden and the need to provide him with untrammelled authority and extensive latitude; they had developed more understanding of the problems Henry Smith had faced than they dared to admit. The long and uninterrupted exercise of a warden's power, they argued, must blunt the sensibilities of that officer. 'It is not to be wondered at, therefore, if the Warden of a Penitentiary ... should become lukewarm in the cause, and harsh in his treatment of men whom he is led to view as incorrigible.' Having enunciated this significant insight, the commissioners turned for a remedy to the principle of responsible government then in the process of being implemented by Baldwin and LaFontaine. Any incumbent warden, they wrote, should understand that he was subject to removal at any moment at the pleasure of the executive and 'without specific charges of maladministration' being brought against him.[24]

But how was the authority of the executive best brought to bear? The commissioners' answer was to replace the old gentry practice of using local worthies as inspectors with the appointment of two paid inspectors also holding office during pleasure and answerable directly to the government. On the principle of 'he who pays the piper calls the tune,' the commissioners envisioned a significant expansion of inspectoral duties. They stressed the need for paid inspectors to watch over financial matters, insisting that had the old board provided 'anything like' a systematic examination of the accounts, 'thousands of pounds' would have been saved each year. Equally important, the new inspectors would open communications with 'philanthropic associations and individuals in other countries' actively engaged in prison-related work. It would be their role to receive and impart valuable information on all aspects of penitentiary management in order to elevate Canadian practices at least to the level of those abroad. Their reports would be replete with 'the statistics of crime and punishment' for the use of legislators concerned with penal enactments. And, not least, the inspectors might do double duty and in addition to the penitentiary turn their attention to the gaols then so desperately in need of reform.[25] In laying down the responsibilities, processes of control, and division of authority between warden and inspectors, the commissioners were propounding new principles of profound importance for the control and governance of bureaucratic bodies.[26]

Other administrative recommendations followed logically. With the warden's primacy assured, it became possible to recreate the office of deputy warden. Improved bookkeeping and accounting procedures were recommended and implemented. One new idea that did not work out well was the creation of the office of overseer to superintend and instruct the convicts in mechanical labour, while the keepers were relegated to responsibility for discipline. No thought, however, was given to providing training for any of the officers. The assumption still prevailed that they would learn on the job. Nor was anything said of the qualifications or remuneration of those who would fill prison positions.[27]

Another omission was the failure to provide even a tentative timetable for completion of construction. With Protestant worship performed in the dining room and Catholic services in part of another large room, the commissioners recommended the early construction of chapels and of a schoolroom. After noting the deplorable accommodation for the female prisoners in the north wing, including the opportunity for 'perfectly unrestrained' communication at night, they urged that a suitable building for women be erected as an absolute precondition of any attempt at reformation, but the assumption was that it would be on the grounds of the existing penitentiary.[28]

There was a good deal that was positive in the commission's report and certainly the commissioners saw themselves as bringing enlightenment to bear. But, as they emphasized, their recommendations largely restated goals for which penal reformers had worked since the day of John Howard; to prove the point they cited extracts from the abortive British penitentiary statute of 1779. The commissioners were correct in this assessment of the traditional nature of their work. They looked more backward than forward, neglecting or rejecting the new currents then emerging, however tentatively, in international correctional thinking. What they hoped to accomplish was the reform of the penitentiary idea of the 1820s and 1830s, rather than the enunciation of new principles of prison management and correctional treatment. As a result, real innovation in Canada's penal practices would derive not from the work of George Brown and his fellow commissioners but from the efforts of E.A. Meredith and his colleagues a decade later, after the failure of the reforms of the early 1850s had become apparent to a new group of prison inspectors.

1851 STATUTORY CHANGES

Like the commissioners' report itself, the 1851 statute did not challenge any of the central assumptions of Auburn. The Act did not address subjects of general importance, such as the purposes of punishment, the role of deterrence, or even the utility of the rule of silence. It was, as its title proclaimed, an Act for the 'better management' of the penitentiary. The Act confirmed the existing penal verities, asserting that convicts were to be clothed 'in garments of coarse but comfortable materials,' fed on 'a sufficient quantity of wholesome food,' 'kept constantly employed' at hard labour, and forbidden 'all conversation not absolutely required in carrying on the work.' It also gave legal embodiment to another prevailing practice, declaring the prison to be for persons sentenced to 'a term not less than two years.'[29]

The first innovation made it the duty of the inspectors to erect up to fifty cells, as the commissioners had recommended, with a workshop attached to each, 'adapted to carry out the "separate" or "solitary" system of discipline.'[30] This instruction proved abortive, partly because it was to take effect only when the annual grant to the institution remained under £6,000. This limitation, included in reference to other construction projects as well, reflected the belief of the Brown commissioners that Kingston could be run far more economically than it had been under Smith. But the failure to proceed with solitary cells cannot be attributed entirely to the issue of cost. There is little evidence in the documentation of the 1850s that either the warden or the inspectors became committed to the scheme.

The second initiative effectively brought responsible government to penitentiary management. It provided that the institution was to 'be governed by two Inspectors' who were to hold office during pleasure. The Act stated that these officers were 'subject to the control of the Governor General in Council' and were 'to obey such orders in Council as shall be from time to time made.' Each inspector was to receive £400 a year. Their duties, outlined in five pages, were extensive. It was not the warden but the inspectors who received the responsibility to ensure that the institution was administered in accordance with cabinet instructions and the best interests of society. They were made responsible 'for the system of discipline and management' and were to make all necessary rules and regulations, to determine the employment to be carried on and the manner in which it should be carried out, to consider the place of secular education and moral and religious training, and to control all punishments. In one interesting initiative, they were to draw up a code of rules and regulations for all employees. They were to inspect the prison regularly and report fully to the government about the institution and the convicts. In their work, they were to reflect on the nature of the penitentiary and its place in the criminal justice system, and to make any suggestions to the government 'for the prevention of crime and the reformation of the criminal they may deem necessary and expedient.' By giving such detailed statutory authority to paid inspectors, the government had two objectives. It was endeavouring to ensure there could never be a repetition of the dereliction of duty that had prevailed in the 1840s and to put in place a new structure of penitentiary authority that fully reflected the far-reaching improvements in Canadian governmental systems achieved in the Union years.[31]

Given the equally important recommendation of the commission that the position of warden be strengthened to the point where he should become the single all-powerful official in the penitentiary, the extent of the authority given to the inspectors seems puzzling and certainly it bemused and annoyed many members during debate in the legislature. John A. Macdonald preferred the old voluntary inspectoral system, arguing that the visits of two paid inspectors 'could have no other effect than to interfere with the Warden in the discharge of his duty.' Many members seemed to agree with Henry Sherwood that the innovation was intended merely to enrich the Baldwin–LaFontaine government's store of patronage. Sherwood asserted that the work could be done better by prominent Kingstonians for no remuneration. Henry Smith Jr objected to the 'arbitrary' and 'despotic' powers being conferred on the inspectors, including the right to suspend the warden, and Colonel Prince from Windsor complained that paid inspectors must be 'but poorly qualified to perform the duties' of gaol inspectors, compared to 'intelligent local Grand Juries.' Macdonald also complained that inspectors could not carry out their functions at the penitentiary if they were 'compelled to travel from Gaspe to Sandwich in the capacity of Gaol Inspectors and Political speculators.' He moved that the penitentiary be placed under a board of five unpaid inspectors.[32]

Regrettably, the clause respecting gaol inspection disappeared; not until 1857 would the central state provide for officers to inspect the local gaols. Doubtless some of the objections to the bill were mere debating points, but the Tories seemed genuinely alarmed at the precedent being laid down by the Reform administration for the expansion of its patronage system and a few members, especially perhaps Macdonald, genuinely viewed the initiative as a serious breach with Canadian traditions of government. So too did the government – that was precisely the point. Solicitor General Sandfield Macdonald argued persuasively that it was no longer appropriate to use the services of members of the local elite, because local feelings could thereby operate in the institution to the detriment of the provincial interest. Even more aptly, Crown Lands Commissioner Price 'objected to employ public officers without paying them; you cannot obtain the necessary control over them.' The extension of this principle to the management of so important a public institution as the penitentiary was a significant legal and administrative advance.

It was never intended that the authority given to the responsible inspectors should entrench upon the 'absolute' power of the warden. The warden, Macdonald complained, like the captain of a ship, 'should have the whole control, as he was always there rather than the Inspectors who would only require to be there 36 days.'[33] In fact, Macdonald's analogy caught the government's intention well. The very clause that vested responsibility in the inspectors vested power in the warden, stating that 'they shall have no executive power, except that of giving instructions for the conduct and management of the Institution ... to the Warden.' As a subsequent clause put it, the warden was the chief executive officer, vested with 'the entire executive control and management' of the institution, subject only to the rules, regulations, and written instructions of the inspectors. In all matters not provided for by statute or regulations, and when the inspectors were not present, he had authority 'to act in such manner as he may deem most advisable.'[34] The statute did not repeat the blunder made in 1834 of defining the warden's role primarily as business manager and giving the deputy warden responsibility for the discipline. By the 1851 enactment, the warden was supreme in the institution.

With Henry Smith's neglect of his duties in mind, the statute laid down in minute detail the warden's onerous daily routine, which included visiting every cell every day, being present at religious services, and attending in fact to everything that went on throughout the institution. Unlike Smith, the new warden could be in no doubt that he was on call and in charge twenty-four hours a day. Similarly, unlike previous inspectors, the new two-man team understood that the government would no longer sit on the sidelines as a relatively uninterested spectator while rival factions inside the institution battled for control. The statute of 1851 embodied the emergence of a new political will to establish and enforce a sense of order on state-funded institutions. It extended the political achievement of responsible government fully into the administrative sphere, thereby carrying forward to a logical conclusion the bureaucratic-political rationalization initiated by Sydenham a decade earlier.

The other principal recommendation of the Brown Commission now put into effect was the appointment of full-time Protestant and Catholic chaplains and a teacher. Each chaplain was to receive a salary of not more than £250, and each was to devote his 'whole time and attention to the religious instruction and moral improvement of the prisoners.' As befit legislation of a Reform administration, the Protestant clergyman was to be chosen from 'any of the Religious Denominations of Protestant Christians recognized by the Laws of this Province.' Public services were to be conducted every day when the prison opened and closed and twice on Sundays. The chaplains were to establish Sabbath schools and to ensure that each convict received a Bible. Many of their obligations were as much secular as religious, encompassing duties which would later be carried out by large staffs of placement officers, psychologists, and social workers. The chaplains were to be diligent in conversing with the prisoners at all reasonable times and administer 'such instructions and exhortations as may be calculated to promote their spiritual welfare, moral reformation and due subordination.' For these purposes, they received 'access at all times, subject to the rules of the Prison,' to the convicts under their care. They were also to take charge of the library and to visit the sick each day.[35]

There was to be no repetition of the Catholic–Protestant bickering and insubordination that had consumed so much inspectoral time in the 1840s. The statute intended that a chaplaincy service be placed unequivocally under the authority of the state, and the chaplains' responsibilities to the government took priority over all religious obligations. They were enjoined to guard against encouraging complaints or communicating improper information to the prisoners. They were to keep the inspectors fully informed of whatever they might learn of prisoner attitudes and to report annually, or whenever called upon, on all aspects of convict conduct, including religious and moral, and to supply 'any other information' the inspectors might require. The chaplains' role as record keepers and sociological investigators was confirmed by a clause requiring them to keep a register of such personal details of each convict's life as education, habits, the crime of which he was convicted, and even to include 'remarks as to the conversations' had with each convict.[36] Finally, the chaplain was to be present when the warden put questions to convicts at the time of discharge relative to the penitentiary experience. Events would soon suggest that the long arm of George Brown was behind these provisions. Before long, it would be clear that the effort to turn the chaplains into subordinate officers who were effectively spies of the administration departed so far from the spirit of prison chaplaincy as to largely destroy the moral and practical power of the office.

The clause providing for the appointment of a permanent schoolmaster was equally disappointing. Brief and vague, its lack of explicitness suggests that little thought had been given to the role of education in the rehabilitative process. A schoolmaster, to be paid £150, was to work under the surveillance of the chaplains and to devote 'his whole time and attention' to his duties. He was to teach only 'such convicts as the Warden may select' in reading, writing, 'and such other branches of secular knowledge, and at such times and hours, and under such regulations as the Inspectors may from time to time designate.'[37] In an era in which many citizens regarded education as a universal panacea and were convinced that ignorance was a principal cause of crime, such restrictive phrasing suggests that those who framed the statute were uncertain as to the place schooling should occupy in the institution.

It seems more surprising that the statute offered little guidance to the employment of convict labour. With the annual grant pegged at a maximum of £6,000, prison officers had no choice but to somehow render the institution remunerative. The Act, however, simply charged the inspectors to 'consider and determine the branches of employment to be prosecuted in the Penitentiary, and the manner in which the same is to be prosecuted.' The warden was to designate the employment of each convict, 'having reference to the capacity and past pursuits and habits' of each, and to 'make all purchases, sales and contracts, under the instructions and advice of the Board of Inspectors, and to superintend the industrial pursuits of the prison.'[38] No limitation was placed on how the warden and inspectors were to carry this out. Obviously, the Hagerman Committee's limitations no longer applied, but the political opposition to convict labour remained strong. In the House, Henry Smith Jr argued that convict labour had 'nearly ruined Kingston' and John A. Macdonald unsuccessfully moved an amendment to limit the sale of convict produced goods.[39]

The section on 'punishment and privations' was more forthright. Henceforth only the warden could award punishments and these were to be recorded in a register to be signed by him. No punishment was to be inflicted for any offence 'until the day after the said offence shall have been committed' and until the warden had entered the details in the punishment book. In emergencies, the warden could segregate a convict and keep him in a cell apart from others 'until the usual hour of punishment shall have arrived.' The inspectors were given the authority to consider what convict acts should require punishment and what form that punishment should take. Where corporal punishment was authorized by the inspectors, 'the Warden shall have recourse to it only in extreme cases, and shall not inflict more than seventy-five lashes for any one offence.' There was to be no physical punishment until the physician certified the convict's bodily fitness, and both warden and physician were to be present; these provisions were carried over from the Smith regime. The most important innovation was a clause ending corporal punishment for women, which was added by amendment during debate. The Tories split on the issue, with High Tory Henry Sherwood moving an amendment to abolish all corporal punishment and moderate conservative John A. Macdonald insisting that it remain for both sexes. The abolition of corporal punishment, Macdonald argued, would 'lead to a great amount of insubordination ... .He thought the discretion of inflicting this punishment should be left with the Warden.'[40] The government held firm and the measure as passed included the abolition of corporal punishment for women.

There were numerous other clauses, none of which effected significant change. Female prisoners, as before, were to be kept 'totally distinct and secluded' from the men, and placed under a matron and assistant matron. The matron's salary was seventy-five pounds per annum, confirming both her own inferior status and that of female prisoners in the institution. As before, convicts were not allowed to have visitors or to communicate by letter. There was a provision to fine anyone who gave the convicts alcohol or tobacco. There was no sign in any of this of a softening of attitude or of a more humane feeling towards the prisoners. Nor was there any effort to define the qualifications of guards; little education and low pay continued to reflect their narrowly custodial role. The physician's responsibilities were spelled out in more detail; once again he was enjoined to 'exercise a general surveillance over the cleanliness and ventilation of the Prison and the diet of the convicts.'

THE NEW ADMINISTRATION

With the revelations of the Brown Commission a recent memory and these statutory provisions in place, Kingston Penitentiary was poised uncertainly on the brink of a new era. The statute offered a reformed Auburn-style prison, one run more efficiently and subject more directly to the authority of the Canadian state. What this would mean for the life of the prison and of the convicts remained to be determined. As much as anything, it would depend on the inspectors and officers who were put in place to make the new system work. By far the most important of these were the inspectors and the warden, and the appointment as inspector of Wolfred Nelson was promising. Born in Montreal in 1791, Nelson trained as a military surgeon and served during the War of 1812. Following the war he established himself in Saint-Denis, where he became a determined supporter of the patriot cause and a colleague of the great Papineau. Elected to the Assembly in 1827, he was radicalized and became a leader of the Reform party. His role in 1837 in a famous patriot military victory earned him a reputation as the hero of Saint-Denis. Although he spent seven months in prison in Montreal, his case never came to trial and he was one of seven patriots banished to Bermuda by Lord Durham's famous ordinance. Released when Durham's ordinance was disallowed, he returned to Lower Canada after a brief period in Plattsburg, New York. In 1844, at the request of his friend Louis LaFontaine he ran for the legislature and served seven years as the member for Richelieu, where he was a leading English-speaking proponent of francophone rights and a supporter of responsible government. Throughout his career, Nelson was admired for his many kindnesses and his support of the cause of ordinary French Canadians. When he left the legislature in 1850, at sixty years of age, the LaFontaine–Baldwin government made him prison inspector 'as a reward for his services.'[41] His political career, however, was far from over. In 1854 Nelson became Montreal's first popularly elected mayor and in that position he urged the appointment of municipal inspectors to regulate several public services and supported public welfare measures to assist indigent citizens. All the while he continued to practise medicine. Of a strong humanitarian bent, Nelson's opposition to capital punishment also affected his attitude to penitentiary administration. His services as inspector between 1851 and 1859 were rewarded when he was continued in his position as a member of the new and expanded Board of Inspectors of Prisons, Asylums and Public Charities, created under 1857 legislation and he became the first chair of that important body. Nelson's political experiences and his period as a prisoner in Montreal gaol added piquancy to the appointment. As he put it, '[m]y sojourn for seven months in the Montreal Jail gave me such a practical knowledge of prison affairs, the accursed abuses that prevailed there ... and the uncalled for miseries that were inflicted on the prisoners [as] induced me to accept.'[42]

Andrew Dickson's qualifications as an inspector were more conventional. For many years he was sheriff of the United Counties of Lanark and Renfrew, where he also served as a lieutenant-colonel of the militia, postmaster, commissioner in the Court of Requests, registrar for the county, and magistrate. Like Nelson, Dickson was on the Reform side in politics and seems to have been well known to such leading Reform politicians as Francis Hincks. He served as inspector until 1858, when he was appointed the first warden of the Reformatory Prison in Canada East, but his career there ended ignominiously when he was charged with improper behaviour with one of the female employees.[43]

Aeneas Macdonell's appointment as warden was confirmed in April 1850, and he held the position until his retirement in May 1869. This long tenure during the formative years of the post-Smith period made him instrumental in shaping the character of the Canadian penitentiary and his strong personal qualities determined that his influence would be enduring. Macdonell was hard-working, conscientious, and dedicated. Fifty-six years old in 1850, he brought considerable strengths to the position. Born in Upper Canada, a member of a prominent Eastern Ontario Catholic family, he had attended John Strachan's school in Cornwall and as a young man served in the British regular forces during the War of 1812, being commissioned an ensign in the 8th regiment and retiring on half-pay in 1817 with the rank of lieutenant. Putting his military experience to good use, he had a long career in the militia, serving actively during the Rebellions. Macdonell served as commanding officer of the Stormont battalion between 1846 and 1850. A justice of the peace for the Eastern District, he was elected to the legislature as a Reformer in 1834 and re-elected in 1836, but had no success in politics in the Union period, suffering defeats in 1841, 1844, and 1847. A man of stern and unbending character, it seems likely that Macdonell was uncomfortable with popular politics in the era of responsible government. There were compensations, however, and he served between 1840 and 1843 as one of the penitentiary inspectors and in April 1848 became Crown Lands agent and sheriff of the Eastern District. When he became acting warden of the penitentiary in November 1848, Macdonell possessed many of the qualifications that the position demanded, as his twenty years as warden amply demonstrated.[44]

In assessing the impact of the new leadership, several major changes in the institution that took place in the 1850s must be kept firmly in mind. Most important, the expansion in convict numbers, which had played so large a role in the 1840s, accelerated. A prison population that stood at 153 in 1840 and reached 368 in 1849 mushroomed to 733 in 1859. With 524 prisoners in the institution at year-end in 1855, officials were scrambling to find cells in which to place them: in 1856 the Executive Council formally considered a recommendation from the inspectors that Canada construct a second penitentiary.[45] In these circumstances, much of the energy of Macdonell and the inspectors was consumed by the task of finding room to accommodate these large numbers.

The pressure was subsequently alleviated by the opening of separate new institutions for the criminally insane and for juvenile offenders, and also by the completion of the penitentiary's basic structure. But in 1856 none of this had yet occurred, and Macdonell in that year noted with alarm that over the course of the year the number of prisoners had increased by more than a hundred, and that with the extent of construction work then in progress, the prison was no longer adequately guarded. In the stone cutters' gang, which contained some 'desperate characters,' the shed was frequently unguarded and the keeper was unable to see what was transpiring outside the shed.[46] The government could not have appreciated the warden stating these facts in such a public way in a published report. But Aeneas Macdonell, facing conditions similar to those Henry Smith had been forced to deal with for thirteen years, may have decided not to be victimized as Smith had been, and so he put himself on public record.

Conditions had improved somewhat by the late fifties, by which time all the basic facilities, including dining hall, workshops, hospital, and chapels, were finally ready for use. It was a significant event in Canadian penal history when the inspectors noted in their 1857 report that, with 810 cells in place, 'the Prison proper may now be considered finished, with the exception of the covering in of the centre, by a dome, which ought to be covered with glass.'[47] Not only could more prisoner labour now be sold to contractors, but with prisoner employment henceforth concentrated in the workshops, the prison would be a far safer place for both guards and convicts.

The earlier return to the penitentiary of James Sampson as physician added an element of stability and experience. Sampson remained at his position with gradually declining energy until his death in 1863. Although he performed competently, his involvement in other activities, including the Queen's school of medicine and the Kingston General Hospital, limited his efforts at the penitentiary and the role of the surgeon settled down into one of routine, which generated little controversy.[48] In terms of new programs and policies, the two chaplains and the teacher were more to the fore in the 1850s. The Catholic chaplain, Angus Mac-Donell, the nephew of the first Catholic Bishop of Upper Canada, had first served in the penitentiary in the early 1840s and when the Penitentiary Act of 1846 provided for a 'Roman Catholic Officiating Priest' he received the appointment. At that point, both chaplains were employed only part-time and in 1849 Acting Warden Macdonell found them so remiss in their attendance that he brought it to the attention of the inspectors. In 1850 George Brown and his inspectoral colleagues pointed to the 'lamentable deficiency' in religious and moral influences, which they believed should be the 'most powerful instrument' of convict reformation.[49] The resignation in 1849 of Reverend Rogers on grounds of ill health, and his replacement in 1850 by an energetic new Protestant clergyman, Hannibal Mulkins, was seen as an important step towards reinvigorating the chaplaincy service. With the legislation of 1851 providing for full-time chaplains, the inspectors believed that the reformed chaplaincy service would make a vital contribution to the achievement of a new era in the history of the penitentiary.

Regrettably, neither Angus MacDonell nor Hannibal Mulkins performed as expected and the chaplaincy failed to develop in the 1850s as a source of strength. Some of the blame lay with George Brown and the government, which hoped to achieve by the 1851 legislation a chaplaincy that would be active yet subservient. Having decided that there should be one absolute executive authority in the prison, Brown saw no place for an independent chaplaincy. The first public indication of the inspectors' determination to keep the chaplains on a tight rein came in 1850. In the course of a generally positive report, Angus MacDonell advocated the appointment of a Catholic matron and pointed as well to the harm done by the indiscriminate exercise of executive pardons. On behalf of the inspectors, Brown informed the priest that such matters were none of his business. This touched off a row in which MacDonell challenged the apparent view of the inspectors that the chaplain should refrain from any activity 'beyond a mere relation of the manner in which the convicts class themselves and recite a certain form of set prayers.' 'If that be your meaning,' said MacDonell, '... you will allow me to differ with you in opinion' and he described the inspectors as 'a queer set of beings.'[50] In fact, he had accurately described Brown's views. No doubt the aggressive Protestant inspector would have liked to have tried the priest for *lèse majesté*.

The issue was joined again over the terms of the 1851 statute. When the bill was under discussion, the Catholic authorities informed Provincial

Secretary James Leslie that it was unacceptable, and they believed they had persuaded the government to bring in amendments. When no amendments were forthcoming, MacDonell in 1852 told the inspectors that to become spies and informers against the convicts was intolerable. He refused to 'acknowledge in the Government any power ... to grant me any spiritual jurisdiction over any portion of the Catholic community.' The government, he argued persuasively, should trust the chaplains to report any plots or conspiracies dangerous to the institution. Most important, 'it is well known, that as soon as it would come to the knowledge of the convicts that such a repugnant duty was imposed upon their chaplain, from that moment they would loose [sic] all confidence in him, and his services would become useless among them.'[51] MacDonell was supported by his ecclesiastical superiors and the subsequent weakness of the chaplaincy in Kingston amply proved that he was correct. Generations of prison chaplains would later concur with all that MacDonell had said about the weakness of a subservient or 'Erastian' chaplaincy. By an unsatisfactory compromise, MacDonell carried on his duties without being sworn while Hannibal Mulkins willingly took the oath. The brevity of MacDonell's subsequent annual reports suggest that he never overcame the alienation that developed as a result of this dispute.

There is also evidence that MacDonell and his superiors were engaged in a broader power struggle, with enormous implications for penitentiary governance. On 3 February 1852, Nelson and Dickson were taken aback to receive a series of formal demands from the priest. He began by asking for three-quarters of an hour of the time of the Catholic convicts twice a week to prepare them for confirmation. The inspectors agreed to half an hour once a week. Then, in response to the inspectors' wish to have morning and evening prayer services, he said this could be carried out only if Catholics and Protestants were segregated in separate wings. Facing a shortage of cells, Nelson and Dickson were greatly annoyed. They did 'not approve' they minuted, the widening of the breach between Catholics and Protestants in a penal institution. 'The next thing likely to be called for would be a separate Dining Hall because Protestants and Catholics could not join in the blessing,' and they noted that 'sectarian officers' had already been requested in the form of separate matrons. The board determined, therefore, that 'so far as they are concerned' the penitentiary would be run 'on broad Christian principles where all can join, and by selecting the best men irrespective of creed or country for Officers.'[52]

If MacDonell was progressively alienated, Hannibal Mulkins, whose reports occasionally reached fifty and sixty pages, seemed the embodiment of enthusiasm and dedication. Mulkins, born in Upper Canada in 1811 or 1812, served as a Methodist minister on several circuits between 1835 and 1840. Converted to Anglicanism, he was ordained in 1842 and was an itinerant until his appointment in 1850 to the penitentiary, a post he held until 1870.[53] In his draft history, A.E. Lavell called Mulkins 'the most outstanding chaplain in the whole history of prisons in Ontario,' and asserted that he was 'broadminded, devoted, efficient and most highly approved by officials and prisoners.'[54] A more accurate judgment is made by Thomas Wilson, who examined the comments in inmate discharge books.[55] Numerous convicts reported there that they had seldom if ever been visited or assisted by Mulkins. There were also a number of complaints that Mulkins was negligent in carrying out his more formal responsibilities. The warden's journal, for example, notes that the Catholic chaplain was present every morning at prayers but, as the inspectors pointed out in May 1856, 'there is no reference to the same office being performed by the Protestant chaplain.' A little later they were infuriated when Mulkins excused his absence by claiming that the prison smelled.[56] Wilson concludes that Mulkins neglected his duties to the convicts to promote his personal interests, partly through the activity of compiling voluminous statistical analyses. Although there is considerable evidence in support of this assessment, Wilson, a prison chaplain himself, was reluctant to take the next step by concluding that it was less individual chaplains, whether MacDonell or Mulkins, but the chaplaincy itself which failed in the pre-Confederation period.

Yet, in the 1850s at least, evidence in the inspectors' minute books makes clear both the unrealistic expectations that were held for the chaplaincy and the disappointment of the inspectors when the chaplains failed to live up to these expectations. In their second report, that of 1852, Nelson and Dickson pointed out that the chaplains acquired insights into the prisoners 'which it is quite impossible for any other person to obtain. They are depositors of secrets none other can know,' and the inspectors were sure that the chaplains could serve the interests of both prisoners and institution without betraying their sacred office.[57] But from 1853 the inspectors' minute book is liberally sprinkled with complaints about their neglect of duty. In conformity with the statute, the inspectors in 1850 had informed the chaplains of the need for introducing a greatly expanded religious program, including morning and evening prayers, a second service each Sunday, and a Sabbath school. At first Mulkins entered enthusiastically into these schemes but MacDonell, who opposed Sabbath schools on principle, resented this interference with what he regarded as his domain, and Nelson and Dickson were not long left in the dark about his intentions to oppose their plans. By 1852 they had reason to 'regret exceedingly' the position MacDonell had taken as to his duties.[58] Mulkins proved equally unsatisfactory, failing to perform morning prayers and generally negligent in the performance of his duties. Commenting on Mulkins's attempt to defend himself the inspectors claimed it would 'if well-founded lead to the conclusion that Religious Services are all but useless in this institution.'[59] As Wilson notes, dereliction of duty on the part of one or other chaplain was cited in 1854, 1856, and 1857, and in the 1859 report the inspectors expressed deep regret that there was not a 'self-sacrificing man' to carry out the responsibilities of the chaplains.[60] As had been true in the 1840s, the chaplains were expected to carry a large burden; but with little prestige and even less authority, MacDonell was soon alienated and Mulkins indifferent. Once again, the 'moral machinery' of the prison was an almost unrelieved failure.

So too, and more surprisingly, was the much-heralded dual inspectorate. Nelson and Dickson understood that as employees of the government it was their responsibility, using the warden as their executive officer, to develop a program that reflected the spirit of the Brown Commission, under the guidelines provided by the 1851 statute. In general, this meant that they had to compensate for a greatly reduced government grant by the increased sale of convict labour, to substantially reduce the numbers of punishments and treat the convicts more humanely and, with the provision of full-time chaplains and a teacher, they must somehow achieve the rehabilitative nirvana that had so eluded Henry Smith. They knew, too, that they were expected to be informed of recent foreign developments and to borrow therefrom whatever improvements seemed appropriate to the Canadian situation. Wisely, they understood they had much to learn and must proceed cautiously.[61]

In the early months the two inspectors had high praise for the state of the prison. In their 1851 and 1852 reports they gave their 'entire approbation' to the new teacher, James Gardiner, and to the matron, and they asserted that 'the industry of the prisoners cannot be surpassed.' Sanitary conditions were 'as perfect as possible' and, in a comment which must have rankled with the members of the late commission, they cited the report of the engineer and architect who had inspected the prison buildings in 1846–8: 'the workmanship ... cannot be excelled for its strength or durability' by any prison in Europe or North America. In an assessment that would be repeated often throughout the decade, they praised the warden for his 'untiring attention and zeal.' He was, they said, 'strict without severity; kind without weakness' and possessed the respect and affection of both guards and convicts. 'With few exceptions,' they concluded, 'the affairs of the penitentiary have progressed in the most satisfactory manner.'[62]

Almost a decade later, with a restructured and expanded board about to assume the functions of the dual inspectorate, Wolfred Nelson, despite many difficulties in the intervening years, retained his pride in Kingston's accomplishments. In a 14 October 1859 inspectoral minute, he reported that 'system, order and able management' prevailed throughout the penitentiary. 'The management and government of the Institution reflect the utmost honour on the Warden and his subordinates.'[63] Nelson's pronouncement said as much about the failure of the dual inspectorate as about the institution itself. Although there was no scandal in the 1850s, a critical examination of the prison in that period demonstrates that surprisingly few advances had been made. Kingston, as the succeeding Board of Inspectors soon concluded, remained an oppressive facility, in which punishment and deterrence prevailed with little room left for either the dictates of humanitarianism or the imperatives of rehabilitation. To some extent this situation may be attributed to the inexperience and confusion of the inspectors and to their failure to agree on fundamental objectives.

Nelson's views were outlined in the final section of a special report prepared in 1852, when the government asked the inspectors to study the circumstances of Canadian gaols. In his discussion of Lower Canadian facilities, Nelson dealt with gaols and the penitentiary indiscriminantly and presented an idiosyncratic melange of views. Drawing on the ideas of such international experts as Jebb, Lucas, De Tocqueville, and the members of the Boston Prison Discipline Society, he endeavoured to approach penology as a science, asserting confidently, if naively, that no prison would ever again be constructed in Canada 'without previously consulting scientific men, and especially the Inspectors.'[64] It was characteristic of Nelson to give priority to the need for decent treatment of prisoners. Although he made no reference to professional training, he insisted that prison workers must be individuals 'of humane, and even benevolent dispositions.' Yet there was little that was distinctive about his specific recommendations. Prisoners should never be idle and whenever possible workshops should be erected in the local gaols. In the work of rehabilitation, 'no agency is so potent as religious instruction' and whenever possible the state should supply chaplains for all prisons. 'There should be a Sabbath-school and day school for those who are not engaged in labour,' but neither education nor religion should 'interfere with the quantum of daily labor.' One duty of the chaplain should be to caution the male prisoners (Nelson could not conceive of female temptation) 'against indulging in the revolting and injurious propensity of self-abuse.' Like many penal reformers before him, he thought it necessary to warn against treating prisoners too well. Convicts must understand 'that they alone are to blame' for their misfortunes. Much attention must be paid to providing a nutritious diet. Prison clothing must ensure that any escaped prisoner was conspicuous to all, and 'some mark should be put upon the worst class of prisoners, that their very dress may indicate the crime of which they have been guilty.' Murderers should be clad in black, adorned front and back with the letter 'M' and shunned as if they were 'a walking pestilence, loathsome lepers.' Others whose crime admitted no mitigating circumstances should be 'imprisoned for ever apart, in some lugubrious shed, whose very aspect should excite ... loathing and dread.' Good conduct prisoners should receive a badge. The lash must be retained for punishment and prisoners made to know it was available, but it should be used only as a last resort. Nelson preferred reduced diet and the dark cell because he believed these were more feared than the whip.

In one respect, Nelson was in advance of the recommendations of the Brown Commission. Breaking with the basic tenet of Auburn that all must be treated alike, he insisted that well-behaved prisoners be rewarded with better treatment in the prison and the chance to earn early release. Unless the prisoner was given something to hope for, he would plunge into despair and 'give loose to all his evil propensities.' Nelson believed that sentences were often too harsh; boldly challenging existing policy, he would 'not hesitate' to set aside court sentences if the prisoner's subsequent conduct was good and if there was evidence of 'sincere repentance' or extenuating circumstances. This expanded role for prison officers he thought was preferable to the existing system, in which convicts used political influence to win early release. The hope of pardons would assist in achieving effective prison governance and would also protect prisoners against the debilitating impact of long-term confinement, including 'complete idiocy ... raving madness, or confirmed wickedness.' Alert to arguments that convicts would abuse the system by feigning reform, he insisted the officers could readily detect such ploys. No convict should be released until he had learned a trade, but once that was accomplished, if his conduct was good, early release should be considered. Such a pardon, he emphasized, would do far more good in encouraging the former prisoner to lead a reformed life than one granted under the old system. The section headed 'Pardons' was the most innovative part of Nelson's report, and sooner than he may have anticipated, Nelson would find himself initiating Canada's first prison-administered early release program.

Nelson was equally progressive in condemning Canadian indifference to what befell the prisoner after release. Like many others, he pointed to the 'excellent example' of the United States. Yet once more, a senior Canadian penitentiary official argued forcefully that at the most critical moment of his existence, the ex-convict was 'spurned at every door' and faced 'the dreadful alternative of sinning again, or dying of starvation.' In Canada, he claimed, it had become 'a crime or a stigma' to help the fallen man and there were 'thousands of cases on record' of ex-convicts shunned by society being driven to further crime. One end of prison government, said Nelson, must be to educate the public to accept the possibility of rehabilitation. This process would be furthered if convicts on release received a certificate of good conduct and a diploma, and Nelson even offered an example of such a document. Many of these ideas had been propounded by the warden and inspectors in the 1840s, but there was some reason to hope that the Baldwin–LaFontaine government would prove more receptive than had W.H. Draper and his Tory colleagues in the previous decade.[65]

One discouraging portent of the new era was the emergence of fundamental disagreements about objectives from within the penitentiary. It began with a dispute in the 1852 report between the two inspectors which escalated into a public brawl, and the issue in question was education. In May 1852 the new teacher, James Gardiner, began his duties, teaching in both French and English. In addition to regular classes Gardener spent time, which was greatly appreciated, in the cells at night. Anxious that secular education not outweigh religious and moral training, the inspectors in 1852 also implemented the statutory provision for the establishment of Sabbath schools. These soon operated 'for one to two hours every Sunday, with 35 classes of four to eight convicts each' and using convict teachers.[66] Soon the Catholic chaplain was complaining about those who 'would wish to see the penitentiary converted into a real Academy, and the convicts employed, instead of at hard labor, in the study of the Arts and Sciences.' This must persuade the convicts that they 'owe their present comfortable position to the commission of their former crimes' and would be an incentive to commit more crimes on release. Some convicts, he claimed, on release were already telling their fellows they intended to return soon to receive 'what they called, a finished education.' Angus MacDonell's choicest venom was reserved for the Sabbath school, which he described as 'worse than useless and ... the sooner an end is put to it the better.' (Facing numerous difficulties, the Sabbath school was closed in 1855, although it had resumed in attenuated form by 1867.) However far-fetched such views may now appear, MacDonell genuinely believed that except for the deprivation of liberty 'the condition of the convicts ... is better, and the means of acquiring knowledge greater, than that of the majority of the children of honest and industrious farmers in many parts of the Country.' He had not the least doubt that the convicts were already 'better fed and better clothed' than many citizens. No one who knew 'anything of the state of the country' could challenge such assertions and he greatly feared the effect all this would have on most ordinary citizens.[67]

James Gardiner's description of the educational state of the prisoners lends little credence to MacDonell's position. Describing the degree of their ignorance as 'incredible,' he heaped scorn on the old monitorial system by which convicts, themselves ignorant, used their best efforts to teach others. Gardiner proceeded to separate the prisoners into classes according to skill level and, beginning at 6 a.m. each day, he instructed them in small groups. There were, he reported, thirty-two classes taught in the dining hall, with four to six in a class, a fifth of that number being taught in French. Evidently convicts employed by contractors were not allowed to participate but he stole time from the contractors by instructing their workers during the noon period on Wednesdays and Saturdays and even during the time allotted for shaving. The female prisoners, however, were totally excluded, except for the efforts of the matron and Mrs Robert Cartwright. Not until the Penitentiary Act of 1868 was legal provision made for a schoolmistress.[68] On Sundays, Gardiner assisted in the Protestant Sabbath school but Angus MacDonell, he reported, had not yet required his services.[69]

In fact MacDonell was deepening his opposition to the new regime. The very purpose of penitentiary discipline, he insisted, was to inflict such punishment on the convicts that 'if not morally reformed, the very dread of it will become a salutary check upon their evil propensities' and deter others from committing crimes. MacDonell went so far as to attribute the increasing crime rate, especially the rise in the number of murders, to the fact that punishment was no longer sufficiently severe. He concluded with an early Canadian denunciation, one of the first of thousands made in the years to come, of the 'maudlin sentimentalities' of prison reformers pushed on by the 'insane clamour' of an 'ignorant press.'[70]

No doubt MacDonell's 'less eligibility' arguments had the support of the silent majority, but many in key positions in government and in the penitentiary also thought in this way. In his 1852 report, Wolfred Nelson supported MacDonell's position, insisting that schooling in a penal facility should impart 'the mere elements of a Common School education' so that its recipients would not aspire to rise above their station, and he condemned the Sabbath school because the use of convicts as teachers breached the rule of silence. Andrew Dickson, however, lashed out angrily, asserting that 'the majority of intelligent men' had abandoned such views as MacDonell's as 'totally repugnant to the feelings of all enlightened men.' A furious Nelson responded that to carry out the system of instruction Dickson seemed to advocate would lead to 'a certain class of people making criminals of their children, that they might obtain gratuitously an education in the Penitentiary.'[71]

Although this discourse reflected contrasting world views, one individualistic, Protestant, and progressive, the other rooted in Catholic traditions of social stability and hierarchy, the institution was not wracked in the 1850s with the bitter divisions over religion which had endured throughout the 1840s. This seems surprising, given the virulence of the above exchange and the fact that the issue reflected polarized ideas of penitentiary discipline rooted in equally contrasting visions of the ideal social order. But at other levels there were substantial areas of agreement and Nelson and Dickson cooperated closely for most of the decade. Perhaps this was because the reformed governance embodied in the 1851 Act worked to good effect; more likely it was because the earlier consensus that the penitentiary must at once serve the purposes of punishment, deterrence, and reform remained in effect and for the most part encompassed the different visions of Catholic and Protestant Canada.

More important than differences in social outlook was the question of the general effectiveness of the new inspectoral arrangements. One piece of evidence is the unrelentingly positive reports made by Nelson and Dickson to the government and the contrast between these and the critical notes struck by the successor board in the 1860s. Typical of Nelson's complacency was the 1859 report, the last to appear under the dual inspectorate. The penitentiary, the report asserted, had succeeded in its punitive function by making the convict 'suffer ... the consequences of his misdeeds' and in its deterrent role by 'establishing a salutary dread of offending in the future.' In rehabilitation it had 'in many cases' achieved reform by developing character and teaching skills. The contractors, who made every effort to conform to prison rules, had played an important role in developing the self-respect and self-reliance of the convicts. As for the state of discipline, the behaviour of the convicts was 'very good, if not exemplary' and, he claimed, there had been no act of violence or attempt to injure any of the officers. Most punishments were minor and 'the whip is only resorted to in extreme cases, and the number of lashes seldom exceeds one dozen.' As for the warden, Aeneas Macdonell had earned 'entire approbation' for his efficient administration.

The biases that infuse this document are significant for what they suggest about the dual inspectorate. Although paid by the government and viewed as the ultimate repository of responsibility, Nelson and Dickson had been co-opted by the institution and by the warden himself. In part this was a consequence of their own inspectoral methods; more often than not it was one inspector and not both who made the rounds with the warden. In contrast to his predecessor, Aeneas Macdonell was conscientious to a fault. Present twenty-four hours a day and almost never away from the prison, he knew its every nook and cranny. It was Macdonell's great achievement that the prison was run honestly and efficiently. This was a considerable accomplishment and the inspectors were rightly impressed. As Nelson had put it in 1859, following 'a searching examination' of the whole institution, the 'able management' which prevailed throughout reflected the 'utmost honor on the Warden and his subordinates.' The initial impression of the successor board, chaired, it should be noted, by Dr Nelson, confirmed the overwhelming impression of administrative efficiency and on one of its first tours it found that everything was 'in most excellent order. The female apartments appear to be particularly well managed.'[72]

In a facility marked by order and governed authoritatively, Nelson and Dickson, often acting singly and dealing with a warden who related to them on a level of equality, began to see matters from his perspective. Unlike their successors, they failed to ask probing questions, to seek out areas of concern and weakness or to look beneath the surface harmony at the larger significance of the impact of the penitentiary experience, whether on individuals or on the world outside the walls. In this way, the warden's will became pervasive until the inspectors suspended their critical judgment. The efficient and conscientious Macdonell was, after all, fully in charge of operations and it was easier that way. Fundamentally, the structure of the reformed inspectorate was at fault. The very language of the inspectors' minute book is revealing. With previous boards in the Smith era, the warden would be invited to attend; but now, as testimony to his elevated status, the minutes simply recorded: 'the warden and Mr. Dickson [or Mr. Nelson] comprising the Board.'[73]

Certainly Aeneas Macdonell contributed to the situation through his painstaking attention to routine. While he began his tenure as the chosen instrument of Brownite reform, as the years passed he gradually demonstrated a marked shift in priorities. In his early days, Macdonell believed that his mandate was to implement a new type of prison government. 'Of late years,' he announced in 1852, 'prison discipline has undergone a great change; the object seems at present to be how to carry out the sentence of the law ... by an effectual system of penitentiary discipline, which, though coercive, may at the same time be humane.' For Macdonell this involved the preservation of health, education 'both moral and secular and as far as possible the acquisition of a trade.'[74]

But from the beginning the crusty old Scot's heart was not with the task of achieving rehabilitation. The reformed system, he noted, was more demanding of administrators, but was worthwhile so long as the warden's authority was never challenged. 'I am of opinion,' he wrote in 1852, that the matter of discipline 'claims the most prominent position in the general business of the institution.' Even in 1852 there was a total of 3,822 punishments recorded and the inspectors could only regret that it was 'necessary to punish for such offenses as speaking and laughing, but it seems impossible to avoid doing so in a congregate prison.' In such circumstances, Macdonell was soon distinguishing between three groups of convicts: those who accepted the rules without question, those who tried to avoid hard labour, and those he described as 'vicious and intractable.'[75] Some in this last group, in addition to being whipped, were chained and secured by leg irons. The kind-hearted Nelson could not withstand the warden's forceful insistence that he must be allowed to exercise his own judgment in inflicting punishments. A board minute of late November 1851 read:

Although the Board deplore that corporal punishment should be found necessary in the preservation of order and regularity in the penitentiary, [they] are of opinion that the Warden should not be deprived of the means which has heretofore been in force to curb the disobedient and vicious Convict and do therefore authorize the warden to use his discretion according to the 40th section of the Act.[76]

It is important to distinguish between corporal punishments, such as the whip, and other forms of chastisement, including the solitary cell and reductions in rations. As the information in Table 5.1 demonstrates, the number of corporal punishments authorized by Macdonell never approached those meted out in the final years of the Smith regime.

TABLE 5.1
Corporal Punishments
Selected Years, 1835–1857

Year	Number of corporal punishments inflicted	Number of punishments
1835	78	78
1836	148	148
1837	263	263
1838	222	222
1839	198	198
1840	225	225
1841	172	172
1842	157	341
1843	388	770
1845	1877	2102
1846	2133	3445
1847	58	6063
1848	12	5714
1851	3	872
1852	381	3822
1855	34	5247
1856	53	6294
1857	92	7657

Source: Annual Reports

Macdonell demanded and received authority to deal quickly and ruthlessly with staff as well as convicts. It was his 'firm opinion' that any officer having charge of a penitentiary 'should have ample power to punish insubordination.' Most of all, decisions as to punishment must be the warden's. The inspectors concurred. A minute of 26 April 1852 practically gave Macdonell carte blanche: 'As the Board have approved of the punishments awarded by the warden in our absence we therefore require him ... to award such punishment as he in his discretion shall consider most beneficial ... during our absence.' Macdonell eagerly grasped such power, arguing that not the existence of unrestricted authority but only 'the abuse of it' would pose problems.[77] Although he claimed that vigilance was more effective than punishment, Macdonell believed that little reliance could be placed on the guards as disciplinarians and he was anxious to minimize contacts between guards and prisoners.

Corporal punishments were imposed only for cases of 'outrage,' violence, or refusal to work, and most punishments did not involve the infliction of lashes. In a separate section on 'Punishment, etc.' in their 1853 report, the inspectors argued that the threat of corporal punishment was primarily a deterrent and as such essential. They pointed out that in 1853 such punishment had been inflicted on only '18 convicts, who collectively received 464 lashes.'[78]

Always stern and unbending, Macdonell, as time passed, became increasingly fearful and preoccupied by the demands of security. More than ever he seemed persuaded that many of the convicts were vicious and he felt increasingly helpless as the contract labour system undermined his authority. In these circumstances, he was convinced that a hard core of convicts, vicious and depraved, could understand only the lash. His descent to hardened inflexibility is dramatically traced in the pages of his daily journal. Always inclined to a bleak vision of human nature, by April 1854 he was writing that,

The more experience I have the more I see the necessity for strict discipline, indulgence in many instances is thrown away. The answers of the Convict Feeley on questioning previous to his departure convince me that indulgence is worse than over strictness. I make this observation on the ground that this man has been well treated ... and has shown a very diabolical feeling on going out.[79]

Again and again we find Macdonell commenting that this convict is a scoundrel, that one an incorrigible rogue. For one man, 'one of the most worthless beings in the penitentiary,' Macdonell ordered 'two dozen inflicted to be repeated the moment that he gives up work and to be continued if necessary.' Another convict was ill-disposed and a recidivist: 'all along his conduct has been notoriously bad and should have been punished with the Cat long since. However on his promise of general good conduct in future only inflicted 36 lashes.'

Macdonell believed that the convicts were always testing the boundaries of authority and that weakness on his part would have catastrophic consequences. Sometimes he ordered punishments to combat convicts' 'various attempts to act the madam.' This practice, he noted, 'is gaining ground in the institution and needs to be seen to. Any effort to sabotage the work process was also certain to lead to immediate punishment. Convict Tappin, Macdonell noted, was 'on punishment for improper conduct while at work. In revenge he broke some of the property of the contractor. This proceeding if allowed would be extremely dangerous' and corporal punishment was ordered.[80]

TABLE 5.2
Number of Life Sentences Admitted, 1835–1857

Year	Number	Year	Number	Year	Number
1835	0	1843	3	1851	3
1836	0	1844	1	1852	11
1837	0	1845	3	1853	8
1838	0	1846	6	1854	6
1839	1	1847	8	1855	6
1840	2	1848	6	1856	9
1841	0	1849	8	1857	9
1842	5	1850	8		

Source: Annual Reports

TABLE 5.3
Percentage of Recidivists, 1837–1846 and 1847–1857

Years	Total Commitments	Total Recommitments	% of Recommitments
1837–1846	1076	72	6.7%
1847–1857 except 1851	1586	151	9.5%

Source: Annual Reports

Macdonell was most fearful of the large numbers of long-term and life prisoners and recidivists. In several reports, both warden and inspectors noted that the number of long-sentenced prisoners was substantially larger than in American penitentiaries. In 1853 the prison held fifty-four lifers, in 1855, forty-six. According to the inspectors, there were more than three times as many convicts in New York state prisons as at Kingston, 'yet there are nearly double the number of life convicts' in the Canadian institution. For this reason, the warden and inspectors frequently tried to persuade the government to increase the number of guards.[81] The recidivism rate hovered consistently in the 10 per cent range for the period 1839–65, hardly a cause for great alarm, but the trend was definitely up, as the data presented in Tables 5.3 and 5.4 demonstrate.

Nelson and Dickson shared the warden's fears. In 1852 they told the government they had deemed it necessary to heighten the wall and to build a new watchtower at the point where 'an attack would likely be

TABLE 5.4
Percentage of Recidivists, Selected Years

Year	Percentage	Year	Percentage
1839	11.49	1857	10.23
1840	10.46	1858	9.51
1841	10.67	1859	11.36
1847	8.33	1860	12.88
1852	10.8	1861	15.18
1853	9.27	1862	14.9
1855	9.87	1863	13.12
1856	9.28	1865	13.44

Source: Annual Reports

made in the event of an insurrection among the convicts.'[82] With an inadequate number of guards and sceptical of their reliability, Macdonell knew nonetheless that he would be blamed for any disorder or escapes. His concern was compounded by the physical condition of the prison. In his 1855 report Macdonell, conscious of how his predecessor had been blamed for circumstances beyond his control, offered this graphic description: 'It is all important that I should bring under your notice the unfinished state of the prison buildings. This is a work that must be done, and the sooner it is undertaken the better. To a stranger entering the centre of the prison building, it has the appearance of a ruin.' Escape, fire, and riot were among the dangers. It was a tribute either to the docility of nineteenth-century prisoners or to the executive capacity of the first two wardens that Kingston avoided disaster. Aeneas Macdonell's unwavering attention to duty should also be credited. Constantly fearful and on the alert, he told his superiors that he did 'not leave the Institution night or day.'[83]

Macdonell had been warden for five years before the first successful escape. In 1855, following the discovery of a widespread escape plot, he and the inspectors again pleaded for more guards. With convict numbers straining facilities beyond the breaking point, Macdonell reported that without more guards it was 'impossible to keep a proper observation and command over them.' As a result, 'vicious and badly disposed convicts had conversed together, hatched plots and disturbed the peace.' Visibly shaken, he told the inspectors that although the inmates had been treated with great humanity, 'in a number of instances they have proved unworthy of the exertions that have been made for their benefit and reformation.' As a precaution, he had 'discontinued the school in the Dining Hall as well as the Sunday Schools, wherein they have frequent opportunities of secret conversation.' The government's response was irresponsible: they noted that the statute gave the inspectors the authority to hire more guards, but there was no mention of increased funding. The warden made his complaints public in his 1855 report. The prison, he insisted, was no longer adequately guarded. In the dome and in the cabinet and blacksmith shops, the number of guards was entirely inadequate. 'It is also important you should know, that the South wing of the main prison buildings is often left to the Convicts, while the guard stationed there is away to the relief of the guard on the North-east tower.'[84]

Although a few more guards were soon added, Macdonell for the rest of the decade believed security was inadequate. His unceasing emphasis on this aspect of penitentiary administration detracted from his earlier and never very active interest in reform and rehabilitation. To his credit, the prison on the level of security functioned marvellously well. In 1859, the inspectors praised him highly, claiming that Macdonell's salutary influence was felt 'in every part of this vast establishment,' not least in the sense of calm resignation and willingness to conform to the rules that characterized convict behaviour.[85] This itself was an outstanding achievement in nineteenth-century penitentiary administration. Aeneas Macdonell, given the limited resources that the government made available to him, had probably chosen the right priorities. If nothing else, the absence of riots and disturbances and the low level of gratuitous violence in Kingston Penitentiary meant that this was a relatively safe, secure, and in some respects a healthy environment for both inmates and officers.

6

'Moral Monsters,' Refractory Females, Children, and Workers

Much of what is interesting about the penitentiary in the 1850s relates to specific problems and particular groups of inmates, especially women and the insane. These groups suffered disproportionately, the mentally ill most of all. For this element, practice and policy were in a state of flux, as different interests and approaches competed for primacy. The result caused considerable disruption of prison routine but the principal victims were the deranged themselves, who suffered and died in large numbers while officials, politicians, and doctors debated their place in the penitentiary.

THE MENTALLY ILL

The Brown inquiry had discussed at some length the treatment received by two mentally afflicted convicts, James Brown and Charlotte Reveille[1] but the commissioners had little to recommend, beyond the construction of separate apartments in the prison to house and treat the insane. Their condemnation of the amount of insanity in the Philadelphia system suggested by implication that there was little to fear on that score from confinement in a well-run Auburn-style prison. In this period, convicts afflicted with insanity were confined in the temporary hospital or in cells as far apart from other prisoners as possible. But it was not far enough and their howling, especially at night, was disturbing and unsettling. This situation occasioned a letter from Warden Macdonell to Provincial Secretary James Leslie, which reported that there was 'no remote place of security in which [the insane] can be kept from disturbing the other prisoners, and their unruly conduct is enough to show the other convicts how easy it is to cause trouble in the prison.'[2] The warden fully supported the efforts made in 1850 and 1851 by the inspectors and the surgeon to persuade the government to transfer insane convicts to the provincial asylum at Toronto. Dr Sampson had argued in 1849 that the 'proper moral management' of the insane could not be accomplished in a penitentiary, and he and the inspectors believed that penitentiary confinement was likely to add to their insanity.[3] Sampson had another reason to desire their removal: a convict he had certified as insane in 1847 became the penitentiary's first suicide. The government responded by including a clause in the 1851 Penitentiary Act which provided for the transfer of a convict to the provincial asylum after he had been certified as insane by a medical board of three persons, chaired by the penitentiary surgeon. The board was to be appointed by the government. If the convict recovered his reason while at the asylum, he was to be returned to the penitentiary for the remainder of his sentence. The new clause was immediately acted upon and seven convicts, including James Brown, were sent to the asylum.[4] By May 1853 convicts were being transferred to the asylum on a regular basis.[5]

What the new policy did not take into consideration was the inadequacy of facilities at the provincial asylum to cope with an influx of the criminally insane. Dr Joseph Workman, head of the asylum, was alarmed to find three murderers deposited on his doorstep. Workman solved his problem by turning to the provision in the legislation which gave him the authority to return to the penitentiary convicts who were cured: all three murderers were soon returned to the penitentiary certified sane. The board in response complained to the governor general that the authorities in the asylum were returning lunatic convicts as cured 'which were no better when they returned here than what they were when sent.' Workman refused to back down and reported to the government that the wards in which he had lodged lunatics sent from the gaols and penitentiary, 'have become notorious ... for their disquietude, and the comparative incurability of their inmates; whilst they are altogether unsafe as places of confinement for criminals; and I find it impossible by any amount of vigilance to prevent frequent quarrels and the infliction of bodily injuries, to say nothing of the incessant uproar and profanity at all times prevailing.'[6] In his report the following year, Workman denounced the practice of sending 'moral monsters' to the provincial asylum as 'an evil of inconceivable magnitude ... an outrage against public benevolence and an indignity to human affliction.'[7]

In response, the warden was instructed by the inspectors to inform the government that the penitentiary lacked the facilities for confining lunatics. It took just one convict, he reported, to subvert the 'quiet and good order' of the institution. Such persons were not responsible for their actions and could not be subjected to the discipline and punishments necessary to maintain order. When this letter went unanswered, the inspectors pointed out that the return of convicts who were still insane violated the 1851 statute and they asked for instructions. They also noted that the housing of insane convicts incurred heavy costs with no return, since such convicts could not perform labour for the institution. In this dispute Dr Workman had his way, and no more convicts were sent to the asylum under the 1851 statute.[8] For their part, the inspectors changed their position in their 1853 report, arguing that Dr Sampson, as a 'regular bred Physician,' was well equipped to deal with the insane within the penitentiary, and they endeavoured to provide suitable facilities in the lower story of the new hospital. Sampson himself was unhappy with this development: it was his view that the mentally ill required treatment by 'Medical Officers well trained' for the task.[9] The inspectors seem to have been persuaded and in their 1854 report they changed their minds again and reverted to support of Sampson's position. The penitentiary, they insisted, was 'a place most unsuitable for Lunatics.' The insane disturbed the order of the prison while the keepers and guards were not qualified to deal with them.[10]

The government had its own agenda. In February 1855, Attorney General John A. Macdonald noted that the quarters formerly occupied by the military 'could easily be fitted up for the reception of the criminal lunatics in the asylum, now 21 in number, as well as those at present confined in several county gaols,'[11] and the government appointed John Litchfield, a medical professor at Queen's College, to look after it. Meanwhile the warden received the approval of the government to place the insane convicts in the west wing as more remote from other convicts and renovations were made in this area. In June 1855, mentally disturbed prisoners from the gaols and the provincial asylum began to be transferred to the penitentiary asylum.[12]

The situation, however, remained unstable. Although Dr Sampson was pleased that a separate facility had been established under Litchfield, the inspectors continued to find the lunatics disruptive. In February 1856 they instructed the warden to tell Litchfield that there were only twenty empty cells in the entire prison and that Litchfield should 'apprise the Government of that fact so that some other place may be provided for the Criminal

Lunatics.'[13] By November every cell was occupied and workers were putting up cells in the west wing where the lunatics were still located. The inspectors told the government they required 'instant possession' of this space.[14] In these circumstances, it was the lunatic convicts who suffered most. The government had imposed them on the penitentiary authorities but the inspectors understandably regarded the maintenance of the Auburn silent system, with each convict housed in a separate cell, as their first responsibility. In a panic, Litchfield told the inspectors it was 'out of his power,' to find facilities and the inspectors said the only available space was in the basement, from which they would 'remove the vegetables elsewhere' if he required it. The insane were therefore removed from the west wing to the basement of the prison dining hall.[15] In 1856, this temporary asylum held thirteen insane convicts and twenty-four others who were not penitentiary convicts. Unhappy with this situation, the inspectors told the government that a separate asylum for the criminally insane was imperatively required. The inspectors were not exaggerating the crisis of overcrowding and in 1856 the government purchased an old mansion overlooking Lake Ontario, the Cartwright estate, and set about remodelling the stables to make room for female lunatics and planning to build a separate asylum facility. The 1857 prison omnibus statute proclaimed that 'an asylum shall be erected or provided in the vicinity of the Provincial Penitentiary ... for the reception of Lunatic Convicts.' The Act, it is important to note, repealed the section of the 1851 statute which had directed that insane convicts might be sent to the provincial asylum.[16]

Under the new system, Dr Litchfield proceeded to convert the Cartwright stables into a temporary asylum for women and he also supervised the male lunatics remaining in the penitentiary basement. But, typically, the government proved slow to begin construction of the new facility promised in the 1857 statute. In February 1859 the penitentiary inspectors recorded that the temporary asylum 'would not admit of more convicts without some detriment to their health, physically and morally. Indeed the extent of sickness which has prevailed there already is but too strong proof that the place where they are now confined is extremely unhealthy.'[17] In Nelson's opinion nothing could be done to 'ameliorate the sanitary condition of this low gloomy place,' and Litchfield reported that its sanitary state was a danger both to convicts and guards. They were not exaggerating.[18] The male lunatics would remain in the penitentiary basement until 1865 and the inspectors repeatedly condemned this abominable arrangement, describing it in 1859 as 'in no ways suited for the residence, even for a brief period, of human beings.'[19] In 1857, of thirty-six lunatics housed in the basement, two thirds were not convicts; in 1858, of forty-seven lunatics, fully thirty-two were not convicts.[20] Efforts to improve physical conditions, such as the drainage of the dining hall, were ineffective and the death rate was appalling. It reached 9.01 per cent in 1864, dropping dramatically to 1.5 per cent in 1865, when all patients had been moved to Rockwood. The deaths in 1864, Litchfield noted, were of those confined in the penitentiary basement for 'successive years.'[21] The decision to build Rockwood gradually, using prison labour, was costly in the lives of the poor creatures, many of whom had been convicted of no crime, swept up from about the province and too often condemned to slow death in the penitentiary basement.

But the government responded less to the death rate than to the inspectors' demand, in the face of the crisis of numbers, that the temporary asylum be restored to penitentiary use. With Rockwood also at capacity, the plea for action again went forward to the government. Fortunately, it coincided with another crisis brought about by economic recession and the failure of contractors to fully employ their convict labourers. In late May 1859 Nelson journeyed to Toronto to impress upon George Cartier and John A. Macdonald, the attorneys general, that for the safety of the prison employment must be found for large numbers of convicts. It was not possible to set them to breaking stones because there was such a large supply on hand that no more could be sold and 'no person would take them away for the mere cartage.' Nelson returned to Kingston with the good news that 'an order-in-council would be immediately transmitted to the Warden to send as many hands as could be spared to make preparation for erecting the lunatic asylum at Rockwood.' The order came just in time. That very day Dr Litchfield informed the board that 'many of the Lunatics were daily growing weaker and attenuated and that he feared the debility ... would continue until they actually died.' Litchfield attributed this to 'the low damp dank place where they are confined' and reported that so long as they remained there 'many untimely deaths will occur.'[22] On 30 November Litchfield also warned the inspectors that any visitations of an epidemic such as typhus or cholera must lead to 'an appalling number of deaths.'[23] Nelson confirmed this view. Neither man knew then that the slow progress of work at Rockwood would allow this tragic situation to persist for years longer.

The situation became worse, as numbers confined increased from fifty-nine in 1859 to sixty-four the following year. There was, however, one significant legal reform. The inspectors had been unhappy with the 1851 legislation which had enabled one man, the superintendent of the provincial asylum, to certify convicts as having recovered their sanity and return them to Kingston, while a three-person board was required to send convicts from Kingston to the provincial asylum. The law was amended in 1857 to give the penitentiary surgeon and the superintendent of the Criminal Lunatic Asylum the authority formerly held by the three-man board.[24]

For the penitentiary itself, if not for the unfortunate lunatics, the opening of the temporary asylum, as Kyle Jolliffe concludes, 'basically solved the long-term problems they faced in the management of insane convicts.'[25] Even during the long wait until 1864 for the opening of the new Rockwood, the warden's problems had been alleviated by the banishing of the deranged to the basement under the authority of Dr Litchfield. When the new board made the trip with Litchfield to the basement in 1861, their only comment was that 'the department ... is as well kept as it can be under the circumstances.'[26] The inspectors, however, understood the dangers of the penitentiary asylum and did what they could to expedite the completion of Rockwood. On 31 May 1862, for example, they ordered architect Coverdale 'to place every available man who can be spared from the penitentiary upon Rockwood Asylum works so that they may be completed at the shortest possible period.'[27] But there was a final irony. Although the treatment of these unfortunates would improve greatly with their transfer to Rockwood in 1864, even this proved to be at best a partial and temporary solution to provincial treatment of the so-called criminally insane. In 1877, the Government of Canada sold Rockwood to the Province of Ontario for use as a general asylum for the eastern part of the new province, and the criminally insane from across the Dominion once again found themselves confined with Canada's convict population in Kingston Penitentiary.

FEMALE PRISONERS

The situation of women in the penitentiary had a good deal in common with that of the insane. A relatively small group whose needs were seen as secondary to those of the main body of prisoners, they suffered many abuses and their behaviour and condition initially called forth an analysis that was decidedly negative. In mid-decade, however, a remarkable change occurred and Kingston's female prisoners progressed dramatically from being viewed as the very worst prisoners in the institution to being seen as among the very best. To the student of nineteenth-century Canadian penology, the reasons for this transformation are both puzzling and significant.

In the Smith period, matrons had been hired and the women hived off to their own little section and largely ignored. Under the new regime, which aspired to reform, they received more attention but most of it was hardly flattering. There was an emerging consensus, strikingly similar to that in other jurisdictions, that female prisoners were the worst of a bad lot. Warden Macdonell referred in his 1849 report to 'the bad situation' of the female prison. 'It has not been in my power,' he asserted 'to conduct it with the order and regularity which ought to be enforced,' but he was optimistic that 'a change can be made that will tend to the quiet and good order of that branch.'[28] The Catholic and Protestant chaplains did not share Macdonell's optimism. They believed that existing problems were attributable less to the physical circumstances of the women's prison, then housed temporarily in the hospital and soon to be moved to the old dining hall, than to the character of the female prisoners. In his 1850, 1851, and 1852 reports, the Catholic chaplain, Angus MacDonell, offered an unremittingly negative view of the women. They were 'the most refractory and unmanageable characters' in the penitentiary, often recidivists, and 'with those, whatever temporary signs of repentance they may occasionally exhibit, anything of a permanent improvement can hardly be expected.' Their management, he continued, 'has always created the greatest difficulty in the Provincial Penitentiary, and, I believe, in every other prison where they have been confined.' Most of them were prostitutes, 'diseased in body and debased in mind,' whose long career in crime meant that they were not susceptible to benevolent influences. With some sympathy, MacDonell explained that all but three of the Catholic women prisoners were Irish in origin, often brought up in poverty and ignorance and unable to find employment. These desperate creatures soon turned to petty larceny and were sent to gaol, where close contact with the most depraved characters confirmed them in careers of crime. But MacDonell introduced a hopeful note. In the existing circumstances, when they landed in penitentiary discipline was 'almost a dead letter,' for the women were attended by inadequate matrons and they could communicate constantly with each other, and even with the male convicts. While improvements must be made in penitentiary discipline, and MacDonell was pleased that a Catholic matron was hired, he believed that the solution for the Catholic women was to remove them entirely from the penitentiary and put them under the control of the Sisters of Providence in Montreal. 'In that asylum, they would be treated with motherly kindness, watched with strict surveillance, and they would, moreover, have constant examples of charity and religion before them.'[29]

The Protestant chaplain and the inspectors shared fully in this bleak analysis. In 1850, the interim board, composed of the Brown commissioners, pointed to the 'great difficulty of maintaining good discipline' in the women's prison; as a remedial measure they had moved the women into the just-completed hospital. A few weeks later, in December 1850, they threw economy to the winds and resolved that it was 'absolutely essential' to discipline that cooking of food and washing of clothes not be done there and that silence must be rigidly maintained while the women were at work. The matron was told to sit the convicts at work in rows face to back; food would be sent in from the male prison; and clothing would be sent out of the prison under contract to be washed, a step that was reversed on grounds of economy by Nelson and Dickson.[30] The warden was unhappy because the women had to be conducted though much of the prison to get to a temporary punishment room (the hospital lacked any suitable facility) and this was disruptive. The inspectors admonished Mrs Cox, the matron, for not maintaining discipline, and she in turn blamed the assistant matron for offering little assistance. The board resolved to dismiss the assistant. Numerous references continued to be made to the deficiencies of the matron and her assistant, but the inspectors do not seem to have drawn the obvious conclusion that a salary level well below that of an ordinary guard was part of the reason for this situation.[31]

Under difficult circumstances, Julia Cox did her best. In 1852 she reported that all thirty-eight of the women under her care were diligently employed. About a third worked for the shoe contractor and the others were making and repairing clothing and bedding and performing other domestic tasks. Their health was good, and most had improved in appearance and manners and, 'with few exceptions, in their behaviour.'[32] Obviously, the matron had a different perception of the women than that of the male officers. But she admitted to problems. In 1848, for example, the board learned that the matron was in desperate fear of one Bridget Donnelly, who had already 'twice committed desperate assaults upon her,' and from whose threats she was 'in bodily fear.' They ordered Donnelly confined to her cell 'until further orders' and if she misbehaved she was to be handcuffed.[33] Mrs Cox was assisted in her task by a remarkable woman, Mrs Robert Cartwright, the widow of Reverend Cartwright, who for many years during the 1840s and 1850s conducted a weekly Bible class and, perhaps more important, demonstrated to the prisoners that she cared deeply about what happened to them.

One indication that prison officers were not entirely successful in efforts to segregate the female prisoners was the occasional pregnancy.

Most frequently, this was a result of contact before the women arrived at the prison, although officers were greatly annoyed on several occasions when it emerged that the intercourse had taken place in the local gaol or even on the trip from gaol to penitentiary. More alarming was evidence of improper behaviour in the penitentiary. Although Kingston, unlike American penal facilities, was not wracked by any great scandal over the sexual abuse and exploitation of women, there was an occasional incident, such as that involving Ann Irvine in 1852. In August of that year Irvine and Bridget Donnelly were violently disruptive: Irvine was sent to another cell after breaking the doors and windows of her own room and Donnelly was sent to a dark cell. 'As everything that has been tried has failed to reform or subdue some of the females,' read the inspectors' minute, 'it is resolved that the Warden order a new mode of punishing the very refractory females by cutting their hair very short.' At the same time it was discovered that Irvine was pregnant and on investigation the inspectors learned on oath from two convicts that Guard Turner had acted 'very negligently if not criminally.' Turner was dismissed. The threat of a haircut was an insufficient deterrent and in May 1853 the board ordered the erection of two dark cells in the basement and two others in the regular female dormitory.[34]

One solution to these difficulties was to move forward quickly with arrangements for a new women's prison. In December 1852 Horsey was ordered to proceed according to a plan approved by Dr Sampson. The new facility was to include a spacious workroom and a hospital facility. By the time of the 1853 report, the new facility was occupied. Completely isolated from every other part of the penitentiary and surrounded by a high wall, the reconstructed women's prison pointed to a new era for women in Kingston penitentiary. For the next couple of years, however, staffing difficulties came to the fore, with continual bickering between matron and assistant matron making it almost impossible to enforce discipline. In January 1856 Dickson visited the female prison to find 'nothing but a continual quarrel going on between the Matron and Assistant Matron which I find is destroying the discipline.'[35] When the assistant was removed, the same situation ensued with another. The breakthrough came in early September 1856, when Martha Walker, described as 'an English widow lady' and 'a female of education, and one who has been brought up in good society' was hired as matron.[36] Martha Walker brought to the prison personal qualities that soon effected remarkable improvements. She submitted a list of by-laws for the governance of female prisoners and greatly impressed the warden. Macdonell reported that Mrs Walker deserved every mark of respect, and expressed regret that although she never left the prison she was paid less than any keeper or even guard.[37] Year after year Mrs Walker and her conduct of the female prison won unrestrained praise, not only in the annual reports but also in the private minutes of the inspectors. In a total reversal of previously accepted opinions, Dr Nelson claimed in 1857 that 'this portion of the Penitentiary is ... most easily governed and the least expensive, requiring but one assistant.' Walker had rendered it remunerative by economical management and by work done for the institution and for the shoe contractor. Nelson might have added that money was also saved because the women did not receive some of the services available to male prisoners, including the schooling offered by teacher James Gardiner.

Improved management aside, the female prison had become overcrowded. The 1857 report listed fifty prisoners, with no fewer than twenty-six Irish born, forty out of fifty being first-time offenders, and twenty-seven under the age of thirty. By 1858, eight of the women were compelled to sleep in corridors. In 1859 Mrs Walker reported an average daily population of sixty-eight.[38] At this point, Dr Nelson returned to the earlier suggestions made by his co-religionist, Angus MacDonell, that some at least of the female prisoners should be treated outside the walls of the penitentiary. Nelson praised such facilities as the Magdalene asylums operated in Lower Canada by orders of nuns. 'Here the poor destitute and outcast women find a kind home, consolation, comfort and support,' while to discipline was added 'the powerful element of encouragement and hope.' Similar successes, Nelson claimed, had been achieved by Catholic sisterhoods in England, and such an approach in Canada would save the state the vast sums needed to erect large penal facilities. But the time had not yet arrived in Canada for such experiments. As had happened so many times before, more cells, about twenty of them, were added in the existing facility.

Nevertheless, Martha Walker had succeeded in bringing creative management and greater humanity to the female prison, and as a reward the attorney general, on the recommendation of the inspectors, approved an increase in her salary from $375 to $535. In his definitive judgment of her work, Nelson reported in November 1859 that Walter deserved 'the highest eulogium for the great ability and intelligence displayed in the Government of this important department.'[39] What seems most interesting about developments in this period is how much Martha Walker was able to achieve by deploying methods that must have been quite different from those used in the rest of the penitentiary. Walker was the outstanding pioneer in Canada of the women's reformatory movement and her work, supported by Kingston's male officials, represented some of the most significant advances of the 1850s.

MILITARY PRISONERS

The third special group whose presence, and then absence, did much to shape institutional life in the 1850s was the military. First admitted in 1839, the number of military prisoners grew rapidly, moving from 129 in 1843 to a peak of 261 in 1848.[40] These numbers are deceiving, however, because most military prisoners were confined for extremely short periods, often only a few weeks. Although the military paid a small fee for their presence, military prisoners worked with the convicts and were placed in cells alongside the general prison populace. Reverend Rogers waged a long and unsuccessful campaign to rid the penitentiary of the military in the belief that the presence of short-term prisoners was both disruptive for the convicts and morally degrading for the soldiers who, often imprisoned for breaches of military discipline such as drunkenness, were locked up alongside convicted felons.

Both the prison authorities and the military establishment seem to have shared this concern. The 1851 Penitentiary Act provided for the establishment of a separate system within the prison to segregate the military from convicts. The inspectors' minute book records a July 1850 meeting with Captain Knight, the superintendent of military prisons for Canada, to discuss how to achieve this goal. Describing the existing situation as 'degrading' for the soldiers, they accepted a plan proposed by Knight involving a separate system of discipline and separate cells for the military. The prison would receive the returns from convict labour and the military would pay a higher rate for each soldier confined. After further discussions, this was accepted in principle and in April 1851 the plan was sanctioned by the governor general and the secretary at war. The warden was instructed to set aside the west half of the south wing for night quarters for the military and to provide an exercise area on the east side.[41]

The reformed system proved satisfactory to both sides and most of the former complaints disappeared from the official record. Once again the numbers of military imprisoned, which had dropped to 115 in 1850, began to rise, reaching 211 in 1853. After that date, however, there was a sharp drop. Early in 1855 the lieutenant general commanding the British forces informed the government that in view of the recent reduction in the numbers of troops in Canada, there was no longer any need for space in the penitentiary and the military quarters were handed back to the warden. This had hardly been done, however, when circumstances changed and in 1856 the military asked to resume the former arrangement. By this point, the overcrowding crisis was at its peak and the prison authorities responded that there was no space available.[42] While it is difficult to gauge the effect of the military presence on prison life and routines, it was hardly beneficial and certainly short-term prisoners can have been of little value to the prison's complex system of contract labour. For some reason, a very few soldiers remained for a few years and the section pertaining to the military remained in a revised penitentiary statute in 1859.

JUVENILES

The other group whose presence added to problems of institutional management was the juvenile offenders. To everyone's relief, they too were banished from the institution with the opening of separate reformatory prisons in the late 1850s. Throughout the 1840s all those associated with the penitentiary had persistently pleaded with the government to remove juveniles. Only when the Brown Commission provided its lurid tales of young children receiving repeated whippings was the government willing to listen, and no legislation was passed until 1857. In the meantime, there were efforts to make things better for young people in the penitentiary. Children aged seven or eleven were no longer beaten repeatedly with the cats in front of the entire prison population. Yet nothing demonstrates the extent to which corporal punishment remained in mid-century as a central tenet of a disciplinary society than the continuing practice of whipping young prisoners for acting like children. Nelson and Dickson suffered no pangs of conscience when they directed the warden in September 1852 to 'scourge' recalcitrant children with a birch rod in the presence of all young prisoners. The practice seems to have become so much a matter of routine that the following year they decided that it was no longer necessary for the surgeon to be in attendance when such punishments took place.[43] Aeneas Macdonell took it all in stride. When, for example, in 1856 a boy named Potter required punishment for 'general bad conduct,' Macdonell noted that this was not a first offence and directed that 'for the least offence he should be scourged,' adding as an afterthought that the boy should also be kindly but sternly admonished. For lesser offences, the children were put on bread and water.[44]

Perhaps the most important improvement for juveniles in the 1850s was the availability of special school instruction from James Gardiner. But it is striking how seldom this was mentioned in the official minutes. On 14 April 1853, the inspectors did decide that the area in which the school was located was unsuitable for the boys and they instructed the warden to find a new location.[45] The lack of interest in what happened to the young people suggests that children, like women, were not of great concern in these years. Yet when it came time to select some boys for the new reformatories, they were suddenly regarded as a valuable commodity. The inspectors' minute of 16 September 1858 expressed regret that a sufficient number of boys was not available from the general population to meet the numbers to be sent to the reformatory so, reluctantly, five children were added from the shoemakers' contract gang. Obviously, children hired out to contractors could not expect the advantages of transfer to the reformatory. The following year, when a father petitioned to have his son, who was sentenced to two years, transferred to the reformatory, the inspectors demurred as he too was working in the profitable shoe gang. They recommended that the petition be refused on the grounds that with the rule of silence in effect, 'no contamination or interference can possibly take place. No Institution in Canada up to this moment can afford similar facilities for imparting moral and industrial instruction.'[46] Such hypocrisy contrasted sharply with the persistent efforts of Henry Smith and his colleagues in the 1840s to remove all the children from penitentiary discipline, whatever the monetary consequences.

Nonetheless, by the end of the 1850s changing circumstances and new initiatives pertaining to all four special groups – the insane, the military, women, and children – had substantially altered the Kingston environment. In the following decade this would greatly simplify the task of governing the penitentiary.

CONTRACT LABOUR

In no area did Warden Macdonell experience more frustration and exhibit more confusion of purpose than in that of convict labour, the issue most important to all aspects of penitentiary life. The daily life of every prisoner from sunrise to sunset continued to be shaped by the regimen of hard labour. As the physical construction of the prison neared completion, the expectation remained that Kingston would soon become self-supporting. As early as March 1848, the old Corbett board had promised that 'the period has at length arrived' when the labour of most of the convicts could be let out to hire, and the Brown commissioners were indecently keen to confirm the Smith administration's incompetence by turning a profit. But

Brown and his inspectoral colleagues soon discovered that where prison labour was involved, all was not as simple as they so naively believed. 'We endeavoured,' they reported with some embarrassment, 'to obtain wholesale orders for various articles to be made by the Convicts, without success.' No doubt purchasers were cautious about the quality of goods produced under the supervision of prison officers. Next they attempted, equally unsuccessfully, 'to induce parties to hire the labour of the Convicts for the prosecution of branches of trade not yet extensively carried on in the Province.' Once again, no entrepreneur could be found willing to hire convicts on such restricting terms. Feeling desperate, the inspectors decided as a last resort to sell convict labour 'for any trade, to any responsible parties who might be willing to contract with us for a term of years.'[47]

At first even these efforts elicited no positive response, serving only to renew the old sense of alarm among Kingston-area businessmen and workers, who feared unfair competition. Eventually, in June 1849, the inspectors closed a contract for the labour of fifty convicts in shoemaking at a rate of 1s.6d. per day for each man, with a possible increase in the number of convicts provided to one hundred. The contractor, E.P. Ross, a New York businessman, would maintain his association with the penitentiary for many years, usually as the largest contractor in the institution. Within days a second contract was concluded with two businessmen, one from Napanee and a second from Auburn, New York, for fifty men to be employed for five years in cabinetmaking, at a price of 1s.6d. per day. 'The Contractors are putting up machinery of the best kind, for carrying on the business, and in a very few weeks the whole will be in vigorous operation.' A half a year passed before a third contract was concluded with two Kingston businessmen for the labour of fifty tailors, also for five years at a price per person of 1s.6d. per day. Part of the inducement here may have been an agreement that the same parties would supply clothing for the penitentiary.[48]

In the 1849 report the warden pondered the relationship between contract labour and rehabilitation. With only the boot and shoe contract then operational and using fifty convicts, he asserted that this manner of employing the convicts would be 'extremely beneficial' to the institution, 'as a certain amount of remuneration can always be depended upon, and the Convicts so employed will derive a lasting benefit, by acquiring a trade, by which, after the expiration of their term of imprisonment, they will be enabled to earn a livelihood by honest industry.' As well, by employing convicts in this way 'the discipline of the institution can be more strictly enforced, than if employed in unproductive labour in the yard, where it is very difficult to enforce the necessary degree of discipline.'[49]

Yet the claims of the penitentiary were regarded with mounting hostility by several elements of the larger community. In 1849 a raft of angry petitions to 'His Excellency' proclaimed the concern of Kingston tradesmen over 'a grievous oppression which bears hard upon themselves and families in the vicinity' and would soon affect 'all classes of Mechanics throughout the Province (if the evil be not timely averted),' leading to depression and even 'the final removal from the Province of many of those who are dependant upon their handiwork for support.'[50] The petitioners seemed in a state of panic. Many of them, they claimed, 'are thrown out of employment, from the ruinous competition produced by thrusting into this market the produce of Convict Labour ... That a variety of establishments are being opened for the sale of articles of convict manufacture, all of which are already manufactured by the honest and industrious mechanic, who has spent a number of years in acquiring his trade at a great expense to himself or guardian.' The tradesmen alternatively suggested that convict labour might 'be profitably employed in the manufacture of such articles as at present the Province is obliged to import from other countries,' such as hinges, cutlery, iron and steel smelting, and a variety of other articles 'not likely soon to come into ruinous competition with the Mechanics of this county.' The petitioners, having some doubt that the government would accede at once to this request, proposed 'as present relief' that products then being sold in the Kingston area be distributed across the province, so that 'all might bear their share of the grievance, which your Petitioners from their proximity to the Institution have imposed on them alone.' This document, bearing several hundred names, was dated 13 November 1849.[51]

The Kingston shoemakers presented a petition of their own, which made a different kind of case. They argued that the system of teaching convicts shoemaking affected their 'standing and respectability in Society as a body.' Shoemakers belonged to a class second to none 'as regards respectability of character' and the introduction into their trade 'of a large number of emancipated criminals will have a tendency to lessen our respectability in the eyes of the public and to prevent us from enjoying that confidence which has hitherto been awarded to us individually and collectively.' Furthermore, parents 'will hesitate to apprentice their children to a mechanical trade, in the exercise of which they will be brought into daily and constant contact with convicted thieves and robbers; respectable mechanics will shun our shoes, and consequently the principal part of the trade will fall into the hands of emancipated felons.'[52]

Once again, the doctrine of less eligibility appeared prominently, the shoemakers complaining that 'teaching criminals a mechanical trade, instead of acting as punishment, is rather offering a premium for crime, as the convicts are better lodged, better fed, better clothed, receive better medical attendance in sickness, and are less severely tasked than the majority of those who serve a regular apprenticeship.' The suggested remedy was to employ the prisoners producing goods for His Majesty's troops in the colony and to use them 'in some of the numerous mines with which Canada abounds.'[53] In voicing these fears and prejudices, the tradesmen of Kingston were acting much as their fathers had in the 1830s. The significance of such attitudes extended beyond the issue of convict labour to encompass all the complexities of rehabilitation and reintegration of former prisoners into community life. If tradesmen and mechanics demonstrated as little actual sympathy for former prisoners as their rhetoric suggests, the outlook for all those released from the penitentiary was indeed as bleak as prison officials so persistently claimed.

The immediate issue rapidly assumed a political dimension. On 11 December 1849, the Mayor of Kingston forwarded the petition of city council to Lord Elgin. This document emphasized the impact of convict labour on the city itself. With most of the products of the penitentiary being sold in Kingston, the result 'will be rapidly to depopulate the place of a large number of its best and most industrious citizens and their families; for it is estimated that on an average, the labour of one convict deprives a family of five persons of their livelihood – so that the employment of four hundred convicts in mechanical labour would displace a population to two thousand persons.' Even under the few contracts then in force, 'the revenue of this city is already sensibly diminished.' In June 1850 another petition to Elgin presented by the mayor and bearing the signature of hundreds of inhabitants claimed that their worst fears had been realized: 'establishments for the disposal by retail within this City, of Convict made boots and shoes, ready made clothing, chains, Cabinet makers wares, Blacksmith's work, and various other articles are now in full operation; this has had the effect of driving a large number of our Mechanics from the City and neighborhood.' Such articles were being sold at a price at which 'they cannot be produced by an honest Mechanic, having a family to support.' The idea of reforming the prisoner 'by his present term of mis-called punishment' the petitioners dismissed as 'one of the philanthropic delusions of the day.'[54]

Anger was mounting. The member for Kingston, John A. Macdonald, moved in the legislature on 16 July 1850 that the city council petition and several others be sent to a special committee for discussion. In the ensuing debate, some members no doubt were alarmist in claiming that the new system of convict labour was threatening the City of Kingston with destruction, but not all their fears could have been expressions of political hyperbole. According to John A., the mechanics, unable to compete with the low rates of convict labour, were 'leaving the city in hundreds.' Macdonald said he had a list of two hundred mechanics who had left the town within the last three months, 'all in consequence of this convict labour.' The problem, he claimed, extended over much of the area, including the town of Belleville. Macdonald repeated several of the suggestions made in the petitions and demanded that the government 'take up the subject.'

Other members put forward a range of views. For the ministry, Inspector General Francis Hincks argued that wherever governments had tried to manufacture and sell prison items themselves they had failed, and 'the only way of employing the convict labour to advantage was by the present system of letting it out.' Others, however, pointed to the enormous expense of the penitentiary and claimed that in the United States such institutions were a source of profit. W.H. Merritt, the Commissioner of Public Works, argued cogently that to do away with competition from convict labour it would be necessary to do away with the labour itself. Merritt did not see how reasonable persons could be opposed to competition. To this Henry Sherwood, the High Tory member for Toronto, rebutted that no one objected to fair competition, but the complaint was about competition from slave labour. When Hincks pointed out that the problem was a relatively new one and pledged that the government would do its best to find a solution, Macdonald withdrew his motion. Yet neither the Reform administrations of 1848–54 nor the Conservative governments that followed were prepared to end the contract system.[55]

For penitentiary officials an equally grave problem arose from allowing contractors and their foremen to supervise the work of the convicts. Because of the absence of market inducements to labourers to work hard, the contractors found it advantageous to implement their own systems of rewards. But prison officers objected to a situation that placed important aspects of discipline beyond their control. Even the inspectoral board dominated by George Brown, which was so anxious to induce businessmen to enter into contracts, found it necessary, in the 1850 report, to admit that the system had led to 'the clandestine introduction of tobacco and other articles, as bribes to the Convicts.' Brown believed that strict provisions should be placed in new Penitentiary Act, then being drawn up, to counter this development, but no such provisions were made. In his 1851 report, the warden lamented his own lack of control. 'I regret to have to state,' he noted, 'that the greed and impatience of the foremen employed by the contractors, has given me a very great degree of uneasiness and trouble.' The foremen used tobacco to bribe the convicts to do more work, and most convicts willingly risked punishment to obtain this highly desired contraband. Despite every effort to impress upon the foremen that they would be punished or dismissed from the prison, these practices continued. The foremen knew the warden could do nothing to jeopardize the continuation of the contract.[56]

In the prison environment, no item was more desperately sought after than tobacco; it is not difficult to imagine the effect of its unauthorized distribution on the penitentiary's power structure and in shaping an inmate subculture which had the potential to undermine the warden's uncertain degree of control. In this context, it is worthwhile to note the later comments of John A. Macdonald that for twenty years Macdonell 'never retired to rest without having his pistols at his pillow; and ... he received a most dangerous wound from a convict who sought his life.'[57]

Hannibal Mulkins, the Protestant chaplain, offered another perspective, arguing that circulation of forbidden articles served to 'render nugatory amongst several convicts all exertions of the Chaplain.' 'The lessons of honesty and religion given on Sunday can have little weight indeed, if the convicts, practically, though clandestinely, are encouraged during the week to violate the laws of the Prison, deceive its authorities, and to practice fraud, lying, cunning and theft.' Far better, he suggested, to allow the forbidden articles 'than to have the convicts corrupted by unprincipled men.'[58] He repeated the charges in the following year and was blunt in identifying the contract system as the source of the problem. The distribution of tobacco had 'a pernicious and most demoralizing tendency' as it trained the prisoners 'in the habitual practices of concealing, deceiving, lying, stealing, and violating the Prison rules; for they are schooled and encouraged in these practices by base men, who, more corrupted than the prisoners themselves, not only violate the regulations which they have solemnly promised to observe, but stimulate the convicts to copy their unprincipled example.' Mulkins believed no officer of the prison 'to be guilty of such depravity.' It was found, he complained, 'chiefly in the Contractors' shop.'[59]

Mulkins's views had no chance of prevailing. The contractors' position remained untouchable and Aeneas Macdonell was expected to do all in his power to accommodate their demands. In December 1850 several contractors asked that during the short days of winter the convicts might breakfast immediately on leaving their cells, instead of being marched to and from the breakfast room, which wasted much time. The board agreed. The warden was also instructed to cut back as far as possible on the number of prisoners employed at institutional tasks, and this was carried out at once; the number of stone cutters, for example, was reduced from forty to twenty-five, and this made it possible to reduce the keepers from four to two. Prison routines were thus increasingly shaped by the demands of the contractors and their foremen. Even when the chaplains asked to hold the morning service after breakfast in the dining hall, immediately before the convicts left for work assignment, the response was that the inspectors would try to 'meet the wishes of the Reverend Gentlemen provided it does not interfere in the discipline or pecuniary interests of the institution.' And when, in November 1855, the contractors asked that the meal hour for convicts be shortened from sixty to thirty minutes, the inspectors ordered Macdonell to shorten the time spent at meals. In April 1856, the work day was extended for the summer, the wake-up bell to ring at 5.30 a.m.; in December, when the contractors complained the convicts were not getting to work early enough, the warden was ordered to use candles in the dining room until the days became longer. The imperatives of the contractors even altered convict punishments. When a contractor decided that the heavy chain attached to William Dill following an escape attempt interfered with his work efforts, the warden was told to use a lighter chain.[60]

It was a matter of some concern when one of the early contractors, the tailor shop, failed. The inspectors reported in 1851 that the warden had advertised in Canadian papers, as well as in some in the United States, 'for Contractors for the labor of the Tailors' gang,' but with no success.[61] By dint of continual efforts by the warden and inspectors, four contracts were in operation by 1856. The largest, the boot and shoe operation, employed 148 convicts; followed by blacksmiths (81 convicts); cabinet-makers (67 convicts); and agricultural implements (61 convicts). Neither the blacksmith nor the agricultural implement contractor was using the full number of workers contracted for. Out of 668 convicts, 357, slightly more than half, were employed in these four contracts. The rest were engaged in institutional work and included 136 labourers, 44 seamstresses (most of the women prisoners), 38 stone cutters and masons, 15 carpenters, an assortment of cooks and tailors, and a barber.[62] By the following year, five contracts were in force, only two of which were using the full complement of workers. Taken together, the two shoe contractors used 250 of the 515 convict workers.

Throughout the 1850s, the warden railed impatiently against the con-

TABLE 6.1
Prison Contracts and Rates as of 1857

Contractor	Number of convicts	Time Period	Rate
Messrs E.P. and A. Ross (shoes)	150	1854–9	1s. 9d.
Messrs T. Drummond and Co. (agricultural implements)	100	1854–9	2s. 3d.
Mr J. Morton (cabinetmaker)	65	1855–9	2s. 7d.
Messrs J.P. Millener and Co.	100	1855–60	2s.
Messrs E.P. and A. Ross	100	1857–62	2s.

tract system and how it eroded his authority. In 1857, he reported that contractors were still trying to extract more labour from the convicts by bribing them with gifts. 'This is not an open proceeding on the part of the Contractor and his Foreman, but is done secretly.' When a convict was caught and deprived of contraband tobacco, it often caused that convict to become extremely agitated and led, said Macdonell, to further punishments.[63] But the warden and the inspectors were desperately anxious both to keep the prisoners occupied and to bring in revenue, and Macdonell's reports helped keep alive the expectation that the penitentiary might become self-sustaining. Typical was the minute of 1 February 1855: 'The board anticipating an increase of convicts from increased population of the province and more especially from the class of people employed on public works conceive that more shops should be erected so as to enable more convicts to be engaged at contract labour, the inspectors believing that it is the most profitable mode of disposing of convict labour.' The inspectors ordered Macdonell to proceed at once and to finish the new workshops as soon as possible. In 1856, the warden reported that the year had seen a satisfactory increase in contract labour, which served 'to give an assurance that on the completion of the buildings, the Penitentiary may be made self-sustaining.' The inspectors were more cautious. The financial returns had not been as anticipated, in part because so many convicts were old and disabled. On record with the opposite claim on innumerable occasions, they now argued that 'even under the best management, Penal Institutions will always prove heavy pecuniary burdens to the Country.' The state 'should not expect to make a gain out of the compulsory labour of its criminal population.' Even so, the political reality required that officials be seen to be doing all in their power to bring in revenue.[64]

When numerous convicts refused to work, the institution recognized that it must put down this challenge to authority, by whip and by lash if necessary. The warden was explicit in his 1853 report, noting that the number of punishments had increased because of the number of 'obstinate culprits who take a position against hard labour.' The remedy resorted to after exhausting his powers of persuasion and trying the dark cell without success was 'infliction of the cats.' Macdonell was clear as to how this process of physical intimidation was used: the convict was tied to the triangles but then he had 'only to say I will go on with my labor' in order to be 'immediately released.' In this way, the warden concluded, 'every precaution is taken against the practice of cruelty'!

A brutal and unequal contest ensued between gaoler and gaoled. In August 1853, when convict Cornwall, after eleven days in the dark cell, still refused to work, the inspectors pointed to his case as showing plainly that the dark cell often proved to be insufficient punishment. After seventeen days, the prisoner had not changed his mind and he was told to conform within two days or receive the whip. Convict Cornelius Ryan was given several opportunities to agree to 'go to work peaceably,' but after much stalling he agreed only to work at any other occupation than the shoeshop. This too was intolerable and the inspectors ordered 'thirty lashes with the cats.' In 1854, when convict Tearney refused work, he was awarded forty-eight lashes but after sixteen he 'promised to do his duty.' Tearney was taken down, with the clear warning that he could expect to receive the remainder 'if he did not perform a reasonable amount of work.' There was also the case of Patrick Ellis, who had a record of doing 'little or no work in former times until he received punishment with the cats.' The inspectors in March 1854 had found that the dark cell and other punishments 'had no effect upon him' and that even the cats worked only for a few months. Now he was becoming 'as bad as ever' and the inspectors were 'reluctantly compelled' to employ the cats 'until he performs his work.' If they were to maintain the discipline as required by statutes, they had very little choice.[65] A dynamic had been created and a contest set in motion to test the authorities' resolve; what was at stake may have been nothing less than control of the prison. Macdonell knew that when the convicts tested the boundaries, they must be shown that he could not be intimidated.

The traditional Auburn imperatives remained firmly in place. Work was far from being a rehabilitative tool, and a few convicts preferred the whip to the prison's routine of endless labour, month after month, year after year. Yet, for most, compliance with the labour regimen seemed easier. Not many convicts likely left Kingston ready to seek out and submit to such a routine of unending labour for the rest of their lives.

As the 1850s progressed, the inspectors and warden continued to face innumerable problems about letting contracts so as to maximize the return to the penitentiary. The crisis came in late 1857. On 28 December an alarmed Andrew Dickson informed the provincial secretary that some of the contractors had 'refused to take into employment the full number of Convicts for which they have contracted alleging for their refusal the deprived state of trade, the difficulty of collecting outstanding dues and the large amount of the product of convict labour now on hand and for which they cannot at present find sale.' The inspectors, 'believing that these allegations were well founded,' were reluctant to enforce the letter of the contracts, fearing that 'such a step might result in the embarrassment of the Contractors, as well as much inconvenience and losses to the Institution.' Even so, the consequences for the penitentiary were serious. 'A large number,' Dickson pointed out, had 'lately been sentenced to the prison,' and a larger proportion of the population had to be set at such institutional work as could be found, no easy task in the winter months.[66]

The issue of contract labour often assumed paramount importance in the minds of the inspectors. 'It will be absolutely necessary for the future,' they pointed out in the 1857 report, 'that more contracts for Convict Labour will have to be entered into, as the quarries within the walls are nearly wrought out.' As early as April 1857 the inspectors were becoming frantic because so many prisoners were not employed under contract and large numbers of new arrivals were anticipated. Yet again the warden was told to advertise extensively and repeatedly in Canadian and American papers 'for tenders to hire out convict labour for five years at any branch of industry fitted to be carried on in the Provincial Penitentiary.' They regretted that there were 'too many convicts labouring in the Yard which it would be desirable to have ... put on contract labour.' They especially deplored the fact that 'many of the most active men' were used as cleaners when they could be used far more profitably under contract.[67]

The trade situation soon undermined the ability of officials to prepare accurate budgetary estimates. In their 1857 report, the inspectors claimed to be 'at a loss in making out an Estimate for the present year' because the depression made it uncertain what contracts the warden would be able to negotiate, and even whether present contractors could live up to their commitments. In late 1857 or early 1858, the contractors submitted a joint petition to the governor general requesting a reduction in the price of contract labour to one shilling six pence or thirty cents a day, the price used earlier in the decade. They also asked to be allowed to reduce the number of convicts employed by a half. The warden, through correspondence, determined that at three United States penitentiaries, Auburn, Sing-Sing, and Columbus, no reduction had yet been made in the price of contract labour, although at Auburn they had decreased the numbers employed on each contract. Acting on their own authority, the inspectors had already allowed the contractors an extension of time before payment was due. They now advised the government that 'the best interests of the Institution would be secured by a reduction in the price of contract labour during the depressed times in the Province, without prejudice to the contracts as they now exist, also that the present numbers on the different contracts shall be kept up as they are.'[68] Macdonell reinforced this perspective in a letter of 6 February to the provincial secretary. 'The great object,' he reiterated, was 'to keep the Convicts emply'd.'[69] The warden provided the government with a brief history of each contract, together with his recommendations. The senior contract, dating back to 1849, was still held by Elmore Ross of New York State. By its terms, 250 convicts were to be employed at boot and shoe production, but only 177 were currently at work. The original agricultural implement contract had failed and been taken up by Thomas Drummond. It had not at any time employed the specified number of one hundred and then stood at fifty-nine. James Morton's cabinetmaking contract was generally satisfactory and was using sixty-five of seventy-five convicts. The blacksmith's contract, which had been entered into in 1855 with a group of New York State businessmen, had 'not progressed so satisfactorily as the Boot and Shoe or Cabinet Contracts.' In the circumstances, Macdonell believed that the agreed-to number to be employed of one hundred was unrealistic and that it should be reduced to seventy, together with a price reduction. In the case of the other three contracts, he recommended a price reduction on condition that more convicts be employed. In making these recommendations, he asked the government to keep in mind that of 682 males then in the institution, only 372 were used for contract labour and he emphasized that the financial interests of the penitentiary demanded that as many as possible be employed under contract. In March 1858, the inspectors finally faced up to their inability to find new contractors and decided to set surplus workers to construct new shops.[70] Accepting reality, the attorney general agreed that for the first six months of 1858 the contractors be charged only the price recommended by the inspectors, on condition that the number of convicts contracted for not be diminished. When a second petition appeared at the end of six months alleging continuing financial problems, Macdonald agreed to extend the price reductions to the end of the year.[71]

By the end of 1858 the situation had deteriorated further. Now the contractors asked for a one-year extension of the reduced rates. The harassed warden pointed out that he was forced to contend with the 'very great difficulty' caused by the fact the contractors were not filling vacancies that occurred at the expiration of convict sentences. The blacksmith, cabinet, and agricultural implement shops together were employing only 171 persons, a reduction of 35. On the other hand, the boot and shoe contractors 'now employ two hundred and fifteen and would take on the full compliment [sic] if there was room in their workshop.' Although the shoe contractor paid the sums owing promptly, Macdonell had been obliged to take 'accommodation notes' from two other contractors and the cabinet-maker was in arrears for over $5,000. Again, however, Macdonell demonstrated how tied the institution had become to the contract system, recommending that the contractors receive the requested continuation of a reduction in rates on condition that they not reduce the numbers employed. This time the Executive Council, after expressing some exasperation, agreed to another six-month extension, on condition that all arrears be paid promptly.[72] The warden was instructed to provide all possible accommodation for the shoe contractor.

Part of the explanation for this determination to keep the contract system going, notwithstanding the horrendous problems it created for discipline, is apparent from the institution's balance-sheet. Officials had often seemed to be grasping after a will-o'-the-wisp in their never-achieved expectation that the penitentiary was about to become self-sufficient. But in fact, the returns from convict labour, and especially from the contract system, were quite impressive. In 1856, a typical year, the proceeds from contract labour were £10,228, while the total cost of running the penitentiary was £24,773. As well a total of 40,967½ days of labour was carried out on behalf of the institution and, setting its value at two shillings a day, its worth was calculated at £4,097. Including other calculations, the inspectors reported that the 'exact cost' to the province of running the penitentiary, after deducting the proceeds from contract and institutional labour, was only £7,413. With an average daily inmate population of 606, the annual cost per inmate was £12.4s.9d. By comparison, in the 1980s the average annual cost for a male prisoner in a Canadian penitentiary was over $40,000, and for a female over $60,000. The comparison prison officers made most frequently at the time was with the gaols. There, it was always noted, the prisoners lived in almost complete idleness and received none of the benefits derived from the penitentiary's rehabilitative apparatus, yet the per prison cost exceeded by several times that of the penitentiary. Even during the 1857 trade recession, contract labour brought in nearly £12,000. No wonder the government viewed the contract system so positively, particularly when Macdonell and most of the politicians had little belief in rehabilitation in any case.

Not surprisingly, hard times led once again to renewed agitation against the sale of merchandise produced in the penitentiary. This time the agitation seemed more widespread than ever. In March 1859 the governor general received printed petitions bearing thousands of names from such widely dispersed communities as London, Napanee, Port Hope, Belleville, Picton and Smiths Falls. Concern had always been voiced not only by 'mechanics,' but by diverse elements of society, and these petitions were explicit on that score. The petition from Belleville, for example, described as being the effort of merchants and tradesmen, included engineers, druggists, barristers, insurance agents, accountants, bankers, yeoman, and a wide range of other occupations. Each petition read as follows:

That the present system of disposing of Convict Labour in our Provincial Penitentiary is an unwise policy; That it is not self-sustaining; That it is Injurious to Mechanical Industry – discouraging to Private Enterprise, and Distructive [sic] to the Best Interests of our Country.[73]

The petitioners, asking that such labour not come into competition with established trades, recommended the establishment of an iron manufactory to keep the convicts busy.

During this period and into the 1860s there was continuing controversy and uncertainty about the nature and role of labour in Kingston Penitentiary. Negotiations with the hard-pressed contractors were not easy, nor were they always successful. When the agricultural implements contract expired, it proved impossible to find satisfactory terms for renewal. In one significant advance the Cabinet did agree to attach to all future contracts the explicit condition that the contractors 'must be amenable to the Rules of the Penitentiary and subject to removal from it for infraction of the discipline.'[74] It may be that this much-needed stringency was the final straw that caused some contractors not to renew. In these circumstances, the warden at times seemed almost terrified as to what to do to keep his charges busy and to raise money. The old excuse that many convicts were needed for construction purposes remained at hand. About a hundred convicts were still at work building Rockwood, and there were always substantial projects at Kingston itself. A new initiative sponsored by Meredith's Board of Inspectors was the establishment of a farm, but the rocky outcroppings of the Canadian shield resulted in disappointing agricultural yields, while the seasonal nature of this work limited its value. It remained for the new board in the 1860s to deal with a situation that had been a major source of frustration for Macdonell since he became warden, and to finally shift the balance against a system that had continually placed the prison in conflict with the community while bringing only dubious benefit to the prison itself.

7

Disciplinary Advances

NIBBLING AT THE EDGES

If the imperatives of labour and security dominated the penitentiary's daily routines during the era of the dual inspectorate, there were nonetheless a few hopeful developments. With much good feeling and an essentially humanitarian outlook, Nelson and Dickson managed to nibble at the edges of the disciplinary monolith established by Macaulay and his colleagues and reinforced by Brown and the commissioners. Internationally, this was an era of innovation. Joshua Jebb did his best to humanize prison life in Britain, working with great devotion to ensure that prisoners received adequate food and medical treatment, and that British prisons were built with good heating and ventilation systems. Under Jebb's enlightened leadership the British temporarily abandoned older notions of unproductive penal labour, such as treadmills and crankshafts, in favour of new public works prisons in which convicts engaged in constructive labour. They also established a ticket-of-leave system by which convicts could return to the community after serving a portion of their sentences. In Ireland, Sir Walter Crofton, the greatest name in nineteenth-century prison reform, was fine-tuning his model of 'reformatory prison discipline,' which brilliantly deployed a sophisticated system of incentives and progressive development to encourage prisoners to work towards early release. In the United States there was an encouraging departure from traditional Auburn rigidities.[1]

In Canada, the portents seemed less favourable. With only a single penitentiary, there was no opportunity to develop a pool of talent in correctional administration or even to educate bureaucrats and politicians in some of the more positive foreign developments. Given the turbulent politics of the Canadian Union in the 1850s, governments had other pressing preoccupations – such as survival. As for the warden and the two inspectors, their own horizons were limited. The stolid Macdonell lacked Henry Smith's interest in searching out and applying recent international advances, Dickson was probably not up to the task, and Nelson, who continued to practise medicine and politics in Montreal, never gave his full attention to the inspectorate. The performance of the two inspectors consisted largely of well-intentioned and humane, if often a little confused, recommendations.

Nelson and Dickson did initiate a gradual humanizing process within the penitentiary. An early example was the warden's decision in June 1849 to order weekly baths, 'with warm water and soap,' for all convicts, while clean shirts and socks were to be issued twice a week, and windows kept open for better ventilation. A more significant innovation was the relaxation of the restriction on visitors. In December 1850 the warden, after receiving several applications from relatives to visit, had asked the Brown board for guidance. The board's response was that 'the spirit of the discipline is the entire isolation of the Convict' and no visits could be permitted.[2] In November 1851, in one of their first decisions, Nelson and Dickson decided that, in the presence of the warden, visits could be allowed for parents and children, that chaplains should be permitted to write letters on behalf of immediate family, and that answers could be received.[3] The warden's daily journal reveals that he was frequently willing to make himself available to permit family visits, most often of the prisoners' wives. The inspectors also reduced the numbers of persons visiting the prison out of 'mere idle curiosity,'[4] and there is considerable evidence in the board minutes that they were genuinely concerned to improve the prison's ventilation and heating systems, and to ensure that the prisoners received nutritious food. And, especially for convicts who were regarded as well behaved, there were acts of individual kindness. When a bill of exchange was sent to the prison with the request that it be invested in an annuity for convict Richard Paul, the warden and inspectors agreed to act on his behalf.[5] Sometimes the warden was even willing to allow visits with convicts by those who professed to have personal business with them. The visiting policy seems to have been interpreted liberally and only the most suspicious characters were refused admission;

the warden reported, for instance, that 'a very rough female' had asked to see one prisoner, 'but as she could not show that she was a particular relative I could not allow her to see him.'[6]

INSTITUTIONAL PARDONS

The most important changes effected in the 1850s related to early release and the pardoning process. In January 1847, it will be recalled, the Corbett board directed the warden to bring forward from time to time the names of well-behaved convicts as fit objects for clemency. Pardons granted on the basis of good behaviour, they suggested, would have a positive effect on the behaviour of the prisoners in general. Unfortunately, in the confusion of the scandal and investigations of 1848–9 this policy was not developed and the Brown Commission unequivocally rejected it. But Nelson and Dickson, in their 1852 report, drew upon French and British sources to advocate the introduction into Kingston of a system of classification using 'marks and badges worn on the dress.' In some English facilities, they pointed out, three degrees of badges had been adopted, leading through simple good conduct to regular perseverance and, at the highest level, 'superiority of demeanor.' To explain the thinking behind a progressive badge system they cited Jebb: 'deprive a prisoner of the element of hope for a long period, and no form of discipline will have a favorable effect on his character.' In France, they pointed out, worthy young convicts could qualify for cash prizes.[7]

Similarly, they urged that consideration be given to creating a sophisticated system of pardons which could be used to minimize the dangers while taking advantage of the benefits provided by the handing down of long sentences. Already, they noted with approval, applications for pardon were being referred to them for information about the convicts' behaviour in prison. It was a logical extension of this procedure that no prisoner 'should have extended to him the Royal Clemency of Pardon, whose conduct in the Penitentiary has not been the most exemplary.' The decision should be influenced by evidence of contrition and the likelihood that the recipient would avoid future crime. Pardons should never be given to short-sentenced convicts, in order to ensure that sentences continue to have their full deterrent effect, and to give prisoners time to acquire a trade. And in no case should a prisoner who had not passed through the three stages and received the successive good conduct badges receive a pardon. There was an important element of institutional self-interest involved in the proposal: pardons would provide 'the means of preventing the Institution from being overthronged,' an important consideration given the rapidly approaching numbers crisis. But the inspectors justified their plan primarily in terms of its salutary effort on the individual, who would receive the all-important 'element of hope.'

Finally, the establishment of a pardon system would mitigate a growing problem of the Canadian penitentiary: the disproportionate number of prisoners sentenced to long terms. This situation, the inspectors argued, had abominable consequences for both the institution and the individual. During a long incarceration a person 'becomes enfeebled both in mind and body.' Let out into the world incapable of earning a living, he must either return to a life of crime or become a mendicant.

Support for these arguments was provided by the Catholic chaplain. As early as 1849, Angus MacDonell had pointed out that his years of experience as chaplain suggested 'great objections ... against the free use of the pardoning power on the part of the Government.' Almost all those who knew anything about prison discipline, he asserted, found the existing system objectionable 'because it has a strong tendency to unsettle the whole machinery of penal enactments, and deprive punishment of much of its terrors by removing all its certainty.' But if early release were 'made contingent on the prisoner's own good conduct,' this would have a salutary effect. MacDonell persisted in these views and in 1852 argued that he would not exempt even the most guilty from 'the hope of their condition meeting with the most merciful consideration of the Government.'[8]

Although there was an unusual unanimity of opinion on the subject within the penitentiary, the extent to which the inspectors were responsible for this initiative is unclear. Up to this point, petitions on behalf of convicts were usually undertaken by relatives or friends and the advice of the trial judge was always far more important than the convict's behaviour while in prison in determining the result. Yet even the Brown board in 1849 seemed to be moving toward a more advanced position. The board had directed the government's attention to several convicts in the belief that 'strongly mitigating circumstances' might exist to justify pardons. The inspectors at this time did not emphasize good behaviour in the prison, noting rather in the case of one Saunders, committed in 1842 for murder, that should the government seem disposed 'to extend the Royal Clemency ... on the merits of his case, his conduct since his incarceration has been such as to strengthen his claim.' Not good conduct in prison but 'strongly mitigating circumstances' seemed necessary to justify release. Thus they noted that one man's crime had been committed while the man was drunk, and in another case that prisoner had a 'large and deserving family.'[9] Nonetheless, the board's willingness in 1849 to take the initiative in bringing cases to the attention of the government constituted a significant breakthrough. The old board's efforts in special cases made it easier for Nelson and Dickson to argue for the development of a new policy on pardons.

Even so, such a policy emerged only gradually, as the case of an Indian, William Anthony, demonstrated. In 1851, George Anthony, a Delaware Chief residing on the Grand River, prepared a petition which indicated that his brother William had been tried at the Niagara Assizes of the previous October before Mr Justice McLean, and convicted of horse stealing. This was alleged to be his first offence and he was sentenced to four years in penitentiary. George Anthony attributed his brother's downfall to liquor; previous to William's addiction 'he had a farm and was very industrious.' More important, George alleged that his brother was innocent: the horse had been stolen by others. The petition was referred to Justice McLean, who pointed out that the facts brought out at the trial had left no doubt of the prisoner's guilt; furthermore, Anthony had been quite sober when he had sold the stolen horse. On the basis of McLean's report, and probably without even asking penitentiary officials about the prisoner's conduct in the institution, the petition was turned down.

A year later, George Anthony petitioned again. This time, the warden responded to a request for a report on William Anthony's conduct with the information that the prisoner's offences had been minor in nature, such as talking at the dinner table. Although William had been in delicate health for several months after his arrival, his condition of late was much improved. Nelson and Dickson covered some of the same ground in a letter to the provincial secretary, A.N. Morin. In their words, they had been asked to consider whether a pardon 'would be beneficial,' but the inspectors concluded that 'at present we can not see anything particular in the case to recommend him.' He was a short-sentenced prisoner who had served only twenty-five months and for most of that period 'he was a bill of expense to the Institution on account of sickness.' The inspectors added that he was 'now at work,' thus intimating that his pardon should be refused at least partly so he could work out his 'debt' to the penitentiary. The provincial secretary responded that 'having procured a report of the case' from the inspectors, it was not one with which the government could interfere.

In Anthony's second petition the negative decision proceeded from the recommendation of the inspectors and no direct reference was made to the earlier assessment of Justice McLean. Perhaps encouraged by their influence in such cases and by their good relationship with members of the Reform government, the inspectors in May 1852 placed before Morin important recommendations pointing towards the development of new pardoning procedures:

In studying every interest of the Provincial Penitentiary we have come to the conclusion that a judicious clemency in extending the Royal Prerogative in granting pardons, has a good effect in keeping alive hope in the minds of many who otherwise would sink into despondency.

And if such pardons were strictly confined to the orderly and well conducted, great good would arise to the Institution by holding out a hope which would be beneficial to the convict as well as the Institution, as it would stimulate him to control his bad temper and bring it into subjection, that after a proper lapse of time he might become a good member of society.

Having briefly put the positive case, the inspectors boldly condemned the existing system. 'Instances are on record,' they pointed out, 'where pardons have been granted through other influences than good behavior.' 'Some have been pardoned in the face of upwards of sixty records in the punishment book against them; others whose conduct has never been inquired into; others have been pardoned while they had only partially learned their trades. Indeed one convict very lately complained to the Warden of being turned out on a pardon before he had completed his trade.'[10] The inspectors left the government in no doubt that, in their opinion, the effect of such a policy on the penitentiary had been thoroughly bad.

   To test their support, Nelson and Dickson placed before the government the names of several men 'whom we conceive by their good conduct and long imprisonment most entitled to Your Excellency's clemency.' These included a case of rape, one of burglary, and one of arson.[11] There were, they noted, others 'whom we would wish to bring under Your Excellency's notice from time to time for pardon if it is Your Excellency's pleasure so that it might stimulate the convicts to good conduct by the prospect of pardon, instead of depending on the exertions and influence of their friends without.' The official reaction was all that the inspectors had hoped for, the requested pardons being granted within days. The government's response referred not only to the convicts' good behaviour in prison but also to 'the salutary effect which such exercise of the prerogative may reasonably be supposed to have upon the other convicts.'

Nelson and Dickson had achieved a major breakthrough. The needs of the institution, it seemed, had become an important consideration in the pardoning process. In confirmation of their new role, the assistant secretary was instructed to add that, 'with reference to the concluding portion of your Report, that H.E. will be happy to receive and give his full consideration to the cases of any of the convicts that you may think proper from time to time to bring under H.E.'s notice.'[12] The triumph seemed complete; just what it would mean in practice, however, remained to be determined.

In the months ahead the inspectors put forward a number of names of convicts whom they considered deserving. Perhaps because of their earlier success, they were now willing to propose convicts imprisoned for relatively brief periods. In August 1852, for example, they presented two men, both of whom worked as stone masons; one had been sentenced to five years' imprisonment, the other for seven years, and both sentences expired in January 1853. Describing these prisoners as two of the most profitable and well-conducted men in the institution, the inspectors regretted that their release would mean a financial loss for the penitentiary. 'But we conceive on the whole there will be a gain ... by inciting others to conduct themselves in an exemplary manner.' Once again, Morin acted positively on the inspectors' recommendation. These and other cases seemed to confirm that an important new policy had been established in the Canadian criminal justice system.[13]

But that was not to be. The return to office of the Conservatives, with John A. Macdonald as Attorney General, Canada West, saw a reassertion of unimaginative traditionalism. The change became apparent in November 1854, when Nelson and Dickson recommended pardons for two convicts convicted of rape. Their recommendation took the form of a petition to the governor general, transmitted through the provincial secretary, Pierre Chauveau. They reported that 'these convicts have been the longest confined of any except three who are in for the crime of murder and both had been well behaved.' The government agreed to the release of one convict, but adhered to an earlier negative decision in the case of the other who, John A. Macdonald explained, 'should be obliged to undergo imprisonment for the full term, as the punishment cannot be considered severe or disproportionate to the offence.'[14] In this case, as in others, Macdonald showed no interest in the institutional considerations that had in part motivated the penitentiary officers and the previous government; for him the verdict of the courts remained sacrosanct.

Only a few extraneous matters could move Macdonald in the direction of a pardon, and of these the ill-health of the convict seems to have been

the most important. In taking advice, Macdonald held the recommendations of the Assize judges in the highest regard and viewed the officers of
the penitentiary as functionaries whose duty did not extend far beyond
the narrowly custodial. They were to carry out the instructions of the government and maintain order in the prison, nothing more. The busy attorney general doubtless had no inclination to read the reports of the officers
of British or foreign prisons, and whether he ever did more than scan the
reports prepared by Canadian prison officers is open to debate. In this
field, the criminal law, Macdonald was supremely confident that he knew
best what should be done; as his scribbled comments on other petitions
indicate, he had little patience for the views of subordinate officers.

In October 1854, for instance, a petition was presented by a Mrs Foley
on behalf of her son Patrick, convicted of manslaughter, who had served
six and a half years of a seven-year sentence. It was supported by a prominent farmer for whom the father had worked for many years. Macdonald's very full report on the case confirmed the type of considerations
he deemed to justify pardons. He looked first to the nature of the crime
and reported that 'the manslaughter was of a most aggravated kind.'[15] As
for Foley's behaviour in prison, Macdonald would say only that 'his conduct is said to have been good.' He had learned the trade of cabinetmaker
'and will I hope [here the sceptical Attorney General had crossed out the
word "expect"] leave the penitentiary a better man than when he entered
it.' Macdonald had little to say about such factors as the family's alleged
respectability, its recent ill fortune, and the support offered for the petition by a leading member of the community, although one suspects that
they may have determined that he would give the case some attention. 'I
cannot recommend his discharge merely because his conduct in penitentiary has been good or because his mother, whose husband is said to be
insane, stands in need of support from her son.' In dealing with petitions
Macdonald consistently refused to consider good conduct or the dire
state of the offender's family as cause to justify release.

On the other hand, the circumstances of the prisoners' families often
weighed heavily with the penitentiary inspectors and when present in
concert with good behaviour in the penitentiary and where the prisoner
had served a substantial portion of a long sentence, a positive recommendation was likely to be forthcoming. In the Foley case, Macdonald did not
even refer to the fact that the prisoner had only a few months remaining
in his sentence. Although he had expressed the hope that Foley might
emerge a better man, it seems not to have been a consideration with him
that, for someone soon to be released in any case, a timely exercise of

mercy and of concern for that convict's family might contribute much to ensuring that he left the penitentiary with a positive attitude. Macdonald was consistent throughout a long career; he believed in deterrence through punishment; rehabilitation was a distinctly secondary and not entirely likely prospect.

Perhaps as part of an effort to persuade members of the government, the inspectors offered a full analysis of the benefits of pardons in their 1855 report. For Nelson and Dickson, royal clemency was properly part of the penitentiary's good behaviour system and as such must be an integrated part of a full institutional program.[16] 'The most powerful auxiliary to the success of prison discipline after "the magic influence of kindness,"' they continued, was the granting of rewards for good behaviour. Showing more regard for the feelings, 'nay, the very rights' of the prisoners would result in great improvement in their conduct. 'For the maintenance of good order, and a profitable government of prisons, and for the furtherance of reformation, the most powerful adjuvant to kind and humane treatment, would be the exercise of the Royal clemency of pardon.' Their experience in dealing with John A. Macdonald may have persuaded the inspectors to urge that the subject be dealt with by legislation, even though 'there might be some difficulty in enacting a law of this kind.'[17]

The prisoners themselves quickly became aware that something significant was afoot. In July 1856 Nelson, while walking through the dining hall, was virtually thronged by convicts 'who were desirous of obtaining pardons.' To all such inquiries he responded 'that if such indulgence would be granted, that it would only be in consequence of very good behavior.'[18] Already, one suspects, the hope of pardon was affecting how many convicts deported themselves. But the attorney general for Canada West remained indifferent to such considerations. There was to be no legislation on the subject and there is no indication that any major change occurred in the formal procedures of the pardoning process.

Nonetheless, in at least one case, that of Elijah Williams, the attorney general alluded to conduct within the institution as a consideration in remission. The provincial secretary's files for 1856 contain correspondence respecting the pardon of six long-term offenders that raises important issues about the procedures being followed at that point. One of the six had been sentenced to death for murder in 1843; his sentence had been commuted to imprisonment for life. A second had been sentenced in 1840 to death for murder, and he too was apparently serving a life term. Another, sentenced to death for bestiality in 1846 was likewise serving a life sentence. What was curious about the matter was that Assistant Secretary Meredith in a July 1856 letter to the warden asserted that he had been unable to locate any information on the other three convicts. 'I shall thank you therefore to advise me as to the nature and date etc., of their respective sentences.' On 6 August the warden responded that the fourth convict had been sentenced to death for bestiality in 1847, which sentence had been commuted to life imprisonment; the fifth had been sentenced to five years' imprisonment for horse stealing in 1852; and the sixth had been sentenced in 1854 to three years' imprisonment for manslaughter. The same day that he supplied this information the warden reported that all six convicts had been released. One wonders who took the initiative and especially whether Macdonald had become more sympathetic towards pardoning even persons convicted of such serious crimes as bestiality and murder.[19]

These pardons may or may not have resulted from political intervention. Certainly, it would be hard to make a case that the process in Canada was ever abused to the extent that it was in some American states. It is difficult to believe that Macdonald on occasion might not have been moved by an appeal from a political friend, or that he might not have taken special notice of a petition signed by local worthies. But, notwithstanding the argument made by the inspectors in 1853 about the illegitimacy of some pardons, there is no evidence that the process was ever subject to gross abuse. Taken together, the many comments written on petition files in John A. Macdonald's hand demonstrate only that he was a hard man to persuade and that he believed, reasonably enough, that the considerations that influenced Nelson and Dickson represented one element, and not the most important element, in a sensitive area of judicial administration.

The annual reports of the chaplains provide data on numbers released and some sense of what influences shaped individual decisions. In 1856 Mulkins reported that, of the Protestant convicts that year, one woman and fourteen men had been pardoned. Of these one was an Indian, and one a black; the rest were white. The black had served about sixteen years of a life sentence for murder. According to Mulkins, the granting of pardons to convicts of different race and nationality proved that the prerogative was being exercised impartially, and that 'the deserving alone have felt its influence.' Yet Mulkins's breakdown demonstrates at least one clear area of bias: those who were married were far more likely to be pardoned than those who were single, notwithstanding that far larger numbers of single persons were in confinement. One convict was a widower, five were single, and nine were married. As for offences, three had committed crimes against the person, including one murder; one had committed a brutal 'unnatural' offence; and 'eleven had committed serious crimes against property.' Most of those released had come to prison 'almost wholly without instruction – intellectually and morally.' In Mulkins's judgment, the penitentiary had succeeded in giving them an education so that 'nearly all of them can write, and all can read the Word of God.' Most had learned useful trades. Judged by their good conduct, all, he believed, would be good citizens 'and some of them sincere Christians'; 'society has no just cause of apprehension from their liberation.'[20]

The relatively small number of those who received this boon, however – in 1858 thirteen Protestant convicts received pardons, in 1859 only eight – probably accounts for the absence of public concern or political opposition.[21] By contrast, the perceived threat posed by ticket-of-leave men in England touched off a furor in the late 1850s and played a role in the development of harsher attitudes toward criminality in the 1860s.[22] The English, and especially the Irish, ticket-of-leave systems represent early examples of pardon being transformed into earned remission programs. In Canada, however, the restricted use of pardoning meant that it had failed to become part of a broad strategy of penal management. The innovations advanced by Nelson and Dickson respecting the prerogative of pardon had been presented as part of a larger system of good conduct classification, and the Conservative government's steadfast opposition to changes in pardoning procedure weakened any impulse towards a good conduct system or any other of the reforms associated with Crofton and Jebb. By mid-decade, the inspectors had lost their initial enthusiasm as they continually saw their proposals ignored by the attorney general and his colleagues. In 1855, in the same report in which they wrote so eloquently of the benefits of an institutionally based system of pardoning convicts, the inspectors remarked that they had 'very few suggestions to make that they have not already made in all their former annual reports; yet very little action has been taken upon their recommendations.'[23]

The final word belongs to Macdonald and demonstrates the extent of the attorney general's influence on the nineteenth-century penitentiary. In 1861 Macdonald explained his views to Chief Justice Robinson. It 'has not been the practice,' he told Robinson, ever since the fall of the Reform government, to review capital sentences that had been commuted to life, 'unless on petition from the convict's friends, or representations from the Judge who tried them, or on evidence of danger to life' from continued imprisonment. Macdonald emphasized that he was 'opposed to second commutations if they can be avoided, lest we might drift by degrees into the American system.' In the United States, he noted disdainfully, 'if a man can only contrive to escape execution, it is of little importance what may have been the nature of his crime, or period fixed for his imprisonment.' For Macdonald, the American criminal justice system had suffered the worst consequence of democratization and politicization and become corrupt. 'In a short time his case is forgotten by the public, and his friends get up petitions to the Governor for his release. Political influence is used and the convict is released.'

The attorney general made it clear to Robinson that his experience had not led him to attach much importance to the convict's behaviour in prison. This depended largely on temperament; the most brutalized man was often docile and obedient behind bars, while the man of imagination was most likely to chafe against confinement and to get into 'the black books of his keepers in consequence.' Having held firm to this belief for almost two decades, Macdonald resolutely maintained his long-standing faith in the sanctity of the courts and the legitimacy of the traditional appeal process. Nothing, certainly not the needs of the penitentiary, which existed to carry out the judgment of the courts, could be permitted to disturb the majesty and certainty of the Crown's judges to try and decide and of the Crown's duty to punish.

Macdonald drove these Beccarian convictions home one final time in the early 1870s in a letter to John Creighton, early in Creighton's tenure as Kingston's warden. The power of release, he told Creighton, 'should be exercised very sparingly. Certainty of punishment and more especially, certainty that the sentence pronounced will be carried out is of more consequence in the prevention of crime than the severity of the sentence.' If anything the passage of time had strengthened the prime minister's contempt for American criminal justice. 'I believe,' he stressed yet again, 'that one great cause of the prevalence of crime in the United States is the ease with which pardons can be obtained from the Governors of the several States through the political process of the friends of the convicts.' For those who shared Macdonald's beliefs, Canada's national system of criminal justice and appointed judges was incomparably superior to the American structure, where control lay at the state and local levels and, finally, with that turbulent popular element that DeTocqueville had viewed so disdainfully in the 1830s. With Macdonald ensconced almost permanently as the keeper of the gate, few Canadian prisoners would make their way to the other side until the expiry of their sentences.[24]

AFTERCARE

If Macdonald had some reason not to hand authority for pardoning over to penitentiary officers, there was less excuse for government inaction in aftercare. The subject had been raised frequently by penitentiary officials in the 1840s, it had figured largely in the proposals of the Brown Commission, and it was a theme to which Nelson and Dickson often turned. In 1852, they seemed satisfied with the role played in this area by the chaplains, who communicated with the friends of the prisoners 'with a view to procuring them a kind reception on discharge, as well as to be prepared with some employment for them.' Although this increased the chaplains' already arduous duties, the inspectors were satisfied that they carried out this function 'with much alacrity and interest.'[25]

These comments notwithstanding, in the following years the inspectors expressed grave concern about what happened to convicts in the critical period after discharge. In 1853, they contrasted the large number of philanthropic associations in the United States with Kingston where there was but one woman who had taken the discharged prisoner in hand, Mrs Robert Cartwright, who visited the female prisoners each week. They had no doubt that the number of recidivists would be much smaller if more citizens would lend themselves to such efforts. Discharged prisoners who had no one to take any interest in them were often victimized by 'human vultures' who lay in wait in groggeries to deprive them of the small sum they received on release. To avoid this regrettably frequent occurrence, the inspectors advocated the establishment of an association to procure lodging and employment for prisoners before their release.

In the same report, Hannibal Mulkins deplored the lack of benevolent associations to aid convicts and lamented that there was no 'House of Reformation' to which they might be transferred in the period prior to their absolute discharge. In these circumstances, Mulkins initiated the suggestion, which was taken up cautiously by the inspectors, that deserving convicts receive a small portion of their earnings as an allowance. This would help them on release and provide an incentive to good behaviour in the institution; some of this money might also be given to prisoners' families or laid out in procuring books so as to be drawn upon over a period of time.[26]

Like most constructive suggestions, these were ignored and in 1856 the inspectors were reduced to a feeble defence of the few efforts that were then being made to help the discharged prisoners. To prevent them from being readily recognized as ex-convicts, they were given 'plain and decent' clothing of a type that all working men wore. To ensure that they did not remain in Kingston, 'where there is such a number of vile resorts for the vicious,' they were conveyed to the railway station and their fare was paid. Furthermore, the warden wrote to each family informing them when the prisoner was to be released, so that some relative 'might come and receive them.' The inspectors 'hoped' that by such methods 'the majority of the released prisoners will escape the toils of the harpies ever on the watch for them.' Beyond clothes, a railway ticket, and a token sum of money, the inspectors offered only the platitude that society had a duty to 'tender the hand of the Samaritan to the fallen man.'[27]

In these comments, Nelson and Dickson again confirmed the views expressed by Henry Smith and the inspectors of the 1840s. Wolfred Nelson did so even more forcefully in six rambling pages of his 1858 report on the subject 'Assistance to Discharged Prisoners,' in which he bluntly claimed that society was 'criminally remiss' in its duties to those persons. With the law's vengeance satisfied, the discharged prisoner found that 'the prejudices of the world are stronger than ever against him.' The result: 'he must perish by starvation, by his own hand [suicide] or he must be guilty ever more.' Nelson claimed that he could offer a thousand examples of such injustices.[28]

This was marvellous Victorian melodrama, provoked perhaps by too literal a reading of Victor Hugo. But was hyperbole based on fact? Was it really the lot of most ex-prisoners to so excite the revulsion of the community? Nelson's claims are astonishingly similar to those made by penitentiary officials during the previous decade. While he may have exaggerated, his comments had a firm basis in reality and as such they offered considerable insight into contemporary attitudes. In mid-Victorian Canada, the convict who had experienced years of penitentiary discipline elicited public fear and loathing, which had seldom been present in the case of those released from gaol. This stigma, like the mark of Cain, was one of the most far-reaching consequences of the penitentiary system. From comments made over several decades it is evident that these feelings cut across all classes. The ex-convict found at least as little, and probably less, sympathy from the working class of society as from other social groups – possibly because the working class aspired to respectability even more passionately than other classes, and feared being tainted by association with those who had spent years in a penitentiary. The working class was also more vulnerable to crime and its consequences.

What seems puzzling is that, while associations to help former prisoners existed elsewhere, they did not in Canada. Nelson, for example, noted in his extended 1858 discussion the role played by philanthropic associations abroad. But he doubted that the explanation for such a conspicuous philanthropic failure lay in the fact that Canada was a young developing country, since many charitable and benevolent societies had been established in other fields. Nelson could find no ready explanation. Possibly the revulsion and sense of moral condemnation with which Canadians viewed the ex-convict was reason enough.

But fear and revulsion can hardly account for the failure to assist helpless children about to be thrown friendless back on their own resources. Teacher James Gardiner was appalled, and cited numerous cases of young boys overwhelmed by anxiety at what might happen to them on release. For example, there was a nine-year-old orphan convicted of petty larceny and sent to the penitentiary for three years. As the date of his release approached, he became despondent. When Gardiner expressed surprise that he seemed unhappy about being released, he confessed that 'I have no one to do anything for me, and the trifle of money which ... each prisoner receives when discharged ... will not be sufficient to pay my way to Montreal where my sisters are now living, and what I am to do I know not.' When Gardiner approached an officer of the penitentiary for assistance for the child, he was rebuffed. On liberation day, in the middle of winter, he took the boy to his own home until he was able to find someone to take him to Montreal.[29]

CRIMINAL CAUSALITY AND REHABILITATION

The penitentiary officers of the 1850s, including the inspectors, chaplains, teacher, and warden, were united to varying degrees in the belief that many convicts could be rehabilitated by institutional programs. They shared, too, the conviction that society had a responsibility to help convicts because many of them, as the inspectors put it, were 'more sinned against than sinners.' The prison officers were charged by statute to make use of their experience to gain insight into the causes of crime. Through daily association with convicts, through questions put to them on entry and prior to release, and through the compilation of masses of statistical data, a duty which fell particularly to the chaplains, they had become better able than most to develop insights into the criminal personality. The results of these efforts to comprehend the causes of crime, however, were of no particular value, and no dominant causal determinant emerged in the minds of prison officials. Officials at Kingston often differed as to which factors were more significant in leading persons to crime. The warden, true to form, seemed most ready to posit a theory of innate evil. Many convicts, he wrote in 1855, 'are guilty of crime from the effects of vicious dispositions, that is a mind prone to evil.' Apart from viciousness of mind, Macdonell regarded the conventional sins of intemperance and idleness as 'the main sources from which this Institution is furnished with so many subjects.' For Macdonell, it was an 'established fact that intemperance is the road to ruin, particularly in families where the parents are addicted to liquor, by which means the children have so unfortunate an example.'[30]

If his wide experience led him no further in his analysis of criminal causality than the commonplaces of the day, Macdonell also remained less optimistic than his colleagues about rehabilitation. Thieving, he argued, was in many instances 'found to be so strong a propensity that it is impossible to conquer it.' He had seen many convicts leave with the best of intentions, but no sooner were they out than they fell into their old practices. Macdonell was persuaded that 'a second theft establishes the character of the perpetrators for life.' His solution was to imprison recidivists for very long periods. Such beliefs did not prevent him, however, from supporting the introduction of a good behaviour system; it may be assumed that he believed both that the institution would benefit from such a reform and that he would be free to punish the recalcitrant as much as to reward the well-behaved.[31]

The inspectors presented a less bleak perspective. In 1855, they indicated that the increase in numbers incarcerated had been less than anticipated, given the decrease in the demand for labour and 'the dearness of every article of consumption.'[32] If it was conventional to see a relationship between the crime rate and the state of the economy, it was also commonplace to point out that the numbers in the penitentiary would be fewer if discipline in the gaols improved. Like the warden, however, the inspectors believed that 'many are born prone to evil from physical confirmation, which the best domestic training cannot always counteract or remedy;' unlike Macdonell they felt considerable sympathy for those born with an hereditary taint. The inspectors were more alert to the fact that 'with not a few, sentiments of villainy are inculcated as points of duty to vicious parents, and obedience to unscrupulous masters; commendation and caresses are bestowed for successful acts of deception and villainy.' It was curious that the inspectors in this analysis did not seem to draw on information gathered in their line of duty; at any rate they seldom referred to the character of individual convicts, to the discharge books, or to other records kept by prison officers; instead, they were content to generalize on the basis of impressions and foreign literature. Possibly more regular contact with the convicts would have led them more towards the warden's scepticism. On the basis of what information they were able to garner, they concluded that many prisoners were 'far more deserving of commiseration than cruel and relentless chastisement.'[33]

The inspectors' most extensive effort to understand the causes of criminality made little reference to the inmate population. It was the product of the enthusiasms of Dr Nelson, who had recently served a term as Reformist Mayor of Montreal. The inspectors announced in their 1856 report an intention 'to impart their views to the whole country' because the fullest cooperation of society was needed to prevent the spread of crime. This was especially the case because there was 'much reason to apprehend' that criminal activities were 'fearfully on the increase.' To this end, the report included a section entitled 'Prevention of Crime,' which argued forcefully and at length that the cause of 'half the mischief so prevalent in the Country is to be attributed to the confined dirty cottages and lodgings set apart for the poor.' The susceptibility of such communities to epidemics carried off the adults and consigned 'tens of thousands' of 'the wretched offspring to fill the future ranks of prostitution, mendicancy and crime.' The inspectors described the 'thronged courts, blind alleys, garrets and cellars, where numerous families live crowded to suffocation, even in the same apartment' as 'the prolific nurseries of the most aggravated vices.' In focusing upon the criminogenic effects of slums, the inspectors were influenced by what they read of social conditions in the great cities of the United Kingdom. After noting the views of British writers, including Matthew Davenport Hill, and applauding the efforts of Prince Albert to erect model housing in London, they cited the chaplain of Pentonville: 'the only sure way to diminish crime ... is, ameliorate the condition of the poor and laboring classes, who supply the vast majority of trespassers.'[34]

Certainly, an analysis of the crimes for which individuals were sentenced to the penitentiary adds weight to the inspectors' socio-economic analysis. Throughout the pre-Confederation period the convict population (excluding the military) was composed primarily of major property offenders (see Table 7.1). It is significant, however, that there was a continual increase in the percentage committed for crimes against the person.

Attributing the propensity of the working classes to crime to social conditions beyond their control represented a substantial advance over earlier opinions, still held no doubt by many, that the poorer classes proceeded to crime through immoral behaviour. As a remedy, however, the inspectors did not advocate change in the relations of capital and

TABLE 7.1
Crimes of All Inmates, 1835–1864, by Five-Year Percentages

Years	Crimes against the person	Crimes against property	Crimes against morality and public order	Other
1835–9	4.33	89.82	0	5.85
1840–4	9.34	79.94	0.52	11.2
1845–9	12.65	78.08	2.9	7.82
1850–4	18.82	73.03	1.98	6.17
1855–9	17.36	73.05	1.31	8.27
1860–4	18.89	72.05	1.37	7.69

Source: Annual Reports

labour; rather, they offered a narrowly paternalist solution. The more favoured members of society, they urged, should take an interest in the well-being of the lower orders by 'an occasional visit to their homes,' in order to 'encourage frugality, and the cultivation of the domestic virtues, inculcate the necessity of school instruction, give a book or two to the little ones.' The inspectors, without being specific, also called for the erection of 'decent tenements' and urged that every class of worker be provided with 'reasonable remuneration.' By directing the attention of the public to the circumstances of the poor, Nelson and Dickson were making the case for social responsibility. The environmentalist approach of late eighteenth century British reformers remained to the fore in mid-century Canada.[35]

Chaplain Hannibal Mulkins was less persuaded than the inspectors of the relationship between crime and economic circumstances. Reporting in 1856 on the seventy Protestant convicts discharged that year, he stated that 'a majority of them had trades, or some stated occupation, and possessed therefore, a means of living which should have placed them above temptation.' Several possessed a degree of education 'which might, and it seems had, secured them employment in respectable positions.' Mulkins admitted that the largest amount of crime, 'as might have been anticipated,' was committed by persons lacking regular employment. 'It is merely possible,' he asserted, 'that the increased expense of living has borne heavily upon this class in the community, and led to the evident increase of crime,' but in Canada cases in which a man could not obtain an honest living 'must be rare.' Furthermore, economic need could hardly explain why some men committed 'the most degrading and appalling crimes.' No fewer than 224 out of 395 Protestant convicts were members of the labouring class and they had committed nearly every crime against the person and the worst crimes against property. Only 171 of the Protestant convicts had trades or fixed occupations. According to Mulkins, about one-fifteenth of the population were members of the labouring class, 'and yet, it produces nearly two-thirds of the criminals, and half of the murderers and most revolting crimes committed amongst us.' 'The labouring population, or more correctly speaking, the population having no stated employment or trades, living from day to day on mere chance occupation, is beyond all dispute the most criminal class among the white population.'

Mulkins's experience led him to conclude that not economic need but deficiencies in education and moral training had led many of that class to crime. Although many were not without some education, this had been sadly deficient and had served 'merely to develop and gratify the lowest propensities, but had neither enlightened the conscience nor expanded the intellect.' Many could not read well enough to understand the meaning of what they were reading. About one-fourth were unbaptised, and all were without sound Christian instruction. 'Not one, on entering the prison, professed himself a Christian in reality.'

Next to class, Mulkins identified national origin as the most important indicator of criminality. Here and in other reports he remarked on how frequently criminals were immigrants. Only 99 of the 395 Protestants remaining in the prison were native-born, and only one-quarter of crime in the country was indigenous. No fewer than eighty-three convicts were natives of the United States: 'Although the American population in Canada is not numerous, being only 56,214, yet one-fifth of the crime in the Province originates with it. The English-born convicts are eighty-two; the English population in Canada 93,929; yet, though nearly double that of the United States, it produces less Criminality. The Scotch population is 90,376, while the number of Scotch convicts in the prison is only twenty-nine.' Finally, there was race: 'It is remarkable that out of a small Negro population, amounting at the last census to 8,000 souls, and probably now to twice that number, one-eighth of all the crime in Canada is produced; a fact that indicates with evident distinctiveness, the terrible demoralization of its victims by slavery.'

It is not surprising that Mulkins reached conclusions about the causes of criminality which emphasized his own role as chaplain and educator in the rehabilitative process. Despite his differences with the inspectors, he too said little of inherited or genetic propensities and remained firmly in the environmentalist camp. At one point he claimed to expect to redeem relatively few of the convicts, but for most of the 1850s Mulkins remained optimistic. The best test of success, he argued, was behaviour after release. With former prisoners dispersed about the country, it was impossible 'to obtain any accurate account of their moral deportment after leaving the Prison.' Yet, 'of one thing we are certain, that very few return on recommitments.' On the basis of his statistical analysis, which remained unequalled until after Confederation, Mulkins was fully persuaded that the penitentiary experience was successful. 'The behaviour of discharged convicts,' he argued, was 'the best test of the institution's moral machinery,' and there were then in the prison only thirty-five Protestant convicts on recommitments.[36]

At mid-century then, although there was a consensus that some proportion of the convict population could not be rehabilitated, there was also agreement that many convicts, perhaps a majority, were susceptible to reform through the inculcation of moral and religious precepts, educational training, and the provision of the skills needed to earn a living. The statistics offered in such profusion by Mulkins to demonstrate the extent of success, if they did not prove this case, must have convinced some. To an extent, the generally hopeful environmentalist analysis present at the institution's birth, which held that people could be remade in controlled environments, continued to prevail into the second half of the nineteenth century.

THE HUMAN EQUATION

There is one school of thought in the literature on nineteenth-century social control institutions which argues that facilities such as prisons and asylums, while genuinely reformative in theory and to an extent in practice, underwent a fundamental transformation within decades, if not years, of their establishment. Confused in intent, starved for funds and, above all, increasingly overcrowded, they experienced a relatively rapid decline in just about every respect. Ceasing to be reform facilities, they became narrowly custodial in nature, warehousing masses of humanity at the cheapest possible price and subjecting their inmates to indignities and cruelties without number.

It is difficult to make this case for Kingston Penitentiary. The penitentiary, as we have seen, was reformist in origin only in the limited sense that it was created by a Tory ruling elite acting on John Robinson's axiom that 'order is heaven's first law.' It was intended to punish and to deter and, as part of this exercise and whenever practical, to reform. But the Tory understanding of human nature was not an optimistic one, and even the moderate Conservatives of the new generation, most obviously John A. Macdonald, never really expected the convicts to be born again. Reformers such as Nelson, Mulkins, and a few others were marginalized, outnumbered even in their own institution by tough-minded realists like Aeneas Macdonell and Angus MacDonell. Moreover, the penitentiary, an expensive operation for a small colonial society, was expected to pay much of its own cost by keeping the prisoners constantly at work, and the imperatives of dawn-to-dusk labour all but buried the rehabilitative impulse. A few politicians, such as Charles Duncombe and George Brown, it is true, possessed a somewhat different and more hopeful vision, but all too often their own proposals for change failed to point in a practical direction. Brown, in particular, proved incapable of transcending the Auburn disciplinary system, which expressed so effectively a rigorous vision of social control achieved through unending labour and lengthy imprisonment.

For these reasons, the changes proposed by the Brown Commission and implemented in the statute of 1851 offered no real prospect of effecting fundamental change, nor were they intended to do so. The compliant inspectors, Nelson and Dickson, and the efficient warden, Aeneas Macdonell, were apt representatives of the narrowly circumscribed reform enterprise of the 1850s. Under their leadership, Kingston Penitentiary became a well-run prison of the old Auburn type, nothing less, nothing more. Under the prodding of the well-meaning Nelson, the warden implemented a few changes which, in minor ways, perhaps made imprisonment more humane for some. Yet even a cursory glance through the penitentiary's minutes and reports makes clear the horrible sufferings of many wretched individuals who lacked the strength or the will to survive in an unrelentingly punitive environment.

The best source for many of these cases is Aeneas Macdonell's daily journal, which records the pathetic efforts of a few poor souls to resist the juggernaut of state power wielded by Macdonell with much efficiency and little human sympathy. In addition to the occasional suicide and the frequent resort to whipping, Macdonell, in flat and unemotional prose, recorded the desperation of human beings whose only means of resistance was often refusing to eat or to work. 'Old Tipple,' for example, 'will neither walk or work – so that he has to be dragged backwards and forwards like a dog.' Cornelius Ryan passed much of his time lying rigidly in the punishment cell, refusing all nourishment. There would be no need of an autopsy, Dr Sampson anticipated, as it was obvious his death would be from starvation. Convict Foster, described by the warden as 'a very bad man' who was 'at the head of a conspiracy to break out of the Toronto Gaol,' was frequently guilty of 'general bad conduct and acting the madman.' Macdonell considered him 'the most debased convict in the institution' and awarded him frequent punishments.[37]

And there was the tragic case of William Dill. A doctor from Dundas, son of a prominent Irish minister, Dill was convicted in 1849, perhaps wrongly, of raping a patient who was alleged to have been his mistress. Sentenced to death, he won a commutation to life imprisonment with the support of such local worthies as Sheriff Cartwright-Thomas of Hamilton, who had noted 'the possibility that there may be circumstances which constitute the crime to be one of less magnitude.'[38] The prison records tell the tale of a man deprived of his senses by long years of silence and hard labour. Perhaps, as a man of education and previously high station, Dill suffered more than those who had never been so privileged; doubtless a convict unjustly convicted suffered most of all. But what contributed most to create despair and a loss of sensibility in convict Dill was the gradual realization that he had no hope of pardon, having once already been the object of mercy. John A. Macdonald made clear in his response to several petitions that there was little prospect for a 'double commutation.' In 1856 the desperate man escaped and made his way to New York state. The years of imprisonment had left their mark, however; he returned to Canada after a few days in a dazed condition and was recaptured. Macdonell ordered four dozen lashes with the cats but Dr Nelson countermanded this, fearing that Dill might not survive, and instructed instead that he be chained in his cell every night for at least six months.[39] Told that he had forfeited any hope of a pardon, Dill lost his will to live. Subject to fits and often unable to work, he died in 1864 a relatively young man. The story of William Dill, with its stark portrayal of the effects of nineteenth-century prison discipline on the human spirit, differed little from that of numerous other convict lives of the day.

But the convicts were not the only ones to spend long years behind the walls. Like many a subsequent warden, Aeneas Macdonell often had more to contend with at the hands of his lower-class and frequently hostile guards than he did from the convicts. Macdonell often felt that the government was forcing him to employ some of the worst dregs of Canadian society, and perhaps the worst of these was his long-time acting deputy warden, one Samuel G. Murray. The warden's daily journal is littered with complaints about Murray who, it seems, was incredibly lazy and spent most of his time avoiding his responsibilities. 'I am sincerely of opinion,' Macdonell wrote on 10 August 1855, 'that there is no greater humbug in the country than this man Murray. He has nothing to do but to go about the Institution and look to the Convicts and it is not done.'[40] Other officers were simply crooked. In November 1854 guard Morris, arrested for stealing penitentiary property and released on bail, absconded before his trial; in November 1855 guard Flanagan was charged by Murray with stealing from the shoe shop and the convicts also claimed he was stealing their food. Flanagan was dismissed. There were almost as many complaints from the contractors about guards as from prison officers about contractors. In April 1856 a guard was dismissed after a contractor complained he was using the convicts to do personal work; in 1857 there was an investigation into pilfering of firewood and also the dismissal of the kitchen keeper for theft involving an elaborate kickback system.

There were occasional references to guards associating with ex-convicts and humiliating them outside the institution.[41] Most serious were reports of brutality against the convicts. The hospital keeper, in particular, was a man of cruelty and the object of numerous convict complaints. Juveniles were afraid to report sick because of fear of him.[42] The most notorious incident occurred in 1857, when the hospital keeper killed a patient. According to board minutes, 'Convict Waterson recollects Convict Berube being brought to the hospital ... the Keeper asked the patient where he felt the pain' and when he pointed to his stomach 'the Keeper then said I will damned soon take that pain out of you and gave him a pretty severe blow in the stomach.' Berube groaned terribly and died a few hours later, with the doctor being called for only at the last moment. Guard Atkins, who evidently observed some of this, described the hospital keeper as a tyrant. The punishment? 'Dr. Nelson reprimanded' the Hospital Keeper and told him 'to be careful for the future as a similar circumstance would lead to his dismissal at once.'[43]

With wages low and formal qualifications non-existent, little could be expected from the guards, and the warden understood as much. Nelson and Dickson worked to maintain discipline and numerous guards were dismissed for such offences as drinking and sleeping on the job, but Macdonell and the inspectors also worked hard to improve conditions for all officers of the prison. They were willing to listen to the guards collectively and they did their best to make their case with the government. Thus on 27 June 1854 the minutes note that 'the warden has again laid before the board the case of the Keepers Salaries, likewise the Guards have waited upon the board as a body to represent the low state of their wages and the high state of all necessaries; the board therefore deem it their duty to again press upon the notice of the Government the necessity of having their salaries raised in a corresponding ratio to other men similarly engaged.'[44] Evidently this effort was unsuccessful and in August, when two senior keepers threatened to leave, the warden was directed again to draw the attention of the government to 'the earnest desire of the Inspectors' that an increase be granted. In January 1856 the guards won a small increase, but salaries remained low and the penitentiary was expected to carry on with a calibre of employee in whom the warden could place little reliance.

Everything considered, the penitentiary under the dual inspectorate functioned as well as could be expected. It performed the unpleasant tasks that politicians and people had given it. It punished and doubtless it deterred although, despite Mulkins's statistical pyrotechnics, deterrence is always difficult to demonstrate. The penitentiary seems to have excited in most of its inmates a desire not to return, and in that sense it contributed to the rehabilitation of an unknown number of criminals. It performed these functions in an environment which, despite occasional inmate violence, was reasonably safe, secure, and healthy; and that was a considerable achievement.[45] It provided some convicts with a smattering of education and some skills which might be of use in finding employment after release. But it did so in a way that created feelings of revulsion in society at large for all who had spent time within its walls, and it failed to offer any guidance or assistance to convicts after release. Moreover, through its disciplinary regimen and the punishments it imposed it broke the health and spirit of many prisoners and left them scarred forever.

Nelson and Dickson, as we have seen, became such an integral part of the institution's life that in the end they were incapable of exercising critical judgment. The revitalized board that assumed control in 1859 viewed the successes and failures of Kingston Penitentiary in a very different light. The assessment of this new board would differ in almost every respect from the self-congratulatory conclusions provided by the dual inspectors.

8

Institutional Rigidities and Punitive Policies: The Penitentiary's Enduring Reality

Just as the 1850s began with a new statute and the prospect of genuine reform, so the 1860s held out an excellent opportunity for progressive change in the penitentiary. This time the impetus came not from a scandal succeeded by legislation, nor from sources inside the institution, but from forceful leadership within the Canadian bureaucracy. Although new statutory provisions passed in 1857 for penitentiary governance provided the framework for change, the forward thrust came from the astute, determined leadership of E.A. Meredith, secretary and later chair of the newly created Board of Inspectors of Prisons, Asylums and Public Charities, assisted by several of his eminent colleagues. But political forces, both local and national, together with the intractable realities of penitentiary life, were powerful enough to defeat the bureaucratic impulse and accompanying pressures towards modernization. And it turned out, the failure of Meredith and his fellow workers to achieve the majority of their goals was decisive. For the remainder of the nineteenth century and the first half of the twentieth, the institutional rigidities and punitive policies that shaped the Canadian penitentiary would prevail. A terrible oppressiveness in the dreary routines of the institution endured from the 1830s to the middle of the twentieth century.

THE BOARD OF INSPECTORS

Wolfred Nelson, who led the inspectoral team of the 1850s, was a strong advocate of extending systematic public inspection to a wider range of social institutions and of providing an expanded inspectorate with important new functions. Writing in 1854 to Reform leader A.N. Morin, he supported the claim of Dr William Rees of Toronto, formerly head of the temporary asylum, to a position on a new type of public authority. 'A Sanitary Board,' he assured Morin, 'is very much wanted equally for the benefit of the sick, the stranger, the alienated and the infirm.' Such a body, he claimed, would save the country thousands of pounds annually and 'would relieve the adminstration of a vast amount of trouble and vexation.'[1]

Rees, although a seeker after patronage, spoke for an ever-widening group of middle-class professionals and urban dwellers who looked to the extension of state authority as a precondition of social progress. As Rees told Morin, for many years there had been an 'almost universal complaint,' expressed most frequently in the newspapers, about the need for improved inspection and administration of public institutions. As a remedy, he proposed the creation of a 'permanent Establishment or Commission to superintend the hospitals, asylums, prisons, and Penitentiary.'[2] Such a system, he said, already existed in most European countries.

But Wolfred Nelson was the most influential proponent of reform. Fresh from his term as mayor of Montreal, where he had advocated the establishment of appointed bodies to address sanitary concerns, Nelson lobbied the new Cartier–Macdonald government in 1856 'on the necessity,' as he put it, 'of establishing a Board of Inspectors for the supervision of our Public, Charitable, Penal and Sanitary Institutions.' Nelson assured Rees that '[o]ur friends the Ministers would reap great popularity and consideration' by establishing such a board.[3]

Pressure for such reform was by no means restricted to the urban middle class and the professional community. Grand jurors charged with the responsibility of inspecting county facilities had equally weighed in on the side of structural change. The most frequent complaints of grand jurors focused on the gaols. The local gaol, said the grand jurors of Ontario County in 1856, exhibited 'a total want of suitability in any respect.' Its condition, they pointed out, 'presents a glaring example of the necessity which exists for general Legislative interference in respect to such buildings' to protect the public 'from the ignorance of the men who project, and the incompetence and jobbery of those who construct them.' To that end, the Ontario County jurors called for 'one general law' to govern the future construction of prisons and the appointment of a commission 'with power to inspect, report on, and if necessary condemn' all existing gaols if they had been erected without 'proper attention to the classification of prisoners, their comfort and safety.'[4]

Other factors also influenced the decision of the government to create a powerful new agency with responsibilities for penal and welfare institutions. The continuing controversies which beset the governance of the provincial asylum and the pressing need to expand the services provided for the mentally ill were much to the fore in local and provincial political circles. And the friction which had emerged between penitentiary officials and Dr Joseph Workman of the Toronto Asylum may have persuaded the government of the value of attempting to achieve greater coordination and integration of existing and emerging welfare services. Doubtless the prospect that Drs Nelson and Rees held out of saving money through increased efficiency had considerable appeal. So too did the possibility of heading off potential political pitfalls by placing penal and welfare matters in the hands of self-proclaimed professionals: Canadian politicians in the turbulent Union years, constantly faced with sectional and sectarian strife, were understandably anxious to lessen their own burden of responsibility.

The 1857 statute that established the Board of Inspectors also advanced various measures of gaol reform and provided for the creation of two juvenile prisons and the asylum for the criminally insane at Rockwood.[5] But it was the granting of extensive powers and responsibilities for both public and private welfare institutions to an appointed board that made this legislation such a bold and progressive measure. Clause 14 stated that it was expedient to establish 'a uniform system for the government and inspection of Public Asylums, Hospitals and Prisons.' The reference to 'government' in addition to 'inspection' indicated that the board was intended to play an active role in developing policy and in supervising the entire range of administrative functions in these institutions. Apparently, too, the authors of the bill and their advisors believed that a commonality of approach was called for in the governance of public facilities. Thus the government did not merely continue the existing prison inspectorate and create a new board for other eleemosynary institutions; rather, it brought all welfare and penal institutions together under a single integrated inspectorate. In the objective, the establishment of 'a uniform system,' one suspects, may be seen the fine hand of the assistant provincial secretary, E.A. Meredith. By virtue of his position, Meredith was aware of the challenges facing not only the penitentiary but all of the country's social institutions, and his experience undoubtedly contributed to the decision to endeavour to achieve the important bureaucratic objectives of uniformity and integration of function and control.

The new inspectors were five in number, including a chairman and a secretary. Holding office 'during pleasure,' they received all the powers and responsibilities then vested in the penitentiary inspectors and in the commissioners of the provincial lunatic asylum. This was essentially a transfer of existing authority. The instruction that the inspectors were to 'visit and inspect all gaols, Houses of Correction and prisons as often as may be determined upon by them or ordered by the Government, and at least twice a year,' constituted a greater break with the past. In carrying out these new responsibilities, they received the power to examine all officers and employees, to inspect all records, 'and to enquire into all matters concerning the said place of confinement.' In addition to collective inspections and reports, each inspector was required to make individual inspections and to file a separate and distinct report. The statute's provisions respecting gaols marked a significant encroachment of central authority over localism and traditionalism. In deference to the continuance of local administration of gaols, the inspectors' authority over those facilities was restricted to inspectoral and limited supervisory and financial powers. But henceforth county councils would have to receive the approval of the inspectors for all new gaols and for additions and alterations.

The statute required the inspectors to consider numerous matters affecting the health, classification, and security of the prisoners, and to frame a comprehensive set of rules and regulations. Other provisions, potentially at least, brought private as well as public institutions more fully under the authority of the state. The inspectors were to inspect every private lunatic asylum whenever required to do so by the government but 'at least once a year.' On receipt of an adverse report the government might revoke that institution's licence. Hospitals and benevolent institutions supported wholly by public money were to be inspected at least twice a year, while institutions supported only in part by state funding (which was the case for most general hospitals) were to be visited by the inspectors as required by the government.

The government's intentions in enacting the 1857 statute are not entirely clear. For one thing, no efforts were made in either 1857 or 1858 to implement the Act. And the consolidated statutes of 1859 included, as Splane notes, a separate Inspection Act containing all the provisions relating to inspection that had been included in the statute of 1857, although presented in a more orderly fashion and at much greater length.[6] The board was established under this second statute on 9 December 1859 and held its first meeting on 27 December. The distinguished membership suggests that the government was fully seized of the importance of the new initiative. It included Wolfred Nelson as chair, until his death in 1863; Dr J.C. Taché, a Conservative politician and man of letters who succeeded

Nelson as chair; and E.A. Meredith, who remained as assistant provincial secretary and became secretary of the board. Meredith, a member of a well-known Anglo-Irish family, had been president of McGill College before joining the government service, where he became one of Canada's most respected public servants. When Taché became deputy minister of agriculture in 1864, Meredith assumed the chair. The appointment to the new board of John Langton, a prominent figure and Canada's first auditor, confirmed the weight and authority of the new board. J.E. Hodgetts described Langton as 'an able, forthright and courageous official' who laid the basis of Canada's 'modern system of budgeting.'[7] Finally, Aeneas Macdonell's appointment to the new board signalled the government's continuing confidence in his administration of the penitentiary.

This was an impressive group. Yet there was some uncertainty as to whether the government fully understood the implications of its own legislation. The government may have supported the measure, as Nelson suggested to Rees in 1854, primarily as a means of heading off larger expenditures and relieving the ministers from having to deal with the details of innumerable social problems. Certainly it refused to let the expanded inspectorate assume effective control of the policy-development function, and the board in the nine years of its existence often found that political support was lacking for its recommendations.[8] Many of its objectives, as Splane notes, 'were not attained.'[9] The board itself entertained no doubts about its role, and in its first report, dated 23 March 1860, complained that it lacked sufficient authority to perform its duties. The board members believed, understandably, that the legislature had given them responsibility for 'the general direction of Public Institutions,' and defined their task as follows: 'To have to watch over the progress of all the penal and charitable institutions of a great country ... to be in a word, charged with the direction and control of every thing relating to the administration of public charity, and with the execution of the punishment inflicted by justice ... to have moreover, to investigate the causes of the sufferings and crimes which afflict society.' [T]o have all these duties to perform,' they concluded, 'is, it will be admitted, to be charged with highly important functions.'[10]

The board expected to exercise those functions with a degree of independent authority that set them apart from ordinary civil servants. Their reports are liberally sprinkled with criticisms of government policy and complaints about restrictions on their powers. By 1866, board members had concluded that few advances would be made in social policy until their own authority was substantially expanded: 'the simple authority to report was all but nugatory, especially when reiterated reports failed to attract attention, or at least to bring about a remedy.'[11] No one, it seems, asked why these responsibilities should reside in an appointed board, rather than being exercised directly by a department of government that could assume both responsibility and authority.

The inspectors misconstrued their true position. Macdonald and his colleagues were willing to allow the board members a degree of latitude, but in the final analysis they were to follow ministerial instructions. Moreover, the policies the board promoted were also subject to all the demands and vagaries of the political process. To the extent that board policies were ignored or rejected, this was attributable as much to the hostility of the elected representatives of local government as to opposition from Macdonald and his colleagues in Cabinet.

Its political difficulties notwithstanding, the board was an impressive achievement, an outstanding manifestation of the public service ideals of Canada's professional gentlemen. For its members, and in particular Meredith, Langton, and Taché, public welfare issues were properly approached through rigorous scientific investigation and the systematic study of foreign advances. The inspectors explained the procedures they intended to follow in a preliminary report and again in their full 1860 report. The first step must be data gathering; only when information had been collected and analyzed would it be 'possible to apply in Canada those important principles connected with the administration of Public Institutions, which the last few years have brought to light in other countries.'[12] To deal with such a formidable task, the inspectors divided their work as much as possible by region and established five permanent committees: accounts, correspondence and records, hospitals and asylums, penitentiaries and prisons, and information and statistics.

Determined to apply rigidly scientific principles of analysis, the board began by studying the substantial volume of materials forwarded 'from the Public Offices, as bearing upon their peculiar duties.'[13] Prominent among this documentation were years of grand jury reports focusing on the gaols. These etched an indelible impression on the inspectoral mind. They concluded that the gaols were 'frightful,' a shameful blot on Canadian society, and this conviction shaped many of their efforts over the life of the board. It was partially responsible for their determination that, except for 'a few well-conducted institutions,' it would be necessary to begin anew.[14] Impatient with the perceived backwardness of facilities that still bore the marks of their pioneer origins, the inspectors were convinced that they alone possessed the mandate and were positioned to acquire the knowledge to bring Canadian social institutions up to international standards.

To create the requisite knowledge base they sent extensive questionnaires to the sheriffs, chaplains, and medical officers of all local gaols. The questions were framed, the inspectors reported, 'to bring out in their true light the main facts connected with these institutions, and at the same time, to form the groundwork of the statistics which the board felt to be absolutely necessary.' The data gathered they condemned as 'most deplorable.'[15] Not a single gaol in Canada carried out the objects for which it was intended; in many there were no rules of any kind for either employees or prisoners. Gaol reform became the inspectors' highest priority.

The inspectors instinctively believed that reform must proceed from the top down, in the form of rules and regulations imposed from the centre on the province's far-flung territories. The perceived chaos of local indifference, if not ignorance, was deplored, and short shrift was given to the stubborn refusal to understand the emerging centrist conviction that timely expenditure was the way to true economy. Backwoods farmers, ill-educated craftsmen, and petty local merchants could not be expected to comprehend this truth; it became the duty of the trained professional to overcome tenacious local resistance and put the modern policy in place.

The inspectors thus vastly preferred the order and symmetry of the large, centrally financed and controlled institution to the frequent disorder and perceived inefficiency of local gaols, municipal poorhouses, and private hospitals. Working in an era before sociological analysis had blackened the reputation of the total institution, they were impressed by the apparent state of order and responsiveness to central dictates exhibited by the penitentiary, the asylum, and other national facilities. Although they admitted there was room for improvement, the inspectors held that 'these large institutions, without exception, presented a marked and most pleasing contrast to the common prisons ... and ... do honour to the country.'[16] In these facilities the Canadian state, via paid officers, made its presence felt through the enunciation and enforcement of fixed rules and firm discipline. Where rules were imposed from above, it was relatively simple, at least in principle, to effect improvements simply by issuing orders and changing the rules. The large institution was a society unto itself, and the new inspectors cherished it as their society. It was a place, above all other places, where the sense of order and regularity so beloved of the centrist mind existed in full measure. If the Cabinet members – and for most of this period that meant John A. Macdonald – could be persuaded to share this vision, then there was no insuperable obstacle to implementing the bureaucratic ideal.

An integral part of the case for extending this controlling vision to the most remote extremities of the Canadian state was the financial saving to society. Localism and disorder, the inspectors loudly proclaimed, were costly features of the old system which their own efficiencies would remedy. By their calculations, the average annual cost of maintaining a prisoner in a gaol was $123.42, whereas in the penitentiary the cost was only $78.85.[17]

But for the new bureaucrats cost, however important, was far from the most essential consideration. What professional insight and scientific knowledge had, above all, to offer was the potential to change and control the way the world operated. Meredith, Taché, and Langton were confident that the combination of education, training, and dedication that they exemplified gave them every opportunity to actually achieve that to which an earlier generation of reformers, the John Howards and Elizabeth Frys, had been able only to aspire. With the support of government, they could bring to bear the best of international practice and achieve the rule of law – their law – in Canadian social institutions. Nor did they hesitate, as Nelson and Dickson had hesitated in the early 1850s, to lay out their goals and objectives. Brilliant and determined, they were rather in a hurry, if only because Meredith believed that he had been seconded to the position for a brief period and on a part-time basis and would soon be returning to other duties.[18]

First they turned to the gaols, described contemptuously as *'public boarding houses'* in which n'er-do-wells could find food, shelter, and comradeship whenever it suited them, 'with the certainty of getting out within a few days of whatever time may suit them.' Most of the inmates, the inspectors believed, 'enjoyed their detention.' Gaols were controlled by the prisoners and run for their convenience, whereas in the penitentiary convicts were classified, put to hard labour, taught a trade, given adequate food and medical attention and, most importantly, received religious instruction, 'without which reformation is impossible.'[19]

The sheriffs' returns, in particular, led the inspectors to conclude that the laxity of the common gaols had nurtured in Canada an entire class of debased and demoralized criminals. Some prisoners had been convicted 'as often as seventy-six times and one, actually one hundred and sixty-three times.' The gaols, they asserted, were 'to a large extent filled by a class of persons who ... systematically take up crime and vice as a profession.' Despite their espousal of statistical analysis and the scientific method, the new inspectors concluded on the basis of little evidence and less analysis that society was beset by a criminal class. Like others of the mid-Victorian generation, the members of the new board were persuaded that society was threatened by a group composed of individuals who began their careers as drunkards, prostitutes, and petty criminals and went on to become thieves and murderers.[20]

The prejudice demonstrated by the board did not, however, undercut the value of their positive program. Central to their scheme of reformation was the idea of the intermediate prison. The existing gaols, they argued, should become 'mere places of confinement for short periods of persons awaiting trial' or for those given brief sentences for minor offences, while new central prisons should be established in the principal cities and serve as 'Houses of Correction' for all those recidivists who were not convicted of major felonies. The inspectors expected to play the leading role in planning and administering the new prisons.[21] Note was also taken of the absence of any penal facility for delinquent girls comparable to the reformatory prisons for boys, and the inspectors recommended the establishment of a girls' reformatory as an essential companion to the male institution.[22]

This was an ambitious agenda to be developed at so early a stage of the board's work. As the principal liaison between the board and the provincial secretary, Meredith pressed this program on a government which must have wondered a little about how to control its own zealous servants. In a February 1861 letter to the provincial secretary, Meredith submitted the board's 'Special Report on the subject of Central Jails,' which argued that central prisons must form 'the basis of the reformation of our Prison system.'[23] And the inspectors emphasized that these central prisons must be designed so as to effect significant changes in the prisoners. Consequently, they required a special organization, an adequate staff of officers, and suitable buildings; and 'ample means of religious and industrial instruction.' Anticipating that many would reject such a system as too elaborate and expensive for a country like Canada, the inspectors claimed that in Canada more than elsewhere conditions determined that reform could be achieved only through centralization of policy and resources: 'the necessity is felt all the more from the fact that the population in most of our Counties and Districts is scanty and their resources but very limited.' Each central prison would therefore receive all prisoners from a group of counties in its neighbourhood committed for more than three months and less than three years. For recidivists, the length of sentence should be increased. Most important, central prisons 'should be placed on a similar footing as to organization and management with the Penitentiary and Reformatories.' In the inspectors' minds, these provisions would ensure an end to the obfuscations of local control.[24]

The reform agenda bore striking similarities to the regional detention centres eventually established under the Robarts and Davis administrations more than a century later,[25] and some features, particularly the more punitive ones, found expression in the establishment of a single central prison in Toronto in 1874. But in the 1860s the proposal to scatter central prisons about the province was too ambitious and too costly. And advocacy of such a program may have done more harm than good, if it caused provincial politicians to question the judgment of Meredith and his inspectoral colleagues.

But E.A. Meredith was nothing if not bold. From the board's commencement, he questioned time-honoured practices which prevailed in the penitentiary. Backed by Langton and Taché and, presumably, by the provincial secretary, Meredith in fact questioned almost everything. By the second quarterly meeting of the new board in May 1860, the warden of Kingston Penitentiary probably began to realize that he was no longer dealing with a compliant inspectorate. For one thing, the inspectors were suspiciously anxious to participate in the questioning of convicts on discharge, and in doing so they exhibited a new and unsatisfactory attitude to the convicts. As a minute of 30 May noted about one man whose five-year sentence had just expired: 'the examination of the man, who seemed intelligent and well disposed, was very interesting.'[26] This was heresy. It betrayed an attitude to the prisoners that would cause the warden no end of annoyance and worry.

Even more disturbing was the inspectors' inclination to challenge Macdonell on vital matters of discipline. At the June meeting Taché and Langton raised the issue of the long-standing ban on tobacco. Notwithstanding the prohibition, they noted that 'the Convicts are frequently supplied with tobacco through the contractors and their foremen' and that 'this leads to a systematic violation of the Prison Rules, and is one of the most frequent causes of punishment of convicts.' While it is not clear whether the inspectors realized the role played by illicit tobacco in the complex functioning of Kingston's prisoner subculture, they understood that its use was 'attended with many other serious evils.' They concluded that they could see no objection to the convicts receiving tobacco 'when it is supplied by their friends or by the Contractors or others' so long as it was always given to the warden for distribution.[27]

Having thus grandly altered the delicate balance of institutional power, the inspectors turned next to the ongoing problem with the chaplaincy. They expressed 'surprise and regret' that communion had never been held in the Protestant chapel and directed Mulkins to proceed forthwith to hold communion. Recognizing how little communication had ever taken place between the convicts and the chaplains, they took immediate steps to increase personal contacts. If necessary, the convicts 'should be called from their several occupations' to receive their religious ministrations.[28] The inclination to place religious needs ahead of convict labour was striking evidence of a new order of priorities.

The strongest challenge to the old regime, however, was the inspectors' growing conviction that many of the guards and keepers were little better than rogues themselves, and that many of them treated the prisoners with wanton brutality. The first official notice of this was taken in the important inspectoral minute of 1 June 1860, on the occasion of the new board's second quarterly visit. The inspectors

observed with regret that in many instances the Convicts complain of the harshness and severity of the Keepers and Guards. Under these circumstances but without adding to these complaints more importance than ought to be attended to them the Inspectors think it incumbent on them to impress on all who are placed over the Convicts the necessity of exercising towards them every kindness and consideration consistent with a due observation of the discipline. To enforce discipline strictly is the first duty of the Officers, Keepers and Guards, but in doing this they should carefully abstain from all unnecessary unkindness or sternness in word or act.

It should also be remembered ever by all who have to do with Convicts that they are men, and men, who, from the trying nature of their position, are peculiarly liable to be softened by kindness or hardened and rendered callous by harshness or want of feeling.[29]

This minute effectively challenged Aeneas Macdonell's administrative style and called into question some of his most cherished beliefs. It resulted before long in a degree of hostility between warden and inspectors that affected everyone in the prison. The board took the unprecedented step of publishing the minute of their meeting and communicating it to all prisoners. To Macdonell this action was nothing short of high treason, but Meredith was delighted at its effect. The convicts, he boasted, had become firmly convinced that the inspectors had their best interests at heart.

The crusty old warden could not contain his rage over some inspectoral initiatives. In May 1861 Meredith and company were hearing out convicts who desired to complain of punishment practices. As Meredith told the story, Macdonell during this exercise, 'displayed a lamentable lack of dignity and temper. He told both of the convicts that they lied and actually with his own hand collared "Murphy" and put him out of the Board Room. Losing sight not only of his own position but of the respect due to the board. The board should have checked him and ordered the convict back, but the age of the warden prevented this step from being taken.' Instead Dr Nelson, as his oldest associate, was deputed to tell Macdonell that he had 'acted in a very unbecoming way and to be more guarded ... in future.'[30]

In Meredith's view, someone who could behave so violently in the presence of the board almost certainly made the convicts' lives miserable when outsiders were absent. His scepticism towards the guards, the warden, and even the former inspector, Dickson, contrasted with his charitable opinion of many convicts, made Meredith an almost unique figure in nineteenth-century Canadian penitentiary life.

In 1862 Macdonell, in an uncharacteristically reckless gesture, made his prolonged displeasure with the board's June 1860 minute public in his annual report. The order, he claimed, had tended 'to draw retorts from convicts when spoken to by the overseers and guards; consequently, altercations at times ensue, which lead to reports of misconduct and insubordination.'[31] Macdonell lectured the inspectors severely, telling them to 'keep in view that well-disposed convicts seldom come into contact with an overseer or guard.' It was those with habitual discipline problems who blatantly broke the rules. Speaking from his vastly superior experience, Macdonell warned the inspectors of the possible consequences of their misguided initiatives. In the Massachusetts State Prison the warden and his deputy had been murdered, and even in England convicts turned upon their warders. A lax state of discipline, he warned, 'is a dangerous experiment.'[32]

But Meredith was not a man to be bullied in this way. The inspectors defiantly reprinted their earlier resolution and they also drew the government's attention to their own by-law, giving every convict the right to be heard by the warden before receiving punishment. This, they claimed, was 'a fundamental principle of justice' and its absence had led to 'ridiculous and painful mistakes.'[33] Meredith was even franker in his condemnation of the Macdonell regime in his private diary.[34]

The new board's practice of holding frequent hearings with convicts to hear complaints or just to gather information yielded much evidence to

Third Gaol, Toronto, 1840–60, Front Street East, between Berkeley and Parliament Streets, 185–? Watercolour by Frederic V. Poole, ca 1912. After a pen and ink drawing by W.J. Thomson.   Metropolitan Toronto Reference Library, J. Ross Robertson Collection T11970

Public execution in Ontario, possibly Windsor or Guelph, date unknown.
Photograph by Frank Kiborn, Windsor, Ontario, loaned to National Archives of
Canada by David G. Perch

The Central Prison of Ontario, Toronto.   Archives of Ontario, L113

Central Prison guards.   City of Toronto Archives SC214 #5

Central Prison, Cordage Mill, 1902, from Ontario, Annual Report, Inspector of
Prisons and Public Charities, 1903

Kingston Penitentiary, convicts at work.   Kingston Picture Collection,
Queen's University

The Andrew Mercer Reformatory for Females and Industrial Refuge for Girls, Toronto.   Ontario Sessional Papers

Carleton City Jail.   National Archives of Canada PA12371

'Polly,' inmate at Carleton Jail, 1875.   National Archives of Canada PA27436

Inmates at Rockwood Asylum.   National Archives of Canada C58821

Aeneas Macdonell, warden, Kingston Penitentiary, 1848–69.
Archives of Ontario

Wolfred Nelson, penitentiary inspector.   National Archives of Canada CB3484

E.A. Meredith, assistant provincial secretary and chair, Board of Prison
Inspectors.   National Archives of Canada

John Beverley Robinson, attorney general, Upper Canada, 1818–29; chief justice, 1829–62.   The Law Society of Upper Canada Archives, Photograph Collection P. 1053

George Brown, publisher of Toronto *Globe* and Reform politician. Metropolitan Toronto Reference Library, J. Ross Robertson Collection T15091

Harriet Dobbs Cartwright, Angel of Mercy. Queen's University Archives,
Grier Collection

John Macaulay. Kingston Picture Collection, Queen's University Archives, copyright Agnes Etherington Art Centre

Hugh C. Thomson. Kingston Picture Collection, Queen's University Archives

John A. Macdonald, attorney general, Canada West.   Kingston Picture
Collection, Queen's University Archives

John Woodburn Langmuir, Ontario prison inspector, in later life.
Metropolitan Toronto Reference Library T32930

confirm Meredith in his opinions. Two prisoners who appeared before the board in May 1861 claimed to have been frequently punished unjustly on the basis of guards' reports 'and that the Warden would not hear them in their own defence.' Meredith had no doubt, 'from the Warden's own confession,' that there was much truth in this. If the convicts were not allowed to be heard and there was no appeal from the reports of the guards, then 'great injustice must often be done,'[35] which in turn, he asserted, would create a brooding sense of injustice among the prisoners. Consequently, Meredith persuaded his colleagues to alter the rules in order to forbid the punishment of any convict before he was given the right to defend himself. In a diary entry in the fall of 1861, Meredith expressed pleasure that Macdonell was now required to investigate all complaints against the convicts before assessing punishment.

During his inspection in the fall of 1861 Meredith became increasingly critical of prison personnel. 'It was clearly shown,' he recorded in his diary, 'that the convicts (especially the life convicts) were in great dread of the guards and keepers, and also that the guards sometimes induce the convicts to steal for them. Money circulates ... very freely among the convicts.'[36] One investigation that caused grave concern involved the women's quarters. The female quarters were overcrowded and conditions had deteriorated greatly. Then came disclosure of a rather incredible prison counterfeiting ring masterminded by the institution's long-time teacher, James Gardiner.

'It would appear,' thundered the *Daily British American*, 'that the institution designed for the suppression of crime and the safe-keeping of criminals has actually afforded facilities for the perpetuation of a most dangerous evil.'[37] An American convict named Spragge, by trade a jeweller, had been sent to Kingston for counterfeiting. While there he was recruited by Gardiner, who held out various promises, including assistance in obtaining a pardon, to induce Spragge to help him to counterfeit American coins. But Spragge, it seems, was shrewder than Gardiner realized. According to his own story, he felt pangs of conscience at what he was doing and decided to confide in the chaplain. The disclosures were finally presented to the county attorney.[38]

While Meredith regarded Spragge as 'a cunning fellow' manipulative enough to fabricate information to win a pardon, he was inclined to believe most of what he said, and especially that corruption in the penitentiary went far beyond the teacher. When Spragge claimed that 'a large portion of the guards are dishonest,' Meredith replied simply, 'I believe him.'[39]

Meredith was discreet and he would not have confided in convicts. Nonetheless, the prison was soon alive with the exciting intelligence that the inspectors could be counted on for sympathy and more. This information must have undermined to a degree the position of the warden and his staff and could have created a genuine crisis in penitentiary management. Increasingly, convicts felt free to bring their complaints to the inspectors and Meredith recorded it all.

The highlight of the board's subsequent inspection was the examination of Eugene McSweeny, a convict about to be liberated. Meredith described the examination as 'very interesting,' noting that it seemed 'most painful' to the warden, who got up and left after a few questions 'saying that he could not stand any longer such a pack of lies.' From Meredith's perspective, 'McSweeny mercilessly exposed the warden's administration,' alleging that he 'must be either a very bad man or a very incapable one.'[40] The testimony of McSweeny and other convicts reinforced Meredith's belief that Macdonell's administration was harshly punitive and hostile to the rehabilitative ideals he believed prevailed in Jebb's English and Crofton's Irish systems.

Both sides in this dispute, warden and inspectors, faced formidable restraints and understood that any early resolution of their differences was unlikely. As the warden and his staff struggled with the board for control, it was clear that the 1851 statute had not resolved the difficult problem of who should run the prison. The inmates were not merely a passive force and the attitude of the new board, whatever its merit, offered an opening which clever men like Spragge and McSweeney were quick to take advantage of. The precise nature of the Kingston subculture, and in particular the extent of its power, remains unclear, but there can be no doubt that it was a force to be reckoned with. The stubborn warden probably had a better grasp of this reality than did the brilliant civil servant. The strong sense of responsibility held by both the warden and the inspectors, however, prevented them from allowing their quarrels to get so out of hand as to paralyse the daily administration of the penitentiary. Perhaps the fear of penal anarchy, the memory of the bad old days of Henry Smith, and the chaos of 1847–8, remained etched in official memory. Or perhaps both factions were competing for the support of a government which had yet to indicate decisively where its own sympathies lay.

In such a competition, each side had advantages and liabilities. Meredith remained a man of place and power who had the ear, if not necessarily the full support, of the highest officers of the state. But the warden was the man of experience who could keep a lid on society's most dangerous institution. There was ample testimony from members of the board itself that the warden was running a tight ship. Taché, for example, following a tour of American prisons, reported that he had been wrong in his earlier negative opinion of Kingston. He now believed that Kingston was 'inferior to none' and that 'with all its faults' it ranked as a 'model institution.' In 1861 Nelson reported that 'this excellent Institution' continued 'to merit entire approbation for its superior management.' Inspector James Ferres the same year said that 'under its able warden its order and discipline was everything that could be desired.'[41]

Meredith remained critical. His individual report of 1861 contained a scathing condemnation of the Kingston regimen, which, he asserted, focused not on reform but on coercion. It was 'one of rigid repression, of uncompromising coercion, one which admits no change or improvement in the condition of the convict in consequence of good conduct. Nothing that the unhappy man can do can secure for him the slightest mitigation of his punishment.'[42] Curiously, the other board members, especially Ferres and Terence O'Neill, although not perhaps Nelson, would have accepted this assessment. In their praise of the warden's regimen, they were referring primarily to the order, cleanliness, and sense of security that Macdonell had achieved through his relentless dedication and unwavering enforcement of penal discipline. This they admired but, perhaps perversely, they followed Meredith's lead in also believing that a coercive and repressive regimen had closed the door on reform.

The extent of the board's commitment to Meredith's reform ideology was initially apparent in two documents forwarded to the provincial secretary in September 1860. These were extracts from the minutes of a 5 September meeting of the board and a magisterial report prepared by Meredith on 'certain changes necessary with a view to make the Provincial Penitentiary more useful as a "Reformatory" Institution.' In this report Meredith set out a comprehensive program for penal reform. It was based on the Irish system made famous by Sir Walter Crofton, which was then enjoying a vogue in Europe and America comparable only to the acclaim received by the Auburn and Philadelphia systems a generation earlier.[43] Meredith's early initiative set the agenda for penal reform for the next decade and ensured that the Crofton system would remain in the foreground as the board's major objective.

It was this program that the extract from the minutes of 5 September so strongly endorsed, including 'a system of Conduct Classification of the Convicts, accompanied by gratuities to the well-conducted Convicts'; the employment of some of the best-behaved convicts on public works, 'with a view to reform and test the character of the Convicts'; and finally, 'the remission of a fixed portion of the Sentence of those Convicts who behave well in the Penitentiary.' The board concurred in these general propositions and proclaimed it desirable to introduce a scheme of classification 'as soon as possible.' Meredith also included a detailed plan for devising and implementing classification and for the keeping of records on convict behaviour. On Meredith's advice, the classification scheme was the only aspect of the proposal set apart for early implementation, and Taché was charged to study the other suggestions. Finally, the board ordered the warden to transmit Meredith's memorandum to the provincial secretary, 'with a view to obtain the assent of the Government to the proposed scheme of gratuities.'[44]

Through sheer force of intellect, Meredith had carried the day. His position as assistant provincial secretary would hardly have been sufficient by itself to persuade his colleagues, if only because he was able to offer no assurances that his proposals would have official support. Indeed, his strategy seems to have been to try to win such support by presenting the government with the unanimous opinion of the full board. Meredith also relied on the prestige of the Crofton system itself, backed by an impressive range of converts in Britain, Europe, and America. It is difficult to recapture the intensity of the excitement that this system ignited among penal reformers. At last, they believed, the cant of the rival American penal systems could be unceremoniously buried; at last it would be possible to reform many convicts and, integral to the process, to persuade society to accept them back into its bosom.

Meredith, proud of his Irish roots, worked skilfully to convince an always sceptical government of the desirability of his program. His 1860 memorandum was the opening volley of a determined campaign, and in his individual report for 1861 Meredith published the principal arguments made earlier in private. He now added, however, that he wished it to be understood that his suggestions were not original: 'They are taken (modified somewhat to suit the circumstances of the country) from the admirable system which has for the last 8 years been enforced with such signal success in the Irish convict prisons.'[45]

Yet Meredith made an unfortunate beginning. In Kingston's discipline, he argued, the objectives of punishment and deterrence had 'apparently, received more attention' than those of reformation, 'yet it can hardly be denied that the "Reformatory" is the highest of these three ends.' Meredith, who knew Macdonald well, should never have flagged this, for the attorney general pounced. 'If by the highest is meant most important to the community,' he scrawled in the margin, 'I would doubt this proposition.'[46] Blissfully ignorant of Mr Attorney's reaction, Meredith pressed on. Reformation, he argued, implied that 'the Institution is intended so to operate on the convict while subject to its discipline, as to restore him to the world, a good man and a useful citizen.' But this was not enough. In common with every other prison inspector Meredith believed that much recidivism was attributable to the hostility society directed toward the ex-convict. It was critical therefore that 'we should endeavour ... to prepare Society to receive the convict on his release.'[47]

To Macdonald this was puerile utopianism. But Meredith, like many other mid-Victorian liberals, retained the earlier belief, shared by utilitarians and evangelicals alike, that evil was not innate, that man was infinitely malleable, and that reform could be achieved through manipulation of a controlled environment. The first generation of penitentiary advocates had faltered not because their environmental analysis was flawed, but because they had been unable to devise a disciplinary system that worked. But Crofton, and to some extent Jebb, appeared to have achieved results which held out the highest hopes. To some degree, the program which Meredith now laid before his political masters had elements of continuity with Auburn. The convict must be taught 'lessons of industry – of the necessity of steady perseverance and providence. We should implant ... feelings of self-respect, self-reliance and self denial.' The convict, Meredith argued, was usually led to crime 'not from any peculiar depravity of disposition, but rather from weakness of character.'[48]

Meredith also believed that the old systems had floundered because their focus was on institutional behaviour and not on the more important reality that one day almost all prisoners would be released. Kingston's discipline was satisfied 'if the convict passed through the term of his imprisonment without any material violation of the discipline of the Institution.' With that as its principal end, the system had become one 'of repression, or coercion, which admits of no change or modification, either in consequence of good conduct or otherwise, from the beginning to the end of the convict's sentence.' While his sentence lasts, 'he has nothing ... to hope for: – Now it is idle to expect any reformation in a convict, unless you give him something to hope for.' Citing the German Von Holtzendorf, who had recently studied the Irish system and concluded that individuals no more than nations could 'be educated to freedom by coercion,' Meredith sadly proclaimed that at Kingston, '[w]e write over our Penitentiary Gate, "Who enters here leaves hope behind."'[49]

The genius of the Irish experiment, however, lay not in fine sentiments;

its success was subject to empirical demonstration, and it was this scientifically verifiable quality that appealed above all to the new inspectorate. As Meredith explained it to his government, the Irish approach, termed 'reformatory prison discipline' by Mary Carpenter, was both a method of prison management and a technique of prisoner reformation based on appeals to self-interest.[50] The scheme which Meredith proposed at this time, however, fell substantially short of the full Irish system, suggesting either that Meredith as yet had an imperfect grasp of the Croftonian program or that he accepted that it could not then be fully implemented in Canada. In Ireland, the prisoner's sentence began with an intensely penal phase of imprisonment in a separate cell in a specially designed facility, Mountjoy Prison.[51] The convict spent the best part of a year there on a reduced diet doing hard and monotonous work. After earning his graduation from this penal phase, he was sent to another prison where conditions improved and where he progressed at his own speed through four distinct levels of classification, with marks awarded for hard work, obedience, and educational aptitude. In the second phase, the convict was paid a small gratuity which increased as he worked his way up to the fourth level. This owed a considerable debt to the great work done earlier in the century by Alexander Maconochie on Norfolk Island. The next phase was more original. On graduation from phase two, the prisoner was sent to one of several 'intermediate' prisons, where he was subjected to minimal restraints and often employed in the community. The intermediate prison provided a marvellous opportunity for the convict to demonstrate that he was worthy of trust. Equally important, it was intended to persuade the public that he was trustworthy.

The fourth and final stage was liberation on ticket-of-leave. Prisoners released under these licences received extensive community supervision. A variation of this system was implemented in England under Jebb's leadership, but less use was made of the intermediate prison phase and release on ticket-of-leave included no supervision comparable to that imposed by Crofton in Ireland. The proposals of Meredith and his colleagues were modest and incomplete in comparison with either Jebb or Crofton. On Meredith's advice the board, in recognition of its own limited authority and in anticipation of resistance from the warden, put into effect only one part of what was intended as a large and integrated scheme of prison discipline, and even that was misunderstood or rejected by prison officers. With some reluctance, the warden implemented a program of convict classification by which well-behaved convicts received badges. But the 1861 report in which Meredith printed most of his 1860 memorandum to the government was curiously silent about how effectively untrained guards were able to administer such a system. The inspectors asserted only that it 'seems to have succeeded very well,' but Meredith's diary, as usual, tells another story. The penitentiary staff, he lamented, was unable or unwilling to grasp the spirit of the new system and did 'not understand the principle upon which it should be carried out.'[52]

Several of Meredith's colleagues were equally anxious to supplement good conduct badges by more substantive rewards, including gratuities and earned remission. But gratuities had to await government action and when this was not forthcoming, the inspectors were powerless to move ahead. The same was true of earned remission. In Ireland the relative lengths of the fixed and changeable portions of the sentence were governed by law and within these limits the prison authorities were given the power to determine the date of release. Spain had adopted a similar system. Meredith did not make a fuller case at this time because he wished to undertake further study and understood that Canadian prison officers, and indeed, the government itself, would have to be educated along these lines before progress could be made.

He was able to say more about the employment of some convicts on public works because he believed the government would be more receptive to a potentially cost-cutting proposal. In Ireland, he noted, the system of employment of convicts in intermediate prisons as the penultimate stage of the discipline had contributed, perhaps more than any other feature, to Crofton's 'signal success.' But he recognized that Irish-style intermediate prisons were beyond the range of the politically possible in Canada, with its farflung territories and a labour market bitterly jealous of convict competition. The answer, it seemed to Meredith, was to employ the convict outside prison walls on public works. In such an environment he could be 'more trusted than when in the Penitentiary.'[53]

Although Meredith, in his published 1861 report, expressed the hope that the board would receive the sanction of the executive and of the legislature for such a system, this was not forthcoming. It is impossible to say whether this was because of the scepticism of members of the cabinet, the success of the penitentiary's existing administrative system, or the warden's hostility to proposals he regarded as dangerous and naive. In his reports of the early 1860s Macdonell continued to demand unconditional support and to argue that strict discipline was the essential condition of safety and security. In a vigorous defence of his administration, Macdonell claimed he used every prudence, especially in the mildness with which he treated occasional minor offenders. Yet there was a class of persons in the prison to whom he would show no mercy, and upon whom 'the good intentions of the board are wholly thrown away.' Macdonell believed that many of this element fully intended to pursue their criminal activities on release and that it was his job to break their spirit while he had the chance. If convicts were not obedient, they must 'be forced to be so.' And this included enforcing strict adherence to the silent system. Backed by the government, supported by public opinion, and running a facility where order and regularity prevailed, Macdonell felt free to tell the inspectors in print that he did not intend to change a system he regarded as already perfect.[54]

In one area of Croftonian innovation there was a measure of agreement between the warden and the inspectors. Macdonell ardently desired the solitary cells advocated by the Brown commissioners, and so too did Meredith. The warden, however, wanted to use them as punishment cells while Meredith wished to deploy them to institute the penal phase of the Irish system. But in this as in so many other areas, Meredith learned that changes that cost money seldom achieved political support, and that penal reform in the politically turbulent 1860s had no profile at all.[55] While the inspectors came to recognize that formidable barriers blocked their path, they refused to back off.

Their 1866 report gave particular emphasis to the need for every convict to endure a solitary phase at the commencement of imprisonment. They noted that solitary cells had been contemplated by the Penitentiary Act itself and called for the construction of about fifty cells at a location outside the walls of the prison. But given government indifference and facing the opposition of the warden, the board was hamstrung. By this date there was some prospect of forcing Macdonell into retirement. In 1866, the inspectors remarked that 'the burden is now too heavy' for his advanced years. Stubborn as always, the old man insisted in his own 1867 report that his health was good. Only nature itself, it seemed, would save the institution from the old warden and in the course of things this could not be long delayed. But the inspectors also had reason to believe that with Confederation about to be achieved and a new statute in the works, the Croftonian day would soon dawn.

In the meantime, their frustration was nowhere more evident than in their powerlessness to end what they had come to regard as the greatest evil of all, contract labour. From its beginning the new board set itself in opposition to the contract system. The productiveness of the labour of the prisoners, they insisted, 'should never be made ... a question of primary interest.'[56] They were not indifferent to the significance of the income derived from convict labour, as their boast in 1860 that the penitentiary was a wonderful bargain, costing a mere $16,000 a year, demonstrated. But they understood the negative implications of convict labour in Auburn-style facilities and recognized that it constituted the principal institutional barrier to all reform efforts. The contract system still held the unwavering support of the politicians because it was by far the most remunerative way of deploying convict labour. It had equally strong support from the warden, who believed quite simply that it was the best way of keeping most convicts busy. The renewal of the contracts, he told the government, was 'of paramount importance.'[57]

By 1861 Hannibal Mulkins, who had railed against the evils of contract labour for more than a decade, was sharpening his attack. The contractors' only objective was to maximize profits. In his 1861 report Mulkins claimed that his close contact with convicts over the years had shown him that the large majority left the prison without having been taught a trade, with only about one in five given the skills needed to find employment. Mulkins related this failure to the extent of crime then prevailing.[58] It was largely owing to the demands of the contractors that the educational needs of the prisoners were almost totally neglected. In 1867 he itemized the numbers who could not read, write, or do simple arithmetic. The school, he insisted, could never 'under existing arrangements, even in a tenth degree, accomplish its purpose.'[59]

Meredith and his colleagues fully concurred in Mulkins's opposition to the contract system and the board's own indictment emerged full-blown in its 1866 report. The contract system had never been widely used in Europe and it had recently been condemned 'by the most intelligent Wardens' in the United States, by the ablest state inspectors and prison commissioners, and most especially by Dr E.C. Wines, one of the special commissioners appointed by the Prison Association of New York State to study North American penal systems. According to the board, the evidence from these sources established 'incontestably' that the contract system was injurious to discipline and hostile to reformation. From their observation of the contract system as it operated in Kingston, the inspectors concluded that it was 'utterly wrong in principle' and 'most objectionable in practice.' It should be replaced by the plan followed in the model prisons of Europe, and especially Ireland, which could take one of two possible forms: work might be carried on inside the penitentiary under the control of prison officers for and on behalf of the state, or the prisoners could be employed on public works. The inspectors favoured the latter alternative as more in accord with the intermediate prison approach of the Crofton system.[60]

Their sense, however, that no progress could be made while Macdonell remained at his post was justified by the warden's adverse reaction to these proposals. The inspectors understood the futility of reply. But they took comfort in the fact that the penitentiary bill then receiving consideration from the legislature 'is so framed as to permit the carrying out of all the foregoing recommendations of the board.'[61] At long last, the goals of the board seemed about to be realized. The reality, needless to say, would fall far short of their hopes and ambitions.

THE PENITENTIARY IN THE NEW DOMINION

In 1866, with Confederation approaching, Meredith campaigned more aggressively to persuade his government to implement the Croftonian system. In January he resubmitted his 1861 paper on penitentiary reform. He reminded the government that only the part relating to convict classification had been put into effect, while other changes 'were, in accordance with my own suggestion, postponed' to allow time for further study and to give penitentiary officers an opportunity to familiarize themselves with classification procedures. But here, he noted, the process had stalled. In a barely disguised allusion to the resistance offered by Macdonell and his staff, Meredith claimed that 'circumstances connected with the internal management of the Penitentiary, which it is unnecessary here to particularize, caused doubts in the minds of the inspectors as to how far the system of classification was carried,' and therefore they had recognized it could not be relied on 'as a safe basis for further changes.' But, he argued, 'the time has now come for urging upon the Government the propriety of amending the law in such a way as to carry out the second recommendation.' Convicts, he proposed, should be given by legislation 'the power of earning by industry and good conduct, an abridgment of a certain stated portion of their sentence.'[62]

What had changed to make Meredith, and presumably his inspectoral colleagues, believe they could achieve their oft-stated objectives? Nothing in the rest of Meredith's submission indicated that the penitentiary staff had become more willing or able to move in the desired direction.[63] Clearly the impending retirement of the old warden combined with the changes in Canadian penal law and circumstances which Confederation would necessarily require provided the opening. The government now turned to its most experienced adviser on welfare issues, who was also its most skilled legislative draftsman, to prepare the impending legislation. Almost inevitably Meredith became the principal author of the 'Act respecting Penitentiaries,' the first penal statute of the new Dominion of Canada, assented to on 22 May 1868, and he took advantage of the opportunity to push forward as much of his program as he dared. The 1868 statute, he later noted ambiguously, was the best that could be achieved in the circumstances.[64]

For the Croftonians, it was very good indeed, the pinnacle of their Canadian success. Such a statute had become necessary, its preamble asserted, because the British North America Act had placed the penitentiaries under the control of the new Dominion government. This included not only Kingston but the smaller facilities in Halifax and Saint John and in little more than a decade would encompass no fewer than five new institutions spread across the vast territories of the Dominion. Section 91 of the BNA Act provided that the Parliament of Canada should have exclusive legislative authority over the criminal law and over 'the Establishment, Maintenance and Management of Penitentiaries.' The provinces in turn received exclusive responsibility for 'Public and Reformatory Prisons in and for the Province' and for hospitals, asylums, charities, and eleemosynary institutions. This division of authority excited much later comment and speculation for two reasons. First, it partially reversed the earlier decision of the Quebec Conference of 1864, which resolved that the local legislatures should have control over both penitentiaries and prisons. Second, it led, together with the provision in the 1868 statute that defined a gaol term as two years less a day (thereby confirming the pre-Confederation practice), to a division of authority in correctional matters which would be condemned by every twentieth-century commission on correctional practices, from Archambault in 1938, through Fauteux in 1956, to Ouimet in 1969, and frequently thereafter.[65] Yet there was a forceful logic to a division of authority which confirmed the traditional status of gaols as local institutions and granted to the new Dominion government, with its responsibility for criminal law, control over a national penitentiary system. Gaols had always been local institutions, serving a range of community purposes, and there was little choice but to confirm this social reality; the penitentiary, on the other hand, had from its very origins served the whole society, and it was equally appropriate that this too was recognized. The decision occasioned little contemporary disagreement and both levels of government moved at once to enforce their new responsibilities.

This division of penal and welfare responsibilities had grave implications for the pre-Confederation Board of Inspectors. Once welfare and gaols became provincial responsibilities, the old board lost the reason for its existence. At the provincial level, Ontario appointed a single inspector to deal with the entire range of provincial penal and welfare functions. The inspector was subsequently granted extensive powers to supervise the construction of new gaols, while the renovation of old ones required him to frame by-laws for all provincial institutions and to provide full financial statements for them, as well as projections of 'the amount of aid likely to be required from the Provincial Exchequer.'[66] The inspector was further asked to prepare full statistical returns and to recommend changes and improvements 'as he may deem necessary and expedient.' The combined responsibility for both penal and welfare institutions was strikingly similar to the powers exercised formerly by the old five-man board.[67]

What of the federal penitentiaries under the new national system? The 1868 Penitentiary Act, although it incorporated key elements of Meredith's cherished Croftonian program, was not otherwise a particularly enlightened or imaginative statute. Necessarily, it worked its way through the dreary routine of functions, powers, and penalties, but the Act neglected to address such critical components of penitentiary discipline as the chaplaincy or educational schemes. Labour programs were mentioned, but only to declare that the convicts were to 'be kept constantly at hard labour, the kind of which shall be determined by the Warden.' The statute assumed that many elements of penitentiary routine and governance would continue to draw on traditions and routines already firmly in place.

The most important change was found in clause 3, pertaining to governance. This provided for the appointment of three directors who, subject to any instructions from the government, were given 'the control and management of all the Penitentiaries in Canada' and also of such other prisons, hospitals, asylums, and other public institutions 'as may from time to time be ordered.' Because of the provincial control of most medical and welfare institutions, the new directors were concerned primarily with penitentiaries. As in the 1851 statute, it was made clear that within the penitentiaries they were to have 'no direct executive power' whatever, except as specifically provided for in the statute. As before, they were to make rules and regulations for the management of the penitentiaries and audit the accounts; they were to be allowed access to every part of the prison to examine all papers and records although, curiously, there was no reference to regular inspections and reports. The government was given the right to appoint the principal officers, although these were subject to suspension by the directors pending an investigation.[68]

Meredith's focus was on several of the Croftonian changes he and his colleagues had been pressing for since 1860 and he was relatively indifferent to other issues. The statute at long last permitted convicts to earn early release by their own efforts: they were given the opportunity to reduce their sentences by up to one-sixth, a significant consideration indeed. The statute further provided that the warden might permit a convict of exemplary conduct to work over hours at 'such work as can be conveniently done in the Institution' at rates fixed by the directors. These earnings could either be paid to his family or held for the convict until release.

Third, it was asserted bluntly that 'no system of discipline in a Penitentiary can be effectual for punishment, or for reformation of the criminal, unless it be combined with strict separate confinement during some period of the time of his imprisonment.' To that end it became lawful for the warden, whenever he deemed it expedient, to order that penal cells be constructed as necessary.

But that was all. There was no reference to the intermediate phase of imprisonment that Meredith had frequently claimed held the key to Irish success, or even to the employment of prisoners on public works, which, he had told the government might be better adapted to Canadian circumstances than intermediate prisons. Nor was there any effort to introduce the final ingredient of the Irish system, release on strictly controlled ticket-of-leave.

Beyond that, other clauses of the Act suggested that the Canadian authorities were doing little to distance themselves from some of the harsher aspects of the Auburn discipline. Thus there was no movement in the direction of paying prisoners even a token amount for their daily performance of hard labour. And the statute reaffirmed the rule of silence, which had numerous negative implications for prison life well into the twentieth century. More positive was the clause regulating punishments. Before awarding any punishment, the warden was required to investigate upon oath the facts of the case, and to present minutes of the evidence to the directors. In no case could more than sixty lashes be inflicted on any prisoner. Other clauses also embodied some of the other changes the board had effected under Meredith's leadership, including procedures regulating the discharge of convicts. With respect to convicts who appeared to be insane, the decision to transfer to Rockwood was to be made by the penitentiary surgeon and the medical superintendent of Rockwood consulting together; the same procedure was to be followed to return convicts once cured from Rockwood to the penitentiary.

The provisions pertaining to the Croftonian system were embodied in 1870 in revised rules and regulations, and should have gone some distance towards fulfilling Meredith's ambitions. But once again, external developments, both British and American, influenced Canadian decision-makers and may have deflected even Meredith from his focus on Crofton. In contrast to the earlier experience, it was the British example which spoke most forcefully at this point. The British in the mid-1860s were abandoning many of the humane policies followed by Jebb in favour of a harsher and more punitive regimen. In part this was the official response to a series of riots and generalized disobedience in British prisons in the late 1850s and early 1860s.[69] Then, a little later, in 1862 and early 1863, there were 'an unusually large number of robberies with violence' some of which were 'garrottings.' Numerous sensational stories in the press contributed to what has been called a moral panic,[70] which in turn resulted in an increased determination in official circles that tougher criminal laws and a more repressive prison regimen was essential to the national safety and security.

These sentiments appeared dramatically in two famous official investigations into the British criminal justice system: a royal commission appointed in 1863, chaired by Lord Grey and including the lord chief justice, was directed to 'Inquire into the Operation of the Acts relating to Transportation and Penal Servitude'; and a Select Committee of the House of Lords on the Present State of Discipline in Gaols and Houses of Correction, which made its report in 1863.[71] That same year the colonial secretary, the Duke of Newcastle, distributed these reports through the British Empire in the hope that the colonies might benefit from the evidence 'so labouriously collected.' The Canadian Board of Inspectors took note of the reports and commented favourably on their contents.[72] Then in January 1865 Colonial Secretary Edward Cardwell addressed circular despatches to the colonies soliciting information as to the state of colonial prisons, 'with a view to ascertain how far they are in conformity with approved models in this country, and what reforms may be required in them.'[73] This demonstration of concern on the part of the mother country served at least to stimulate local interest in recent British thinking on penal matters.

It is difficult to determine the extent to which Canadian prison authorities were influenced by the tough new British approach. Certainly the Canadian prison inspectors had reason to be pleased with the British dispatch, for every aspect of their work was warmly endorsed. The inspectors were praised for the zeal with which they carried out their duties and for their efforts to improve the state of the local gaols: 'the Penitentiaries and reformatories are in most respects in happy contrast with the county prisons. They are liberally managed and efficient, so far as a still imperfect penal system allows.' The colonial office shared fully the inspectors' own sense that they deserved far stronger support from the central authority. The executive government, it concluded, 'appears not to have felt justified in using all the powers conferred' by the 1859 Prison Act 'in support of the inspectors.'[74] This ringing endorsement of his efforts prompted Meredith to assert in a February 1865 letter to Provincial Secretary William McDougall that the circular despatch 'strongly corroborates the views of the board set forth in their Memorandum and in the printed pamphlet which accompanied it and that in particular it assumed "That the separate system must now be accepted as the foundation of Prison Discipline."'[75]

In claiming that the British government endorsed the approach pursued by the board, Meredith enlisted British prestige on the side of his own program. But in doing so he neglected to direct his government's attention to the striking differences between British and Canadian approaches. The 1865 circular despatch expounded the views of both the House of Lords Select Committee and the Royal Commission on Penal Servitude to the effect that penal discipline must be transformed in the direction of harshness and rigour. According to the Lords' Committee, industrial labour should form part of the discipline at certain stages but, in general, 'the chief means of exercising a deterrent influence' must be such strictly penal devices as the crankwheel and the treadmill. The Lords expressed scepticism as to the economic and social value of industrial labour, dismissing claims both as to profitability and to rehabilitative benefit as too difficult to measure.[76] With respect to prison discipline, they said the matter of strict separation or association was most important; the separate system had been tested over many years and was accepted by 'the highest authorities' as the critical element of prison discipline, not only for penitentiaries but also for county and borough gaols.[77]

They also claimed that the dietary should 'form part of the punishment.'[78] Nor was there the slightest doubt as to the efficacy of physical punishments: 'The most experienced witnesses are unanimous as to the wholesome influence of corporal punishment.'[79] The same rigid attitude shaped the discussion of rehabilitation. The Lords' Committee was 'compelled to admit that the reformation of individual character by any known process of prison discipline is frequently doubtful.'[80]

Finally, the Lords' Committee endorsed a memorandum prepared by the lord chief justice, which had been attached to the Royal Commission on Penal Servitude. In it the chief justice stated that society's interest must necessarily lie in deterrence far more than reformation. The reformation of the offender, he asserted, 'is in the highest degree speculative and uncertain, and its permanency, in the face of renewed temptation, exceedingly precarious.' On the other hand, the chief justice was certain that 'the impression produced by suffering, inflicted as the punishment of crime, and the fear of its repetition, are far more likely to be lasting.'[81]

For the next three decades, the British penal system unrelentingly opted for severity.[82] But there seems to be little evidence that Canadian policy makers were strongly influenced by this dark phase of British penology. In part this was because the Canadian government continued to return negative replies to inspectoral requests to visit Britain and Europe to study developments there and direct contacts were infrequent. Whatever the reason, it is impossible to discern in Canada at this time any sharp turn in the punitive direction then being taken in the mother country.

It remained cheaper and more convenient to look to the United States – but here the message was mixed and confusing. In the 1860s the New York Prison Association, which had assumed the mantle of leadership from the defunct Boston Prison Discipline Society, appointed a commission to investigate penal methods across the United States and Canada. Headed by E.C. Wines, a Protestant cleric and educator, and Theodore Dwight, the dean of Columbia University Law School, this body in 1867 produced an authoritative 570–page report which had 'an impact on penal developments in America and Europe second only to John Howard's *State of Prisons*.'[83] Wines and Dwight found little to praise in the prisons they visited. Instead, as American prison historian Blake McKelvey argues, they held up the Croftonian system 'as the most worthy model' for Americans to follow, and they were able to find aspects of Crofton being deployed only in a few reformatories and in the Detroit House of Correction. This institution was headed by Zebulon Brockway, already embarked on the innovative career that won him recognition as America's outstanding warden of the nineteenth century. Brockway recognized that there were many positive features in American prisons; the difficulty was 'to find them, combine them, and apply them.'[84] The American prison reform movement, McKelvey concludes, was effectively re-established in 1865 with the tour by Dwight and Wines and was greatly advanced that same year by the establishment of the American Association for Promoting the Social Sciences. The movement was furthered in several states, most notably New York, Pennsylvania, and Massachusetts, by the efforts of state prison associations and boards of charities. The members of these several boards and associations 'came to regard themselves as professional penologists.'[85] A number of states published schemes for model prisons and gaols and by 1869 the majority of the northern states had passed legislation permitting the commutation of sentences for good behaviour.

The United States prison reform movement culminated in 1870 when some 130 delegates gathered in Cincinnati for the first national congress of an American prison association. The declaration of principles adopted by the Congress set the agenda for prison reform well into the next century. It included the full Croftonian program, including the progressive stage system, earned remission, and indeterminate sentences. It focused also on intermediate reformatories, institutions for juveniles, and even separate institutional facilities for women. In practice, most American prisons in the years ahead, as David Rothman argues, failed to achieve many of these objectives.[86] Yet the American reformers provided a vision of enduring significance and some striking examples of creative innovation and of legal initiatives. These ideals became part of a wider criminological debate in the late nineteenth and twentieth centuries and influenced the objectives and aspirations of prison reformers everywhere. For practical reasons, American influences were stronger than the British in late nineteenth century Canada, yet it is difficult to determine the extent to which either did much to shape Canadian experience.

NEW LEADERSHIP

When James Ferres assumed the post of warden of Kingston on Macdonell's retirement in 1869, the new warden at last had the opportunity to put into effect the strategy of kindness which the old board had believed would soften and humanize the convicts, rendering them more susceptible to rehabilitative influences. Ferres's service as warden was brief and he died early in 1870, but his successor, John Creighton, who served until his own death in 1885, proved equally humane in his attitude to the convicts.[87]

Together Ferres and Creighton did what they could to make life a little better. In 1867, good conduct prisoners had been confined in a special cell block with lighting to allow them to read until nine o'clock, and in 1871 lamps were placed outside their cells. Convinced that it was denigrating to every prisoner to receive another's clothing after laundering, Ferres stamped each item with a number and had it returned to its owner. In

1869, exercise was permitted on Sundays, non-religious books were purchased for the library, and more liberal letter-writing privileges were granted. In 1871, the directors purchased a steam-cooking apparatus to relieve the monotony of prison food. They also approved the introduction of church music into religious services and the best-behaved prisoners became eligible to join a new church choir.[88] These cosmetic changes, all Croftonian in inspiration, portended a revolution in the treatment of convicts but for many reasons they were soon stalled. Convict life in the 1880s and 1890s indeed had more in common with conditions a half a century earlier than with prisoner life in the second half of the twentieth century. Why this should have been the case is suggested by a letter John A. Macdonald, still minister of justice, sent to John Creighton in 1871. Creighton had insisted that 'if a convict's physical comforts are neglected, you cannot convince him that you have any great concern for his moral welfare.' Macdonald responded that he feared that the warden's 'natural kindness of disposition' would lead him to forget that the primary purpose of the penitentiary was punishment:

You say that you desire to feel that you are the means of making five or six hundred of your fellow creatures more happy than they have previously been in the Penitentiary. I could quite sympathize with your desire if it were to make them less miserable ... rather than more happy – happiness and punishment cannot and ought not to go together. There is such a thing as making a prison too comfortable and prisoners too happy.[89]

Nonetheless, Creighton, who had the advantage of being a personal friend of both Macdonald and of Sir Alexander Campbell, who also served as minister of justice, was given some latitude in softening the discipline.

While the Canadian penitentiary in the late nineteenth century was never as self-consciously and unrelentingly punitive in approach as the British system under Edmund Du Cane, it never became as progressive as Wines, Brockway, and the Cincinnati reformers aspired for American penitentiaries. In their 1867 survey of North American prisons, Wines and Dwight commented that Kingston's notoriously small cells were 'the smallest we met with anywhere.' In 1869, the directors finally recognized that constant confinement in such a small space 'is bad for the convicts physically, and bad for them morally,'[90] but the cells remained unaltered until the 1890s. An even greater barrier to humanitarian reform was the administration's unthinking adherence to the rule of silence. This oppressive requirement operated much as it had in the pre-Confederation period to create a stifling, unnatural environment. In many senses in the late nineteenth century the traditional punitive structures played out their grim role, continuing to ensure that convict life must be filled with all but unrelieved pain and suffering. There is every reason to confirm the conclusion of two students of Canadian penal history of this era that little emerged from Confederation to century-end that was liberal or hopeful. According to Richard Zubrycki, 'it cannot be said that this was a period of dramatic changes or advancement. It was a slow, plodding development, rich in rhetoric but impoverished regarding its application.' And for William Calder, 'the direction of later post-Confederation penal evolution was largely determined by the theory and practice developed during the early years of penitentiary operation,' while for the convicts 'the essentially punitive nature of prison life altered little in the period' 1867–99.[91]

Two important features dominated the developments of the period and greatly affected prison life. One was the far-reaching administrative and structural changes that accompanied the spread of the Canadian penitentiary system across the Dominion, from Atlantic Canada to British Columbia. The second was the playing out of that great reform impulse, the belief that prison experience could effect beneficial changes on even the most hardened of felons. This impulse had inspired the program of the penitentiary's earliest statesmen in Canada, including Thomson, Macaulay, Duncombe, and even Smith, and been taken up anew and with different inspiration by E.A. Meredith and his colleagues of the 1860s. Regrettably, however, there was little accomplishment either in developing an adequate administrative structure, or in finding a formula for rehabilitation. Failure in both these areas had dire consequences and the repressive old system simply lurched forward into the twentieth century until, finally, its bankruptcy was fully revealed in the penetrating analysis of the Archambault Commission in 1938.

On the administrative side, the pre-Confederation balance between a powerful Board of Inspectors and a warden with unquestioned executive authority did not endure. The 1868 statute, in its failure even to mention the department of justice, was characteristically vague as to the focus of governmental authority and this proved increasingly unsatisfactory in the circumstances of the new Dominion. In September 1867 Meredith and Ferres were despatched to inspect the newly acquired prisons in Halifax and Saint John. Ferres was appalled by what he encountered. The conditions, he reported, differed 'but little from the Common Gaols' in Canada which the inspectors had so frequently condemned. The prison at Saint

John was horribly overcrowded, while conditions at Halifax were so dreadful that Ferres assumed personal control on the spot.[92] The Dominion faced a formidable task of construction and reconstruction and over the next decade heroic measures were taken to build a national system from coast to coast, using Kingston as the model. The Board of Directors, with James Moylan in the foreground, was actively involved in the establishment of the new penitentiaries of St Vincent de Paul, which opened in Quebec in 1873; Stony Mountain in Manitoba (1877); the British Columbia Penitentiary at New Westminster (1878); and Dorchester in New Brunswick, opened to serve Atlantic Canada in 1880.

To cope with these transcontinental responsibilities, the Penitentiary Act of 1875 replaced the three-man Board of Directors with a single inspector of penitentiaries and explicitly transferred full and comprehensive authority to the Department of Justice, thereby relieving the inspector of most of his power. James Moylan, who had become secretary-director of the old board, now became inspector of penitentiaries, a post he held with some distinction. Although Moylan retained considerable latitude, there was necessarily a new emphasis on centralization and bureaucratization. Moylan's staff was small; he received a full-time clerk in 1876 and in 1888 his operation was composed of 'two officers, an accountant and a third class clerk.' His authority was further limited when an accountant of penitentiaries was appointed in 1879 as a Department of Justice watchdog.[93] One pre-Confederation tradition that continued to prevail was the government's tendency to ignore inspectoral recommendations. In his annual reports, Moylan frequently lamented the failure to send a representative to the international penal congresses which had assumed considerable significance in this period, or even to follow the example of Ontario, which sent its officers to observe American penal operations. Moylan's recommendations that the department hold regular meetings of wardens and institute formal staff training were also ignored. Moylan was blunt about the failings of guards and the damage they were doing to efforts to reform prisoners, but his hands were tied. His concern for female convicts and his recommendation that a separate women's prison be constructed also failed to find favour with Justice Department officials.[94]

With an inspectorate reduced to a single official who lacked the prestige of the old board and who had been reduced in status to departmental functionary, the situation of the wardens was vulnerable. Not only were all major staff appointments made by the department, but all policy initiatives proceeded from the minister through the inspector. The wardens, reduced to bureaucratic functionaries, required authorization for even the most minor expenditures. At times, the influence of the Department of Justice bureaucracy was limited by practical considerations. Distance from Ottawa mattered a great deal and at one point the warden of the British Columbia penitentiary complained that it had been seven years since Moylan had even inspected his facility.[95] Inevitably, the first-hand experience of the warden and his staff in the daily life of the institutions ensured that they could never be mere ciphers. In countless ways the officials on the spot had to make the hard daily decisions and they still set the tone of their own institutions. Even so, bureaucratization had come, the warden's institutional authority had been truncated, and as the system became larger still in the early decades of the twentieth century, there would be yet more erosion of the power of local staffs and of their ability to assert leadership. As successive ministers of justice obviously had other priorities and little interest in penitentiary affairs, the possibility of effecting significant reforms diminished to zero.

Under these circumstances, few important advances were achieved in the Canadian penitentiary system in the last quarter of the nineteenth century or in the first decades of the twentieth. Even the progressive stages of the Croftonian approach allowed for by the 1868 statute were eroded. First to fall was the critical provision calling for the construction of a prison of isolation. The minister of justice requested plans and estimates for the construction of such a facility and in 1869 Cabinet approved an inquiry into the workings of the silent system at Philadelphia. A year later, the government formally approved construction and by July 1870 work had commenced at a location near Kingston.But the prison as planned at this time was never built. Not until the 1890s was a prison of isolation constructed on Kingston's grounds, and its design and use were wrenched from Croftonian purposes. Kingston's soon notorious prison of isolation was nothing more than a unit designed to deal with recidivists and trouble-makers. It was never used as a mechanism through which all prisoners must proceed as they worked their way up the classic Croftonian ladder.[96]

The system envisaged in 1868 of making special payments to hard-working and well-behaved prisoners suffered a similarly sad fate. In 1873 Warden Creighton was asked to prepare a report on the gratuity system; in it he explained that the best behaved and most industrious convicts could earn up to fifty cents a month for six months and if they maintained their good record they could proceed over the next two years by stages to the point at which they could receive $1.50 a month. Creighton concluded that the system was a great incentive to industry and proper deportment and 'works admirably.' One year later he changed his mind. Citing the case of two men who had received pay for overtime labour and on release had failed to seek employment until all their money had been spent, he told Moylan in a private letter that others had earned substantial sums in the shops only to squander it in taverns and on prostitutes. In response, the gratuity payment was scaled down. In the 1880s, when contract labour itself was ended, the system of over-stint payments was not extended to the new state-use labour system which was then implemented.[97]

Earned remission, however, established itself as an indispensable part of the Canadian penitentiary system. After being confined for six months, the convict could begin to earn a maximum of five days a month remission. Nonetheless, by a statutory change in 1883 the system on Creighton's recommendation was extended and it remained in place as the outstanding achievement of late nineteenth century penal reform.[98] Although remission was widely acclaimed, Moylan was not able to persuade the Department of Justice that the law should be amended to permit officials to deal with repeat offenders by means of indeterminate sentences. Like many late nineteenth century prison administrators, he became increasingly concerned with the problem of recidivism but Canada, unlike Great Britain, did not in these years pass a Habitual Offenders Act.[99]

Without a penal prison, with payments to prisoners in disfavour, and in the absence of anything resembling the intermediate phase of prison discipline so admired by Meredith and his colleagues, it is apparent that the Croftonian system was never implemented in Canada in any meaningful sense. In his 1877 report James Moylan commented in detail on the extent to which Crofton had been or could ever be put into effect under Canadian circumstances. Realistically, he pointed out, the costs of the Irish system would be too great, separate prisons could not easily be built under Canadian geographic conditions to house convicts during different phases of discipline, and it would be impossible to provide the close supervision of convicts that would be required either on prison farms or after release on ticket-of-leave. But he continued to insist that convict reformation must be the leading objective of prison policy. To that end he argued that Croftonianism in any case was too rigorous for Canadian convicts, who responded better to kind treatment and to inducements to become 'self-respecting, self-reliant and industrious.' And Moylan claimed with scant justification that convicts in Canada were treated more humanely than in many other jurisdictions. The fact of imprisonment itself, he insisted, was punishment enough and the convict, while confined, was 'the ward of the state, whose duty it is to treat him humanely.'[100]

Not surprisingly, it proved difficult to translate such a general humanitarianism into practical programs. Moylan was able to effect a few improvements, including an increase in the size of Kingston's notoriously small cells, and there was also a continuing de-emphasis on corporal punishment in the late nineteenth century. And as Moylan's own comments suggest, there is little evidence that Canadian prison administrators in this era were influenced by the rigid biological determinism associated with such European theorists as Cesare Lombroso, who argued that entire groups or classes of individuals were born criminals and not susceptible to reformatory influences.[101] Although a few Canadians, including the distinguished alienist Richard Bucke, were attracted to positivist criminological theories, most concerned with the punishment of crime continued to accept an essentially environmental analysis of criminal causality and to believe that there was some hope for rehabilitation in the prison environment. The failure of Lombrosianism to make substantial inroads is probably attributable to the small number and relative intellectual isolation of Canadian prison administrators. James Calder is certainly right to conclude that 'there is no evidence that federal prison authorities ever squarely faced the theoretical challenge which heredity as a factor in criminality posed to their efforts.'[102] By the same token, there is little evidence that the harsher biological theories ever impacted negatively on the administration of the late nineteenth century penitentiaries.

There was, however, one practical change which sharply differentiated the late nineteenth century institution from the penitentiary as it had existed under Smith and Macdonell. Like his predecessors in the inspectorate, James Moylan abhorred the contract system of managing convict labour and he was even more antagonistic to the British attachment to unproductive penal labour. By this time, there were strong intellectual currents, not only in Canada but in much of North America, against maintaining the contract approach and to these were added a new militancy on the part of trade unions. Organized labour was beginning to emerge as a force of some influence by the late 1870s and 1880s. As economic change made the future of many of the old artisanal trades precarious, and as the pace of industrialization quickened, the trade unions became more powerful and politicians, both federally and provincially, became inclined to listen to their complaints about unfair competition from prison labour. The coincidence of strong opposition from both prison administrators and from newly legitimated union leaders meant that the contract system was finally doomed. In any case, each year it was becoming increasingly more difficult to find contractors willing to risk the vagaries of employing prisoners in circumstances in which the industrial process was increasingly complex and convicts less able to meet the demands of employers. It came as something of an anti-climax when the Macdonald government announced in 1883 that no new contracts would be signed. The last existing contract ran out in 1887.[103]

The declining income received from contracts had simplified the government's decision, but the convicts had to be employed somehow. Although the government was no longer hopeful about raising enough revenue to offset operating costs, there was still pressure to gain as much from convict labour as possible. In the circumstances, the best solution seemed to be to produce goods for sale to other government institutions. As well, there was some effort to use 'the piece-price system,' by which businessmen supplied raw materials and convicts working under prison supervision produced goods under contract. Neither alternative was satisfactory. With Canadian penitentiaries poised to enter the twentieth century, the question of how best to use convict labour remained as troublesome as ever.

As Croftonianism failed to gain more than a foothold, and in the absence of significant new intellectual theories, there could be little significant change in the style and substance of the Canadian prison. The late nineteenth century was characterized by the administration of previously established routines, by intellectual sterility, and by the continued maintenance of a system founded and run on the solid pillars of parsimony, prejudice, and indifference. The bankruptcy of reform ideology, the stultification brought about by an over-centralized administrative structure, and the final failure of the contract system together destroyed any semblance of a sense of purpose in the nineteenth-century penitentiary. In these circumstances, there was little if any hope for rejuvenation. The Canadian penitentiary system could only deteriorate further, and it did, as investigations revealed in 1914 and confirmed in 1938. All Canadians, those who did time in a penitentiary and those who did not, were ill-served by the heritage of this nineteenth-century institution which had started with much hope but now endured with none.[104]

Part III

Alternative Sanctions and Reform Initiatives

9

'The Government Boarding House': Upper Canada's Gaols in the Age of Progress

THE UNION YEARS

The Union of the Canadas in 1841 was a point of departure in colonial development. The next quarter of a century saw unprecedented progress and social growth. It was marked by great population expansion, economic diversification, and social change. In his definitive survey of the period, J.M.S. Careless described the Union years as characterized most of all by the emergence of the institutions that would play central roles in the development of modern Canada, including responsible government and a reformed structure of moderate political parties, new systems of state schooling and welfare administration, and the construction of transportation networks, especially the railway, which brought the age of iron and steam to the furthest reaches of the Canadian wilderness. Canadians of this era confidently believed that they were living through an unprecedented period of economic development and social progress. As one writer put it at the beginning of the Union years, 'THANK HEAVEN! we live in the nineteenth century in an era of unparalleled improvement in science, in art, in literature, morals and religion. Never before did such glorious days as these dawn upon the human race.' And D'Arcy McGee, the prophet of national destiny, proclaimed in the 1860s that 'the law of our youth is growth, the law of our growth is progress.'[1]

Canadian gaols did not share in this progress, although they were affected in various ways by the aspirations which inspired it. Assistant

Provincial Secretary E.A. Meredith and his inspectoral colleagues worked assiduously to achieve reform, but they fell far short of their objectives. During Canada's mid-Victorian years of progress and development the gaols remained in place as glaring symbols of social failure. The failure was one of political will and commitment. Meredith and the board offered indisputable evidence of the extent and nature of the problem and provided reasonable and affordable options for change. But Canadians in the Union years had other priorities and their political leadership, both local and provincial, preferred to tinker with the gaols, while leaving in place most of the elements of the system that Meredith found so repulsive.

Canadians were by no means ignorant of the abuses that existed. In the mid-century years more than in any other period the local gaols faced a barrage of criticism. The attacks, which came in waves, were often provoked by one of the countless escapes which, typically, were blamed not on the negligence of the gaoler but on the disrepair of the facility and the refusal of the municipal government to maintain it adequately. Grand juries, as we have seen, habitually used blunt language to point to innumerable deficiencies. Officials, such as gaol surgeons, or even ordinary citizens would occasionally raise their voices in protest. But most significantly, perhaps, it was the distinguished judges of the Court of Queen's Bench and, after 1849, of the new Court of Common Pleas, who took the lead in condemning the local gaols as both nurseries of crime and places that were criminally dangerous to the health of all confined in them.

Considering the numbers confined therein, as well as the different categories of prisoners, this situation should have been deeply disturbing to community leaders. It is difficult to be precise about numbers confined in the 1840s and 1850s. The most reliable, and the most devastating, comment on contemporary gaol statistics was made in 1849 by Walter C. Crofton in his paper prepared for the Board of Registration and Statistics. Crofton, endeavouring to prepare a set of tables on the state of crime in Canada since 1841, experienced only frustration. 'Unfortunately,' he reported, 'our gaol registers have been so imperfectly kept and without any regard to uniformity, that they afford not any sufficiently correct data on which to ground any calculation as to crime.'[2] The only statistical resources he found useful were the annual penitentiary returns.

The deficiencies of contemporary statistics, however, cannot disguise the large role the gaols continued to play in Ontario life for the rest of the century. Far more than the penitentiary, the gaols were in the front line of the criminal justice system, with thousands of persons of every sort and description passing through them annually. Local communities continued to regard the gaols in an almost proprietary way as all-purpose facilities essential to local life and culture. It is important, then, that Ontario's gaols did not change significantly either in social mission or in physical circumstances from the end of the Upper Canadian period in 1840 to the close of the century. Improvements, to be sure, were made as local communities grew in population and in wealth and as the decrepit old pioneer structures were replaced by new buildings of brick and solid stone. But as numerous grand jury presentments and, after 1859, inspectoral reports, make clear, Ontario's counties rarely succeeded in providing decent and adequate structures to house their criminal and indigent populations.

THE PRE-INSPECTORAL ERA

They did especially poorly in the 1840s and 1850s, in the period before the establishment of the reformed Board of Inspectors. With no central inspection, and with numerous financial and administrative problems standing in the path of reform, the gaols remained, as Meredith asserted in 1852, a disgrace to the country. This state of affairs cannot be attributed to any malignity or incompetence on the part of those most directly concerned with their administration, the sheriffs and gaolers, or even to indifference on the part of the municipal politicians and county councils; rather, it was attributable to various unsolved problems of local administration and to the failure of provincial politicians to assume responsibilities that were regarded as local in nature.

The first difficulty lay in the failure of the Board of Gaol Commissioners appointed under the 1838 statute to function as intended. By the mid-1830s the many deficiencies of Upper Canada's gaols had attracted the attention of colonial office officials and, in the colony, of high court judges. With the 1838 statute an attempt was made to use the powers of the central authority to effect significant changes. The Board of Gaol Commissioners, composed of the chief justice, the vice-chancellor, the Queen's Bench judges, all the sheriffs, and several others appointed by the lieutenant-governor, was to supervise the construction of new gaols and the repair of old ones and to frame rules and regulations for their administration. As we have seen, while the board demonstrated some initial energy it soon disappeared from view. In the absence of any Canadian tradition of strong bureaucratic support, such a body had no prospect of carrying out its legal responsibilities. In a sense, the board was the last of a long line of victims of the weaknesses of Upper Canadian state authority.

In early 1840 reference was made to its efforts in the report of commissioners appointed to investigate the state of the several public departments of the province, including the state of public gaols. This group carried out its investigations conscientiously, offering brief comments on thirteen gaols and finding a wide range of conditions. Many of the new gaols, especially Newcastle and Simcoe, received positive reports. The severest condemnation went to the London gaol, which was considered unsafe and inadequate, with cells described as 'loathsome.' The committee, composed of justices Sherwood, Macaulay, Jones, and McLean, spoke from first-hand experience of the conditions they described. Once again, judicial wisdom held that there was an 'imperative necessity' to place these facilities 'under a well-regulated and wholesome discipline, and subject to the constant superintendence of some active and efficient inquisitorial power.' The judges were equally well placed to know what had happened to the Board of Gaol Commissioners, being among its leading members. They pointed out that the provisions of the statute establishing the board 'do not seem to have been regularly complied with.' The committee recommended that a local commissioner or commissioners be appointed to carry out thorough inspections of every gaol in the province and to report thereon to the executive government. The government would transmit these reports to the Board of Gaol Commissioners, which would make recommendations as to any further action. Finally, the committee recommended that the executive government be given the authority to order the district magistrates to carry these recommendations into effect and to impose a rate on the district to defray expenses.[3] This scheme offered a practical remedy to the defects of the 1838 statute. But the new proposal was flawed, for the government was not about to pay commissioners across the country to interfere with what had traditionally been regarded as a local responsibility.

In any case, this was a period of fundamental restructuring in the Canadas, as Charles Thompson, soon to be Lord Sydenham, pushed ahead in a sweeping effort to reform and modernize the machinery of government. The part of the Sydenham administrative revolution most relevant to the gaols, the District Councils Act of 1841,[4] transferred much of the responsibility for local government from appointed magistrates to popularly elected councils. Although under this statute both the district warden and the treasurer were to be appointed by the central government (until an 1846 amendment provided for these officers to be appointed by the council), the measure introduced a new popular element into gaol administration. Unfortunately, the change was more apparent than real. In many districts the immediate result was a substantial rise in the local tax burden. As one rural supporter wrote to Robert Baldwin in 1843, 'farmers taxes that was five Dollars last year is twenty this and no one understands it.'[5] The inefficiency of the new municipal system and its perceived cost ensured that few local leaders were anxious to contribute to even larger increases in the rate by undertaking improvements to the gaol.

However, in 1849 the famous Municipal Corporations or Baldwin Act[6] introduced a completely responsible system of local government and laid the basis for the more efficient performance of local functions. By creating the systems of townships, counties, and urban municipalities that characterized local administration in Ontario for more than a century, the Baldwin Act seemed to make possible the achievement of numerous essential reforms in the local gaols; unfortunately, reality fell far short of the promise.

To understand the reasons for these several political-administrative failures it is necessary to probe the various circumstances that prevented effective change. At first, local officials were puzzled that the gaol commissioners were so little in view about the province. In October 1840, for example, we find the grand jury of the Niagara District noting that they did 'not understand that this District has been made acquainted with the proceedings of the Commissioners' under the 1838 statute. They were not even sure that recent changes made in the Niagara gaol had been sanctioned by the commissioners and they feared that in these circumstances recent expenditures might have been largely wasted.[7]

One reason the government failed to take up the suggestion of the 1839–40 committee investigating public departments that the 1838 board be rejuvenated was the expectation that Sydenham's new Board of Works would be a more efficient instrument of gaol reconstruction. The board was created in 1840 outside the regular structure of government departments and, as Sydenham's 'most prized project,' it was given extensive authority and substantial funding. In 1852 Assistant Secretary Meredith, endeavouring to understand the reasons for the disappearance of the gaol commissioners, noted that 'the Judges and other Statutory Commissioners under the above Act appear to have considered that their authority to examine plans of Gaols etc. was superseded by the establishment of the Board of Works.'[8] But the Board of Works was preoccupied with the reconstruction of the Canadian canal system. Under the inspired but erratic leadership of Hamilton Killaly it had a troubled existence until, in 1846, it was transformed into a Department of Public Works with expanded responsibilities. Given the stormy career of the board under Killaly, it was not realistic to expect that the local gaols would receive significant attention.

Meredith made it clear to the provincial secretary that the demise of the Board of Gaol Commissioners and the problems with the Board of Works meant that there had been no provincial leadership in gaol reform. Referring to the Baldwin Act, he noted that in 1849 the new municipal councils had assumed the responsibility for erecting gaols and keeping them in repair but that the government failed to provide the necessary supervision. For Meredith the result was predictable: 'the Council naturally put up the gaol at the smallest possible cost without reference to the health or reformation of the prisoners.' The consequences were deplorable. Many gaols were so unhealthy 'that the Judges are unwilling to sentence the prisoners to the length of imprisonment' that their offences would justify. Further, 'many gaols are so unsafe that to prevent prisoners from effecting their escapes the Sheriff and Gaoler are compelled to resort to methods of securing the prisoners by [means] injurious to their health.' Finally, 'not a solitary gaol allows of any proper classification of the prisoners confined.'[9]

Meredith's acknowledgement that the municipal authorities could never be relied on to pay adequate attention to the needs of the gaols was the logical conclusion to be drawn from several recent studies of their condition. This circumstance had of course been noted by the Brown Commission, which had spent little time on the gaols but nonetheless described them as 'nurseries of crime and vice.' So long as the gaols remained in their existing state, the commissioners argued, there could be no effective reform of the penitentiary, and they recommended that they 'be placed under the control of Government Inspectors.'[10]

Walter C. Crofton's report confirmed the commission's critical assessment. After deploring the shoddy systems of gaol record keeping, Crofton documented the usual litany of sins, including the lack of classification, the inability to implement labour programs, and the frequent committal of juveniles, which almost invariably made their circumstances worse rather than better. There followed the inevitable judgment: Canadian gaols were 'little better than nurseries of crime.' It was apparent 'to the most casual observer ... what little attention has been paid to prison discipline either by the Executive, the Parliament or the Officers entrusted with the administration of the Law.'[11] But this neglect, it seemed, was about to change. With the Reform government of Baldwin and LaFontaine soon to take action on the recommendations of the Brown Commission, it appeared that superior arrangements for the gaols would be achieved as part of a comprehensive prison reform package.

For reasons which remain unclear but probably reflected the government's sense that the gaols must continue to be local institutions shaped by local needs, the government deferred action. The 1851 statute made no reference to the gaols and failed to take advantage of the opportunity to give the newly appointed penitentiary inspectors any responsibility for their supervision. Not until 2 March 1852 did Nelson and Dickson even receive letters directing them to 'inquire into the discipline and pecuniary management of the several Gaols throughout the Province.'[12] They divided the work. Dickson visited twenty-two gaols in Canada West, with predictable results. His condemnation was sweeping: he found 'little or no discipline or classification,' and badly ventilated and frequently subterranean cells. In every gaol in the province, male and female prisoners could easily converse with each other and in some they had direct association in the day room. In many the prisoners had ready contact with friends and strangers through cell windows, and alcohol and anything else could readily be passed through. Dickson found 'few or no safe yards' where prisoners might exercise or perform work, and none of the gaol returns showed any proceeds from the labour of prisoners, except the largest gaol, that of Toronto, where prisoners did stone-breaking. There was 'no uniformity in the expenses of the different Gaols.'

Dickson was especially condemnatory of the gaol at Hamilton which, in 1851, held 419 prisoners in cells 'eight feet nine inches by nine feet nine inches, partly underground, with one small loop-hole for light and air; the door opens into a dark passage; six human beings are incarcerated in each of these cells night and day, with a tube in place of a water-closet.' The prisoners were vermin infested and the sheriff, Cartwright-Thomas, refused to visit them 'unless specially called upon to do so, being in a state of *disgust* with the condition of the Gaol, and wholly unable to ameliorate the condition of the prisoners, either morally or physically.' Dickson believed that three months in the Hamilton Gaol 'must shorten life more than a sentence of three years in the Provincial Penitentiary.' Toronto had the best conducted gaol 'and that is far from what it ought to be.' The gaoler, Mr Allan, was a man of energy and ability who attempted some primitive classification, albeit with limited success. Dickson concluded that he had found the gaols in Canada West fully as bad as was anticipated, and Wolfred Nelson reached similar conclusions for Canada East. Dickson recommended that the existing gaols be used as places of detention for only the briefest possible period; that houses of correction and new penitentiaries be built; and that one or more juvenile prisons be established. With railways even then under construction, he believed it would soon be feasible to transport prisoners to the appropriate institution anywhere in the province. In any case, Dickson warned, Canadians must recognize that they must pay a price to effect such improvements: 'no great good can be effected without cost.'[13]

The collective portrait that emerges from grand jury reports and judicial comments confirms in every respect the scathing criticisms of Crofton, Dickson, and Nelson. In 1840, the Niagara grand jury found the district gaol 'offensive and insufficient' and called for a new facility 'on a well designed plan.' In May 1841 the London District grand jury found the local gaol deficient in so many respects that they concluded that 'confinement in it in many cases, amounts to greater punishment than is intended by the law,' a view which Justice Macaulay hastened to tell Provincial Secretary S.B. Harrison was entirely accurate. Macaulay also complained that he and his fellow judges were often embarrassed in awarding punishments because the means of enforcing hard labour did not then exist in a single gaol yet many crimes did not warrant a penitentiary sentence. Indeed, officials of the London District had already submitted plans for a new gaol to the Board of Works for approval, a process which the London grand jury in May 1843 stated was 'required by law.'[14]

Chief Justice Robinson had an even harsher view of the situation. In April 1843 grand juries of the Gore and Niagara Districts had returned scathing presentments.[15] Robinson waited nearly half a year before forwarding these presentments to the government, delaying until the legislature was in session in the hope that any submission from the executive branch would thereby be more likely to engage the attention of the members. The problems of the gaols, Robinson admitted, were incapable of being addressed 'except by measures, which it rests with the District Councils to take.' But he added that he had concluded 'while I was in the Districts, that recourse to the legislature would be necessary.'[16]

If judges, grand jurors, and others in the early 1840s understood this so clearly, why was no provincial action taken for almost two decades, until the Prison Inspection Act passed the House in 1859?[17] The only possible answer, it would seem, is the lack of political will to present legislation, spend the money required, and interfere with entrenched local rights when all that was at stake was the health and welfare of members of the underclasses. Throughout the 1840s and most of the 1850s, grand jurors and judges constantly made the same case, reinforced, as we have seen, by occasional special reports such as those of Crofton, Dickson, and Nelson, but to no avail.

One common complaint was that the absence of a wall and the poor quality of construction required the gaoler to place prisoners in irons to prevent their escape. In 1853 the Frontenac, Lennox, and Addington grand jurors found the gaol 'so insecure as to offer little, or no impediment to the escape of the prisoners,' with the result that 'additional and unnecessary restraint has been rendered unavoidable to the detriment of the health of the prisoners confined.' When the Ontario County jurors inspected the 'new and scarcely finished Gaol' they were appalled 'how any Architect could be so wanting in a knowledge of his profession, as to recommend the construction of a Gaol' without a water closet in the entire building. They were equally astounded to find that 'the outer walls are so built and constructed as to present but little or no obstacle to the escape of the prisoners, and that nearly all the partitions are of the most frail description.'[18]

Many municipal leaders blamed provincial politicians. Not only had the Board of Gaol Commissioners and the Board of Works failed abysmally, but the municipal reforms embodied in the district councils had merely substituted new inefficiencies for old ones. There was now also an element of legal and political uncertainty with which to contend, including the apparent legal requirement that plans be approved by the Board of Works. Chief Justice Robinson believed that not even the Executive Council could remedy the situation.[19]

Robinson's assessment indicated that the Sydenham municipal reforms had done little to remedy the inadequate taxing authority and relative poverty of the municipal authorities. The cry of municipal poverty was the most frequent explanation given throughout the Union years for the local failure to build improved prisons. Independent observers had little patience with such excuses. In April 1850 the grand jurors of Wentworth and Halton argued that it could not be claimed 'that the credit and resources' of such wealthy and prosperous counties 'are in such a crippled condition as to render it inexpedient or impracticable' for the council to act.[20] Robinson shared these views. In 1851 he referred to the many attempts made over the years to persuade Wentworth and Halton to loosen their purse strings to provide 'a remedy for evils which ought not to exist in any part of Canada, and certainly not in Counties so populous and wealthy.' With the municipal council, as Robinson put it, 'unable or unwilling to take any effectual measures,' the time had come for '[l]egislative interference, or the interference of the Government.'[21]

The local authorities, even with a small tax base and considerable rural poverty, could have acted more responsibly. However, throughout the 1840s the district unit of government had been volatile and unstable. As the population of Canada West increased rapidly, growing from about 480,000 in 1841 to 952,000 in 1851 and reaching 1,396,091 in 1861, no level of government was more fundamentally affected than the districts. With local boundaries shifting constantly, municipal leaders were reluctant to invest in facilities that might soon be made obsolete by altered political boundaries and by the new county structure established by the Municipal Corporations Act of 1849.

This difficulty appeared in extreme form in disputes between incorporated municipalities and the surrounding counties. In October 1852 Robert Spence, warden of the United Counties of Wentworth, Halton, and Brant, made an extended defence of his council's difficulties to the provincial secretary. Feeling aggrieved, he insisted that 'the censure so harshly heaped by public functionaries, and by Grand Juries, on the Municipal Council of these United Counties is not altogether deserved.' In 1850 and again in 1851 Wentworth and Halton on several occasions had investigated the need for a new gaol, as did the United Council in 1852; prior to that the Gore District council had devoted considerable attention to the matter. In 1848, the district council held a special meeting, plans were approved and steps taken to carry the project into effect, 'but through opposing influences the designs of the Council were frustrated.' Subsequent efforts had likewise resulted in failure and Warden Spence reported that the difficulty of reconciling conflicting interests had prevented any progress:

Amongst other hindrances, not the least was found to be those relating to the territorial division scheme, introduced by the Government in 1850, and which, so far as relates to these counties, is not yet completed. The County of Brant, one of these United Counties, is about to be declared a separate county, having provided her own Court House and Gaol. The County of Halton, also one of these United Counties, will probably soon be separated from the senior County ... In view of changes of this description, the selection of a site, and the extent and nature of Gaol accommodation, are subjects quite proper for the consideration of the County Municipality. These considerations, from the constant agitation of County Division schemes, and the uncertainty of having permanent County limits, have to a considerable extent, retarded the adoption of a plan which should prove suitable.[22]

Although the Wentworth dispute dragged on, the bitter struggle between the City of Toronto and the Council of the United Counties of York, Ontario, and Peel best illustrates the relationship between jurisdictional wrangles and the failure to attend to pressing social concerns. The Municipal Corporations Act of 1849 authorized the city's use of the county prison until the city should direct otherwise. This led to prolonged clashes between county and city authorities. In January 1853, Joseph Gould, chair of the United Counties Committee on Property and Gaol Management, responded at length to a communication from Provincial Secretary A.N. Morin urging the council to early action. Every step had been taken at successive meetings of council during the previous two-and-a-half-years, Gould claimed, to reach a reasonable agreement with the city to extend and improve the gaol, but all without effect. According to the counties, the city was legally entitled to send its prisoners to the county gaol and such prisoners 'usually comprise the great bulk of those confined.' It was the county committee's position that there must be a reasonable division of costs, with the city council agreeing to occupy the improved gaol for ten years from the date of the extension being completed. As city prisoners outnumbered those from the counties by more than six to one, the counties felt that the city prisoners were entirely responsible for the need for an addition. To make matters worse, the County of York might soon be saddled with the entire cost of the gaol, as the counties of Ontario and Peel were expected soon to become separate jurisdictions. The haggling went on interminably and, as usual, it was the prisoners who suffered.[23]

For Justice Burns it was precisely this situation of population expansion and the rapid creation of new county political units that rendered provincial intervention imperative. Burns refused to consider the matter as merely a temporary difficulty of local administration. In his view, it was a basic flaw in the division of powers to impose on the local authorities the responsibilities of gaol administration. This was a matter, he continued, 'that does not merely affect one particular County, but it affects the whole Province, and its society, from the one end to the other. One efficient system of prison discipline, and one proper mode of constructing Prison buildings, should be adopted, and in my opinion the Government should have the power of compelling all Counties to adopt that one system and mode.'[24]

Burns was persistent, pressing his views in numerous charges to grand juries, letters to government officials, and conversations with politicians from all levels of government. In a December 1853 letter to Provincial Secretary P.J.O. Chauveau, he argued that one reason why gaol reform was proving difficult was because county courthouses and gaols often occupied the same building. The counties, he suggested, should be able to exercise whatever discretion they wished with respect to embellishing their courthouses, and this could be facilitated if the gaols were placed in separate quarters and maintained to provincial standards. Of course the county, he told Chauveau, should provide the means for the erection of the gaol, 'but I believe it would be much better if a Board of Commissioners were appointed' to do all the necessary planning and were enabled by law to compel the county to build a structure in conformity with such a plan. At present, each county did as it saw fit, 'and I need hardly remind His Excellency and the Executive Government of the inexperience of these bodies in such matters, and of their unwillingness to expend the necessary means.'[25]

It was not Burns but the Chief Justice of the Court of Common Pleas, James B. Macaulay, who, in May 1854, only months before his death, provided a conclusive demonstration of the legal and judicial confusion that existed over the status of the gaols. In transmitting to the government a series of grand jury reports for the western counties, Macaulay pointed out that in the Norfolk gaol, which had recently experienced a homicide, there was no code of prison regulations in effect. Since Macaulay had once served as a member of the Board of Gaol Commissioners, which long ago had formulated gaol regulations, this piqued his curiosity. 'I was under the impression,' he told Chauveau, 'that the Inspectors of the Penitentiary were also appointed Inspectors of all the County Gaols, with power to make rules and regulations for the Government, and management thereof.' But after a search the chief justice was unable to 'find any such authority conferred upon them.' Many years previously, he noted, gaol regulations had been framed under authority of the provincial statute of 32 Geo. III, c. 8, s. 16, 'and I have on several occasions examined and sanctioned rules prepared' under that statute. It had been superseded in 1838, however, by 1 Vict., c. 5, s. 6 and by subsequent municipal Acts and therein lay the problem: 'I am not aware that any general system of rules for the government of the Common Gaols was ever established under the 6th section. I rather think it was lost sight of, and not acted upon.' Therefore, he concluded, he had 'on several former occasions, suggested the expediency of a series of Prison Regulations being declared by Act of the Legislature' and 'with provision for enforcing the prompt observance thereof.'[26] If the chief justice had so entirely lost sight of existing penal ordinances, it was hardly surprising that others were equally confused.

By the mid-1850s the sheer volume of reports from grand jurors, judges, municipal councils, and special commissioners made an impression on the provincial government. Judge Burns, that conscientious advocate of provincial intervention, deserves the last word. Burns told Chauveau in November 1854 that "Her Majesty's Government, should, without delay,' withdraw the superintendence of gaols from corporate bodies and vest it in the government 'as part of the Administration of Justice.' 'A Municipal corporate body, is, I think, on account of its ever changing character, an improper tribunal to be entrusted and invested with powers connected in any way with Prisons, further than providing the ways and means for the expenses ... At present, the responsibility of a Municipal Corporation is nothing, and rests upon nobody's shoulders.' Again Burns restated his conviction that the executive should appoint a board of commissioners with the power to construct prisons, 'and then there would be some responsible persons to whom to look for the proper administration of Justice.'[27]

Although the bleak picture these documents paint of conditions in the gaols in Canada West in the 1840s and fifties is generally accurate, it should be understood that neither in the correspondence received in the provincial secretary's office nor in the inquiries carried out by judges and grand juries is there any significant reference to cruelty on the part of gaolers and sheriffs. The grand jury reports frequently noted that the prisoners did not blame their keepers for the hardships they were suffering, and were often grateful for many kindnesses offered by gaolers and turnkeys.[28] Partly because of a similarity in class origins, gaolers and turnkeys felt considerable empathy with their charges. Possibly, too, nineteenth-century prisoners were so accustomed to hardship and penury that they were more accepting of privations than modern prisoners would have been.

The occasional exception seems to prove the rule. There were in this period a few instances of unrestrained rage which, as noted earlier, had sometimes led to destruction of gaol furnishings and much sullen resistance in the 1830s. Prisoners seldom expressed their feelings in writing, as James Radcliffe did in 1858. Recently released from the London gaol, Radcliffe wrote his 'most graishes Exelency' to inform him of 'the evil that is caried on' in 'the Devils den.' '[W]hat I don there my self i broke a fore leged bed sted i cut up the rope of the bed i broke a new table of oke i broke the iron that was on the hot air hole i broke a wash basin i brock a tin Dish i brock a window sash I brock two long tin disheses i tore up three blankets.' The purpose of Radcliffe's letter was to let the governor general know precisely why he had engaged in this orgy of destruction:

this is not the work of Draimes or of crayesenes it is don on the account of the traitment i receive in London gail a hell up on hearth a hell in London city the 'Devils Den ... i shall now let you know how i was treted in London gaol they give me whiskey mixed with poison to make a skeleton of me ... today i went to show my skin and bones to a doctor he told me i could get damiges of them for the way i was ill yoused by the men that was over the prisoners in London gaol the serve the devil all the week and mock god on Sunday the ware a fraid to let me to church on Sunday afraid i should expose them may god ... protect the poor prisoners in Canada gaols.[29]

If few prisoners complained of their gaolers, part of the reason was that no attempt was made to enforce penitentiary style discipline. The records, with minor exceptions, are free from references to the infliction of punishments. No doubt confinement in unhealthy subterranean caves was punishment enough.

Some prisoners were put in leg irons, but this was used less as a punishment than to prevent their escape. Given the large number of escapes in the 1840s and 1850s and the flimsy conditions of the gaols, it seems surprising that more prisoners did not suffer the use of irons. The official correspondence to the governor through the provincial secretary chronicles the ease of escape and the frequency with which prisoners, often large numbers at a time, made off from the prisons. When Sheriff Simon Fraser of the Dalhousie District reported to His Excellency on the escape of four prisoners in 1847, his cry of anguish would have been echoed by just about every sheriff in Canada. 'For my own part,' he began,

I can only repeat that I have remonstrated with the Magistrates and the Municipal Council upon the insecurity and the insufficiency of the Prison to secure the safe keeping of prisoners, that I have brought this matter under the notice of the Government, that I have applied to the Commander of the Forces for a guard to watch over this Prison but all of no avail, and I now assert without fear of contradiction from any quarter ... that every prisoner in that gaol may be at large before tomorrow morning if they choose to apply themselves to the means at their disposal.[30]

Not even the ball and chain were always adequate restraint. Sheriff James Hamilton reported from London in 1849 that a prisoner sentenced to six months' hard labour had made his escape 'with ball and chain attached.'[31]

Sheriffs like Hamilton and Simon Fraser were more fearful of the escape of debtors than of criminals, because of their direct financial liabilities. This explains why many debtors complained of hard treatment. 'It is very hard,' Fraser reported, 'if I am ruined if mulcted in damages if the debtors should make their escape and I have now some in custody for very heavy sums and had one last summer for 6000 pounds or upwards and for whose safe-keeping I was responsible.'[32]

In 1850 the use of cruel expedients to prevent escapes finally caused apprehension at the provincial level. In January a petition from the London gaol informed His Excellency that,

we subjects of Canada know [sic] undergoing Sentence in this Gaol of Petty Larceny of hard Labour Sentenced by Judge Small, that we have a Iron ball ... and a chain 5 feet long ... we have them riveted on with a Shackle above the Ankle and we can not take of our Socks or Pantaloons, that we are unable to keep ourselves clean with having to keep them on both day and night we are unable to keep from getting lousey ... we can not find out by whom this Extra Punishment is Afflicted by, the Judge says he has nothing to do with this extra punishment.[33]

They humbly begged therefore that His Excellency should determine 'if it is an Act of Law' to impose the ball and chain in addition to hard labour.

With gratifying speed, James Leslie asked Sheriff Hamilton for an explanation a few days later. On 5 February the sheriff reported that the gaol was without a yard or even a room for prisoners to work in and the principal portion of labour had to be done 'outside the precincts.'[34] Genuinely anxious to alleviate suffering, Sheriff Hamilton told the government that an alternative to the ball and chain might be to allow the prisoner's family to post monetary security as a guarantee against escape.[35]

The government found the use of ball and chain unacceptable and in February 1850 appointed County Court Judge James Small to conduct a formal inquiry. While emphasizing that the sheriff had done all in his power to ameliorate the condition of the prisoners, Small concluded that 'no circumstances exist sufficient to warrant its continuance without the authority of Law.' At the same time, he admitted that the sentence of hard labour could not be carried out within the prison under existing conditions. Like many others, Small found that 'there appears to be an apathy on the part of the County Councils generally to expending the county funds upon the completion and securing of County Prisons as well as for any portion of the administration of Justice.' He recommended that the province pass legislation to appropriate 'a certain percentage of the general assessment in each County to the above purposes to be expended under the direction of a Joint Committee of the County Council and the commissioned magistrates.'[36]

Small's report received a positive response from Solicitor General Sandfield Macdonald. Macdonald minuted on 2 April that he could find no justification at all for the practices followed in the London gaol, and added that Judge Small's suggestion that there be a general enactment appropriating a percentage of the general county assessment 'to be expended in repairing and securing County prisons and the yards attached thereto, would seem in respect to the County Gaol of Middlesex to deserve early consideration.' The provincial secretary's office responded by telling Sheriff Hamilton that the practices used in Middlesex since 1837 'should hereafter be relaxed in so far as the superaddition of the sentence of hard labour, to that of confinement, in the Gaol, is concerned,' unless that labour could be carried on within the precincts of the gaol. The use of ball and chain to secure prisoners while at labour must be discontinued. At the same time, James Leslie advised his Cabinet colleague, Inspector General Hincks, that the government had the state of the gaols under consideration and that 'a general enactment is necessary appropriating' a percentage of the general county assessment to completing and securing these facilities. Hincks was instructed to consider the matter 'in connection with the measures in contemplation' affecting the provincial penitentiary.[37] And there it seemed to rest. The government moved ahead in 1851 with its penitentiary statute and reserved action on the gaols at least until Nelson and Dickson had completed their reports.

The innumerable reports made by sheriffs to the provincial secretary almost invariably attributed escapes to the failure of the county to provide adequate resources. Perhaps the most frequent cause of escape was the failure to hire enough guards. From the Midland District Sheriff Corbett reported an escape in 1848 which occurred because the keeper was obliged to take at least two prisoners outside the walls on a regular basis to fetch water. Another example occurred in Guelph, in 1853, when the gaoler let a prisoner out to gather some wood and the man ran off.[38] Urgent and dangerous circumstances sometimes led to the pleas of a desperate sheriff actually being heeded. In Sandwich in 1852 the county sheriff reported that 'he ha[d] in custody five of the worst characters in America.' When the sheriff at Detroit warned him that members of a gang intended to liberate their friends by force, he applied to the military for assistance. They promptly sent him a number of armed pensioners and all was well.[39]

The ease of escape, although it frequently led to increased suffering through the use of irons, also worked to the advantage of some prisoners, and the abominable physical conditions of many gaols often had the same effect. When prisoners petitioned for early release because their health was being undermined, the attorney general and his colleagues had voluminous evidence on hand as to actual conditions. Perhaps they felt that some of the responsibility for this state of affairs rested with their own government. Even John A. Macdonald was frequently sympathetic on grounds of health. When pregnancy was an additional factor, an early release was virtually assured, as John Robinson's speedy release of a prisoner from the London gaol confirmed in 1858.[40] In such cases, what was occurring was less the exercise of mercy, however, than a use of the pardoning power as a convenient safety valve.

Another revealing circumstance of mid-century gaols was their continuing use as congregate facilities to house the poor, the old, and the mentally ill. The 1837 House of Industry Act had attempted to address this problem, but the desired facility could not be erected under this statute until three successive grand juries had recommended the measure to the district magistrates assembled in Quarter Sessions. Splane argues that the Act was attacked by Reformers as a Tory measure which was far too costly and it was 'never implemented,' although private houses of industry came into being through other means.[41] Evidence of ongoing opposition to the statute in the mid-1840s came from the Midland District Council, in a document that raised several significant issues.[42] It was the jurors' recommendation that the district establish a house of industry which most agitated the district councillors. They were

not aware of any existing cause which would render it more necessary to have a Poor House or House of Industry within its limits than within the limits of any other District of the Province excepting such cause as may arise from the circumstance that the incorporated Town of Kingston is so situated as to be visited by a great portion of itinerant poor on their way through the Province, and that this Council cannot perceive the justice of heavily taxing the industry of the Agricultural Population of the back townships to meet the exigencies of this casualty peculiar to the City of Kingston.

If that seemed harsh, the council pointed out, not unreasonably, that it regarded the needs of the itinerant poor 'as having an equal claim on the charity of all Districts in the province.' The council passed a motion of opposition to the 1837 Act and expressed itself as willing to support its own poor.

For many districts this meant placing them in gaol. At its best, this arrangement suited both the municipality and the indigent population tolerably well. Many counties allowed prisoners confined as indigent to come and go at will. This practice outraged some of the province's more legalistically minded officials. In 1858, the district sheriff of Norfolk County reported to Provincial Secretary T.J.J. Loranger that he had discovered on his appointment 'that a number of paupers have been in the habit of finding an asylum' in the gaol. The gaol committee, he continued, had no authority to convert the gaol into a poorhouse; 'nonetheless they have been compelled on many occasions either to open its doors to the destitute diseased poor, or to allow them to perish on the streets.' In most cases, the township councils absolutely refused any assistance to their own poor, 'who are thereby driven into the Town to seek relief, and the Committee have felt themselves compelled in some instances to lock [them] up and furnish support.' The committee felt justified in admitting such people only in cases 'of great and urgent distress' when the unfortunate persons might otherwise perish, but they knew they were departing from the letter of the law. The problem had become progressively more serious 'and the expenditure incurred without authority of law has become an important item.'

John A. Macdonald cut through the verbiage. The municipalities, he noted, 'have the power of providing for the District poor and the whole responsibility of doing so rests upon them.' The gaol, he pointed out, 'ought not to be made a Poor House and the Sheriff should refuse to receive any person not legally committed to his custody.' This message was communicated to the sheriff, but without evident effect.[43]

A similar circumstance arose out of the absence of paid inspectors. No one either at the local or the central level was immediately responsible for addressing gaol problems; no level of government and no official or functionary was willing to accept responsibility. Consequently, the dozens of grand jury presentments prepared each year on the state of the gaols were usually ignored. The judge would forward them to the provincial secretary who in turn sent them back to the sheriff who could do little more than place them before the council for consideration, and the whole circular process tended to lead nowhere.

Let us conclude this account of the pre-1859 years with an assessment by the august Chief Justice of the Court of Queen's Bench, John Beverley Robinson. In 1858 Robinson received a presentment from the grand jury of Middlesex which was 'of so startling a nature' that he 'took the earliest opportunity' of inspecting the gaol and conversing with the prisoners about the treatment they had received. Robinson was relieved to find conditions in the London gaol no worse than in many others, but they were 'well below what the judges would deem satisfactory. The magistrates of the counties can no longer ... be relied upon for reforming abuses,' or even for providing the necessary supplies for the gaol, because they now lacked the power to do so. In Robinson's experience, the new municipal councils 'cannot be got to attach that importance to matters of this kind' that they should. The complaint of the sheriffs and magistrates was 'that the Councils cannot be got to sanction the expenditure which is necessary.' Robinson noted that previously the members of the municipality – presumably he meant the magistrates – had made frequent inspections, but 'for some time past' these had been discontinued, leaving the prisoners 'without means of redress against any evils they may be made to suffer.'[44] In Robinson's judgment the old system of appointed JPs had worked better than that of elected councils because the justices had taken their responsibilities more seriously. Conditions in the gaols in some respects had thus actually deteriorated as a consequence of municipal reform. But the legislature, Robinson believed, had at last understood the significance of this state of affairs and had passed the Prison Inspection Act of 1857 in response. As we saw earlier, a revised version of the Act was proclaimed in 1859, and John Robinson and his fellow judges believed that gaol reform would soon be achieved. Nonetheless, during much of 1858 and 1859 the expectation that a new Board of Inspectors would soon assume responsibility for gaol administration actually delayed change. Since it was understood that all gaol reforms would need the approval of the new board, and since there was some expectation of central government funding, many county councils did nothing until the new board was in place.

THE BOARD OF INSPECTORS

When the board was finally appointed in 1858, a new era was underway for the gaols of the United Canadas. For the first time, the central government had assumed adequate inspectoral and administrative authority to reform and modernize the Canadian institution which, more than any other, desperately required active statist intervention. For a moment, enthusiasm and hope prevailed. The board, appalled by what its preliminary investigations revealed, gave the gaol problem top priority. Persuaded that the condition of Canadian gaols lay at the core of the threat posed by criminality and deviance, the inspectors were determined to use their authority to reform the criminal justice system at its weakest point.

And they had been given broad authority to do just that. E.A. Meredith and his colleagues in 1860 summarized their statutory powers in their first full report as follows: either singly or together, to inspect every gaol at least twice a year; to ensure that every gaol was built according to a plan approved by the inspectors and sanctioned by the government; and to visit every gaol erected or being erected to ascertain whether it satisfied provincial requirements. The critical section 18 of the statute directed the warden of every county in Canada West to appoint a 'special committee' to confer with the inspectors on what would be required to make the local gaol conform to provincial standards. As a balance to this apparently sweeping assumption of central authority, the board itself was required 'to make as few and inexpensive alterations in the Gaol as in their opinion the requirements of the Act will allow.' The county councils were directed to raise by direct taxation or to borrow the sums required to make the necessary alterations and additions, while the government might pay from the 'Upper Canada Building Fund' 'a sum not exceeding one half of the expense of the same,' up to a maximum of $6,000. Finally, the inspectors were directed to frame rules and regulations for the governance of the gaols and to submit these to the government for approval.[45]

In their remarkable preliminary report the inspectors expressed shock that the gaols were even worse than anticipated. There were, they noted, thirty-one county gaols in Upper Canada and twenty-one district gaols in Lower Canada. The inspectors concluded that '[t]he defects of our prisons are of every possible kind ... Defects in superintendence, defects in discipline, defects in construction ... defects in the sanitary arrangements, defects, above all, in the means of reforming; defects everywhere.' Six gaols had but a single officer 'to do everything,' while another twenty-two had but two, a gaoler and a turnkey, even though some of them held up to forty prisoners at a time. In such circumstances, the authority of the officers 'exists by the sufferance of the prisoners.' In thirteen there were no rules of any kind. Escapes seemed actually encouraged as 'a great number of the buildings used as Gaols, stand directly on the public road, and afford the prisoners every facility for communication with those without.' The prison buildings presented 'an insurmountable obstacle' to any effort to classify prisoners. Finally, 'no provision is made for the religious wants of the prisoners, and yet, without religion, reformation is impossible.' The inspectors were certain that Canadian gaols failed in all the objects of prison discipline: 'We do not punish, or we punish improperly. We do not deter from crime, and we do not reform the criminal.'[46]

Unlike the grand jury reports, the board's main focus was not on the horrors of the gaols and their effect on the health of the prisoners, although that note was struck. What the inspectors emphasized was the way in which a population of drunks, vagrants, prostitutes and n'er do wells was exploiting society, lodged at public expense in an atmosphere of no restraint and no reformation. Their unmeasured denunciation of 'the government boarding house' contained little if any effort to understand the social circumstances that had led so many Canadians to life in gaol.

The inspectors approached one aspect of the evidence hesitantly and then only to express puzzlement. In the midst of this 'chaos of promiscuous intercourse,' in the depth of dens mostly closed to air and light, with as many as twenty-five prisoners herded together and 'breathing, in many instances, an atmosphere poisoned by the adjoining privies, the prisoners enjoy good health.' Of thirty-nine prisons, only seven, and those 'to a trifling extent,' were exceptions to this rule. Furthermore, apart from forty-five escapes and about thirty additional attempts during the same three-year period, the inspectors had been able to discover a mere three cases 'of serious breach of prison discipline.'[47]

Meredith, Nelson, and the others were astounded by these perverse facts. They eventually attributed the general absence of violence and the good health of the prisoners to the circumstances they had already noted, namely 'that the majority of the inmates in our Common Gaols enjoy their detention in these establishments, and are fully alive to the advantages of these asylums, where they can recruit their strength and invigorate themselves for fresh crimes.'[48]

These conclusions were bizarre. In this period many members of the middle class, in Britain and the United States as well as in Canada, became persuaded that the numbers of paupers and criminals were expanding at a rate beyond any previously recorded. Failing to reflect on how the vast array of new municipal by-laws pertaining to moral and public order offences had combined with the expansion of professional policing to swell the numbers of short-term prisoners, such critics overreacted to this perceived moral crisis. In Canada, the prison inspectors failed entirely in their self-proclaimed role of scientific analysts and social engineers, merely adding their authoritative voices to the growing chorus and swelling the sense of fear and loathing which 'the dangerous classes' increasingly inspired. Meredith should have known better, and so too should have such experienced officials as Nelson and Taché.

If there was any excuse for their exaggerated fears, it was found in the statistics to which the mid-Victorians gave an unwarranted prestige and weight. The numbers seemed impressive. Each year the statistics presented a more frightening picture of how a deviant culture had captured the gaols and turned them to their own wicked purposes.

The numbers confined in gaol in the United Canadas were 10,483 in 1858 and 11,131 in 1859. It was sad, said the inspectors, to find 11,000 prisoners in a population of less than three million 'in a country where land is fertile and abundant, and where honest industry and persevering toil are sure to be well repaid.' And it was 'more sad to find that upwards of a third' of these were women (3,503) and children under the age of sixteen (414 boys, 171 girls). Almost all the women, they alleged, were prostitutes for whom the prisons served 'as boarding houses and places of shelter.' In the rural districts, this class of prisoner, the inspectors claimed, was 'almost unknown.' Of the 6,586 in 1859 who came from Upper Canada, 1,558 were recidivists. The existence of repeat offenders, they concluded, demonstrated a defect in the criminal code: those who were convicted repeatedly should either be committed forever as dangerous and incorrigible or sent to a lunatic asylum. Finally, no fewer than 321 lunatics had been imprisoned over the previous three years, 'in defiance of the dictates of justice and humanity.'

The inspectors were as upset at the cost to the taxpayer of supplying 'boarding house' services as they were at the social consequences of these abuses. As we saw in the previous chapter, the annual cost for each prisoner in the common gaol was $44.57 greater than for each prisoner in the penitentiary.[49] In the statistical return dealing with revenue from prisoners' labour, not a single gaol in Upper Canada listed anything under earnings. This, said the inspectors, was outrageous.

Having once reached these conclusions, they never abandoned them. Each successive inspection of individual facilities over the next eight years, together with agonizing negotiations with local politicians, reinforced their conviction that the gaols constituted nurseries of crime and undue burdens to the taxpayer. From the beginning the inspectors were certain about the remedy. The gaols, to be sure, must be reformed, but the inspectors were determined that these local institutions be used only for those confined for brief periods, either awaiting trial or sentenced for matters not involving any proof of a fixed habit of vice or degradation. For those they defined as the criminal class, the recidivists who flouted conventional morality, they would establish a new institution. In the principal Canadian cities all misdemeanants and recidivists from the adjoining counties or districts would be confined in district or central prisons.'[50]

Seldom have Canadian bureaucrats expressed such exalted hopes only to see them come crashing down for lack of political support. Thus began a bizarre three-ring circus with the inspectors, the government, and the county councillors all pursuing generally conflicting objectives. In January 1860 the inspectors sent the counties a circular asking them to appoint their special committees to begin the planning process. Soon a committee of the board had prepared plans for a model gaol and in May these were circulated with a statement of the objectives of prison discipline. The board stated its gratification that the county councils and others, 'almost without exception,' had expressed approval.[51]

With the work proceeding, the inspectors obtained meetings with the special committees. On these occasions, members of the board would inspect the gaol, hold discussions with the committee, and leave behind a written statement of the alterations and additions they deemed necessary. These were brought before the county councils for consideration. Final plans were returned to the inspectors and then to the government for approval, and a large number were considerably modified. In a flurry of activity, the board approved and the government sanctioned plans for new gaols in Toronto, Ottawa, and Walkerton, while alterations were approved for gaols in twelve other communities. The Toronto gaol presented special problems. Plans had been approved and the project sent out to contract before the board had come into existence. Its architect had modelled the facility on Pentonville, the English model prison, but the inspectors believed that 'the extreme views then held regarding the merits of the solitary system have been very greatly modified, if not altogether exploded.' The city co-operated, the architect altered his plans, and the changes received the sanction of the board and the government. The inspectors believed that the Toronto city gaol and a new gaol in Quebec City might serve as prototypes for their network of central prisons.[52]

In this early hopeful period the inspectors promulgated new rules and regulations for the gaols, printed in seven pages of the 1860 report. These proposals embodied the inspectors' progressive vision and humanitarian sentiments; they expressed as well the efforts of this central government agency to impose uniformity and order on local diversity. The rules were what one would expect from well–intentioned bureaucrats. They confirmed that full authority by law was vested in the sheriff as chief executive officer of every county prison and that it was his duty to see the rules 'strictly observed.' In every prison, however small, there must be at least a keeper (the new name was significant) and an assistant keeper. The keeper was envisaged as almost an employee of the inspectors, with a responsibility to keep extensive records and to inform them of every aspect of prison life. In a further assertion of inspectoral authority, all matters relating to heating, drainage, and even 'the mode of procuring the Prison supplies' were to be left to the decision of the board. In all city prisons, and whenever the inspectors deemed it necessary, there must be a matron; where no matron was in residence, the sheriff must always secure females to attend female prisoners. In the larger prisons, the inspectors envisaged the appointment of chaplains who, in addition to performing religious services, would 'devote a considerable portion of their time to visiting and instructing the prisoners.' Similarly, medical officers were to have an expanded function to 'frequently inspect every cell' and to regularly report to the inspectors on such matters as heating, ventilation, clothing, quality of the food, and any other matter which 'may be likely to prejudice the health of the prisoners.'[53]

There were also significant changes to be applied in penal practices. The most important asserted that prisoners might be classified under several heads to include those charged and those convicted; first offenders and others; civil prisoners (mostly debtors) and criminals; and those deemed to be of disgusting habits and degraded appearance. Juveniles were to be kept completely separate. The sheriff was to provide for the removal of lunatics to an asylum at the earliest opportunity. In addition to this refined system, the prisoners might be divided into two broad categories. Both the best and the worst prisoners were to be kept completely separate from all others at all times; other prisoners could mingle during the day but must be given separate cells at night. There were to be different dietaries for the different classes, especially those employed at hard labour. But there was to be no effort to replicate penitentiary-style discipline by enforcing the rule of silence. In a further departure from penitentiary standards, the sheriff was to make 'such rules as he may think proper' to govern the sending and receiving of letters and admission of visitors. Finally, the gaol officers were directed while enforcing the rules to treat the prisoners 'with kindness and humanity.' They were always to bear in mind that 'the great object of prison discipline is to reform the Prisoner,' in part by acquiring a moral influence over him.[54]

The principal area in which the inspectors seemed hesitant about imposing their wishes on local authorities related to hard labour. They noted that such labour, compulsory for all who received it as part of their sentence, was 'optional for all other prisoners.' The keeper was directed to invite this group to such labour 'with a view alike to their reformation and their health,' but there was no effort to propose particular forms of work and notably absent was any reference to the British preference for penal unproductive labour. Realistically, it was laid down that the kinds of labour 'will be determined according to circumstances, by the Sheriff and Keeper of the Gaol.'[55]

The implementation of these rules presumed a large extension of central authority over institutions whose construction and operating costs were paid for locally. The inspectors probably had enough political insight – and if not they would soon be jolted awake – to understand that under these circumstances their ideal rules would be honoured more in the breach than in the observance. In their judgment, the want of adequate staff, especially teachers and chaplains, and the difficulty in achieving an adequate classification or a labour regimen 'seemed to preclude' the hope of converting them into reformatory institutions. The experiences of their first year had made them feel even 'more strongly the great necessity of "Central Gaols."' These facilities would be for all those currently sentenced to the penitentiary for less than three years, thereby relieving that institution of overcrowding by removing from it between one-half and two-thirds of its prisoners. Notorious repeat offenders and all others deemed unsuitable for the local gaols would also be housed in the central prison, which would be fully staffed with officers comparable to those of a penitentiary. In their 1861 report, the inspectors again asserted hopefully that the new gaols in Toronto and Quebec City would 'soon be available for the inauguration of this indispensable part of the penal system of Canada.'[56] But in 1862 they had to renew their earnest entreaties to hasten ... the establishment of Central Gaols, and to obtain a change in the Criminal Law, by which the recurrence of crime ... should be deemed a fault of an aggravated nature, and punished accordingly by imprisonment ... at hard labour,' in prisons specially designed for the purpose. The construction of 'local penitentiaries' would, they acknowledged, entail heavy expenses but with the rapidity of Canadian development there must also be more crime to deal with. Any funds allocated to the control of social problems would be returned to the state 'in the salutary check thus imposed upon the increase of vice.' From the government's perspective, however, the cost and the political risks of building mini-penitentiaries were simply too great. There was frustration in the board's next comment: 'The remedy rests with the Executive, and it is not to be expected at the hands of the Board.'[57]

In 1861 the board printed its new rules in pamphlet form and distributed copies to every sheriff, with instructions to see that they were enforced so far as local circumstances permitted. Copies were also sent to the judges of the superior courts and frequently endorsed by them. And to add even more official weight, the provincial secretary's office sent copies to the warden of every county, 'for the information of the County Council,' indicating that the rules had been 'confirmed by His Excellency the Governor General in Council, under the provisions of the 22nd Vic., cap.110sec.22.' The wardens were told to take such steps 'as may be necessary' for putting them into effect. The inspectors did not expect their rules to be 'carried into full effect at once'; they admitted that enforcement would encounter some opposition, 'involving as it does, an entire departure from long-standing practices, interfering also with certain vested interests, and exacting ... greater vigilance ... and greater expenditure on the part of the Municipal Councils.'[58]

But even with limited expectations, the inspectors were not prepared for what they found on their inspection tours and they lamented that 'little or nothing had been done to enforce the code.' When local authorities claimed that most of the rules could not be put into place in the existing prisons, the board addressed another circular to the sheriffs pointing out that while some rules could not be enforced, others could be, either in part or in whole.[59] Nonetheless, the inspectors had succeeded to the extent that the new rules and regulations had become the standard to which all counties must to some extent aspire. As the campaign to build new and reconstruct old gaols continued, there was every prospect that an ever-expanding number of counties would gradually achieve substantial parts of the provincial standard.

Politically, the most interesting aspect of this process of disseminating centrist and bureaucratic values throughout the province came in the form of extended confrontations between the inspectors and municipal leaders. A few examples of these disputes will make the point. On 14 February 1861 William Cook, the Warden of Haldimand County, petitioned His Excellency on behalf of the county council that the county should not be required to make a large expenditure to remodel the old gaol and build a new one, as the board was demanding. The council pointed out that the county was 'still considerably in debt' for erecting the existing gaol and courthouse, and the tax level was already 'very burdensome' to the community. The petition emphasized that there was 'no desire ... to evade any reasonable expenditure for enlarging the Gaol if unhappily it were necessary, but ... no such necessity exists.' There had been no more than three prisoners in the gaol at any time over the previous half-year, and no reason to suppose there would be any more. Cook informed the government that 'a very strong and general opinion exists throughout this County' against any additional expenditure, 'especially as contemplated by the said plans involving as they do a very large outlay.' John A. Macdonald forwarded this document to the board and Meredith replied that the board saw 'no reason to depart from the views already officially notified.'[60] Meredith's failure to give reasons earned the board no friends in Haldimand.

Elgin County Council made the same case in July 1861 about the St Thomas gaol. The government, as usual, referred the case back to the inspectors and negotiations continued. In August 1862 an exasperated Elgin Council again went over the board's head and petitioned the government, pointing to the limited number of prisoners and the county's indebtedness. An angry Meredith told the provincial secretary that 'this gaol is in every important essential so defective that the board cannot recommend that the County Council of Elgin should be permitted to postpone the work of altering it' in conformity with the statute. Three years later, the county council was still pleading poverty and the inspectors were still trying to persuade the government to take executive action. Clearly, a determined county council, by delaying and outright refusal, could all too easily balk the inspectors and do just about as they pleased.[61]

The matter of the Hastings County gaol in Belleville revealed other dimensions of conflict. The council's position, as outlined in a letter of 30 July 1863 to the provincial secretary, was common enough. The county was financially embarrassed because of large expenditures on gravel roads and felt that in any case there was no imperative necessity to alter the gaol. But the members of council also challenged the role played by successive grand juries: 'the presentments of Grand Juries are not always based upon the most intelligent consideration of facts and their complaints are often a repetition of previous presentments and made often as a matter of form.' By this time county councils were disinclined to remain passive in the face of criticisms from irresponsible jurors and bureaucrats whom they considered indifferent to local needs and priorities. The matter remained unresolved well into 1865, when the board's persistence prevailed and the Executive Council approved alterations to the Belleville gaol under the provisions of section 15 of the Prison Inspection Act.[62]

But progress was slow. Many of the defects that had been so obvious in Canadian gaols in the 1840s and 1850s remained unremedied throughout the board's tenure and were inherited at Confederation by the Province of Ontario. Grand jury reports and correspondence in the provincial secretary's office continued to document that escapes were as frequent as ever, there appear to have been few changes in staffing, there was no evidence of more frequent attendance of ministers, and the provision of food and clothing still varied from county to county. The counties also continued to give access to the gaol facility on the basis of need rather than criminality.[63]

There was also, of course, a good deal of progress, thanks to the determination of the inspectors. Since 1859 new gaols had been built in Toronto, Ottawa, and Lindsay, and alterations had been carried out in eleven gaols, including London, with plans for changes approved in twelve more. But 'nothing has been done,' the inspectors lamented, in Belleville, Hamilton, Kingston, Owen Sound, Peterborough, Sandwich, Stratford, and Welland. They were hopeful about making progress with most of these, with the exception of Hamilton, where the city and the county council were engaged in their interminable dispute over financial responsibility.[64]

The Perth County gaol at Stratford saw some of the most prolonged resistance. In July 1865 Meredith, in forwarding a critical grand jury presentment to the provincial secretary, informed him that all the board's efforts to persuade the county to make alterations to satisfy the Prison Act had 'hitherto proved unavailing.'[65] By 1867, the matter had progressed to the point that Meredith and the county gaol committee were quarrelling over rival plans for the erection of a new facility. Finally, a special county committee appointed in December 1868 to 'report on the actual condition of the oft-condemned gaol' claimed that all could soon be set in order through a few renovations. The committee vented its anger at 'the fears excited at the reports of the prison inspector, interested officials, and irresponsible grand jurors' in condemning the old gaol 'without sufficient foundation in fact.' The necessary alterations would have been made long ago, had it not been for the pressure to compel the county to erect a new gaol. The committee pointed to the inspectors' most recent report which, as usual, had condemned the gaol in very general terms without, they claimed, specifying precisely what was needed to improve it. In any case, in view of the proposal to erect central prisons, one of which 'ought to be located in Stratford,' the special committee insisted that only the most moderate expenditures should be made on improving the old prison. The report was adopted unanimously at council.[66]

More constructively, the Perth Council appointed a committee on central prisons which, on 18 December 1868, reported that these institutions would be vastly superior to the existing penal system, most of all in enforcing a system of hard labour. They suggested that three central prisons be built, in Kingston, Toronto, and Stratford, 'provided the expenditure in their construction is moderate, and the most accessible, and central locations selected.'[67] On another point the Perth County gaol committee was in agreement with the inspectors. On 29 January 1869, after inspecting the gaol, they lamented that, with several strong and healthy males confined, there was no way to use their labour to advantage. The inspectors' admonitions had had some effect, for the gaol committee now suggested that the county purchase pants, blankets, shoes, jackets, and other supplies. Finally, they expressed the belief, also shared by the inspectors, that 'many persons confined, consider it a boon to have the privilege of being so confined – one stated that he was committed for ten days, and felt sorry that it was not for a month.'[68]

The strongest concern that runs through the documentation dealing with the board's relationship with county councils was cost. It was the constant refrain of county wardens that the local taxpayer could not bear the financial burden of gaol repairs and additions. The issue was partly one of spending priorities, combined with resentment of appointed bureaucrats pre-empting the county's own authority in this area. But money in this capital-scarce society was a critical consideration. Many counties, when they applied for assistance from the 'Upper Canada Building Fund,' discovered that the rules were applied strictly and their appeals were not granted.

If the government had fully supported the objectives of its own inspectors, this fund might have been used flexibly to encourage counties to proceed, but that does not appear to have happened. Take, for example, the 1865 request of Victoria County, which in 1862 had expended $20,000 on a new gaol. This had included an additional storey for workshops, which the inspectors had insisted upon before giving their approval. The county council cited section 21 of the statute to the effect that they could apply for funding support for any 'alterations or additions.' When its request for $6,000 was denied because funding was not available for new gaols, the council felt it was being discriminated against: 'the Government [had] granted the sum of $24,000 to assist in erecting the new Gaol in Toronto, and they subsequently paid one half of the cost of erecting what might be very properly termed a new Gaol in Peterboro.'[69]

One illustration of a county council digging in its heels over costs can be found in Lennox and Addington in 1865–6. Meredith had inspected the gaol and made numerous suggestions for improvements to the sheriff and his deputy, who were receptive. The sheriff appointed an assistant keeper and requested the county council to make provision for his salary. The result was an appropriation of $150 a year, 'a sum so insignificant that the Assistant at once resigned his appointment, and no person can be found at that salary to take his place ... I am fully persuaded the small sum of $150 was voted with the intention of getting rid of the Assistant.' Furious at having responsibility without power, the sheriff asked Meredith to 'instruct me what to do.' Meredith referred the matter to the attorney general, but apparently no action was taken. In short, the sheriff and the inspectors were ignored; democracy had again prevailed.[70]

In Hamilton in 1866, when a gaoler was partly responsible for an escape,

Sheriff E. Cartwright-Thomas told the provincial secretary he was 'reluctant to dismiss [the gaoler], feeling that for the small amount of remuneration awarded to him ... it will be difficult to supply his place efficiently.'[71] Cartwright-Thomas, one of the most experienced and well-connected sheriffs in the province, was reduced by 1866 to throwing up his hands in frustration. In June of that year he told Meredith that the gaol held far too many prisoners, many of whom in his view belonged more properly in a city house of correction. Attached to his letter was an extract from Meredith's 1861 report, which had described Wentworth gaol accommodation as 'perhaps the very worst in Upper Canada'; Meredith further noted that the board had repeatedly condemned this gaol. Attorney General Macdonald directed that the correspondence be forwarded to the warden of Wentworth and the mayor of Hamilton requesting their 'immediate and earnest attention.'[72] Typically, Macdonald refused to challenge the municipal authorities directly. This deference to local authority would prevail in Ontario for another century in the field of gaol administration.

With their legal powers rendered largely nugatory, the inspectors could only bluster. In these circumstances the board made its case to the best of its ability. In their individual reports between 1862 and 1866, which was the last full year in which the members of the old board dealt with local gaols, two inspectors, Terence O'Neill and James Ferres, often reflected on the larger social implications of maintaining these unreformed institutions. In 1862 Ferres argued persuasively that the old shibboleth that gaols were 'nurseries of crime' was literally true. The new Toronto gaoler, Mr Allen, regarded as a highly efficient officer, provided Ferres with figures for 1860, 1861, and 1862, comprising 587 recidivists, which demonstrated a remarkable record of reconviction. Shocked at such figures, Ferres claimed that the failure of the law and the judges to deal with the problem of recidivism served 'to foster crime, and to train up families of criminals to the second and third generations.' Moreover, the cost of 'frequent commitment systems' was appalling. In Toronto in 1862, 380 persons were tried 1166 times and in Montreal 649 'worthless vagrants' were tried 2146 times. 'These recommitments proceeded from the Recorder's and the Police Courts, and if we reckon the expense of the police, the witnesses and the clerks, and assume them at the moderate rate of $5 for each arrest and trial, we have the sum of $16,560 expended in producing crime, instead of repressing it.' These circumstances, Ferres claimed, prevailed across the country, in the smaller gaols as well as the larger. Ferres would solve the problem by combining longer sentences for recidivists with a system of hard labour at public works.[73]

TABLE 9.1
Toronto Recidivists, 1860–1862

Persons Committed	Times Committed	Persons Committed	Times Committed
182	2	2	17
107	3	4	18
62	4	5	19
43	5	3	20
36	6	7	21
23	7	6	22
14	8	2	23
18	9	4	24
13	10	1	25
7	11	4	26
9	12	4	27
5	13	3	28
9	14	1	30
8	15	1	31
5	16		

Source: Annual Reports

Terence O'Neill, for his part, spent as much time attacking municipal politicians as condemning the criminal class. More than half of the gaols he found were in conflict with legal requirements and it was shocking that the municipal authorities were 'so insensible to their responsibilities.' The false economy of the counties was unpatriotic and injurious to morals. Like Ferres, O'Neill believed that recidivism had created a threatening and dependent criminal class, and he argued that the only response was the rigid enforcement of hard and punitive labour. He found some satisfaction in noting in his 1864 report a very sharp drop in the recidivism rate in the new Toronto gaol, which he attributed to the imposition of what he called 'real "hard labour."' In 1862, he noted, out of 2,091 committals, no fewer than 1,420 were recommittals; for the new gaol in 1863, out of 1,961 committals, but 291 were recommittals. The criminal class, he believed, was on the run.[74]

Persuaded nonetheless that society continued to face both moral degradation and the crippling costs associated with large increases in the numbers of the criminal class, Meredith and his fellow inspectors continued to make the rounds of the counties to cajole or bully the local politicians to action. Their 1863 and 1864 reports offer a chronicle of gradual progress. By 1864, the annual list of alterations and improvements in Upper Canada's gaols showed that Hastings and Grey Counties had evinced a desire to cooperate, leaving only Elgin, Halton, Perth, Prince Edward, and the United Counties of Stormont, Dundas, and Glengarry as 'recusant' counties. In all these cases, the board urged the government to force compliance, but the government as usual was reluctant.[75]

Several gaols posed special problems. The old county gaol located in Toronto at Front and Berkeley streets, the third Toronto gaol, had been in use since 1840. The perpetual dispute between the city and the county over the sharing of cost accounted to some extent for the earlier failure to attend to pressing problems. Meredith was assured by officials that when the new Toronto gaol opened the board's rules would be enforced in both facilities. The Don Gaol, to be operated by city council, had been under construction since the late 1850s and received its first prisoners in 1864. The inspectors were delighted with what they described as this 'handsome' new gaol, with its extensive facilities for classification and for the implementation of work programs. They fully believed that through the strict enforcement of prison rules 'the number of habitual frequenters of the gaol will ere long be materially decreased.'[76]

MEREDITH'S DIARY

The best source of uncensored comment on gaol conditions in the 1860s is Meredith's personal diary. There was no gaol that he condemned more vividly than that of Ottawa. His loathing of this horrible old place leaps from the page. In October 1861, he wrote, he

went through the wretched Gaol with the Gaoler. It is truly a very mockery of a prison. All the windows of the cells, and ... day rooms are all perfectly accessible to the public. While I was there several persons came to the window to talk to the prisoners who were all gathered around the window ...

The dingy cells off the corridor are damp dark and unwholesome. The privy ... was over-flowing with abomination and sends out a stench which poisons alike the prison and the Court House. There is but one cell for women off this corridor, and the Gaoler had one woman ... in the same room with some male prisoners upstairs, intended for debtors, being afraid to leave her in the abominable hole below. There were 6 young boys in the corridor below with the men whose minds must have been poisoned by the moral atmosphere as their bodies were by the physical atmosphere in which they were living. The Cells and Corridors need white washing very much. I could not allow myself to leave Ottawa without writing a letter to the Warden urging him to instruct the County Council (I should like to throw them into the Gaol!) to have the privies cleaned.[77]

Fortunately, a new gaol was under construction. In their 1863 report, the inspectors asserted with audible relief that the new gaol was 'probably the best in Canada, and the old gaol was probably about the very worst.'[78]

A few counties simply refused any cooperation; others, including Wentworth, faced genuine difficulties in carrying out the directives of the board. The majority, however, made an honest effort to comply. When he visited the St Thomas gaol in September 1861, Meredith encountered only three prisoners, a circumstance which made many counties reluctant to spend money remodelling underused facilities. The Elgin Council had been uncooperative until Meredith met personally with its members. This interview, he related, 'confirmed me in the opinion which I have always entertained since my appointment to the board, that to effect anything with the Councils' it was necessary to see them and to reason with them. The County Council of Elgin had been most resistant in correspondence, 'and yet after half an hours quiet conversation' they were willing 'to do anything that was required of them' and decided on the spot to advertise for tenders.[79]

Meredith was proudest of the changes effected in the Woodstock gaol, which he inspected in September. The plan adopted for altering this gaol had 'succeeded beyond [his] hope.' Best of all, 'the County Council appears very desirous to aid the board in enforcing the Rules.' They had already supplied clothing and appointed a matron and the food, now supplied by contract, was costing seven cents a day as opposed to between thirty and forty under the old system. The county council was delighted with the savings and the chair of the gaol committee reported that the prisoners were 'quite satisfied with their fare.'[80]

It seems unlikely, however, that the prisoners could genuinely have been satisfied with food purchased at a fraction of previous cost. In a revealing section in the 1863 report, the inspectors boasted that the prisoners vastly preferred the old unreformed gaols to the new streamlined models. Wherever new gaols had been built or the old ones altered to permit the implementation of the board's prison rules, 'there was a marked falling off in the number of prisoners confined in the gaol.' In Ottawa the number of prisoners had dropped from 416 in 1861 to 232 in 1862. The board concluded that the dislike of the new gaols, which had increased their deterrent power, was attributable most of all to improvements in classification. 'In the old gaols the cells might be filthy, the air pestilential, and the food bad ... but at least the prisoners could spend the day together round the stoves in the day rooms, and enjoy the unspeakable comfort of sleeping at night three or four in a cell.'[81]

ADMISSION OF FAILURE

The most useful summary of the results of the board's gaol reform efforts appeared in a Special Appendix to the 1864 report prepared by Meredith. Dismissing the board's not inconsiderable achievements as largely ineffectual, Meredith cut to the heart of the problem with an almost ruthless social judgment. In the area of prison management, he asserted bluntly, 'the labors of the board in this matter have had no practical results.' Still needed, he argued, was far greater provision for the separation of prisoners and more efficient means to establish systems of hard labour that could play a deterrent role. There were, said Meredith, four changes requisite to the establishment of a sound system of prison discipline which were still absent. These were frequent and thorough inspection; an adequate staff of good officers; buildings adapted to enforce discipline; and a uniform system of discipline enforced by a common code of rules and regulations. To remedy many failings of the existing system, he advocated above all the establishment of central prisons and the strict enforcement of the principle of individual separation.[82]

In enunciating this credo, the inspectors' thinking had advanced considerably over 1860. They now recommended that separation be given priority over hard labour, in part because of problems in carrying out such labour, but also because they believed separate confinement as advocated by English authorities in 1863 was a more severe form of punishment. If it were instituted, they suggested, 'the ordinary length of sentence should be reduced to about one-third of that now imposed' to compensate for this greater severity. Separate confinement would add to the deterrent effect, end the existing moral contamination of free association, and more than double the capacity of existing gaols.[83] A further refinement of this approach appeared in their 1865 report. Here the argument was made that to the extent that hard labour continued to be imposed, it should be penal in nature and involve the performance of unpleasant tasks primarily for their deterrent effect, such as treadwheel and shotdrill.

But there was also a more progressive side to their evolving views. As a strong proponent of frequent inspections, Meredith in 1864 reiterated his earlier proposal that local voluntary boards, composed of the county warden, the mayor, and the district judge, carry out regular inspections and report to the board. But this scheme was not supported by his fellow inspectors, allegedly on the ground that it might create local jealousies. Meredith persisted, however, arguing that several local magistrates could also be asked to participate in the inspectoral process. From travelling about the province he had formed the conclusion that public indifference and ignorance were the greatest barriers to the establishment of a humane and efficient prison system. The organization of local boards, he argued, would contribute to the establishment of an informed public opinion on prison matters. Until 'such a public opinion has been formed,' and 'until the public mind has been educated ... any great or important reform in our Prison system will be almost impossible.'[84] At such moments, Meredith's fertile mind transcended the customary limitations of the bureaucratic approach to comprehend the larger basis for effective public action. Unfortunately, he could convince neither his colleagues nor the politicians of the need to enlist a broader public in a prison reform movement.

Meredith clearly recognized that although the board's labours would make some difference, apathy and ignorance, together with the lack of political will, both locally and centrally, must eventually defeat its efforts. The board could only, 'remonstrate and entreat' the counties to comply with the statute dealing with alterations to the common gaols; it could not compel them to do so. And while recusant counties could be brought to the attention of the executive, where no action was taken the efforts of the board were 'consequently paralyzed.'[85]

The following year, in their 1865 report, the inspectors printed as a 'Special Appendix' the circular despatch dated 17 January 1865, which Colonial Secretary Edward Cardwell had sent to all British colonies on the subject of prison discipline. This document, it will be recalled, was based on the 1863 report of the House of Lords on British gaols and on the Royal Commission on Penal Servitude of the same year. The inspectors expressed their admiration for Cardwell's despatch in its advocacy of strict discipline, centralized control, corporal punishment for juveniles, a reduced dietary, penal unproductive labour and, above all, of a classification system designed to maximize separation. Probably because this coincided closely with many of their own ideas about how to deal with 'the criminal class,' it seems to have strengthened the more repressive aspects of their thinking.[86] In any case, the influence of British thinking, as it had evolved since 1863, replaced for a brief period the earlier Canadian inclination to look to the United States as a source of ideas and practices.

And there matters rested until the board's demise in 1868. Undoubtedly the Board of Inspectors appointed under the 1859 legislation represented a big step forward in Canadian welfare administration. The board had many accomplishments to its credit and the efforts of successor boards at the federal level in post-Confederation Canada pale by comparison, although Ontario's remarkable prison inspector, J.W. Langmuir, did some outstanding work. It was not the least of the old board's achievements that it understood the limitations to its power and its successes, even as it chafed against them. In 1866 the American prison reformers E.C. Wines and Theodore Dwight would refer admiringly to the efforts of the Canadian board, regretting that the Canadian government had failed to support it more generously.[87] But perhaps after all Meredith was wrong and John A. Macdonald right. The restraints on bureaucratic authority were necessary and proper. To a considerable extent the board's failure at critical points reflected the narrow economic priorities of pre-Confederation society and pointed to aspects of the new democracy which delegated real power to popularly elected municipal politicians. Nonetheless, the strongly expressed view of Burns and other judges that control over all prisons should always have been lodged in the central rather than the municipal authority had much force, although it did not gain acceptance in Ontario until the 1960s.

As E.A. Meredith clearly understood, penal reform in general, and the state of the gaols in particular, intersected closely with prevailing social and intellectual mores. Neither state formation conceived as a centralist function nor the extension of bureaucratic values could negate that prevailing reality. Despite all efforts to the contrary, the gaols in many essentials remained primarily local institutions, responsive to local values and serving democratic needs. It remained to be seen whether the establishment in 1867 of the new Province of Ontario and the relegation of all gaol matters to a single powerful inspector would somehow alter and reshape that fundamental reality.

10

The Persistence of Community: Ontario's Gaols in the Industrial Era

Between Confederation and century-end, Ontario experienced its first industrial revolution. In that same period Ontario's gaols were caught uncertainly between the old and the new, as they struggled to adapt to the demands of the emerging industrial age. The gaols, as we have seen, had in some respects been left behind in the modernization and institutional growth that embodied the social dynamic of the 1840s and 1850s. While state formation, bureaucratization, and the emergence of large institutional structures focused provincial attention on the penitentiary and the asylum, the gaol during the Union years retained the communitarian characteristics that had shaped its role in the Upper Canadian period. These local facilities had proved resistant to even the most insistent urgings of the new inspectoral board of the 1860s. Now they would similarly resist the determined assault of Ontario's single powerful inspector of the post-Confederation era, J.W. Langmuir.

But there was one major difference in the situation of the gaols in post-Confederation Ontario. Now they were left to play out their anachronistic role in a society feeling the full effects of industrial transformation. To what extent could industrial capitalism permit an institution redolent of the old order of rural, local, and decentralized structures of power to carry on as though nothing had changed? The gaols continued to house a congregate population and to serve the local counties as cheap and convenient all-purpose facilities. They also received, and in some measure protected, the casualties of industrialization: tramps, vagrants, prostitutes, and other dropouts and victims of the industrial struggle.

Further changes were also transforming the province. This was a period of unprecedented political stability; the Liberal Party ruled for more than three decades and Ontario, under its astute premier, Oliver Mowat, achieved a myriad of reforms, including manhood suffrage, temperance legislation, and factory and workers' compensation Acts. Ontario also experienced rapid urbanization and much rural depopulation. Urban numbers grew from 14 per cent in 1851 to 35 per cent in 1891. The population of some cities soared, most of all Toronto, whose population increased from 86,415 in 1881 to 376,471 in 1911. The criminal justice system, including the gaols, was affected by these transformations in numerous ways; at the same time, what went on in the gaols and other prison facilities contributed to the shaping of late nineteenth century Ontario.

To position the situation of the gaols within this wider panorama of social and political change is a task of infinite complexity, but three themes will emerge in this chapter. Firstly, the tensions between the forces of centralization and bureaucratization and powerful local and community interests that were characteristic of the earlier period continued. Although the old Board of Inspectors died with Confederation, the new Ontario inspector, J.W. Langmuir, armed with extensive authority, was a host in himself. Langmuir was determined to rationalize and reform every aspect of Ontario's prison and welfare systems. In pursuing this goal he was fully in harmony with the powerful thrust of late nineteenth century political change: the Mowat administration, controlled by middle-class business and professional elements, embarked on sweeping campaigns to impose order and rationality on almost every aspect of provincial life.

Secondly, John Langmuir, like the Meredith board, proceeded to base his reform program on the firm foundation of statistical analysis. He charted 'the movement of gaol populations' with unremitting care, drawing conclusions and devising policies on the basis of carefully calculated numbers. Langmuir's statistics (and others calculated within this chapter) demonstrate both change and continuity in Ontario's penal culture.

Thirdly, the gaols continued to serve the Ontario community as refuges, shelters, asylums, and poorhouses. But they did so in ways distinctly different from the experience of the Upper Canadian years. In a society criss-crossed with railway lines, dotted with industrial smokestacks, and beset with the social conditions characteristic of life in substantial cities, many of the gaols that housed this congregate population of the aged, the ill, and the poor seemed to have lost the sometimes benign local characteristics that had shaped custom and practice in a more rural province. In the urban and industrial age, how did these neglected populations fare in the continued absence of other facilities purpose-built to meet pressing social needs?

LANGMUIR AND ADMINISTRATIVE REFORM

Langmuir's first two reports demonstrated the intractability of the problem as viewed from Queen's Park. Like Meredith, he noted that even those gaols that tried to conform to inspectoral directives remained horribly defective. Classification was 'almost, if not altogether, *a dead letter* in the Common Gaols of this Province.' With the exception of 'occasional jobs' there was no system of hard or penal labour, despite 'the solemn farce' of sentences to hard labour continually being handed down by the courts. Langmuir placed emphasis too on the urgent need to achieve the old board's goal of a uniform dietary at a much reduced cost, one in which the gaoler was to have no pecuniary interest. And he adopted as the cornerstone of his own policy the long-standing inspectoral commitment to establish central hard labour prisons in the west, centre, and east of the province, under provincial control, for those sentenced to between sixty days' and two years' confinement.

If there was a new emphasis at all, it was in Langmuir's commitment to improving conditions for female prisoners. He pointed out that fully 2,530 of the 8,015 gaol commitments over the previous fifteen months had been female. Three-quarters of these were prostitutes and he pointed to 'the most painful fact' that 340 of them were girls under sixteen. It was, he believed, the urgent moral duty of the province to establish a reformatory for young women to ensure that none would ever again suffer the horrors of imprisonment in a common gaol.[1]

Langmuir soon discovered, as his second report indicated, that the 'recusant counties' were as determined as ever to resist central authority, and he was 'unable to report any actual progress' in moving them to action. Beyond that, the system was plagued in this period with escapes and irregularities. Determined to achieve comprehensive change, Langmuir announced that a commission had been issued 'authorizing me to make inquiry into all matters connected with Gaols.'[2] During his years in office, Langmuir conducted a substantial number of such special investigations, usually resulting in recommendations for improved security or staff changes.

Langmuir quickly achieved enormous prestige and authority, first within the Sandfield Macdonald government, and then with the Liberals who came to power in 1871. The Liberals admired his enormous energy and respected his judgment, and he never experienced the rebuffs that had been Meredith's lot. Adding to these fortuitous considerations were the expanded powers given the inspector under the province's 1868 inspectoral legislation. The British North America Act of 1867, as noted earlier, assigned to the provinces broad welfare responsibilities, including 'Public and Reformatory Prisons' and 'Hospitals, Asylums, Charities and Eleemosynary Institutions.' The 1868 'Act to Provide for the Inspection of Asylums, Hospitals, Common Gaols and Reformatories in this Province' established the legal framework for inspectoral activities.[3] In conformity with pre-Confederation practice but in contrast to what was now done at the national level, the Ontario statute grouped a range of correctional and welfare functions under a single inspectorate. Instead of five inspectors, however, there was now only one man, and he would receive a salary and expenses about a third less than that given any single inspector before Confederation. Considering the range of functions and the heavy duties of the position, such parsimony was curiously shortsighted. The statute dealt with three types of inspectoral activity: areas falling fully under provincial control, especially asylums for the mentally ill; areas that were privately controlled but in receipt of some provincial funding, such as poorhouses and hospitals; and areas in which responsibility was shared between the municipalities and the province, especially the gaols.

In this latter field the provincial inspector, possibly in response to the frustrating experiences of the old board, was given expanded legal powers to deal with recusant counties. If the inspector discovered that any gaol was not built or maintained according to provincial standards, he was to 'forthwith report the fact' to the government, and to furnish a copy of such report to the county or city council, which would appoint a committee to confer with the inspector to arrange all necessary changes or repairs. If no agreement was reached between the inspector and the council, it became the duty of the government to decide between the two parties and the council might then be ordered to proceed. In default, the council 'may be proceeded against by Mandamus' issued out of a superior court at the instance either of the attorney general or of any private prosecutor.

The statute of 1868 seemed to provide the legal hammer that Meredith and the old board had lacked. It forcefully restated the right of the inspector to make rules extending to every aspect of the life of the gaols and requiring him to approve the plan of every new gaol in accordance with an extensive list of criteria. With extended powers and enhanced prestige, J.W. Langmuir commanded respect and spoke with an authority that required the most independent of municipal politicians to take heed. The municipalities in the post-Confederation period were also in some respects more clearly subordinate to the new province than they had ever been to the Province of Canada during the Union years. All this portended much for gaol reform – but once again achievements fell short of expectations.

This was not immediately apparent and was hardly the fault of the inspector. J.W. Langmuir was a remarkable public servant. When one early writer remarked upon the formidable responsibilities given to the inspector under the 1868 statute, he commented that many believed 'that the work of the office was too great for one man, but Mr. Langmuir showed that it depended on the kind of man.'[4] Born in Scotland in 1835, Langmuir migrated to Canada West in 1849 at the age of fifteen, settling in Picton and in Kingston where he engaged in mercantile activities, especially the grain trade. Successful in these activities, he acquired the Picton branch of his employer's business in 1853 and in 1858 became mayor of Picton. Like many others on the rise, he became active in militia affairs, attaining the rank of major and seeing service during the Fenian raids of 1866. It is not known why this formidable young man turned his back on his business successes and sought the position of prison inspector in 1868. Although a Liberal, he received the appointment from the 'Patent Combination' of Sandfield Macdonald and held it during the critical period when the new Province of Ontario, free at last to develop its own social policies, put in place what Langmuir regarded as all the elements of a complete program of welfare and penal services.[5]

Langmuir chose the occasion of his tenth annual report in 1877, the beginning of Ontario's second decade as a province, to reflect on what had been achieved. He noted that by Confederation 'a good deal had been done to improve the condition and discipline of the common gaols,' yet a large majority remained 'faulty in construction, defective in arrangement, wanting in the means of classification, loose in discipline, and, worse than all, associated idleness with all its evils reigned supreme.' But according to Langmuir, enormous strides had been taken over the past decade to mitigate the effect of enforced idleness, and the means of reformation had 'largely increased.' Every common gaol, with but one or two exceptions, 'had either been rebuilt or reconstructed, in order to comply with modern views' and to meet the requirements of the Prison Inspection Act.[6]

Langmuir was proud of what Ontario had accomplished in other welfare areas as well, especially the expansion in the asylum system. Through the Charity Aid Act of 1874,[7] funding was systematically made available to private institutions, including poorhouses and hospitals, which accepted provincial inspection and were doing work that had provincial approval and maintained acceptable standards. At Langmuir's urging Ontario opened an institution for the deaf at Belleville in 1870 and, in 1872, a facility for the blind at Brantford. In the area of mental illness, he pointed to the establishment of three new asylums, including one at London which held about a thousand patients, and an associated asylum 'for Idiots.' When the press of numbers overwhelmed available space at London, a separate facility, the Ontario Asylum for Idiots, was opened in Orillia in September 1876. With the opening of the Central Prison in Toronto in 1874, Langmuir achieved the dearest objective of the old board, the establishment of mini-penitentiaries, and he was the driving force behind the opening in 1880 of a separate women's prison in Toronto, the Mercer.

Notwithstanding the accomplishments listed in the 1877 report, Langmuir was privately far from satisfied. Most of all he chafed under the restrictions imposed by the need to seek the cooperation of municipal politicians. More than a decade later Langmuir's reservations were confirmed by the findings of the 1891 prison commission which he himself chaired. The commissioners were told repeatedly by sheriffs and gaolers of the distressing consequences that arose when counties refused to pay the salaries needed to hire competent staff or to undertake essential repairs or supply the most basic prisoner needs. Many observers agreed with H.C. Corbett, the gaoler at Kingston, that 'the whole foundation of the county gaol system is rotten from the bottom upwards.'[8] Once again the commissioners made recommendations to reform the gaols, but again political and financial exigencies and the indifference of public opinion to the plight of the prisoners determined that little would change. In essence, the gaols of Ontario remained unreformed institutions at the end of the century, confirming the old view that they were nurseries of crime and a disgrace to the province.

Between 1874 and 1899, the lowest number in the gaols was 8,203 (1899), and the highest was 13,481 (1877); throughout the period the recidivist rate hovered between a quarter and a third of all those confined.[9] Facing such large numbers, Langmuir's priority was to ensure that all gaols met provincial standards and that counties that did not were brought into line.

One of the worst offenders was still the county council of Perth. In his 1870 report, the inspector announced that the attorney general had applied for a writ of mandamus to compel Perth to provide the accommodation required under the Act. Apparently this had the desired effect and the warden promised to submit a by-law 'providing for the expenditure of $20,000 in the erection of a new Gaol.' Similar action had to be taken to deal with the Wentworth County Council and the Victoria County Council.[10] As early as 1871 Langmuir expected to 'shortly be able to report the provisions of the Inspection Act, in reference to the state and condition of Gaols, as fully complied with throughout the province.'[11] But this was far too optimistic. In 1891, almost a quarter of a century after Langmuir's original appointment, the prison commission he chaired pronounced most of the province's gaols unsuited to the demands of classification and reform.[12]

There were nonetheless a few achievements. Always cost conscious, Langmuir was as offended as his predecessors by the inefficiency and the impropriety of relying on gaolers with a financial interest to supply their prison with food. He triumphantly reported in 1875 that he had ended irregularities and imposed the official system across the province, and that this had 'greatly reduced gaol expenditures.'[13]

There was some reason for this concern with cost. The 1868 inspection statute had ended the pre-Confederation system by which counties altering or repairing their gaols had been able to receive funding for up to half the cost, to a maximum of $6,000, from the Upper Canada building fund. When some counties, for example Essex, now claimed they needed provincial financial assistance, they received no sympathy from the inspector. 'I reminded the Special Committee,' he reported in 1869, 'that Government assistance *had* been offered to them, in common with other counties, through the provisions of the late Act, which, although it had been in existence for nine years, the County of Essex failed to take advantage of it, although repeatedly urged to do so.'[14] The counties, however, persisted in their efforts to get provincial assistance.[15] Langmuir realized that it would be infinitely easier to achieve his objectives if the province proffered the carrot as well as the stick. Through an 1874 statute revision, Ontario provided assistance 'towards the construction and alteration of, and additions to County Gaols.' According to Langmuir's comprehensive calculations, $67,210.30 would also be required to liquidate claims of counties for work already done. The new policy made several recusant counties less so and generally expedited the reform program.

Alert to the practical advantages of providing financial assistance, the province soon also offered support for an entire category of prisoners.

The statistical section of the annual reports included a column headed 'Actual cost of prisoners,' showing costs for each gaol. In 1869, for example, this totalled $100,739 for all thirty-seven gaols. Langmuir's tidy mind was offended less by the total cost than by the variations from county to county and he was determined to achieve and enforce uniformity. The 'confusion and want of uniformity in expenditures,' he asserted, must continue, 'as long as direct authority and supervision is not vested in the Government.'[16]

In 1870 the statistical tables differentiated between two classes of prisoners: those 'chargeable to Criminal Justice Fund' and those 'chargeable to the County.'[17] The assumption by the province of the complete cost of some prisoners seems to have been an innovation and it strengthened Langmuir's hand as he manoeuvred to gain wider authority over internal operations and management. This change was eased by a reform of the court system under which persons charged with offences could waive some of their rights and be tried before a county judge without a jury in 'Interim Sessions Courts.' According to the 1870 report, these courts had 'operated very favourably in relieving many of the Gaols from being overcrowded, by the almost immediate discharge of persons found not guilty of the offence for which they were sent to Gaol' or their removal to other institutions. The table that followed showed that 644 prisoners had elected to be tried at the Interim Sessions Courts.[18] The 1871 report included a table showing that the maintenance of 4,739 prisoners was paid for by the counties, while 1,876 were paid for by the province 'out of the appropriation for Criminal Administration.'[19] Although numerically county prisoners were in excess of provincial ones, the latter were confined for longer periods of time. That this distinction between provincial and municipal prisoners was an innovation seemed confirmed when Langmuir promised that in future returns he would provide detailed information on the total days' custody of each class. In the 1872 report he noted an average stay of forty-one days for provincial and twenty-four for county prisoners. In his 1877 report Langmuir explained that provincial prisoners were those convicted for indictable offences and whose maintenance was provided for by funds voted by the legislature.

Gradually, Langmuir endeavoured to tighten the screws of central authority. In 1876 he expressed his frustration that numerous escapes had resulted from the incompetence of local officers. Many local officials, he complained, were 'confiding and unsuspicious to the verge of simplicity' and the only remedy was more direct government control.[20] Appointments of gaolers and turnkeys were vested in the sheriffs, who were appointed by the province, yet salaries were fixed by the county, and 'too often at so low a rate that it is impossible' to procure suitable officers. The problem of escapes and of 'culpable neglect' on the part of subordinate officers could be remedied only 'by the adoption of a uniform system of government in the Common Gaols, and the strict enforcement of whole-some regulations by one controlling authority.'[21]

Over the next several years, Langmuir still believed he would have his way by means of a complete provincial takeover. Not until 1880 or 1881 was he told by his superiors that this would not happen. Baulked at least temporarily, he and his successors became increasingly peremptory in issuing orders to sheriffs to follow instructions, frequently demanding the dismissal of incompetent officers and ordering county councils to make essential improvements. In the 1890s, for example, orders were issued that non-criminal prisoners be provided with civilian clothing and special diets. In this gradual way, provincial authority was increasingly felt throughout the system and a new degree of efficiency and standard-ization was achieved. It was, however, far from complete, and the 1891 commission would once again demonstrate the extent to which divided authority and local initiative continued to adversely affect efforts to establish decent and province-wide standards.

The least satisfactory circumstance for Langmuir and many other middle-class Ontarians was the failure to implement systems of remun-erative labour. Year after year almost every gaol had nothing to report in the column outlining revenue from prisoner labour; one exception was Toronto which, in 1868, listed $632.84, of a province-wide total of $725.33. In 1877, Langmuir reported over $77,000 derived as revenue that year from government-owned institutions, including over $21,000 from the Toronto asylum, but only $2,120.86 from labour in the gaols.[22] While the economic loss rankled, this situation was unacceptable primarily because it offended the moral sensibilities of many respectable persons. 'Enter the corridor of any of our gaols,' Langmuir wrote in 1869, 'and the first thing that strikes an observer is the *utter idleness* that prevails'; not the wearing, silent idleness of solitary confinement but '*vitiating associated* idleness.' To this, said Langmuir, could be traced 'all the vicious and demoralizing effects of our Common Gaol System.' Better to return to the crank and the treadwheel than to continue a system that contributed so greatly to 'the nurture and spread of vice and crime.' Ontario's gaols, he concluded, 'whether examined from a penal, reformatory, or economical standpoint must be pronounced a delusion and a failure.'[23]

Year after year, Langmuir and his successors laboured without success to introduce work programs into the province's gaols. In his 1870 report he calculated that the return on a potential of 146,400 days in prison labour had been a paltry twenty-five cents for each prisoner for the entire year. Comparing this with returns in other countries, he calculated a loss to the province of $49,560.[24] The only solution, Langmuir believed, was the establishment of intermediate prisons on the model of the industrial reformatory. Ironically, not even the establishment of a big industrial prison in 1874 solved the problem, and the province's moral guardians continued to express outrage at the idleness that still prevailed in the local gaols. Some wood chopping, stone breaking in a few, and a little maintenance work were about the most that was ever achieved, although there were occasional, often short-lived, exceptions. In the Ottawa gaol in 1872, for instance, 'upwards of sixty tons of stone' were broken for a profit of $300 and female prisoners were busily picking oakum, with a considerable quantity to market. But efforts to keep prisoners employed were sporadic and the revenue column for most county gaols, and even for the big city gaols, usually remained blank.

In his frustration, Langmuir failed to consider that some positive consequences could be attributed to the unwillingness to enforce punitive labour. Prisoners who spent their time socializing and playing cards had better dispositions than those forced to break stone, and this accounts in some measure for the absence of major disturbances and harsh punishments. There were very few exceptions, one occurring in Toronto in 1889 when the inspector encountered 'a considerable disturbance,' probably staged for his benefit, when prisoners moving earth inside the yard refused to labour.[25]

The most innovative effort in this area was to employ prisoners in public works outside the walls of the gaol. In numerous reports, faced with an embarrassing number of prisoners who walked off while gathering wood or employed in a similar task, Langmuir made it clear that it was illegal for gaolers to allow prisoners to work outside the prison limits. Any sheriff who permitted such activity was informed that he personally would be held responsible for any escapes.[26] But the attractions of a system of extramural employment proved irresistible. In 1877 the federal government passed legislation to permit prisoners convicted more than once to be so employed, but apparently this did not apply to offenders convicted for non-indictable offences.[27] In 1877, Langmuir urged the provincial secretary to enact a provincial law applicable to such offenders.[28] By this time he was increasingly frustrated that the question of employment for prisoners sentenced to hard labour 'remains to be solved.' It was 'not to be wondered at' that there was a problem in the rural gaols, 'but that little or nothing should be obtained for them to do in places like Toronto and Hamilton seems incredible.' For Langmuir the problem was a disciplinary one, and with 7,000 of 8,470 prisoners sentenced the previous year committed for two months or under, the difficulty of providing work was greatly compounded.[29]

The press, as Stephen Connor has indicated, often expressed outrage at the prevailing idleness. Faced with an escalating committal rate, the Toronto *Mail* referred to the 'reign of terror' of the criminal element and insisted that the gaols be made truly deterrent. In 1868 the *Ottawa Citizen* had demanded a return of the treadmill and similar sentiments now surfaced elsewhere: the Perth *Courier* called in 1879 for the infliction of corporal punishment to reduce crime, reflecting sentiments which doubtless were widespread.[30] In the same year that he promoted extramural labour, Langmuir found it necessary to combat the idea that the gaols had gone soft. The notion was 'frequently expressed, that we have gone rather too far in the improvement of gaols ... some even go so far as to say that they are luxurious.' These canards, said Langmuir, 'I emphatically deny. On the contrary, the great object aimed at ... has been the provision of hard labour.' But he had to admit that this had been accomplished only in the Central Prison.[31]

In response to such criticism the government in 1878 passed legislation for the desired extension of extramural labour. Mowat emphasized that this was not an attempt to make the law more harsh or punitive, but merely to carry out existing sentences to hard labour.[32] Although the 'chain-gang' statute was popular with the legislators, there were difficulties in putting it into effect. Langmuir had tried to prepare the ground in his 1878 report by presenting elaborate regulations. At the discretion of the sheriff, the guards attending to prisoners employed outside the prison might be furnished with firearms, any prisoner who attempted escape might be secured with a ball and chain, and prisoners might be chained together. But in the same report Langmuir noted that the counties were not taking advantage of the statute, perhaps because the municipal politicians feared the hostility of free labour.[33] It was fortunate that Ontario was spared the excesses of chain-gang labour which darkened the record of many American state penal systems, but this additional failure demonstrated once again that it was beyond the ability of local officials to find a satisfactory solution to the hard labour problem. Langmuir's own conclusion was that 'these troubles furnish a further reason why the Common Gaols should be taken over by the Government.'[34] In his 1878 report,

Langmuir again urged the legislature to 'follow the example of England and assume the entire management and control of the Common Gaols.'[35]

By 1881 he knew this would not happen. For several years, he reported, he had been delaying the implementation of new rules and regulations to replace those of the old Meredith board until the government decided whether it would emulate the English example. But now he had been officially informed it would not. As his valedictory, therefore, he put in place a comprehensive set of gaol rules which differed in important respects from those of the Meredith board. Most importantly, discretion was no longer available to dilatory municipal officials. The rules were approved by Cabinet on 15 December 1881, and the counties were instructed to begin enforcing them at once. A gaoler, turnkey, matron, and medical officer were required in every gaol; the sheriff was to make most appointments, subject to government approval; and he or his deputy were to make regular fortnightly inspections. No fewer than one hundred clauses and many subclauses governed all possible situations, including such perennial Langmuir concerns as diet and prison clothing. Perhaps most noteworthy was the continuation of the existing policy of not resorting to such harsh physical punishments as existed in the penitentiary and Central Prison. Punishments available were restricted to the hard bed, a bread and water diet for a period not exceeding five days, and confinement in the dark cell for a period not exceeding three days.[36]

On the administrative side, in the decade following Langmuir's retirement there seems to have been some regression. Shortly before he left office, the burden of work necessitated the appointment of an assistant to the inspector in the person of Dr W.T. O'Reilly. From 1881 to 1890 O'Reilly was responsible for the inspection of hospitals and asylums. In 1882 a second inspector was appointed, Robert Christie, who became responsible for penal institutions and houses of refuge. Richard Splane argues that this division of responsibilities led to 'an immediate and important loss.' The province's social programs were no longer 'viewed in their entirety' by a single inspector who acquired a comprehensive overview of provincial requirements.[37] This may have been true. There is no longer a sense that the inspectorate is headed by someone with a feeling of urgency and a commitment to social betterment or even to achieving the maximum degree of responsiveness and efficiency. The social commentary becomes brief and routine. Above all, there is no sense that the inspector is at the leading edge of social change. After Langmuir, the inspectorate largely assumed a routine administrative function and some old problems began to reappear.

The absence of aggressive inspectoral leadership contributed to the situation encountered by the prison commission in 1891. As Langmuir had warned, in circumstances of divided legal authority problems were likely to fester and to recur. Many of the sheriffs and gaolers who testified before the commission were blunt in their condemnation of county administration. Once again they confirmed the reluctance of the counties to spend money on necessary upkeep and repairs. Gaol officials usually believed the blame lay not so much with local councillors as with public hostility to increased expenditures. James Gillespie, the sheriff of Prince Edward County, pointed out he had 'almost to threaten' the councillors to pay his gaoler 'a sufficient amount to keep him from starving.' The councillors, he noted, were elected annually and if they increased the gaol expenditure 'they are afraid they will be kicked out when they seek re-election.'[38]

Those who believed the existing system worked well were in a distinct minority. William Allan, the gaoler in Milton, had 'no complaint at all' to make of the county council, and William Grant of Perth (Lanark County) also had no problems with council. However, H.C. Corbett, the Kingston gaoler, echoed a position taken by E.A. Meredith three decades earlier: 'I think the inspectors are overworked men and have no time to make a proper inspection of the gaols ... The inspector comes here by train and is anxious to take the next train back again.'[39]

Most of the witnesses would have agreed with Sam Roether, the Walkerton gaoler. Members of the county council, Roether noted, 'are not permanent enough to acquire sufficient experience' of gaol matters. About half of the councillors were new each year and the gaol committee 'generally consists of men who have no knowledge of gaol requirements. They live in the country and never even see the gaol except when the Council is in session.'

The inspector himself, Robert Christie, was less sanguine that full provincial control would be beneficial. With every gaol different, efforts to achieve uniformity, he warned, might be prohibitively expensive. Christie was even dubious about the old notion of grouping several counties together for gaol purposes, since the cost of transfering prisoners over long distances was prohibitive. Christie told the commissioners that the existing situation should probably not be disturbed. He had been able to effect improvements in several gaols, and he had 'never found the authority of the inspector directly disputed, except in the case of Ottawa.'[40]

By 1891, the Mowat government, long in office, was being subjected to increasing criticism for trampling on local authority and for grasping too much power to itself at Queen's Park. In 1894 the provincial election would be fought largely on that issue, and the election of seventeen Patrons of Industry represented a forceful voice of protest from rural Ontario against the trend to centralization. Sensitive to these currents, the government, and the commission itself, reacted cautiously to the views of the sheriffs and gaolers, especially since differences of opinion did exist.

In their recommendations respecting gaols, Langmuir and the other commissioners had astonishingly little to say. Langmuir, still alert to the political exigencies of the Mowat Liberals, had become cautious about his old favoured solution of a provincial takeover. Theoretically, he admitted, provincial management might be ideal, but clearly further efforts at gaol reform were no longer a priority with the province, the inspectors, or even with Langmuir and his colleagues on the prison commission.

GAOL POPULATIONS: THE STATISTICAL RECORD

In his annual reports, Langmuir commented extensively on gaol statistics and used them as a basis for policy formulation.[41] The early reports contain extensive information on the gaol population. Data on the religion, national origin, literacy, drinking habits, occupation, and marital status of the prisoners was recorded, although this information is of dubious accuracy since it came from the prisoners themselves. Other material is more reliable, including data on numbers of the insane, escapes, deaths, costs, gender, labour performed, and trial results and sentencing of offenders. Recidivism data present special problems, given the unreliability, in an era before finger-printing, of tracking efforts, and also a lack of clarity as to how different gaolers chose to record recidivists in their registers.

Early lists of offences made no effort to break them down into crime categories but in the 1875 Annual Report some attempt was made at classification:

Offences Against the Person: assault, attempted suicide, abduction, cutting, stabbing and wounding, manslaughter, murder, rape, shooting and intent.

Offences Against Property: arson, burglary, counterfeiting, destroying property, embezzlement, forgery, fraud, livestock stealing, housebreaking and robbery, larceny, receiving stolen goods, trespassing.

Public Morals: bigamy, indecent assault and exposure, inmate and freqenter of and keeping house of ill-fame, perjury, prostitution, seduction.

Public Order and Peace: abusive and obscene language, sedition and threatening, breach of peace, breach of by-laws, carrying unlawful weapon, escaping, obstructing court, deserting employment, selling liquor without permit, drunk and disorderly, vagrancy, unlawful shooting, giving liquor to Indians.

Other: contempt of court, cruelty to animals, debtors, detained as witnesses, lunatics, bail and sureties offences, misdemeanors, misc.

Many of the published tables were presented on a cumulative basis, which encouraged consistency over time in record keeping. The cumulative data provided the foundation for much of the work of the 1891 prison commission.

The principal deficiency of these published aggregates is their failure to relate data on such matters as age, religion, gender, and nativity to type of crime. Using only the aggregates, it is impossible to determine, for example, whether a particular type of crime was committed disproportionately by members of particular ethnic, religious, or age groups. These deficiencies are partially compensated for by computer-assisted analysis of the gaols of the counties of York (Toronto), Wentworth (Hamilton), Wellington (Guelph), and Ontario (Whitby), for the period 1881–91. For York County, one entry in ten was coded (3,320 cases out of 33,391); for Wentworth the same was done for one in eighteen entries (1,042 out of 18,958 cases); and for Wellington County three out of four entries (653 out of 872 cases). Ontario County was coded in its entirety. While this effort supplied some interesting correlations not available to the late nineteenth century inspectors, it would not have altered by much the general statistical profiles available to Langmuir and his successors.

In general, the data did not present a very alarming picture of the state of criminal activity in late nineteenth century Ontario. The most basic information provided by the published aggregates is simple numbers confined, broken down by age (over or under 16) and gender.[42] The figures show some fluctuations but suggest a crime rate that did not expand significantly between Confederation and century-end. Using decanal census data adjusted and projected for non-census years, Table 10.1 presents the numbers provided in the annual reports (including those confined and subsequently found not guilty) to establish a crude provincial crime (or more accurately committal) rate for the period 1867–99. Table 10.2, taken from the inspector's annual report, 1902, breaks the figures down by age and gender. The number of boys under age sixteen incarcerated dropped from 294 in 1869 to 216 in 1902; the corresponding figures for girls were 82 and 15. The number of women imprisoned dropped from 1,680 in 1869 to 1,193 in 1902 and the overall figures suggest that numbers alone did not account for the decision to open a women's prison in the late 1870s.

These data demonstrate a striking increase in the number of committals

TABLE 10.1
Gaol Committals and Rates, 1867–1899

Year	Population	Total Committals	Rate per 100,000
1867	1,530,947	5,073	331.6
1868	1,553,423	5,978	384.9
1869	1,575,889	5,655	369.0
1870	1,598,375	6,379	399.2
1871	1,620,851	6,615	408.3
1872	1,651,458	6,958	421.4
1873	1,682,065	7,877	468.3
1874	1,712,672	9,488	554.2
1875	1,743,279	10,073	577.9
1876	1,773,886	11,236	633.7
1877	1,804,493	13,481	747.3
1878	1,835,100	12,030	655.6
1879	1,865,708	11,220	601.6
1880	1,896,314	10,700	564.3
1881	1,926,922	9,229	479.2
1882	1,945,661	9,620	494.6
1883	1,964,400	9,880	503.1
1884	1,983,139	12,081	609.2
1885	2,001,878	11,426	571.0
1886	2,020,617	10,645	527.0
1887	2,039,356	11,017	540.3
1888	2,058,095	12,454	605.2
1889	2,076,834	12,531	603.6
1890	2,114,321	11,810	558.7
1891	2,121,183	10,423	491.4
1892	2,128,045	9,011	423.5
1893	2,134,907	8,619	403.9
1894	2,141,739	9,450	441.4
1895	2,148,601	9,380	436.7
1896	2,155,463	9,058	420.3
1897	2,162,325	8,884	409.6
1898	2,169,187	8,256	375.9
1899	2,176,049	8,203	376.9

Source: Annual Reports

during the 1874–80 period. In 1859, 6,586 persons had been committed to the gaols of Upper Canada, and committals remained steady for more than a decade, reaching 6,958 only in 1872. By 1874 they had jumped to 9,488 and they remained at a relatively high level throughout the rest of the 1870s and the 1880s. In 1890, however, they began a gradual drop,

TABLE 10.2
Men, Women, and Children Committed to Gaol, 1869–1902

Year	Men over 16 years of age	Boys under 16 years of age	Women over 16 years of age	Girls under 16 years of age	Total
1869	3,599	294	1,680	82	5,655
1870	4,215	319	1,737	108	6,379
1871	4,586	329	1,642	58	6,615
1872	5,006	281	1,615	56	6,958
1873	5,745	323	1,735	74	7,877
1874	7,298	377	1,746	67	9,488
1875	8,048	389	1,566	70	10,073
1876	9,005	434	1,727	70	11,236
1877	11,053	542	1,824	62	13,481
1878	9,537	480	1,959	54	12,030
1879	8,995	416	1,756	53	11,220
1880	8,229	549	1,863	59	11,300
1881	7,007	468	1,681	73	9,229
1882	7,236	522	1,750	62	9,620
1883	7,858	423	1,551	48	9,880
1884	9,858	458	1,719	46	12,081
1885	9,419	450	1,507	50	11,426
1886	8,831	352	1,424	38	10,645
1887	8,996	409	1,574	38	11,017
1888	10,060	551	1,778	65	12,454
1889	10,349	451	1,685	46	12,531
1890	9,622	461	1,677	50	11,810
1891	8,469	421	1,501	32	10,423
1892	7,177	446	1,335	53	9,011
1893	6,798	368	1,399	34	8,619
1894	7,785	278	1,350	37	9,450
1895	7,912	284	1,154	30	9,380
1896	7,622	265	1,147	24	9,058
1897	7,533	235	1,069	47	8,884
1898	6,974	284	969	29	8,256
1899	6,846	267	1,057	33	8,203
1900	7,063	298	1,291	42	8,694
1901	7,059	262	1,198	27	8,546
1902	6,850	216	1,109	15	8,280

Source: Annual Reports

and by 1899 the rate per hundred thousand was almost back to what it had been in Confederation year.

In order to provide insight into the larger significance of what was hap-

TABLE 10.3

Crime Rates per Hundred Thousand by Offence Category, 1874–1899

Year	Crimes against the person		Crimes against property		Crimes against public morals and decency		Crimes against public order and peace		Other	
	N	Rate	N	Rate	N	Rate	N	Rate	N	Rate
1874	939	54.9	1843	107.6	213	12.4	5751	325.4	742	43.3
1875	968	55.6	2253	129.2	315	18.0	5876	336.5	661	37.9
1876	1128	63.6	2494	140.6	331	18.6	6533	368.5	750	42.3
1877	990	54.9	2772	153.7	415	23.0	8544	473.6	749	41.5
1878	1009	55.0	2686	146.3	519	28.2	7066	385.0	750	40.9
1879	847	45.2	2523	135.2	449	24.1	6700	359.2	701	37.5
1880	904	47.7	1963	103.5	492	25.9	6600	348.1	741	39.1
1881	853	44.3	1990	103.3	399	20.7	5388	279.7	599	31.1
1882	920	47.3	2175	118.8	466	23.9	5391	277.2	688	35.4
1883	859	43.7	1989	101.2	366	18.6	6068	308.8	628	31.9
1884	933	47.0	2676	134.9	418	21.1	7341	370.2	713	35.9
1885	1043	52.1	2614	130.6	376	18.8	6671	333.4	722	36.1
1886	907	44.9	2314	114.5	346	17.1	6350	314.3	728	36.0
1887	838	41.1	2183	107.1	401	19.6	6886	337.7	709	34.8
1888	923	44.8	2812	136.6	446	21.7	7514	365.1	759	36.8
1889	968	46.6	2636	129.9	434	20.9	7722	371.9	772	37.2
1890	870	41.2	2623	124.1	429	20.3	7123	377.4	755	35.7
1891	865	40.8	2475	116.7	333	15.7	6046	285.0	704	33.2
1892	723	34.0	2274	106.9	327	15.3	5077	238.6	608	28.5
1893	651	30.5	2197	102.9	374	17.5	4836	226.6	561	36.2
1894	771	36.0	2701	126.2	442	20.6	4949	231.2	587	27.4
1895	673	31.3	2746	127.8	393	18.3	5016	233.5	552	25.6
1896	674	31.3	2623	121.7	370	17.2	4833	224.3	558	25.9
1897	716	33.1	2545	117.5	373	17.4	4711	218.0	537	24.8
1898	649	29.9	2784	128.4	354	16.3	3962	182.6	507	23.4
1899	638	29.3	2396	110.1	247	11.4	4316	201.1	546	25.1

Note: Breakdowns by crime category are not available on a province-wide basis prior to 1874.

Source: Annual Reports

pening to criminal activity in Ontario, these figures need to be broken down by crime category, a procedure which was undertaken in each of the provincial reports from 1875. As one looks first at crimes against the person, what is most striking is the consistent drop in the rate. It reached its peak for the entire period between 1874 and 1878 and dropped consistently, moving from the mid-50s per hundred thousand to 29.3 in 1899. Ontario, it would seem, was becoming a less violent society.

The fluctuation in the rate of property offences is less both for the entire period and for the beginning and terminal dates. It increased from 107.6 per hundred thousand in 1874 to 110.1 in 1899. There was a high of 153.7 in 1877; the three highest years for the entire period were 1876 to 1878. The recession years 1873–78 also saw high rates for crimes against the person and for public order offences. A case can be made for a positive relationship between depressed economic conditions and the high committal rates of the 1870s, but the fluctuating rate of the 1880s and 1890s calls into doubt any simple economic interpretation of these changes.

More significant is the downward trend in committal rates overall between the mid-1870s and late 1890s. This seems to conform to the analysis of Gatrell and Hadden, showing significant drops in the British crime rate for the same period. Gatrell and Hadden suggest that the drop in rate may be attributable to such factors as improved policing, which acted as a deterrent, and to a variety of social reforms.[43] In Ontario one might point to the social control effect of state education, including the enforcement after 1891 of compulsory attendance, to advances made by the temperance movement in controlling excess consumption of alcohol, and to numerous other social and political reforms of the period. But before too much is made of these changes it is necessary to note that there was strikingly little change in the rate between the period 1867–72 and the late 1890s.

Both the consistency over time of the proportion of offences accounted for by each crime category and the predominance of public order offences for the entire period is clearly revealed in Table 10.4, which provides the percentage committed for each crime category between 1874 and 1899. The breakdown of crimes by type changed remarkably little between 1874 and 1899, apparently remaining relatively impervious to the great social and economic changes of the late-century years.

What emerges most clearly from this data is the continuation of a trend dating from the 1830s, the large expansion of what a later generation would call 'victimless' offences, especially drunk and disorderly and vagrancy. As Langmuir and his colleagues complained endlessly about

TABLE 10.4
Percentage Distribution of Gaol Inmates by Type of Offence, 1874–1899

Year	Crimes against the person	Crimes against property	Crimes against public morals	Crimes against public order	Other
1874	9.9	19.4	2.2	60.6	7.0
1875	9.6	22.4	3.1	58.3	6.6
1876	10.0	22.2	2.9	58.1	6.8
1877	7.3	20.6	3.1	63.4	5.6
1878	8.4	22.3	4.3	58.7	6.3
1879	7.5	22.5	4.0	59.7	6.3
1880	7.7	24.9	4.2	56.7	6.3
1881	9.2	21.6	4.3	58.4	6.5
1882	9.6	22.6	4.8	56.0	7.0
1883	8.7	20.1	3.7	61.4	6.3
1884	7.7	22.1	3.4	60.8	5.9
1885	9.1	22.9	3.3	58.4	6.3
1886	8.5	21.7	3.3	59.6	6.7
1887	7.6	19.8	3.6	62.6	6.4
1888	7.4	22.6	3.6	60.3	6.1
1889	7.7	21.0	3.5	61.7	6.1
1890	7.4	22.0	3.6	60.4	6.4
1891	8.3	23.7	3.2	58.0	6.7
1892	8.0	25.2	3.6	56.3	6.8
1893	7.5	25.5	4.3	56.1	6.5
1894	8.1	28.6	4.7	52.4	6.2
1895	7.2	29.3	4.2	53.5	5.9
1896	7.4	29.0	4.1	53.4	6.2
1897	8.0	28.6	4.2	53.0	6.0
1898	7.9	33.7	4.3	48.0	6.1
1899	7.8	29.2	3.0	53.3	6.7

Source: Annual Reports

how the gaols were filled with what they regarded as the cast-offs and misfits of society, the courts continued to sentence vagrants and drunks in appallingly large numbers. As Table 10.6 reveals, women were sentenced for vagrancy in numbers about equal to men, for being drunk and disorderly even more frequently, and in very large numbers for prostitution-related offences. Taken together, these offences amounted to fully 70.5 per cent of all female committals. Thus the top five crimes for which men were committed to gaol accounted for 77.5 per cent of all crimes for which men were committed. The top five crimes for which women were committed accounted for 82.0 per cent of all crimes for

TABLE 10.5
Top Five Reasons for Committal to Ontario Gaols, 1875–1899

Offence	Percentage of cases out of all offences		Conviction rate per type of offence	
	N	%	N	%
Drunk & disorderly	82,111	31.5	50,800 / 68,633	74.0
Vagrancy	52,608	20.2	43,285 / 52,608	63.7
Larceny	38,544	14.9	20,105 / 31,873	62.8
Assault	12,840	4.8	6,954 / 10,666	65.2
Lunatics	9,686	3.8	Not applicable	
Other	64,518	24.8	12,321 / 43,780	28.1
Total	261,307	100.0	133,375 / 207,560	64.3

Source: Derived from the 'Gaol Statistics of the Province of Ontario' published in the *Ontario Sessional Papers*, 1875–99

which women were committed to gaol. And the top five crimes for which people of both sexes were committed accounted for 77.1 per cent of all crimes for which people of both sexes were committed to gaol.

For the Ontario inspectors, the numbers assumed their greatest significance when placed in the context of longer time periods. By the mid-1870s Langmuir was expressing alarm over what the figures seemed to reveal about the activities of those he increasingly regarded as forming a habitual criminal under-class. As early as 1871, he noted increases of about 10 per cent in numbers committed more than three times. He described this group as representing 'a further addition to the already large list of habitual offenders who are almost constant inmates of our Gaols.' Of 6,615 prisoners, 2,063 were recidivists. Many of these were vagrants and at this point the inspector seemed sympathetic to their plight. Many, he said, had committed no offence, being guilty only of poverty and old age. The commitment of such persons to gaol was 'entirely at variance with the dictates of humanity' and interfered with the work of the gaol, preventing classification and turning it into a poor-house and a hospital. Many were committed under the Vagrancy Act for two months and formally recommitted, while in other cases 'the farce of attempting to legalize such an act is waived, and the person is kept in continuous confinement for months and years.'

Langmuir's commitment to the establishment of inebriate asylums for

TABLE 10.6

Top Five Crimes for Which Men and Women Were Committed to Gaol, 1881–1891*

| Male | | | Female | | | Total | | |
Crime	N	%	Crime	N	%	Crime	N	%
Drunk & disorderly	36,614	35.1	Drunk & disorderly	7,552	41.4	Drunk & disorderly	44,166	36.5
Vagrancy	18,679	18.2	Vagrancy	3,231	17.7	Vagrancy	21,910	18.1
Larceny	14,879	14.5	Prostitution-related	2,086	11.4	Larceny	16,531	13.6
Assault	7,180	6.9	Larceny	1,652	9.1	Assault	7,603	6.3
Trespass	2,345	2.3	Assault	423	2.3	Prostitution-related	3,163	2.6
Total	79,697	77.0	Total	14,944	81.9	Total	93,373	77.1

*Does not include lunacy or 'others' (i.e., crimes not specified in official records).
Source: Annual Reports

chronic drinkers was made in this early period, with three-fifths of those admitted to gaol being intemperate in their habits. From the data he concluded that while commitment to gaol was 'a fearful penalty' for occasional drunkenness, nonetheless it was 'wholly inadequate for punishment' and, more to the point, 'insufficient for reformation.' In Langmuir's mind the figures also proved 'conclusively' that an individual's marital state had 'an important bearing upon the morals of a community,' with fully 65.42 per cent of those confined unmarried. So too did literacy: one-fourth of the prisoners committed during the year could neither read nor write.[44]

In 1873, with committals jumping by 13 per cent to 7,877, there was no departure from established trends. Again Langmuir saw the gradual increase as an urban phenomenon, noting that the five city gaols of Toronto, Hamilton, Kingston, London, and Ottawa had 'as usual, been the largest contributors,' while 'many of the rural gaols exhibit a marked diminution.' Prescott and Russell, for example, with a population of almost 36,000, sent seven persons to gaol for criminal offences; Bruce County, whose population was over 48,000, likewise sent only seven people to gaol.

As before, Langmuir focused on recidivism, which he situated firmly among those convicted of moral offences and which he increasingly saw as deriving from idleness and drunkenness. Of the 5,745 male prisoners, 'no less than 3,124' had been sentenced to under two months' confinement, and he estimated that more than three-quarters of these were confined for drunkenness, disorderly conduct, and vagrancy. Many of those imprisoned as vagrants, he suggested, were in gaol only because of the absence of a poorhouse. But a still greater number, through chronic drunkenness and demoralization, had become 'criminal vagrants' and their experience in gaol was turning them into life-long criminals. 'These classes, with those committed for drunkenness and disorderly conduct,' constituted 80 per cent of the 2,821 recommittals; 1,185 had been committed over three times and must be deemed incorrigible.[45]

High gaol committals prevailed for the rest of the 1870s. Each year Langmuir expressed alarm, focusing on the urban nature of crime and the threat posed by recidivism and vagrancy. Langmuir particularly deplored the brevity of gaol sentences. Of 7,011 sentences passed on prisoners in 1876, 5,479, or over 75 per cent, were under sixty days and 3,032 were under thirty days. There were 3,283 recommittals, and nearly 1,000 of these were of persons sent to gaol between four and twenty times. Habitual offenders were a nuisance to society, and Langmuir noted that with three-quarters of them unmarried it would be no hardship to their families to confine them for longer periods in the Central Prison. Only in the Central Prison was discipline adequate to achieve 'the entire subordination of the will of every prisoner to constituted authority'; 'the very first lesson that these men have to learn on entering the prison is implicit submission.'[46]

With an 'enormous increase' of criminal commitments in 1877 (from 11,236 to 13,481, a 20 per cent rise), Langmuir's commitment to statistical analysis developed proportionately. Now he insisted that the 'best, and perhaps only' way to ascertain the causes of a dangerous situation was through 'a critical analysis of the crimes and offences committed ... and by making a comparison of such offences ... with those of previous years.' Langmuir carried out this analysis by providing a comprehensive list of specific crimes, presented in the traditional categories, and comparing them for the years 1869, 1875, 1876, and 1877. Not surprisingly, this exercise confirmed the inspector's sense that the threat was posed primarily by habitual criminals, recidivists, and members of the criminal classes.

'Offences against public order and peace' caused the greatest alarm. Committals had risen roughly 200 per cent, from 2,886 in 1869 to 8,554 in 1877. 'The committals for drunkenness and disorderly conduct have increased from 1,793 in 1869 to 4,032 in 1877; vagrancy committals rose from 783 in 1869 to 3,888.' Combined, these represented an increase of 208 per cent in eight years.[47]

No doubt Langmuir, in common with other middle-class Ontarians, was genuinely offended by repeated evidence that tramps and vagrants were making such good use of 'the government boarding house.' Nonetheless, Langmuir understood that tight-fisted municipal councillors preferred to house such populations in gaols rather than to establish purpose-built facilities, because the former alternative was incomparably cheaper. He recognized, too, that the figures were inflated by local circumstances, particularly since many municipalities did not have lock-ups. Many vagrants and tramps were committed to the gaol for the night and discharged in the morning.[48]

The very nature of the tramping phenomenon, given easy access to the freight trains which, by the late century, served almost every Ontario community, and the still-primitive nature of criminal justice identification techniques, determined that recidivism statistics were truly problematic. Men simply could not be identified as they moved from community to community and gaol to gaol. The fine points of statistical analysis, however, did not matter a great deal to contemporaries. In most communities the repeat vagrant would be a well-known local figure, while the presence

TABLE 10.7
Percentage of Recidivists in Ontario Gaols, 1868–1891

Year	%	Year	%
1868	32.4	1880	34.7
1869	33.6	1881	35.1
1870	29.1	1882	33.9
1871	31.1	1883	32.8
1872	33.8	1884	33.0
1873	35.8	1885	32.2
1874	33.1	1886	24.8
1875	22.9	1887	26.4
1876	29.1	1888	27.7
1877	26.8	1889	27.1
1878	29.8	1890	27.4
1879	30.9	1891	27.7

Source: Annual Reports

year after year of numerous tramps infuriated local worthies. It is interesting, then, to note that published recidivism figures for the 1868–91 period are remarkably consistent. Beginning at 32.4 per cent in 1868, they reached a high point of 35.8 per cent in 1873 and thereafter fluctuated, declining to 27.7 per cent in 1891. To a degree, reporting errors must have cancelled each other out. Above all, the statistics suggest that Langmuir's increasing concern in the late 1870s was unnecessarily alarmist.

However anxious he may have been about recidivist data, Langmuir seldom expressed much concern about the ethnicity or religion of those sent to gaol. He muttered from time to time, it is true, about American riff-raff, the weakness of extradition laws, and the perceived problem caused by the immigration to Ontario of too many diseased and uneducated immigrants from the British Isles. But he never focused on the Irish Catholics as a source of the problem, and generally he seems to have adopted the common perspective that crime was brought about by a multiplicity of environmental factors, even though the data might have supported a different interpretation. Both Irish and Americans were in fact heavily over-represented in Ontario gaols, as the data in Table 10.8 demonstrate. This became even more important, as we shall see, when Langmuir, as chair of the 1891 prison commission, rejected out-of-hand the racial extremism and hereditarian analysis then being propagated by advocates of Lombrosian criminology.

TABLE 10.8
Index of Over- and Under-Representation in All
Ontario Gaols by Country of Origin, 1880–1900*

Country of origin	All gaols
Canada	0.6
England and Wales	2.0
Ireland	3.3
Scotland	1.3
United States	3.1
Other	1.6

*The index was created by dividing the percentage
of inmate population made up by an ethnic group
by that group's percentage representation in the
Ontario population. A score of less than 1.0
indicates that a group was under-represented in
the gaols, while a score of more than 1.0 indicates
that the group was over-represented.

In their statistical profiles the Ontario inspectors also brought to the
public attention a mass of other data which may have influenced policy
formulation but which, in its general contours, would have surprised no
one familiar with criminal justice statistics in any country. The data, as
noted above, were dependent largely on the (dubious) veracity of the
prisoners themselves as well as on the (equally dubious) accuracy of local
record keepers. They include the usual sort of material (so fascinating to
Hannibal Mulkins during his years as Kingston chaplain) on social habits,
education, marital status, class, and religion. They were printed each year
in the annual reports, with no effort to relate them to Ontario population
profiles. The data are offered in Tables 10.10 to 10.13 only in cohorts and
will assume greater significance in Chapter 11, when a fuller analysis is
offered and comparisons are made between prisoners in the gaols and
those in Ontario's new intermediate prisons.

THE GAOLS AS ASYLUMS

For Langmuir there was no more significant issue connected with the
gaols than their indiscriminate use as congregate facilities. Almost every
inspection of every facility throughout his years in office resulted in
adverse comment on the presence of those he regarded as social victims
and his successors carried on the same crusade.[49]

TABLE 10.9
Distribution of Four-Gaol Sample, Numbers by Class (Toronto,
Hamilton, Whitby, and Guelph Gaols), 1881–1891*

Class	Four-gaol sample	
	N	%
High-status business and professional	21	0.03
Small business and clerical	517	8.5
Skilled labour	1,451	24.1
Semi-skilled labour	496	8.2
Unskilled labour	2,572	42.6
Not Classified	970	16.1
Total	6,027	100.0

*This class division is based upon the occupational classification by
Theodore Hershberg et al., 'Occupation and Ethnicity in Five
Nineteenth-Century Cities: A Collaborative Inquiry,' in *Historical
Methods Newsletter* 7 (June 1974)

TABLE 10.10
Drinking Habits, 1868–1898

Year	Temperate	Intemperate
1868	3020	4879
1878	4135	7895
1888	3732	8722
1898	3436	4820

Source: Annual Reports

TABLE 10.11
Marital Status, 1868–1898

Year	Married	Unmarried
1868	2669	5346
1878	3960	8170
1888	4446	8008
1898	2742	5514

Source: Annual Reports

Table 10.12
Educational Status, 1868–1898

Year	Literate	Illiterate
1868	5,348	2,667
1878	8,968	3,062
1888	10,076	2,378
1898	6,871	1,385

Note: Literate – could read and write.
Illiterate – could neither read nor write.
Source: Annual Reports

TABLE 10.13
Religious Denomination, 1868–1898

Year	Catholic	Anglican	Presbyterian	Methodist	Other
1868	3037	2652	850	962	454
1878	4720	3704	1503	1454	564
1888	4499	3925	1590	1646	794
1898	2782	2202	1116	1433	723

Source: Annual Reports

Not only was the gaol's use as a multi-purpose facility frequently illegal, it also interfered with its principal purpose, the safe custody of prisoners. The inspectors documented numerous cases in which the necessity for the gaoler to tend to the needs of old people or of the insane endangered security and threatened the lives of its officers. But the humanitarian aspect weighed most heavily. The inspectors' Victorian sensibilities determined that it was simply wrong for helpless people to be forced to spend their declining years in prison, when they should have been looked after by friends or family or lodged in some more caring and purpose-built facility.

THE MENTALLY ILL

Of the several classes of unfortunates present in such numbers, the mentally disturbed suffered the grossest indignities. Under law individuals deemed dangerous to be at large could be committed to a gaol if certified by a justice of the peace and two doctors, to remain there until further examination determined how they should be dealt with; others found not guilty of an offence on grounds of insanity might also be retained in a gaol unless it could be determined that they would benefit from asylum treatment; and still others became insane while imprisoned.[50] It was the inspector's responsibility to ensure that the provisions of the law were respected and to make recommendations for the further disposition of insane prisoners. Langmuir was conscientious in attending to these responsibilities. He did all in his power to minimize the suffering of prisoners in various phases of mental distress and to facilitate their placement in the most therapeutic environment available. Nonetheless, his reports demonstrated a shortage of proper asylum facilities, and the reluctance of families to assume responsibility. The local gaol, however unsatisfactory it might be, remained home to large numbers of ill and unbalanced persons. It will be recalled from Table 10.5 that 'lunatics' represented the fifth largest category committed between 1875–99. No fewer than 9,686 lunatics were committed, representing 3.8 per cent of the total gaol population.

The use of the gaol to house those contemporaries referred to as 'idiots,' or sometimes 'imbeciles,' was also questionable. Although there were facilities for this populace at the London asylum and, by the mid-1870s, in a separate institution at Orillia, the mentally retarded continued to be housed in gaols throughout the late nineteenth century. In Pembroke in 1869 Langmuir found no criminal prisoners, only 'a poor unfortunate imbecile who has been here for the past three years.' Perhaps more than any other group, the retarded, often regarded as untreatable at least in an ordinary asylum, spent long periods in prison confinement. Langmuir made it a priority to establish care and treatment facilities for retarded persons at the new London asylum; and he was also successful in persuading the government to establish the completely separate facility at Orillia. Beyond that, he sensibly recognized that many retarded persons could function well in a home environment, often making significant contributions to the family economy. It is not clear how frequently this expedient was used or to what extent home care harmed or benefited this class of persons. Soon after the opening of the London asylum, the available space was filled. In May 1874, for instance, Langmuir wished to recommend the transfer of two 'female idiots' from the Napanee gaol to 'the Idiot Asylum' but reported that there was no room, 'nor likely to be for a long time.' While the opening of the Ontario Asylum for Idiots at Orillia relieved the pressure, it did not solve the problem; mentally retarded persons continued to spend long periods of time in the province's gaols.[51]

The use of the gaols to house 'harmless imbeciles' as well as some cases of chronic insanity put great strains on many ill-equipped local gaols. Thus, when Langmuir inspected the St Catharines gaol in February 1869 he found it 'in a fair state' of cleanliness and order, 'considering that there are several insane people under confinement, some of whom are very filthy in their habits.' Every year of his inspectorate, he made similar findings. It was clear, he concluded, that there was an urgent need to change the mode of certifying insanity, 'as well as the mode of committing persons as dangerous lunatics.'[52]

On the other hand, Langmuir ensured that those who were dangerous were removed to Rockwood or elsewhere in short order. When he found five dangerous lunatics out of thirteen prisoners in the Cobourg gaol during an 1870 inspection, he dealt with these cases with his usual expedition. One, William Powers, 'was so very violent and dangerous that he has to be put under restraint by bandaging the hands.' The same day he recommended that Powers be sent to the Toronto Asylum and asked the surgeon to examine the others with a view to their discharge or removal.[53]

For those charged with a criminal offence and acquitted on grounds of insanity, Langmuir usually ordered a medical report and on its basis made a recommendation to the government as to placement. A case with interesting legal implications was that of a man in the Walkerton gaol in January 1872 who had been found not guilty of assault on grounds of insanity. Shortly after the trial his mental condition improved, and Langmuir followed the procedure of having him examined by the gaol surgeon, another doctor, the chair of Quarter Sessions, and another JP. His condition was described as 'temporary insanity' and his discharge recommended.[54]

Sometimes expert opinions did not concur. Langmuir's reports include several cases in which doctors certified prisoners as insane and the legal establishment begged to differ. In the case of Charles King, committed as a dangerous lunatic, the county judge refused to confirm the medical finding of insanity. After seeing the man in the Brockville gaol in September 1873, Langmuir agreed with the judge that he was 'evidently a quiet harmless imbecile' who would derive little benefit from asylum treatment. Nonetheless, 'for future guidance I would ... beg to submit this case for the decision of the Hon. the Attorney General.'[55] The self-confident inspector did not hesitate to comment on his sense of whether individuals of evidently deranged mind had received a fair trial.

By 1874, Langmuir was hopeful that the cottages for chronics in the London asylum would relieve the pressure. Doubtless they did so but the law still ensured that many lunatics initially at least were handled through the gaols and many helpless chronics continued to spend long periods of time there. He offered some sense of the dimensions of the problem in his 1877 report: 'With regard to the 333 lunatics and idiots committed during the year, 272 were transferred' to asylums, 30 recovered their sanity while in gaol and were released, and 31 remained at year end. He noted that most of the latter were not suitable for asylum treatment, but that steps had been taken to transfer the rest as soon as possible.[56]

For the rest of the century little changed. Throughout the 1880s and 1890s the prison reports document numerous sad cases of untrained gaol staff struggling to deal with disturbed inmates. In August 1881 a prisoner of unsound mind committed suicide by beating his head against the bars; the coroner's jury recommended that all gaols have padded cells. Langmuir disagreed, arguing that existing mechanical restraints such as chairs fastened to the floor and leather muffs were more effective.[57]

The evidence given during the 1891 commission hearings confirmed that not even the rapid expansion of the province's asylum system had relieved the pressure. The Belleville gaoler reported he had to use criminals to take care of dangerous lunatics. The Cobourg gaoler reported that thirteen persons had been committed as lunatics and although he believed all of them should have been transferred to an asylum, some remained for long periods because of a lack of asylum space. Big city gaolers had to cope with very large numbers of insane prisoners, in 1891, twenty-one in Ottawa, twenty-one in Hamilton, and eighty-seven in Toronto, where they were placed in a corridor with the drunks.[58] The commissioners reported that in 1889 a total of 437 persons had been committed as lunatics:

The evidence shows that of the persons so committed a large proportion are merely imbeciles who should be cared for in a poor house, and that these generally remain a long time in the gaols because they are not regarded as fit subjects for a lunatic asylum. Of those who should be sent to an asylum some, when the accommodation in the lunatic asylums was insufficient, remained in the gaols for months; and in some instances lunatics still remain in the gaols longer than they should because the proper means for procuring their removal are neglected.[59]

After all this testimony, the commissioners offered two brief recommendations. First, 'when at all possible' lunatics should be admitted to an asylum directly on the certificate of physicians. No lunatic should ever be sent to a gaol 'unless in case of absolute necessity' and with everything possible being done to ensure that any person amenable to cure be transferred to an asylum. Second, if a lunatic committed to gaol was found not fit for transfer to an asylum 'because incurable, or merely imbecile and harmless,' the examining authorities should establish whether the lunatic might safely be entrusted to his family. If this was possible, 'the family shall be required immediately to take change of such insane person, unless it be shown that they are unable to furnish proper maintenance and care.' In such cases transfer to a poorhouse should be arranged whenever possible.[60] These recommendations seem complacent and unimaginative and they left enormous scope for continuing neglect and abuse.

Because of the larger numbers involved, the problems posed by the use of the gaols to house the ill, the poor, and the elderly posed an even graver problem, but it was one which had a somewhat more satisfactory resolution by the century's end. Again every year and in almost every individual gaol report, the inspectors pointed with regret to the way in which the local authorities were using the gaols as alternatives to poorhouses, houses of refuge, and even hospitals. Once again they presented horrific accounts of individual suffering. Yet in contrast with the situation of the insane, there was a distinct change in tone in the official reports and in other documentation as the numbers of those confined in these circumstances grew.

VAGRANTS

As the 1870s began, Langmuir's comments on the vagrants he encountered were generally sympathetic, emphasizing the legal irregularities often involved in their incarceration and regretting the failure of the counties to provide poorhouses or other facilities for their care. In May 1870, when he found only four criminal prisoners out of sixteen inmates in the Barrie gaol, he pointed to 'considerable irregularity' in the incarceration of vagrants.[61] The federal vagrancy statute passed in 1869 provided for a sentence of a fixed time not to exceed two months, yet many of those in the Barrie gaol were there for an indefinite period.[62] Often, too, those who were merely ill and unable to take care of themselves were imprisoned on charges of vagrancy. In April 1870 the Carleton grand jury pointed to the case of a young man 'guilty only of the misfortune of being epileptic and of falling in the streets' who was confined on a vagrancy charge 'for the purpose of securing his maintenance.'[63] Not only the ill but the elderly were swept up under the new statute. When he inspected the Perth gaol in April 1870, Langmuir found that five out of nine prisoners were elderly vagrants. Under the Vagrancy Act, he noted, 'this class of inmate may legally occupy the Gaol but it is very clear that Gaols were not built for them.' Nonetheless, he was 'very glad to find their wants are strictly attended to and every comfort extended them that can be in their position.'[64]

Local officers were manipulating the statute for their own purposes. In Peterborough in 1871 Langmuir discovered that 'the practice obtains in this County of committing habitual Vagrants to the Gaol and keeping them, in continuous custody by placing a new Committal in the hands of the sheriff before the expiration of the previous sentence.' Langmuir hastened to point out that the provisions of the Vagrancy Act did not sanction this practice.

Neither inspectoral disapproval nor the illegality of such situations ever persuaded local authorities to mend their ways entirely. For the next quarter of a century and longer numerous poor people continued simply to show up at Ontario's gaols and present what amounted to tickets of admission. In June 1872 a coroner's inquest into the death of a ninety-year-old woman in the Frontenac gaol, where she had been admitted 'without the commission of a crime by her, and, apparently, from no other cause than that of poverty,' concluded that she was illegally recommitted until the day of her death. The provincial secretary's office informed the sheriff of the government's 'grave displeasure' at the role of the sheriff and other officials in participating in such illegal activities; they were admonished not to do it again.[65] Such cases were clear examples of conflict between the centralized and legalistic values being implemented throughout the province by the urban businessmen and lawyers who controlled the Mowat government and older traditions of localism and self-help. To ordinary people in many Ontario counties, the gaol remained a community facility intended to serve local needs. Bureaucrats and lawyers from Toronto were unwelcome intruders. In the 1894 election, the provincial Liberals would learn just how deep these currents of resentment ran in much of rural Ontario, and their reaction to this election helped immobilize the Liberal government for many years until its final defeat in 1905.

Municipal officials often tried to do better in response to such stern admonitions, but in the absence of a poorhouse the temptation was often too great. Municipal leaders simply had their own sense of what was required. In his 1879 report, Langmuir printed the standing order issued by one mayor to the keeper and his assistant: 'Any vagrants or parties asking admission to the Gaol after nightfall, and admitted as having no place to remain during the night, and as being dangerous to be allowed to remain out, may be discharged in the morning, without being first brought before me, or any other magistrate sitting in the Police Court, if no charge has, in the meantime, been laid against them.' In this case, the outraged inspector went straight to the attorney general, and 'as a result instructions were given to discontinue the practice.'[66] Nonetheless, law and circumstances tended to encourage such practices.

The penalties laid down by the 1869 Act Respecting Vagrants provided for 'imprisonment in any gaol or place of confinement other than the Penitentiary, for a term not exceeding two months and with or without hard labour, or by a fine not exceeding fifty dollars, or by both.' An 1874 amendment extended the term of imprisonment to six months and another change in 1881 gave additional emphasis to the imposition of hard labour. In 1886 a new statute, the Public Morals and Public Convenience Act, provided a list of alternate institutions to which vagrants might be sent, including a house of industry or a workhouse, but these alternatives were dropped in 1892 in the new Criminal Code. As well, Ontario's municipalities could also enact by-laws to restrain and punish vagrants.[67] The successive statutes and by-laws were so sweeping in their definition of vagrancy that it became possible for police and local authorities to cast their net as widely as they wished. Among those defined as vagrants by the 1869 statute were all idle persons not having a visible means of maintaining themselves, those able to work who wilfully refused employment; those begging or receiving alms without a signed certificate indicating that he or she was deserving of charity; those who loitered in the streets and caused a disturbance; and all common prostitutes, nightwalkers, keepers, and frequenters of houses of ill-fame unable to give a satisfactory account of themselves. With the 1874 extension of the term of imprisonment, it became even easier for the authorities to use the gaols to hold non-criminal prisoners. It was a matter of convenience and economy for the local authorities to pursue a variety of casual and illegal procedures, including, most commonly, the practice of simply admitting individuals who committed no crime and never appeared in court.Langmuir and his successors alternated between condemning and condoning the imaginative uses to which municipal politicians put the gaols.

The inspectors found several features of the system particularly offensive. Regularly, for example, they encountered truly aged men and women, some in their nineties. There were also cases from time to time of hospitals refusing to receive critically ill persons, presumably because they could not pay, and this was denounced as an outrage against

TABLE 10.14
Number of Vagrants Sentenced to Ontario Gaols,
1869–1889

Year	Number	Year	Number
1869	783	1882	1449
1875	1641	1883	1554
1876	2128	1884	2130
1877	3888	1885	2445
1878	2524	1886	2243
1879	2536	1887	2192
1880	2210	1888	2301
1881	1580	1889	2164

Source: 1891 Commission Report

humanity.[68] Yet many of those confined, usually able-bodied men whom the inspectors deemed anxious to avoid work, received little sympathy. In 1880 Langmuir noted that too often the sentence of such vagrants did not include hard labour and he protested that 'it is most desirable that they should be so sentenced,' noting that this could be done under 37 Vict. c. 43.[69] In 1880, possibly after reading Richard Dugdale's famous account of the criminal activities of the Jukes of New York State, he expressed concern about the presence in the Napanee gaol of a family including three children who had spent two successive winters in the gaol. 'If some action is not taken the community will be charged with the care of a large family of confirmed tramps who will soon become in the natural order of things, criminals.' The children, he suggested, 'should be sent to one of the Homes and the mother and the father ... should be compelled to earn their living ... most certainly it was never contemplated under the Vagrant Act that whole families should be sent to Gaol.'[70]

By this time Langmuir had become genuinely alarmed by the growing extent of the vagrancy problem. The numbers of vagrants in Ontario gaols had grown from 783 in 1869 to an astounding total of 3,888 in 1877, a result doubtless of economic recession. This as it turned out was a peak, but the sense of alarm it caused did not soon abate and was reflected in Langmuir's 1877 report, in which he asserted that 'the unprecedented increase in the commitment of the vicious, depraved and vagabond classes, generally known as vagrants and tramps, calls for prompt action.'[71]

To some extent the presence of such fears in Ontario reflected developments in the United States. There the term 'tramp' first found widespread use during the 1873–4 recession, which has been characterized as 'the first major, nationwide industrial economic contraction' in the United States. Soon the word tramp was being used 'almost indiscriminately to describe different categories of people,' including hoboes, beggars, and vagrants, all of whom were widely regarded as work-shy, often travelling from place to place, begging to survive, and engaging in petty theft and intimidation.[72] The perception in the United States that the large numbers of tramps on the road posed a serious threat to life and property led to the passage of a series of 'tramp laws,' beginning in New Jersey in 1876. Within twenty years only four states had failed to enact such legislation. Although the tramp laws varied in harshness and rigour, they represented a significant expansion of the use of the criminal law to control the poor, the jobless, and the homeless.[73] Promoted primarily by leaders in the Charities Organization Society, whose objective was to organize 'charities scientifically to prevent indiscriminate almsgiving from demoralizing the working class and encouraging laziness,' the fears they reflected were echoed by many middle-class Canadians. The conviction that the too-liberal distribution of charity would destroy the work ethic and tend to the creation of an entire class of worthless tramps and paupers was perfectly captured in a famous Toronto *Globe* editorial of 1874: 'Promiscuous alms giving is fatal ... it is the patent process for the manufacture of paupers out of the worthless and improvident. A poor law is a legislative machine for the manufacture of pauperism. It is true mercy to say that it would be better that a few individuals should die of starvation than that a pauper class should be raised up with thousands devoted to crime and the victims of misery.'[74]

Although such extreme views never shaped public policy in Ontario, they were not without effect. In the 1880s in Ontario the Associated Charities worked to achieve private and public programs similar to those advocated in the United States by the charity organization societies. And Langmuir demonstrated a growing determination to ensure that tramps and vagrants not be allowed to resort, without fear of penalty, to the pleasures of 'the government boarding house.' In his numerous and fervent denunciations of recidivism and in his determination to enforce hard labour, including the extramural employment of convicts in street gangs, the Ontario inspector demonstrated the extent to which Ontario officialdom shared the class fears that inspired American tramp legislation. In Ontario neither law nor practice fully encompassed the punitive spirit of American anti-tramp measures.[75] This was probably because here the threat remained primarily to the taxpayers' pocketbooks, and even then was hardly excessive and never led to incidents of riot, social protest, and industrial unrest comparable to what was occurring in Chicago, New York, and other American urban centres.

As a result, there was a moderate and desultory quality to the Ontario debate. Even while gaolers and inspectors complained about the presence of tramps and wastrels, they denounced the failure of municipal authorities to establish poorhouses, homes for the elderly, and other facilities. Langmuir, to be sure, did make distinctions between those who were unemployed through no fault of their own and others who allegedly had no interest in honest labour. But so too did almost all middle-class Ontarians who had occasion to articulate their feelings, and Langmuir never let his concern with the threat of the 'criminal classes' detract from an overriding commitment to the systematic provision of provincially funded and purpose-built facilities to replace the use of the gaols to serve those populations.

This was the constant refrain of his inspectoral reports and of those of his successors as well. After the death in 1874 of a woman in the Owen Sound gaol, Langmuir argued that Grey County should provide a house of refuge and industrial farm with apartments for lunatics, the aged, and the indigent. The law passed in 1867–8, which permitted counties to establish such facilities should, he urged, be made compulsory, a view he continued to express and repeated again almost two decades later as chairman of the 1891 prison commission.[76]

More than anything else, it was the statutory amendment passed during the 1867–8 session which determined that the county gaols would continue to be used to serve a mixed and congregate population. In 1866, it became compulsory for all counties with a population of over 20,000 to establish a house of industry or refuge, and counties below that population figure were to do so in combination with another county. For reasons which can only have been financial and a response to pressure from local politicians, the province rescinded this mandatory provision in its 1867–8 amendment, thereby delivering a death-blow to the principle of requiring counties to make provision for poor people and the elderly.[77] Although counties, townships, and villages had the authority to spend funds for relief purposes, including outdoor relief, most preferred to save money by placing those in need in the county gaols.

Thus while Langmuir's indignation was justified, many Ontarians saw the issue from other perspectives. The vagrants themselves often found the provision of a secure haven too attractive to resist, particularly when officials were unable to enforce hard labour. It was a boon for men on the tramp to know that local politicians would hand out certificates of entry to gaols located across the province. The Toronto gaol was a favourite refuge and so were several others located on convenient rail routes, especially Kingston and Milton. There was considerable truth to Langmuir's comment, made in 1872 after finding that about three-quarters of the sixty-two prisoners in the Hamilton gaol were vagrants or drunks, that for such persons the gaol was not regarded as punishment 'but in many instances what they really desire.'[78]

Increasingly, Langmuir began to distinguish between different groups and classes of vagrants, between county residents and tramps, and between the 'deserving' and the 'undeserving' poor. The usual criterion in making these distinctions was recidivism. In his 1872 inspection of the Hamilton gaol, for example, Langmuir noted that one drunk had been committed 153 times and all the drunks except one were recidivists. Almost all vagrants, he insisted, were also drunks. One vagrant had been committed ninety-three times and only six of the vagrants were there for the first time.

ALTERNATIVE FACILITIES

Faced with a burgeoning population of the ill, the unfortunate, and the deviant, most Ontario counties continued to regard the gaol as an all-purpose facility available to serve the diverse needs of the community. In these circumstances county leaders were unlikely to respond favourably to the entreaties of the provincial inspector to establish poorhouses and houses of refuge. It was the province, after all, which had repealed the mandatory provisions of the 1866 legislation and, in the absence of provincial leadership, local politicians saw little reason to take the initiative. As a result, the growth of alternative facilities was agonizingly slow. Under the Charity Aid Act of 1874 private institutions conforming to certain standards could receive some public funding on a formula basis and by 1893 there were no fewer than thirty-three private institutions classified as houses of refuge. These facilities offered care for a variety of individuals, including old people, poor people, incurables, widows, and orphans. But the prison inspectors' reports demonstrated the extent to which the gaols continued to hold large numbers of unfortunates from all these classes.

Private facilities and the community itself were criticized from time to time by the provincial inspectors for refusing admission to some of the most needy cases. In 1889, when a vagrant died in the Port Arthur gaol, the acting sheriff reported that an attempt had been made to have him removed to the hospital, 'but owing to the strenuous opposition of the hospital authorities our efforts were not successful.'[79] The available private facilities often restricted admission according to religion and were reluctant to accept some of the worst cases; as well, they were far from covering all parts of the province and they often refused to accept responsibility for strangers.

As Splane notes, the private facilities, however incomplete and unsatisfactory they may have been, had nonetheless been put in a preferred position by the terms of the Charity Aid Act.[80] This enabled them to receive provincial financial support, while no equivalent aid was offered to the county facilities. One effect of the Act seems to have been to actually discourage counties from establishing their own homes for the poor and the elderly. The absurdity of this situation could not help but attract criticism. In 1889 Goldwin Smith, a socially prominent writer and critic, joined with other representatives of the Associated Charities of Toronto to urge the government to address what they regarded as an intolerable social problem. It was highly regrettable, they insisted, that 'persons of unsound mind,' the aged, the infirm, and the destitute continued to be committed to gaol. They demanded that gaol be reserved for criminals and urged the government, if it needed more information, to appoint commissioners to gather evidence, an idea which would soon see fruition.

In its 1890 throne speech the Mowat government announced that it would introduce a Houses of Refuge Act: 'Public attention,' the throne speech pointed out, 'has of later years been directed to the inadequate provision by County Municipalities for the care and support of the aged, helpless and poor.' Only nine counties had established houses of industry or refuge. In the larger centres of population 'organized philanthropy' had provided old age homes, assisted by provincial grants. But this was not enough and the government, responding at last to the views of its own prison inspectors, as well as to pressure from prominent individuals active in philanthropic work, including officers of the Prisoners' Aid Association, had finally mobilized itself. 'With a view of encouraging the erection of County Houses of Refuge in connection with Industrial Farms and of thereby relieving the gaols of this unfortunate class of their inmates,' the province, by an 1890 statute, would provide a grant of up to $4,000 to any county or counties wishing to establish such facilities. Equally important, financial assistance was promised to those counties which had already established houses of refuge. The Act itself went somewhat further then this, making funds available to municipalities other than counties and it also provided for the inspection of all houses of refuge. Yet the statute remained permissive and the financial assistance provided was not equal that given either to private houses or even to the local gaols.[81] Not surprisingly, then, the statute did not go very far towards eliminating the presence of the old and the poor from the county gaols and it remained for the 1891 commission to urge the province to more vigorous action.

The Ontario prison commission carried out a thorough investigation of the use of province's penal facilities for welfare purposes. On the basis of testimony before the commission it seems probable that most vagrants in the county gaols were now strangers, frequently foreigners who were on the tramp. Such persons either preferred gaol to the poorhouse or found it easier to gain admission to the gaol than to a house of refuge. 'Do many poor who come casually into the county find their way into the poor house?' was the question put to the Elgin County gaoler. 'Very few,' he replied. 'They are admitted on the certificate of the reeve of the municipality or the magistrate, and these are very careful about whom they give certificates of admission to.' Other officials confirmed this assessment. The gaoler at Hamilton reported that 'a great many vagrants wander through the county coming from the United States and they cannot get into a refuge because they are not citizens and the magistrate, if they apply to him, must send them to gaol.'[82] Clearly, a primitive sorting process was at work and gaols and houses of refuge received substantially different clienteles.

There was a firm consensus that the numbers of tramps and vagrants being institutionalized should be controlled by enforcing hard labour. James Ogilvie, the Hamilton gaoler, reported that once for a month there had been no stone to break. 'The news spread rapidly, and we never had so many prisoners in gaol as we had during that month.' According to Robert Davis, the sheriff of Haldimand, 'vagrants and tramps constitute the vast majority of those who come to us.' The county, he continued, attracted large numbers of these classes because the Grand Trunk and Canadian Pacific railways both had through lines. It was also important, he suggested, that the tramps knew there was no poorhouse in the area, only a gaol. This encouraged them to 'either ask to be committed to gaol or commit some offence for which they must be committed, in order to obtain food and shelter for a few days.' Few of the tramps and vagrants in the gaol were residents.[83] John Edward Pell of Toronto's Associated Charities was asked to address the concern that the mandatory creation of county poorhouses might 'bring forth a large number of people who would otherwise work.' Pell responded that this would not happen if the poorhouse system was carefully regulated, with work enforced at every institution.

Nonetheless, there were alarmists, such as the Reverend A.H. Baldwin. Baldwin, an Anglican priest, testified with a distinguished group including the Hon. G.W. Allan, a wealthy businessman, Professor Goldwin Smith, and former Toronto Mayor W.H. Howland, all representing the trustees and managers of the Toronto House of Industry. He provided statistics that purported to prove 'that in cities of the United States which have three times the population we have, there is only a tithe of the number of vagrants.' For Baldwin it was 'incredible' that the Toronto House of Industry had 1,481 tramps last winter, with all but 350 staying for more than one night. The only labour the house had been able to provide was the cutting of a little wood. 'We could not send them to the Toronto gaol, as because that would be simply making criminals of them.' In any case, once sent to gaol they would find it 'ten times more comfortable than our quarters' because of 'the loafing system that is now going on there.' According to Baldwin, the answer was 'to make men who won't work, work, whether they like it or not.' His colleague Goldwin Smith argued that the gaol 'should under no circumstances be used as an almshouse or place of refuge. It ought to be used as a penal institution.' His proposal was to preserve the house of industry for the old, the feeble, and the disabled, but to add a casual ward which could enforce a work test for the class of tramps who were causing so much trouble, a solution soon implemented in Toronto.[84]

David Archibald of the Toronto police force was even more outspoken. He complained that 'the philanthropic people of Toronto, in providing homes and shelter for the professional tramps, have done infinitely more harm than good.' He was speaking, he explained 'of the majority of the people who do a little work in the country in the summer and then drink their earnings and live in the gaols in the winter.' The situation, he thought, had improved somewhat because more tramps were being sent to the Central Prison for six months' hard labour. 'That class of people don't like hard work.'[85]

David Archibald's perspective represented a common but by no means predominant opinion among those who testified. The chief constable of Kingston, for example, drew a clear distinction between the tramping class and many people who were desirous of finding work and merely passing through town. James Ogilvie testified that many vagrants confined to the Hamilton gaol could not work because of physical disability. And many witnesses agreed with Haldimand sheriff Robert Davis that destitution was the principal cause of vagrancy and with Louis Appleby, the gaoler of Belleville, that most vagrants were of the deserving poor, unable to work because of ill health or old age.

On the basis of this testimony, the commissioners distinguished between several types of tramps and vagrants. Drawing not only on the testimony of witnesses but on Langmuir's expert knowledge of gaol conditions, they insisted that care be taken to discriminate between honest, industrious people reduced to poverty by age or misfortune and those who were 'reckless and improvident.' This latter group must be required 'to give full value in work for the shelter and food they receive in gaols or other institutions.' Professional vagrants, they insisted, should be treated most severely of all and if they persisted in their vagrancy should be sent to the Central Prison for long terms. The commissioners were persuaded that 'the honest tramps who desire to obtain employment' were few in numbers and the problem they posed would largely disappear, 'if they were treated as they should be.' As for those addicted to drink, they should not be sent to gaol at all but to an inebriate asylum for terms of not less than six months.'[86]

There was little understanding in these conclusions of the effects of an industrial recession on the labouring classes or of the extent of the demoralization of many farm labourers and workers brought about by the displacement experienced during the transition from rural to urban environments and from artisanal to industrial modes of work. Satisfied that the problem was susceptible to simple solutions, the commissioners recommended that county councils be compelled to ensure that the means be provided to enforce hard labour as part of every gaol sentence imposed on any tramp or vagrant. After a second commitment of such persons to a gaol, the sentence must be to the Central Prison for a period commencing at six months, to be increased for each additional commitment. On the other hand, those who were merely homeless and destitute, whether from old age or illness, should be sent to a poorhouse, the establishment of such a facility to be made compulsory in every county. Following the opening of a poorhouse in a county, 'it shall be unlawful ... for a magistrate or justice to commit to a common gaol as a vagrant any homeless and destitute person who seems to be physically incapable of working, unless such person has committed some offence.'[87]

While these recommendations did not address the larger problems of structural unemployment or offer any insights into the personal tragedies of those displaced individuals who constituted the tramping classes, they would at least have effected some improvement in the state of the gaols.

Unfortunately, the province again failed to provide leadership. One small indication of provincial concern was the decision of the legislature in 1892 to order a census of the numbers confined to gaol for vagrancy or insanity, but the government itself was not moved to act.[88] That old prejudices persisted among many Ontarians was suggested by the publication in 1898 of Thomas Conant's study, *Upper Canada Sketches*, in which the author argued almost violently against compulsory county poorhouses. 'In a land of plenty like ours,' Conant asserted, there should be no need for such institutions and if they were established they would always be filled. Beyond that, ought the hard-working and thrifty to be taxed 'to provide for the lazy and thriftless. Or again, is it wise to foster the growth of a class of persons whose filth and foul diseases are the result of laziness and their own vices?'[89]

The Liberal government did not pass a Houses of Refuge Act until 1903.[90] This statute required each county or union of counties to build such a structure. By 1911 a comprehensive system of houses of refuge was in place across Ontario, and there is little doubt that the impassioned and courageous advocacy of the gaol inspectors in the 1890s made an important contribution to the achievement of this objective.

CONCLUSION

Not even the establishment of houses of refuge in every county solved the problem. A quarter of a century later, in 1930, another commission, chaired by journalist P.D. Ross, reported on Ontario's welfare system. The Ross Commission was scathing in its condemnation of Ontario gaols and other welfare institutions, pointing to idleness, lack of proper classification, gross overcrowding, and inadequate inspection. 'As regards the Corrective Institutions particularly, there is an unassorted, unstandardized, unstudied system of commitment, transfer and admission, which results in an overflow of delinquent population in these institutions, consisting of a mixture of normal, mentally deficient, light and very grave offenders, and unplaceables.'[91]

What had gone wrong? Had all the efforts of E.A. Meredith, J.W. Langmuir, and their colleagues and supporters had little or no effect? That was simply not the case. The physical and administrative reforms that had been achieved beginning in 1859 with the establishment of the Board of Inspectors and continuing for the rest of the century had been considerable. Without this effort, conditions would have been immeasurably worse, and the reform achievement should not be underestimated. There is something to be said, too, for the perspective of local politicians, reflecting community values, that the gaols as congregate facilities filled certain needs, however inadequately. There is almost no evidence of brutality or mistreatment of prisoners by gaolers; the opposite was more often the case with a number of gaolers suffering physical beatings and, in a few cases, even death at the hands of the incarcerated. As well, physical conditions in most gaols had been raised to meet at least minimal standards of creature comfort so far as warmth, ventilation, and diet were concerned, although, sadly, there was also much backsliding. Most of all, perhaps, it was revealing of contemporary attitudes and conditions that many sought entrance to gaol because they could survive better there than in the community. The published statistics revealed few deaths and the willingness of many vagrants and tramps to admit themselves to these facilities represented a statement on their part. There was, to be sure, much suffering as a result, but Ontario's gaols never reached the depths of those in some American jurisdictions.

Still it could not be denied by anyone, least of all the 1891 commissioners, that enormous room remained for improvement, and in this sense at least the results of the commission's work were profoundly disappointing. Their comments on gaol conditions reflected their own sense that while more remained to be done, much had been achieved, and that there was no crisis. As a result, their recommendations were few and conservative and their reform program, as it affected the gaols, depended primarily on what the government chose to do in other correctional and welfare areas. And that is at least part of the reason why gaol reform was not achieved to any significant extent in Ontario in the 1890s or later, and why the Ross Commission in 1930 found so much to condemn. Thorough-going reform of Ontario's gaols would be achieved only in the more affluent and progressive 1960s, and even then only through the instrumentality of the complete provincial takeover that John Langmuir had once advocated but which he failed to place before the government, even as an option, in 1891. For better and for worse, in nineteenth-century Ontario bureaucratic reforms achieved limited results and community standards prevailed. Instead of gaol reform, the province addressed one aspect of the perceived problem by establishing intermediate prisons for male and female recidivists.

11

Terrorizing the Underclass:
The Intermediate Prisons

INTRODUCTION

The 1860s and 1870s were a period of mixed portents for penal development. In England, the moral panic known as the garrotting crisis combined with growing disillusionment with what was regarded as the naive policies of Joshua Jebb led to an era of repression. In Ireland, the progressive-stage system implemented by Sir Walter Crofton achieved international acclaim. Croftonianism was a major breakthrough, and left the old verities of the Auburn–Philadelphia systems in an intellectual backwater. But it possessed as well a narrowly punitive side which placed impossible demands on all convicts and punished severely those who did not measure up. This negative aspect of Croftonanism was exemplified by the regimen of the most famous of late nineteenth century American wardens, Zebulon Brockway. The Croftonian and positivist ideals of American prison reformers enunciated at Cincinnati in 1870 were given physical and institutional embodiment at New York State's Elmira reformatory, under Brockway's leadership. Elmira implemented educational and skills training programs that allowed prisoners to advance through stages to earn early release under an indeterminate sentence law. Elmira, and other American reformatories modelled on it, worked assiduously, and in retrospect ruthlessly, to rehabilitate what was regarded as the most hopeful class of prisoners, first offenders aged sixteen to thirty. The downside to Elmira, as Alexander Pisciotta has demonstrated, was that prisoners who could not or did not conform were subjected to sometimes violent physical punishments and endured intense psychological pain.[1] In England, by contrast, most elements of the progressive stage system, based as it was on medical analogies and notions of the possibility of treatment and cure, were rejected out of hand. In that country the later decades of the nineteenth century were characterized by an unrelenting harshness and an emphasis on administrative efficiency in which all convicts, in theory at least, received precisely the same treatment. In the United States, conditions in state and local facilities varied tremendously, but few states made any significant effort to implement the positivist program enunciated at Cincinnati.

In Ontario neither positivism nor the reformatory movement more generally had any significant impact. The two intermediate prisons that were established, the Central Prison for Men in 1874 and the Mercer Reformatory for Women in 1880, were created on entirely different principles. At the federal level, as we have seen, there was some effort to implement aspects of the Croftonian and positivist programs at Kingston Penitentiary but little progress was made in either direction. As a consequence, the penitentiary enterprise in Ontario stumbled on, achieving some successes and experiencing more failures, with amazingly little reference to international ideas or practices.

What then did the opening of the Central Prison and the Mercer Reformatory for Women portend for penology in Canada? This chapter examines Ontario's two new intermediate prisons in a comparative perspective. Assessed in terms of their ability to reform or rehabilitate, there is little doubt that both institutions failed. For example, in 1890, during the hearings of the commission established to study the province's penal system, there were claims that no one had ever been rehabilitated in the Mercer. As well, there was a consensus that the objective of the Central Prison had always been deterrent – to serve, as one witness told the commission, as 'a terror to evil-doers.'

Yet to argue so bluntly that both institutions were designed primarily to deter and to punish is to miss important distinctions between the male and female facilities. The Central Prison was an unrelentingly punitive facility designed to terrify the repeat offenders who were crowding the province's gaols. As such, it had little in common with facilities such as Elmira, which owed their existence to a reform impulse and which at least attempted to rehabilitate and not merely to punish. The Mercer Reformatory, on the other hand, both in its origins and in its administration under its first superintendent, Mary Jane O'Reilly, was influenced by the ideological values of middle-class feminism and by the idealism of a group of influential American prison reformers. The history of the Mercer in its early decades was consequently quite different from that of the Central Prison. If the objective of the Central Prison was almost entirely punitive, to inspire 'terror in evil-doers,' the Mercer established a quite different regimen. Its purpose, to use the language adopted by many of the advocates of all-female facilities, was 'to govern by kindness,' and the results achieved by this strategy were more positive by far and entirely distinctive from those which characterized life in the male facility.

THE CENTRAL PRISON

In its origins, the Central Prison owed little to the reform impulse which had inspired the Cincinnati Declaration. The prison was designed to fill a gap in the new Province of Ontario's correctional system by holding prisoners sentenced to less than the two years that were served in what had become the Dominion penitentiary, but to more than the brief period which was to be served in the local gaol. The prison embodied a long-felt need. Although the Board of Prison Inspectors in the 1860s had made the construction of several central prisons the cornerstone of their reform policy, they had never been able to persuade the government of the Province of Canada to embark on such an expensive reconstruction of the prison system. What brought the central prison program within the realm of practical politics were the social changes that had been transforming Canada throughout the Union years. In the 1840s and 1850s, many newly incorporated towns and cities passed by-laws designed to hold in check forms of behaviour that had previously excited little concern. The migration to Canada West in the 1840s of thousands of poverty-stricken Irish immigrants posed a new kind of threat to those who lived in such cities as Toronto, Kingston, and Hamilton and led to strict by-laws aimed at drunks, vagrants, and other persons guilty of unruly behaviour. A Hamilton by-law of 1843 directed that: 'All vagrants, vagabonds, or other persons of ill-fame, or persons who are drunk or so conducting themselves to be a nuisance and found wandering in the Town at night shall be liable to be arrested and upon conviction thereof shall be liable to a fine of 30 shillings for each offence or in non-payment, 30 days in the District Gaol.' This particular measure, as John Weaver has demonstrated, led to as many as 50 per cent, or 516 of 1,105, of Hamilton's share of committals to the Gore District gaol between 1843 and 1851.[2] The figures would not have differed significantly for any urban gaol across the province.

Municipal by-laws enforcing new standards of social behaviour were part of a larger movement to assert social control. This included the passage in 1845 of provincial Sabbatarian legislation, the proliferation of temperance societies and the tightening of local licensing laws and, most of all, the movement to establish more efficient policing. Although the province had rejected centralized policing in 1856, gradual reform continued, with the result that stronger local police forces charged with enforcing municipal by-laws arrested increasing numbers of persons whose behaviour in the earlier era had escaped official notice.

Yet if the expanding social control net swept ever larger numbers of petty offenders into the local gaols, the crisis that led to the creation of the Central Prison was not primarily one of gaol overcrowding. In some parts of the province, especially in the cities, gaols did suffer from the press of numbers, but in such cases newer and larger facilities were built, as in the case of Toronto's Don Gaol in the 1850s. In the more rural parts of the province, existing gaols were readily able to accommodate the number of committals. By the mid-1850s, however, a strong sense developed in both city and countryside that the confinement of drunks and vagrants in county gaols under conditions of idleness was serving more to encourage than to deter this persistent and annoying class of criminals. When Mr Justice Robert Burns submitted the reports of several county grand juries to the provincial secretary in 1854, he told the minister that there was an urgent need to make fundamental changes in the system of punishing criminals. 'The County Gaols,' he noted, 'do not afford the means of employing convicts at any useful or profitable employment. There is a large class of convicts which it is not desirable should be consigned to the Penitentiary, and yet there are no means by which a proper reformatory punishment can be inflicted by incarceration in the County Gaols.' Burns's remedy was to erect two or three 'houses of correction'[3] in different parts of the province; in other presumably more rural areas, counties should unite to construct larger, more efficient gaols.

In the years ahead, judges, grand juries, sheriffs, and other judicial officers regularly expressed outrage about society's inability to enforce sentences of hard labour in the local gaols, and usually they suggested some variation or other on the theme of central prisons. In 1865, for example, W.H. Draper, the distinguished Chief Justice of the Court of Common Pleas, reported to the provincial secretary that he received 'frequent representations from Sheriffs, that they found it extremely difficult to carry into effect in the County Gaols sentences of imprisonment coupled with hard labour.' Draper pointed out that it would probably be too expensive to equip county gaols with the means to enforce hard labour. In many counties the number of prisoners was so small that the burden of establishing a labour system would be disproportionate to any benefits. Yet there was still no middle ground between a short gaol sentence and imprisonment in the penitentiary for at least two years, and for that reason, the chief justice lamented, 'many offenders will escape with inadequate punishment, a heavy and most unprofitable burden will continue to be cast upon the community and there will not be that wholesome dread of punishment which might operate to check the repetition and increase of crime.' A full eight months passed before Attorney General John A. Macdonald responded to his old chief's complaints. On 27 August 1866, Macdonald minuted in reference to the grand jury reports and the comments of the chief justice, 'Worthy of all consideration, but in consequence of the speedy alteration in the political system, no action is at present expedient.'[4]

Although the state of politics in the early 1860s was hardly conducive to prison reform, it is striking how prescient the old Board of Inspectors was in reinforcing the case which grand juries and judges had been making for more than a decade about the use of the gaols to house what they regarded as a permanent class of debauched offenders. For this class, the inspectors repeated at every opportunity, the gaols were 'a harbour of refuge and, a few weeks in the Government boarding house forms a pleasant change in their street life; here they are treated gratuitously for the ailments contracted by excesses in intemperance or vice.' The inspectors worked themselves into a state of high dudgeon as they denounced the sloth and cynicism of the criminal classes: 'The majority [of gaol inmates] enjoy their detention [and are] fully alive to the advantages of these asylums, where they can recruit their strength and invigorate themselves for fresh crimes.' This was particularly true of the female offenders, who in 1859 constituted no fewer than 3,503 of a total of 11,131 persons confined that year in Upper and Lower Canadian gaols. Almost all the female offenders, the inspectors wrote, were prostitutes, and for them the prisons were nothing but a resource in distress, a refuge during the inclement season.

What the statistics revealed, the inspectors emphasized, was 'the actual state of petty crimes among us.' The number of persons imprisoned in the penitentiary in 1859 for more serious crimes came to a total of only 791 compared to 11,131 persons confined in the gaols. Minor offenders presented the community with a significant social and financial burden for, as we have seen, it cost much more to maintain a prisoner in the county gaol than it did to confine him in the penitentiary.

For the inspectors, the most disturbing statistic of all was the number of recidivists. For Upper Canada alone, out of a total gaol population of 6,586, no fewer than 1,558 were repeat offenders. Repeated convictions, said the inspectors, 'argue a settled habit – a fixed purpose of doing wrong. It constitutes of itself, an aggravation of the offence, calls for a more severe punishment, and proves the necessity of more energetic measures of repression.' The detailed comments provided by sheriffs offered even greater cause for alarm on this score than did the statistical aggregates, for these indicated that the same persons were returning to gaol time after time. Such persons should be classed either as dangerous and incorrigible and 'never be allowed to leave jail' or as monomaniacs who should be treated in an asylum.

For the inspectors, then, the gaols were filled 'by a class of persons who ... systematically [took] up crime and vice as a profession.' Furthermore, under the existing situation of the gaols, there was 'no hope for any improvement among this unfortunate class.' The board's solution was for the government to establish 'in our principal cities District or Central Prisons, in which would be confined all misdemeanants and recidivists from the adjoining counties or districts.' Furthermore, changes should be introduced in the criminal law to define the 'inveterate offender' or recidivist and to ensure that he was sent to a new central prison. Although the board made it clear that discipline in the new institutions would be rigorous, with the rule of silence firmly enforced, they believed as well that religious instruction and steady employment would rehabilitate prisoners in a way that the miserable county gaols never could. The Board of Inspectors never deviated from this position. They pressed it on successive governments until the Confederation settlement of 1867 altered the situation fundamentally by giving responsibility for the gaols to the new provincial governments.[5]

J.W. Langmuir, the man who did most to shape the Central Prison, dominated correctional work in the province until his retirement in 1882. Langmuir's energy, determination, and intelligence were instrumental to the development of the Ontario system. Although he has been described as a reformer whose purpose was to 'place inmate rehabilitation ahead of punitive impulses,' his primary purpose was to put in place an efficient and businesslike system.[6] Open to influences from abroad, he sought out approaches that he regarded as modern and effective wherever they might be found. Langmuir was familiar with the work of the Cincinnati Congress and also with the massive study, published in 1867 by E.C. Wines and T.W. Dwight, of prisons and reformatories in the United States and Canada. This famous document condemned almost all existing prisons but praised the work being done by Zebulon Brockway, at that time warden of the Detroit House of Correction.[7] At Detroit Brockway had established elaborate educational programs, a sophisticated chaplaincy service, separate facilities for women, and a grading system that allowed the best-behaved inmates to spend the final stage of their confinement in a secondary facility which served as a kind of halfway house. John Langmuir made pilgramages to Detroit in 1869 and 1871; he described Brockway's efforts as 'a monument of perfect Prison administration.'

There is little in Langmuir's work in establishing the Central Prison to indicate that he had a very sophisticated grasp of the real nature of Croftonian 'reformatory prison discipline' or even of Brockway's work at Detroit. His principal interest was in what Detroit, as an industrial prison that administered rigorous discipline and also turned a tidy profit, had to teach Ontario. In his 1869 report, in which he strongly urged Ontario to establish an industrial reformatory, Langmuir emphasized only two considerations. First, he took up the old theme, made familiar by a generation of critics, that the gaol system was 'a delusion and a failure.' Juveniles and those awaiting trial were contaminated by association with old offenders who 'lounge their time out in idleness and sloth.' Not only did the gaols cost more than $100,000 a year to maintain and bring in only $700 in return, but over a third of the population were recidivists. Second, all Langmuir was able to see in Detroit was its balance sheet: it had turned a profit each year since opening in 1862 and had achieved a favourable balance of $56,000. If Ontario established an industrial prison, he promised, it would be self-sustaining if the average inmate could earn as little as forty cents a day. Langmuir was sanguine about the demand for prison labour and about his ability to dispose of the products it produced. He believed that the plan under which the province itself controlled the convict workers and disposed of all goods produced was 'far superior' to the contract system by which private businessmen purchased the labour of the prisoners. The politicians were persuaded. When Premier Sandfield Macdonald presented a Central Prison bill in February 1871 he concluded a brief debate by commenting that he expected that the new institution would save the province money.[8]

The statute was brief and unimaginative, a framework to allow the government to develop the new prison as it saw fit.[9] The government was authorized to buy land somewhere in the province and build a prison. Much was left to the inspector's discretion. The inspector was 'to make rules and regulations for the management, discipline and police' of the prison and for 'prescribing the duties of the warden and every other officer,' subject to Cabinet approval. The rhetoric of rehabilitation that had characterized earlier Canadian prison statutes was notable by its absence and, in another striking departure, there was no provision for a chaplain. About the only evidence of progressive thinking was a clause that made it lawful for the inspector, 'in order to encourage good behaviour and industry,' to make rules so that an accurate record of the conduct of each inmate should be kept, 'with a view to permit such criminal to earn a remission' of a portion of his term. The statute made ample provision for employing the convicts at hard labour, whether within or outside prison walls. And the provincial secretary was given the authority to transfer any prisoner sentenced to gaol for a period of not less than fourteen days to the new prison. Most notably, there was no effort to restrict the prison to those most likely to be rehabilitated and it could be argued that the very reverse was true. And the prison was not designed for young men below age thirty, as Elmira soon would be.

With that statutory framework in place, the decision was made to build the new institution in Toronto on Strachan Avenue south of King Street, a location served by two major railway lines. The prison was a three-storey building consisting of a main section one hundred feet wide with wings on each side and large workshops in the rear of each wing. There were cells for 336 prisoners. Its first warden, William Prince, a veteran of the British Army, had served as chief of the Toronto Police for fifteen years, earning a reputation for 'arrogance and arbitrariness.'[10] His principal assistants were a chief guard, James Beaumont, and a deputy chief guard, Richard Stedman. On Langmuir's recommendation all three men were sent on brief visits to industrial prisons in the United States to learn the fundamentals of their new duties. Most of the men hired as guards had previous police or military training, and the practice of arming guards with rifles or handguns strengthened the prison's military appearance.

Because the prison was designed as an industrial facility, Langmuir's most important task was to establish industry in the new institution on a financially sound basis. When the Canada Car Company, which manufactured railway cars, offered to use all the labour not needed for prison domestic functions, Langmuir abandoned his earlier opposition to contractors and jumped at the opportunity. Prison workshops were completed and machinery installed to the specifications of Canada Car. For Langmuir the central, if not exclusive, place occupied by hard labour in the prison's regimen was readily justified. In numerous reports he argued that hard labour served several purposes equally well: it served as punishment; it provided industrial training; it inculcated an appreciation of the value of work; and it raised funds for the prison. For Langmuir and most of his contemporaries, there was no suggestion of incompatibility among these several objectives. Ever sanguine where his own projects were concerned, Langmuir was euphoric in his 1874 report about the success of his industrial project and he liberally quoted officers of the Canada Car Company to the effect that prison workers were at least as good as free workers and in many ways better.

But within months the company was bankrupt, a victim of the trade recession of 1875. The years ahead saw Langmuir and his successors struggling with a variety of approaches to prison labour, including the contract system, the state-use system, and the two in combination. With the Canada Car Company in debt to the province for $45,000, a three-man commission composed of two Canadian businessmen and Zebulon Brockway was appointed to investigate the thorny issue of prison labour. The words of its 1876 report must have been a bitter pill for Langmuir to swallow. They challenged the quality of prison labour in general and doubted in particular its financial value for the Central Prison because of 'the class of prisoners confined, and the duration of their terms of sentence.'[11] Such conclusions called into question the very rationale Langmuir had used to sell the prison to his political masters. In response he campaigned even more aggressively to persuade politicians and judges to take steps to stock the prison with healthy young men with longer sentences. This objective, as we will see, was never attained, and for the rest of its history the prison was beset with financial and labour problems. One reason cited prominently when it was closed in 1915 was the failure of the industrial system to achieve any of its objectives.[12]

Mired in the morass of woes arising out of the bankruptcy, Langmuir seized on these difficulties as an excuse for his failure to implement the earned remission system referred to in the statute. The subsequent history of earned remission in the prison, however, throws further doubt on the extent of his understanding of and commitment to reformatory principles. At this time remission was part of the rehabilitative apparatus in Kingston penitentiary, and in 1877 a federal statute clarified the province's authority in this sphere. This Act allowed a remission of up to a sixth of the sentence for Central Prison inmates and, as a concession to the view that sentences were already too short, judges received the authority to add another four months to the previous maximum of two years less a day. In presenting the measure, Justice Minister Edward Blake stressed not its rehabilitative but its disciplinary purpose. According to Blake the prospect of a four-month remission was more likely than the fear of the dark cell to make prisoners orderly. To an interjection from John A. Macdonald he responded that the government 'had another thing in view besides the reformation of the prisoner, viz., the good of the institution itself.'[13] But remission even as a disciplinary instrument failed to take hold in the Central Prison. In 1884 James Massie, Prince's successor as warden, bragged that convicts preferred longer sentences in Kingston to a period in the Central Prison, because 'there is no remission earned here.' In contrast to many late nineteenth century institutions, inmates in the Central Prison were there for the duration of their sentences. Remission and pardons were seldom granted, even for special cases. In 1894, 1895, and 1896, there were two, one, and six remissions respectively and six, fifteen, and zero pardons.[14]

Other rehabilitative methods common in the nineteenth century were equally weak or absent. Chaplains played a significant role in Kingston Penitentiary, not only offering religious sustenance but carrying out many of the functions performed by trained treatment personnel in twentieth-century penal establishments. Probably ignorant of the chaplain's role in federal institutions, Langmuir believed the Central Prison could rely on volunteers. To this end, he encouraged the establishment in 1874 of the Prisoners' Aid Association and solicited attendance by local clergymen. These volunteers were expected to provide religious services and to run a Sabbath school. For several years divine services and the school could be provided only on alternate Sundays because not enough clergymen offered their services. Notwithstanding the propensity of prisoners to participate in any activity to relieve the tedium, the school in 1877 was attracting an average attendance of only thirty-five inmates. A measure of reform came in the 1880s, when the Toronto Ministerial Association was paid $700 annually and the Catholic church $350 for performing these services, but there was no attempt to institute a full-time chaplaincy.[15]

Educational training received equally short shrift. Not until 1879 was a night school for illiterates even considered. Whatever the deficiencies of educational programs in Kingston Penitentiary, they were at least available to all prisoners, and the nature of the education to be provided was the subject of lively debate among penitentiary officials. When the Central Prison night school finally began operations in the 1880s, it was available only as a privilege. Attendance remained small, with the teacher reporting attendance in the winter months of between forty and fifty prisoners. Nor did officers place much importance on the prison library. When the few books available became too dilapidated to be read, the warden could only suggest that money to replace them be raised by charging fees to visitors to the prison. Somewhat later occasional lecturers came to preach to the prisoners on uplifting topics, including the dangers of masturbation, much to the delight of the prison physician, who argued at length in several reports that this practice was the source of all evil.[16]

CENTRAL PRISON STATISTICAL PROFILE

The Central Prison's lack of interest in traditional rehabilitative processes, as they existed, for example, in Kingston Penitentiary, is striking. When one considers as well the acclaim that Zebulon Brockway received in the late 1870s for his efforts at Elmira to reform a select group of first offenders aged sixteen to thirty, the reactionary character of the Ontario institution becomes even more glaring. The Ontario facility, however, had not been established as a reformatory to rehabilitate younger or more hopeful offenders. Its purpose, as a statistical analysis of its population confirms, was to deter habitual minor offenders by punishing them with a maximum of rigour.

The most important single characteristic of the inmate population was its lower-class nature. As Table 11.1 demonstrates, out of a total of 8,243 inmates from the 1874–1900 period, fully 92.4 per cent fell into the three categories of unskilled, semi-skilled, or skilled workers. This compares to Michael Katz's calculation that in Hamilton in 1871 a total of 73 per cent of the entire male working population fell into these three categories.

Unskilled workers were most grossly over-represented, representing 47.1 per cent of the total Central Prison population, while Katz calculates that this group represented only 15 per cent of Hamilton's total male working population. Of the five most common occupations cited in the annual reports, labourer leads at 46.5 per cent, followed by tailor at 3.9 per cent (see Table 11.2).

Skilled labourers made up fully 35.8 per cent of the population of the Central Prison, but only 24.1 per cent of four sample gaols' population and 0.08 per cent of the Mercer Reformatory (Table 11.3). Apart from what this suggests about the place of women in the late nineteenth century, it is apparent that prison officials were actively transferring workers with job skills to the prison to further institutional ends.

The type of crime committed provides another measure of the nature of the prison population. The most common offences by far were crimes against property, mostly minor, with larceny leading the list at 36.7 per

TABLE 11.1
Occupation of Central Prison Inmates, 1874–1900

	1874–5		1876–80		1881–5		1886–90		1891–5		1896–1900		1874–1900	
	N	%	N	%	N	%	N	%	N	%	N	%	N	%
Professional	0	0.0	15	0.5	4	0.1	2	.06	2	0.1	15	0.5	38	0.2
Semi-professional	61	7.7	277	9.1	258	7.0	232	6.4	215	8.0	248	8.0	1291	7.4
Skilled	274	34.4	1165	38.1	1263	34.5	1330	36.9	1105	33.5	926	29.9	6063	34.6
Semi-skilled	64	8.0	336	11.0	435	11.9	419	11.6	321	9.7	302	9.8	1877	10.7
Unskilled	397	49.9	1262	41.3	1705	46.5	1626	45.1	1651	50.1	1602	51.8	8243	47.1

Note: The table has been compiled primarily from the published annual reports of the Prison Inspectors.

TABLE 11.2
Five Most Common Occupations of Central Prison Inmates, 1874–1900

	1874–5		1876–80		1881–5		1886–90		1891–5		1896–1900		1874–1900	
Occupation	N	%	N	%	N	%	N	%	N	%	N	%	N	%
Labourer	449	56.4	1123	36.8	1687	46.0	1626	45.1	1651	50.1	1602	51.8	8138	46.5
Tailor	21	2.6	90	2.9	134	3.7	170	4.7	180	5.5	89	2.9	684	3.9
Carpenter	46	5.8	134	4.4	166	4.5	148	4.1	85	2.6	77	2.5	656	3.7
Painter	44	5.5	102	3.3	98	2.7	169	4.7	127	3.9	105	3.4	645	3.7
Sailor	39	4.9	116	3.8	135	3.7	97	2.7	60	1.8	66	2.1	513	2.9
All others	197	24.7	1490	48.8	1445	39.4	1399	38.8	1191	36.2	1154	37.3	6876	39.3

Source: Annual Reports

TABLE 11.3

Distribution of Sample Inmates by Class: Toronto, Hamilton, Whitby, and Guelph Gaols, 1881–1891, Ontario Central Prison, 1874–1891, and Mercer Reformatory, 1880–1890

	Four-gaol sample		Central Prison		Mercer Reformatory	
	N	%	N	%	N	%
High status business and professional	21	0.03	5	0.04	0	0
Small businessmen and clerical	517	8.5	83	7.5	32	4.4
Skilled labour	1451	24.1	393	35.8	7	0.08
Semi-skilled labour	496	8.2	122	11.1	21	2.5
Unskilled labour	2572	42.6	488	44.5	51	6.1
Not classified	970	16.1	2	0.01	723	86.7
Total	6027	100.0	1095	100.0	834	100.0

Table 3 is derived from a computer analysis of four sample gaols, the Central Prison register and the Mercer register. Sample sizes were as follows: Toronto Gaol, approximately 1 in 10 (3320 out of 33,391); Hamilton Gaol, approximately 1 in 18 (1042 out of 18,958); Guelph Gaol approximately 3 in 4 (653 out of 872); Central Prison approximately 1 in 11 (1095 out of 11,783); Mercer Reformatory, 1 in 2 (834 out of 1,668). All 1,012 gaol register entries from Whitby Gaol between 1881 and 1891 were included.

cent (see Table 11.4); vagrancy at 15 per cent, assault at 10.1 per cent, and drunkenness at 7.5 per cent. At first this would seem to suggest that the prison was primarily used to protect society from property offenders rather than from crimes against the person or moral offences. And in fact for the whole period, no fewer than 55.7 per cent of all committals were for property offences. This impression gains strength from Table 11.5, which groups offences by type and indicates changes at five-year intervals. This shows an increase in committals for property offences from 46 per cent in 1874–5 to 63.5 per cent in the period 1896–1900, and a correspondingly sharp decline in public order committals (primarily drunkenness) from 27.4 per cent in 1874–5 to 17.7 per cent in the period 1896–1900.

Percentage changes are far less distinct when considered for all five-year intervals, and in any case the common crime categories hide a good deal about the nature of the inmate population. It was natural, as V.A.C. Gatrell has demonstrated for the English situation, that property offenders should receive longer sentences than offenders against the person or morals offenders.[17] Assaults were often regarded as momentary aberrations or crimes of passion; property offences were more likely to be carried out by professional criminals. Gatrell appears to conclude that there was considerable justice to these sentencing considerations, and he argues that they give the lie to any 'crude class interpretation' which suggests that the harshest punishments were unfairly meted out to the property offender. Because the gaols were intended for the shortest-term offender, it seems inevitable that committals to the Central Prison should include so many property offenders.

Furthermore, officials seldom differentiated between petty thieves and drunks. It is true that the published statistics showed that only 19 per cent of Central Prison committals between 1874 and 1900 were for public order offences, a figure confirmed by our prison register analysis, which placed public order offences at 19.3 per cent for the period 1880–1900. (By contrast, 57.4 per cent of all gaol committals, 1880–1900, were for public order offences.) Yet officials, noting that fully 77.9 per cent of Central Prison inmates were intemperate, believed that the vast majority of prisoners were drunks and vagrants who repeatedly committed minor offences. In their analysis, the distinctions between minor larceny, vagrancy, and drunkenness did not loom large. All were attributable to the same lack of character and motivation in the offender population. The real significance of the higher proportion of larceny committals for the Central Prison is that occasional drunks went to gaol and habitual drunks

TABLE 11.4
Five Most Common Offences Committed by Central Prison Inmates, 1874–1900

Offence	1874–5		1876–80		1881–5		1886–90		1891–5		1896–1900		1874–1900	
	N	%	N	%	N	%	N	%	N	%	N	%	N	%
Larceny	266	33.4	1376	45.0	1298	35.4	1439	39.9	1303	39.6	751	24.3	6433	36.7
Vagrancy	209	26.3	402	13.2	551	15.0	509	14.1	535	16.2	421	13.6	2627	15.0
Assault	80	10.1	365	11.9	387	10.6	364	10.1	301	9.1	270	8.7	1767	10.1
Drunkenness	76	9.5	220	7.2	562	15.3	323	8.9	117	3.6	9	0.3	1307	7.5
Theft	–	–	2	0.07	–	–	–	–	52	1.6	500	16.2	554	3.2
Other offences	165	20.7	690	22.6	867	23.7	974	27.0	986	29.9	1142	36.9	4824	27.5

Source: Annual Reports

TABLE 11.5
Offences Committed by Central Prison Inmates, by Category, 1874–1900

Offence	1874–5		1876–80		1881–5		1886–90		1891–5		1896–1900		1874–1900	
	N	%	N	%	N	%	N	%	N	%	N	%	N	%
Crimes against the person	116	14.6	459	15.0	436	11.9	464	12.9	378	11.5	361	11.7	2214	12.6
Crimes against property	366	46.0	1789	58.6	1742	47.5	1964	54.9	1926	58.5	1963	63.5	9750	55.7
Crimes against public morals	12	1.5	67	2.2	131	3.6	145	4.0	170	5.2	191	6.1	716	4.1
Crimes against public order	218	27.4	485	15.9	746	20.4	667	18.5	669	20.3	549	17.7	3334	19.0

Source: Annual Reports

TABLE 11.6
Sentence Length of Central Prison Inmates, 1874–1900

Sentence length	N	%
1 month and under to 6 months	12,811	73.2
6 months, 1 day to 12 months	2,815	16.1
12 months, 1 day to 24 months	1,816	10.3
2 years, 1 day to 5 years	70	0.4

Source: Annual Reports

or drunks who committed another offence as well would wind up in the Central Prison.

No issue was of more continuous concern to prison officials than length of sentence. Although these officers argued unconvincingly that longer periods of incarceration were needed to give the prison an opportunity to work its rehabilitative magic, their primary consideration was the needs of the prison industries. Despite numerous urgent pleas from inspectors and wardens, Ontario judges proved unwilling to bend their sentencing practices to accommodate the correctional philosophy of prison administrators. Stubbornly, the judges continued to believe that petty crimes deserved brief sentences. Fully 73.2 per cent of the inmate population was sentenced to six months' imprisonment or less (see Table 11.6).

The analysis of the national origin of inmates is particularly revealing, providing little support for the popular stereotype that the hard-drinking Irish were disproportionately represented in the criminal class. Like other work, the Central Prison study confirms that immigrant status was far more important than national origin in contributing to crime. The proportion of Canadian-born inmates increased gradually from less than 40 per cent in 1874–5 to over 67 per cent in the period 1896–1900 (see Tables 11.7 and 11.8).

Calculating the relationship between committal rates by national origin and the place of birth of the entire provincial population is somewhat difficult, since the census did not report the place of birth of men and women separately. The figures for the Central Prison and the Mercer Reformatory have therefore been added together. Because the census did not consider the country of birth of women and children separately either, these figures are somewhat misleading, since they compare the adult-only prison population to the entire provincial population. Nonetheless, the results of these calculations as presented in Table 11.9,

TABLE 11.7
Country of Origin of Central Prison Inmates, 1874–1900

	1874–5		1876–80		1881–5		1886–90		1891–5		1896–1900		1874–1900	
	N	%	N	%	N	%	N	%	N	%	N	%	N	%
Canadian	313	39.3	1420	46.5	1777	48.5	1882	52.1	1962	59.6	2077	67.2	9431	53.9
English & Welsh	140	17.6	544	17.8	626	17.1	557	15.4	445	13.5	329	10.6	2641	15.1
Irish	178	22.4	517	16.9	587	16.0	477	13.2	305	9.3	200	6.5	2264	12.9
Scottish	56	7.0	143	4.7	184	5.0	163	4.5	120	3.6	86	2.8	752	4.3
American	86	10.8	347	11.4	385	10.5	405	11.2	345	10.5	327	10.6	1895	10.8
Other	23	2.9	84	2.7	106	2.9	125	3.5	117	3.6	74	2.4	529	3.0

Source: Annual Reports

TABLE 11.8
Canadian and Foreign-Born Inmates in Central Prison, 1874–1900

	1874–5		1876–80		1881–5		1886–90		1891–5		1896–1900		1874–1900	
	N	%	N	%	N	%	N	%	N	%	N	%	N	%
Canadian	313	39.3	1420	46.5	1777	48.5	1882	52.1	1962	59.6	2077	67.2	9431	53.9
Foreign-born	483	60.7	1635	53.5	1888	51.5	1727	47.9	1332	40.4	1016	32.8	8081	46.1

Source: Annual Reports

TABLE 11.9

Country of Origin, Central Prison and Mercer Inmates
Compared to All Residents of Ontario, 1881, 1891

| | 1881 | | | | 1891 | | | |
| | Ontario | | Central Prison & Mercer | | Ontario | | Central Prison & Mercer | |
Country of Origin	N	%	N	%	N	%	N	%
Canada	1,499,414	77.8	464	48.0	1,710,932	80.9	444	56.1
England	139,031	7.2	142	14.7	151,301	7.2	126	15.9
Ireland	130,094	6.8	189	19.6	102,986	4.9	94	11.9
Scotland	82,173	4.3	53	5.5	70,157	3.3	23	3.0
United States	45,454	2.4	98	10.1	42,702	2.0	67	8.5
Other	30,756	1.6	20	2.1	35,243	1.7	36	4.6

Source: Annual Reports

seem persuasive. In 1881, 77.8 per cent of the Ontario population was Canadian-born, as compared to only 48 per cent of the population of the two intermediate prisons. Between 1881 and 1891 the Irish dropped from 6.8 per cent of the total population and 19.6 per cent of the prison population to 4.9 per cent and 11.9 per cent, respectively. By comparison, the English, between 1881 and 1891, went from 7.2 per cent of the total population and 14.7 per cent of the prison population to 7.2 per cent of the total population and 15.9 per cent of the prison population. The analysis of aggregate statistics does not indicate very significant differences between Irish and English immigrants in criminal tendencies. The American immigrants stand out, moving from 2.4 per cent of the provincial population and 10.1 per cent of the prison population in 1881 to 2.0 per cent and 8.5 per cent in 1891, confirming the literary evidence, which included innumerable complaints by prison officials about the cost of confining American ruffians operating across the frontier.

The differentiation by place of birth stands out most clearly, however, in Table 11.10, an index of Over- and Under-Representation by country of birth for the period 1880–1900 in all Ontario gaols, the Central Prison, and the Mercer. A score of less than one means that a national group was under-represented, a score of more than one means that it was over-represented. In this table, Canadians in the Central Prison score 0.7, the English 1.9, and the Irish 2.0; the Americans achieve the huge figure of

TABLE 11.10
Index of Over- and Under-Representation in All Ontario Gaols,
the Central Prison, and the Mercer Reformatory, 1880–1900

Country of Origin	All Gaols	Central Prison	Mercer Reformatory
Canada	0.6	0.7	0.7
England & Wales	2.0	1.9	1.8
Ireland	3.3	2.0	2.9
Scotland	1.3	1.1	0.8
United States	3.1	4.9	4.0
Other	1.6	1.8	1.0

Source: Annual Reports

4.9. So much for the notorious criminal propensities of the wild Irish! Again, the figures help to clarify the literary evidence, for not only are there frequent complaints in the prison annual reports about the Americans but there is a remarkable absence of comment on English and Irish immigrants. Indeed, Ontarians in this period seldom made the connection between ethnic origins and crime. The Americans were regarded less as immigrants than as rootless drifters, tramps who came with the season, thus confirming the habit of Central Prison officials of thinking of their inmate population in terms of class, not ethnicity.

Other calculations round out the picture. Understandably, those counties with large cities were most likely to send inmates to the Central Prison, and York and Wentworth with their cities of Toronto and Hamilton sent 41.3 per cent of all inmates between 1880 and 1900. In terms of religion, Roman Catholics were over-represented, contributing 34.3 per cent of the inmate population, although only about 16 per cent of the Ontario population was Catholic, providing further confirmation of the prison's lower-class constituency. The age breakdown shows 57.4 per cent of the population at thirty or under and three-quarters under forty, confirming impressionistic evidence that this was a relatively young group. With respect to marital status, only 29.1 per cent of inmates of the 1874–1900 period were married. Most surprising, perhaps, was the literacy analysis. For the period 1880–1900, 79.5 per cent of the inmates were recorded as being able to read and write; another 5.6 per cent could read only. While this was less than the provincial 1891 rate of 93.7 per cent, it was high enough to call into question the argument of those who equated ignorance and crime. For prison officials, perhaps the most strategically significant statistic of all was the recidivism rate. The prison register analysis between 1881 and 1891 demonstrates that fully 30.1 per cent of the inmates had been imprisoned in the Central Prison at least once before. With so high a recidivism rate, it might be argued that the prison was failing in its most basic purpose. More realistically, it confirms that the Central Prison was a facility designed specifically to hold this group.

From the above analysis it is clear that this was a relatively young, disadvantaged working-class population, convicted of minor property and public-order offences and sentenced to brief periods of incarceration. In particular, those convicted of crimes against property predominated and grew proportionately between 1874 and 1900. Certainly there was enough here to sustain the belief of the criminal justice officials, rooted in the pre-Confederation era and continuing into the later nineteenth century, that these people represented a hardened and degraded criminal class deserving of little sympathy and much hard punishment. Although the same figures provided ample room for a more sympathetic judgment, few who came into contact with Central Prison inmates seemed willing to offer sympathy and support. In the circumstances, and considering the original financial rationale for the institution, the failure to commit scarce resources to traditional rehabilitation is understandable.

CENTRAL PRISON DISCIPLINE

One of the most succinct statements of Langmuir's correctional philosophy appeared in his 1876 report, following a series of investigations into the prison's internal administration and discipline. To protect society, punish crime, and reform the criminal, Langmuir wrote, 'the very first step' must always be 'the entire subordination of the will of every prisoner to constituted authority.' At first glance, this determination to begin the rehabilitative process by breaking the prisoner's will was nothing more than an echo from the 1820s and 1830s, when America's earlier generation of penitentiary ideologues had expressed precisely the same view. There was, however, a difference, which made Langmuir's assertion far more brutal and repressive than any the pioneers of the Auburn and Philadelphia systems had ever voiced. In the earlier day, penitentiary administrators, motivated by genuine idealism, were persuaded that subordination was a necessary part of a far-reaching rehabilitative process. For those who shaped the Central Prison, however, repression and punishment were ends in themselves, part of a program of deterrence aimed at the criminal class both within and beyond the walls of the Central Prison. Langmuir expressed this frankly and forcefully in 1876:

The lives of habitual offenders having been one continued revolt against law and order, with little or no subjugation of the will, or exercise of moral restraint, the very first lesson that these men have to learn on entering the Prison is implicit submission. Failing that, the application of reformatory measures to those of this class who are not beyond such influences, must prove abortive – whilst deprivation of liberty only, to those who are, is no punishment whatever, unless it be accompanied by strict prison discipline and enforced hard labour.[18]

For Langmuir then – to reverse a famous twentieth-century penological dictum – men were sent to the Central Prison not as punishment but for punishment. Yet not even this correctional philosophy, together with an inmate population regarded as being composed of the dregs of society, can fully explain the Central Prison's harsh regime.

Langmuir and his colleagues never grasped the need to come to terms with the power of the inmates as expressed through prison subcultures. Elsewhere, harassed prison governors saw the value of a range of techniques, including early release and payments for over-stint industrial production, in maintaining order but Langmuir believed such methods had little application to the short-term and demoralized inmate population of the Central Prison. The result ensured that life in the Central Prison would be characterized by a maximum of violence and a minimum of goodwill or cooperation.

This pattern emerged in the first few years of the prison's operation and was accompanied by such serious administrative problems that they almost resulted in chaos. Senior guards functioned at cross-purposes and with slight evidence of control or direction from the warden. The chief guard, James Beaumont, himself a former prisoner in an Upper Canadian gaol, over-indulged in alcohol, often in the prison itself, and lost all semblance of control over his fellow guards. Administrative staff, such as the bursar and the cook, refused to follow orders from senior guards and fraternized with the prisoners to the detriment of discipline.[19] The responsibility for some of this lay with Langmuir, who had decided not to establish rules and regulations for the prison until he had had an opportunity to observe the routine as it actually functioned. In the absence of clear rules enforced by experienced administrators, the situation deteriorated to such an extent that several internal investigations, conducted of course by Langmuir himself, had to be carried out into the activities of the chief guard and related problems.

In one of these reports, Langmuir admitted that the failure of the administrative staff to follow orders had led to undue familiarity with convicts, causing some of them to become unmanageable. The alcoholic chief guard was dismissed along with some of his co-workers, and the former deputy chief guard, Richard Stedman, was promoted and evidently instructed literally to whip the institution into shape. Stedman, a powerful and determined man, proceeded to do so, leaning heavily on the prisoners and earning the dislike of many guards. Langmuir belatedly established a comprehensive code of rules, enforcing such essentials of the Auburn system as the rule of silence, the lock-step shuffle, and a restriction on inmate letter writing to once a month and on visits to once every two months. In the area of punishment, the operative principle was 'the discretion of the Warden' and no protection was offered prisoners against unfair or cruel treatment. Numerous escapes had occurred during the prison's first year and this discretionary authority gave Stedman every opportunity to overawe the prisoners and punish them at will. There was a progression of punishments from solitary confinement through ironing to the wall and, finally, whipping. Stedman also used more direct methods, and many a prisoner received on-the-spot beatings from the burly chief guard.[20]

By early 1876 charges of maladministration and cruelty were a source of newspaper comment, and Langmuir and the minister to whom he reported, Provincial Secretary S.C. Wood, carried out an investigation. Unlike some American inquiries, this one did not allow prisoners to testify. Testimony from such persons as the bursar, the bailiff, the storekeeper, and even the acting chief guard, made it obvious that many prisoners had experienced brutality, much of it at the hands of Richard Stedman. The cook, for example, saw the chief guard kick one old man repeatedly; the bailiff, who had conveyed another prisoner beaten by Stedman to the insane asylum, related that the doctor there was shocked at how the prisoner had been mistreated; in another case the storekeeper had heard the screams from prisoners beaten after an escape attempt, and reported, 'I was unwell for two or three days after this from the effects, having never seen anything of the kind before.' The formal report exonerated the prison administration in every respect, while in a covering letter to his Cabinet colleagues the provincial secretary commented that the Central Prison was 'second to none in America.' Any laxity of discipline, he asserted, would 'result in insubordination and mutiny.' If the prison was 'to be considered a place where crime was punished,' it was 'imperatively required that strict discipline be enforced.' Although the report praised Stedman as being 'in many respects a good officer,' it did admit that on occasion he had been 'unnecessarily severe,' and his resignation was accepted.[21]

More revealing than these confident assertions of official rectitude, however, were clear indications in the report of prisoners' resistance to authority. Many of the prisoners subjected to harsh punishments were being disciplined for attempted escapes, and in the prison's first year nine prisoners had actually escaped. Other prisoners had collected an assortment of weapons, including knives, and it was admitted that the prisoners had managed to defy the rule of silence and to communicate frequently among themselves. In subsequent reports there were many references to fires breaking out in the workshops and elsewhere about the prison. Most important, the day after Stedman's removal, Langmuir was forced to report that 'the insubordination of a large number of the prisoners ... became so general yesterday, as to amount to a preconcerted mutiny.' The disturbance had started in the dining hall as a protest over inadequate food. Langmuir had reasserted control by rushing to the prison and having three ringleaders whipped on the spot. Henceforth, to eliminate one obvious point of prisoner interchange, the convicts were served their meals in their cells. Following these events, the prison's officers asserted a firmer control over the prison community.[22]

We are given an unusual glimpse into the inner working of the prison in the late 1870s in letters written by a young guard, Gilbert Hartley, to his fiancée, Mary, in Hamilton. Hartley came to the prison in 1877 and before long was put in charge of one of the largest prison industries, the broom shop. From the correspondence he emerges as a sensitive, well-read young man, ultra-respectable, and a devoted Christian. His letters throw light on several aspects of the prison's operations, but what emerges most forcefully is the growing contempt he felt for the prisoners themselves. He was appalled, for example, that the Episcopal minister would conduct a communion service for such riff-raff, but he could hardly keep a straight face himself when the first convict seized the communion wine and 'drank almost the entire contents' before it could be seized from him. He complained:

I see their daily conduct and I have no hesitation in saying that they are at best liars and thieves. I get so disgusted with them when I see much that is vile and evil among them. Heaven forbid that I should disparage Christian work among them or set myself up as a model of purity. I should be glad indeed if they could be converted to a man for it would save a great amount of vexation and work. I do wish that I was in a purer element. There is nothing that is elevating and refining all is base and vile. I cannot believe a word any of them says. I have often seen them doing things distinctly and when accused of it would deny it.[23]

A few months later Gilbert described to Mary the administration of a whipping. He began by informing her that several of his charges had just been punished by forty-eight hours in the dark cell:

Do not think I am cruel but I find the only way to manage the thieves and roughs who number about three hundred and fifty is by stern measures, kindness to most of them is like throwing pearls to swine. At nine a.m. on Tuesday a prisoner named Kennedy was flogged getting fifty lashes. On Sunday last during Sunday-school he struck one of the guards. Flogging is not a very refining medium but it is one that cools down a man very quick.[24]

After edifying his fiancée with a vivid description of the mechanics of the operation, he related that for the first ten or twelve lashes, 'it was fearful to hear him cry and beg and twist around' but after that he was silent. 'His shoulders were all purple and blistered, a sore place for many a day to come. This marks the third time for him.'

A little later he told Mary of another whipping, that of a man whose escape plans had been discovered. This prisoner took forty lashes, 'without a murmur. His feet are now shackled and will remain so for near two years.'[25] From this respectable young man, who could urge his fiancée to read Milton and Macaulay and write movingly of the sunset on Toronto Bay, there was no expression of sympathy for any of his charges, only dislike and contempt.

Any prison that relied for its efficient administration on fear, punishment, and hard labour was bound to experience untoward incidents. In 1885 the Irish Catholic Benevolent Union charged prison officers with cruelty, ill-treatment, and excessive punishments, especially towards Irish prisoners, and following extensive publicity a three-man royal commission was appointed to investigate.[26] One of the commissioners, inevitably, was the retired inspector, J.W. Langmuir, and he dominated its work. Unlike the previous investigations, this one allowed prisoners to testify, but their testimony was treated with unrestrained contempt. Again and again, the commissioners simply justified whatever punishment had been administered. In the case of William O'Neill, kept in his cell for three months on bread and water and then declared insane, they found the punishment 'certainly not as severe as might have been meted out.' Michael Wynne, a thirty-year-old recidivist, kept forty days on bread and water for refusing to work, was pronounced to be thoroughly bad. He had brought his punishment on himself, and if he had been released with neither clothes nor money, that had been the result of his own behaviour. In the case of a convict from Albany, New York, who had threatened the warden, the lash had not been used because the physician had expressed doubts about the convict's sanity. The commissioners had no such doubts; they pronounced the man incorrigible and regretted he had not been flogged. In the case of a young man who had received fifteen punishments, the commissioners commented, '[t]he recurrent jailbird of this prisoner's type is worthy of no consideration,' and '[t]here need be no very great concern on the part of society if the very hardest usage under prison rules is meted out to him.' In the case of a man who had been placed on bread and water for seven weeks for refusing to work, the commissioners commented, 'We do not think that a man should be starved into submission.' Instead, they advised that he be beaten into submission.[27]

All in all, the report of the 1885 royal commission is a remarkably revealing document. The warden's administration was fully exonerated and the status quo staunchly defended. The state, the commissioners advised, was 'not bound to treat vicious members so daintily in prison that they would be better off by reason of their vice, or to make unexceptional lodging for them, while many of its virtuous members outside [were] suffering from hunger.' The commissioners were greatly concerned that 'the vagabonds and criminal class' not be advised of the fact that comfortable lodging and first-class food were 'to be furnished by simply breaking the law.' Most of all, they reaffirmed the contrast between the penitentiary environment in which prisoners serving long sentences could be induced to obey the rules through the prospect of receiving good conduct remission, and the different circumstances of the Central Prison. In penitentiaries, they pointed out, prisoners might receive such luxuries as tobacco and newspapers, but 'for the class of offenders who seek to make the Central Prison their occasional or permanent resting place, the Government should render this Prison as undesirable and as uninviting as the most rigid discipline, added to the hard labour contemplated by law, can make it.' The Central Prison, they concluded, was entirely different from the penitentiary, for in the prison 'a large majority of the inmates are drunkards, vagrants and petty criminals who are almost constant residents of one prison or another ... The lives of many of these prisoners have been almost one continued revolt against law and order, and the first lesson they have to learn on entering the Central Prison is to subjugate their wills to prison authority.'

That this conception of the Central Prison's role in Ontario society should prevail through several investigations and be restated so forcefully time and again suggests emphatically that the prison was not the creation of any one man or the instrument of a few prison officers. And, despite Langmuir's early praise for Brockway's Detroit and his occasional references to the ideals of American prison reformers, the prison owed little if anything to foreign influences. Its origins are to be found in the changing definitions of crime and conceptions of criminality developed in the pre-Confederation era and expressed forcefully in the 1850s and 1860s by numerous sheriffs, grand jurors, judges and, most eloquently, by the old Board of Inspectors. The Central Prison reflected fundamental values and impulses rooted deep in Ontario society. In establishing a prison designed to punish and deter, Langmuir was no more and no less than the voice of old Ontario. This was a society with a strongly authoritarian strain, still largely agrarian in its values, and deeply committed to a traditional work ethic. Most Ontarians, whether urban middle class or farmers, were deeply affronted by evidence of the existence of a class of men and women who refused to conform. As this element filled the gaols and became an increasing burden to the pocketbooks of respectable citizens, there were few who would have disagreed with the comment of an Ottawa newspaper in 1880 that 'criminals must be recognized as a class, and brought under a system of control.'[28]

A few years later, in 1891, evidence given by numerous individuals before the famous Commission to Enquire into the Prison and Reformatory System of Ontario again served to underline the broad foundation of support for the deterrent prison. Numerous sheriffs, gaolers, police chiefs, and others involved in the criminal justice system applauded the deterrent prison with unrestrained enthusiasm. The gaoler at L'Orignal expressed the view of all when he confidently asserted that a prison should be 'a terror to evil-doers. I know that they dread the Central Prison and that many of them don't go into evil again.'[29] In late Victorian Ontario, the Central Prison was an apt expression of middle-class beliefs, an institution applauded by most and all but impervious to criticism and scandal. It was only the prisoners who suffered and, as the 1885 commissioners saw it, few of them deserved the consideration or sympathy of their fellow Ontarians.

THE MERCER REFORMATORY FOR WOMEN

The members of the 1891 commission, supported by the testimony of sheriffs and gaolers from across the province, found much to praise in the deterrent role of the Central Prison. A different attitude seemed to exist towards the Mercer Reformatory for Women. During the hearings members of the commission expressed concern that no formal code of rules was in place to govern inmate behaviour, and Lucy Coad, the deputy superintendent, claimed the women were allowed far too much liberty, which made it all but impossible to maintain order. Coad regretted that the rule of silence was not enforced and painted a picture of an absolute babble of noise and confusion. When one of the commissioners, Charles Drury, asked whether the institution was carrying out the kind of rehabilitative work for which it was intended, Coad's response was damning, 'no, it is just simply a place of detention.' Another witness, Robert Laird, the bursar, confirmed that there was little if any reformation and suggested that stricter discipline and a better staff were greatly needed. And in reaction against the very essence of the facility, the control exercised by female staff, Laird asserted that it would be 'very advisable' to interest an 'advisory board of gentlemen' in the management of the Mercer.[30] These criticisms do not appear to have been taken entirely to heart by the commissioners, who had little to say about the Mercer in their report. Most notably the commission report issued no challenge to Mary Jane O'Reilly, who had served as superintendent from the beginning.[31] In part this is testimony to O'Reilly's skilled leadership. Despite the complaints of Lucy Coad, which were probably motivated by ambition or jealousy, there had been no riots or even outbreaks of violence, and the facility seemed quiescent and well governed.

It was significant that the 1891 commission was chaired by J.W. Langmuir, under whose leadership the Mercer had opened and who from the beginning had demonstrated a solid understanding of the principal objectives of the women's reformatory movement. If Langmuir's contribution to the Central Prison was narrowly based on the economic program befitting an industrial reformatory, and upon his stern disciplinary vision, the role he played in establishing and maintaining the Mercer was reflective of broader and more humane reform aspirations.

When Langmuir visited the Detroit House of Correction in 1869 and 1871, he would have observed the efforts there of Emma Hall, the matron of the House of Shelter, an adjunct to the House of Correction. According to Warden Brockway, whose own ideas about a women's reformatory had been influenced by a Massachusetts school for delinquent girls, 'we are profoundly convinced that little can be done to reclaim fallen women except through sisterly care, counsel and sympathy of their own sex.'[32] Under Hall, the Detroit facility was described as a family; it emphasized religious and educational training and moral and domestic influences. Langmuir made it clear in his annual reports that he was influenced by

Detroit and by related aspects of the American prison reform movement of the early 1870s. Certainly the inclusion in the Cincinnati Declaration of a strong statement in support of separate facilities for female prisoners helped shape the Ontario inspector's commitment to the separate prison ideology. Langmuir's advice to the Sandfield Macdonald government was unambiguous:

Respecting the advisability of confining both sexes in the same prison, the very highest authorities in the specialty of prison administration have declared themselves in favour of separate establishments for women, and the National Congress on Penitentiary and Reformatory Discipline, which met at Cincinnati, Ohio, in their "Declaration of Principles" adopted and promulgated this principle, and already several States have passed laws creating separate prisons for women.

Langmuir was totally convinced of the rightness of the American position. It was 'not to be doubted,' he had told Sandfield, that the separate principle was the correct one and the time was not far distant when 'Ontario will found an industrial reformatory for women, with the official staff attendants, keepers and instructors of the same sex. Then, and only then, will women be fully able to exercise and wield their great power and influence, in practical ways towards reclaiming the criminal and fallen of their sex.'[33] For most of the next decade, however, successive Ontario governments ignored Langmuir's advice and there is no indication of any movement of public opinion in support of such an initiative.

Part of the reason for this indifference was the simple fact that the female criminal was perceived to pose no serious threat to the public safety. For a while, to be sure, there was a growing number of female prisoners in the local gaols. In 1868, in his first report, Langmuir pointed out that women were a 'large and increasing proportion' of gaol inmates. Of 8,015 commitments over the previous fifteen months, 2,530 were females. He estimated that three-quarters of the women were prostitutes and expressed alarm that 140 were under sixteen years of age. Gaol imprisonment, he pointed out, offered neither employment nor education and 'very often, through contamination, the evil sought to be remedied is aggravated and increased.' Most of all, he suggested, the women regarded gaol terms as no punishment at all, as 'a large portion of females of this class are committed to Gaol from twenty to twenty-five times before they attain the age of twenty-five.' Langmuir's first priority was the female juvenile and he urged the province to establish a reformatory 'somewhat of the character of a Magdalene Asylum' for those under sixteen if there was to be any hope at all of saving them from a life of crime.[34] In the 1870s middle-class Ontarians were thinking actively of establishing industrial schools and of moving on several fronts to address more aggressively what many saw as an approaching crisis of juvenile criminality.

At this point the more general problem of adult female crime presented itself forcefully. When Langmuir inspected the Toronto gaol in 1868, he encountered sixty women and sixty-one men; the following year there were eighty-six women and only sixty-one men. Yet over the next several years the proportions of male to female prisoners in the gaols fluctuated so considerably that numbers alone can scarcely account for the decision to establish a women's prison. In his 1874 report, the inspector noted that there had been no appreciable increase in the numbers of females committed since 1869. Five years later, in 1879, he pointed to a small but significant increase. The number of males sent to prison dropped from 11,595 in 1878 to 10,017, while the number of females increased from 1,886 to 2,013. Yet the 1880 report, which provided eleven-year averages, demonstrated that commitments for women between 1869 and 1880, the very years that a prison for women was under active consideration, 'did not increase in anything like the same proportion as those of the men.' The increase for women was 11 per cent, for men 145 per cent and female commitments went from 1,680 to 1,863. The decline continued into the 1880s, the inspector's 1886 report showing substantial decreases in the percentages of female prisoners to the total of gaol commitments from 1869, when the women represented 29.7 per cent; to 1874, 18.41 per cent; 1879, 15.65 per cent; 1884, 14.22 per cent; 1885, 13.19 per cent and 1886, 13.28 per cent. Yet if Ontario was experiencing no dramatic expansion in female criminality, the increasing numbers of women confined in city gaols such as that of Toronto at least made the problem highly visible. As Langmuir put it in his 1878 report, 'the fact that the annual commitments have reached 2,000 is sufficiently alarming to warrant the adoption of the most progressive measures known in prison reform, in regard to that class of our prison population.'[35] Clearly, then, there was no sudden or rapidly escalating crisis of female criminality to account for the government's belated decision to follow Langmuir's almost decade-old advice. Given the extent of the inspector's influence in the provincial government, it seems likely that for most of the 1870s he himself, although a supporter of a women's prison, had other and more pressing priorities, including the reformation of Penetanguishene Reformatory and the opening of several new asylums for the mentally ill. Then, in 1878, when the province came into a windfall of $100,000 from the estate of Andrew Mercer and Premier Mowat asked his inspector how the funds might best be spent, the time for a women's reformatory had at last arrived. In his considered response Langmuir's justification was not the increasing extent of female criminality, but rather the great merit of differential treatment as enunciated by American experts. Langmuir filled the premier in on the background in an 1878 letter, telling him that his own experience in the decade since he had recommended a women's prison to Sandfield had confirmed his earlier views. Langmuir's report to his political masters was a complete brief statement of the women's prison ideology: for a reformatory for women to fulfil its promise, he all but lectured Oliver Mowat, 'it should be completely isolated' from any men's prison. 'The buildings, their interior arrangements, the disciplinary management, industrial pursuits and general surroundings of a Reformatory for females, are altogether different from those for males.' And, in an after-thought dear to the hearts of Ontario's late nineteenth century politicians, he assured the premier that women's prisons, both in construction and administration, were 'of a far less costly character' than men's prisons.[36] Mowat was persuaded; Ontario at long last would have its women's prison.

DIFFERENTIAL TREATMENT

What did Langmuir understand by the concept of a totally different 'disciplinary management'? Seeking to deepen his knowledge he made another trek south to visit several American facilities but he was unimpressed by how Americans were putting into practice the separate but equal ideology enunciated at Cincinnati.

He reported that the Ingleside Home for Women at Buffalo, whose inmates were primarily prostitutes, had failed because it possessed no 'structural means' of enforcing discipline. He was critical even of the famous reformatory at Framingham, Massachusetts, because the buildings were too scattered to permit adequate supervision. This, he said, was essential: in a female facility 'influence and example are the most powerful factors in the reclamation of the inmates.'[37] This emphasis on role models was an important insight of the women's reformatory movement, which differentiated its approach from that used in traditional male custodial institutions, where guards had no role at all in any rehabilitative process.

Langmuir also was an ardent supporter of what American reformers had postulated about the architectural distinctiveness of the female reformatory. It was 'of the utmost importance,' he argued 'that the structure should externally, be as free as possible from prison appearance' in order to add to the home-like atmosphere most apt to assist the rehabilitative process.[38] With its attractive design and ornamental towers, the Mercer was a large and rather handsome building which could easily have been mistaken for a hospital or an educational facility. As Langmuir had wished, this was a compact structure, three storeys high, with a raised basement. Wisely, it was built not by convict labour but under contract. It contained 147 cells and rooms and 49 isolation cells in the basement, enabling it to hold 196 women. The Industrial Refuge for Juveniles was located in an entirely separate wing, with space for fifty girls.

But the part of the Mercer design most reflective of its reformatory function was its interior arrangements. The Mercer was built, as Langmuir proudly reported, so as to obtain 'as perfect a system of classification as it is possible to have ... There are twelve distinct corridors or wards in the building, to each of which is attached a separate workroom, and in addition the general workshop is divided into two flats and five distinct apartments ... and there are also four distinct yards for airing and exercise.' The objective was to provide distinct and separate accommodation for four grades of prisoners. On arrival, each inmate was to be placed in a small cell, which Langmuir described as 'prison-like,' from whence she might be 'promoted' to better and larger cells and improved surroundings. Continued good conduct could be further rewarded by transfer to a single room in another wing. After another period of good conduct which demonstrated 'marked evidence of reformation,' the prisoner could be moved for a final time to an area 'in which few or no prisoner surroundings' were evident and where every inmate would 'be furnished with a good sized single room and a window opening in each.'[39] With its system of two levels of cells and two of rooms, the Mercer was equipped with the most advanced system of reformatory prison discipline available in any nineteenth-century Canadian prison.

For reasons which are not readily apparent, the commitment to classification and grading that had been incorporated into the Mercer's original design never assumed a large role in actual practice. The original intention that all the inmates would be required to earn their progress through two types of cells and two types of rooms seems to have been entirely lost to view. About all that was done was to try to separate older, hardened offenders from the younger women. There is a suggestion in the 1882 report that madames were taking advantage of their stay in the reformatory to actively recruit young girls. The report that year announced that women under twenty-one would be separated 'from the wretched women in whose houses they have led lives of sin.'

At this time Mercer superintendent Mary Jane O'Reilly instituted the practice used in some American and British reformatories, by which new arrivals were placed in isolation for a month, partly in order to allow officers to gain 'a knowledge of the character and capabilities of the new prisoner.'[40] Two years later, however, the inspector reported that this system was being discontinued; henceforth new arrivals would be admitted at once to the general ward and the space previously reserved for them was used for the refractory class. This significant change was put into effect at once. The objective, as expressed by the inspector, was to encourage new prisoners 'to maintain their position by good behaviour' and to place them in the refractory ward only if they faltered.[41] Although the annual reports provide scanty information about subsequent classification procedures, this apparently meant that the inmates began their stay with most available privileges, and that they could lose them as a form of punishment. From this point on about all that was done in the area of classification was to appoint an attendant to keep girls under eighteen separate from older women. In 1887 there was so little evidence of any classificatory system that a grand jury called it a disgrace that women who were penitentiary graduates or insane were being allowed to mix with young girls. Mercer officials indignantly denied this charge, yet it is noteworthy that their rebuttal said not a word about what arrangements for classification actually did exist.[42] Certainly the elaborate scheme envisaged when the Mercer was established had failed to materialize.

STAFFING

There was little in the thirty-one brief clauses of the 1879 Andrew Mercer statute to convey to the public any sense that an interesting social experiment was being launched. The statute simply proclaimed the establishment of the new prison, described officially as the Andrew Mercer Reformatory for Women, and asserted that the lieutenant-governor might appoint a female superintendent and schoolmistress, with no reference being made to the sex of other officers and guards. The role of women managers was potentially challenged by the authority given to Langmuir as inspector to 'make rules and regulations for the management, discipline and police of the said Reformatory, and for fixing and prescribing the duties and conduct of the Superintendent and every other officer or servant,' as well as for every other aspect of the prison's life.[43]

Yet if ultimate statutory authority rested with the inspector, there is no doubt that the Mercer's first superintendent had full control over the daily life of the prison, and she maintained it virtually unchallenged for the next two decades. The statute gave her the same authority as a male prison warden. She was to live in the institution and, as chief executive officer, under the direction of the inspector, to have 'the entire execution, control, and management of all its affairs.' Possibly the strong-willed Langmuir would have been tempted to interfere but he retired in 1882 and none of his successors seems to have been inclined to question O'Reilly's management. The prison, of course, functioned as part of a wider welfare bureaucracy in which financial control was tight. Mrs O'Reilly, for example, had to make a case for even the smallest expenditures, such as a few dollars for books, or money to paint the chapel. Within those constraints, however, she was in charge and one suspects she revelled in the challenge and responsibility. Mary Jane O'Reilly shaped the Mercer in the image of a model women's reformatory.

O'Reilly herself was a perfect example of a female superintendent. Genteel and upper middle class, the widow of James O'Reilly, a prominent Kingston lawyer and Tory member of Parliament, she possessed all the qualities of breeding, judgment, and firmness which the position was deemed to demand.[44] Perhaps, too, as a Roman Catholic of Irish descent she had some special sympathy for many of those under her protection. Not even the dull formality of two decades of official reports to Queen's Park can disguise the warmth and caring that Mary Jane O'Reilly offered her charges and wards. If the Mercer Reformatory ultimately failed to fulfill the aspirations of its founders, it was not because of any lack of dedication or mismanagement at the top.

Nor was it because the institution's staff fell short of the ideal of being entirely female. The bursar, Robert Laird, who also performed the duties of storekeeper, as the husband of the assistant superintendent lived in an apartment in the building. There was also a male engineer and a night guard, and by the late 1880s this position was held by James Kenny, a former sergeant-major in the Royal Artillery. Another constant male presence was Dr John King, the institution's physician. Yet the assistant superintendent was always a woman, as was the school teacher and most of the guards. Most important, there was never any doubt that it was Mary Jane O'Reilly who established priorities and shaped the discipline which distinguished the Mercer so sharply from the Central Prison.

Perhaps Mrs O'Reilly faced more of a struggle to retain control than is apparent in the official reports. One sign of a lingering reluctance to place confidence in a female administration appeared in 1880 over the appointment of a Sunday School superintendent. The position was a significant one because of the important place volunteer activities were to occupy in the prison's rehabilitative machinery and S.H. Blake, the long-time president of the Prisoners' Aid Association, had serious reservations about giving it to a woman. He spoke to Langmuir and gave him, as Langmuir explained to the provincial treasurer, 'some strong reasons why the proposition for the Sunday School at the Reformatory to be controlled by a lady should be modified so as to allow of the appointment of a male superintendent.' It was Blake's judgment that 'if a man were appointed, his business habits and knowledge of discipline and general management, would enable him to take a practical and common sense view of matters, which a woman would not perhaps always do.' The name of William Howland, a future Toronto mayor well known for his philanthropic efforts, was suggested, and Langmuir recommended 'that Mr Blake's request be acceded to.'[45] As a result, Howland became superintendent of the Mercer Sunday School program. There was, undeniably, a strong and influential male presence in Ontario's model women's prison.

COMMITTAL AND RELEASE

Feminist historians agree that 'the heart of the women's reformatory model lay in its assumptions about commitment.'[46] These procedures, it is argued, differed fundamentally from past practices. While men convicted of most public order and morals offences were sent to a local gaol or not incarcerated at all, women now began to be sent to reformatories. As well, those American states which opened women's prisons instituted sentencing schemes that made it possible to imprison female misdemeanants for relatively long periods of time. Women's reformatories, Nicole Rafter asserts, created a category of female prisoner that had no male counterpart: they were 'based on acceptance – indeed, willing embrace – of differential standards for the imprisonment of women and men.' Those American states which instituted reformatories, it is argued, 'gave legal force to a double standard that punished women more severely than men who had committed the same offences.'[47]

These practices, it is suggested, originated in the intent to create a reformatory environment geared to rehabilitation. The first committal law in the Massachusetts Reformatory permitted it to receive only women who had committed minor offences; and the overwhelming majority of committals during the late nineteenth century were for petty moral offences. New York's practices were even more exclusive. That state's two late nineteenth century women's reformatories accepted only women convicted of petty larceny, habitual drunkenness, and prostitution and it also legislated an age limit which rejected older women deemed unlikely to be receptive to reformative influences. Notably, too, almost no black women were admitted.

As for sentence length, the reformatories of the north eastern United States pioneered in the use of indeterminate sentences. This reflected the belief that even in the case of minor offenders, reformatory discipline needed an adequate time in which to achieve behaviourial changes. The law establishing the Massachusetts Reformatory set a two-year maximum for many offences which had previously carried a six-month maximum, but it set no minimum, and many prisoners continued to be released in less than a year. When reformers objected to this, an 1880 law set one year as a minimum sentence. New York State established the astounding maximum for minor offenders of five years, but some judges refused to commit women on this basis. Reformatory officials countered that the courts did not understand that the objective of long sentences was to help women achieve rehabilitation. Still, in 1899, the maximum was lowered to three years.[48]

The interpretive consensus about these committal and release practices is that, however well-meaning they were in intention, they resulted in forms of differential treatment which effected a double standard which discriminated against women. Rafter's conclusion is typical. Even after New York's reduction of the maximum for female minor offenders from five to three years, she writes, 'female minor offenders were still liable to far longer imprisonment than before the reformatories were founded, and ... no similar extension of state control occurred in the case of men convicted of petty crimes.'[49] Even in the new reformatories, it seemed, women had once again emerged as victims.

Using this analysis for purposes of comparison, did law and practice in the province of Ontario reveal similar inequities? According to Carolyn Strange, it was Langmuir's intention to complement the motherly discipline provided by the female staff by sending to the institution 'daughterly subjects' who were 'the most suitable persons for Reformatory discipline and treatments.'[50] In fact, there is little evidence to suggest that the Mercer in this respect replicated the American reformatory ideal. When the Mercer was discussed by the Public Accounts Committee in 1879, Tory Leader W.R. Meredith asked the inspector, 'what class of women do you expect to get in that Reformatory?' The answer was unequivocal: 'the same kind of offences as warrant the commitment of men to the Central Prison.'[51] In his reports of the previous decade, Langmuir had frequently pointed to the presence in the gaols of a hardened class of female recidivists and this was the element which soon filled the Mercer. Out of the first group of thirty women sent to the Mercer, the annual report noted that 'in nearly every case, the women were habitual offenders ... and the lives of many of them had been largely spent in Common Gaols.' To the Public Accounts Committee Langmuir described them bluntly as 'the criminal class.'[52]

In his 1879 report Langmuir emphasized the similarity between Mercer committal clauses and those for the Central Prison. If Langmuir had intended to populate the Mercer with 'daughterly subjects' deemed most suitable for correction, he would have written the statute differently. Instead, the Mercer, like the Central Prison, was soon filled by the most notorious repeat offenders from the local gaols.

That this indeed was the intention is suggested in Langmuir's 1881 report. There he commented that a year's observation of the actual working of the new institution had led him to conclude that the Mercer was fulfilling its original objectives 'in a very satisfactory way.' This was especially the case, he continued, 'when it is considered that a large number of the prisoners for whom it is intended furnish perhaps the very worst material to work upon with a view to reclamation.' In Langmuir's judgment, it was demoralized offenders and recidivists who were most in need of the lengthy sentences that could be better enforced in a prison than in a gaol.

One of the most persistent themes in the annual reports was the request of Mary Jane O'Reilly for longer sentences. These were deemed absolutely essential for the prison program to be effective.[53] It is important to note, however, that such requests were consistently ignored by the sentencing authorities. Nearly 65 per cent of Mercer inmates received sentences of six months' confinement or less. The most common sentences were for between three and six months, representing 57.7 per cent of all sentences.

Still, a greater proportion of Mercer inmates (35.4 per cent) received sentences longer than six months than did Central Prison inmates (26.8 per cent).[54] One can only speculate as to the reasons for this. It is hard to believe that judges across the province were more willing to listen to the superintendent of the Mercer than to the warden of the Central Prison in this respect. The differential might reflect a lingering sentiment among criminal justice officials that women were harder to reform than men;

TABLE 11.11
Sentence Length of Central Prison and Mercer Inmates, 1880–1900

	Central Prison		Mercer	
	N	%	N	%
1 month and under–3 months	4,436	31.2	182	6.9
3 months, 1 day–6 months	5,976	42.0	1,517	57.7
6 months, 1 day–9 months	629	4.4	69	2.6
9 months, 1 day–12 months	1,592	11.2	406	15.4
12 months, 1 day–18 months	790	5.6	150	5.7
18 months, 1 day–24 months	755	5.3	288	11.0
2 years, 1 day–5 years	43	.3	17	.6
Total numbers	14,221		2,629	

Source: Annual Reports

TABLE 11.12
Sentence Length of Central Prison and Mercer Inmates, 1880–1900

	Central Prison		Mercer	
	N	%	N	%
1 month and under–6 months	10,412	73.2	1,699	64.6
6 months, 1 day–12 months	2,221	15.6	475	18.1
12 months, 1 day–24 months	1,545	10.9	438	16.7
2 years, 1 day–5 years	43	.3	17	.6
Total numbers	14,221		2,629	

Source: Annual Reports

equally, it may represent a feeling that women were more reformable than men, and therefore worth the investment of a longer sentence.

What is most significant about these figures, however, relates to the argument of American feminist historians about the double standard inherent in significantly longer sentences given to women convicted of minor offences. The sentences of most women imprisoned in the Mercer were brief, between three and six months, despite the continual plea of the woman who headed the Mercer that they be made longer. Mercer inmates most emphatically were not sentenced to long periods of incarceration for minor transgressions. And there were no indeterminate sentences available to make it possible for reformatory officials to retain prisoners until they deemed their behaviour satisfactory or their prognosis good.

It is true, nonetheless, that women were sentenced to the reformatory for crimes that were less serious than those which landed men in the Central Prison. As an analysis of offence patterns demonstrates, over two-thirds of the inmates were convicted of public order and morals offences. The relatively harmless nature of most female offences is emphasized by the low proportion of Mercer women sentenced for assault or other crimes against the person. For the whole period 1881–1900, only sixty-four women, or 2.5 per cent of the total population, were committed for such crimes. By comparison, even in a period when women were more actively entering the labour force and frequenting other formerly male preserves, they remained much less prone to violent activities than men.

Similarly, there continued to be a great disparity between the numbers of men and women imprisoned for property offences. Between 1881 and 1900, 745 women, or 20.4 per cent of the population, were there for property crimes. This compared to 7,595 men in the Central Prison; for the 1874–1900 period, 55.7 per cent of Central Prison inmates were there for property crimes. The difference is striking. Presumably men in need stole while women sold their bodies.

A total of 32.9 per cent of the Mercer women, compared to 4.1 per cent of the Central Prison men, were committed for public morals offences. Since morals offences included prostitution, this is far less striking than the male-female disparity in crimes against public order, which accounted for 33.7 per cent of female committals and only 19 per cent of male committals. This encompassed vagrancy and drunk and disorderly, but not drunkenness, which was listed under 'other' offences. The disparity is explained by the number of female vagrants who were prostitutes. In the Table 11.14 list of five most common offences, vagrancy is well in the lead at 26.5 per cent. Put another way, the total of public morals and public order offences is 66.6 per cent for women, compared to 23.1 per cent for men. In late nineteenth century Ontario, men, it seems, specialized in property offences and crimes of violence, women in morals-related offences.

It is true, therefore, that the offences for which women were sent to the Mercer could be regarded as 'less serious' than the offences that sent men to the Central Prison. But perhaps they were just different, which is hardly surprising because they reflected what society for centuries,

TABLE 11.13
Offences Committed by Mercer Inmates, 1881–1900*

	1881–5		1886–90		1891–5		1896–1900		Total	
	N	%	N	%	N	%	N	%	N	%
Crimes against the person	12	1.4	17	2.6	16	2.8	19	3.6	64	2.5
Crimes against property	160	18.9	350	20.8	112	19.7	123	23.0	745	20.4
Crimes against public morals	283	33.4	214	33.0	197	34.6	162	30.3	856	32.9
Crimes against public order	268	31.6	245	37.8	197	34.6	165	30.9	875	33.7
Other offences	125	14.7	37	5.7	47	8.3	65	12.2	274	10.5
Drink-related offences only	169	19.2	78	12.0	67	17.8	73	13.7	387	14.9
Prostitution-related only	278	31.7	209	32.3	190	33.4	155	29.0	832	32.0
All other offences	401	49.1	361	55.7	312	54.8	306	57.3	1380	53.1

*Figures for 1880 are not available.
Source: Annual Reports

TABLE 11.14

Five Most Common Offences Committed by Mercer Inmates, 1881–1900*

Offence	1881–5		1886–90		1891–5		1896–1990		Total	
	N	%	N	%	N	%	N	%	N	%
Vagrancy	206	24.3	180	27.8	164	28.8	140	26.3	690	26.5
Larceny	142	16.7	115	17.7	93	16.3	110	20.6	460	17.7
Keeping/inmate house of ill-fame	126	14.9	83	12.8	102	17.9	71	13.3	382	14.7
Drunkenness**	123	14.5	36	5.6	41	7.2	62	11.6	262	10.1
Keeping/inmate disorderly house	90	10.6	49	7.6	39	6.9	42	7.9	220	8.5
Total	687	81.0	463	71.5	439	77.2	425	79.6	2014	77.5
All other offences	161	19.0	185	28.5	130	22.8	109	20.4	585	22.5

*Figures for 1880 are not available.
**Includes those convicted of simple drunkenness.
Source: Annual Reports

whether fairly or unfairly, had recognized as widely different patterns of male and female criminality. But it is simply inaccurate to insist that somehow this pattern of committal should be attributed primarily to the women's reformatory movement. It originated centuries earlier and reflected a bewildering variety of enduring gender-based attitudes and social circumstances, including society's different perceptions of improper behaviour in men and women, as well as changes brought about by processes of industrialization and urbanization which gradually altered male and female spheres of social and economic activity. To suggest that this represented a double standard either achieved or exaggerated by the maternal feminism of women's reformatory advocates is to distort a far more complex reality. A double standard did indeed exist, but it was one which rewarded and punished both men and women in numerous different ways, and committal practices, at least as they existed at the Mercer, did little, much to Mary Jane O'Reilly's regret, to fundamentally reshape that reality.

If there is little in the Mercer's committal practices to substantiate the argument that this facility was designed specifically to deal with 'daughterly subjects' who had gone temporarily astray, it was equally true that there was nothing about the Mercer's discharge procedures to distinguish it from male facilities. Under the American system, the deployment of indeterminate sentences was premised on the idea that well-behaved young women could earn early release from detention through good conduct and by offering other evidence of rehabilitation, while those who were undeserving would be retained for longer periods.[55] In Ontario, clause 7 of the Mercer statute asserted the desirability of putting an earned remission system in place 'in order to encourage good behaviour and industry,' yet no remission system was implemented in this period. In 1881, Langmuir supported remission in principle, pointing out that many women were 'anxious to know whether good conduct would earn for them a remission of a portion of their sentences.' Yet he noted that nearly every woman in the Mercer was a hardened offender and that sentences were already too brief to achieve rehabilitation. He was therefore at that time not prepared to recommend 'that full effect be given to that portion of the law providing for the shortening of a sentence on account of good conduct.' All he was willing to do was to make special recommendations in the case of deserving individuals. In the same report O'Reilly pointed to the great benefits of remission systems used in other countries and expressed regret that nothing had been done to reward good behaviour in the Mercer. She must have been disappointed by

Langmuir's decision, because it placed discretionary power entirely in the inspector's hands and was no substitute for a full-scale program shaped around institutional needs and standards.[56]

Over the years O'Reilly returned to the question of remission many times. Many of the best behaved inmates, she reported, 'frequently ask me if there is any probability that some of their time will be remitted for good conduct,' and she found it frustrating to be able to offer no hope. 'Every year since this Reformatory has been in operation,' she asserted in 1886, 'I have hoped that those vested with authority would introduce a law, by which our inmates could merit this remission of sentence.' Such clemency, she argued, would be recommended only for first offenders sentenced to at least one year. 'The hope of having the sentence short-ened, ever so little, by their own efforts would I feel sure prove a strong incentive to good conduct.' Fully a decade later O'Reilly had made no progress and repeated the customary plea. 'If the hope of time being remitted for good conduct were held out to them,' she suggested plain-tively, 'it would be a strong incentive to good behaviour.'[57] A remission system was at this time in effect in Kingston Penitentiary and the failure to make use of an approach that had proven its utility is difficult to explain. Possibly provincial officials did not want to hold out such a pros-pect to the type of repeat offenders who were in the Central Prison and believed it inappropriate to employ a system in the Mercer which they were not prepared to use in the male facility. Certainly they regarded remission as inappropriate for short-term prisoners. In any case, the per-sistent failure to heed O'Reilly's advice placed an important limitation on her ability to manage the Mercer in her own fashion.

At the same time, O'Reilly's efforts continued to be constrained by the statutory obligation to accept and retain all prisoners for the term sent to the Mercer by the sentencing authorities. Repeatedly she did her best to educate or persuade the judicial authorities to consider the institutional implications. Short sentences, she argued in 1886, were particularly regrettable for addicts. Habitual drunkards, who usually received six months, were invariably released with their appetites sharpened. In Mas-sachusetts, she noted with approval, a term of two years had been estab-lished for women with prior convictions for drunkenness.[58] Following a visit in 1890 to reformatories in the United States, she suggested that longer sentences there contributed a great deal to institutional order. The discipline received had time to take root and she did not observe there 'that restlessness and excitability I have seen among the women sent for shorter terms to this Reformatory.'[59] The inspector concurred, arguing in

1898 that little would be achieved in the Mercer 'until commitments are for a longer period, or what would be better still an indeterminate period.'[60] Canada, he urged, should follow American practice and enact the important reform of the indeterminate sentence. At the very least, O'Reilly believed, it would serve as a deterrent if the sentence length were increased for each successive conviction. Yet, in contrast to the American model, Ontario during O'Reilly's tenure neither effected longer sentences nor legislated earned remission or indeterminate sentences.

Throughout her tenure O'Reilly's belief in the good work done in the Mercer was balanced by her consciousness of the extent of recidivism. The 1882 report, for example, noted that 212 women had been admitted during the year, and 35 of these were recommittals; in 1886 O'Reilly reported that 27 out of a population of 88 were recidivists. Offsetting the high rate of recidivism, however, was a consistent drop in total numbers confined. The number in custody was 262 in 1885, and dropped to 167 in 1898. Nonetheless, neither O'Reilly nor James Noxon, the inspector, had become any more willing to make claims of rehabilitative success. Noxon emphasized in 1899 that structural changes were finally being made that would permit a superior system of classification to be put in place. But even when a complete classification was possible, Noxon asserted, the Mercer would remain 'a reformatory only in name, being impotent because of the short term of sentence, to influence the lives' of the inmates for permanent good. At this point Noxon took an extreme view, asserting that if any faith still existed 'in the possibility under favourable conditions' of reforming the lives of at least some of the inmates, then every effort must be made to secure the indeterminate sentence. According to Noxon, this was 'the all important organic change absolutely necessary to successful reformatory efforts in Ontario's two intermediate prisons.'[61]

INDUSTRIAL PROGRAMS

In one other respect, the Mercer and the Central Prison shared a common characteristic: each was established as an industrial reformatory and represented the province's concerted attack on the state of idleness that prevailed in the common gaols and which was so offensive to middle-class Ontarians. Thus Langmuir habitually referred to the Mercer as an industrial reformatory and O'Reilly also regarded the work program as central to the prison regimen. She fully accepted the conventional wisdom about the relationship between idleness and crime, asserting that 'of all wretched women the idle are the most wretched.'

'We try to impress upon them the importance of labor, and we look upon this as one great means of their reformation.'[62] To ensure that there should be no misunderstanding about this, Langmuir, with the Mercer about to open, asked the premier to address a circular to all sentencing authorities outlining the objectives of the Mercer. Mowat obliged by telling the judges and magistrates that normally no woman should be sentenced to the reformatory for less than six months, and that '[n]o one should be sentenced to this Reformatory where hard labour is not intended to be imposed or without the certificate of the Gaol Surgeon that the convict is physically and mentally capable of performing ordinary day labour.' If there was any doubt, the woman should be sent to the local gaol for possible future removal to the Mercer. 'Of course,' he concluded, 'no one who is not sentenced to hard labour will be removed to the Reformatory.'[63]

For Langmuir, in the period when the Mercer was being organized, the manner in which the inmates were to be employed was 'perhaps the most important problem in connection with this institution, which has to be solved.' He took it for granted that it would be 'an act of folly' to congregate large numbers of women in prison without furnishing suitable employment. The statute, he noted, 'very properly' made provision for the enforcement of sentences of hard labour.[64] For Langmuir this encompassed not only discipline and punishment but was also a means of ensuring that prisoner labour relieved the government of much of the institution's operating expenses. The income received was not very significant. In 1882, for example, institutional costs were $29,105.21 and the proceeds of labour came to $3,076.46. The figures did not change dramatically over the course of O'Reilly's tenure. In 1899, operating expenses were $23,635.74 and total revenue $4,212.06. With daily costs per inmate running at about 50 cents to an annual total of about $182 per inmate, the financial burden assumed by the province was hardly excessive.[65]

There was one fundamental difference between approaches to labour in the Mercer and the Central Prison. In the former there was a strong initial effort to make the work regimen part of a wider program of good behaviour classification. 'There should be a variety of labour,' Langmuir indicated in his 1879 report, 'commencing with that of a more menial order, such as washing etc., so that the continued good conduct of an inmate might be rewarded by advancement to a higher grade of work, such as machine-sewing etc.' The inspector advised the government to establish facilities for a range of work, including shoemaking, paper box making, tailoring, and sewing by both machine and hand. He also intended to allow private contractors to make proposals to come into the prison and hire the inmates for different types of labour.

All this came to little. There were problems finding contractors to employ the Mercer women, and before long a single task, laundering, dominated all others. To a lesser extent, sewing, knitting and prison domestic work were also carried out. It is difficult to know why Langmuir's original plan failed so completely. No doubt it had a good deal to do with the character of the inmate population and the lack of any semblance of the work ethic. O'Reilly and her colleagues seem to have quickly concluded that the vast majority of Mercer prisoners were working-class women fitted only for the most menial tasks; they rationalized their position by arguing that the provision of training in the basic skills required of a domestic servant was most likely to lead to post-release employment.[66]

In fact, the Mercer population was even more strongly working class than that of the Central Prison. In Table 11.15 an amazing 87.5 per cent of the inmates were reported as holding occupations. Of this group, only 4 per cent held positions which could be described as middle class, although the position listed as 'housekeeper' in the domestic category poses a problem. It is possible that this refers to what today would be called a housewife. But even if it is assumed that such persons were not gainfully employed, there still remain 75.3 per cent reporting occupations. The category, 'no occupation,' which accounts for 12.5 per cent of the inmates, is equally problematic in attempting to determine class, but there is no reason to believe that any substantial proportion of this category was other than working class. If this is so, it appears that almost 96 per cent of the population was working class. But what sets the class composition of the Mercer most dramatically apart from the Central Prison is the larger proportion of unskilled workers. Unskilled workers, including both domestics and prostitutes but omitting those with no occupation, made up 82.3 per cent of the inmate population, compared to 47.1 per cent in the Central Prison.

Some explanation is needed for the decline in the number reporting the occupation of prostitute from 29.7 per cent in 1881–5 to just 5.6 per cent in 1896–1900. While this may reflect the success of police anti-prostitution campaigns, the extent of the change suggests it may be more logically attributable to a labelling change, as the authorities became increasingly reluctant to dignify prostitution by calling it an occupation. Also noteworthy is the increase in the number of domestics, from about 57 per cent in the 1886–90 to 70 per cent in the period 1891–1900, further confirming

TABLE 11.15

Occupation of Mercer Inmates, 1881–1900*

Occupation	1881–5		1886–90		1891–5		1896–1990		Total	
	N	%	N	%	N	%	N	%	N	%
Domestic[1]	490	56.6	365	56.3	398	69.9	374	70.0	1627	62.6
Industrial[2]	7	.8	7	1.1	9	15.8	6	1.1	29	1.1
Prostitutes	252	29.7	171	26.4	59	10.4	30	5.6	512	19.7
Other[3]	35	4.1	20	3.1	28	4.9	22	4.1	105	4.0
No occupation	64	4.0	86	13.3	75	13.2	101	18.9	326	12.5

* Figures for 1880 are not available.

[1]Includes charwomen, cooks, housekeepers, laundresses, servants, domestics, washerwomen, and ladies' maids.

[2]Includes lace makers, box makers, basket makers, book makers, book binders, book folders, brush makers, factory girls, labouring women, presser in dye works, rag pickers, weavers, paper-box makers, spinners, white washers, cane-chair makers, and knitters.

[3]Includes clerks, dressmakers, furriers, milliners, pedlars, seamstress, tailors, teachers, waitresses, nurses, market women, second-hand dealers, store keepers, hotel keepers, midwives, and telegraph operators.

Source: Annual Reports

the popular impression that the Mercer was home to a population composed primarily of members of the servant class.

Table 11.16, which itemizes the five leading occupations of Mercer inmates, further highlights the low number of Mercer women reporting skills. The leading four occupations, representing 79.4 per cent of all inmates, were all unskilled. The fifth largest category, dressmaker, seamstress etc., accounted for only 2.9 per cent of the inmates. Clearly, in late nineteenth century Ontario unskilled women were far more likely to turn to criminal activity than unskilled men.

While O'Reilly's judgment of the skill level and abilities of the inmates may have been a realistic one, the work training offered in the Mercer undeniably confirmed and reinforced their position at the lowest level of Ontario society. Probably the decision taken was the only one possible and best suited the social circumstances and post-release needs of Mercer graduates. O'Reilly stated frankly in 1891 that 'we have tried to keep discharged inmates in view, and provide situations for those who are willing to go into service.'[67]

There is no doubt that many of the Mercer women were entirely uneducated and, as the 1882 report put it, 'almost wholly ignorant of the plainer duties of domestic work.' Differences in status and opportunities explain the enormous disparity between male and female prisoners in the level of literacy. Almost four-fifths of the men were recorded as literate, in contrast to barely more than half the women. The literacy level given for men, however, seems surprisingly high. In this regard it is significant that evidence from the Mercer prison register suggests that Mrs O'Reilly exercised considerable care in examining incoming inmates. Her conclusion that only about half the inmates could read and write may well be a more accurate measurement of the literacy abilities of late nineteenth century Canadian prisoners generally than that provided by Central Prison records. There was, then, much practical justification for putting the prisoners to work at domestic drudgery.

But considerations of class, status, and ability were not the sole factors in determining that the Mercer never took up the challenge of training its inmates in a broader range of work activities. The 1882 inspection minutes made a claim which, if true, is a tragic commentary on the social circumstances as well as the medical condition of many distressed and lower-class women in late nineteenth century Ontario. 'Owing to their mental and physical debasement,' they indicated, 'not more than one-fourth of the women when committed to the Reformatory are capable of doing any kind of work properly.' In these circumstances, it was an

TABLE 11.16

Five Leading Occupations of Mercer Inmates, 1881–1900*

Occupation	1881–5		1886–90		1891–5		1896–1990		Total	
	N	%	N	%	N	%	N	%	N	%
Servant/domestics	355	41.9	258	39.8	262	46.0	209	39.1	1,084	41.7
Prostitutes	252	29.7	171	26.4	59	10.4	30	5.6	512	19.7
Housekeepers	70	8.3	59	9.1	72	12.6	115	21.5	316	12.2
Charwomen	41	4.8	33	5.1	42	7.4	36	6.7	152	15.8
Seamstresses, tailoresses, Dressmakers	30	3.5	12	1.9	19	3.3	14	2.6	75	2.9
Total	748	88.2	533	82.3	454	79.8	404	75.7	2,139	82.3
All other occupations	100	11.8	115	17.7	115	20.2	130	24.3	460	17.7

* Figures for 1880 are not available.

TABLE 11.17
Literacy of Central Prison and Mercer Inmates, 1880–1900

	Central Prison		Mercer Reformatory	
	N	%	N	%
Read and write	11,300	79.5	1,401	53.3
Read only	802	5.6	545	20.7
Illiterate	2,119	14.9	683	26.0

Source: Annual Reports

achievement of sorts to be able to assert, as the inspector did in 1882, that 'quite a number' of women left the Mercer well-trained and able to earn a good living.[68]

Altogether the state of work in the Mercer contrasts favourably with the disciplinary and practical problems which occurred in the Central Prison. In 1887, a typical year, revenue earned consisted of $2,090.63 from laundering, $740.22 from making clothes for inmates, $521.58 from sewing, and $243.50 from knitting. Although efforts were made, with some success, to obtain orders for prison products from private business, these were often hard to come by. The 1889 report pointed out that laundry had become the principal employment because it had become difficult to obtain needlework of any description and there was 'no immediate prospect of securing large orders for clothing, etc.' At this point, the prison's meticulously kept statistics showed that the laundry that year had completed 87,064 pieces for the Central Prison, 61,856 for various groups in the city, and 22,809 for the CPR. By this time, too, the garden, not part of the Mercer's original design, was producing great quantities of vegetables for internal consumption. Despite the difficulties, especially the failure to relate work programs to good conduct classification, 'women's work' seemed easier to provide and simpler to carry out than the occupations found at the Central Prison. The Mercer women, as the peaceful state of the facility and the lightness of punishments suggests, showed little of the resistance to work routines which was so prominent a part of the cycle of violence in the Central Prison.[69]

COMPLETING THE INMATE PROFILE

Other aspects of the inmate profile highlight both similarities and distinc-

TABLE 11.18

Nativity of Mercer Inmates, 1880–1900 (by Country of Origin)

	1880–5		1886–90		1891–5		1896–1900		Total	
	N	%	N	%	N	%	N	%	N	%
Canadian	407	46.4	358	55.2	350	61.5	354	66.3	1,469	55.9
English & Welsh	132	15.0	98	15.1	75	13.2	53	9.9	358	13.6
Irish	211	24.0	105	16.2	79	13.9	60	11.2	455	17.3
Scottish	23	2.6	22	3.4	14	2.5	16	3.0	75	2.9
American	85	9.7	52	8.0	47	8.3	44	8.2	228	8.7
Other	20	2.3	13	2.0	4	.7	7	1.3	44	1.7

TABLE 11.19

Nativity of Mercer Inmates, 1880–1900 (Canadian-born/Foreign-born)

	1880–5		1886–90		1891–5		1896–1900		Total	
	N	%	N	%	N	%	N	%	N	%
Canadian	407	46.4	358	55.2	350	61.5	354	66.3	1,469	55.9
Foreign-born	471	53.6	290	44.8	219	38.5	180	33.7	1,160	44.1

TABLE 11.20
Religion of Central Prison and Mercer Inmates, 1880–1900

Religion	Central Prison		Mercer Reformatory		Ontario Population, 1891	
	N	%	N	%	N	%
Episcopalian	4,510	31.7	917	34.9	706,838	17.6
Roman Catholic	4,916	34.6	897	34.1	679,139	16.9
Methodist	2,183	15.4	449	17.1	1,245,536	31.0
Presbyterian	1,764	12.4	217	8.3	871,461	21.7
Baptist	461	3.2	121	4.6	212,718	5.3
Other	387	2.7	28	1.1	299,390	7.5

tions between male and female prison populations in the 1880–1900 period. Thus Tables 11.18 and 11.19, which contain the analysis of national origin of inmates, confirm earlier work on the Central Prison demonstrating that immigrant status was a far more powerful indicator of criminal propensity than ethnicity. As the Ontario population became gradually more Canadian in origin between the 1881 and 1891 census years, so too did the female criminal population. Unfortunately, the census did not consider the nativity of men and women separately, but overall between 1881 and 1891 the Canadian-born increased from 77.8 per cent of the population to 80.9 per cent. In the same period, the percentage of Canadian-born in the province's two intermediate prisons went from 48 per cent to 56.1 per cent. The group of women demonstrating the greatest decline in level of imprisonment over the period 1880–1900 is the Irish, reflecting the decreasing numbers of Irish emigrating to Canada in the late nineteenth century. Nonetheless, Irish women were imprisoned at a much higher rate than Irish men. For the 1874–1900 period, 12.9 per cent of the inmates of the Central Prison were Irish, compared to 17.3 per cent of Mercer inmates for the 1880–1900 period. Throughout most of the century, both literary and quantitative evidence continually confirmed that Irish women were imprisoned in the entire range of correctional facilities at rates higher than men.

The same is true for religious comparisons. One feature of the inmate profile of both prisons is the over-representation of Catholics (see Table 11.20). This might tend to reinforce the popular stereotype of an underprivileged and alienated Catholic proletariat largely segregated from the Protestant population and manifesting its alienation by a far higher crime rate. What offsets this image, however, are the figures for Episcopalians,

TABLE 11.21
Age of Central Prison and Mercer Inmates, 1880–1900

Age	Central Prison		Mercer Reformatory	
	N	%	N	%
Under 18	810	5.7	369	14.0
18–20	1,422	10.0	316	12.0
21–30	5,929	41.7	938	35.7
31–40	2,933	20.6	504	19.2
41–50	1,719	12.1	324	12.3
51–60	975	6.9	120	4.6
61+	433	3.0	58	2.2

Source: Annual Reports

who were over-represented in both prisons in almost the same proportion as Catholics. On the other hand, Methodists and Presbyterians were
particularly law-abiding.

If existing nativity and religious data can reveal few distinctions
between Mercer and Central Prison inmates, age, marital status, and
drinking habits do highlight more substantial differences. As the data
presented in Table 11.21 demonstrate, the inmates of the Mercer tended
to be younger. Fully 14 per cent were under eighteen years of age, compared to 5.7 per cent for the Central Prison. Almost two-thirds of the Mercer women were age thirty or younger, and 81 per cent were forty or
younger. The relative youth of Mercer inmates probably helped to sustain
official belief in the facility's reform potential. On the other hand, the
youthfulness of the Mercer's population is not unrelated to the high proportion of the inmates who were prostitutes, not the most likely group to
be rehabilitated.

The fact that 43.4 per cent of Mercer women were married, compared
to 29.5 per cent of Central Prison men (Table 11.22) also seems suggestive.
For men it would seem that the married state contributed to stability and
lessened inclinations to crime. For women, often left destitute by the
death of a spouse, ill-treated or abandoned, marriage did not necessarily
bring economic security. Many married women may have been forced to
resort to crime to support themselves and their families.

One can only speculate as to why a significantly higher proportion of
the men were reported as intemperate than of the women (Table 11.23).

TABLE 11.22
Marital Status of Central Prison and Mercer Inmates, 1880–1900

	Central Prison		Mercer Reformatory	
Marital status	N	%	N	%
Single/widowed	10,029	70.5	1,489	56.6
Married	4,192	29.5	1,140	43.4

Source: Annual Reports

TABLE 11.23
Drinking Habits of Central Prison and Mercer Inmates, 1881–1900

	Central Prison		Mercer Reformatory	
	N	%	N	%
Temperate	3,021	22.1	1,098	42.2
Intemperate	10,640	77.9	1,051	57.8

But once again, it may reflect significant economic differences between men and women in late-nineteenth-century society.

To summarize, the Mercer inmate population was younger, less literate, more temperate, and more likely to be married than the male population in the Central Prison. Also, it was serving somewhat longer sentences. Almost no women were imprisoned in the Mercer for crimes against the person; two-thirds of the inmates were there for public morals and public order offences. As was true of the Central Prison inmates, immigrant status was far more important than ethnicity in accounting for criminality. But the most pervasive reality shaping the Mercer inmate profile was class. The Mercer housed a population composed almost entirely of the unskilled and the disadvantaged, women who had little to lose from engaging in criminal activities.

GOVERNING BY KINDNESS

If neither work discipline nor committal and discharge procedures were strikingly different between the Mercer and the Central Prison, it might seem necessary to conclude that herein lies the explanation for the willingness of conservative Ontarians to establish and support a women's prison. The institution, it seems, except for the prominence given to women in its administration and some statistical differences in inmate profile, essentially replicated the familiar procedures of the Central Prison. Men held several important positions in the prison and the male inspectors were probably perceived as being finally in control. But such a dismissive conclusion misunderstands the extent of Langmuir's commitment to the social feminist vision of prison administration and misses a great deal about what went on in both of Ontario's late nineteenth century prisons. It is at this point that the words and actions of O'Reilly and her colleagues must be taken very seriously, for when looked at closely it soon becomes evident that the Mercer as managed by Mary Jane O'Reilly had almost nothing in common with the punitive male prison.

Contemporaries were clear in their own minds about the differences between the Central Prison and the Mercer. The former was planned and run with the objective of deterrence; it was designed, as some put it, to inspire terror and it achieved this objective. Men were sent to the Central Prison for punishment and women to the Mercer, as O'Reilly explained it, for discipline in the context of kindness, friendship, and support. It is impossible to imagine any official associated with Ontario's men's prison setting out objectives similar in any respect to those O'Reilly regularly enunciated for the Mercer. As she put it in 1881, her purpose was to inspire the inmates 'with a feeling of self-respect, and to teach them that they can cherish pure thoughts, perform good actions and live soberly, impressing upon them the fact that true reformation must begin with themselves. Our aim has been to govern with kindness, and we have found this the most effectual way of influencing them, treating them as human beings who have a claim upon our charity as well as upon our justice.'[70] Perhaps because both officers and prisoners understood and to a degree accepted these modern objectives, O'Reilly was able to run the facility without resort to frequent punishments or other harsh disciplinary tools. The absence of scandal or riot meant in turn that O'Reilly seldom faced the threat of outside interference. As a result, the praise offered by the inspectors in the annual reports for O'Reilly's administration is as frequent as O'Reilly's own praise for both the inmates and the members of her staff. In innumerable ways, then, O'Reilly's expressed intent 'to govern by kindness,' however difficult it is to document, was felt and experienced by all members of the the prison community. And it contributed to an exceptional administrative success which made the Mercer in this period one of the most harmonious prisons anywhere.

During her tenure Mary Jane O'Reilly would prove again and again that her administration lived up to her carefully articulated goal of governing by kindness as fully as the Central Prison did to its own repressive mission. Consider, for example, the evidence offered by two decades of prison reports. Such documents must always be regarded critically, for in general they reflected only what their authors wanted to be known about the life of the prison. Almost always, however, they reveal rather more than a superficial reading would suggest and this is true of O'Reilly's Mercer reports. At first they seem to offer little to compel attention or to suggest that the prison was the setting for a worthwhile social experiment. Certainly there was little of the sense of drama or danger which even the casual reader gains from most reports of life in male prisons. Year after year, the government inspector could find little to comment upon; there were no life-threatening issues and apparently no great achievements in the work of reforming the inmates. About the most O'Reilly ever claimed was her 1881 comment that perhaps 'good seeds have been sown among the briars and weeds.'[71] Moving beyond metaphor, the place was clean, the food fairly acceptable, and the prisoners relatively compliant. In a typical comment, the inspector told the government in 1893 that there was 'nothing of importance to report.'

With the benefit of hindsight, it would be more accurate to conclude that the complacent male bureaucrats who succeeded Langmuir in the inspector's office simply lacked the insight to understand what was really happening in the Mercer. On one level of vital importance to life in any prison, O'Reilly's achievement was enormous. Under her leadership, there were no scandals, riots, charges of brutality, or other incidents characteristic of punitive prisons everywhere. The contrast between the ambience of the Mercer and the unruly, often violent, behaviour that Kingston Penitentiary officials complained had characterized female behaviour in that institution in the 1840s and early 1850s is striking. Although the extent and precise nature of violence in the nineteenth-century female prison remains largely unprobed, and although the gendered nature of such violence doubtless differentiated it from that in male prisons, its existence should be neither doubted nor underestimated. As Philip Priestley notes for England, women 'were by no means immune' from such outbreaks. In the punitive institution, prisoners react to official oppression, contempt, and brutality by returning it in full measure and they develop a subculture that helps them cope with the pains of imprisonment and which is reflective of the anger and hatred which pervade such facilities.[72] The official comments about the Mercer that there was 'nothing to report' strongly suggest that this institution was not characterized by a subculture of resistance and hatred.

In the more traditional areas of rehabilitative endeavour the Mercer, in common with women's reformatories elsewhere, made a substantial effort to provide both educational programs and religious succour, with far more success in the latter area than in the former. Although the Toronto Ministerial Association assumed responsibility for nominating clergymen to attend the Mercer on a part-time basis, the work among Protestant prisoners was formally directed by the Prisoners' Aid Association of Toronto (the PAA).[73] In the absence of a resident chaplain, it became the responsibility of Mrs O'Reilly or the deputy superintendent to conduct the daily reading of prayers, while more formal services were performed by the clergymen sent by the Ministerial Association on Sundays and on one weekday. O'Reilly reported that the rule obliging inmates to be present at religious services was 'rigidly enforced' and claimed that much that was positive about the Mercer was attributable 'to the good influence these religious services have on the minds of the inmates.'[74]

The Prisoners' Aid Association asserted its influence on the Mercer primarily through the Sabbath school under William Howland. As well, as the Association report put it, 'the government decided, for various reasons, that the staff of teachers should consist entirely of ladies' and 'a Lady Superintendent was also appointed' in the person of Elizabeth Harvie.[75] The school opened in 1881; each week an average of thirteen teachers, some of them experienced veterans from the Central Prison, instructed the inmates in Christian homilies, distributed religious tracts, and encouraged recitations. Not surprisingly, the choir, which enabled the women to have some contact with children from the Industrial Refuge, the attached children's wing, was a popular feature. School attendance was voluntary and in 1881 it averaged fifty-nine from the Reformatory and eleven from the Refuge.

Year after year, the reports of Howland and Harvie proclaimed their own marvellous success. The women, it seemed, paid rapt attention, never causing the slightest disturbance. Their behaviour was always 'orderly and correct in every respect,' and they had frequently shown 'by the quivering lip and starting tear, that not only has the attention been arrested but the heart impressed.' The 1882 report, which claimed that 'not even one case of bad conduct or even inattention' had occurred, was repeated year after year.[76] Perhaps this was all true. The women of the Mercer, young, poor, uneducated, and in trouble, may have been overawed by the formidable ladies of the Sabbath School Association and may have eagerly accepted the message that through belief and cooperation they would achieve salvation and even temporal success. Or perhaps they were responding primarily to the evident interest and kindness being offered and a kind of feminine bonding was being achieved through friendship and solicitude. Or possibly the prisoners regarded it all as entertainment, a welcome diversion from the drudgery of the laundry, while ignoring or rejecting the message itself. Scattered evidence does suggest that this approach reached a more receptive audience in the Mercer than in the Central Prison, where religious ministrations occasionally led to unpleasant incidents.[77] There was a practical side, however, to the proffered hand of friendship, which doubtless accounts in some measure for the receptiveness of the Mercer women to the efforts of the Sabbath ladies. The teachers provided clothing and other necessaries on release, they made gifts of crochet needles and other supplies which could be used for recreational purposes, and they met the women 'at the prison gate' and helped them find lodging and work.

The volunteers of the Prisoners' Aid Association worked diligently on behalf of men as well as women; a sharper contrast between the milieus of male and female prisons is found in the attitudes and approaches of the paid employees of the respective facilities. In the old-fashioned custodial prison, especially the men's prison, it was axiomatic that the guards, poorly trained and ill educated, would be allowed to have almost no contact with the inmates. In theory at least, guard and inmate were not even to converse other than on a limited range of absolutely essential matters. The staff's role in the Mercer, as laid down in the 1882 report by the inspector, reversed the normal practice in every possible respect. To effect inmate reform, the inspector announced, it would be necessary to select only such attendants 'as are likely to be thoroughly interested in their work ... The fact that the inmates are daily and hourly in contact with these attendants, and have the opportunity of consulting with them for their benefit, is sufficient evidence that in the hands of the staff rests, one, if not the chief, agency' for inmate reformation.

It was one thing to assert this ideal of guard as role model, another to put it into practice. In addition to the natural constraint between gaoler and prisoners there were formidable barriers of class between the Mercer inmates and middle-class women like O'Reilly and Deputy Superintendent Lucy Coad. Whether real bonding ever took place or could occur between a woman like O'Reilly and a frightened and ignorant young prostitute is almost impossible to determine. But to an extent unequalled by any other nineteenth-century Canadian prison, O'Reilly and her staff made the effort. And it helped a good deal that there was a practical side to much of the assistance rendered. This applied especially to some extraordinary initiatives in the neglected field of aftercare. In her 1881 report, O'Reilly pointed out that of 108 discharged inmates, jobs had been obtained for 15 by officers of the reformatory, and 17 were 'taken in charge' by the Sunday school staff, while others had been directed to such institutions as the Toronto Magdalene Asylum and a local convent. O'Reilly suggested that twenty women seemed to have returned to their former activities. 'As in former years,' she noted in 1884, 'we have continued to keep up a correspondence with discharged inmates, visiting from time to time with those within our reach.' Through visitations and correspondence, O'Reilly was able to provide estimates of how many girls managed to keep out of trouble and hold down jobs. In 1886 she reported that 23 of 137 discharged inmates seemed to have fallen back into their old ways, but the others were doing well. O'Reilly's comment that 'we strive to keep the discharged inmates in view as far as we can,' was no idle boast. 'Every member of the staff,' she asserted proudly, 'does her utmost to help and encourage discharged inmates.'

Not all institutional programs met with the same degree of success. At first O'Reilly had believed that a considerable dint could be made in the institution's high illiteracy rate by compulsory secular education. As the 1881 report expressed it, the plan was to try to ensure that all women confined for longer sentences emerged able 'to read and write a little.' In contrast to the Central Prison, where no provision was made for a teacher until a school was finally established by the PAA, the Mercer was able to use the teacher employed at the Industrial Refuge to offer regular night classes. The resulting program was not a success. In 1884 O'Reilly concluded that 'it is utterly useless to compel women over thirty years of age to attend school. With few exceptions they are unwilling to be taught.' The night school continued on a voluntary basis and a new program began during the morning for younger women and for one hour in the afternoon for older women anxious to learn to read and write. In 1889, O'Reilly confirmed that the number of illiterates was 'the same as usual, about three-fifths,' but she had not changed her opinion that compulsion was useless.

In the prison environment, small kindnesses assume considerable significance. It was important that O'Reilly understood that those inmates who could read would be unlikely to have any interest in the five hundred volumes donated to the Mercer library by the Department of Education, which she described as 'far beyond the comprehension of the majority.'[78] In 1886 she complained that the library contained only Bibles, catechisms and school books but, as 'almost all young girls have a craving for fiction' she urged that a judicious selection be made in this area. In 1887 she reported that a special appropriation for the library was 'much appreciated.' Beyond a willingness to acquire novels for the library, O'Reilly essayed several other unusual steps to relax the oppressive prison environment. In 1893 she urged that a boardwalk be constructed in the yard for use during bad weather. This was 'the only opportunity these poor women have of breathing the fresh air and getting some outdoor exercise.' In 1898 she asked for the addition of 'a recreation room for the inmates ... where they could meet' for the two-hour daily period of freedom from labour. For inmates unable to read, 'some harmless amusement could be provided.'

The essential humaneness of O'Reilly's approach was even more apparent in her attitude to punishment. She immediately grasped that the enforcement of frequent punishments would undermine any prospect of winning the cooperation of the inmates. 'We seldom use the dark cells,' she wrote astutely in 1882, 'for our experience has taught us, that to degrade a woman for some trivial offence, when an admonition would suffice, is injudicious.' O'Reilly may have found it politic to say little in her reports about the relaxation of the rule of silence, but it is clear that she obviated much of the need to inflict harmful punishments by permitting the inmates to engage in a wide range of social discourse. At times the resulting clamour alarmed some of the more traditional members of her staff, and in 1887 she clamped down somewhat. 'I have striven,' she wrote, 'to enforce stricter discipline requiring perfect silence in the workshops.' The implication is that even at this point the women were allowed to converse freely among themselves on most other occasions. The statistics confirm the infrequency of punishments. Over the whole of 1884 only forty-three inmates were punished and a total of 131 punishments administered. According to O'Reilly, these statistics proved 'that the number of refractory women is small, and that a very large number are never guilty of any breach of the Reformatory rules.'[79] Even under the tighter discipline administered in 1887, the number of offences totalled only 171. O'Reilly was vague as to what these punishments entailed, but they seem to have amounted to little more than reprimands, the withdrawal of privileges, and occasionally being placed in a solitary cell. The dark cell was used only fourteen times in 1885, three times in 1886, and six times in 1887. In 1890 she reported proudly that there had been no dark cell punishments at all. Such an achievement offers a startling contrast with the painful reality that pervaded all male prisons of the era.

Further evidence of a kindly and nurturing approach to the inmates was evident in the work of the institution's long-time surgeon, Dr John S. King. Often the doctor becomes one of the most hated authority figures in the prison, because he regards it as his special task to search out malingerers and send them back to work at the first possible moment. By contrast, so far as it is able to tell from official reports, John King was genuinely concerned about the state of health of the inmates, which he often found to be deplorable, and over the years he worked conscientiously to do all in his power to be of assistance. On admission, each woman received a physical examination, and during the period of incarceration Dr King often referred with some pride to weight gains and other evidence of physical improvement. King regarded it as his responsibility to ensure that the prisoners received a nutritious diet and that the facility was well heated and ventilated, and the regular inspections he carried out helped to make the Mercer a healthy place in which to live. The prison avoided such medical emergencies as epidemics, its death rate was low, and it seems likely that the doctor was accurate in his judgment that most of the women were healthier inside the prison than they had been in the world of poverty and alcohol which they knew outside.[80]

Dr King's reports provide a sad commentary on the life of disadvantaged women in late nineteenth century Ontario. He described many women on admission as 'wholly unfitted' for any work but knitting, either from general debility or disease. Some were so weakened 'from debauch, disease or want of nourishment' as to be totally incapacitated. The most serious problem was syphilis. It affected thirty-two inmates in the prison's first year and was prevalent throughout its early history. Rigid segregation was imposed and those infected were confined in a separate ward. In King's judgment, Mercer's inmates came almost entirely from two classes: prostitutes and chronic drunks.[81]

One of King's responsibilities highlighted the distinctiveness of the women's prison. In the early years, King delivered two or three babies annually. Occasionally the numbers increased and in 1893 he reported eleven births and the arrival of a number of new inmates with child in arms. Mercer officials had mixed feelings about this situation. The presence of mothers with children had a humanizing effect on institutional life, but it also disrupted routines and at one point thought was given to closing the nursery. The presence in a separate wing of the Industrial Refuge for Girls also distinguished the Mercer from the Central Prison. On occasions, such as during choir practices, there was contact between the Mercer women and the girls in the Refuge, surely another softening feature of reformatory life.

By the mid-1880s Dr King was pointing in his reports to the presence of increasing numbers of persons he regarded more as unfortunates than as criminals. In 1884 he regretted that every year 'several insane cases are sent to the Reformatory.' The institution, he commented, was 'forced into becoming a sort of refuge for old and debilitated cases.' Soon both King and O'Reilly were commenting regularly on the increasing numbers who were severely retarded or of such low intelligence as to be unable to perform the most menial tasks. Although O'Reilly found such women far more difficult to deal with than ordinary criminals, she believed that 'these poor unfortunates are not as responsible as others more gifted by nature,' and she expressed grave fears that 'when they regain their liberty they will fall back into their old ways.' By the early 1890s O'Reilly was conscious of the fact that the Mercer was becoming, like the gaols, a congregate facility housing a disparate population of the criminal, the destitute, and the ill. 'A number of incapables are sent to us every year,' she pointed out in 1893, 'old women charged with vagrancy guilty of no crime, subjects for a home rather than a reformatory. We have also in the house at the present time two insane women, besides some half-dozen who are weak-minded. The infant population also is largely on the increase.'

THE SUCCESS OF THE MERCER

There are two critical questions pertaining to the early history of the Mercer: the nature of the differential treatment and the issue of success. The first of these is more easily dealt with. The Mercer, as we have seen, did not follow the pattern of the American women's reformatory in several important respects. That is hardly surprising since there was no common trajectory; each jurisdiction had its own distinct traditions and priorities and reformatory institutions evolved somewhat differently everywhere. The Mercer naturally reflected the political priorities and social values of the Ontario elite and, equally inevitably, the administrative style of the powerful inspector, Langmuir. As such, it was a prison administered by a woman; its committal policies required it to accept women who were frequent offenders; and it had only very modest expectations as to rehabilitation. Nonetheless, it applied disciplinary methods that were gender specific and distinctly feminine and it created an environment that distinguished it in important respects from its male counterpart, the Central Prison.

Any discussion of differential discipline, however, leads inexorably to the larger question: just what did this discipline achieve? Most feminist scholars have followed the lead of Estelle Freedman, who argued in *Their*

Sisters' Keepers that the ideology of separate spheres which attempted to achieve rehabilitation through the application of a prison discipline that drew on the nurturing qualities inherent in the female character contained within itself flaws and contraditions which severely limited its success. In Freedman's view, this social or maternal feminist strategy, like the separate but equal ideology of racial segregation, 'rested on a contradictory definition of equality. The nineteenth century prison reformers did seek to expand women's rights ... But at the heart of their program was the principle of innate sexual differences, not sexual equality.'[82] This kind of differential treatment, while not without some benefits, served to channel women into sexually stereotyped programs of character training and skills development, thereby reinforcing the very disadvantages which had led women to crime in the first place. In any case it was just too much, Freedman and others concluded, to believe that the nurturing qualities of maternal feminism could succeed in the inherently hostile environment of the prison in which relationships were shaped by the crude realities of class and power. In this environment, the notion of sisterhood based on gender identity inevitably yielded to new relationships reflecting the unbreachable distance between middle-class and working-class values, between gaolers and prisoners.

Such conclusions reflect the approach of scholars who have investigated the women's prison in large measure for what it has to tell us about change and evolution in the place of women in nineteenth-century society. For the criminal justice historian, however, the primary focus must not be on gender but on the entire range of influences that shaped the prison experience. From that more encompassing point of view, the contribution made by Mary Jane O'Reilly and other maternal feminists to the prison enterprise can be considered from a different and more positive perspective. When the women's prison is compared, for example, to the experience of male institutions, it is impossible not to be struck by the extent of the contrast at many critical points. From this point of departure what becomes most interesting in the women's reformatory is not the alleged spectacle of feminism constrained but rather the relatively enlightened objectives and the substantial humanizing achievements of the Ontario Reformatory for Women.

One can gain further insight into this perspective by returning to the testimony given to the 1891 Ontario Prison Commission and to the evidence provided by Mary Jane O'Reilly. When concern was expressed about the state of discipline, O'Reilly replied confidently that 'there are no more than half a dozen at all refractory that I cannot manage without punishing,' and even those 'eventually succumb to discipline.' Commissioner Timothy Anglin responded that some female convict prisons in England were notorious for 'periodical revolts' in which the women 'destroy property, smash the furniture and break the windows.' Such cases had been very rare in the Mercer, said O'Reilly, and had not involved any number of women acting in concert. Given the absence of such outbreaks, O'Reilly was able to respond with confidence when the commission chairman, John Langmuir, seemed perturbed by the absence of printed rules. 'Cast-iron rules,' she replied firmly, 'do not always work well.' She made sure that all the women understood the general rules when they came in, and in any case, she added, it would be of little use to post printed rules with a majority of the inmates unable to read.

The other critical issue the commissioners raised was rehabilitation. Could much good be done, they wanted to know, in the absence of a better system of classification? Given the prison's design, she responded, it was 'not easy to classify them as we would wish'; and it was always impossible to prevent contamination in a prison environment by any system short of complete solitary confinement, an approach of which she decidedly disapproved. In an ideal structure, she argued, the women would be housed in cottages and classified according to age, character, and nature of their offence.

O'Reilly's intelligence and confidence were apparent in the way she responded to several perplexing yet naive questions. Asked whether she was accomplishing everything she could, given the Mercer's flawed design, she told the commissioners 'that is a pretty hard question to answer.' Asked next how many of the eighty-five women then imprisoned she could hope to reclaim, she rebutted, 'you ask me one difficult question, and then you follow it up by asking another.' Still, some response was required and she told the commissioners that 'with the modes of treatment that we adopt now we are doing a great deal of good, and ... a good many never come back to us after they are released.' The staff followed up on what happened after release as far as possible, and while 'there are very many who do well for a few months ... afterwards a good few of them fall away.' She refused to take credit for a recent decrease in the average annual inmate population. 'I do not know how to account for it.'[83]

The commissioners were not sufficiently impressed by the views expressed by O'Reilly's critics to challenge her administration. Perhaps the women's prison, so long as it was efficiently administered, did not interest them very much. Probably John Langmuir, as the founder of the

Mercer, retained some memory of the feminist ideals present at the beginning and understood the truly reactionary implications of the disciplinary proposals advanced by Lucy Coad and Robert Laird. In their brief recommendations the commissioners proposed improved classification, the use of the indeterminate sentence for recidivists or their committal for longer periods, and the diversification of the work program, all goals Mrs O'Reilly had herself advocated many times in the past.[84]

Mary Jane O'Reilly carried on as superintendent for another decade. In subsequent annual reports the provincial inspector was again generous in his praise of her efforts. For O'Reilly, this was no mean achievement. As Canada's first female prison superintendent, she had established the Mercer in her own image and for two decades had responded to all challenges and administered it without scandal, riot, or even sustained criticism. Under O'Reilly the Mercer was indeed a reformatory for women run by women and there is little doubt, as she herself so cautiously claimed, that many of those unfortunates who lived for a time under her roof benefited from the experience.

If the Mercer could be described as a failure in any sense, it was surely not because it proved impossible to apply feminist methods in a prison environment. The Mercer was, after all, a prison, and the limitations inherent in that reality would survive so long as prisons themselves. But within institutions of that description there existed almost every possible kind of horror and cruelty and, far less frequently, occasional glimmers of hope and humanity. Prisons, like every other human institution must be judged and assessed in all their variety and cirumstances, not condemned generically by formula or ideology. It is scarcely possible to miss the point more totally than to condemn a prison for being a prison.

When considered as an historical institution and in the context of the social values of its own day, the Mercer's history makes it problematic, even ahistorical, to emphasize its failures over its achievements. In many ways it is remarkable that the women's prison went so far as it did to devise and apply gender-specific methods appropriate to the contemporary female condition. To add yet one more example, Matilda Elliot, who was in charge of the Industrial Refuge, provided the 1891 commissioners in a rather matter-of-fact way with an interesting piece of information. After pointing out that the Refuge, like the Mercer itself, had no hard and fast rules and that her objective was 'to bring the girls up as if they were at home,' she added that 'I never lock up my rooms. The front door is always open and Mrs O'Reilly's quarters are the same, and have been the same for all these years.'[85] For anyone knowledgeable about Ontario's nineteenth-century male prison, it is impossible to conceive of a more significant or of a more symbolic contrast between the Mercer and the Central Prison than Mary Jane O'Reilly's door which was kept open 'for all these years.' By itself, this was, quite simply, an astounding, indeed a symbolic, commentary on the truly profound differences between the world of the Mercer and that of Kingston Penitentiary and the Central Prison. And as such it represents a glowing tribute to Mary Jane O'Reilly, to her colleagues, and, perhaps most of all to her charges, the petty thieves and prostitutes of late nineteenth century Ontario.

In all these ways, then, the Mercer did not fail either as a women's prison or in its efforts to apply feminist principles in a prison environment. The failure of the Mercer rather related to the failure of Langmuir, Noxon, and all those other male bureaucrats who were so utterly unable to even consider much less comprehend that there might be a larger social significance to the Mercer's accomplishments, one which had relevance for penal strategies generally. The Ontario community had much to learn from the efforts of Mary Jane O'Reilly and her colleagues in the Mercer, if only it had tried to understand. Its failure to make the effort contributed not a little to the enduring tragedy of Canadian prison life poised to enter the twentieth century with harsh, rigid, and unspeakably cruel structures still firmly in place. The failure of recent scholarship equally to appreciate the nature and extent of this late nineteenth century achievement of a few middle-class women and a lot of prostitutes and pilferers is perhaps less understandable and even more regrettable.[86]

12

Aftercare and the Ambiguities of Reform

The Prisoners' Aid Association of Canada (PAA) carried out a range of activities centred in Toronto between 1874 and 1915. Controlled by a group of wealthy and socially prominent Torontonians, the Association appears as almost a prototype of the comparable bodies which proliferated in this period in many North American and European communities whose efforts seemed to be directed at the control and modification of deviant and criminal behaviour on the part of the less privileged and lower class members of society. Studying the relationship between PAA workers and prisoners in Ontario's gaols and prisons sheds considerable light on social and class relationships and the actual functioning of social control and behaviour modification processes. The greatest challenge in correctional history, however, is to employ the abundance of official or semi-official documentation to understand the feelings and values of convict populations. Regrettably, most of what we know about prisoner life must come from such sources as the annual reports of prison inspectors and other officials. Materials generated by prisoners themselves are few in number and suspect in purpose, while statistical materials offer only limited insight into those qualities of spirit and personality that touch the core of prisoner life. The availability of documentation generated by voluntary and philanthropic agencies such as the PAA does not at first glance offer much of a corrective to these problems. All that survives of

PAA records are official reports and a few scattered pamphlets; the reports did include snippets from prisoner correspondence from time to time, but these were carefully selected by PAA officers to serve propagandistic ends.

In this selective quality, however, extant prisoner correspondence is no different from the bulk of official reports of wardens, asylum superintendents, and other officials, which were equally manipulative in intent but nonetheless yield much useful information. If analysed critically, a great deal can be teased out of this documentation, and from PAA reports as a whole. The prominent clerics, lawyers, businessmen, and civil servants who served long periods as PAA officers were among the few members of their class to interact in a sustained way with that element of Ontario society sometimes described as the 'dangerous' or 'criminal' classes. Their behaviour in these encounters was remarkably, indeed suspiciously, similar from one individual to another and even from one decade to another, and for that reason can be seen as expressing not personal attitudes but class values.

Just as revealing as the comments of prominent members of the PAA executive, such as Samuel Hume Blake, Hamilton Cassels, and W.H. Howland, were those of the rank-and-file workers, people like Thomas Croxton, James Lee, Mrs Scott, Mrs Graham, and all those students from Knox College who served as Sunday school teachers. These hitherto anonymous toilers in the field lacked the social cachet of PAA leaders and for that reason their contacts with the prisoner class offer a different perspective. At times a relationship, even a bond, developed between worker and prisoner, and it was far easier for the ex-prisoner after release to feel a degree of comfort when invited, as sometimes happened, to the home of Henry Coombes or S.C. Schook than into the mansions of Sam Blake or Senator George Allan. Another set of relationships existed among PAA staff members such as the agent, Henry Softley; the Bible woman, Maude Keith; the matron, Laverna Bellamy, who ran the Home for Girls; and the prisoners who were in receipt of these services. The comments provided by these early Canadian social workers add a distinctive dimension to the contents of PAA reports.

The reflections of all associated with the PAA assume their fullest significance in conjunction with prisoner correspondence. Occasionally written while in prison, but more commonly after release, prisoner letters offer an unrelenting chorus of praise for the services offered by the PAA and sometimes indeed for the entire prison experience. The language is fulsome, the gratitude cloying, and the reader gasps at the ability of PAA members to be swept along by the torrents of their own propaganda. Certainly these published extracts were carefully selected and reflected months of careful indoctrination; the prisoners who wrote them shrewdly committed to paper precisely what they knew their erstwhile teachers wanted to read. Still, even so questionable a source can be revealing. Although the letters were published anonymously, they were retained in the PAA offices and were open for public inspection. If used with these considerations in mind, they offer a preliminary excursion into the largely uncharted territory of relationships in late nineteenth century Ontario between persons of widely differing class and circumstances.

Prisoner letters present only one dimension of the PAA's role in Ontario life. The Association carried out numerous programs both within and outside prison walls, involving personal visiting, Sunday school classes for convicts, and aftercare work. The significance of these efforts, including the motivation that inspired them and their effect on prisoners, can be understood only within the larger context of the international circumstances of late-nineteenth-century prison life. There was a hardening of attitudes in many North American and European societies in this period, a loss of confidence in rehabilitative programs, and a determination to reinforce the deterrent effect of the prison. These conditions were reflected in the harsh dynamic of Ontario's Central Prison, in many American state penitentiaries and, most strikingly, in the English convict system associated with the rigorous regimen of Edmund Du Cane. In Ontario, PAA efforts ran counter to these general trends. In a recent analysis of the decline of the reformative ideal in late-nineteenth-century British prisons, W. J. Forsythe demonstrated that pessimism about rehabilitation was prevalent among British prison officials and that the few prisoners able to make their voices heard were almost unanimously of the opinion that individual reformatory attempts were entirely absent. The prisoners saw themselves as trapped in the hands of a brutal and impersonal bureaucracy in which little effort was made 'to engage them on the basis of example or instruction.' 'They took pains to relate in great detail occasions when staff did enter into personal discussion, recalling words spoken or actions taken,' and they were anxious to record 'the identities and words of staff who ... showed kindness or fairness and justice in dealing with them.'[1] In Ontario more than in many jurisdictions the work of the PAA determined that prisoners were the object of personal attention and acts of kindness. Part of the purpose of this chapter will be to explain the reasons for this and to assess its significance in nineteenth-century Ontario prison life.

THE CHALLENGES OF AFTERCARE

Organized prisoners' aid work developed in Canada somewhat late in the day. During the first several decades of the life of Kingston Penitentiary, officials of that institution regularly lamented the absence of such efforts. As we have seen, they used cataclysmic language to note the dire prospects facing convicts on release, asserting that the only choice available for some was starvation or a return to crime. Despite the emotional pleas of prison officials, almost nothing was done to rectify this until the establishment of the PAA in the 1870s. The failure of aftercare organizations to emerge earlier owes something to the prevalence in a pioneer society of a sense that those sent to the penitentiary deserved severe punishment and that whatever problems they faced on release were of their own making. Yet the extent of prisoner aid work in more advanced industrial societies such as Britain and the United States can easily be exaggerated, and in those societies such efforts were restricted primarily to the large urban centres.[2]

Nevertheless, the failure to develop prisoners' aid work at an earlier date requires explanation. In many of his reports of the early 1840s, the Kingston chaplain, Reverend Robert Rogers, described the prejudices faced by convicts after release and pointed urgently to society's duty to offer aid and succour. Other officers of the institution during the first decade and a half of its existence, including warden and inspectors, made similar appeals, always without result.[3] As the 1840s ended, the Brown Commission, impressed by the work performed by philanthropic organizations in the United States, made a concerted appeal to private charity in Canada, but this too fell on deaf ears.[4] In the 1850s, during the inspectorate of Wolfred Nelson, a similar call was issued and this was repeated in the 1860s by E.A. Meredith and his colleagues on the reconstituted Board of Inspectors, but with less apparent conviction than in the earlier period.[5]

If this was the situation with respect to the highly visible penitentiary at Kingston, the deplorable circumstances in local gaols in the county towns are hardly surprising. Occasionally a dedicated cleric would attend regularly to offer religious services, sometimes to assist in the composition of petitions for mercy, and to provide more practical help. Regrettably, there are too many comments in the surviving sources to the effect that men of the cloth seldom darkened the doors of the local gaol to encourage a belief that any group in the community was moved to render any organized measure of assistance to prisoners or their families. Reasons for this are readily suggested but difficult to confirm. In a society emerging from pioneer conditions, both governments and private individuals had other priorities. Undeniably there was a lack of sympathy for, or at least understanding of, the challenge of readjustment facing former convicts, a reflection perhaps of a conservative political culture combined with the ingrained individualism characteristic of rural communities. Still, a somewhat more liberal tradition, one in which volunteer efforts had emerged in such fields as temperance and anti-slavery work, existed by the 1850s in the more urbanized communities of Canada West, and the failure of philanthropists to pay any attention to prisoner needs is mildly surprising.

The development of organized prisoners' aid work in the 1870s came at a special point in the evolution of the province's religious life and can be directly related to evangelical fervour. Such PAA officers as W.A. Howland and S.H. Blake were prominent leaders of the Toronto evangelical community, devoted to good works with those in need and to converting their fellow citizens to their own activist form of Christianity. In the last quarter of the nineteenth century organized religion reached new heights of power and prestige.[6] This effervescence was marked by the establishment of national structures for Presbyterianism in 1875 and Methodism in 1884, by the Gothic revival period of church architecture, by the proliferation of a powerful religious press, and by an unprecedented level of lay involvement in missionary and religiously based social service work.[7] John Grant describes what was happening as 'a sort of lay religion,' characterized by indifference to doctrinal distinctions, a simplistic Biblicism, and an overweening confidence in the ability of the human will to consecrate itself to Christ. In social outlook the new evangelicals were sympathetic to the poor but inclined to seek the solution of their problems through conversion and moral reformation, rather than by any radical change in the economic system.[8] The origins of the PAA are to be found in this milieu. Led by evangelicals and staffed by workers consumed with religious passion, it served its clients by working for their conversion.[9]

From 1868 a low church and evangelical group, which included J.G. Hodgins of the Education Department as its president and Sheriff Fred Jarvis as treasurer, had run a Mission Sunday school in the Toronto gaol. This had come under the notice of Langmuir, who heartily approved of these efforts. Like every thoughtful person who had any contact with prisoners, the inspector grasped the obvious fact that for most prisoners the critical moment came on release. In his 1873 report Langmuir pointed to the often overwhelming difficulties former prisoners faced in finding shelter and employment and in gaining community acceptance. He urged that philanthropists provide organized assistance in the new Central Prison.[10] In response, the group at the Toronto Jail Mission organized a meeting in June 1874. Chaired by Sheriff F.W. Jarvis, and with clergymen playing a prominent role, the gathering expressed its willingness to act in accordance with Langmuir's wishes.

One important initiative was the decision, as J.G. Hodgins put it in a letter to Langmuir, 'to employ an agent who will devote his whole time to the welfare of prisoners.'[11] Those present adopted the name 'Prisoners' Aid Association of Toronto,' and elected Dr Hodgins as president; three vice-presidents, including Dr A.M. Rosebrugh, who would serve the association faithfully for more than two decades; and a board of managers. Dr Hodgins set the new organization in motion by sending a circular to every clergyman in Toronto. After pointing out that the PAA represented 'the various Evangelical Religious Bodies of the City,' he urged the clergymen to cooperate by volunteering to preach in the prison several times a year and to suggest the names of Sunday school teachers. Receiving a positive response, Hodgins was asked by Langmuir to work through a body called the Ministerial Association to attend to Sunday services for the Protestant prisoners. From the outset Hodgins believed that the most effective part of the new Association's program would be not preaching but Sunday school work.[12] Langmuir offered a more secular perspective. He believed such an organization should 'visit every convict previous to his discharge, to ascertain from him his necessities, the state of his clothing, where he proposes to go when liberated, what are his wishes, prospects, plans etc., and having gained the necessary information, to supply his needs, procure railway tickets to send him to his home if he so desire; procure employment if he wishes it, and give him counsel and sympathy.'[13] When the decision was made to place much of the responsibility for the expanded effort of the new Association in the hands of a paid agent, provincial support was expected.[14] No grant was forthcoming, however, and the lack of adequate resources acted as a constraint throughout the life of the PAA.

This is surprising, given the prominence in Toronto society of several of the PAA's long-time officers. Samuel Hume Blake, Hodgins's successor as president, came from a distinguished political and legal family and, like most of the PAA officers, combined business and professional success with a lifelong devotion to evangelical causes. W.H. Howland was equally well known and prominently connected. As Reform Mayor of Toronto from 1886 to 1888 he became the leader of an alliance of moral reformers and prohibitionists.[15] The same could have been said of many other PAA officers.[16]

Almost without exception, the board members were Protestant, well educated, and active in the professions or business. Although members of the leading churches – Methodist, Presbyterian, and Anglican – their involvement in welfare and social service activities reflected their deep commitment to a compelling evangelical perspective. On the basis of these facts, it becomes possible to hypothesize as to their motivation. For some, including Howland, Hamilton Cassels, and Liz Harvie, who dedicated themselves to these efforts Sunday after Sunday, year after year, such a sustained effort can hardly be explained by concern over crime rates and social order, and certainly not by a desire to assert continuing leadership in the challenging new social structure of urbanizing and industrializing Ontario. The PAA charter group was firmly at the top of Ontario society and its members had no fear of being displaced. It makes more sense to accept at face value the urgency of the evangelical impulse, combined with a genuine sympathy for some of the less fortunate of their fellow men and women, whatever the psychological origins of such a commitment may have been. Given the social composition of the leadership, however, and the fact that its efforts were directed at modifying antisocial behaviour, it may be unwise to entirely discount a perceived need to control the social environment and render it more safe. Yet nowhere in several decades of annual reports and other documentation did the PAA itself emphasize any threat to urban order or social harmony. There was no discussion at all in these extensive reports of insecurity of property or of the dangers posed by rowdyism and disorder. The only concern, it would seem, was to bring these wayward men and women to Christ for the sake of their everlasting souls and to permit them to lead healthy and productive lives.

Considering the high profile of its board of managers and the desire of the provincial government to encourage its work, it is rather astounding that the PAA struggled, with little success, for financial resources. It is equally surprising that its habitual ambition to extend its work beyond Toronto to much of the rest of Ontario met with abject failure. Was there some defect in the Association's organizational structure that hampered its work? Or did social and professional elites in late nineteenth century Ontario truly have so limited an influence and power? Not until the 1883 meeting did the PAA announce it would seek incorporation under the Benevolent Societies Act, and this change in status had little effect on its activities.[17] The Association's constitution was published in the 1882

Report. Now called the PAA of Canada, its 'central point of operation' was, realistically, declared to be Toronto. Article II asserted that the Association had three goals: the reformation of offenders during confinement and their welfare when discharged; the prevention of crime; and prison reform. Although the latter two objectives suggested new directions, crime prevention was largely encompassed within efforts to reform the offender and it would be several years before the PAA redirected its energies towards prison reform.

Article II enjoined the PAA to 'endeavour to organize similar Associations throughout Canada.' For years no headway was made in this task. With the provincial prisons for men and women located in Toronto, much of the Association's work centred there. Yet there was also a pressing need to serve prisoners in the local gaols and to look after those who left Toronto to return home after release from the Central Prison and the Mercer. Year after year, hope was expressed that local initiatives would take place and branches appear.[18] In 1890, meetings were held in London among interested parties and it was decided to invite W.H. Howland 'and other gentlemen experienced in prison work' to offer advice. A branch association was established and a constitution adopted. In the 1891 PAA report, the secretary of the new branch informed the Association that many 'warm-hearted friends' had since been active conducting Sunday school services in the London gaol and providing other forms of assistance.[19] Yet the London branch was not a great success and there were no more local associations established to the end of the century. The PAA's failure to organize beyond Toronto represented a verdict by public opinion in Ontario on the work of the Association. The PAA never did become a Canadian or even an Ontario organization; it remained no more than a Toronto group of zealous evangelicals.

Association budgets were small. For the first year of operation receipts totalled $764.53 and disbursements were $764.33, leaving a balance of 20 cents. The agent, Henry Softley, collected $54.41 of this amount. Softley's salary was $321.75 and he disbursed $61.26 on discharged prisoners. PAA revenue came from 259 subscribers, including eight Sunday schools. The subscribers, whose names were published in the report, contributed amounts ranging from $10 to 50¢. More than half the subscribers, or 129, donated one dollar. At this point, no money was received from any level of government.[20]

Softley did not like fund-raising, objecting that it took too much of his time, but he must have been persuasive. In 1875–6 he raised $698.58, with all other amounts received that year totalling only $119.39. The PAA found it difficult to survive on this amount, and by 1879–80 governments were beginning to help. Income that year was $1,079.58, with $723.22 from private subscriptions, $300 from the City of Toronto, and $50 from York County. The Ontario government paid the cab fares of the Sunday school teachers and apparently considered this a sufficient commitment. By 1881 this was reflected in a budgetary item of $700. The province also made a payment to the Ministerial Association for the regular Sunday services and a commensurate grant to the Roman Catholic Church. In concurrence with Langmuir's expressed views about leaving the initiative to private philanthropy, it made no contribution to the PAA's many projects.

Significant shifts in the Association's priorities in the 1880s were reflected in the budgets. In 1881, $156.62 was spent on discharged prisoners and $600 on the agent's salary; in 1883 the salary was $514.37 and $750.14 went for aid to prisoners. By 1891, there were substantial increases in government support. The province, in addition to $700 for cab fares, provided $1,000, mostly to pay for the Central Prison night school run under PAA auspices. By this time the City of Toronto was contributing $600 annually and other municipal and county commitments totalled $325. Yet the PAA had not succeeded in generating more public support, and subscriptions from that quarter came to only $431.50, now representing a much lower proportion of the total budget. By 1899–1900, some advance had been made in extracting county contributions, but this was more token than real. The budget now included a list of grants from twenty-two counties, the majority contributing $10 and even York just $50. Toronto was the only city to give anything and it continued to contribute $600. Over the decade the total budget showed no appreciable growth. In the face of various PAA appeals, this reflected a demonstrable failure to impress or engage the public.[21]

Expenditures continued to reflect fairly significant shifts in priorities. Salary expenditures reached $1,711.25, a mark of increasing bureaucratization and expansion of functions. On the payroll were the agent, the night school teacher (the positions were often combined), the Bible woman, the matron of the home for girls, a typist, and an assistant secretary. There were fewer budgetary categories for prisoner aid; the major one, meals and lodging, came to $556.99. The PAA had moved a long way from its original emphasis on spending its income on direct assistance to prisoners. The most important sign of change was a category labelled 'Prison Reform account,' which included salaries and printing, postage, and travelling costs, reflecting the PAA's determination to transform itself into a prison reform society whose energies were directed at lobbying governments and converting public opinion.[22]

Much of the early responsibility for administering the Association's efforts rested with the agent. Little is known of the background of people like Henry Softley, Edward Taylor, Finlay Spencer, and other PAA agents, of Maud Keith (the Bible woman), or of Laverna Bellamy, the matron of the cottage home for girls. These were paid employees but there were other, less demanding, ways to earn a living and it is reasonable to believe that the evangelical impulse represents a large part of the explanation for their commitment to service activities. Probably an engagement in prisoner aid work and the attendant association with members of the Toronto elite brought with it a more elevated status. And work it was, hard and unrelenting. Henry Softley regularly visited prisoners in their cells, and every Sunday afternoon he held services at the Toronto gaol. He maintained close contacts with the Bible and Tract Society, reporting in 1874–5 that he had distributed 30,720 copies of their publications in prisons and other likely places. Softley believed that his visits to the prisoners in the cells sometimes enabled him to gain their confidence. In 1875–6 he reported that he had received thirty testimonies in writing from prisoners in their cells that they had been converted, and fully sixty-nine in the Central Prison that year had professed conversion.[23] In his first year as agent he made 880 calls on behalf of prisoners. Softley dealt with pawn tickets and contacted friends and relatives; he collected clothing or arranged for it to be dropped off at his home or with a friendly baker on Jarvis St and a confectioner on Bay St. He wrote numerous letters to prospective employers and arranged jobs for 134 ex-prisoners at release. He found lodgings for 102 and boarding houses for 40. Sometimes he found tools and implements to assist the ex-prisoner in keeping a job. Another much appreciated form of assistance was the thirty-three pairs of spectacles provided free of cost by a caring optician. Sometimes assistance amounted to no more than an occasional meal; sometimes it involved visiting the home of the prisoner to offer comfort to the parents and to bring news back to the prison.

What was the impact of some of these visits? Was Softley heavy-handed in conveying the evangelical message to modest homes and grieving parents? His impression of prisoners' families was blunt: they were often drunkards and could easily be behind bars themselves, so he used the opportunity of the visit to deliver, as he put it, 'a timely word of warning' to such persons. This was probably resented, but in most cases the visit itself from a person of substance and the chance of news of the loved one in prison may have outweighed any negative feelings. Softley spent considerable time with prisoners after discharge. 'It is necessary to visit them as frequently as possible, and correspond with those who are at a distance.' In return he received many letters of thanks.[24]

Each year, for almost a decade, Henry Softley carried on with these demanding tasks. Often he was on the road, spending nights in hotels, visiting the prisoners in the local gaols. Softley's comments provide insights into the circumstances of those in receipt of assistance. In 1881, he reported that 'a very large proportion' of the prisoners were discharged either insufficiently clad or wearing cast-offs provided by the PAA. 'It is certainly very hard to preach Christianity to an erring brother on the eve of his departure from Prison, and still leave him to face the world again in rags.'[25]

In focusing on the threat posed by the demon rum and in urging prisoners and their families to take the pledge, Softley typified the strategy followed by most PAA workers. Many inmates shared in the official view that they were in prison because of over-indulgence. 'I never was so glad for anything,' an ex-prisoner wrote Softley from Brantford, 'as for signing the pledge that day I came out of prison. I meet with many temptations, but I pray to God for strength to resist it, and He helps me. I hope that all that come out, will go and see you and sign the pledge.'[26] The powerful evangelical message persuaded some prisoners that continuing abuse of alcohol would lead them to roast in hell. If only he had seen earlier the folly of intemperance, a prisoner lamented in 1878–9, for this would have saved him 'many bitter hours of anguish, pain and remorse.' Rather than return to his old ways, he 'would rather remain an inmate of this place.' Such discourses reflected the calculated strategy of the prison evangelists.[27]

One of the agent's functions was to run the PAA shelter at 148 Bay St and at times he lived in this residence. The decision to establish a shelter resulted from years of experience of trying to place ex-prisoners in cheap boarding houses. The willingness to commit scarce resources to a permanent home represented a more secular departure for the Association. In furtherance of this practical approach was the linking of the provision of temporary shelter with an expanded program of assistance in finding employment. In making the case for a permanent shelter, the 1881 report asserted that the PAA felt 'confident from our past experience if work could be procured for the prisoners upon their discharge not one in ten would ever return to a life of crime.'[28] As for numbers given shelter for a few days, the Association's reports were equally vague, but the objectives were clear. The 1883 report asserted that the establishment of the shelter had enabled the PAA to open a broom factory, so that only those prisoners willing to earn their keep would henceforth be provided with shelter.[29] The imposition of a work test was not out of character for the PAA. For all their sympathy with the fallen, Association workers went to enormous lengths to impress upon a sceptical public that they were no pushovers for those who refused to do a day's honest labour.[30] The belief that all men were sinners and that all were capable of being saved did not lead PAA workers to romanticize the prisoners. It was the PAA, for example, which worked successfully to ban tobacco from the Central Prison, even though prison officers probably regarded this indulgence as relieving the tensions of the prison environment. It is suggestive of the degree of resistance to the Association's paternalistic approach that few ex-prisoners availed themselves of the new shelter. Over the first months of operation the numbers in the broom factory averaged only five a night and there seems to have been no dramatic expansion over time.[31] The rented facility on Bay St was eventually replaced by the Association's own home on Simcoe St, but the punitive milieu continued to deter potential users. By 1898–9, the decision was taken to dispose of this facility. The excuse given was the establishment of 'good cheap lodging houses where men could be sent to be in respectable company.' A more insightful note was struck when it was pointed out that there was one disadvantage of keeping discharged men in a PAA home: they were thereby labelled or, as the Association put it, 'ear-marked' and discriminated against by others.[32]

If the decision to dispose of the shelter brought to an end an effort of dubious value, the deterioration of a comparatively forward-looking project is more difficult to explain. The loan scheme emerged informally when the agent and some of the Sunday school teachers began to assist a few prisoners financially in small ways. In 1881, for example, one woman wrote her former teacher that she was sending her ten dollars 'to put in the Savings Bank,' as part of an effort to save fifty dollars by Christmas. In 1883, Edward Taylor, the new agent, found it 'encouraging' that several ex-prisoners had placed parts of their earnings in his hands for safe-keeping, and this now amounted to sixty dollars. He also reported that he had advanced the ex-prisoners, 'by way of loans, to enable them to begin housekeeping, or to start them in some small way of business, the sum of $268.97, of which $121.50 have been already repaid.'[33]

Over the next decade, the sums involved grew considerably. In 1886, the PAA advanced $455 to prisoners and $325.40 was repaid. In spite of this success, the amounts advanced dropped off throughout the decade and the 1899–1900 report noted loans in the amount of only $23.97. By this time there were other urgent demands on PAA funds, but it is curious, if the loans were being repaid, that so praiseworthy a project would be virtually eliminated.[34]

In contrast to the shelter for men and the loan plan, the cottage home for girls emerged in the 1890s as one of the Association's most heavily funded and successful projects. This facility owed its existence to the work of Laverna Bellamy. A do-gooder of the type well known in this period, Laverna did indeed do much good. As Officer Chapman of the Toronto Police Department explained in 1901, Laverna was a discovery not of the PAA but of the police. The Morality Department had been puzzled, he related, when one of the 'most disreputable and vicious women' in Toronto suddenly disappeared from her usual haunts in the streets. Then it was discovered that she was spending her time attending church with Laverna Bellamy. This led to the Morality Department sending some of its most difficult cases to her. Bellamy was subsequently discovered by the PAA and it opened a home under her direction. According to the admiring policeman, many children, some of them forced into prostitution at an early age, had been 'saved' by the home, where Laverna acted 'as mother, father, advisor, confidential friend, magistrate and police.'[35] The PAA believed its cottage home for girls to be one of its outstanding achievements. Laverna and her assistant, a Miss Kelly, became familiar figures to the court and its customers, attending every morning, often taking home young women who were released to their care. They visited the Mercer and the gaol several times a week, as well as the hospitals and other institutions where women in distress were to be found. The cottage home proved far more popular as a temporary abode than the men's shelter ever had. In the 1900–1 report it was noted that over the previous year a total of 162 girls had been in residence or, counting repeat stays, 272. A large number of these were said to have found situations in 'respectable families' or had returned home and were 'completely reclaimed.'[36]

Like comparable facilities detaining women and children in other countries, the PAA home claimed the right to keep their charges confined indefinitely: 'the girls of this class remain with us until we think they are fit to take situations.' What would happen if a woman insisted on leaving is not stated. Possibly the institution's coercive authority derived from the threat to return them to the magistrates or the police court if they failed to behave. There is no way to judge whether abuse of authority ever or often occurred. The reports noted that few stayed any length of time. Probably the caring and common sense amply demonstrated by Mrs Bellamy served to mediate between legal ambiguity and the need of many young women for shelter and friendship. 'After the girls go to situations,' the 1901 report claimed, 'they come to us if they have an after-noon or evening out.' The PAA was delighted by the cottage home's success, partly because it appeared to be fulfilling a commitment to preventive reform which had become increasingly important to PAA leaders. Even though the home was expensive to maintain, costing about $1,200 in 1900, the Association refused to either cut back or close it, preferring to try (with limited success) to raise more funds by special appeals. The decision to carry on, compared to the willingness to close the refuge for men, reflected the prevailing belief that women and children deserved more attention than adult males, because they were less recalcitrant and more open to positive influences. More cynically, the home's success reflected its usefulness in serving as an employment agency placing its clients as servants in 'proper homes.' It seems interesting that so many middle-class families proved willing to accept into their homes young women who had been in trouble with the law.

Good works such as the shelters for men and women carried on outside prison walls were highly visible PAA ventures, but one of the Association's most significant projects remained entirely inside the Central Prison. Encouraged by a grant from the province, the PAA established a night school in 1883, with attendance contingent on good behaviour. The Central Prison school offers the most prominent example of the way in which the PAA was able to effect changes in internal prison routines. The secular school was established at least in part because the Sunday school teachers could see at first-hand how desperately many of the prisoners required basic instruction. In the 1878–9 report, A.D. Stewart, the superintendent of the prison Sunday school, pointed to the urgent need for a night school: 'It is painful to notice how many there are who stand in need of the simplest elements of education.' Hindered in their own efforts by the ignorance and illiteracy of many prisoners, the PAA teachers drew on deeply rooted evangelical traditions to advance the cause of secular education in the prison environment. The teacher, J.J. Pritchard, had nothing but praise for the students. Of 141 students present in the first few months, all but four or five, he claimed, had worked to the best of their abilities and most were full of gratitude for the opportunity to learn.[37]

Later the relationship between the school and the Association became even closer when the agent assumed the teacher's duties. By the early 1890s the night school was receiving more attention in the PAA reports than the Sunday schools, and Association officials were anxious to advance the secular road to prisoner reformation.[38] Thanks to the PAA, the night school had become an important humanizing element within an institution known primarily for unrelenting harshness. In another innovation, a day school was put in place in the Toronto gaol by 1889, which offered elements of secular education to prisoners under conditions far more adverse even than those in the Central Prison.

Nonetheless, the Sunday school program remained the focus of PAA energies. There were three separate Sunday schools, one in the Toronto gaol dating from the late 1860s' and those in the Central Prison and the Mercer Reformatory, in place from the opening of those institutions. The reason for the Association's faith in its Sunday school work was stated succinctly in the 1883 report. These missions represented the PAA's 'most productive field of usefulness' because, 'week after week the prisoners meet with the same teachers, and thus a kindly intercourse is kept up, sympathy is felt and expressed, and undoubted testimony can be given of the abiding character of the work which has been accomplished.' Was the Association's own assessment of the value of its Sunday school work justified? One man in a position to make a judgment was James Massie. Himself a PAA member and a dedicated teacher in the Sunday school, Warden Massie had nothing but praise for the Sabbath program. 'When a prisoner, stained with crime, is seated face to face with a teacher, who is inspired with the truth of the message he brings, and hears that message pointedly delivered to himself, he is much more likely to give heed to it than if spoken to the whole body collectively.'[39]

According to Hamilton Cassels, the superintendent of the Central Prison Sunday school, the objective was to have one teacher for every five prisoners, although to Cassels's regret that had not been achieved by 1881.[40] In its first report, the Association recorded that in 1874–5 between twenty-four and forty teachers had worked each Sunday in the Central Prison. The following year there was an average teaching staff of ten in the gaol and twenty-five in the prison. By 1881, there was an average of thirty-four teachers in the Central Prison during the winter, dropping to twenty-one in the summer, when theology students from Knox College were not available as teachers. Attendance was voluntary. In 1883, about 40 prisoners attended each Sunday in the gaol and in the Central Prison an average of 31 teachers worked with about 205 prisoners. At the Mercer the same year average attendance was seventy-four and there were thirteen children from the Refuge.[41] On occasion the reports expressed regret that it had been difficult to attract the desired number of teachers. At the annual meeting of 1882, it was admitted that the practice of holding Sunday services in the gaol corridors for prisoners not allowed out of their cells had been suspended from time to time because of want of assistance.[42] In general, several dozen teachers attended Toronto's gaols and prisons. Both men and women taught at the gaol and at the prison but, because the teachers are identified in the reports only by their initials, it is not possible to know the respective numbers of each sex. In the Mercer Reformatory the teachers were all women, except for the superintendent.

If the teachers achieved intimate communion with some portion of their prisoner audience, this was partly because they truly saw themselves as instruments of God's work. 'I have never been so deeply interested or actually blest in my work for Christ before,' exclaimed one teacher. Central Prison Superintendent Hamilton Cassels affirmed that the teachers 'universally become more deeply interested in their labour at the Prison than any other religious work.'[43] The opportunity to labour among guaranteed sinners inspired the teachers to heights of religious passion. One teacher described the prison as 'one of the richest corners of the Lord's vineyard' in which to carry forward a Christian mission. Another, an experienced Methodist class leader, reported that 'in no place ... have I seen the bright prospects that I realize in this work.' The closeness of sin was a powerful aphrodisiac for the youthful teachers. 'Everyone in my class,' one man enthused, 'is under deep penitential sorrow for sin, and resolving with God's help to do better in the future.'[44]

Both teachers and officials used the annual reports to highlight conversions, but there was no sure way to be precise about numbers. A typical assessment appeared in the 1875–6 report. 'In the class I am now teaching I have good reason to hope that several men had really been converted. I put the question to them personally and five or six of them intimated to me, that they would lead a new life.' That the sincerity of such commitments was in question is clear from the same teacher's remark that after release, 'their subsequent conduct is known only to the Searcher of hearts.'[45]

Other evidence of success that the PAA brought to the public attention included letters from former prisoners who had left Toronto and from their families. 'We have the family altar set up in our house since my return home,' reported one man, 'and we always remember you [Softley] in our prayers.' Many parents thanked PAA workers for the apparent miracles performed on their wayward offspring. From Leamington a father reported, 'my son is quite a different man since his return home, and goes regular to church; he has also joined the temperance lodge.' A delighted father wrote from Dundas, 'it made my heart leap for joy when I heard my son Richard say he had consecrated his all to Jesus.'[46]

One teacher explained why the teachers could feel encouraged even when few conversions were achieved. Not once during the year had any of the teachers met with a single insult or rebuff, and this theme pervaded the reports year after year. For over a quarter of a century not a single teacher pointed to unruly, threatening, or even disrespectful prisoner behaviour. Evidently neither the thieves nor drunks in the Central Prison, nor the hardened prostitutes of the Mercer, nor even the hopeless recidivists in the Toronto gaol ever abused the trust or elicited the animosity of their teacher. If teacher comments are to be trusted, there could have been no more respectful and cooperative a group of students anywhere in Ontario. One veteran of five years' teaching in the Central Prison reported in 1878–9 that his charges were 'invariably respectful and attentive,' adding proudly that not a single one of his students had ever been recommitted. The same year another teacher described his students as 'quiet, respectful and attentive.' What was true of the men's prison also applied to the Mercer. In 1882 Howland and his colleagues reported that 'the deportment of the pupils has been all that could be desired, not a single case of improper conduct, or even of inattention having been reported to the Superintendent.'[47] Clearly the one-sided nature of this discourse raises the possibility that the real achievement of PAA workers was more to reinforce their own religious commitment than to achieve any lasting conversion on the part of their charges, so frequently recognized as 'unpromising soil.' In this sense, the relationship between teacher and prisoner was not symbiotic but emotionally exploitative.

If the prisoners without exception were seen by their perhaps unworldly teachers as respectful and cooperative, another claim repeated just as frequently in the PAA's reports seems equally astounding. In the Association's first report, officials were delighted to claim that several prisoners were 'thankful that they were ever sent to prison.' A teacher reported that one of his class 'thanked God for his incarceration'; instead of a prison it had become 'a place where liberty has been proclaimed to the captive.' The following year Henry Softley announced that 'a great number' of prisoners had expressed thanks at being sent to prison.[48] Such comments possessed an irresistible emotional appeal for PAA workers desperate for affirmation. 'I thank God that I was sent to the Central Prison,' one inmate claimed, 'before I got so steeped in crime that I could not see the love of the Lord.'[49] No prisoner would have seen his or her situation in quite that way, had that individual not been subjected over a period of time to the persuasive powers of a respected teacher. It adds somewhat to the credibility of such comments that they were usually made in letters written after the prisoner's release, when there was little to be gained by attempting to manipulate the teachers. 'I am *a new man*,' wrote one former prisoner, 'I cannot but think it was a blessing that I was sent to the Central Prison.'[50]

Were the PAA workers really contributing, as they believed, to the reformation of some criminals and doing so in large measure by converting them to Christianity? And if so, why should that have been the case? Were prisoners in late-nineteenth-century Ontario especially susceptible to the evangelical appeal, or was it the skill with which the workers went about their task or some other combination of factors that allowed the PAA to claim some degree of success? In order to answer these questions, it is necessary to probe the relationship between PAA methods and the working-class nature of their constituency. A teacher, rejoicing at several conversions in the Central Prison, offered one insight: 'As is often the case, the simplicity of the plan of salvation staggers them.'[51] This seems plausible. Here were people with little education, deeply in trouble with the law, and having recently experienced the degradation of being introduced into a prison environment which, in many cases, stripped away what remained of their sense of worth and personality. Sad, fearful, sometimes demoralized, they were inculcated week after week with the message that they would be forgiven their sins and saved. All they had to do in return was to give their hearts to God.

Members of the prisoner class, poor and uneducated, must have been particularly susceptible to the hellfire and brimstone approach that infused much revivalist theology. It may be that some in the privacy of their prison cells succumbed through fear and dread. Significantly, there is nothing in the teachers' reports to indicate that the apocalyptic approach was ever emphasized. The focus was gentler, more constructive. The teachers described themselves as imitating Christ through 'a sincere desire to aid in the work of Him who came "to seek and to save that which was lost."' They professed to believe that this meant that they must be caring and understanding in all contacts with prisoners. 'Whenever Christ came in contact and dealt with the criminal,' said one teacher in 1883, 'it was in a spirit full of tenderness and love.' Christ 'clearly drew the distinction between sin and the sinner.' He denounced the sin 'in the most uncompromising terms' but had 'nothing but infinite compassion' for the sinner.[52]

Unlike many Central Prison guards, who often felt little but contempt towards the prisoners, the teachers endeavoured to cross barriers of class and circumstances to forge bonds of sympathy. In contrast with most criminal justice officials and with most of the province's population, they saw the prisoners as more sinned against than as sinners. They were, said A.D. Stewart, superintendent of the Central Prison Sunday School, 'a class on whom the world has turned its back, but for whom the blood of Christ was shed on Calvary.'[53] A.E. Lavell, for decades a leader among Ontario prison reformers, proclaimed, 'the convicts are our kinsmen.' Lavell assured the annual meeting of the PAA in 1901 that the vast majority 'were not really different from other men.' They were 'a very ordinary lot; ordinary in ability, in sin, and in aspiration.'[54]

Although official reports are always written to a purpose, it is possible to deconstruct them to penetrate their language and to develop a sense of the attitudes and prejudices of their authors. What appears year after year in the PAA discourse is abiding sympathy and true caring. 'There are a good many bright, fine looking girls at the Reformatory now,' reported the Bible woman in 1899. 'I have lost sight of none of the men who have been in my class,' said a teacher in 1878–9, and she claimed that 'they all write to me and indicate at least a desire to lead new lives.' Another teacher saw to it that one of her charges was admitted to the General Hospital on release and she visited her regularly in that institution, while others opened their homes to provide temporary lodgings for those without shelter.[55]

These and other examples of apparent empathy and compassion are consistent with the PAA's refusal to accept any analysis that placed full blame for their condition on the prisoners themselves. In 1882 Hamilton Cassels suggested that the experiences of the past year in the Central Prison had strengthened the conviction that teaching the men in prison was 'but part of our duty towards them. The very serious difficulties they meet with upon their discharge, by reason of the taint upon their character, and their poverty and helplessness, demand a far more complete and extensive system of extending to them aid.' Cassels had a perceptive understanding of the negative impact of the prison environment. He and other PAA members, through intimate contact with the inmates, developed real and subtle insights into the consequences of incarceration. No one, he argued, 'can have any conception of the amount of moral strength that is requisite to enable prisoners who desire to reform, to withstand the incessant efforts to make foul and keep foul, which the hardened criminals put forth.'[56] Such comments were never mere posturing or cant, yet ultimately the evangelical appeal provided an inadequate basis on which to establish a widely based prisoners' aid movement in an increasingly secular society. Gradually in the 1880s the PAA leadership came to understand the need to transform a religious crusade into a more far-ranging and, finally, more secular effort.

THE SALVATION ARMY

First, the PAA faced a new challenge, one mounted by a vigorous movement of evangelicals whose appeal to the working-class constituency of prisoners seemed far more urgent and personal than the older Association was able to mount. When Toronto in 1900 cut its grant to the PAA from $600 to $300 in order to give half that amount to the Salvation Army, it gave formal recognition to an organization that had been doing outstanding work in Canadian prisons for more than a decade.[57] The Army, which originated in Britain in 1865, reached Canada in 1882. The Salvationists shared a common evangelical tradition with the PAA and like it directed their efforts first to conversion and then to the provision of material assistance. But in its personal aid approach the Salvation Army better reflected working-class values and, in its early years at least, it carried out its work with more empathy and imagination than the somewhat staid and predominantly middle-class PAA had ever been able to muster. Its military-style organization – Army members were ranked as privates, corporals, colonels, and generals – not only provided administrative efficiency but, together with uniforms, martial music, and marching bands, it seized the attention of an entertainment-hungry populace. In its first year, the Army organized corps in no less than twelve Ontario cities; its official publication, *War Cry*, launched in 1884, achieved within a year a circulation of almost 33,000. By the end of the decade the organization had extended across Canada and into Newfoundland.[58] The Army's expansion was part of that outburst of late-nineteenth-century religious enthusiasm that has been described by S.D. Clark as 'the Great Revival of the City.'[59] The organization appealed to many of the working-class English immigrants then pouring into the country and, as the offspring of revivalist Methodism, it filled a need that the older institutional churches no longer seemed able to meet.

It was natural that the Salvation Army should take up prisoners' aid work. In England, the Army's unorthodox methods and the intrusion of its bands and marches into public space had led to numerous arrests, and some Army members, recruited from the underside of city life, were also veterans of the courts and the gaols. In Canada, too, Salvationists from the beginning had frequent encounters with the law. In June and July 1884 in London some twenty Army members charged with 'beating a drum in a public street,' 'playing a tambourine,' and otherwise disturbing the peace, were sentenced to between ten and twenty days in gaol.[60] Similar sentences were handed down over the next several years in Brockville, Brantford, Walkerton, and other Ontario communities. In January 1887 the Victoria *Warder*, the local Lindsay paper, described how practically the entire Army corps in that community was thrown into gaol.[61]

In response to the social problems that inspired its establishment and fuelled its expansion, the Army in Canada in the late 1880s and 1890s established an impressive array of institutions to assist the poor and downtrodden. 'By 1900 the Salvation Army in Canada was operating eleven rescue homes, thirteen men's hostels, two women's hostels, five coal and wood yards, two enquiry departments, one farm colony, one children's home, and a maternity home and slum post requiring the full-time services of more than a hundred trained officers.'[62] As in England, a special feature of the Army's social program was prison work. The Army, said founder William Booth, 'has at least one great qualification for dealing with this question ... I am in the proud position of being at the head of the only religious body which has always some of its members in gaol for conscience' sake ... We, therefore, know the prison at both ends.'[63] The Army was never in any danger of regarding men and women in prison as a 'dangerous' class to be feared or blamed or shunned.[64] Army members established a 'prison-gate' mission with shelters in close proximity to the gaol so that all in need might find a haven; they sent officers to the courts to divert deserving prisoners away from institutionalization and into their care; and they created enterprises that allowed ex-prisoners to earn money and to receive skills training.

In these endeavours, the Army's militance contrasted with the more sedate approach of the PAA. Apparently the Army's first contact with Canadian criminals occurred at the London gaol in February 1883. 'A detachment of the Salvation Army consisting of about 20 soldiers, principally women, made a sudden and determined attack on the jail today, taking turnkey Kelly so completely by surprise ... It is understood that they intend visiting that institution weekly hereafter.'[65] A similar incursion occurred in Hamilton: 'a service was held in Barton Street jail to the satisfaction of the prisoners. Hallelujah Bertha presented the prisoners with 25 War Crys. Many of the soldiers also put papers into their hands as the Army marched out of the grounds singing a salvation hymn. Captain Eastwood's address to the prisoners was very effective.'[66]

To a greater extent than the PAA, the Army made a special effort to serve female prisoners. Many of its soldiers and officers were female and the Army worked to achieve separate courts for women and better segregated facilities in the local gaols. In 1886, one of the Army's outstanding workers, a young woman, Captain Jones, started work in Toronto with 'fallen

women' by making the rounds of the police court and gaol, diverting prostitutes into her custody. 'She would put up such a fuss and be so convinc-
ing, that she never had a shortage of girls with whom to work.'[67] Another
worker, Sister King, professed to observe the remarkable effect of her min-
istration on the prisoners at the London gaol: 'tears were seen to start and
hearts were bowed beneath their load of sin, and as we again gripped hold
of God for souls we felt His presence very near, and oh, hallelujah.'[68]

The establishment of prison-gate homes was critical to the Army's aftercare work. The first home in Toronto was established in 1890 at the corner
of Yonge and Eglinton. The former inmates were given shelter and coun-
selling, taught trades, and received the exhortations of Army members.[69]
The Army's van, named 'the Deliverer,' was painted red and made the
rounds of the gaol and the men's prison, bringing discharged prisoners to
the home. After the Toronto home was fairly started, others were opened
in Hamilton, Kingston, Montreal, Winnipeg, Victoria, and Vancouver.[70]

The members of the PAA must have envied the ability of the Salvationists to achieve goals, particularly the establishment of branches across
Canada, which had always eluded them. The Army's period of greatest
expansion, the 1880s, occurred just at the point when the PAA was being
forced to recognize that its own methods were failing to appeal to a wider
public. Ironically, the Army's successes may have contributed to a transition within the PAA during the eighties. The PAA increasingly understood that a more activist program of practical assistance, most obviously
in the shelter for women and the work of diversion carried on in the
courts, must supplement its traditional evangelical message. The Association proceeded to attempt the difficult transformation from a dedicated
band of ministers and teachers into something more sophisticated and
more secular.

The initial surge of support for the Salvation Army did not endure,
and the 1890s was a decade of crisis for both organizations. For the Salvationists, 'the wave of enthusiasm had reached its peak and was, in fact,
receding.'[71] One disgruntled former officer concluded the Army must
henceforth put its energies into mass evangelization and not social work.
It was self-defeating, he claimed, to focus on 'a few miserable specimens
of humanity picked up for the most part at the police courts, and who for
nearly all their lives have been drifting between jail and the Mercer
Reformatory.' In many smaller communities 'the Army was forced to
withdraw and, in many instances, sell its property.'[72] The diminishing
tide of zeal did not affect the PAA, which had never expanded so
dramatically.

THE REFORM PROGRAM AND THE LANGMUIR COMMISSION

By the late 1880s the Prisoners' Aid Association understood that it could no longer rely on personal evangelism to achieve its goals. Many of its supporters were frustrated that neither the politicians nor the public seemed interested in their efforts. One event that may have persuaded PAA leaders of the need to strike out in new directions was the meeting in Toronto in September 1887 of the National Prison Association of the United States.[73] Rutherford B. Hayes, Association president, struck the note that may have influenced the PAA to reassess its approach. In all probability, Hayes argued, in Toronto as elsewhere 'the majority even of the intelligent and well-disposed have not considered' prison reform seriously. Hayes told the delegates that the Congress's leading objective was 'to induce people to study the subject, to become informed about it, and thus to create that enlightened and favourable public opinion which is the essential precursor of successful reform.'[74] For the next decade, this was precisely what the PAA attempted.

The old guard was forced to such a public relations effort by irrefutable evidence that the evangelical appeal had failed to achieve its objectives. Puzzlement and disillusionment are among the dominant notes struck by PAA reports in this period. 'We are sorry,' the 1890 report proclaimed, 'to find our penal and reformatory institutions have failed to accomplish the work for which they were designed, but there is nothing to be gained by hiding the facts.'[75] The prevailing malaise dominated the 1892 annual meeting. Even the enthusiasm of volunteer Sunday school teachers and Association officers seemed to wane. The reports of the superintendents from the three Sunday school missions were increasingly perfunctory.

There was a note of desperation in the PAA's efforts to appeal to the larger public. Religious tracts had always been provided to inmates, but now the Association moved from the distribution of religious works, which often had been donated by other evangelical bodies, to the large-scale production and distribution of primarily secular materials such as petitions, pamphlets, and press releases. The 1894 report gratefully acknowledged a special provincial grant to help the Association distribute literature on county gaol reform and on municipal refuges for the poor. From October 1893 to October 1895 the PAA printed and distributed 413,630 pages of prison reform literature and claimed that this effort had already influenced two counties to begin constructing refuges for the poor.[76] The Association's propaganda was directed at elite groups most likely to advance reform objectives. The pamphlet 'County Paupers and

County Houses of Industry' was sent to 11,000 potential supporters, including municipal politicians, members of the legislature and the House of Commons, sheriffs, judges, gaolers, teachers, school inspectors, and church bodies.[77] Other PAA pamphlets followed, including, in 1896, Lyman Abbott's 'How to Treat the Criminal Classes' and Sam Blake's 'Our Faulty Jail System' and, in 1901, Alfred Lavell's 'Our Prison Problem.'[78] It took years for Association officers to grasp the extent of public indifference. In 1897, Sam Blake pronounced it 'incomprehensible' that the politicians had failed to put into effect the sensible reforms advocated by the PAA.[79]

The leadership pressed on, and following the 1887 example of the National Prison Association, it launched a series of public conventions. The first, held on 26 November 1889 and chaired by Mayor W.H. Howland, was held for the purpose of carrying forward the agitation begun by the PAA several months earlier to persuade the provincial government to establish a commission to conduct a wide-ranging enquiry into crime and punishment.[80] To this end, the Association compiled a list of principles that foreshadowed the recommendations made almost two years later by the famous 1891 Prison Commission chaired by John Langmuir. The number of social and religious organizations present at the Reform Conference gave grounds for hope that at last public opinion had become mobilized. In addition to numerous church groups, the meeting attracted provincial Cabinet ministers, police officers, gaol, prison and penitentiary officials, and representatives of houses of industry, the Humane Society, the Associated Charities, the YWCA, and the Victoria Industrial School. In his address as chair, William Howland described the complete failure of Ontario's prison system. 'The ordinary working of prisons,' said Howland, 'was to take hold of men not wholly bad and to turn them out wholly bad.'[81] The most important new idea was a reformatory for young men, aged sixteen to thirty, to be established by the province 'and conducted in accordance with the most advanced principles of modern penological science.' The facility led by Brockway at Elmira, New York, was to be the model.

The real purpose of the conference, however, was to request that the Ontario government appoint such a prison commission. The Mowat government agreed to this request and the resulting inquiry turned out to be the most sophisticated investigation in the history of nineteenth-century Canadian corrections.

It is impossible to encapsulate the work of the justly famous Commission Appointed to Enquire into the Prison and Reformatory System of the

Province of Ontario. Many of its efforts have already been noted. That the commission was chaired by ex-Inspector J.W. Langmuir ensured that this would be a thorough and professional undertaking. Langmuir and his colleagues were appointed on 3 July 1890. Their terms of reference could hardly have been broader. The commissioners were 'to collect information regarding Prisons, Houses of Correction, Reformatories and the like, with a view of ascertaining any practical improvements which may be made in the methods of dealing with the criminal classes in the Province.' They were directed to consider such open-ended concerns as the causes of crime, the rescue of children, sentencing, and 'any improved way of dealing with tramps and habitual drunkards in the Province.'[82] Langmuir was joined in this endeavour by four colleagues, including Dr A.M. Rosebrugh, the workhorse of the PAA.

Langmuir's efficiency and intellectual grasp enabled the commission to undertake a wide-ranging investigation and submit a comprehensive report within ten months. The report includes 225 pages of the commissioners' analysis of the issues and 575 pages of appendices, principally verbatim transcripts of witness evidence. While the value of such material is self-evident, its worth was immeasurably increased by its mode of investigation and analysis. The commissioners held hearings in major Ontario cities, visited institutions in Massachusetts, New York, Michigan, and Ohio, and studied literature from the United States, Britain, and Europe. They attracted to the hearings an impressive array of eminent Canadian and foreign experts from the entire field of social welfare. As Don Wetherell has argued, the result was a report that gave Ontarians the best of all possible worlds. The commissioners studied the international context, they studied the existing Ontario system in unique and vivid detail, and they made specific recommendations which reflected their mandate to avoid all 'unworkable theories' and to submit 'the most advanced, but at the same time the most practical methods of dealing with vice and crime.'[83]

The commission's procedures reflected its chairman's commitment to systematic investigation. Langmuir drew on his sweeping knowledge to prepare comprehensive sets of questions to be put to particular categories of witnesses, while another series intended for all dealt with general themes. The questions were both broad – 'What, in your opinion, are the chief causes of vice and crime?' – and specific, which ensured that the commission would generate a valuable body of comparable data. Provincial bureaucrats were put to work preparing statistical analyses on crime and deviance in post-Confederation Ontario. John Langmuir approached this work not merely as one more official responsibility in a long and distinguished career, but as a unique opportunity to grapple with some of the most challenging issues shaping social relationships.

The most useful summary of the commission continues to be that of Richard Splane, who emphasizes those recommendations which led to early legislation, especially in the field of juvenile delinquency.[84] From a different perspective and as representing an extension of the work of the PAA, other aspects are equally significant. The commission proved to be the culmination of the PAA's attempt to recast the discussion of crime and punishment in Ontario and to develop a higher level of public and official consciousness. The leading theme in the commission's work, and the one with the greatest potential for breaking down entrenched patterns of thought, was its treatment of the causes of crime. The report described this as 'the most important of the subjects' into which the commissioners had been directed to enquire. Again and again the question was put to witnesses. Those who lived in the cities held views quite different from those from rural districts. Some who had been active for years in reform movements had developed decided opinions, yet many 'of great experience who have devoted many years to the study of this and kindred questions ... spoke with doubt and hesitation.'[85] Even though the commissioners recognized the limitations of this type of questioning, they reached a bold conclusion: *'The neglect of its duties by the State and by society in all its other forms of organization, is largely responsible for the prevalence of vice and crime.'*[86]

By arguing this rather astounding case, the commissioners effected something of enduring significance. Earlier in the century the older demonological interpretation of criminal causality had been replaced by the pervasive belief that the individual's moral propensities were shaped by the circumstances of his or her immediate environment. This conviction, accepted unquestioningly at all levels of society, had reinforced the traditional belief that criminal acts were primarily an individual responsibility. This classical tradition of free will had been reflected in the Brown Commission's conclusion in the 1840s that criminals were shaped by such 'environmental' factors as parental neglect, educational and moral deficiencies, and family traditions of idleness and drink, far more than by broader socio-economic circumstances such as slums and poverty. Here was one of the most enduring beliefs of Ontarians throughout the Victorian era. The most important consequence of this was the oft-expressed opinion that criminals must be held personally responsible for their actions and punished accordingly.

Ironically, the emergence in the second half of the century of intellectual theories that pointed to genetic and racial causes for criminal impulses did not challenge the prevailing belief in individual as opposed to social responsibility. The most important development of the 1870s and 1880s was the emergence of the Italian school of criminology associated with the positivist doctrines of Cesare Lombroso.[87] Lombroso in *Criminal Man*, published in 1876, established the anthropomorphic approach to criminology which claimed that career criminals were a distinct physical type, characterized by low foreheads, large ears, small eyes, receding jaws, and other distasteful physical characteristics believed to be passed on from generation to generation. Criminal types were thought to develop in a poisoned atmosphere of alcoholism, syphilitic diseases, and moral degeneracy. The popularization of such theories proceeded rapidly, especially in societies experiencing such consequences of too rapid urbanization and industrialization as poverty, unemployment, and urban slum life. The publication in the United States in 1876 of Dugdale's study of the notorious Jukes family, which counted among its number two hundred criminals and deviants descended from a single woman, was cited by innumerable commentators, including members of the Langmuir Commission, and made a profound impact on the popular mind.

There was nothing inherent in positivist criminology or in the new emphasis on genetics and heredity that led inevitably to the promulgation of more repressive theories of deterrent punishments, but the tendency was there. If the criminal culture was linked scientifically to moral degeneracy, including alcoholism, idleness, and promiscuity, and if society was increasingly victimized by deviants and degenerates incapable of comprehending the traditional virtues of religion, hard work, and thrift, then it was morally justified in pursuing whatever course was required to protect itself. For the habitual criminal, this might mean an indefinite sentence to a harshly penal environment, in which a full range of corporal punishments would be deployed. In many ways, then, and for many reasons, there was considerable potential in the early 1890s for the provincial government to be influenced by the newer intellectual theories and to succumb to a climate of opinion that placed deterrence and repression ahead of rehabilitation in theories of crime and punishment. Langmuir himself, as prison inspector in the 1870s and early 1880s, had often expressed concern and anger at how individuals refused to work, evidently preferring the care and ministrations offered by 'the government boarding house.'

Now, however, and perhaps surprisingly, the commissioners offered an analysis fully in harmony with the relatively progressive beliefs promulgated by the PAA. Rejecting the extreme position that bad heredity made rehabilitation almost impossible, and rejecting as well the view that wrongdoing was primarily a consequence of the moral turpitude of 'the criminal classes,' they argued that the individual convicted of criminal activity could often be rehabilitated, and they recommended numerous reforms to achieve this end. Led by Langmuir and PAA officials, Ontario had developed a dissenting body of opinion on these subjects, one which was thoughtful and informed and, most important of all, was prepared to challenge popular prejudice and conventional wisdom.

Such a positive perspective on crime and the prison problem was apparent in the conclusions the commissioners reached about criminal causality. The commissioners began their discussion with an analysis of the most prestigious international literature, especially the recent volume by Havelock Ellis, *The Criminal*. Ellis, like other students of this period, had laid out several categories of criminals, including political criminals; criminals by passion, who act under stress and never become recidivists; occasional criminals, who act out of moral weakness; and, most threatening to society, instinctive criminals. He described the latter group as moral monsters lacking all normal social impulses. In establishing such a classificatory scheme and in designating some criminals as moral monsters, Ellis, the commissioners argued, had departed sharply from the once prevailing orthodoxy – that moral weakness existed in all individuals – and was moving towards an interpretation of criminality that brought hereditary factors to the fore. But even Ellis, they pointed out, did not go as far as some theorists and contend that 'nothing can be done to save the children of criminals from a life of crime.'[88]

The commissioners returned frequently to the problem of the genetic transmission of criminal tendencies. In this period large numbers of children were being brought to Canada from the slums of London and other British cities by Dr Barnardo and the British child-saving movement. Considerable controversy had been generated about the alleged contribution of slum children to the growth of crime and deviance in Ontario, and witnesses underwent close questioning on this score. There was a wide range of opinion on an issue of such complexity. Dr Barnardo himself maintained that of 2,905 children sent to Canada since 1882, no girls and only ten boys, or 0.34 per cent of the total, had ever been convicted in a Canadian court. Environment, he argued persuasively, 'is much stronger than hereditary taint.' Barnardo nonetheless was typical of most witnesses in his view that 'the tendency to crime and vice is derived and strengthened as the result of heredity.' Thomas McCrosson, the superintendent of the Penetanguishene Reformatory, was distinctly in the minority in maintaining the older perspective that it was entirely surroundings that shaped a child's character. McCrosson supported this thesis by claiming that fully two-thirds of the boys in the reformatory were the off-spring of 'honest, careful, thoughtful parents.' Poverty, McCrosson insisted, was the leading cause of crime.[89]

The opposite argument was advanced by Dr Richard Bucke, author, mystic, and superintendent of the massive London Asylum. For Bucke, 'heredity governs everything.' When asked if he could imagine individuals with no hereditary taint who might acquire an appetite for drink and become confirmed drunkards, Dr Bucke spoke with great certitude: 'I do not think that people become vagrants, drunkards, criminals, prostitutes, however, unless there is a hereditary taint – unless they are born defective ... I do not believe that persons who are really good hereditarily ever become drunkards or vagrants.' For Bucke the decision to bring out 'gutter children' from British slums was incomprehensible: 'this is scandalous and outrageous ... These people might as well collect small-pox and typhoid fever and send them out ... These are not only savages, but they are nearly all diseased savages.' Bucke believed that there was a class largely devoid of moral nature. In the great chain of evolution, this class was recruited by atavism, a lapse or throwback in the evolutionary process and little if anything could be done to assist or rehabilitate those afflicted. Dr Bucke cited with approval the views of a friend who, after visiting hundreds of gaols, had concluded that 'there is no such thing as reformation.' One response was to control marriages so as to 'prevent [the criminal class] from bringing others of their kind into the world.' It would be worse than useless, Bucke contended, to send many such persons to gaol, or even to punish them in any way. They were not responsible for their actions: 'I look upon all punishment as simply revenge.'[90]

Listening to Bucke's testimony, John Langmuir must have reflected on that part of the commission's instructions directing it to avoid all impractical theories. Langmuir and his colleagues were determined to make recommendations, as the report put it, which embodied 'the most advanced, but at the same time the most practical methods of dealing with vice and crime.'[91] In this spirit they worked through masses of contradictory testimony to finally reject the pessimistic prognosis offered by Richard Bucke. Some of the witnesses, they noted, 'shared in a vague way the old and still popular belief as to good and bad stock,' yet 'nearly all' held that the children of even the worst criminals, 'if removed in time from the evil environment and properly educated may be saved.' Of those witnesses who could be regarded as expert, only Dr Bucke, they noted, 'held the extreme doctrine of heredity.' Pointing to the vast reduction of crime in Britain and Ireland, they argued that this had been achieved by 'the timely removal and the judicious training of such children, and not to what Mr. Dudley Warner calls the "elimination of a vast amount of bad blood from the body politic" by numberless executions of criminals.' After sifting the evidence of witnesses and assessing the recent literature, the commissioners concluded firmly that '[a]ny theory which leads to the conclusion that some are formed by nature for a life of crime and must, no matter what their education, be criminals ... will not find general acceptance although it may be true that "criminals present a far larger proportions of anatomical abnormalities than the ordinary European population."'[92] This was as far as Langmuir and his colleagues were willing to go in the direction of Lombrosian theory. It was not very far at all.

After dismissing the extreme posture of Bucke and of positivist criminology, they presented their own conclusions. The chief causes of crime, they claimed, were 'the want of proper parental control; the lack of good home training and the baneful influence of bad homes ... and the evil effects of drunkenness.' As well, it was 'the almost universal opinion' of all who gave testimony and of all the literature studied, that the great majority of criminals began their careers in early youth and only methods directed at young offenders could prevent the formation of large numbers of adult criminals.[93] Entirely conventional in ascribing the occurrence of crime to drink, idleness, and bad homes, the commissioners nonetheless were alert to the complexities of social causation. They agreed, for example, with Havelock Ellis that 'the relation of alcoholism to criminality is by no means so simple as is sometimes thought; alcoholism is an effect as well as a cause. It is part of a vicious circle.' Similarly, the commissioners concluded of idleness that 'it is sometimes difficult to decide whether it should be regarded as cause or effect.' The commissioners were unwilling to dismiss the effects of poverty as a significant cause of crime merely because 'many very poor persons lead honest, virtuous lives.' The reality, they asserted, was that, especially in cities and towns, the poor were often compelled to live in crowded lanes and alleys and in a foul moral atmosphere to which children were especially vulnerable, exposed constantly to corrupting influences. In these circumstances, the commissioners concluded, only the state had the power and authority to take preventive action. The government, they insisted, had not done its duty by providing police and courts and gaols, or even school systems.

'All this system of dealing with criminals and offenders rests upon the exploded principle that crime can be prevented, and criminals kept in check, only by deterrent agencies.' They insisted boldly and with no equivocation that 'much more can be done by the State and by associations to save those who are in danger.'[94] The onus of responsibility, it seemed, had undergone a change of radical dimensions. More realistically, however, the commissioners must have understood that words alone, even when representing informed opinion, must prove insufficient when confronted by massive ignorance and indifference.

Nevertheless, the rest of the work of the commission, including its forty-eight specific recommendations, flowed from the conviction that the government had a solemn duty to pass advanced legislation to address the crime problem. The methods advocated were both preventive and remedial, and they were based on the commission's rejection of the excesses of genetic theory and recent hereditarian thought. From this point, the commission's work became an exercise in assessing the several approaches that had been coming to the fore in correctional thinking in recent years, and most especially in the neighbouring republic at the meetings of the National Prison Association. There was much cross-fertilization between American and British thinking and emerging Canadian practice, and it is not possible to disentangle all the ideas and practices that the commissioners considered in order to credit them to specific authors or sources. The recommendations fell into twelve categories: juvenile criminality; the Mercer Reformatory; Drunkards; Tramps and Vagrants; Homeless and Destitute Prisoners; Insane Prisoners; Young Criminals–First Offenders; Sentences; Good Time System; Lock-ups and Police Stations; and Jails and Prison Labour. Most attention was given to juvenile crime and the commission's influence contributed soon to the passage of the important Children's Protection Act of 1893.[95] Langmuir and his colleagues recommended the compulsory expansion of the industrial schools system, the removal of Penetanguishene Reformatory to a more suitable location and its establishment on a cottage system, the separation of the Refuge for Girls from the Mercer Reformatory, and the establishment of a reformatory for young first offenders along the lines of the Elmira system.[96] They suggested the establishment of special facilities for tramps and vagrants and of poorhouses for the homeless and destitute, and the removal of all insane persons from gaols. They favoured the widespread use of the system of indeterminate sentences. They did not, as we have seen, advise that the province take over control of the county gaols, but they did recommend improved classification in the gaols, that these facilities be used only as places of detention for prisoners before trial, and that all gaols be conducted on the separate or cellular system. In the area of prison labour, they suggested an end to the contract system and its replacement by a provincial account system in which the province would assume full control over all industrial operations. Little was said about either staff training or inspection methods. Not surprisingly, given Langmuir's role, no support was given to establishment of a new Board of Prison Commissioners. Instead, it was argued that the existing system of a provincially appointed inspector was more in harmony with British traditions of responsible government.[97]

Most of these recommendations reflected ideas already commonplace in British and American prison reform circles. Some had been advocated recently by the PAA, and the rest soon would be. In this sense, the commission's investigation represented everything the PAA could have wanted. The reaction of Association officers seems to have been the delighted conviction that with this endorsement the provincial and federal governments could no longer remain indifferent to the growing demand of informed opinion for substantial changes.

Disillusionment soon followed. Association officers were loath to admit that governments could remain indifferent to their wishes any longer, and at several annual meetings in the early 1890s, the view was expressed that circumstances had never been better for prison reform. The PAA had learned much over the years about the priorities of democratic politicians. They knew enough about public opinion and the vacillations of government to recognize that they would have to organize to persuade the Mowat administration to act on recommendations as costly as those made by the Langmuir Commission. It was the old and familiar story. Not only did prisoners and their supporters have little political influence, but any expenditure on their behalf incurred political risks: that at least had remained a constant over the course of the century. The PAA nonetheless girded itself for battle, and it was the moving force behind a second Prison Reform Conference. Held in Toronto on 27 November 1891, its sole purpose was to endorse the recommendations of the commission and to impress the government that elite opinion was firmly resolved in favour of the Report.[98]

In 1892 the same group, still committed to the mobilization of elite opinion, held yet another Prison Reform Conference.[99] A delegation was sent to meet Oliver Mowat who pointed to the government's difficulty in dealing with county councils 'and urged the necessity of taking steps to secure their cooperation.' Over the next several years the province took substantial action only in the area of child reform, with such measures as the enforcement of truancy provisions and the passage of the Children's Protection Act of 1893. Even in this field, however, the Mowat government did not fully carry out the approach recommended by the Langmuir Commission. There was no early effort to move the reformatory to a more suitable location or to separate the Girls' Refuge from the Mercer; there was no legislation to encourage counties or municipalities to establish industrial schools; and the Children's Act of 1893 was itself primarily an effort to enlist voluntary activity.

Frustration pervades the PAA reports over the next decade. Nonetheless, the Association continued to disseminate pamphlets and reports, and more than ever speakers at the annual meetings raised broad issues of social policy which bore the imprint of the Langmuir Commission.

A focus on the relationship between crime and poverty had become a leading PAA theme. 'The Poorhouse Question in the County of Bruce,' the address of Mr Justice Robertson to the grand jury and the jury's presentment, was featured prominently in the 1897–8 report.[100] On several occasions the Association printed material reproduced from the Prisons and Police Department of the Ontario Women's Christian Temperance Union's (WCTU) annual report. Travelling committees of WCTU members visited gaols in many counties regularly, holding 'evangelistic services,' distributing literature, finding employment for prisoners, and in some cases, taking them into their homes.[101] In this way, the WCTU, in close cooperation with the PAA, performed the outreach function that had remained beyond the capacity of the PAA itself. By this time, too, the Association was having a little more success in its effort to involve more communities outside Toronto in its work. The 1894–5 report listed such towns as Picton, Kemptville, Arnprior, and Walkerville as making small financial contributions. Another innovation partly attributable to PAA influence was the establishment in 1898 of the Canadian Conference of Charities and Corrections, which served as an umbrella national organization.[102]

The Prisoners' Aid Association ceased operations in 1915, although it did not surrender its charter until 1927. According to J. Alex Edmison, an executive director of the John Howard Society, which later took up the task abandoned by the PAA, its failure was in many ways an old story and not an unusual one. The old guard died or moved away and the Association's reports in the years leading up to World War I were 'a lesson in futility.' Discouragement, financial problems, and the absence of a strong central organization able to cooperate with similar groups in other provinces are among the reasons advanced by Edmison for its demise.[103]

According to John Kidman, who took up prison reform work in Montreal after World War I, Dr Rosebrugh's death in 1915 marked the effective end of the Toronto Association; despite an assiduous search Kidman was able to turn up no records relating to the Association after that date, 'either by report, or in the city directory.'[104]

With the passing of the original group, the religious impulse that had once inspired the PAA's efforts was no longer sufficient to persuade a younger generation to take up the torch. This was hardly surprising. Although the PAA had carried on a vigorous program throughout the 1890s, including its campaign of community mobilization on behalf of the Langmuir report recommendations, the failure of the Liberal government to enact the reform program had confirmed the Association's political impotence. In Ontario in this period, the public imagination was excited by a range of causes, everything from the Riel and Equal Rights agitations to good works on behalf of children and animals. At some point it became clear to the members of the PAA that their cause lacked both public and political support.

The Liberal government's own campaign literature put this most bluntly. The Liberal platform of 1898, 198 pages in length, said little about prisons beyond praising the Reformatory for Boys, while almost contemptuously dismissing efforts to rehabilitate those confined in the Central Prison and the Mercer. Such prisoners, it seemed, were regarded as hardened criminals and 'it would be too much to expect a similar state of progress in reformatories for adults.'[105] It is difficult to blame the lack of public interest in adult prisoners entirely on financial stringency. These were relatively buoyant times for the province, and the government accumulated a budgetary surplus of over five million dollars between Confederation and 1897. Furthermore, the same piece of Liberal campaign literature pointedly remarked that in Ontario in 1898 the government had spent $806,131 on asylums and prisons, an amount, it was claimed, that was over two and a half times that spent by Quebec. Obviously, a parsimonious administration dominated by rural voters was not about to embark on new costly programs on behalf of 'the criminal class.'[106] If such essential facilities as the University of Toronto and the province's many hospitals were starved for lack of sufficient funding, the Ontario Liberals were not prepared to be perceived as lavish spenders on behalf of those who were regarded as the least deserving members of the Ontario community. In turn of the century Ontario, the old concept of less eligibility died hard.

An equally plausible explanation for the failure of the prison reformers to gain political support is found in the apparent drop in the occurrence of crime in late nineteenth century Ontario. The period from the early 1890s to the mid-point of the first decade of the twentieth century was a time of declining commitments to Ontario's correctional facilities. Inspectors and prison officers speculated on the reasons for this decline in the annual reports. Sometimes they attributed it, in part at least, to the marked success of existing correctional systems. In these circumstances, it was difficult for the PAA to persuade governments to adopt costly new programs. This argument could of course be turned around. In an era when citizens did not feel threatened by burgeoning crime rates, they should have been more willing to experiment with the positive reform programs advocated by the PAA. Regrettably, the process did not work that way. In any case PAA officials, doubtless with a rising feeling of anger at their impotence, tried to make the opposite case. Resorting in their 1893 report to alarmist sensationalism, the Association asserted that the criminal class 'is increasing ... it is costing millions of dollars of the public chest ... it is a menace to our homes; a menace to our cities; a menace to our civilization.'[107] Few were convinced. Not many Ontarians felt threatened. The only real menace provoked by such rhetoric was to the credibility of the PAA.

More credence was given to those who exalted, often in glowing terms, existing social conditions in the great Province of Ontario. When Thomas McCrosson tried to explain the decline in numbers at Penetanguishene Reformatory, he itemized the increase of religious influences, the existence of strict liquor licensing laws, and the spread of educational opportunity.[108] Many late nineteenth century Ontarians held similar views about the state of their society. When Toronto Alderman S. Morley Wickett published his study *City Government in Canada* in 1902, he sang the praises of Ontario's progressive and balanced society, a community well policed, well governed, and at harmony with itself.[109] This was preeminently a self-satisfied society, one which could happily ignore the prisoner class.

In the correctional context the same self-gratulatory note was struck by J.J. MacLaren, a Toronto lawyer, in his 1897 address to an American body, the National Conference of Charities and Corrections, that met in Toronto. Echoing McCrosson, MacLaren pointed to religious influences and alcohol regulation, noting too the efforts of the morality department of the Toronto police and the child-saving movement led by J.J. Kelso. To his American audience, MacLaren preached that in Ontario there were 'no slums, no tenements ... no immigrant population, so that many of the problems which are perplexing to you ... are unknown to us.'[110] The PAA had little prospect of making headway in such a complacent society.

What then can be said of the actual achievements of the PAA in the four decades of its existence? What can be said of prison reform generally? The PAA helped hundreds of prisoners and their families by providing temporary shelter, loans, clothing, and assistance in finding employment. The annual reports, especially of the Sunday school classes and extracts from prisoners' letters, demonstrate that some positive relationships developed between PAA workers and prisoners. The presence in the prison environment of PAA workers who offered compassion, advice, and personal attention on a continuing basis helped to offset the narrowly punitive environment of the late Victorian prison. Nonetheless, the PAA's own reports often expressed regret that so many refused the proffered 'hand of friendship.' Association workers need not have been surprised at this. Only occasionally was it possible to break through the barriers of class and differences in values and status.

Perhaps more could have been achieved by workers able to take the allegedly value-free and non-judgmental approach of the modern social worker. But such a conclusion would be anachronistic. When aftercare work did emerge in Canada in the 1870s, it did so through an organization driven and inspired by the evangelical impulse, and the accomplishments of the PAA cannot be separated from the religious spirit of the age. The religious values that infused the PAA's early efforts did not prevent it from moving in a more secular direction in the 1890s. It is equally apparent that the broader prison reform program of the 1890s, despite its short-term failure, did leave a mark on informed opinion and helped set the agenda for a future generation of correctional work. In the 1890s the Association's leaders demonstrated a sophisticated understanding of the socio-economic context of crime, and the specific reform proposals advanced in the 1890s, especially probation, parole, indeterminate sentences, and the advocacy of a reformatory modelled on Elmira for the sixteen to thirty age group, reflected forward-looking insights. This was an organization with solid accomplishments to its credit. It did much to articulate the characteristic program of twentieth-century corrections.

Conclusion

Prisons and gaols had always existed, but mostly for purposes of detention before trial. In Ontario, the major transition from an old regime system of shaming punishments to one that relied overwhelmingly on imprisonment culminated in the 1830s. Although the opening of Kingston Penitentiary has always symbolized that shift, the change began a decade earlier, with the increasing number of gaol sentences handed down by Assize judges. In fact, it was imprisonment itself and not any particular form of restraint which marked the change, and the continuing role of the local gaols assumes a large interpretive significance in helping to explain the incomplete nature of the transition to modernity.

By the same token, the reform impulse of the 1830s cannot be understood merely as a new willingness to resort to institutionalization, whether propelled by growing class tensions or by fear of crime. If the penitentiary had something in common with the other new institutions that were established in the 1830s and 1840s (asylums and poorhouses), there were also profound differences in its purpose and structure. The ritual of punishment as it evolved in Ontario is better understood not as an impulse to institutionalization alone but as part of an ongoing continuum of criminal justice issues. To understand the penitentiary and its role, one must look equally to the circumstances of the gaols, to the urgent need to reform the criminal law and, as the propellant of change, to the perceptions and experiences of justices of the peace and Assize court judges.

The legal–judicial revolution of the 1830s, however, fell far short of total success. The justices and judges who pushed hardest for change were not administrators or politicians and their program did not fulfil expectations. Most obviously, the penitentiary faced formidable structural problems. These were being addressed by the late 1840s and 1850s, but they were not solved and proponents of change were no longer primarily Tory ideologues but members of an emerging and powerful middle-class elite. Unlike the gaols, the penitentiary was fully expressive of the values of the new commercial and professional classes; it represented in almost pure form the ideals of centralization, standardization, bureaucratization, and rule of law. But the uncertainties and weaknesses of central state authority combined with ambiguities about the very purpose of the new institution to lead to hesitation and confusion about Kingston's role. However, it must always be understood that the critics, whether James Buchanan, who had challenged the very idea of the penitentiary, or E.A. Meredith and a few of his inspectoral colleagues, who regarded the institution as purely repressive, always represented a small minority. Almost all of those in authority, and almost certainly the vast public whose views mattered only indirectly, supported Kingston precisely for its repressive and punitive features. In these terms, Ontario's nineteenth-century penitentiary was an unquestioned success, and Aeneas Macdonell was a model warden. He enforced stern discipline, allowed few escapes, and provided a reasonably healthy and secure environment. It is particularly significant that the most astute Canadian politician of the day, Macdonald, firmly supported the punitive style of administration. John A. never saw the penitentiary as anything other than an instrument of punishment and deterrence.

Perhaps surprisingly, the gaols were more complex and in some senses more interesting institutions. In the face of the reform impulse so strongly embodied by men like J.B. Robinson, J.B. Macaulay, and later, Meredith and Langmuir, they continued to exemplify many of the older, pre-industrial values. Expressing the forces of localism and of numerous traditional community needs, they remained throughout the century as stubborn symbols of the old era. Firmly in place, resisting almost all efforts to achieve the newer management styles of the emerging professional–commercial elites, they drove the central bureaucrats – the judges and civil servants – to rage and distraction.

Nonetheless, there was another side to the story of the gaols. Embodying local control, exemplifying parsimony, and representing the one and often only community resource centre available for an array of social needs, they played an undeniably significant role in local life. First JPs, and after 1849, locally elected councils used the gaols to house a congregate population of the aged, the poor, the mentally ill, the local bum, and the habitual drunk. In a society whose rural values were pervasive and one with minimal surplus wealth, there was little prospect of providing a range of alternate social and institutional services for non-conforming populations. Without the gaol, there often was only the street, and sometimes death by cold and starvation. In these circumstances, local reeves and aldermen sometimes ignored the law to house both a habitual and a floating population of indigents and unfortunates. No doubt the righteous anger of the bureaucrats was justified and other services, developed along modern, centrist lines, would have been vastly preferable. No doubt, too, gaol conditions were often horrible and those forced to resort to those services frequently suffered terribly in facilities that destroyed the soul and attacked the body. It is a commentary on Ontario society that many of the old dungeons survived into the 1960s and beyond, to be replaced by provincially administered regional detention centres with agonizing slowness. Fortunately, by that time a range of other social services had undercut the gaol's nineteenth-century role as a congregate facility, but that of course was also a gradual development.

In the face of local resistance and this ongoing struggle between traditional community and emerging central authority, there was, nonetheless, change – if not necessarily progress. By the mid-1880s, Ontario finally, half a century after the triumph of institutional punishment, had in place a full-range of purpose-built facilities for its adult population of law-breakers. In addition to the gaols for the petty offenders, the drunks, prostitutes, and petty thieves, and the penitentiary for major property offenders, murderers, and rapists, there were the intermediate prisons. The idea of the central prison had emerged in the mid-century years and was championed especially by many of the judges and by the Meredith board. A long time in realization, it assumed somewhat different forms for men and for women. For the male population, the Central Prison was directed at the repeat offender, sometimes simply those perceived as drunk, dissolute, and wastrel, but more often those also convicted more than once of larceny, who were regarded as representing a danger to respectable society. The discipline of the Central Prison was harsh and deterrent and its work program was designed as the essence of that deterrence, as a punishment of a type that had never been enforced in the local gaols. There was work also in the Mercer, but the discipline was distinctly different, feminist in origin and practice. Its inmate population was equally distinct, a group composed primarily of offenders against the moral code of late-nineteenth-century society.

With this range of institutions in place, most Ontarians were satisfied with their penal system. Thus, they felt free largely to ignore the well-meaning efforts of such reformers as the men and women of the Prisoners' Aid Society, which gradually moved from providing assistance to prisoners to promulgating an impressive program of prison reform. Ontarians were not only uninterested in these efforts, they were more than a little hostile. In a society with a remarkably low crime rate and in which the number imprisoned was actually dropping, the average citizen saw little need to expend hard-earned resources on criminal and deviant populations. There are many indicators of this indifference, including the frustration of the PAA and its ultimate disappearance. It was of more than symbolic significance that the province's two political parties, Liberal and Conservative, in their election platforms of the late-nineteenth century period, all but ignored the question of crime – it was indeed a non-issue – and the needs of the prisoner population.

That ignorance and lack of interest included as well most matters relating to the actual character and consequences of societal punishments. All students of the nineteenth-century Ontario penitentiary agree that the facility was remarkably static and unchanging over the entire period. Don Wetherell, for example, notes that it was 'rare for anyone to challenge the assumption that men could be made better by imprisoning them,' and that there were few changes in attitudes towards prisoners between Confederation and 1914.[1] William Calder saw few innovations and little that might be described as new programs between the 1830s and century-end.[2] In truth, the efforts of reformers like Meredith, Ferres, and Warden Creighton came to little, as did the attempts to graft Croftonian hope onto the essentials of oppressive Auburnism. The basic features of Auburn remained in place to century-end and beyond, particularly the rule of silence, although enforcement became more a bad joke than a reality. In such circumstances, there could be little more than lip-service paid to the ideals of rehabilitation. The penitentiary, to the extent that it worked at all, did so only as a punitive and deterrent institution. In some ways there was even regression as the long and troubled story of efforts to employ the convict population productively fully demonstrated.

In these circumstances, and considering the absence of most modern means of intimidating convict populations, the relative safety of the facility and the absence of riot and extreme violence seem surprising. Either nineteenth-century convict populations were more docile than those of the twentieth century, or prison officers were shrewder and more manipulative than at first appears. Even so, by century-end this was changing, as the riot at St Vincent de Paul Penitentiary in 1886 demonstrated and the full-scale inquiry into the abominable conditions in that facility confirmed.

What stands out most of all in the chronicle of nineteenth-century prisons is how unreflective most prison officers and officials seem to have been about the consequences of prison life, and how indifferent the general populace was to most of those consequences. There was, to be sure, a fear and abhorrence of the ex-convict on the part of many ordinary people, especially perhaps members of the working class. There is no more haunting commentary on the period than the frequent refrain of prison officers that too often the released prisoner had no choice but to repeat his or her offence or face starvation. The revulsion that the ex-convict inspired is positively reminiscent of Marx's well-known contemptuous attitude towards the criminal population and doubtless explains why the Prisoners' Aid Society was never able to win widespread support. Not only was there revulsion, but there was also little effort to gain understanding. An occasional individual (Hannibal Mulkins and E.A. Meredith come to mind), might demonstrate a more reflective stance, but even this did not go very far. Meredith seemed to feel instinctively that to confine men and women for long periods and offer them no hope must be utterly destructive of their personalities, and he had the foresight to understand that society would pay a price, if only on release. But certainly John A. Macdonald's sense that to reform it was enough to punish harshly was typical; he and others never really believed that the prison experience could make bad men good. Far more representative was the revealing slogan, often repeated across the century, that it was enough if prison should remain 'a terror for evil-doers.' And more typical at the bureaucratic level was John Langmuir's sense in the 1880s, inspired by the example of Auburn, that the essential role of the Central Prison was to break men's spirit and enforce obedience and social conformity through terror. To some extent, the Mercer Reformatory for Women was an exception to this mindless brutality and far from benign indifference.

Yet it remains true for all facilities that the actual effect of the prison experience, let alone the consequence of 'prisonization' as it later came to be understood, interested almost no one. In this, Ontario prison administrators were in no way unique. But Ontarians seemed more isolated intellectually than most Europeans and Americans, and Ontario society paid a price for its parochial self-satisfaction in suffering and scarred lives. In this respect, the more advanced ideas of some members of the PAA stand out as rare beacons in a dark and dreary sky.

None of this is surprising. The realities of prison life, and especially the nature of prison populations, conformed simply and starkly to pre-existing stereotypes. Ontario's prison populations across the nineteenth century consisted overwhelmingly of young, working-class males, and officials chose to emphasize the extent to which this was a population of recidivists. As well, the statistics compiled by prison officials tended to confirm the bias of those who believed that a disproportionate number of offenders were of Irish and American origin. Interestingly, those who analyzed these statistics did not dwell on any perceived threat posed by particular ethnic or national groups, understanding no doubt both the challenge that immigrants faced in a new land and the vital role they played in Canadian development. Their focus was on class rather than ethnicity, on the danger to community values posed by a recidivist population of drifters and low life. Increasingly, the inspectoral reports expressed a vision of the threat presented by an apparently permanent population of the dangerous and criminal classes. At the same time, however, that threat was perceived less in terms of public safety than of the fiscal burden to the local taxpayer. Perhaps that is why Ontarians in the nineteenth century never became truly alarmist about any alleged danger posed by the so-called criminal class. It is particularly noteworthy that the 1891 Prison Commission rejected out of hand the race-based and hereditarian Lombrosian interpretation of the nature of the dangerous classes and proposed constructive, moderate, and pragmatic solutions to the social problems of crime and punishment. In nineteenth-century Ontario, there was no moral panic and no repressive solutions analogous to those adopted in Britain and the United States.

Perhaps it was this relative absence of pressure and concern, this ongoing sense of public and official complacency, that largely accounts for the extent to which the solution of imprisonment for so long dominated official Ontario attitudes to crime and punishment. Change came to the nineteenth-century structure with excruciating slowness and alternatives to imprisonment were adopted more reluctantly than was the case for many other jurisdictions. Ticket-of-leave or parole legislation which existed in England and Ireland from the 1850s, did not come to Canada until 1899 and in any case was never regarded as an alternative to prison. Parole in Canada long had limited applicability and was seen primarily as a mechanism of prison management and as a form of mercy which gradually replaced the older system of offering royal pardons. Full-scale parole did not come to Canada until the establishment of a National Parole Board in 1958. In Ontario, a ticket-of-leave system started in 1910 and extended in 1916 had limited applicability and required reference to the federal authority for final permission.[3] Far more relevant as an alternative to prison sentences was the establishment of a system of probation, but for many years this applied primarily only to juveniles under the Juvenile Delinquents Act of 1908.[4] A few first-time adult offenders convicted of minor offences were eligible, but adult probation did not make significant inroads across Ontario until the late 1950s.[5]

There were, of course, other changes in the penal structure. The closing of the Central Prison in 1915 and its replacement by the Guelph Reformatory and the prison farm at Burwash near Sudbury represented some advance towards a more rehabilitative, less punitive approach. In general, however, there was no significant challenge to the nineteenth-century focus on the prison as the dominant method of punishing offenders until the second half of the twentieth century. And in the same period there was little evidence that Ontarians had much interest in developing more flexible or constructive approaches within the confines of imprisonment, or even a better understanding of the individual and social implications of imprisonment.

The long-term results of the emergence in the nineteenth century of the dominant forms of imprisonment were deep and enduring. Although innovation and change eventually came to Ontario, the province and its people are still feeling the consequences of the nineteenth-century punitive equation.

Notes

PREFACE

1 Douglas McCalla, *Planting the Province: The Economic History of Upper Canada, 1784–1870* (Toronto 1994)
2 John Foote, quoted in Peter Oliver, *Unlikely Tory: The Life and Politics of Allan Grossman* (Toronto 1985), 175

CHAPTER 1: UPPER CANADIAN PUNISHMENTS

1 *The Statutes of Upper Canada* [hereafter *Upper Canada Statutes*], An Act for the further introduction of the Criminal Law of England, c. 1 (1800)
2 *Upper Canada Statutes* (1792)
3 James H. Aitchison, 'The Development of Local Government in Upper Canada, 1780–1850' (PhD thesis, University of Toronto 1953), 619
4 Douglas Greenberg, *Crime and Law Enforcement in the Colony of New York, 1691–1776* (Ithaca, NY 1974), 125
5 Adam J. Hirsch, *The Rise of the Penitentiary: Prisons and Punishments in Early America* (New Haven, CT 1992), 7
6 Ibid., 47, 57–8
7 Margaret DeLacy, *Prison Reform in Lancashire, 1700–1850: A Study in Local Administration* (Stanford 1986), chap. 2, Prison Populations, esp. 59–60
8 Quoted in Aitchison, 'Local Government,' 620
9 Ibid., 621–2; Edith G. Firth, ed., *The Town of York, 1793–1815* (Toronto 1962), 92

10 Firth, ed., *The Town of York*, 93

11 Alexander Fraser, ed., *Minutes of the General Quarter Sessions of the Peace for the Home District*, 1800–11 (Toronto 1933), 9, 16

12 Ibid., 26, 36, 61, 90, 105, 148–9, 182, 186, 203–4

13 Ibid., 51, 54. The term Bridewell derives from the London, England hospital, formerly a Royal palace, which was converted in the middle of the sixteenth century into a disciplinary facility primarily for vagrants and the idle poor. By the early seventeenth century, these institutions, often called Houses of Correction, had spread across most of England. See Joanna Innes, 'Prisons for the Poor: English Bridewells, 1555–1800,' in Douglas Hay and F. Snyder, eds., *Labour, Law and Crime* (London 1987).

14 *Upper Canada Statutes*, c. 5. (1810)

15 Ibid.

16 David Murray, 'The Cold Hand of Charity: The Court of Quarter Sessions and Poor Relief in the Niagara District, 1828–1841,' in W. Pue and J.B. Wright, eds., *Canadian Perspectives on Law and Society* (Ottawa 1988)

17 Fraser, *Home District Minutes*, 186, 98, 104

18 Ibid., 109–10

19 Alexander Fraser, ed., *Minutes of the Court of General Quarter Sessions of the Peace for the London District*, 1800–9 and 1813–18 (Toronto 1934), 139, 145

20 In addition to local and county histories, material on early gaols may be found in Marion MacRae and Anthony Adamson, *Cornerstones of Order: Courthouses and Town Halls of Ontario, 1784–1914* (Toronto 1983), and in C.K. Talbot, *Justice in Early Ontario, 1791–1840* (Ottawa 1983), Pt. III, 'The District Jails and Provincial Penitentiary of Upper Canada, 1791–1840.'

21 MacRae and Adamson, *Cornerstones of Order*, 24

22 Talbot, *Justice in Early Ontario*, 251–3

23 Ibid., 238–42

24 The travails of the London District gaol are readily traced through the excellent index to Fraser, ed., *London District Minutes*.

25 The Gore District gaol is well described in several works by John Weaver, including 'Crime, Public Order and Repression: The Gore District in Upheaval, 1832–1851,' *Ontario History* 78 (1986); and see *Journal of the House of Assembly of Upper Canada* [hereafter *Journal of the House of Assembly*] (1826–31), Session 1826–7, 'Report of the Select Committee to Whom Was Referred The Several Petitions Relative to The Erection of a Jail and Court House in The District of Gore,' J.B. Robinson, chairman, 1 February 1827.

26 Aitchison, 'Local Government,' 620

27 For a sketch of the design of the Midland District gaol see Talbot, *Justice in Early Ontario*, following page 242.

28 National Archives [hereafter NA], RG5, Series A–1, Upper Canada Sundries, circuit report, William Campbell, 25 September, 1816.

29 Upper Canada Sundries, Robinson to Hillier, 25 October 1824. For a description of the Upper Canadian justice on circuit see Ontario Archives, Pamphlet, 1922, #40, W.R. Riddell, 'A Criminal Circuit in Upper Canada A Century Ago.'

30 Fraser, ed. *London District Minutes*, 1 July 1816, 154. This was typical sentencing practice in England for games offences. See Peter Munsche, 'The Game Laws in Wiltshire, 1750–1800,' in J.S. Cockburn, ed., *Crime in England 1550–1800* (Princeton, NJ 1977). A fuller analysis of sentences handed down at Upper Canadian Quarter Sessions for the entire 1791–1840 period and beyond is greatly needed, but was beyond the capacities of this project.

31 Fraser, ed., *London District Minutes*, 195

32 Ibid., 119

33 Ibid., 174–5

34 Ibid., 9, 71, 83

35 Ibid., 83

36 Ibid., 19. In 1803 Rice was also found guilty of 'Throwing down the Stocks' and was sentenced to one half-hour in them. See page 52. He seems to have been an experienced offender. For the 1818 case, see 183–4.

37 Fraser, ed., *Home District Minutes*, 170

38 Ibid., 11

39 Ibid., 30

40 Ibid., 47

41 Ibid., 115–16

42 Ibid., 136, 156

43 Ibid., 196

44 Michael Ignatieff, *A Just Measure of Pain: The Penitentiary in the Industrial Revolution, 1750–1850* (New York 1978), 90; Greenberg, *Crime and Law Enforcement*, 223

45 Michelle Corbett, 'Corporal Punishment and the Criminal Justice System of Upper Canada, 1800–1841' (graduate essay, Department of History, York University 1985), 18–19, from Archives of Ontario [hereafter AO], RG22, Series 134, *Assize Minutebook Criminal*, vol. 1, 1798. And see *Upper Canada Gazette*, 1 December 1798, for a report on the Hawkins whipping.

46 *Assize Minutebooks*, vol. 4, 1818, as cited in Corbett, 'Corporal Punishment', 24

47 *Assize Minutebooks*, vol. 4, 1815, and vol. 5, 1830, as cited in ibid.

48 See Corbett, 'Corporal Punishment', Table 1, 'Sentences Handed Down at the Criminal Assizes of Upper Canada, 1792–1853.'

49 Upper Canada Sundries, Powell to Major Hillier, 3 November 1820

50 Ibid., D'Arcy Boulton to His Excellency, 6 November 1820; petition of William

Stoutenburgh, 31 October 1820; petition of Luke Stoutenburgh, 11 January 1819; petition of William Stoutenburgh, 1819; letter, D'Arcy Boulton, 11 January 1819

51 Ibid., Grant Powell to secretary, 22 May 1816
52 Ibid., petition, John Willson to Sir Peregrine Maitland, n.d. [September 1818]
53 Ibid., Blewett to John Strachan, 21 April 1822; Campbell to Major Hillier, 25 April 1822; Strachan to Hillier, 24 April 1822
54 Ibid., petition of William Laird, 1822
55 Ibid., William Campbell to Hillier, 1 December 1824
56 MacRae and Adamson, *Cornerstones of Order*, 14–15
57 Corbett, 'Corporal Punishment,' 25–6 and Table I
58 Ibid., 26
59 See Myra C. Glenn, *Campaigns against Corporal Punishment: Prisoners, Sailors, Women and Children in Antebellum America* (Albany 1984); and J.R. Dinwiddy, 'The Early Nineteenth Century Campaign against Flogging in the British Army,' *English Historical Review* (April 1982).
60 Ignatieff, *A Just Measure of Pain*, 90
61 For the Rolph bill see *Journal of the House of Assembly*, 5 April 1825, 86; for the Bidwell bill see ibid., 15 December 1826, 14; and see the discussion in Corbett, 'Corporal Punishment,' 32–3. For Robinson's comments see *Upper Canada Herald*, 2 January 1827. See also *Journal of the House of Assembly*, 25 January 1827, 63, and, for an abortive bill to abolish female whipping, 9 January 1829, 5. I am indebted to Michelle Corbett for these references.
62 Corbett, 'Corporal Punishment,' 36; *Assize Minutebooks*, vol. 5, 1824
63 Corbett, 'Corporal Punishment,' 37, from E.C. Guillet, *Early Life in Upper Canada* (Toronto 1933), 111. Corporal punishment did not disappear from Canadian law and remained in the criminal code until 1972. See Graham Parker, 'Corporal Punishments in Canada,' *Criminal Law Quarterly* 7 (1964–5), 195.
64 Corbett, 'Corporal Punishment,' Table 1
65 See J.M. Beattie, *Crime and the Courts in England, 1660–1800* (Princeton 1986), 468.
66 Upper Canada Sundries, Elliott Buck (or Bush) to His Excellency, 16 June 1835; gaoler, York Gaol, and John Strachan, 14 October 1822
67 W.J. Blacklock, 'The Prosecution of Crime in Upper Canada' (MA paper, University of Toronto 1987), 105–6
68 *Upper Canada Statutes*, c. 24, s. 31 (1841)
69 *Journal of the House of Assembly* (1831), 'Report of Select Committee on the Expendiency of Erecting a Penitentiary,' H.C. Thomson, chairman
70 Upper Canada Sundries, Smith to Sherbrooke, 20 October 1817
71 See Corbett, 'Corporal Punishment,' Table II. And see Table 1.1 above, at page 14.

72 Upper Canada Sundries, petition, Henry Ryan to Sir Peregrine Maitland, 26 August 1819

73 For examples of limited banishment, see J.E. Jones, *Pioneer Crimes and Punishments in Toronto and the Home District* (Toronto 1924), 14–16. Upper Canada Sundries, Sarah Gilbert to lieutenant-governor, 28 December, 1834

74 *Upper Canada Statutes*, An Act to reduce the number of cases in which capital punishment may be inflicted, etc., c. 4 (1833)

75 Upper Canada Sundries, Robert Jameson to Colonel Rowan, 16 December 1834

76 *Upper Canada Statutes*, An Act respecting the Transportation of Convicts, c. 7 (1837)

77 Blacklock, 'The Prosecution of Crime,' 117

78 Corbett, 'Corporal Punishment,' Table 1, and see Table 1.1, above, at page 14.

79 Upper Canada Sundries, Robinson to Hillier, 25 October 1824

80 See P. Romney, *Mr. Attorney: The Attorney General for Ontario in Court, Cabinet and Legislature, 1791–1899* (Toronto 1986), 140, for the Collins case.

81 Ibid., 141

82 Upper Canada Sundries, Niagara justices to lieutenant-governor, 5 June 1809

83 Ibid., Powell to lieutenant-governor's secretary, 1 May 1810

84 Ibid., Niagara magistrates to lieutenant-governor, 17 April 1810

85 Ibid., petition of Thomas Davison, 5 September 1820; fiat, J.B. Robinson to sheriff of the Johnstown District, 19 April 1821

86 Ibid., fiat, J.B. Robinson to sheriff of the Home District, 19 April 1821

87 Ibid., W.D. Powell to lieutenant-governor's office, 1 May 1810

88 Ibid., W.L. Mackenzie to Rowan, 8 July 1834

89 Ibid., clerk of the peace, the Gore District, to His Excellency, 20 October 1835

90 Ibid., George Hamilton, chairman of Quarter Sessions, Gore District, to civil secretary, 24 September 1835

91 These figures were compiled by my research assistant, John Choules.

92 See Constance Backhouse, 'Nineteenth-Century Canadian Rape Law 1800–1892,' in David H. Flaherty, ed., *Essays in the History of Canadian Law*, vol. 2 (Toronto 1983).

93 For a full discussion of the evolution of the law on infanticide see Constance Backhouse, 'Desperate Women and Compassionate Courts: Nineteenth-Century Infanticide in Canada,' *University of Toronto Law Journal* 34 (1984).

94 For Burley see Robert Fraser, *Provincial Justice, Upper Canadian Legal Portraits* (Toronto 1992), 296–8, and Upper Canada Sundries, J.B. Robinson, circuit report, 4 September 1830; for Vincent see Robert Fraser, 'Michael Vincent,' *Dictionary of Hamilton Biography*, vol. 1 (1981), 203–6, and John Weaver, *Crimes,*

Constables and Courts (Montreal and Kingston 1995), chap. 1; for Kennan and Bird see John Choules, 'The Periodic Necessity of Example: Deterrence and the Dramaturgy of Public Executions in Ontario, 1792–1869' (graduate research paper, Department of History, York University [n.d.]); Dr Fraser's comment on the gallows casting 'a short shadow' appeared in his biography of Michael Vincent.

95 Upper Canada Sundries, Samuel Smith to Sir John Sherbrooke, 30 October 1817

96 Metropolitan Toronto Historical Board, pamphlet, 'The Life of William Kain,' (printed at the *Herald* office, 1830)

97 *Upper Canada Statutes*, c. 4 (1833). For similar English practice dating from the mid-eighteenth century see Beattie, *Crime and the Courts*, 525–30.

98 For the United States experience see, *inter alia*, Louis P. Masur, *Rites of Execution: Capital Punishment and the Transformation of American Culture, 1776–1865* (New York 1989), 157–9; see also David B. Davis, 'The Movement to Abolish Capital Punishment in America, 1787–1861,' *American Historical Review* 63 (October 1957).

99 Kingston *Chronicle*, 7 September 1833

100 *The Church*, as cited in Choules, 'Public Executions,' 49

101 *The Christian Guardian*, 18 December, 1837, and the Toronto *Globe*, 10 March 1862; as cited in Choules, 'Public Executions,' 50–1

102 See for example NA, RG5, C–1, vol. 252, petition to Lord Elgin, January 1849. The name Montreal is crossed out and that of an Upper Canadian community written in on each petition; in this case Goderich was inserted.

103 Elizabeth Gibbs, ed., *Debates of the Legislative Assembly of United Canada* (1850), 503, 1203

104 Toronto *Globe*, 9 December 1869

105 Upper Canada Sundries, petition of Thomas Blewitt, February 1816

106 Ibid., petition of James McArdle, 25 August 1835

107 Ibid., petition of William Orr, 14 September 1825

108 Ibid., petition of Anne O'Bryon, 29 July 1835

109 Ibid., W.L. Mackenzie to civil secretary, 8 July 1834

110 Ibid., petition of Moses Pattison, 10 September 1835

111 Ibid., petition of (illegible), 2 August 1821

112 W.J. Blacklock notes that the Niagara District treasurer's accounts for 1838–9, when gaol imprisonment was in ever-wider use, showed that about 20 per cent of that district's funds went to the gaol. See Blacklock, 'The Prosecution of Crime,' 73.

113 Firth, ed., *The Town of York*, 107; Upper Canada Sundries, petition of Catherine Sharply, 23 November 1823

114 Upper Canada Sundries, petition of Reuban Woodworth, a U.S. citizen, 21 October 1826

115 Ibid., petition of John Wirick, 28 January 1835

116 For a persuasive discussion of McSwiney's shrewd manipulation of the petitioning process, see Robert Fraser, *Dictionary of Canadian Biography* [DCB], vol. 5, at 557–9.

117 Upper Canada Sundries, F.F. Robinson to Major Foster, 13 June 1815

118 Ibid., Sheriff Macdonnell, Cornwall, to secretary, 29 April 1823

119 Ibid., Thomas Merritt to chairman, Quarter Sessions, Niagara District, 1809; Samuel Street to His Excellency, 14 April 1809

120 Ibid., Thomas Ridout, clerk of the peace, Home District, to His Excellency, 26 April 1810

121 Ibid., Archibald McLean, chairman, Quarter Sessions, Eastern District, 27 January 1817

122 Ibid., Sheriff Ridout to Edward McMahon, 25 August 1821

123 Ibid., John Beikie, late sheriff, Home District, to McMahon, 12 May 1815

124 Ibid., F.F. Robinson to Major Foster, 13 June 1815

125 Ibid., William Campbell to lieutenant-governor, 11 November 1820; *Journal of the House of Assembly* (1836), Statement of the Grand Jury of the Home District, 5 April 1836

126 Ibid., William Campbell to His Excellency, 11 November 1820

127 Ibid., William Botsford Jarvis to Sir John Colborne, 1830

128 Ibid., Sheriff Leonard to private secretary, June 1829 and 8 and 14 July 1829; 18 June 1830; Sheriff, Niagara District, to lieutenant-governor, 13 December 1834

CHAPTER 2: THE GAOL AND THE COMMUNITY

1 Margaret Angus, 'Health, Emigration and Welfare in Kingston, 1820–1840,' in Donald Swainson, ed., *Oliver Mowat's Ontario* (Toronto 1972); David Murray, 'The Cold Hand of Charity,' in W. Pue and J.B. Wright, eds., *Canadian Perspectives on Law and Society: Issues in Legal History* (Ottawa 1988)

2 NA, Upper Canada Sundries, John Alma, JP, to J. Joseph, Government House, 24 October 1836; certificate, F.W. Porter, MD (?) To John Alma, 19 October 1836. Someone from the government office wrote on the file, 'Too humane perhaps,' and Attorney General Jameson responded that while Alma was within his rights to commit her, so too were the magistrates who released her. See Report of Robert Jameson, 26 October 1836.

3 *Journal of the House of Assembly of Upper Canada* (1830), Appendix, 'Report of the Committee on Petition of Prisoners in Gaol at York,' W.L. Mackenzie,

chairman, 17 February 1830; *Upper Canada Statutes*, An Act to authorize the Quarter Sessions of the Home District to provide for the relief of Insane destitute persons in the District, c. 20 (1830). See also Thomas Brown, '"Living with God's Afflicated": A History of the Provincial Lunatic Asylum at Toronto, 1830–1911' (PhD thesis, Queen's University 1980); and Rainer Baehre, 'The Ill-Regulated Mind: The Making of Psychiatry in Ontario, 1830–1921' (PhD thesis, York University, 1985).

4 *Upper Canada Statutes*, An Act to continue an Act passed (in 1830) and to extend the provision of the same to the other Districts of this Province, c. 46 (1833)

5 Upper Canada Sundries, Grand Jury, Johnstown District, 11 November 1835; the 1835 cost figures appear in the *Journal of the House of Assembly* (1836), Appendix no. 44, Gaol Reports, 'Report of the Chairman of the Quarter Sessions,' D. Boulton, Home District, 9 March 1830. For comments on the four insane prisoners, see also Appendix no. 117 (1836), 'Gaol Reports as Returned for the last four years,' Report of Sheriff W.B. Jarvis.

6 Tom Brown, 'The Origins of the Asylum in Upper Canada, 1830–1839,' *Canadian Bulletin of Medical History*, 1 (1984), and see generally the comments by magistrates in the published 1835 and 1836 Gaol Reports, above, note 5.

7 *Journal of the House of Assembly* (1836–7), Appendix no. 11, 'Reports of Grand Juries of the Midland, Johnstown, Eastern and Bathurst Districts, on the state of their respective Gaols,' J.B. Macaulay to J. Joseph, 22 September 1836

8 The Bathurst District, for instance, regretted the presence of Patrick O'Rourke, confined for many months, but it expressed the view that 'it would be dangerous to society, to set him at large.' Ibid. Gaol Reports 1836–37, Report of Grand Jury, Bathurst District, 25 August 1836

9 Upper Canada Sundries, clerk of the peace, Niagara District to Rowan, 25 October 1834; Report of Grand Jury, 23 October 1834, and Report of Chief Justice Robinson on Patrick Donnelly (also spelled Donally) [n.d.]

10 Upper Canada Sundries, Report of Grand Jurors, 26 October 1840

11 Ibid., circuit report, J.B. Macaulay to provincial secretary, 26 October 1840

12 Ibid., J.N. Gamble to Jarvis, 23 April 1840

13 *Upper Canada Statutes*, An Act to authorise the erection of an Asylum within the Province for the reception of Insane and Lunatic Persons, c. 11 (1839)

14 *Journal of the House of Assembly* (1836) Appendix, Charles Duncombe, 'Report to the Honourable the Commissioners Doctors Morrison and Bruce, and the Honourable the Committee appointed upon the subject of Lunatic Asylums, etc.'; Sam Shortt, *Victorian Lunacy: Richard M. Bucke and the Practice of Late Nineteenth-Century Psychiatry* (Cambridge 1986), 26. It is necessary to keep in mind the distinction between the insane and the criminally insane, although at this point the difference was not always clear in their actual treatment in gaol.

15 *Journal of the House of Assembly* (1836) Appendix no. 117, 'Gaol Reports As Returned For the Last Four Years'

16 Evelyn Kolish, 'Imprisonment for Debt in Lower Canada, 1791–1840,' *McGill Law Journal* 32(3) (1987), 630. Fecteau's figures are taken from ibid.

17 *Journal of the House of Assembly* (1836) Appendix no. 117, Gaol Reports

18 For a splendid analysis of an English debtors' prison see Joanna Innes, 'The King's Bench Prison in the later Eighteenth Century: Law, Authority and Order in a London Debtors' Prison,' in John Brewer and John Styles, eds., *An Ungovernable People: The English and their Law in the Seventeenth and Eighteenth Centuries* (New Brunswick, NJ 1983).

19 Richard B. Splane, *Social Welfare in Ontario, 1791–1893: A Study in Social Welfare Administration* (Toronto 1965) 119

20 For John Rolph's bill, see the long report of Rolph's speech in the Assembly in the Kingston *Chronicle*, 14 March 1829.

21 For the slow reform process in the English law of debt see Bruce Kercher, 'The Transformation of Imprisonment for Debt in England, 1828 to 1838, '*Australian Journal of Law and Society* 2(1), 62

22 *Upper Canada Statutes*, An Act for the Relief of Insolvent Debtors, c. 7 (1805)

23 *Upper Canada Statutes*, An Act to make further regulation respecting the Weekly maintenance of Insolvent Debtors, c. 8 (1822)

24 *Upper Canada Statutes*, An Act Assigning Limits to the Respective Gaols, c. 6 (1822)

25 J.F. Pringle, *Luneburg or the Old Eastern District* (Belleville 1972)

26 Upper Canada Sundries, Captain Matthew Leech [1823]: *Journal of the House of Assembly* (1825)

27 Upper Canada Sundries, Jackson to Hillier, 3 January 1823

28 Ibid., (illegible) to Hillier, 26 June 1825

29 Ibid., James Gray to Colonel Rowen, 1 March 1834 and 28 June 1838

30 Ibid., James Gray, letter, 28 June 1838

31 Ibid., James Bergin to Bond Head, 4 October 1836

32 Ibid., Leonard Dickenson, James Tauset, and William Stiles, letter, 16 November 1833

33 Ibid., John MacLean to Hillier, 1 February 1827; Dr James Geddes (?) deposition, 27 January 1827; Robert Richardson, JP, deposition, 31 January 1827; Elias Dulmage, gaoler, deposition, 11 February 1827

34 Ibid., Magistrate Pringle, deposition, 31 January 1827

35 Ibid., James Nickalls, deposition, 1 February 1827

36 Ibid., Elias Dulmage, deposition, 1 February 1827

37 Ibid., Lester Farrand to Maitland, 1821; Charles Walsh to Sir Francis Bond Head, 2 August 1836. For Gray see notes 29 and 30, above.

38 Ibid., Sheriff Maclean to Hillier, 1 February 1827

39 Ibid., 'Memorial of Debtors confined in York Gaol,' June 1832; letter, Dickenson, Tauset, and Stiles, Kingston, 16 November 1833

40 Ibid., clerk of the peace, Newcastle District, to His Excellency, 28 April 1835

41 Ibid., petition of John Newall, 18 February 1835; sheriff, Newcastle District, to His Excellency, 28 February 1835

42 Ibid., 'Memorial of Debtors in York Gaol,' 1832; petition, 28 June 1832

43 Ibid., see minute on above petition; see also Government House, 30 June 1832 'Reference to the Chief Justice.'

44 See *Upper Canada Statutes*, An Act to afford Relief to persons confined on Mesne process, c. 3 (1834); An Act to continue and amend the Law for Attaching the Property of Absconding Debtors, c. 5 (1835); An Act to mitigate the Law in respect to Imprisonment for Debt, c. 3 (1835).

45 *Journal of the House of Assembly* (1836), Appendix no. 44, Gaol Report, George Hamilton to J. Joseph, 9 February 1836

46 Ibid., D. Boulton, 9 March 1836, and S. Washburn, Office of the Clerk of the Peace, 10 March. See especially page 18.

47 Ibid., John Macaulay to Rowan, 30 December 1835

48 Ibid., William Young, chairman, Quarter Sessions, London District, 31 December 1835

49 Ibid., D. Bethune, chairman, Quarter Sessions, Prince Edward District, 7 March 1836

50 Upper Canada Sundries, petition to Sir George Arthur of debtors in the Hamilton Gaol, (?) June 1838; Alan Macdonell to S.B. Harrison, 11 July 1839

51 See *Journal of the House of Assembly* (1836), Appendix no. 136, 'Second Report on the Administration of Justice'; National Archives [hereafter NA], RG5, C–1, vol. 522, petition of the municipal council of the County of Lambton to the governor general in council, 18 June 1857

52 NA, RG5, C–1, vol. 552, Petition of the Inhabitants of Galt to Sir Edmund Head, 17 March 1858

53 NA, RG5, C–1, vol. 537, Report of the Grand Jury of General Quarter Sessions, Middlesex County, 12 December 1857

54 NA, RG5, C–1, vol. 364, Elizabeth Hart to Lord Elgin, [4 September 1852]

55 *Journals of the Legislative Assembly of the Province of Canada* (1851), Appendix L.L., 'Return of debtors confined in Upper Canadian prisons, and of those released to the limits,' Sheriff Cartwright-Thomas, 10 June 1851; Sheriff James Hamilton, 9 June 1851; sheriff Thomas Corbett, 9 June 1851; sheriff's office, Niagara, 10 June 1851

56 *Journals of the Legislative Assembly of the Province of Canada* (1857) Appendix no. 44, 'A Return [showing various information about debtors], since the 1st January, 1855, 9 June 1857. This return requires far fuller analysis than is offered

here. It includes information on the court that issued the writ, the amounts of the debt, whether or not an arrest was made, and on the individual committed to gaol.

57 *Upper Canada Statutes*, c. 37 (1834); c. 24 (1836–7); and c. 11 (1839)
58 This interpretation is advanced by Tom Brown in 'The Origins of the Asylum in Upper Canada, 1836–1839,' *Canadian Bulletin of Medical History* 1 (1984).
59 Upper Canada Sundries, Report of Grand Jury, Johnstown District, 18 May 1821; and 'Rules and Regulations for the Gaoler of the Johnstown District,' 24 February 1821
60 Upper Canada Sundries, petition of the magistrates, grand inquest and other inhabitants of the Eastern District, Cornwall, 29 January 1825; Report of Grand Jury, London District, 13 August 1831
61 Ibid., Report of Grand Jury, London District, 13 August 1831
62 Ibid., Report of Grand Jury, Johnstown District, 11 November 1835
63 Ibid., presentment of grand jurors, Gore District Assizes, 5 August 1834
64 Ibid., John Clark and Niagara magistrates to Colborne, 30 January 1835
65 Ibid., presentment of grand jurors, Niagara District, 16 March 1839
66 Ibid.
67 *Journal of the House of Assembly* (1830), Appendix, 'Report of Petition of Prisoners in Gaol at York,' W.L. Mackenzie, chair, 17 February 1830
68 See R.J. Burns, 'W.B. Jarvis, DCB, vol. 9, 411–12 for a brief biography.
69 For extracts from Colborne's letter see Upper Canada Sundries, Powell to Rowan, 26 July 1834.
70 Upper Canada Sundries, Jarvis to Colborne, 17 June 1834, and Powell to Rowan, 26 July 1834
71 Ibid.
72 For the Hoff case see Niagara *Gleaner*, 24 July 1830, and *Canadian Freeman*, 29 July 1830; *Canadian Freeman*, 24 June 1830, 11 August 1831. Collins, convicted of libel, had spent forty-five days in gaol.
73 *The Colonial Advocate*, probably 12 June 1834. With the political pot boiling, the state of the gaols had emerged as one of the leading issues of the day. In particular, a bitter dispute broke out between Mayor W.L. Mackenzie and the gaoler, Charles Barnhart. For a spirited account of the dispute see Paul Romney, 'Rebel as Magistrate: William Lyon Mackenzie and His Enemies,' in Jim Phillips et al., eds., *Essays in the History of Canadian Law*, vol. 5, *Crime and Criminal Justice* (Toronto 1994). The Upper Canada Sundries contain numerous letters on this episode.
74 The Upper Canada Sundries contain several letters on this incident. For a summary see Robert Fraser's DCB biography of McCarthy, vol. 6, at 425–6.
75 Upper Canada Sundries, sheriff's office, remarks on petition of McCarthy and

Roony, 26 January 1835; petition of McCarthy and Roony, [n.d.]; petition on behalf of McCarthy and Roony, 20 January 1835; Sheriff's Office to Rowan, 26 January 1835; report, Judge Macaulay, 29 January 1835

76 Ibid., Report of Grand Jurors, 28 August 1835; Letter, sheriff's office, 31 August 1835

77 Ibid., Judge Macaulay to Rowan, 29 August 1835. I thank Robert Fraser for the references to Glenelg's views.

78 Quoted in Fred Landon, *An Exile from Canada to Van Dieman's Land* (Toronto 1960), 89.

79 Upper Canada Sundries, 'Representation of the Judges Respecting Treatment of Prisoners,' 22 December 1835. This document was printed as part of the *Journal of the House of Assembly* (1836), Appendix no. 44.

80 Ibid., 'Message From His Excellency with Despatch On the Subject of Prison Discipline,' 7 March 1836, and Gaol Reports

81 Ibid. Subsequent references in the text are to these Gaol Reports.

82 *Journal of the House of Assembly* (1836), Appendix no. 92, Statement of Grand Jury, Home District, with Charge of Judge Robinson, April 1836

83 *Journal of the House of Assembly* (1836–7), Appendix no. 11, Gaol Reports, John Macaulay, 30 December 1835

84 *Upper Canada Statutes*, An Act to regulate the future erection of Gaols in this province, c. 5 (1836); for the throne speech commitment, see *Upper Canada Gazette*, 14 January 1836, as cited in Splane, *Social Welfare*, 124.

85 *Journal of the Legislative Assembly of the Province of Canada* (1839–40), Appendix, vol. I, Part. I, 'Report of the Commissioners of Gaols'

86 See Patrick Brode, *Sir John Beverley Robinson: Bone and Sinew of the Compact* (Toronto 1984), 227–8; for the Sydenhamite reforms see J.E. Hodgetts, *Pioneer Public Service* (Toronto 1955).

87 *Journal of the Legislative Assembly* (1839–40), Appendix, vol. II, 'Report of the Commissioners Appointed to investigate and report on the state of the several Public Departments of this Province'

CHAPTER 3: 'ORDER IS HEAVEN'S FIRST LAW'

1 J. Alex Edmison, 'The History of Kingston Penitentiary,' in *Historic Kingston* (1953–4), 30

2 Charles Dickens, *American Notes*, quoted in G.F.G. Stanley, 'Kingston as Early Tourists Saw It,' *Historic Kingston* (January 1974)

3 For Dalhousie's proposal see Rainer Baehre, 'Imperial Authority and Colonial Officialdom of Upper Canada in the 1830's,' in Louis A. Knafla and Susan W.S. Binnie, eds., *Law, Society and State* (Toronto 1995), 186; and see NA, MG24, A12, vol. V, 22 December 1822

4 Kingston *Chronicle*, 29 September 1826
5 J.J. Bellomo, 'Upper Canadian Attitudes towards Crime and Punishment,' *Ontario History* 64 (1972)
6 Tom Brown, 'The Origins of the Asylum in Upper Canada, 1830–1839, *Canadian Bulletin of Medical History* 1 (1984)
7 J.M. Beattie, *Attitudes towards Crime and Punishment in Upper Canada, 1830–1850: A Documentary Study* (Toronto 1977)
8 Rainer Baehre, 'Pauper Emigration to Upper Canada in the 1830's,' *Histoire sociale/Social History* (November 1981), 355–6
9 Ibid., 357
10 For the use of the gaol as a temporary asylum, see Rainer Baehre, 'The Ill-Regulated Mind: A Study in the Making of Psychiatry in Ontario, 1830–1921' (PhD thesis, York University 1985), 79–85.
11 Baehre develops these views in the works listed above (notes 3, 8, and 10). His emphasis on the international context receives fullest treatment in 'Imperial Authority and Colonial Officialdom of Upper Canada in the 1830s,' in Knafla and Binnie, eds., *Law, Society and the State*.
12 H. Pearson Gundy, 'Hugh C. Thomson: Editor, Publisher and Politician, 1791–1834,' in Gerald Tulchinsky, ed., *To Preserve and Defend: Essays on Kingston in the Nineteenth Century* (Montreal 1976), 216. For Russell Smandych's interpretation see 'The Upper Canadian Experience with Pre-Segregative Control' (PhD thesis, University of Toronto 1989), and two articles, 'Beware of the "Evil American Monster": Upper Canadian Views on the Need for a Penitentiary, 1830–1834,' *Canadian Journal of Criminology* (April 1991); and 'Tory Paternalism and the Politics of Penal Reform in Upper Canada, 1830–34: A Neo-Revisionist Account of the Kingston Penitentiary,' *Criminal Justice History* 12 (1991). Professor Smandych and I are in agreement as to the dominant role played by Tory paternalism.
13 Kingston *Herald*, 10 August 1833; Kingston *Chronicle*, 6 November 1830
14 John Macaulay, Kingston *Chronicle*, 5 May 1832; Charles Eliot, to Western District Quarter Session Grand Jury, *Canadian Emigrant and Western Advertiser*, 19 January 1832
15 Cited in Kingston *Chronicle*, 29 September 1826. For Beccaria see Marcello Maestro, *Cesare Beccaria and the Origins of Penal Reform* (Philadelphia 1973).
16 *Farmer's Journal*, St Catharines, 18 March 1829
17 For an interpretation that emphasizes Colborne's role far more than Thomson's, see Smandych, 'Pre-Segregative Control,' chap. 9, esp. 356–7. See also Gundy, 'Thomson,' 219; J.B. Robinson, charge to Niagara grand jury, 3 September 1832, cited in Donald J. McMahon, 'Law and Public Authority: Sir John Beverley Robinson, and the Purposes of the Criminal Law,' *University of Toronto Faculty of Law Review* 46 (1) (Winter 1988), 404

18 See Smandych, 'Beware of the "Evil American Monster",' 138–9, for the division of opinion in 1830 on the need for a penitentiary.

19 The 1833 law reform statute itself (see note 20, below) represented one of the clearest expressions of Robinson's views. See also the important criminal law reform statutes of 1841, which further reduced the number of capital offences to eight, and which made punishment by imprisonment virtually the only punishment for all non-capital offences. These substantial statutes in effect constituted a criminal code for the new Province of Canada. They completed the modernization of criminal law by abolishing the pillory and by failing even to mention the anachronistic punishment of whipping. The supplemental 1842 statute further reflected the predominance of imprisonment over every other non-capital punishment. See esp. 4 & 5 Vict., cc. 24, 25, 26, and 27. By a supplemental statute of 1842, any prisoner sentenced to penitentiary under these statutes might alternatively be sent to gaol for 'any term not exceeding two years.' The use of two years to distinguish between gaol and penitentiary imprisonment dates from these statutes.

20 *Upper Canada Statutes*, c. 4 (1833)

21 For Sir John Colborne's address see *Journal of the House of Assembly of Upper Canada* (1833), 112–13 and 140.

22 A useful discussion of the Constitutional Act is found in the standard work by Gerald Craig, *Upper Canada: The Formative Years, 1784–1841* (Toronto 1963), chap. 1.

23 Richard B. Splane, *Social Welfare in Ontario, 1791–1893: A Study in Social Welfare Administration* (Toronto 1965), 66–7

24 Smandych, 'Pre-Segregative Control,' esp. chap. 7.

25 The classic account of poor relief in Upper Canada remains that provided by Richard Splane in *Social Welfare*.

26 Rainer Baehre, 'Paupers and Poor Relief in Upper Canada,' *CHA, Historical Paper* (1981), 60

27 Patrick Brode, *Sir John Beverley Robinson; Bone and Sinew of the Compact* (Toronto 1984), 25

28 McMahon, 'Law and Public Authority,' 401; Grand jury charge, Toronto, 1836

29 McMahon, 'Law and Public Authority,' 403

30 Ibid.; Grand jury charge, Gore District, 23 August 1830

31 Brode, *Robinson*, 114

32 McMahon, 'Law and Public Authority,' 406, Charge, London, 1836; 410, Charge, Sandwich, 1833; 415, Charge, Western District, 1836

33 McMahon, 'Law and Public Authority,' 403

34 Ibid.

35 Ibid. For English reforms see Sir Leon Radzinowicz's monumental *History of*

English Criminal Law, esp. vol. 5, by Radzinowicz and Roger Hood, *The Emergence of Penal Policy* (London 1986).

36 *Journal of the House of Assembly of Upper Canada* (1831), 211–12, 'Report of Select Committee on expendiency of erecting a penitentiary,' H.C. Thomson, chairman, February 1831

37 Ibid.

38 W. David Lewis, *From Newgate to Dannemora: The Rise of the Penitentiary in New York, 1796–1848* (Ithaca, NY 1965), 101, and David J. Rothman, *The Discovery of the Asylum* (Glenview, IL 1971) 101. The idea of 'less eligibility' was one of Jeremy Bentham's favourite notions.

39 *Journal of the House of Assembly of Upper Canada*, (1832–3), 'Report of the Commissioners appointed ... for the purpose of obtaining Plans and Estimates of a Penitentiary to be erected in this province' [hereafter Thomson–Macaulay Report], 12 November 1832

40 For fuller discussion of Auburn and Philadelphia, see Lewis, *From Newgate to Dannemora*; Rothman, *The Discovery of the Asylum*; Blake McKelvey, *American Prisons: A History of Good Intentions* (Montclair, NJ 1977), and Adam J. Hirsch, *The Rise of the Penitentiary: Prisons and Punishment in Early America* (New Haven, CT 1992).

41 Thomson–Macaulay Report

42 NA, Upper Canada Sundries, Macaulay to Colonel William Rowan, 26 October 1835. He made similar comments in a letter dated 23 December 1836

43 Thomson–Macaulay Report

44 Thomson–Macaulay Report, correspondence between William Powers and the commissioners: John Macaulay to Powers, 31 July 1832, and Powers to commissioners, October 1832

45 Thomson–Macaulay Report

46 *Upper Canada Statutes*, An Act granting to His Majesty a sum of Money to Defray the Expense of Erecting a Penitentiary in this Province and for other purposes therein mentioned, 44 (1833)

47 A Select Committee on the Report of the Penitentiary commissioners, chaired by Henry J. Boulton, reported to the House of Assembly on 15 January 1833 (*Journal of the House of Assembly* (1832–3)). The Boulton Committee recommended the adoption of Colonel Powers's proposals and suggested the penitentiary be built either in Kingston or Hamilton. They recommended an appropriation of £12,500 for the commissioners to proceed with such a work, and the 1833 statute provided this sum of money.

48 Ibid.

49 For a discussion of the early opposition of mechanics see Bryan Palmer, 'Kingston Mechanics and the Rise of the Penitentiary, 1833–1836,' *Histoire sociale/Social History* 13 (1980). For a fuller discussion of James Buchanan's

opposition, see Smandych, 'Pre-Segregative Control,' 370–8, to which I am indebted for the Buchanan reference.

50 *Journal of the House of Assembly* (1836) Appendix no. 59, Sundry Reports, 'Report of the Select Committee on the Message of His Excellency and Docments Relative to the Provincial Penitentiary,' C.A. Hagerman, chairman, 28 March 1835 [hereafter Hagerman Committee Report]

51 See Palmer, 'Kingston Mechanics,' 13.

52 Ibid.

53 *Journal of the House of Assembly* (1835), petition of C. Armstrong and 379 others, 19 February 1835

54 Ibid., petition of Wm. Ketchum and 870 others, City of Toronto, 16 March 1835, 247

55 Ibid., Appendix, 101, 5 February 1835, petition of George Oliver and 578 others, Town of Kingston

56 Hagerman Committee Report, 28 March 1835

57 Palmer, 'Kingston Mechanics,' 15

58 Kingston *Chronicle and Gazette*, 2 October 1830

59 W.L. Mackenzie, quoted by Palmer, 'Kingston Mechanics,' 16, 15

60 *Journal of the House of Assembly* (1835), Appendix no. 20, 'Report of the Commissioners of the Provincial Penitentiary'

61 *Upper Canada Statutes*, c. 37 (1834); *Journal of the House of Assembly* (1836–7), Appendix, 'Report of the Penitentiary Inspectors (No. 10) Rules and Regulations of the Penitentiary,' 19–26

62 NA, Upper Canada Sundries, John Macaulay to Colonel Rowan (lieutenant-governor's office) 10 July 1834; and 30 July 1834

63 Ibid. Dr James Sampson to Rowan, 11 May 1834

64 *Upper Canada Statutes*, An Act to provide for the Maintenance and Government of the Provincial Penitentiary, erected near Kingston, in the Midland District, c. 37 (1834)

65 J.F.C. Harrison, *The Early Victorians, 1832–1851*, as cited in Seán McConville, *A History of English Prison Administration*, vol. 1, *1750–1877* (London 1981), 301–2. See also Splane, *Social Welfare*, 25, 27.

66 This conflict is fully discussed in Baehre's *The Ill-Regulated Mind*, 143–83.

67 See note 61, above.

68 Upper Canada Sundries, Macaulay to Rowan, 30 July 1834. See also Macaulay to Rowan, 11 January 1834.

69 The disputes between Smith and Powers receive full attention in the first report of the Brown Commission's investigation of penitentiary affairs. See *Reports of the Commissioners Appointed to Enquire into the Conduct, Discipline and Management of the Provincial Penitentiary* (Montreal 1849), 'History of Penitentiary,' 4–5.

70 See the Statute and the Rules, above, note 61.

71 Ibid.

72 Ibid.

73 *Journal of the House of Assembly* (1836), Appendix no. 19, 'Report of the Penitentiary Inspectors,' 1835. The report reprints at some length extracts from the Crawford report.

74 In a letter to Rowan (Upper Canada Sundries) dated 26 October 1835, Macaulay thanked the governor for sending him a copy of the Crawford Report, which, he said, provided 'a great deal of information' previously beyond the reach of Canadians.

75 Penitentiary Inspectors' Report, 1835

76 *Journals of the House of Assembly* (1836–7) Appendix no. 10, 'Report of the Penitentiary Inspectors'

77 Upper Canada Sundries, Macaulay to J. Joseph (governor's secretary), 19 October 1836

78 Ibid., Macaulay to Joseph, 23 December 1836 and Inspectors Gray, Cartwright, and Pringle to Joseph, 3 November

79 Ibid., Henry Smith to Rowan, 5 August 1834

80 Ibid., Henry Smith, letter 4 May 1835

81 *Penitentiary Inspectors' Report*, 1835

82 *Journal of the House of Assembly* (1836), Appendix no. 71, 'Report of Commissioners on the Subject of Prisons, Penitentiaries etc.,' Charles Duncombe, acting commissioner for obtaining certain information etc.; and *Journals of the Legislature Assembly of Upper Canada*, (1839), Appendix, 'Commissioners on the Removal of the Penitentiary from Kingston to Marmora,' (i) A. Manahan and G.A. Ridley, and (ii) Isaac Fraser

83 Rainer Baehre, 'Origins of the Penitentiary System in Upper Canada,' *Ontario History* (September 1977), 195–200

84 Duncombe *Report* (1836), 183

85 Report, Commissioners on the Removal of the Penitentiary (1839)

CHAPTER 4: 'THE REFORMATION OF CONVICTS IS UNKNOWN'

1 *Reports of the Commissioners Appointed to Enquire into the Conduct, Discipline and Management of the Provincial Penitentiary* (Montreal 1849) [hereafter Brown Commission Report], 120, 258

2 J. Alex Edmison, 'The History of Kingston Penitentiary,' *Historic Kingston* (1953–4), 28; Sydney Shoom, 'Kingston Penitentiary: The Early Decades,' *The Canadian Journal of Corrections* (July 1966); Bryan Palmer, 'Kingston Mechanics and the Rise of the Penitentiary, 1833–36,' *Histoire sociale/Social History*, 13 (1980), 16

3 Donald Creighton, *John A. Macdonald*, vol. 1 (Toronto 1956), 159–60; J.M.S. Careless, *Brown of the Globe*, vol. 1 (Toronto 1959), 78–87. For Henry Smith Jr see Donald Swainson, DCB, vol. 9.

4 W.G.C. Norman, 'A Chapter of Canadian Penal History: The Early Years of the Provincial Penitentiary at Kingston and the Commission Inquiry into its Management, 1835–1851' (MA thesis, Queen's University 1979), 203

5 Peter Hennessy, 'The Prison at Kingston, Canada West, "So Irksome and So Terrible,"' *The Beaver* (February/March 1991)

6 A.E. Lavell, 'History of Prisons in Ontario 1792–1932' (unpublished manuscript, 1937). A copy of the Lavell manuscript is in the Queen's University Archives.

7 See Norman, 'Early Years at Kingston,' 73–4.

8 Brown Commission Report, 4, Sullivan to the commissioners, 1 June 1848

9 Ibid.

10 J.E. Hodgetts, *Pioneer Public Service* (Toronto 1955), chap. 3, 'Lord Sydenham Disposes,' and also 80–1

11 Ibid., 14–15

12 *Upper Canada Statutes*, c. 37 (1834), cl. 38

13 NA, Upper Canada Sundries, W.L. Mackenzie, letter, 4 September 1834; see also extract from the Calendar of Prisoners Convicted at the Mayor's Court, City of Toronto, 2 September 1834

14 Ibid., Richard Beasley, chairman of Quarter Sessions, to Rowan, 12 August 1834

15 The penitentiary reports are full of complaints from inspectors and warden about these circumstances.

16 Brown Commission Report, 273–80; 80

17 Ibid.

18 Upper Canada Sundries, Smith to Rowan, 15 August 1834

19 Ibid., letter, F. Bickerton, clerk, 23 April 1835

20 Ibid., Macaulay to Rowan, 7 May 1835

21 NA, Warden's Letter Book, Smith to inspectors, 4 May 1835

22 Ibid., Smith to inspectors, 6 April 1836

23 Ibid., Smith to J. Joseph, 30 April 1836; Upper Canada Sundries, Macaulay to Joseph, 25 May 1836, and see NA, Warden's Letter Book, Smith to Macaulay, 25 June 1836

24 Ibid., Smith to board, 13 December 1836

25 Ibid., Smith to James Nickalls, 11 April 1838

26 Ibid., Smith to Nickalls, 10 October 1838; 4 February 1839, Smith to T. Asken. For an example of 'shameful' provisions, see the entry of 13 January 1842

27 Norman, 'Early Years at Kingston,' 26

28 NA, Warden's Letter Book, warden to Michael Ackman, 6 February 1839

29 Ibid., Smith to Strachan, 8 August 1837

30 Ibid., Smith to Nickalls, 29 June 1839

31 Ibid., Smith to Nickalls, 31 July 1839

32 Ibid., Smith to Nickalls, 17 March 1840; NA, Board of Inspectors' Minute Book [hereafter Inspectors' Minute Book], Minute of 27 February 1840

33 Ibid., Inspectors' Minute Book, letter from governor general's secretary, J.W.C. Murdock, 21 August 1840, and Nickalls to Murdock, 28 August

34 Ibid., 14 February 1841

35 *Journals of the Legislative Assembly of the Province of Canada* (1842), Appendix H, 'Annual Report,' Provincial Penitentiary, 1841 [Annual Reports of the Inspectors of the Provincial Penitentiary appear hereafter as AR, followed by the year of the report.]

36 Ibid.

37 *Journals of the Legislative Assembly of the Province of Canada*, Appendix, Report for 1842 and 1843

38 Inspectors' Minute Book, 5 September 1842; 17 September 1844

39 Douglas McCalla, *Planting the Province: The Economic History of Upper Canada, 1784–1870* (Toronto 1994), 167–71

40 Norman, 'Early Years at Kingston,' 17. Norman provides a good account of the struggles between Smith and his deputies. These are also summarized effectively in the Brown Commission Report in its historical survey beginning on page 4.

41 Brown Commission Report, 290

42 Upper Canada Sundries, Nickalls to J. Joseph, 3 October 1837

43 Ibid., Hagerman opinion, 13 February 1838

44 AR 1836; AR 1837

45 The Powers–Smith dispute is discussed fully in the Brown Commission Report, 7–9.

46 Upper Canada Sundries, Pringle letter, 14 July 1839

47 Ibid., part of a John Macaulay letter (Document #124410) [n.d.]

48 Ibid., Nickalls to S.B. Harrison, 11 July 1839

49 Ibid.

50 Brown Commission Report, 7

51 AR 1839, 58

52 Brown Commission Report, 8–9; Upper Canada Sundries, Nickalls to Harrison, 10 October 1839; Government House to Nickalls, 2 September 1840; Nickalls to Harrison, 17 September 1840

53 For this characterization, see Norman, 'Early Years at Kingston,' 36

54 Inspectors' Minute Book, 5 September 1842. The board, 'in consequence of the

satisfactory manner in which Mr. Smith has discharged the onerous duties of his situation,' recommended a salary increase.

55 Richard B. Splane, *Social Welfare in Ontario, 1791–1843: A Study in Social Welfare Administration* (Toronto 1965), 138; Norman, 'Early Years at Kingston,' 36

56 Ibid., 44–6

57 *Journals of the Legislative Assembly of the Province of Canada* (1846), Appendix G; AR 1845, Board of Inspectors, Report of the Warden, 15 October 1845

58 Inspectors' Minute Book, 19 March 1844, and numerous other entries

59 AR 1845

60 Inspectors' Minute Book, 12 March 1845

61 Norman notes that at this point there were no reliable punishment statistics, but the board was dissatisfied with what it regarded as laxity and rumours circulated that the inmate population could only be controlled by more corporal punishments. 'Early Years at Kingston,' 58

62 AR 1845

63 AR 1842; AR 1844

64 Canada, *Statutes*, An Act to consolidate and amend the Laws relating to the Provincial Pentitentiary, c. 4 (1846)

65 See Norman, 'Early Years at Kingston,' 58–63, for a fuller discussion of the board's resignation.

66 There is a good account of these matters in Norman, 59–63. For the board's perspective, see their minute book for 25 July 1846.

67 The sociological literature from the 1930s to the 1950s on prison subcultures emphasizes that prisons are usually governed through complex sets of compromises between prisoners and officers. See, for example, the famous discussion of Gresham Sykes, *Society of Captives: A Study of a Maximum Security Prison* (Princeton 1958).

68 Toronto *Globe*, cited in Norman, *Early Years at Kingston*, 70

69 Inspectors' Minute Book, 4 November 1846

70 For Frank Smith's trial by the new Corbett board, see Brown Commission Report, 16, 29 October 1847.

71 AR 1841. Rogers was at this time temporary chaplain during Herchmer's leave.

72 Thomas E. Wilson, 'An Historical Study of the Relationship of the Anglican Church of Canada to Kingston Penitentiary, 1835–1913' (PHD thesis, University of Ottawa 1979), 21–2

73 AR 1837

74 Wilson, 'The Anglican Church and the Penitentiary,' 61. And see AR 1839.

75 Ibid.

76 AR 1837

77 Ibid.
78 AR 1839
79 AR 1837
80 AR 1839
81 AR 1842
82 AR 1839
83 AR 1840
84 Wilson, 'The Anglican Church and the Penitentiary,' 48
85 Ibid.
86 AR 1840
87 Ibid.
88 Ibid.
89 AR 1843
90 AR 1840
91 AR 1844
92 AR 1845
93 Ibid.
94 AR 1840
95 Ibid.
96 AR 1844
97 AR 1846
98 Wilson, 'The Anglican Church and Kingston Penitentiary,' 18
99 Smith referred to this American recidivist legislation in several reports. See AR 1839 and 1840.
100 AR 1841
101 NA, RG5, C–1, File 9496, Warden Smith to Henry Smith Jr, 17 December 1844. This important letter contains many of Smith's suggestions for substantive change in the penal system.
102 AR 1839; Inspectors' Minute Book, 7 July 1840
103 NA, RG5, C–1, File 9496, Warden Smith to Henry Smith Jr, 17 December 1844
104 AR 1839; Warden Smith to Henry Smith Jr, 17 December 1844. These reports were printed following a complaint made by the warden in his 1838 report that he had been unable to reciprocate following receipts of reports of other institutions.
105 NA, Warden Smith's Letter Book, Smith to Reverend Louis Dwight, 4 January 1843
106 Warden Smith to Henry Smith Jr, 17 December 1844; AR 1845
107 NA, Warden Smith's Letter Book, 3 March 1842, in answer to questions posed by commissioners from Lower Canada; see also Lewis, *From Newgate to Dannemora*, 41–5; figures compiled by Brown Commission Report, 6.

108 NA, Warden's Letter Book, 13 March 1839; and 19 July 1837, Smith to John McKenzie of Bath

109 For Smith's understanding of Maconochie's convict mark system, see AR 1843; see also Warden Smith to Henry Smith Jr, 17 December 1844

110 AR 1844

111 Ibid., and see Warden Smith to Henry Smith Jr, 17 December 1844

112 AR 1844

113 For the repressive views of Lynds, Wiltse, and others, see Lewis, *From Newgate to Dannemora.*

114 The fullest statement of MacDonell's views on less eligibility and the dangers of too much schooling appeared in the 1852 report, in which he asserted that no one could doubt that the convicts were 'better fed and better clothed' than most ordinary citizens. AR 1852, 33

115 Cesare Beccaria, *Of Crimes and Punishments,* trans. Henry Paolucci (Indianapolis 1978), 47

116 Lewis, *From Newgate to Dannemora,* 32–3 and 102–3. There is an excellent literature on the prison labour question. Close analysis of the Canadian experience suggests that there is considerable merit to the traditional Marxist accounts (George Rusche and Otto Kirchheimer, *Punishment and Social Structures* (New York 1939), and Dario Melossi and Massimo Paverini, *The Prison and the Factory* (London 1981)), and I have no doubt that the labour system followed at Kingston was broadly a reflection of North American socio-economic circumstances. I have also benefited from the more particularist studies: Glen A. Gildemeister, *Prison Labour and Convict Competition with Free Workers in Industrializing America, 1840–1890* (New York 1987); Christopher R. Adamson, 'Hard Labour and Solitary Confinement,' in *Research in Law, Deviance and Social Control* 6 (1984); Dorothy Chunn, 'Good Men Work Hard; Convict Labour in Kingston Penitentiary, 1835–1850,' *Canadian Criminology Forum* (Fall 1981); and Gordon Hawkins, 'Prison Labour and Prison Industries,' *Crime and Justice: An Annual Review of Research* 5 (1983)

117 AR 1836

118 Ibid.

119 Ibid.

120 Ibid.

121 Ibid.

122 AR 1837

123 AR 1839

124 Smith worked hard to persuade the government that internal prison labour was accomplishing the goal of saving money. NA, Warden's Letter Book, 17 August 1836; 20 April 1837; AR 1839 and esp. 1840

125 Brown Commission Report, 26–39
126 Ibid., 82–98
127 Brown Commission Report, 106; NA, RG5, C–1, vol. 236, Smith to Provincial Secretary James Leslie, 4 October 1848
128 Ibid., 104–5, 'Protest of Warden Against Proceedings,' 9 October 1848. On 9 October Smith attempted to have Alexander Campbell, a lawyer, act for him, but Campbell was refused admission. Campbell was a law partner of John A. Macdonald. Subsequently his son, Henry Jr, was allowed to be present but not to speak.
129 Ibid., 113. This occurred on 20 November 1848
130 Ibid., especially 116–69
131 Ibid., 182–208
132 Ibid., 103
133 Ibid., 189–90
134 Ibid.
135 Inspectors' Minute Book, 12 March 1845
136 The question of corporal punishment was discussed by both warden and inspectors in the 1847 Annual Report. Punishments with whip and cats had been temporarily suspended in 1846, when the warden sought clarification of his responsibilities in this area from the government. See NA, RG5, C–1, vol. 191, 'Report of a Committee of the Executive Council,' 12 October 1846. The new rules prepared by inspectors and warden were discussed in late 1846 and supported by the government. See NA, RG5, C–1, vol. 195, 'Report of a Committee of the Executive Council,' 28 December 1846. Government and inspectors struggled to refine the rules for much of 1847. Norman notes that the cats were restored in February 1847, 'but the Board emphasized the salutary effects of alternative forms of punishment.' 'Early Years at Kingston,' 76. At this point the box became a principal instrument to deal with serious infractions. The entire issue left no doubt that responsibility lay far more with the inspectors and the government than with Smith. For the October 1847 Resolution, see the Brown Commission Report, 183.
137 Brown Commission Report, 195–8
138 For punishments of children, see the Brown Commission Report, 190–5; for women, 190. For the Charlotte Reveille case, see 203–8. The Jane Brown and Charlotte Reveille cases pertain to punishment of allegedly insane persons.
139 Ibid., Dr Sampson's testimony, 184–5, 188, 197, 199, 201, 205
140 Ibid., 188, for testimony of Hopkirk, Kirkpatrick, and Sheriff Corbett
141 Ibid.; NA, Warden's Letter Book, innumerable entries, 1835–1840s
142 Brown Commission Report, 169–82, esp. 173, 180
143 Ibid., 174, and see Appendix.

144 Ibid., 98–9
145 Ibid., 174
146 Ibid., 142–69. Of course similar contraband, as numerous studies indicate, exists in almost every modern prison.
147 For evidence that Smith's notion of correct prison discipline was more lax than that of the inspectors, see the lengthy report of the Kirkpatrick board's efforts to enforce stricter rules on both staff and prisoners, documented in numerous pages of the Inspectors' Minute Book, 1841–6. Of course, this could also mean that Smith was simply not doing his job efficiently, but there is little evidence that the Kirkpatrick board ever held this view.
148 Again, the Minute Books and Letter Books contain numerous references to disputes with Rogers, but these are primarily with the inspectors. In his testimony in the Brown Commission Report (120–2), Rogers made it clear that his complaints were not merely against Smith, but perhaps even more against the inspectors and, by implication, against the government. Many of these are also present in Rogers's formal 1847 Annual Report.
149 Brown Commission Report, 122
150 Ibid., 116
151 Ibid., 116–17
152 Ibid., 117

CHAPTER 5: NEW BEGINNINGS

 1 Report of the Commissioners Appointed to Enquire into the Conduct, Discipline and Management of the Provincial Penitentiary (Montreal 1849), 281
 2 Ibid.
 3 Ibid., 282–7
 4 Ibid., 282–3
 5 Ibid., 285–7
 6 Ibid., 288
 7 Ibid.
 8 Ibid., 294
 9 Ibid., 295
10 Ibid.
11 Ibid.
12 Ibid.
13 Ibid., 296
14 Ibid., 292
15 Ibid.
16 Ibid., 292–4

17 Ibid., 294
18 Ibid., 284, 282, 288
19 Ibid., 288
20 Ibid., 283, 287
21 Ibid., 287
22 Ibid., 289
23 Ibid., 290
24 Ibid.
25 Ibid., 290–1
26 For the American experience see Blake McKelvey, *American Prisons: A History of Good Intentions* (Montclaire, NJ 1977), 70–4.
27 Pages 291–2 of the Brown Commission Report deal with staffing.
28 Ibid., 296, 'Prison for Females'
29 *Statutes of Canada*, An Act for the better Management of the Provincial Penitentiary, c. 2 (1851)
30 Ibid.
31 Ibid.
32 Elizabeth Gibbs, ed., *Debates of the Legislative Assembly of United Canada*, vol. 10, Parts I and II (1851), 733–5, 794–5, 907–10, 974–80
33 Ibid., 735
34 *Statutes of Canada*, An Act for the better Management of the Provincial Penitentiary, c. 2 (1851) cl. 9; 15
35 Ibid., cls. 18, 26, dealt with salaries.
36 Ibid., cl. 17
37 Ibid., cl. 20
38 Ibid., cl. 10; cl. 15. One innovation established by cl. 18 was the appointment of an 'overseer' or 'master tradesman' for every twenty-five convict workers, and the relegation of keepers to more supervisory and disciplinary tasks. This innovation was not successful. It created jealousies and soon disappeared.
39 Gibbs, ed., *Debates of the Legislative Assembly* (1851) 733–5, 794–5, 907–80
40 Ibid.
41 DCB, vol. 9, John Thompson, 'Wolfred Nelson,' at 593–7
42 Ibid., 596
43 There is no DCB entry for Dickson. He provides some information on his experience in a letter of 25 November 1857 to Assistant Provincial Secretary E.A. Meredith, in which he was responding to certain charges about his behaviour made during a personal dispute. See NA, RG 5, C–1, vol. 528. For the episode which led to his dismissal from government, see *Sessional Papers* (1861), no. 24, 'Return to Two Addresses of the Legislative Assembly.'
44 DCB, vol. 10, J.K. Johnson, 'Donald Aeneas MacDonell,' at 469–70 (although his

name in the DCB is spelt with a capital 'D', it appears more frequently in public documents with a lower case 'd'); Thomas E. Wilson,' *An Historical Study of the Relationship of the Anglican Church of Canada to the Kingston Penitentiary*,' 1835–1913 (PhD thesis, University of Ottawa 1979), 142–3

45 NA, RG1, E 1, Reel C–118, Executive Council, 13 December 1856

46 *Journals of the Legislative Assembly of the Province of Canada* (1857), Appendix no. 7, 'Penitentiary Report for the Year 1856'

47 *Journals of the Legislative Assembly of the Province of Canada* (1858) Appendix no. 11, 'Provincial Penitentiary Report, 1857'

48 For a fuller discussion of the prison doctor's role see Charles Kyle Jolliffe, 'An Examination of Medical Services at the Kingston Penitentiary, 1835–1856' (MA thesis, Queen's University 1983). I am indebted to Kyle Jolliffe for sharing his research materials with me.

49 NA, Inspectors' Minute Book, Warden's Report, 1 September 1848; and see *Journals of the Legislative Assembly of the Province of Canada*, Appendix R.R., 'Provincial Penitentiary Annual Accounts for 1849'

50 Canada, Legislative Council, *Sessional Papers* (1851), no. 2, vol. 10, Appendix W, 'Provincial Penitentiary Annual Accounts for 1850,' which prints this correspondence.

51 NA, RG5, C–1, vol. 347, Angus MacDonell to the Inspectors, 6 February 1852. Part of the MacDonell–Brown correspondence was published in the 1850 Annual Report, after being laid before the legislature. In a very lengthy 1852 report, MacDonell gave his version of the origins of the disputed clauses of the 1851 statute, and asserted they were introduced into the bill by 'a reformer in words, a tyrant in practice' (meaning George Brown), out of 'hatred to the Catholic religion' and 'personal hatred towards myself.'

52 Inspectors' Minute Book, 3 February 1852

53 There is a lengthy discussion of Mulkins's antecedents in Wilson, 'The Anglican Church and the Penitentiary.' And see DCB, vol. 10, J.J. Talman, 'Hannibal Mulkins.'

54 Queen's University Archives, A.E. Lavell, manuscript history

55 Wilson, 'The Anglican Church and the Penitentiary,' 153–4

56 Inspectors' Minute Book, 9 May 1856; 7 November 1856

57 AR 1852

58 Inspectors' Minute Book, 7 February 1852

59 Ibid., 2 August 1856; 7 November 1856

60 Wilson, 'The Anglican Church and the Penitentiary,' 159–60

61 AR 1851

62 Ibid., 1851 and 1852

63 Inspectors' Minute Book, 14 October 1859

64 *Journals of the Legislative Assembly of the Province of Canada* (1852), Appendix H.H., Wolfred Nelson, 'A General Review of Prison Economics,' 4 August 1852, 115, 102, 107, 108, 107, 105, 111–14

65 Ibid., 111–14

66 Gardiner's ability to teach in both languages was one of the few overtures in recognition of the fact that the prison now served the population of Canada East. Another was the specific requirement, referred to in inspectoral minutes, that the Catholic chaplain also be bilingual. See AR 1852, Andrew Dickson to His Excellency, 9 February 1853 for comment on the Sabbath school.

67 AR 1852. Angus MacDonell's reports were usually brief, less than a page. On this occasion he was clearly agitated and submitted an eleven-page report covering many important subjects. See pages 31 to 41 of the Report.

68 AR 1852, 55–7; see also Wilson, 'The Anglican Church and the Penitentiary,' 193.

69 AR 1852, 56

70 AR 1852, 33

71 Ibid., 4. Although this comment was issued under the signature of both inspectors, Dickson made it clear in his rebuttal that he did not share this view. See ibid., Dickson, 14–19, and Nelson's response, 84–9, esp. 84. One can only applaud the publication of a document that revealed in so frank a fashion many fundamental disagreements. This contrasts sadly with the sanitized nature of the majority of later nineteenth century reports, in Ontario and in most other jurisdictions.

72 See Inspectors' Minute Book, 14 October 1859 and 11 February 1860.

73 See Inspectors' Minute Book, 13 May 1854, for an example.

74 AR 1852, 25–6

75 Ibid., 26. For the inspectors' approach, see the separate section devoted to that subject in the 1853 Report.

76 Inspectors' Minute Book, 23 November 1851

77 AR 1852, 25–6; Inspectors' Minute Book, 26 April 1852

78 AR 1853, 'Punishment, etc.'

79 NA, Warden's Letter Book, 26 April 1854

80 Ibid.; see entries of 27 and 28 April, 4, 6, and 17 May 1, 19, and 20 June, 7 and 12 August 1854, etc.

81 AR 1853 and 1855

82 NA, RG5, C–1, vol. 361, inspectors to His Excellency, 13 August 1852; AR 1855

83 For the warden's comments on his attendance see AR 1867. In his 1862 Report, the warden noted the recent murder of both warden and assistant warden of the Massachusetts State Prison and asserted that lax discipline must lead to truly dangerous situations. This theme increasingly pervaded Macdonell's reports in the 1860s.

84 NA, RG5, C–1, vol. 396, warden to Provincial Secretary P.J.O. Chauveau, 29 October 1853 (re Oliver Dawsey); RG5, C–1, vol. 446, Wolfred Nelson to G.E. Cartier, 16 June 1855 and warden to inspectors [n.d., but attached to an accompanying letter, warden to Dr Nelson, 12 June 1855]; government response, E.A. Meredith, 20 June AR 1855
85 AR 1859

CHAPTER 6: 'MORAL MONSTERS,' REFRACTORY FEMALES, CHILDREN, AND WORKERS

1 See especially Chapter 4, 182, 186.
2 Quoted in Charles Kyle Jolliffe, 'An Examination of Medical Services at the Kingston Penitentiary' (MA thesis, Queen's University 1983), 153, 156
3 Ibid., 156–60 and AR 1849
4 Ibid., 158–60. For the list of names, see NA, Inspectors' Minute Book, 19 December 1851
5 Inspectors' Minute Book, 17 November 1853
6 Jolliffe, 'Medical Services,' 166
7 Ibid., 167, and Tom Brown, 'Living with God's Afflicted: A History of the Provincial Lunatic Asylum at Toronto, 1830–1911' (PhD thesis, Queen's University 1981) 182
8 Jolliffe, 'Medical Services,' 169–70
9 AR 1853. The inspectors included a separate section, entitled 'Insane.' Dr Sampson also embarked on an extended discussion, wondering openly whether those convicted and then given a commuted sentence on grounds of insanity should be in prison at all.
10 AR 1854, and Jolliffe, 'Medical Services,' 172
11 Ibid., 173. For the Macdonald letter see J.K. Johnson, ed., *Letters of John A. Macdonald*, 2 vols. (Ottawa 1969), 1:249.
12 Inspectors' Minute Book, 13 March 1855
13 Ibid., 4 February 1856
14 Ibid., 4 November 1856
15 Ibid., 9 November 1856
16 *Statutes of Canada* (1857), especially cls. 28, 29, and 31. See also Catharine Anne Sims, 'An Institutional History of the Asylum for the Insane at Kingston, 1856–1885' (MA thesis, Queen's University, 1981), 16
17 Inspectors' Minute Book, 3 February 1859
18 Ibid., 4 February 1859
19 Sims, 'The Asylum for the Insane at Kingston,' 18–19; Inspectors' Minute Book, 4 February 1859 and esp. 30 May

20 Jolliffe, 'Medical Services' 181–2
21 Ibid., 183–4; and for figures see Sims, 'The Asylum for the Insane at Kingston,'
   19–20.
22 Inspectors' Minute Book, 30 May 1859
23 Ibid., 30 November 1859
24 Jolliffe, 'Medical Services,' 186–7
25 Ibid., 186
26 Inspectors' Minute Book, 25 February 1861
27 Ibid., 31 May 1862. Apparently Rockwood was done on a gradual basis, some
   inmates arriving before 1864. See Inspectors' Minute Book, 30 May 1862
28 AR 1849
29 AR 1850, 1851, and esp. the lengthy discussion in 1852
30 AR 1850; Inspectors' Minute Book, 9 December 1850
31 Ibid., 25 April 1851
32 AR 1852, Report of Julia Cox
33 Inspectors' Minute Book, 3 March 1848. Apparently this was Mrs Cox's second
   tour of duty. See Inspectors' Minute Book, 3 November 1847.
34 Ibid., 7 August 1852; 13 August 1852; 18 May 1853
35 Ibid., 9 January 1856
36 Ibid., 11 September 1856. Walker replaced Cox.
37 AR 1856
38 The statistics on women in the 1857 Report were particularly full. See also the
   1858 and 1859 Reports.
39 Ibid., 30 November 1859
40 The Annual Reports provide full information on the military prisoners. See
   also the useful discussion in Thomas E. Wilson, 'An Historical Study of the
   Relationship of the Anglican Church of Canada to the Kingston Penitentiary
   1835–1913 (PhD thesis, University of Ottawa 1979), 124–6 and 245–8, and the
   table on 383.
41 Inspectors' Minute Book, esp. 11 July 1850; 7 and 9 December 1850; 25 April
   1851; and see NA, RG5, C–1, vol. 365, Colonel Bruce, Military Secretary, to Provincial Secretary A.N. Morin.
42 NA, RG5, C–1, vol. 432, military secretary to 'The Civil Secretary' 6 February
   1855; and vol. 482, Major Griffin, assistant military secretary, to provincial secretary, 24 June 1856, and warden to provincial secretary, 10 July.
43 Inspectors' Minute Book, 27 September 1852
44 Ibid., 1 August 1856
45 Ibid., 14 April 1853
46 Ibid., 16 September 1858; 29 January 1859
47 NA, RG5, C–1, vol. 222, Corbett to R.B. Sullivan, 25 March 1848, AR 1849

48 Ibid.

49 Ibid.

50 NA, RG5, C–1, vol. 277, complaints of Kingston tradesmen about the education of convicts in some skilled and semi-skilled trades, 13 November 1849.

51 Ibid.

52 NA, RG5, C–1, vol. 277, petition of Kingston Shoemakers, 2 November 1849

53 Ibid.

54 Ibid., city clerk, Kingston to provincial secretary, 11 December 1849, enclosing petition of City Council, 11 December and RG5, C–1, vol. 297, petition of the inhabitants of Kingston [n.d.] received 21 June 1850

55 For the debates, see Elizabeth Nish, ed., *Debates of the Legislative Assembly of United Canada*, 16 July 1850, 1237–49.

56 AR 1850, 1851; Warden's Minute Book, 28 June 1854

57 For Macdonald's comment see Canada, *Debates*, House of Commons, 17 June 1869

58 AR 1851

59 AR 1852

60 Inspectors' Minute Book, 9 December 1850; 10 December 1850; 23 November 1852; 14 November 1855; 19 April 1856; 17 December 1856; 7 February 1857

61 AR 1851

62 AR 1856, 1857. The 1856 figures were provided in the Warden's Report with slightly different figures in that of the inspectors.

63 AR 1857

64 Inspectors' Minute Book, 1 February 1855; NA, RG5, C–1, vol. 443, inspectors to governor general, 12 May 1855; AR 1856

65 Inspectors' Minute Book, 22, 23–9 August 1853 (Cornwall); 3 February 1854 (Tearney). The warden's journal for June and July 1854 contains numerous entries about Cornelius Ryan, who followed up his refusal to work by refusing to eat.

66 NA, RG5, C–1, vol. 537, Dickson to T.J.J. Loranger, 28 December 1857

67 AR 1857; Inspectors' Minute Book, 4 April 1857; 29 and 30 April

68 RG5, C–1, vol. 543, warden to provincial secretary, 12 February 1858; warden of Auburn to Macdonell, 8 February; clerk, Columbus to Macdonell, 8 February; warden of Sing-Sing to Macdonell, 18 February. See also RG5, C–1, vol. 596, inspectors to provincial secretary, 6 February 1858

69 Ibid., warden to provincial secretary, 6 February 1858

70 Ibid., 'Remarks of ... Warden ... on the Petition of the Contractors,' 6 February 1858; and updated 29 July

71 Ibid., Report of a Committee of the Executive Council, 10 Sepember 1858

72 NA, RG5, C–1, vol. 596, 'Petition of the Contractors in the Provincial Penitentiary,' to governor general, [n.d. – December 1858?]; Dr Nelson to provincial

secretary, 3 December (?) 1858; 'Report by the Warden ... for the information of His Excellency,' [n.d.]; Report of a Committee of the Executive Council, 19 February 1859

73 AR 1856, 1857. For gaol comparisons, see the early reports of the post-1859 Meredith board; and see NA, RG5, C–1, vol. 608 for the petitions. It has not been possible to state definitely which Ontario communities possessed stores that sold penitentiary-made goods, or even how popular penitentiary products were with the public. In Toronto, even prosperous lawyer Robert Harrison was willing to shop at the penitentiary store for furniture. See Harrison diaries, AO, 9 April 1859.

74 NA, RG5, C–1, vol. 620, Meredith to warden, 21 April 1859

CHAPTER 7: DISCIPLINARY ADVANCES

1 For British developments I am indebted to the standard works, including Seán McConville, *A History of English Prison Administration*, vol. 1, 1750–1877 (London 1981) and, most of all, the theoretically flawed yet superbly informative work of Sir Leon Radzinowicz and Roger Hood, *A History of English Criminal Law and its Administration from 1750*, vol. 5, *The Emergence of Penal Policy* (London 1986). There is no comparable work on American penology, but Blake McKelvey, *American Prisons: A History of Good Intentions* (Montclair, NJ 1977) provides a useful introduction.

2 NA, Inspectors' Minute Book, 7 June 1848; 5 December 1850

3 Ibid., 22 November 1851

4 Ibid., 22 November 1851; Warden's Daily Journal, 10, 14 May, 29 June 1854. The letter-writing efforts of the warden are also referred to by the inspectors in the 1856 Annual Report.

5 Ibid., 22 November 1851; 22 March 1854; and 5 February 1858

6 Warden's Daily Journal, 1 July 1854

7 AR 1852

8 Ibid.

9 AR 1849, 1850, 1852

10 NA, RG5, C–1, vol. 340, David Thoburn, Special Commissioner to the Superintendent General of Indian Affairs, 2 October 1851; petition of George Anthony, a chief of the Delaware Nation to Lord Elgin, 9 July 1851; Judge Maclean Report, 26 December 1851; E.A. Meredith to Superintendent of Indian Affairs, 5 January 1852; Meredith to warden, 19 November 1852; warden to provincial secretary, 23 November 1852; inspectors to A.N. Morin, 24 November 1852; Morin to superintendent, 13 December 1852. And see NA, RG 5, C–1, vol. 355, inspectors to Lord Elgin, May 24, 1852.

11 Ibid.

12 Ibid., Meredith to inspectors, 4 June 1852 and Morin to warden, 4 June

13 NA RG5, C–1, vol. 361, inspectors to A.N. Morin, 11 August 1852; inspectors to Lord Elgin, 11 August; E.A. Meredith to inspectors, 25 August

14 NA RG5, C–1, vol. 425, inspectors to P.J.O. Chauveau, 20 November 1854; inspectors to Lord Elgin, 20 November; Meredith to inspectors, 5 December; Minute by J.A. Macdonald

15 NA RG5, C–1, vol. 422, Nelson to Chauveau, 21 October 1854; petition, Mrs Foley to Lord Elgin, 19 October 1854; J.A. Macdonald Report, 30 October 1854. (Modern readers will notice the commendable speed with which all official parties acted in this matter; Macdonald, it seems, was a highly efficient administrator.)

16 AR 1855

17 Ibid.

18 Inspectors' Minute Book, 30 July 1856

19 NA RG5, C–1, vol. 486, Solicitor General Henry Smith to ?, 27 July 1856; E.A. Meredith to Henry Smith, 31 July; warden to Meredith, 6 August

20 AR 1856–9

21 Ibid.

22 See Radzinowicz and Hood, *English Criminal Law*, vol. 5, *Penal Policy*.

23 AR 1855

24 Macdonald to Robinson, 2 January 1851, quoted in J.K. Johnson and C.B. Stalmack, eds., *The Letters of Sir John A. Macdonald 1858–1861* (Ottawa 1969), 285–6; Macdonald to Creighton, cited in William Teatero, 'The Tragic Life of Dr. William Dill,' Kingston *Whig Standard Magazine*, 19, 26 June; 3 July 1982. This did not mean that Macdonald opposed a mark system for good conduct. He told Robinson in his 1861 letter that the inspectors were considering just such a system. Any system, however, would have had to be made to conform to Macdonald's overriding objectives.

25 AR 1852

26 AR 1853 and 1854

27 AR 1856

28 AR 1858

29 AR 1858

30 AR 1853 and 1854. For Macdonell's comments see AR 1855.

31 Ibid.

32 Ibid.

33 Ibid.

34 AR 1856

35 Ibid.

36 Ibid.

37 Warden's Daily Journal, 4 July 1854; 12 and 14 July
38 For an excellent account see William Teatero's articles in the Kingston *Whig-Standard Magazine*, 19, 26 June and 3 July 1982, 'The Tragic Life of Dr William Dill.'
39 For accounts of Dill's escape and recapture see Inspectors' Minute Book, 1, 2 October 1856. It was several months later, 7 February 1857, that Dill was given a lighter chain, following the cabinet contractor's complaint that he was being impeded in his work. See Inspectors' Minute Book.
40 Warden's Daily Journal, 10 August 1855; Inspectors' Minute Book, 17 November 1854; 10 November 1855; 7 April 1856; 29, 30 July and 1 August 1857
41 Ibid., 27 February 1861
42 This charge was made by the teacher, and the inspectors cautioned the hospital keeper. Inspectors' Minute Book, 28 April 1858
43 Inspectors' Minute Book, 30, 31 July 1857
44 Ibid., 27 June 1854; 30 August 1854; 17 January 1856
45 Although there is occasional evidence in the minutes of knives being seized and of other threatening behaviour, most of the violence seems to have been legal in nature, directed by officers against prisoners. In the absence of modern weaponry, the extent of official control seems remarkable and should offer many insights into nineteenth-century prison life and culture.

CHAPTER 8: INSTITUTIONAL RIGIDITIES AND PUNITIVE POLICIES

1 NA, RG5, C–1, vols. 425 and 520, Wolfred Nelson to A.N. Morin, 23 November 1854
2 Ibid., Rees to Morin, 5 December 1854
3 Ibid., vol. 425, Wolfred Nelson to W. Rees, 25 September 1856
4 NA, RG5, C–1, vol. 473, 29 March 1856, presentment of grand jury of Ontario County
5 Canada, *Statutes*, An Act for Establishing Prisons for Young Offenders, for the better government of Public Asylums, Hospitals and Prisons, and for the better construction of Common Gaols, c. 28 (1857)
6 Richard B. Splane, *Social Welfare in Ontario, 1791–1893: A Study in Social Welfare Administration* (Toronto 1965), 35–6; and see Canada, Consolidated Statutes, c. 110, An Act respecting Inspectors of Public Asylums, Hospitals, the Provincial Penitentiary of Canada and of all Common Gaols and other prisons.
7 J.E. Hodgetts, *Pioneer Public Service* (Toronto 1955), 90–1
8 It would seem that the self-assured attorney general never entirely abandoned the hostility to the paid inspectorate he had expressed in 1851, and he remained unwilling to surrender the authority he regarded as the prerogative

of Cabinet into the hands of a board of bureaucrats. In Macdonald's eyes, the board was suspect from the beginning.

9 Splane, *Social Welfare*, 39
10 Canada, *Sessional Papers* (1860), no. 32, 'Preliminary Report of the Board of Inspectors of Asylums, Prisons etc.,' 1859, 4
11 Ibid., 22; *Sessional Papers* (1868), no. 40, 'Sixth Annual Report of the Board of Inspectors of Asylums, Prisons etc. for the year 1866,' 21
12 'Preliminary Report,' 1859, 6
13 Ibid.
14 Ibid., 6–5
15 Ibid., 6–9
16 Ibid., 14
17 Ibid., 13
18 Meredith made this clear in his memorandum of 29 August 1860 on the provincial penitentiary.
19 'Preliminary Report,' 1859, 10–11; 12
20 Ibid., 12, 21–2
21 Ibid., 21–2
22 Ibid., 20–1
23 NA, RG 5, C–1, vol. 673, 'Special Report on the subject of Central Jails,' 15 February 1861, Meredith to provincial secretary.
24 Ibid.
25 For a brief discussion of the regional detention centres in the late 1960s see Peter Oliver, *Unlikely Tory: The Life and Politics of Allan Grossman* (Toronto 1985), 186–8
26 NA, Inspectors' Minute Book, 30 May 1860
27 Ibid., 1 June 1860
28 Ibid.
29 Ibid., 1 June 1860 and see NA, MG29,E15, E.A. Meredith Papers, Meredith Diary, October 1860. The information about the effect of the board's minute came from McSweeney. Meredith's diary sometimes is unclear as to date of entries; I have done my best, using internal evidence, to supply accurate dates.
30 Meredith Diary, May 1861
31 Canada, *Sessional Papers* (1863), no. 66, 'Third Annual Report on Asylums, Prisons etc.,' 1862
32 Ibid.
33 Ibid.
34 Meredith Diary, September, 1861; October 1861
35 Ibid., May 1861, 26 August, 2 September 1861
36 Ibid., 22 September 1851

37 For references to the counterfeiting ring see the Meredith Diary, 22 September 1862. And see NA, RG5, C–1, vol. 785, copy of an article in the *Daily British American*, 28 October [no year] 'Crime in the Penitentiary ... Astonishing Developments'; Meredith to provincial secretary, 5 November 1863; and Report by Terence O'Neill on the counterfeiting affair [n.d.].

38 Meredith Diary, 22 September 1862, and O'Neill Report

39 Meredith Diary, 22 September 1862

40 Ibid., 1 September 1861 (or 62?)

41 See AR 1862, 'Extract from Minutes, Sitting 1st June, 1860'; and Meredith Diary, 26 August–2 September, 1862

42 AR 1861 and 1862

43 NA, RG5, C–1, vol. 664, D. A.E. Macdonell to provincial secretary, 'Extracts from Minutes made by the Board' 5 September 1860; 29 August 1860, E.A. Meredith, 'Memorandum as to certain changes necessary with a view to make the Provincial Penitentiary more useful as a "Reformatory Institution"'

44 Ibid.

45 AR 1861, 'Memorandum on the Provincial Penitentiary,' 31 March 1862

46 Macdonald, marginal note on Meredith's 29 August 1860 memorandum

47 Meredith Memorandum, 31 March 1862

48 Ibid.

49 Ibid.

50 Ibid., and AR 1861

51 For a useful introduction to the Irish system see Mary Carpenter, *Our Convicts*, 2 vols., (1864), and Meredith's 1860 memorandum. There is a good discussion of reformatory prison discipline in William Arnold Calder, 'The Federal Penitentiary System in Canada, 1867–1899: A Social and Institutional History' (PhD thesis, University of Toronto 1979), esp. chap. 1.

52 Meredith Diary, October 1860 and 25 August–2 September 1861

53 See Meredith's memorandum, 29 August 1860.

54 AR 1861, 'Remarks on the necessary degree of discipline maintained in the provincial penitentiary during 1861'

55 See, for example, AR 1864, 16. There is little discussion of solitary cells in Meredith's 29 August 1860 memorandum. But by 1865 the inspectors were arguing that solitary confinement was 'the basis of all discipline.' See the extended discussion in AR 1865, 15–16. The British influence had become far stronger than the American at this point in time.

56 AR 1864, 55, 56. 88, 89; 1865, 15–16; 1866, 6–7

57 AR 1866, 6–7, 4; AR 1867, 6, 10; AR 1866, 6

58 AR 1861

59 AR 1867

60 AR 1866
61 AR 1867
62 NA, RG5, C–1, vol. 832, Meredith to provincial secretary, 26 January 1866, and accompanying memorandum; and Meredith to the board, 17 January 1866
63 Ibid.
64 Inspectors' Minute Book, Meredith to J. Murray, 21 January 1868; and Meredith to Franklin Sanborn, 25 April 1868, as cited in Calder, 'The Federal Penitentiary System,' 50–1
65 For an extended discussion of the possible reasons for this division of authority see Richard M. Zubrycki, 'The Establishment of Canada's Penitentiary System: Federal Correctional Policy 1867–1900' (MSW thesis, University of Toronto 1980), esp. 19–28.
66 Ontario, *Statutes*, An Act to Provide for the Inspection of Asylums, Hospitals, Common Gaols and Reformatories in this province, c. 21 (1868)
67 See Chapter 8 for a discussion of the 1868 statute and the role of the new Ontario inspector.
68 Canada, *Statutes*, An Act respecting penitentiaries, and the Directors thereof, and for other purposes, c. 75 (1868)
69 Radzinowicz and Hood, *The Emergence of Penal Policy*, 522–3
70 Ibid., 703–4
71 See *Prison Discipline, Digest and Summary: Answers from Colonial Governors, Circular Despatches sent out by the Secretary of State on the 16th and 17th January, 1867*, prepared by Direction of the Secretary of State (London 1867); NA, RG5, C–1, vol. 785, E.A. Meredith to provincial secretary, 19 September 1864; and also Meredith to William McDougall, provincial secretary, 17 February 1865; Edward Cardwell to Viscount Monck, 17 January 1865, enclosing circular, 16 January; and various circular despatches, January 1865, 'addressed by Her Majestey's Principal Secretary of State for the Colonies to the Governors,' 2 January 1867. See also AR 1865, 40–4, Special Appendix, for Cardwell's despatch and the Board of Inspectors' response.
72 AR 1865, 40–4
73 See note 71 above, Edward Cardwell to Monck
74 Circular despatch, North American Department, 2 January 1867, esp. 24–8
75 Meredith to McDougall, 17 February 1865
76 Circular despatch, January 1865, 68, 69
77 Ibid., 4, 65
78 Ibid., 73
79 Ibid., 77–80
80 Ibid., 78

81 Ibid., 87
82 See Seán McConville, *A History of English Prison Administration*, vol. 1, 1750–1877 (London 1981) and Radzinowicz and Hood, *The Emergence of Penal Policy*, chap. 16, 'Turning the Screw of Repression.'
83 Blake McKelvey, *American Prisons: A History of Good Intentions* (Montclair, NJ 1977) 68–70
84 Ibid., 69
85 Ibid., 74
86 Rothman, David *Discovery of the Asylum*, chap. 10, 'The Legacy of Reform,' and *Conscience and Convenience: The Asylum and Its Alternatives in Progressive America* (Boston 1980), 31–8; and see Alexander Pisciotta, 'Scientific Reform, The "New Penology" at Elmira, New York, 1876–1900,' *Crime and Delinquency* (October 1983).
87 In June 1863, on Dr Nelson's death, Dr Taché had become board chairman. At this point there were only four members. Taché left the board in 1864 and Meredith assumed the chair. F.Z. Tasse was appointed to replace Taché. For insight into John Creighton and the late nineteenth century generally I am indebted to the work of Calder, 'The Federal Penitentiary System' and Donald G. Wetherell, 'Rehabilitation Programmes in Canadian Penitentiaries, 1867–1914: A Study of Official Opinion' (PhD thesis, Queen's University 1980). For Ferres see Lorne St Croix, DCB, vol. 9; for John Creighton, see H. Pearson Gundy, DCB, vol. 11. Gundy noted that Creighton went to grammar school with John A. Macdonald. He argues that Creighton 'believed that the first step towards moral reformation of the inmates was improvement of their physical condition.' For the policy of 'kindness' see Calder, 203–4. For James G. Moylan see Peter Oliver, DCB, vol. 13.
88 See Calder, 'The Federal Penitentiary System,' 203–5, and AR 1869, 1870, and 1871.
89 Calder, 'The Federal Penitentiary System,' 202, also 264, citing Macdonald to Creighton, 31 October 1871; cited more fully in Zubrycki, 'Canada's Penitentiary System,' 47–8
90 See E.C. Wines and T. Dwight, *Report on the Prisons and Reformatories of the United States and Canada* (1867, reprinted Montclair, NJ 1976) and AR 1869. For extracts pertaining to Canada see Appendix E of the prison inspectors' Annual Report for 1869.
91 Zubrycki, 'Canada's Penitentiary System,' 74; Calder, 'The Federal Penitentiary System,' Abstract and IV
92 The 1866 *Annual Report* of the Board of Inspectors included a 'Return To an Address of the House of Commons, dated 26th March, 1868,' asking for the

Report of the Prison Inspectors on the Prisons of Nova Scotia and New Brunswick. The 1867 Reports of Meredith and Ferres were printed in the 1866 Annual Report. The 1866 Report was printed in 1868.

93 Calder, 'The Federal Penitentiary System,' 108, and see generally Calder's excellent chap. 2, 'The Framework: Institutions, Staff and Administration, 1867–1899.'

94 See AR 1881, xix; 1882, ii; 1891, xiii; 1892, xi. For a convenient summary of Moylan's thinking on these and other subjects, including his role in planning new federal penitentiaries, see what was in effect his farewell report AR 1894.

95 The British Columbia penitentiary opened in 1878. In the 1882 Report Moylan noted that he knew 'nothing officially of this penitentiary consequently, I have not much to say about it.' It was inspected in 1885. See AR 1886, xxi.

96 Calder, 'The Federal Penitentiary System,' 81–3

97 Ibid., 205–10

98 Wetherell, 'Rehabilitation Programmes,' chap. 4, deals with remission (119–27).

99 For Moylan's support of indeterminate sentences, see Canada, *Sessional Papers* (1889), no. 12, 'Thirteenth Annual Report of the Inspector of Penitentiaries,' 1888, xiv

100 See AR 1877, 12–15 for Moylan's full analysis of Canada and the Crofton System; see also AR 1883, 12–13.

101 Lombroso's thought is discussed in almost every standard criminology text. For his own work see Gina Lombroso-Ferrero, *Lombroso's Criminal Man* (Montclair, NJ 1972).

102 Bucke made some statements in his evidence before the 1891 Prison Reform Commission which were pure Lombroso. See also Calder, 'The Federal Penitentiary System,' 153.

103 The labour issue is discussed at length in both the Calder and Wetherell theses. James Moylan gave it extensive attention in most of his Annual Reports. See esp., 1887, xvii – xix and 1888, xvii–xviii. Moylan believed that labour was vital to the interests of prisons and prisoners and suggested that any attempt to radically confine such work represented 'a return to sheer barbarism.'

104 Those who regard this judgment as harsh should study the 1914 and 1938 reports. See Canada, *Sessional Paper* (1914) no. 252, *Report of the Royal Commission on Penitentiaries* (Ottawa 1914) and Canada, *Report of the Royal Commission to Investigate the Penal System of Canada* (Archambault Commission) (1938).

CHAPTER 9: 'THE GOVERNMENT BOARDING HOUSE'

1 J.M.S. Careless, *The Union of the Canadas: The Growth of Canadian Institutions,*

1841–1857 (Toronto 1967); Laurence S. Fallis, Jr, 'The Idea of Progress in the Province of Canada,' in W.L. Morton, ed., *The Shield of Achilles* (Toronto 1968), 170–1

2 Canada, *Sessional Papers* (1849), Appendix B, Walter C. Crofton, 'Crime and Prisons'

3 *Journals of the Legislative Assembly of the Province of Canada* (1840), 'Report on the Public Departments of the Province,' 10–13

4 Canada, *Statutes*, c. 10 (1841–42)

5 C.F.J. Whebell, 'Robert Baldwin and Decentralization 1841–1849,' in F.H. Armstrong et al., eds., *Aspects of Nineteenth-Century Ontario* (Toronto 1974), 53

6 Canada, *Statutes*, c. 81 (1849)

7 Canada, *Sessional Papers* (1856), Appendix no. 34, 'Copies of Reports of the Judges of the Superior Courts for Upper Canada and Presentments of Grand Juries and other papers on the subject of Gaols,' presentment of grand jury, District of Niagara, 22 October 1840

8 For an excellent discussion of Sydenham's administrative reforms see J.E. Hodgetts's *Pioneer Public Service* (Toronto 1955), chap. 3. For the Board of Works, see page 176. For Meredith's view, see comments by Meredith [n.d, 1852 or 1853] attached to grand jury documents, including charge of Mr Justice Burns to the grand jury of the United Counties of York, Ontario, and Peel, 11 October 1852.

9 Ibid.

10 Brown Commission Report, 287

11 Crofton, 'Crime and Prisons'

12 Canada, *Sessional Papers* (1852), Appendix H.H. 'Report of one of the Inspectors of Gaols for Canada West,' 11 September 1852

13 Ibid.

14 NA, RG5, C-1, 'Judges' Report and Grand Jury Presentments,' grand jury presentment, Niagara, 2 October 1840; grand jury presentment, London, 14 May 1841; Judges' Reports, Macaulay to Harrison, 29 May 1841; extract of a letter from Macaulay, 3 June 1843; presentment of grand jury, London District, 19 May 1843

15 Ibid., grand jury presentments, Gore District grand jury, 27 April 1843; presentment of Niagara District grand jury, spring Assizes, 1843

16 Ibid., Judges' Reports, J.B. Robinson to S.B. Harrison, 30 September 1843

17 Canada, *Statutes*, An Act respecting Inspectors of Public Asylums, Hospitals, the Provincial Penitentiary of Canada and of all common Gaols and other Prisons, c. 110 (1859)

18 Ibid., grand jury presentments, Frontenac, Lennox, and Addington Counties, fall Circuit, 1853; Hastings County, fall Assizes, 1853; Ontario County, April

1854. Judges' Reports, Robert E. Burns to Provincial Secretary P.J.O. Chauveau, 3 June 1854

19 Ibid., Judges' Reports to Provincial Secretary S.B. Harrison, 30 September 1843

20 Ibid., grand jury presentments, Wentworth and Halton Counties, 23 April 1850

21 Ibid., Judges' Reports, Robinson to Mr Secretary Leslie, 1 May 1851

22 Ibid., grand jury presentments, Warden Robert Spence to provincial secretary, 7 October 1852

23 Ibid., grand jury presentments, Report, 'Standing Committee ... on Gaol Management to Council,' 28 January 1853

24 Ibid., Judges' Reports, charge of Mr Justice Burns to the grand jury of the United Counties of York, Ontario, and Peel, 11 October 1852

25 Ibid., Judges' Reports, Burns to Chauveau, 3 December 1853

26 Ibid., Judges' Reports, J.B. Macaulay to Provincial Secretary Chauveau, 19 May 1854

27 Ibid., Judges' Reports, Burns to Chauveau, 9 November 1854

28 NA, RG5, C–1, vol. 359, presentation of grand jurors of Middlesex and Elgin, 11 July 1852; presentation of grand jurors of Norfolk, January 1853

29 NA, RG5, C–1, vol. 587, James Radcliffe to His Excellency, 17 October 1858. On reading this document, someone in the government queried whether Radcliffe was insane. The sheriff responded that the Mayor of London had imprisoned him twelve times for being drunk and disorderly, and that he appeared insane because of 'excessive drinking.'

30 NA, RG5, C–1, vol. 208, Simon Fraser to Dominick Daly, 24 January 1847

31 NA, RG5, C–1, vol. 253, James Hamilton to Provincial Secretary James Leslie, 24 February 1849; 14 April 1849; 14 June 1849

32 See note 30, above.

33 NA, RG5, C–1, vol. 282, petition to His Excellency, 21 January 1850

34 James Leslie to James Hamilton, 30 January and reply 5 February

35 Ibid.

36 Ibid., James Small to James Leslie, 27 February 1850

37 Ibid., Sandfield Macdonald, 2 April 1850; Provincial Secretary, 10 April James Leslie to Francis Hincks, [n.d.]

38 NA, RG5, C–1, vol. 225, Sheriff Thomas A. Corbett to R.B. Sullivan; and vol. 385, Sheriff, Wellington County, to Provincial Secretary A.N. Morin, 25 April 1853

39 NA, RG5, C–1, vol. 360, Provincial Secretary's office to Major Sullivan, Toronto, 28 August 1852, and attached correspondence

40 NA, RG5, C–1, vol. 668, Chief Justice Robinson to T.J.J. Loranger, 28 March 1858

41 Richard B. Splane, *Social Welfare in Ontario, 1791–1893: A Study of Social Welfare Administration* (Toronto 1965) 70–1

42 NA, RG5, C–1, vol. 128, Committee of Midland District Council, n.d., responding to a letter from the provincial secretary accompanying an April 1844 presentment of the grand jury.

43 NA, RG5, C–1, vol. 570, Sheriff A. Norfolk to T.J.J. Loranger, 18 June 1858; chair of county gaol committee to sheriff, 14 June; Minuted by J.A. Macdonald, 12 July

44 NA, RG5, C–1, vol. 668, Chief Justice Robinson to Provincial Secretary, 2 April 1858

45 Canada, *Sessional Papers* (1861), no. 24, 'First Annual Report of the Board of Inspectors of Asylums, Prisons, etc.' (1860). These reports were usually unpaginated. And see Canada, *Statutes*, c. 110 (1859)

46 *Sessional Papers* (no. 32), 9, 10 'Preliminary Report of the Board of Inspectors of Asylums, Prisons, etc.,' 1859.

47 Ibid., 10, 11

48 Ibid., 11

49 Ibid., 11, 12, 13, and see above, 288

50 Ibid., 21. The district or central prison solution was first tentatively noted in the Preliminary Report and advanced in detail in subsequent reports.

51 AR 1860

52 Ibid.

53 Ibid.

54 Ibid.

55 Ibid.

56 AR 1861

57 AR 1862, see section entitled 'Central Gaols.'

58 See AR 1861 for a discussion of the rules. The new rules were annexed to the 1860 report as Supplement B. And see NA, RG5, C–1, vol. 685, secretary's office to county wardens, 6 July 1861.

59 AR 1861

60 NA, RG5, C–1, vol. 673, William Cook to governor general's secretary, 15 February 1861; petition, 14 February minute, John A. Macdonald, 11 April

61 NA, RG5, C–1, vol. 685, petition of county council, 3 July 1861; vol. 717, Elgin county clerk to provincial secretary, 5 August 1862, and petition 14 August; E.A. Meredith, November 1862; Elgin council to governor general in council, 26 January 1865

62 NA, RG5, C–1, vol. 752, warden, Hastings County to provincial secretary, 30 July 1863; vol. 811, Report of the Executive Council, 13 July 1865

63 See for example, AR 1865, 52; and NA, RG5, C–1, vol. 811, Report by J.M. Ferres to the Board of Inspectors, 'Irregular Commitments to Jail at Goderich,' 20 June 1865

64 AR 1862, 'Alterations to Jails in U.C.'

65 NA, RG5, C–1, vols. 805 and 810, Meredith to provincial secretary, 4 July 1865, and Ferres's notes, 20 June

66 Stratford, Perth County Archives, Report of the Jail committee, 7 June 1867; Report of the Special Committee on the Condition of the Stratford Jail, December 1868

67 Ibid., Report of Special Committee on Central Prisons, 18 December 1868

68 Ibid., Report of the Jail Committee, 29 January 1869

69 NA, RG5, C–1, vol. 810, petition, County of Victoria to Viscount Monck, 9 June 1865

70 NA, RG5, C–1, vol. 834, Sheriff to E.A. Meredith, 9 February 1866

71 NA, RG5, C–1, vol. 850, Sheriff to provincial secretary William McDougall, 3 July 1866

72 NA, RG5, C–1, vol. 856, E. Cartwright-Thomas to E.A. Meredith, 18 June 1866; Meredith to provincial secretary, 16 June; Macdonald minute, 18 June

73 AR 1862, individual report of James Ferres

74 AR 1864, individual report of T. O'Neill

75 AR 1864, 27

76 Ibid.

77 NA E.A. Meredith Papers, Diary, October 1861

78 AR 1863, 'Alterations of Gaols in Upper Canada'

79 Meredith Diary, 1861, 1862

80 Ibid., September 1861

81 AR 1863, 'Alterations of Gaols in Upper Canada'

82 AR 1864, Special Appendix, 30–5, E.A. Meredith

83 Ibid., 29, 32

84 AR 1864, 34

85 Ibid., 33

86 AR 1865, Special Appendix, 41–4

87 AR 1866. The Board printed extracts from the Wines–Dwight Report dealing with Canada as Appendix E of their own 1867 Report.

CHAPTER 10: THE PERSISTENCE OF COMMUNITY

1 Ontario, *Reports of the Inspector of Asylums, Prisons etc., for the Province of Ontario, 1867–68* (Toronto 1868), 4

2 Ontario, *Second Report of the Inspector of Asylums, Prisons, etc. for Ontario* (Toronto 1869), 3, 4

3 Ontario, *Statutes*, c. 21 (1868)

4 J.W. Langmuir, *The Newspaper Reference Book of Canada* (1903), 463. For a summary of Langmuir's career see Peter Oliver, 'J.W. Langmuir,' DCB (vol. 14).

5 AR 1877, 1–5; and see Ontario, *Statutes*, c. 21 (1868), An Act to provide for the inspection of Asylums, Hospitals, Common Gaols and Reformatories in this Province.

6 Ibid., 3

7 Ontario, *Statutes*, c. 33 (1874)

8 *Report of the Commissioners Appointed to Enquire into the Prison and Reformatory System of Ontario* (Toronto 1891), 331

9 For a comparison with penitentiary recidivism, see Tables 5.3 and 5.4

10 AR 1870 (1870–71), 8

11 AR 1871 (1871–72)

12 *Prison Commission Report*, 145–7

13 AR 1875, 108, as cited in Stephen B. Connors, 'John Woodburn Langmuir and the Development of Prisons and Reformatories in Ontario, 1868–1882' (MA thesis, Queen's University 1982), 63

14 AR 1869

15 In 1873 Elgin County appealed to Cabinet; in 1874 the United Counties of Stormont, Dundas, and Glengarry made their bid and many other counties did the same. See NA, RG8, Ontario, Provincial Secretary, County Council of Elgin to the members of the Executive Council, February 1873; memorial, Municipal Council, Stormont, Dundas, Glengarry, 4 February 1874; and memorial, Oxford County 31 October 1879. For a full report by Langmuir on county claims, with recommendations for provincial funding, see *Sessional Papers* (1875), no. 4, 'Supplementary Report Upon Common Gaols.' The new provincial policy of assisting counties financially with gaol costs should be seen in the context of the Mowat government's politically astute settlement of the long-standing municipal indebtedness problem. See Margaret Evans, *Sir Oliver Mowat* (Toronto 1992), 79.

16 AR 1870, 7. In a separate section of his 1870 report dealing with 'Gaol Expenditure,' he noted that the total expenditure for the past year, including all salaries, food, and repairs, was $102,320 or $16.03 per prisoner, with the average cost for food, fuel, and clothing alone being $8.15 per person. After noting huge disparities from county, to county both in costs and in functions, he concluded that 'the whole administration of Gaol affairs ... is devoid of *system*, owing to the division and variety of authority having control.'

17 Ibid., 25

18 Ibid., 26

19 AR 1871, 5, 6

20 AR 1876, 76

21 Ibid., 77, 4
22 AR 1877, 5, 6
23 AR 1869, 203
24 AR 1870, 4
25 AR 1889, 66–7
26 Many of the annual reports had separate sections on escapes, in which Lang-muir, after investigations, ordered the dismissal of negligent officials. See for example AR 1876, 72–7
27 Canada, *Statutes*, An Act to Provide for the Employment without the Walls of Common Gaols, of Prisoners Sentenced to Imprisonment therein, c. 36 (1877)
28 AR 1877, 66, 67
29 Ibid.
30 Connors, 'Langmuir,' 69–70
31 AR 1878, 62
32 Toronto *Globe*, 18 January 1878, as cited in Connors, 'Langmuir,' 72; and see Ontario, *Statutes*, An Act to Provide for Employing Persons Without the Walls of Common Gaols, c. 24 (1878)
33 AR 1878, 74–6
34 Ibid., 76
35 AR 1878
36 NA, RG 8, Provincial Secretaries' Papers, Special Series, Langmuir to provincial secretary, 17 November 1881. Although no systematic study has been done of gaol punishments in this period, impressionistic evidence suggests a remark-able absence of official brutality in the late nineteenth century gaols, for which inspectors like Meredith and Langmuir deserve considerable credit.
37 Richard B. Splane, *Social Welfare in Ontario, 1791–1893: A Study of Social Welfare Administration* (Toronto 1965), 52
38 *Report of the Commissioners Appointed to Enquire into the Prisons and Reformatory System of Ontario* (Toronto 1891), William Patterson, 326–7; James Gillespie, 327–9; James Thompson, 369–70; Will Dickson, 499–500, 502; Nelson Moore, 511–15
39 Ibid., William Van Allan, 626–7; William Grant, 370; H.C. Corbett 331–5. Because of the cesspool which seeped into his basement from the gaol, Corbett lost two of his children to typhoid fever, one of his officers died from it, and another lost a child.
40 Ibid., Sam Roether, 492–5; James Wright, 346–7; John White, 359–61, Robert Christie, 662–78
41 In Europe, 'social statistics' had been deployed for these purposes since the 1830s and the efforts of Guerry and Quetelet had elevated their study into a predictive science. In Canada, similar efforts undertaken by the Board of

Inspectors after 1859 had been truncated by the early demise of the board. After Confederation there was a hiatus, but in 1875 a Dominion statute established a program (housed in the Department of Agriculture) of collecting national criminal statistics, which demonstrated the importance statistical analysis was assuming at both provincial and national levels.

42 Even this, it should be noted, is not unproblematic. It is not clear, for example, whether vagrants, often readmitted more or less automatically at regular intervals, were counted once or several times.

43 See V.A.C. Gatrell and T.B. Hadden, 'Nineteenth Century criminal statistics and their interpretation,' in E.A. Wrigley, ed., *Nineteenth-Century Society: Essays in the Use of Quantitative Methods for the Study of Social Data* (Cambridge 1972), 336–96; and V.A.C. Gatrell, 'The Decline of Theft and Violence in Victorian and Edwardian England,' in V.A.C. Gatrell et al., eds., *Crime and the Law: The Social History of Crime in Western Europe since 1500* (London 1980), 238–337. In his diary Ontario Chief Justice Robert Harrison included the report of his 11 January 1876 charge to the York County grand jury, in which he offered a telling comment on the state of gaol statistics in Ontario: 'There is an impression that crime ... is rapidly on the increase ... Whether this impression is well or ill founded, it is impossible in the absence of judicial statistics absolutely to determine.' An application by the chief justice to the deputy sheriff for York County had elicited a minimum of information, and, 'as to the nature of the crimes, the nationality or sex of the criminals, their ages, how disposed of, how many convicted and how many acquitted, I am unable to say.' As a member of parliament between 1867 and 1872, Harrison had strongly advocated a statute requiring the keeping and publication of national criminal statistics, and the establishment of national statistics in the late 1870s owed much to his efforts. See AO, Harrison Diaries, 11 January 1876

44 AR 1871; 1872, 104, 105

45 AR 1873

46 AR 1876, 67, 70, 81

47 AR 1877, 53–6

48 Ibid., 56

49 In a typical report, on examining the Barrie gaol in March of 1871 Langmuir found fifteen prisoners, included one insane person, four 'idiots' and two weak-minded females. At least two of the above he deemed fit for an 'idiot asylum' and the rest for a poorhouse. NA, RG8, Provincial Secretaries' Papers, Barrie Gaol, 20 March 1871; Hastings County, 20 April 1873

50 For legal procedures respecting the mentally ill, see Rainer Baehre, 'The Ill-Regulated Mind.'

51 NA RG8, Provincial Secretaries' Papers, Woodstock Gaol, 17 May 1869; Pem-

broke, 17 June 1869; Walkerton, 3 July 1869; Peterborough, 18 April 1870, (for Harriett Clement see also the published version of this report); Owen Sound, 27 June 1871; Napanee, 17 May 1874; Cobourg, 21 April 1873, and see published report.

52 Ibid., Ottawa, 2 November 1870
53 Ibid., Cobourg, 24 October 1870
54 Ibid., Walkerton, 2 January 1872, and Sheriff William Sutton to Provincial Secretary Peter Gow, 2 January
55 Ibid., Brockville, 26 September 1873
56 AR 1877, 57
57 NA, RG8, Provincial Secretaries' Papers, Belleville Gaol, 19 May 1880; J.W. Langmuir to Provincial Secretary, 15 August 1881
58 Ontario Prison Commission Report, 122, 123, 127, 131, 132, 134, 142
59 Ibid., 146
60 Ibid., 220
61 NA, RG8, Provincial Secretaries' Papers, Barrie Gaol, 17 May 1870
62 Canada, *Statutes*. An Act Respecting Vagrants, c. 28 (1869)
63 NA, RG8, Provincial Secretaries' Papers, Report of Grand Jury, Carleton County, 21 April 1870, Thos. C. Keefer, foreman. Forwarded to the attorney general for consideration.
64 Ibid., Perth, 2 April 1870.
65 Ibid., Kingston, 12 June 1872, coroner's inquest
66 See for example the Ontario Prison Commission Report, 626, 361; AR 1879 (unpaginated)
67 Ibid. Tramps and vagrants are discussed on pages 107–14 of the Ontario Prison Commission Report. And see Canada, *Statutes*, An Act Respecting Vagrants, c. 28 (1869); An Act to Amend 'An Act Respecting Vagrants,' c. 43 (1874); and An Act to Remove Doubts as to the power to imprison with hard labour under the Acts respecting Vagrants, c. 31 (1881).
68 See, for example, NA, RG8, Provincial Secretaries' Papers, Memorandum for Attorney General [n.d.], signed J.W. (Langmuir?), on difficulty in sending ill vagrants to hospital.
69 Ibid., Goderich, 18 February 1880
70 Ibid., Napanee, 27 January 1880
71 AR 1877, 4. For an account of tramping in late nineteenth century Ontario, see Richard Anderson, '"The Irrepressible Stampede": Tramps in Ontario,' *Ontario History* (March 1992).
72 Sidney L. Harring, 'Class Conflict and the Suppression of Tramps in Buffalo, 1892–1894,' *Law and Society Review* (Summer 1977)
73 Ibid.
74 Splane, *Social Welfare*, 99

75 In New York state, for example, misdemeanours committed by others became felonies when committed by a tramp, with penalties of three years' imprisonment at hard labour. See James Pitsula, 'The Treatment of Tramps in Late-Nineteenth-Century Toronto,' Canadian Historical Association, *Historical Papers* (1980), 119; and Sidney Harring, 'Tramps in Buffalo.'

76 NA, RG8, Provincial Secretaries' Papers, Napanee, 13 May 1872; Cobourg, 4 March 1872; Simcoe, 14 July 1873; Berlin, 31 March 1873; Owen Sound, 12 December 1874, coroner's inquest.

77 Splane, *Social Welfare*, 79

78 NA, RG8, Provincial Secretaries' Papers, Hamilton, 13 March 1872

79 Splane, *Social Welfare*, 84; AR 1884, 50; NA, RG8, Provincial Secretaries' Papers, Port Arthur, 17, 19 August 1889

80 Splane, *Social Welfare*, 98

81 Ibid., 98–102

82 Ontario Prison Commission Report, Nelson Moore, 511–15; James Ogilvie, 245–53

83 Ibid., Ogilvie, 245–53; Dr Rosebrugh, 260–4; Robert Davis, 283–5

84 Ibid., John Edward Pell, 613–16; Reverend A.H. Baldwin, 682–5; Goldwin Smith, 685–7

85 Ibid., 701–8

86 Ibid., 113–14

87 Ibid., 219–20

88 Ontario, *Sessional Papers* (1892), no. 91

89 Thomas Conant, *Upper Canada Sketches*, cited in Splane, *Social Welfare*, 113

90 Ontario, *Statutes*, An Act Respecting Municipal Houses of Refuge, c. 38 (1903).

91 See the discussion of the Ross Commission in Peter Oliver, *G. Howard Ferguson, Ontario Tory* (Toronto 1977), 317–21.

CHAPTER 11: TERRORIZING THE UNDERCLASS

1 See Alexander Pisciotta, *Benevolent Repression, Social Control and the American Reformatory Prison Movement* (New York 1994).

2 John Weaver, 'Crime, Public Order, and Repression: The Gore District in Upheaval, 1832–1851,' *Ontario History* 78(3) (1986) 186–7

3 NA, RG8, Provincial Secretaries' Papers, Justice Robert Burns to provincial secretary, 3 June 1854

4 NA, RG8, Provincial Secretaries' Papers, Justice W.H. Draper to provincial secretary, 13 November 1865, including minute by Macdonald

5 Canada, Board of Inspectors of Prisons, Asylums and Public Charities, *Preliminary Report* (Ottawa 1859)

6 Stephen B. Connors, 'John Woodburn Langmuir and the Development of Pris-

ons and Reformatories in Ontario 1868–1882' (MA thesis, Queen's University 1982), ii. D.G. Wetherell also emphasizes the rehabilitative thrust of Langmuir's work. See Donald G. Wetherell, 'To Discipline and Train: Adult Rehabilitation Programmes in Ontario Prisons, 1874–1900,' *Histoire social/Social History* 12 (1979), 145 and 'Rehabilitation Programmes in Canadian Penitentiaries, 1867–1914: A Study of Official Opinion' (PHD thesis, Queen's University 1980).

7 Blake McKelvey, *American Prisons, A History of Good Intentions* (Montclair, N.J.: 1977), 68

8 Connors, 'Langmuir,' 81–2

9 *Ontario Statutes*, 'An Act to Provide for the establishment and government of a Central Prison for the Province of Ontario,' c. 17 (1871)

10 Nicholas Rogers, 'Serving Toronto the Good: The Development of the City Police Force 1834–84,' in Victor Russell, ed., *Forging a Consensus: Historical Essays on Toronto* (Toronto 1984)

11 Ontario, *Report of the Royal Commission appointed to enquire into the value of the Central Prison Labour* (Toronto 1877)

12 For a fuller account of the Central Prison and the labour question, see Joseph Berkovits, 'Prisoners for Profit: Convict Labour in the Ontario Central Prison, 1874–1915,' in Jim Phillips et al., eds., *Essays in the History of Canadian Law*, vol. 5, *Crime and Criminal Justice* (Toronto 1994).

13 Canada, House of Commons, *Debates*, 28 February 1877

14 Figures taken from Annual Reports of the Inspector. For Massie's comment see AR 1884

15 Ontario, Annual Report of the Inspector, 1877 [hereafter AR]; and see 1880 Report.

16 Ibid., 1881, 1882, 1886

17 See V.A.C. Gatrell, 'The Decline of Theft and Violence in Victorian and Edwardian England,' in V.A.C. Gatrell, et al., eds. *Crime and the Law* (London 1980), 299

18 AR 1876

19 AR 1875, 1876

20 Ibid., 1876

21 Ibid.

22 See AR 1877, 1878

23 City of Toronto Archives, Gilbert Hartley Papers, Gilbert to Mary, 9 February 1879

24 Hartley Papers, Gilbert to Mary, 19 December 1878

25 Ibid., 17 May 1879

26 Ontario, *Sessional Papers* (1886), 'Royal Commission Appointed to Enquire into Certain Charges Against the Warden of the Central Prison and into the Management of the Said Prison'

27 Ibid.

28 Ottawa *Journal*, 24 February 1880, as cited in Connors, *Langmuir*, 77

29 Ontario, *Report of the Commissioners Appointed to Enquire into the Prison and Reformatory System of Ontario*, 1891 (Toronto 1891)

30 Ibid. The pages of testimony dealing with the Mercer are 730–8 and 744–52. See esp. 757 and 752.

31 For the commission recommendations see 217–18 of the Report. The pioneering and still most perceptive study is Estellle B. Freedman, *Their Sisters' Keepers: Women's Prison Reform in America. 1830–1930* (Ann Arbor, MI 1981). A more recent and also perceptive study of the American experience is Nicole Hahn Rafter, *Partial Justice: Women Prisons and Social Control*, 2nd ed. (New Brunswick, NJ 1990); see also Rafter 'Prisons for Women, 1790–1980,' *Crime and Justice: An Annual Review of Research*, vol. 5. Good accounts of the British experience are found in R.P. Dobash, R.E. Dobash, and S. Gutteridge, *The Imprisonment of Women* (Oxford 1986) and Lucia Zedner, *Women, Crime and Custody in Victorian England* (Oxford 1991). See also Lucia Zedner, 'Women, Crime and Penal Responses: A Historical Account,' *Crime and Justice: A Review of Research*, 14 (1991). For Canadian accounts see Carolyn Strange, '"The Criminal and Fallen of Their Sex": The Establishment of Canada's First Women's Prison, 1874–1901,' in *Canadian Journal of Women and the Law*, 1 (1) (1985), and 'The Velvet Glove: Maternalistic Reform at the Andrew Mercer Ontario Reformatory for Females, 1874–1927' (MA thesis, University of Ottawa 1983); see also Jennifer Brown, 'Influences Affecting the Treatment of Women Prisoners in Toronto, 1880–1890' (MA thesis, Wilfrid Laurier University 1975), and Ellen Adelberg and Claudia Currie, *Too Few to Count: Canadian Women in Conflict with the Law* (Vancouver 1987).

32 For Emma Hall and the Detroit House of Shelter, see Rafter, *Partial Justice*, 24–8. For references to Langmuir's visits to Detroit see Ontario AR 1869, 1870, and 1871. For a fuller analysis of American influences on the establishment of intermediate prisons in Ontario see Peter Oliver, '"A Terror to Evil-Doers": The Central Prison and the "Criminal Class" in Late Nineteenth-Century Ontario,' in Roger Hall et al., eds., *Patterns of the Past* (Toronto 1988).

33 AR 1878

34 AR 1868

35 AR 1878

36 Ibid. The 1878 order-in-council on the Mercer did offer one suggestive hint as to contemporary Ontario thinking when it asserted that the Mercer would be 'maintained and managed in the same way as the Reformatory at Penetanguishene, and be for the reception of females, irrespective of age' (AR 1878). It was characteristic of much late nineteenth century social legislation that women and children were equated as being legally and physically disadvan-

taged and in need of special legislative protection. For a discussion of the problems at Penetanguishene in the late nineteenth century, see Andrew Jones and Leonard Rutmen, *In the Children's Aid: J.J. Kelso and Child Welfare in Ontario* (Toronto 1981).

37 AR 1878
38 Ibid.
39 Ibid.
40 AR 1882
41 AR 1884
42 AR 1887
43 Ontario, *Statutes*, An Act Respecting the Andrew Mercer Reformatory for Females, c. 38 (1879). For the establishment of the Industrial Refuge, the attached children's wing, see *Statutes*, Ontario, c. 39 and also the 1891 Prison Commission Report, 96–8.
44 I thank Mrs Margaret Angus of Kingston, Ontario for biographical information. Mrs O'Reilly received about the same amount of training for her work as had Colonel Prince when he was appointed warden at the Central Prison. The 1880 Annual Report notes that O'Reilly was sent to visit the Women's Reformatory at Framingham and the assistant superintendent was sent to Indianapolis. As the ever-confident Langmuir put it, they were 'thereby enabled to enter upon their duties with the confidence which can only be gained from practical knowledge.'
45 NA, RG8, Provincial Secretaries' Papers, Special Series, Box 6, Langmuir to the provincial treasurer, 12 October 1880
46 Rafter, *Partial Justice*, 35
47 Ibid., 36
48 Generally, see Rafter, *Partial Justice*, chap. 2.
49 Ibid., 38
50 Strange, 'Canada's First Women's Prison,' 86
51 Ontario, *Journals of the Legislative Assembly*, 1879 Session, vol. XII (no. 1), 30–3
52 Ibid.
53 For example, see AR 1890.
54 I thank my research assistants, Michelle Corbett and John Choules, for their invaluable efforts in preparing the statistical analysis of the first twenty years of the Mercer and the comparisons with the Central Prison. The analysis used both published statistics and materials taken from the prison registers. Of course, prison statistics must be used with caution but from their very nature data such as sentence length and nature of offence are far more reliable than, for example, statistics dealing with such difficult subjects as the amount of crime in society.

55 Rafter, *Partial Justice*, 37–8
56 AR 1881
57 AR 1896
58 AR 1890
59 Ibid.
60 AR 1898
61 AR 1899
62 AR 1881
63 AO, RG8, Provincial Secretaries' Papers, Langmuir to Provincial Secretary A.S. Hardy, 26 August 1880; and Circular, Attorney General Oliver Mowat, 21 September 1880
64 AR 1879
65 AR 1899
66 AR 1891
67 Ibid.
68 AR 1882
69 See the Central Prison case files in the Ontario Archives for repeated evidence of determined resistance to work programs in the male prison.
70 AR 1881
71 Ibid.
72 Studies of prison subcultures have evolved from the early efforts of sociologists writing in the 1930s – 1950s period, who offered a functional analysis, to the 'importation' theory posited by most studies published since the 1960s. See esp. Donald Clemmer, *The Prison Community* (New York 1940) and Gresham Sykes, *Society of Captives* (Princeton, NJ 1958) and, as the most influential example of importation theory, John Irwin, *Prisons in Turmoil* (Boston 1980). There is as yet no satisfactory study of an Ontario facility; W.E. Mann, *Society behind Bars: A Sociological Scrutiny of Guelph Reformatory* (Toronto 1967) is flawed but useful. James B. Jacobs, Stateville (Chicago 1977) is the best study of an American prison, drawing on both functional and importation theory while Rose Giallombardo's *Society of Women: A Study of a Women's Prison* (1966) is the classic attack on functionalism in the environment of the women's prison. Modern studies rely on participant-observer methodology, while nineteenth-century studies present a far greater challenge. For an introduction to aspects of the subculture of the nineteenth-century prison, see my article on the Central Prison. See also Philip Priestley, *Victorian Prison Lives: English Prison Biography, 1830–1914* (London 1985), 21.
73 Oliver, 'Central Prison,' 219
74 AR 1884, 1889. Mrs O'Reilly argued that religion made it easier to enforce discipline and, above all, that it was critical to rehabilitation. In the 1889 Report

she insisted that 'we realize more and more that religion alone will produce a true reformation of character.' Many men in the Central Prison were disruptive and contemptuous during religious services. See, Oliver, 'Central Prison'.

75 PAA AR 1881. For Harvie see John R. Graham, 'The Haven 1878–1930: A Toronto Charity's Transition from a Religious to a Professional Ethos,' *Histoire sociale/Social History* 25 (November 1992), 501.
76 PAA AR 1882
77 See esp., 1886, 1891, and 1893, Mercer ARs.
78 Mercer AR 1881
79 Mercer AR 1884
80 In 1882, for example, Dr King noted that 143 of 177 inmates discharged during the year had gained weight.
81 Mercer AR 1882
82 Freedman, *Their Sisters' Keepers*, 47
83 Ontario Prison Commission Report, 730–5
84 Ibid., 217–18
85 Ibid., 738
86 I have examined both the Central Prison and the Mercer more fully in previously published work. For the Central Prison see Oliver, 'Central Prison'; for the Mercer see '"To Govern by Kindness": The First Two Decades of the Mercer Reformatory for Women,' in Jim Phillips et al., eds., *Essays in the History of Canadian Law*, vol. 5 *Crime and Criminal Justice* (Toronto 1994)

CHAPTER 12: AFTERCARE AND THE AMBIGUITIES OF REFORM

1 William James Forsythe, *The Reform of Prisoners, 1830–1900* (London & Sydney 1987), 213, 207, 208
2 A useful discussion of English aftercare in Sir Leon Radzinowicz and Roger Hood, *A History of the English Criminal Law and its Administration from 1750*, vol. 5, *The Emergence of Penal Policy* (London 1986), 603–17, argues that progress was slow until the mid-eighties.
3 See Canada, *Sessional Papers* (1844–5), *Statement of the Accounts and Affairs of the Provincial Penitentiary for the year 1844*.
4 *Reports of the Commissioners Appointed to Enquire into the Conduct, Discipline and Management of the Provincial Penitentiary* (Montreal 1849), Second Report, 288
5 Aftercare was not in fact a priority of the new Board of Inspectors, and it seems to have been discussed largely in the context of E.A. Meredith's admiration for the Crofton system in Ireland. For an illustration see Canada, *Sessional Papers* (1862), no. 19, 'Second Annual Report of the Board of Inspectors,' 1861, Separate Report of E.A. Meredith.

6 John W. Grant, *A Profusion of Spires: Religion in Nineteenth-Century Ontario* (Toronto 1988), 152–3

7 Ibid., 179, 170

8 Ibid., 182

9 Ibid.

10 AR 'Prisons, Common Gaols and Reformatories in Ontario,' 1873 and 1874

11 J.G. Hodgins, President, Prisoners' Aid Association, to J.W. Langmuir, in AR, 'Prisons, Common Gaols and Reformatories of Ontario,' 1874

12 Ibid.

13 AR 1874

14 Ibid.

15 Desmond Morton, *Mayor Howland* (Toronto 1973), 17

16 For a discussion of the nature of reform leadership in Toronto in this period see Terrence R. Morrison, 'The Child and Urban Social Reform in Late Nineteenth Century Ontario' (PHD thesis, University of Toronto 1971), chap. 2. I draw on this thesis for data about individual reformers.

17 AR, Prisoners' Aid Association of Canada (hereafter PAA AR), 1884

18 PAA AR 1891, 18

19 Ibid., 1892, 20, 35–7

20 Ibid., 1874–5, 11–14

21 All figures are taken from published Annual Reports. In 1898 Hamilton Cassels was at a loss to explain this reduced level of public support. See PAA AR, 1898–9, 29–30

22 PAA AR 1901, 27. Speaking for the association, Reverend A.E. Lavell 'deprecated the extreme folly' of a City of Toronto decision to give half the previous PAA grant to the Salvation Army. He admitted the Army was doing good work, but claimed it was 'a bad precedent' to vote city money to any denominational organization.

23 PAA AR 1874–5, 1; 1875–6, 4–7

24 The above comments all come from Softley's reports in PAA AR between 1874–5 and 1882, his final full year as agent.

25 PAA AR 1882, 14

26 Ibid., 1875–6, 5–6

27 Ibid., 1878–9, 8

28 Ibid., 1881, 5

29 Ibid., 1883, 8, 15–16

30 See for example, PAA AR 1891, title page

31 Ibid., 1883, 16

32 Ibid., 1898–9, 29

33 Ibid., 1883, 16

34 Ibid., 1899–1900, Treasurer's Report, 24

35 Ibid., 1900–1, 31–5
36 Ibid., 1900–1, 17, 31–5
37 Ibid., 1883, 17
38 Ibid., 1892, 32
39 Ibid., 1833, 7; James Massie, cited in PAA AR 1889, 9
40 Ibid., 1881, 7
41 Ibid., 1883, 11–15
42 Ibid., 1882, 8
43 See PAA, various reports, 1874–5 and early 1880s, esp. 1875–6, and 1878–9
44 PAA AR 1875–6, 9; 1874–5, 5
45 Ibid., 1875–6, 7
46 Ibid., 1875–6, 4–7
47 Ibid., 1878–9, 12, 13; 1882, 12
48 Ibid., 1874–5, 3–7; 1875–6, 4
49 Ibid., 1878–9, 7
50 Ibid., 9
51 Ibid., 1878–9, 12
52 Ibid., 1883, 10
53 Ibid., 1878–9, 11
54 Ibid., 1899–1900, 31. The meeting, held in January 1901, was for the 1899–1900 period.
55 Ibid., 1899–1900, 15; 1878–9, 14; 1881, 11. According to the 1881 Report, a 'Prison Gate Mission' had recently been established to assist discharged female prisoners, and a home called the Haven was established in connection with this Mission. See pages 8–11. The Haven was referred to frequently in subsequent reports. See John R. Graham, 'The Haven, 1878–1930: A Toronto Charity's Transition from a Religious to a Professional Ethos,' *Histoire sociale/ Social History* 25 (November 1992).
56 Ibid., 1882, 9–10
57 PAA AR, 1900–1, 27
58 R.G. Moyles, *The Blood and Fire in Canada: A History of the Salvation Army in the Dominion, 1882–1976* (Toronto 1977), 9–11
59 S.D. Clark, cited in Moyles, *The Salvation Army*, 13
60 Moyles, *The Salvation Army*, 49
61 Ibid., 50–1
62 Ibid., 71
63 William Booth, excerpt from *Darkest England and the Way Out* as cited in Jamie Cheslo, 'The History of the Prison Work of the Salvation Army in Ontario, 1886–1910' (undergraduate research paper, York University, Department of History 1987), 6

64 Ibid., 12
65 Cheslo, 'Prison Work of the Salvation Army,' 16
66 Ibid., 17
67 See ibid., 19.
68 Ibid., 20
69 Ibid., 25, 26, and see Moyles, *The Salvation Army*, 66.
70 Cheslo, 'Prison Work of the Salvation Army,' 26–7
71 Moyles, *The Salvation Army*, 121
72 Ibid., 122
73 For a summary of Congress proceedings see *The International Record of Charities and Correction*, 2(7) (October 1887)
74 Ibid.
75 PAA AR 1890, 8–9
76 Ibid., 1894–5, 18
77 Ibid.
78 Ibid., 1901–2, 56–7
79 Ibid., 1895–6, 5
80 AO, Prison Reform Conference, 'Report of Proceedings of Meeting held in the Education Building,' Toronto, 26 November 1889, 5
81 Ibid., 7
82 Ontario, *Report of the Commissioners Appointed to Enquire into the Prison and Reformatory System of Ontario*, 1891 (Toronto 1891), 5–7
83 Donald G. Wetherell, private manuscript, copy in possession of the author.
84 Richard B. Splane, *Social Welfare in Ontario, 1791–1893: A Study in Social Welfare Administration* (Toronto 1965), chap. 6
85 Ontario Prison Commission Report, 34
86 Ibid., 44
87 For discussions of positivist criminology see Hermann Mannheim, ed., *Pioneers in Criminology* (Montclair, NJ 1973).
88 Ontario Prison Commission Report, 36–8
89 Ibid., Dr Barnardo, 432–51; Thomas McCrosson, 452–71
90 Ibid., Dr Bucke, 530–36
91 Ibid., 214. The phrase was part of the preamble to the Commission's recommendations.
92 Ibid., 39–40
93 Ibid., 109–22
94 Ibid., 44
95 Ontario *Statutes*, An Act for the Prevention of Cruelty to, and better Protection of Children, c. 45 (1893)
96 Ontario Prison Commission Report, 214–25
97 Ibid., 225

98 AO, 'Report of the Prison Reform Conference,' held in Toronto, 27 November 1891
99 AO, 'Report of the Prison Reform Conference,' held in Toronto, 18 December 1892, 9
100 Ibid., 1897–8, 40–2
101 See, for example, Ontario WCTU, Department of Prisons and Police, in PAA AR 1895–6, 36–9
102 Ibid., 1898–9, 6. It is important, too, that the PAA was now reaching out beyond Toronto to establish a relationship with the recently established PAA of Montreal. The 1897–8 report printed in full the prison reform platform of the Montreal organization.
103 University of Toronto, Centre of Criminology Library, Address, J. Alex Edmison, Q.C., to annual meeting, John Howard Society of Ontario, 29 April 1964, 'Prisoners' Aid Profiles – Past and Present,' 14
104 John Kidman, *The Canadian Prison: The Story of a Tragedy* (Toronto 1947), 12
105 Liberal Platform, 1898, cited in W.S. Dart, 'The Penal Reform Movement in Ontario (1891–1916); A Story of Failure' (graduate research paper, York University, [n.d.])
106 Ibid.
107 PAA AR 1893, 6
108 Ontario Prison Inspector's Report, 1895, as cited in Dart, 'The Penal Reform Movement,' 97
109 S. Morley Wickett, 'City Government in Canada,' in Paul Rutherford, ed., *Saving the Canadian City* (Toronto 1974), 288–302
110 Dart, 'The Penal Reform Movement,' 98–9

CONCLUSION

1 Donald B. Wetherell, 'Rehabilitation Programmes in Canadian Penitentiaries, 1867–1914' (PhD thesis, Queen's University 1980), 302–3
2 William A. Calder, 'The Federal Penitentiary System in Canada 1867–1899: A Social and Institutional History' (PhD thesis, University of Toronto 1979), chap. 8, esp. 382–5
3 For a full discussion of the ticket-of-leave system see A.E. Lavell's unpublished history of Ontario prisons, deposited in the Queen's University Archives. Lavell played a key role in ticket-of-leave activities in Ontario.
4 Canada, *Statutes*, c. 40 (1908). For the new 'social' approach to delinquency see Neil Sutherland, *Children in English-Canadian Society: Framing the Twentieth-Century Consensus* (Toronto 1976).
5 See Peter Oliver and Michael D. Whittingham, 'Elitism, Localism and the Emergence of Adult Probation Services in Ontario, 1893–1972,' *Canadian Historical Review* (1987).

Index

W.H. Morrow, ed., *Northern Justice: The Memoirs of Mr Justice William G. Morrow*

Beverley Boissery, *A Deep Sense of Wrong: The Treason, Trials and Transportation to New South Wales of Lower Canadian Rebels after the 1838 Rebellion*

1996 Carol Wilton, ed., *Essays in the History of Canadian Law: Volume VII – Inside the Law: Canadian Law Firms in Historical Perspective*

William Kaplan, *Bad Judgment: The Case of Mr Justice Leo A. Landreville*

F. Murray Greenwood and Barry Wright, eds., *Canadian State Trials: Volume I – Law, Politics, and Security Measures, 1608–1837*

1997 James W. St.G. Walker, *'Race,' Rights, and the Law in the Supreme Court of Canada: Historical Case Studies*

Lori Chambers, *Married Women and Property Law in Victorian Ontario*

Patrick Brode, *Casual Slaughters and Accidental Judgments: Canadian War Crimes and Prosecutions, 1944–1948*

Ian Bushnell, *The Federal Court of Canada: A History, 1875–1992*

1998 Sidney Harring, *White Man's Law: Native People in Nineteenth-Century Canadian Jurisprudence*

Peter Oliver, *'Terror to Evil-Doers': Prisons and Punishments in Nineteenth-Century Ontario*

Date Due